ASPECTS OF EDUCATIONAL TECHNOLOGY XX

FLEXIBLE LEARNING SYSTEMS

Aspects of Educational Technology Volume XX

Flexible Learning Systems

Edited for the Association for Educational and Training Technology by
Fred Percival, David Craig and Dorothy Buglass

General Editor
A J Trott *Bulmershe College*

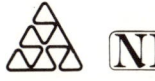

Kogan Page, London
Nichols Publishing Company, New York

LB
1028.35
.F5
1987

First published in Great Britain in 1987
by Kogan Page Ltd,
120 Pentonville Road,
London N1 9JN

Published in the USA by Nichols Publishing Company,
PO Box 96, New York, NY 10024

Copyright © The Association for Educational and Training Technology 1987
All rights reserved

British Library Cataloguing in Publication Data
   Aspects of educational technology.
   Vol. 20 : Flexible learning systems
   1. Educational technology
   I. Percival, Fred   II. Craig, David
   III. Buglass, Dorothy
   371.3'07'8   LB1028.3

   ISBN 1-85091-220-3 (UK)
   ISBN 0-89397-261-4
   ISSN 0141-5956

Typeset in 9pt Baskerville by Columns of Reading
Printed and bound in Great Britain by
Robert Hartnoll Ltd
Bodmin, Cornwall

Contents

Author Index		x
Editorial		xiii

Section 1: General Issues and Aspects of Flexible Learning

1.1	**Opening Keynote Address** **Learner-Centred Learning: The Key Issues (or Seven Deadly Sins which Frustrate Facilitation)** *J Cowan*	2
1.2	**'Flexibilities' – A Simulation on the Resource Implications of Flexible Learning Systems (Workshop Report)** *G Manwaring*	9
1.3	**Innovation in Teaching: Educational Technology as Opportunity vs. Educational Technology as Constraint** *D Ryan*	13
1.4	**Involving Learners in Open Learning Materials** *J Meed*	21
1.5	**Training Authors to Write Open Learning Materials** *T Burton*	28
1.6	**MARIS-NET: The Development of an Online Information Service for Open Learning** *M Dunnett and K Fraser*	35
1.7	**OTTSU – The Development of a National Open Learning Consultancy Service 1983-86** *J Coffey and J Simms*	40
1.8	**Successful Development of Flexible Learning Systems – The Selection and Training of Personnel** *C Stoane*	48
1.9	**Tutoring in Flexible Learning Systems (Workshop Report)** *C Stoane*	56
1.10	**Thinking: Can It Improve the Quality of Student Learning?** *D Fordyce*	58
1.11	**Cognitive Considerations in Developing Courseware Reflective of Adult Learning Needs in Computer-based Training** *R D Spillman*	67
1.12	**Open Learning: The Student's Perspective (Workshop Report)** *C Togneri and N E Paine*	73

1.13	**The Manchester Open Learning Delivery Scheme** *S Rowlands*	77
1.14	**Theory into Practice** *A Henderson*	82
1.15	**Open Learning and Modular Vocational Education: Some Problems in Practice** *C Togneri*	87
1.16	**The Concept of Open Tech and the Reality of Implementation within a Local Education Authority** *A S Donald*	93
1.17	**Resistance to Innovation in Traditional Organizations and Institutions: Bleak Prospects for the Implementation of Open Learning Systems** *J W Gritton and A Jackson*	98
1.18	**Promoting Independent and Informal Learning for Adults (Workshop Report)** *D Hall and V Smith*	106
1.19	**Structure and Organization in Instructional Text** *A M Stewart*	110
1.20	**Multimedia Learning Packages** *K L Kumar*	118
1.21	**Flexible Learning in a Multimedia Environment** *P Barker, J Lees and D Docherty*	123
1.22	**The Ubiquitous Trigger: A Flexible Resource** *N J Rushby, S Weil, A Schofield and G Delf*	129
1.23	**Interactive Learning Systems and the Learner** *D J Morrison*	134
1.24	**Interactive Open Learning – Is it on Line for Branching Out?** *C L G Sangster*	139
1.25	**Open Learning and Information Technology** *J Whiting*	145
1.26	**Flexible Learning through Computer-Mediated Communications: Opportunities and Limitations** *G McI Boyd*	150
1.27	**Presenting Computer Aided Design (CAD) to the Distance Learner** *K J Adderley and P J Lucas*	156
1.28	**Videotex – Interactivity is Flexibility: The Canadian Experience** *D J Gillies*	164
1.29	**Clear, Foggy and Black Boxes: Towards an Adaptable Environment for Novice Programmers** *P M Goodyear*	170
1.30	**Electronic Banking and Home Banking Services** *I Graham and J Stewart*	175

1.31	**Working with Copyright** *C W Osborne*	181

Section 2: Flexible Learning and Training

2.1	**Keynote Address** **Flexible Learning: Developments and Implications in Training** *D Tinsley*	188
2.2	**Identifying Training Needs – An Iterative Answer** *R Matheson and A Garry*	194
2.3	**The Business Analyst – A Client-Centred Approach to Training Needs Analysis** *J Coffey and L Wilcock*	200
2.4	**Open Learning and Training within Small Businesses: A Case Study** *T Moffat, R Laidler, E Polden and B A Gillham*	205
2.5	**Industrial Dimensions of Open Learning: A Comparison of Approaches Adopted by Lucas Industries plc and the Austin Rover Groups** *S Perryman and M Freshwater*	212
2.6	**The Development of a Large County-Wide Open Learning Service: Devon Open Tech** *C Greenwood*	220
2.7	**Distance Learning Programmes for the Offshore Industry** *A Watson, J A Ford and J T J Orr*	225
2.8	**Considerations on the Co-ordination of Flexible Learning Initiatives in the Agricultural Industries** *A R G Tallis and J St J Groome*	232
2.9	**Flexible Learning Systems: Process Technology – Glass** *A Hirst, A Hearsum and M Cross*	239
2.10	**The Application of Flexible Learning to Training in Craft Courses** *J G Taylor*	244
2.11	**A Flexible Learning Scheme for the Training of Non-Craft Industrial Job Evaluators within the United Kingdom Atomic Energy Authority (UKAEA)** *H I Ellington, E Addinall and J G McBeath*	250
2.12	**Industrial Updating in Software Engineering via Distance Learning** *J Chapman and D Saunders*	260
2.13	**Professional Training by Distance Learning: The YMCA/NELP Certificate Course for Youth and Community Workers** *L D Richardson*	265
2.14	**Flexible Learning and Youth Training – A Case Study of Educational Development** *R Houlton, J Hill and D Partington*	272

2.15 **Social Work Education and Open Learning**
R Brewster, M Lever and D Fordyce 281

2.16 **A Flexible Learning System in Nurse Education**
P I Pleasance and J Juett 287

2.17 **Flexible Learning in Hospitality Crafts**
T Baum 293

2.18 **A Training Package in Support of a Training Aid**
C I B Skellern 299

2.19 **Open Learning in Further Education and Industry**
G N Burrows and D Tyldesley 303

2.20 **Flexible Qualifications for Flexible Learning**
P Ellis 308

2.21 **Flexible Learning for Examination Purposes**
J W James 312

2.22 **Trainer Training – A Changing Role**
C R Thorpe 318

Section 3: Flexible Learning and Education

3.1 **Keynote Address**
Flexible Learning: Developments and Implications in Education
M Roebuck 326

3.2 **To Each According to His Needs?**
A Garry and J Cowan 333

3.3 **What Technologies Matter in Primary Education?**
J Oakley 338

3.4 **Flexible Learning Systems – Developments in Secondary Education**
P Waterhouse, J Monaco and R Rainbow 344

3.5 **Some Problems of Computers and the Individualization of Learning in Bulgarian Schools**
A Pisarev and R Pavlova 352

3.6 **How to Promote Student-Centred Learning with Simple Video Technology (Workshop Report)**
D Eastcott and R Farmer 355

3.7 **Flexible Learning Systems: Another Gimmick or What? Implications for Nigerian Education**
A Akinyemi 362

3.8 *Inside Information* **– A Joint BBC and City and Guilds Study Course on Information Technology**
C Loveland 367

3.9 **Peer Group and Self-Assessment of Essays: Their Correspondence with Tutor Assessments, and their Possible Learning Benefits**
N Falchikov 370

3.10 **Directed Self-Learning in Liberal Studies for Science Undergraduates: An Experiment in the Management of Learning**
S M Cox — 376

3.11 **Medical Text and Student Strategies of Learning**
S C Driver — 381

3.12 **A Programme Development for Educational Technology Courses in Teacher Education**
M Inoue, K Kojima and F Shinohara — 388

3.13 **Some Recent Microcomputer-Based Innovations in a Well-Established Micro-Teaching Programme for Teacher Trainers**
J Oakley and M Arrowsmith — 393

3.14 **Reading Skills: A Psycholinguistic Approach to Computer Assisted Learning (CAL)**
M D Vinegrad — 399

3.15 **Illustrative Characteristics of the Figures in Science Material and Construction of Educational Computer Graphics**
I Kitagaki — 404

3.16 **The Computer as a Learning Tool in University Physics Courses**
H Kühnelt — 408

3.17 **Learning Linear and Integer Programming in a Mathematics Laboratory**
T D Scott — 411

3.18 **An 'Intelligent' Approach to Computer Aided Learning: G**
M F W Meurrens — 417

3.19 **A Competence-based Learning Strategy**
P M Roxburgh — 420

Closing Address
The Significance of Flexible Learning Systems
N E Paine — 425

Author Index

Adderley, K J 156
Addinall, E 250
Akinyemi, A 362
Arrowsmith, M 393
Barker, P 123
Baum, T 293
Boyd, G McI 150
Brewster, R 281
Burrows, G N 303
Burton, T 28
Chapman, J 260
Coffey, J 40, 200
Cowan, J 2, 333
Cox, S M 376
Cross, M 239
Delf, G 129
Docherty, D 123
Donald, A S 93
Driver, S C 381
Dunnett, M 35
Eastcott, D 355
Ellington, H I 250
Ellis, P 308
Falchikov, N 370
Farmer, R 355
Ford, J A 225
Fordyce, D 58, 281
Fraser, K 35
Freshwater, M 212
Garry, A 194, 333
Gillham, B A 205
Gillies, D J 164
Goodyear, P M 170
Graham, I 175
Greenwood, C 220
Gritton, J W 98
Groome, J St J 232
Hall, D 106
Hearsum, A 239
Henderson, A 82
Hill, J 272
Hirst, A 239

Houlton, R 272
Inoue, M 388
Jackson, A 98
James, J W 312
Juett, J 287
Kitagaki, I 404
Kojima, K 388
Kühnelt, H 408
Kumar, K L 118
Laidler, R 205
Lees, J 123
Lever, M 281
Loveland, C 367
Lucas, P J 156
McBeath, J G 250
Manwaring, G 9
Matheson, R 194
Meed, J 21
Meurrens, M F W 417
Moffat, T 205
Monaco, J 344
Morrison, D J 134
Oakley, J 338, 393
Orr, J T J 225
Osborne, C W 181
Paine, N E 73, 425
Partington, D 272
Pavlova, R 352
Perryman, S 212
Pisarev, A 352
Pleasance, P I 287
Polden, E 205
Rainbow, R 344
Richardson, L D 265
Roebuck, M 326
Rowlands, S 77
Roxburgh, P M 420
Rushby, N J 129
Ryan, D 13
Sangster, C L G 139
Saunders, D 260
Schofield, A 129

Scott, T D   411
Shinohara, F   388
Simms, J   40
Skellern, C I B   299
Smith, V   106
Spillman, R D   67
Stewart, A M   110
Stewart, J   175
Stoane, C   48, 56
Tallis, A R G   232
Taylor, J G   244

Thorpe, C R   318
Tinsley, D   188
Togneri, C   73, 87
Tyldesley, D   303
Vinegrad, M D   399
Waterhouse, P   344
Watson, A   225
Weil, S   129
Whiting, J   145
Wilcock, L   200

Editorial

The twenty-first annual Educational Technology International Conference (ETIC) was held in Edinburgh from 8-11 April 1986. The conference was hosted by Napier College, Edinburgh and used Heriot-Watt University's Riccarton Campus as a venue. Around 250 delegates from 20 different countries attended. *Aspects of Educational Technology XX* represents the proceedings of the ETIC 86 conference.

'Flexible Learning Systems' was chosen as the theme primarily because of the amount of national and international activity in this area. The theme reflects the increasing awareness of the importance of matching educational and training experiences to the particular needs and circumstances of the learner rather than to those of the institutional base. This trend towards learner-centred approaches has been motivated by both theoretical and practical considerations. While certain large-scale initiatives such as the Open University and the Open Tech programme in the UK have been prominent, much has been happening internationally at all levels of education and training – from primary schools to higher education, and from community education to industrial and commercial training and ongoing professional development.

Increased flexibility can include elements of choice and independence in the time, pace and place of study. Contributions to ETIC 86 included consideration of the nature of the learner and the learning experience, cost-effectiveness, end-user requirements, and delivery systems including the role of information technology.

In addition, ETIC 86 provided an opportunity for educational and training technologists to discuss some other matters of current concern. However, it was a feature of the conference that the vast majority of contributions were directly related to the main theme.

Aspects XX is split into sections which reflect activities in educational and training areas. In many cases, however, there is considerable overlap. Presentations at the conference took the form of formal papers, workshop activities and poster sessions.

The social programme (a feature of Scottish ETICs!) included a trip to the Burrell Collection in Glasgow (via the Trossachs), a visit to the Edinburgh Crystal Glass Factory, a walking tour of Edinburgh (and a chance to get hypothermia!), a visit to the Bank of Scotland Computer Centre, an ETIC 21st birthday party, a ceilidh, and a conference dinner, addressed (with acclaim) by Dr Peter Clarke, the Chairman of SCOTVEC, and Lord Howie of Troon, the President of AETT.

The post-conference evaluation indicated that ETIC 86 had been extremely successful and enjoyable. Several delegates commented particularly that the conference had been the most humanistic ETIC conference in recent years, which is what one would hope for in a conference where learner-centred strategies are put in the spotlight.

Fred Percival, David Craig and Dorothy Buglass
Napier College, Edinburgh

Section 1:
General Issues and Aspects of Flexible Learning

1.1 Opening Keynote Address

Learner-Centred Learning: The Key Issues (or Seven Deadly Sins which Frustrate Facilitation)

J Cowan
Heriot-Watt University, Edinburgh

Introduction

Principles are easier to put into words than to put into practice. I have long been convinced of the need for truly learner-centred learning wherever higher level or affective objectives are concerned. But I must frankly admit that my efforts to put theory into practice have encountered appreciable difficulties during the past 15 years, and have seldom created the educational environment which I hoped for. My only consolation is that these problems and frustrations are apparently shared by others who bring more ability and experience to this important challenge than I can do.

I therefore regard myself as a spokesman for the participants in this conference, charged to identify the issues which presently confront teachers as we strive to bring a greater measure of flexibility and autonomy into the processes of learning and development. I do not propose to play the fool who can so effortlessly ask the questions which wise men find it difficult to answer; instead I intend to pinpoint the questions which will be in my mind during the conference – and which I hope may contribute to the rigour of the presentations and discussions, if we all keep them in our minds.

I must admit that I had originally intended to identify what facilitators should ideally be doing; perhaps I even had vague hope of being able to present ten commandments of good practice in learner-centred learning. But my examples (being drawn from my own work) led me to formulate negative rather than positive statements of advice; and inspiration failed me sooner than I expected. As a result I eventually produced a curtailed list of the seven deadly sins which tempt people like me from the straight and narrow path of facilitating learner-centred learning in an acceptable way.

The Seven Deadly Sins which Trouble Me when I Facilitate Learning

Learner-centred learning, by definition, implies a situation in which the learners exercise appreciable control over at least parts of the process. Often they make unsound judgements in that decision-making, or they encounter difficulties which frustrate their learning, or they opt for priorities other than those which their teachers would advise. It is then difficult for the teacher to rectify the situation without at the same time removing the direction from the learner, and making the learning teacher-centred rather than learner-centred. Yet the alternative is to succumb to temptation and allow the learning environment to be afflicted by one or more of these weaknesses in facilitation:

1. Aimlessness
2. Ineffectiveness
3. Inefficiency
4. Narrowness
5. Shallowness

6. Lack of inspiration

or, worst of all,

7. An impersonal approach.

The Dilemma

So what are we to do? Should we accept learning with some or all of these serious weaknesses; or should we abandon our attempts to centre the learning on the learners and take some of the direction out of their hands? I must confess that neither option appeals to me; I long to discover a third possibility in which none of my seven sins need be committed by the facilitator, while the learner remains consistently in charge of the major learning decisions.

Before considering the feasibility of discovering such a solution, I will first set out and briefly explore a number of assertions which make sense to me, and which each lead to a challenge question that my conscience often asks me about that particular facilitative sin.

1. Aimless Learning is Unacceptable in Education or in Training

One of the principles for which this Association has stood since the APLET years is the need for clearly defined objectives. 'If you don't know where you're going, any bus will do' is as true of learning progress as it is of any other journey. In an aimless situation some learning may ensue fortuitously – but unless it is in accord with our expressed purposes, it is irrelevant to the process of education or training which we claim to facilitate.

Learner-centred activity is often regarded – and evaluated – as an aim in itself. Perhaps some teachers are so relieved to get a scheme working without problems that they are tempted not to define their purpose or to disregard or to forget it. Certainly we are too often assured that learner-centred learning is virtually impossible to evaluate, since the outcomes are so diverse and so complex. The inference is that the learning cannot be compared with the aims, for one reason or another. These claims are probably correct – but not for the reason given; and they are certainly irresponsible.

For, as teachers and trainers, we are all responsible for creating situations within which our aims, or at least significant parts of them, should be achieved by learners. And we are equally responsible for monitoring the consequences of our planning and effort, because if we do not know what learning takes place, we cannot possibly improve our courses or identify the outstanding needs which should have our attention. Consequently we cannot regard aimless learning as the purposeful development which we are charged to promote.

So, as I scrutinize my own work, and as I examine what others are doing as a source of both inspiration and of ideas which I can plagiarize, my first criterion should be to obtain a satisfactory answer to the blunt question:

Is this learner-centred learning purposefully directed towards the intended aim?

2. Ineffective Learning is not Redeemed by Having Worthwhile Aims

As an engineer I draw a meaningful distinction between efficiency (which I will cover in my third point) and effectiveness. Effectiveness is the extent to which an ideal is realized. A sledgehammer, although accepted as an inefficient way to crack a nut, is nevertheless indisputably effective when used for that purpose.

The foremost reason for encouraging learner-centred learning is the belief (founded on pedagogical argument) that it should prove a more effective way to achieve important aims than an instructional style of teaching and learning. If an appraisal does not show a satisfactory improvement in effectiveness (measured as the ratio of performance to aspiration) then the justification for learner-centred learning virtually disappears.

I am perturbed by the tendency to judge many educational innovations (including my own) on their effectiveness for the more able or the more successful learners in the group. And I am unhappily aware that many low achievers are without motivation in well established learner-centred situations. This environment consequently seems to me to be much less effective, for them at least, than an authoritarian regime would be. The fact that neither situation is particularly effective does not detract from my worry that learner-centred learning may be less effective than the status quo. It is that thought which leads me to the wording of my second question, about a sin which my conscience prompts me to answer quantitatively:

How effective is this example of learner-centred learning – for both high and low achievers?

3. Inefficient Learning is Unacceptable in the Present Situation

During a period of declining resource allocations, attention inevitably focuses on efficiency, which is or should be expressed as the ratio of output to input. Notice that the same units of quantity need not be used in the numerator and denominator of this ratio: we are happy, for example, to express the efficiency of a car in miles per gallon.

Learner-centred learning is particularly open to the criticism of being too time-consuming for today's busy course programmes, or too inefficient in terms of the staff input which is required to sustain effective learning. But, although efficiency is seen as a critical issue, we still tend to be very naive in our quantification of it – despite increasing pressures from our funding authorities to formulate quantitative estimates of efficiency in an objective manner. Without doubt this is a difficult task – but our lack of success so far in producing defensible estimates is surely a direct consequence of our lack of effort. It only requires a few educational institutions to approach this task competently, as some are now trying to do, for the excuses to be revealed for what they are.

To obtain meaningful figures which are of use in pinpointing inefficiency, we need to compare efficiencies in circumstances where the comparison is informative. For example, learner-centred or other learning which demands an inefficient tutorial commitment of teachers for one particular topic or activity should be thoroughly evaluated for that topic or activity only. (Incidentally, estimates of efficiency should also consider the commitment required from the learners, whose time, though unpaid, is nevertheless a valuable and accountable commodity.)

Statements about efficiency are not particularly meaningful when they encompass entire courses with dissimilar aims, as in the present practice where we pretend to measure efficiency in terms of student/staff ratios. Comparisons based on overall performance are as meaningful as comparisons of petrol consumption for a two litre car towing a caravan over acute gradients in the Scottish highlands, and a small hatchback travelling long distances on motorways with a top speed of 50mph.

Perhaps the first step we should all take is to begin to compare efficiencies for elements of the learning process. For it is meaningless to talk about efficiency or to aspire to improve it unless we can pinpoint the aspects of our work or of our students' learning which appear to be inefficient, and then investigate the possibility of improving that efficiency. For that reason I constantly force myself to answer this question:

What are the efficiencies in the various parts of my learner-centred scheme, how does it compare overall with the status quo, and what implications can I draw from these findings?

The final choice between one teaching option and another should never be made primarily in terms of efficiency. It is deceptively easy to be more efficient in what you do, by merely lowering the standard of your aims. My wish would be to achieve acceptably demanding aims at optimum efficiency.

4. Subject-Specific Learning Tends to be Narrow and of Restricted Utility

One of the hazards of learner-centred learning is that motivated learners can devote considerable effort in good faith to the business in hand – as they see it. They can then concentrate entirely on one topic, without digressing to explore the transferability of their learning, its relationships with other topics and its interdisciplinary worth. They can readily neglect or reject as irrelevant the vision and experience which a teacher can insist on introducing when the situation is teacher-dominated. In consequence their learning concentrates more on the chosen subject matter than on either the process of specialization or on abilities which have a utility outwith that specialization.

As the knowledge explosion progresses, the world increasingly requires knowledge-handling abilities and interdisciplinary perspectives rather than the storage and mastery of knowledge, however specialized. Indeed narrowly specialized knowledge, which so rapidly becomes an anachronism, is in itself of little more than fleeting value. Teachers naturally welcome the learning experience and development which specialization can bring – provided there is an awareness of process and a development of interdisciplinary competence. But this generally requires a separate consideration of these issues – and that is something which the learner-centred approach often finds no time for, because the learners' interests are directed elsewhere.

With an eye on the need for Education for Capability, I must constantly beware the sin of facilitating merely narrow learning, and ask myself:

To what extent is the learning here narrow and specialized and what transferable abilities and learning are acquired and deliberately developed?

5. Shallow Learning is a Trivial and Unacceptable Outcome, in any Situation

One of the many noteworthy findings of the Gothenburg researchers is the ease with which it is possible to divert a learner into surface processing, even where the learner is naturally inclined to favour deep processing. When the learner discerns certain aspects of the curriculum as encouragement or pressure towards quick assimilation, trivial understanding and hence surface processing will probably ensue. But unfortunately the reverse is not true; the stimulation of deep processing is difficult to achieve – especially since the means of doing so have not been identified.

The circumstances which lead to deep learning, rigorous thinking and appropriately demanding standards tend to involve structured interactions between learners, or between learners and others. These interactions usually involve confrontation or challenge, which few learners will deliberately seek or initiate for themselves. There is thus a real danger that learner-centred learning may remain or become self-satisfied and somewhat superficial – in the absence of external intervention. Yet such intervention is difficult to achieve if the situation is to remain learner-centred in the perception of the learner.

Insofar as learner-centred learning is frequently advocated or adopted as a suitable strategy to facilitate meaningful and deep learning, I constantly feel obliged to check:

Is the learning deep or shallow; and how can I achieve the former in this learner-centred situation?

6. A Learning Scheme is Unlikely to be Successful Unless it Generates or Harnesses Motivation

Learners who direct their studies to the extent of selecting their objectives and study styles can hardly claim lack of motivation or commitment, without being immediately aware of the reason for that failure – and of the person who should be blamed, and who should rectify matters without delay.

However, this argument presupposes learner-directed learning. And that need not necessarily be a feature of learner-centred learning, since the teacher may retain authority for overall direction while still centering all that happens on the individual learners. In the latter case motivation may well be a critical issue.

Learners who have been given greater status and autonomy are understandably more ready to express dissatisfaction with what is on offer to them. Such criticisms, freely expressed within the learner-centred situation, can be a powerfully negative influence on learning. Where learners do not consider or challenge motivation, they may well be prepared to tag along after their teacher, even if in a somewhat lethargic way. But once they have formulated their dissatisfaction and lack of motivation, they are unlikely to progress at all until they feel their complaint has been satisfactorily answered.

One of my principal responsibilities as a teacher or a facilitator is to secure motivation. Failure to do so is perhaps the most serious sin in my list. And so I constantly ask myself:

Is the level – and range – of motivation here sufficient to ensure acceptable learning, compatible with the aims?

7. Learner-Centred Working is Impossible without Genuinely Individualized Treatment of the Learners

All learners differ – and these differences are significant. Each of us has our own idiosyncratic and highly personal assembly of prior learning. Any new learning must be linked to that in an individual way, through active learning in a personally appropriate style. Individuality in learning therefore implies more than catering for different times and rates of learning in a standard scheme. Truly individualized learning takes account of the fundamental differences between learners, by making purposeful efforts to identify them and then to respond to them proactively.

Most of the so called learner-centred schemes do not set out to determine the prior learning and learning needs of each learner. It is thus questionable that they merit the title 'learner-centred', other than as a distinction between individualized learning in detached isolation and mass instruction in a standardized format, as in a lecture.

This is my greatest worry about the pitfalls into which a facilitator of learner-centred learning may fall. Hence the gravest of my seven deadly sins in facilitation has been left to the end of my list. Possibly my reason for so doing is that this weakness is the one which seems to me to exist in virtually every scheme which is currently on offer.

I would maintain that I cannot rightfully describe a scheme as learner-centred without being able to give an affirmative answer to my last question:

Does the scheme identify and respond to individual differences in prior learning and preferred learning style?

In my opinion there are presently no cost-effective situations which can genuinely claim to satisfy this criterion – and only a few which make the appreciable effort in this direction which I would be prepared to accept as a minimum demand under this heading at present.

Is it Possible – and Feasible – to Avoid all of these Weaknesses?

I can see no fundamental reason to preclude the creation of a scheme in which all of my seven deadly sins are avoided by the facilitator – and where the learning is rewarding and commendable. But this is unlikely, in my opinion, for a number of reasons, including that which I expressed at the end of the last section and those which I will summarize here.

- ☐ Deep commitment cannot be guaranteed without passing over authority for direction to the learners. They will at first be as ineffective and inefficient in part of their learning as player-managers tend to be in parts of their sporting activity. So long as the onlooker sees most of the game, self-direction must inevitably be second best in certain situations. Yet learning from the mistakes which arise as a consequence of our own direction of our learning is essential – if our experience is to accrue and deepen. It seems that a certain amount of ineffectiveness and inefficiency is inevitable if deep commitment and worthwhile aims are to be achieved.
- ☐ A genuinely individualized approach cannot be achieved if we are restricted to using today's methods and strategies, within today's staffing and resource norms and in today's ignorance of the nature of individuality in learning.
- ☐ Deep processing demands an adequate allocation of time; it also requires a hidden curriculum within the assessment scheme which is seen to value this type of learning. Since these features are not available in the status quo, comparisons with conventional situations are unlikely ever to be valid, since the conditions and the outcomes are both dissimilar.
- ☐ The more demanding and worthwhile our aims, the lower the effectiveness and the efficiency which we can aspire to demonstrate.

And, most importantly:

- ☐ It is difficult for both learners or facilitators to cope adequately with a large number of comparable but dissimilar criteria within one situation.

With the last of these statements very much in mind, my own solution to this problem has been to look for an acceptable accumulation of strategies and situations within a given course. I believe that it is possible to find an aggregate which will provide the features we require. Failure of one strand to satisfy each and every one of my headings would not then exclude it from use or consideration in the total scheme – but would indicate a deficiency which should be made good by one of the other strands, perhaps deliberately chosen for that purpose. This may be a defeatist approach to the problem; certainly it is a less than ideal solution. But it at least offers the possibility of avoiding each of my seven deadly sins somewhere within a total curriculum.

The question which should then perhaps be asked, but which I will not add to my list, is whether or not it is acceptable to have a curriculum which somewhere or other provides the features I am seeking – or whether the presence of any of my listed weaknesses somewhere in the course is a valid criticism of the entire course.

What, then, are the Key Issues in Learner-Centred Learning?

These are the key issues which seem to me to be giving difficulty to those who facilitate learner-centred learning:

1. The purposeful specification of aims.
2. The selection of effective learning strategies.
3. The need to operate efficiently within available resource provision, and to increasingly demanding requirements.
4. The avoidance of over-specialization and the disregard of process on the part of the learners.
5. The encouragement of deep processing without unacceptable interventions by the facilitators.
6. The generation of motivation and the sustaining of commitment.
7. The identification of individual needs and the discovery and use of suitable

strategies through which to respond adequately to these needs.
8. The integration of the elements of a curriculum into an overall framework within which all of these issues can be adequately if not entirely resolved.

One item is missing from my list, and yet implicit in all that I have written. This is the training and development of the facilitators of learner-centred learning, whose preparation for their demanding work is presently woefully inadequate. It concerns me that there is so little in the literature and such a sparse provision in staff development programmes for those who seek to develop their skills in facilitative teaching. But that is another issue – or at least a topic for another paper, much longer than this and written by someone who can offer answers to questions rather than merely ask them.

1.2 'Flexibilities' – A Simulation on the Resource Implications of Flexible Learning Systems (Workshop Report)

G Manwaring
Dundee College of Education

Abstract: This paper describes the use of a simulation ('Flexibilities') to stimulate discussion and decision-making about open learning. The simulation allows participants to see the resource implications of opening up some dimensions of courses. For example, one flexible approach to assessment is to allow the learner to negotiate the format of the assessment. This may have positive benefits in terms of learner motivation, but it may be harder to mark and may produce more work for both tutor and learner. It may also cause problems for an external moderating body in establishing equivalence.

Introduction

Flexible learning systems, often included in the generic term 'open learning', are student-centred approaches involved in removing barriers. Open learning schemes increase access routes so that individuals can learn where, when and what they want at their own pace. They can include a variety of methods and approaches such as distance learning, resource-based training, flexistudy, negotiation of curricula, practical training facilities, learning by appointment, and study circles. They are frequently delivered via a mixture of learning packages, student support systems and structured learning. They give greater freedom and responsibility to the learner, but often do not fit neatly into the administrative frameworks and procedures within institutions.

Learning systems may be made more flexible in several different ways. The resource implications of putting particular 'dimensions of openness' into practice were explored in this workshop using a simulation called 'Flexibilities'. Participants worked in small groups of about five, each group having a set of playing materials. The simulation was run twice with the same groups. The aims were to make the participants more aware of the resources needed for open learning, of the resources that may be released by open learning, and of the interactions of decisions about open learning. Resources were deliberately limited and acted as a constraint on the decisions.

The Simulation

The participants were set the task of advising an institution about making its courses more flexible and student-centred. At the start some resources had already been committed for the scheme, while others were available from the institution.
The resources being considered were:

- ☐ Tutors – all academic staff involved
- ☐ Materials – learning packages
- ☐ Facilities – rooms, equipment, money
- ☐ Secretarial support – for distribution of materials, record-keeping etc.
- ☐ Institutional support – flexibility needed in timetables, enrolment dates, and so on
- ☐ Favourable attitudes – essential from all involved: learners, tutors, administrators, secretaries
- ☐ 'Jokers' – these could represent any of the six resources listed above.

Resources were represented by coloured cards with the type of resource printed on them. The total number was fixed at the start, but the resources cards were moved between 'committed resources' and 'available resources' during the simulation.

The groups were also given a pile of 11 flexibilities cards, each one representing one dimension of openness. In each case a change from a traditional approach to a more flexible approach was offered.

- fixed starting date → learners may start at any time
- set sequence of course from topic A through to topic Z (ie A, B, C, . . . Y, Z) → variable sequences. Learner chooses route and selects relevant topics (eg C, D, P, A, Y, T)
- support provided by college tutor → learner selects from a variety of support systems, eg college tutor, local mentor, supervisor, friend

The groups considered each flexibility card in turn, this discussion process being one of the main learning vehicles of the simulation. If they decided they wanted to include a particular flexibility, then, and only then, did they turn the card over to reveal the resource implications of that decision.

If there were enough resources to meet the requirements, they moved the resources cards as directed and placed the flexibility card on the 'selected' pile, as shown in Figure 2.

At the end of the simulation, the flexibilities cards had been placed into rejected, selected or unattainable piles. Most resource cards had been moved to the committed piles. As is usually the case, there were too few resources to meet the needs of all the desired flexibilities.

At this point, the groups completed a record sheet indicating the positions of the cards, identifying which resources ran out and summarizing the strengths and weaknesses of the schemes they had planned.

Conclusions

Most individuals found the workshop enjoyable and relevant, and it stimulated a great deal of useful discussion about managing open learning. The following points emerged.

1. The groups learned the importance of systematic planning and many started the second run by choosing priorities and identifying key flexibilities.
2. Some found it useful to try to predict the resource implications before looking at them.
3. By far the most popular flexibility was the freedom to study anywhere: at work, home or at a distance from the college. Out of 31 groups, 23 selected this and none rejected it.
4. The resources that ran out most quickly were secretarial support, institutional support and materials.
5. Some flexibilities were clearly related, eg 'start any time' and 'finish any time'; 'negotiated content/methods' and 'negotiated assessment'. Some groups tried to identify clusters so they could implement a matched set of dimensions of openness.
6. Some groups found they had increased the flexibility of the course for existing students but had not increased access. Others found they had improved access routes but the new clients were offered little freedom or negotiation in their curriculum.

'FLEXIBILITIES' 11

FRONT

> 6
>
> learners study in the college
>
> ↓
>
> LEARNERS STUDY WHEREVER THEY CHOOSE eg AT WORK, AT HOME OR IN THE COLLEGE.

BACK

> 6 COMMENTS
> Materials will be needed for learners to use at a distance.
> Secretarial support needed to organize and deliver materials, keep records etc.
> Rooms eg lecture rooms, laboratories etc in the college will be made available for use by other courses/clients.
>
> | RESOURCES | NEEDED | RELEASED |
> |---|---|---|
> | Tutors | | |
> | Materials | 2 | |
> | Facilities | | 1 |
> | Secretarial Support | 2 | |
> | Institutional Support | | |
> | Favourable Attitudes | | |

Figure 1. *A Flexibility Card*

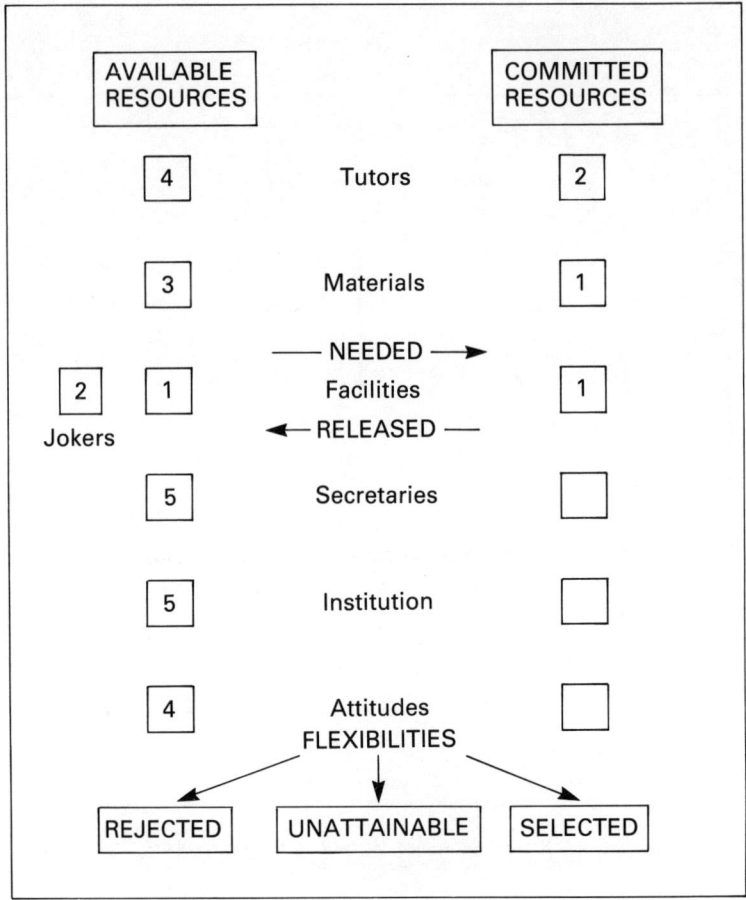

Figure 2. *Layout of cards at the start of the simulation*

7. Some individuals expressed a wish to use the simulation as a staff development tool in their own institution. They then planned to focus on the selected flexibilities and the resource restrictions for future planning meetings and staff training.

It is intended to publish the simulation. Details are available from the author.

1.3 Innovation in Teaching: Educational Technology as Opportunity vs. Educational Technology as Constraint

D Ryan
Higher Education Foundation

Abstract: This paper argues: (a) that promoters should remember that educational technology has social aspects ('software') as well as technical aspects ('hardware'); and (b) that new technology is always in competition with established technology, which may have powerful if unobserved software reasons for continuing to exist despite being technically outclassed. These arguments are illustrated from four teacher-developed innovations. The concluding discussion tries to derive some general principles to guide educational developers.

In what follows I shall argue for a sociologically extended conception of 'educational technology', one which takes account not only of the new hardware which is so striking, but also of those implicit features of educational technology which we tend to minimize, if not ignore. I shall then illustrate the usefulness of this conception from some unpublished interview research on innovation in the Scottish Central Institutions.

The Argument

Before illustrating how my conception may be applied, the concept of 'educational technology' itself needs to be drawn out, in two directions: first, in its *character*, secondly, in its *scope*.

1. Educational technology is social as well as technical and includes not only the machine but also the organization which it requires.

The impressive part of educational technology is the 'hardware', the visible objects: chalkboards, books, OHPs, tape-slide machines, videodiscs, computers, laboratories, and so on. When a post in higher education is advertised referring explicitly to 'educational technology', it is understood that dealing with these objects will be one of the principal duties of the appointee. Even where 'educational technology' has been supplanted by 'educational development', it is rare for the developer to escape all responsibility for educational devices. Since we live in a high technology civilization, and have an appropriately mechanical view of the world, we privilege hardware. In privileging hardware we neglect the associated 'software', the sociotechnological organization which each piece of hardware needs to be most effective.

I take 'sociotechnology' to mean an institutional arrangement where technical and social factors are mixed to form a purposive ensemble focused on some objective specific to that kind of institution. Farms and factories, police forces and hospitals, are no less sociotechnologies than schools and colleges. In each case, hardware is *originally* a good idea which is *then* made practical by being embodied in real materials (scythe or lathe, truncheon or scalpel); the software is the theory of use which makes the hardware effective. What differentiates educational institutions is their commitment to transforming the capabilities and attitudes of learners; their software exists because educational objects are not effective on their own, any more than a scalpel would be without anatomical knowledge. A bookstore requires a classification system and other rules of usage to become a library; a timetable and a curriculum make an assortment of classrooms, teachers, and pupils into a school; a specified training experience prepares a teacher to assume an educational role; an educational system is articulated both by a formal legal framework and by the informal expectations of a host of ancillary actors, such as parents, employers, and the public at large. These abstract entities – with very real effects – are what I mean by 'software'. They combine with the hardware to make a sociotechnology. Sociotechnology has as many aspects as organization itself; it contains a spectrum of significant features running from the real and tangible, through the social and interpersonal, to the abstract and invisible.

Seen in this perspective, a modern educational institution is a complex system for the application (including self-application, eg libraries) of a range of technologies to individuals and groups so as to foster learning. Proper analysis of such institutions, therefore, has to bear in mind that the hardware-software link is reciprocal. Not only does the classroom presume a teacher, or the TV presume appropriate programmes, but in their turn the timetable presumes classrooms, the curriculum presumes books or gymnastic apparatus, teacher training presumes appropriately-equipped classrooms with pupil role players working within a largely shared cultural repertoire.

While mismatches between the hardware and the software are obvious sources of educational inefficacy (eg the 'talking head' video), it is the reciprocal influence between the hardware and the software which makes problems of increasing flexibility in learning so difficult to identify. Hardware problems can often be straightforward; software problems are very rarely so. It was their tendency to neglect the software in the search for a neat technical solution which gave the first generation of educational technologists their reputation as *terribles simplificateurs*, pushy enthusiasts more interested in the sale of their services than in the client's problem. Their one-eyed stance discredited by contamination the technology-based systems approach to the analysis of educational systems, an approach with a rehabilitation now overdue.

2. New technology is never introduced into a non-technological world. There is always a sociotechnology there already, however rudimentary.

The high visibility of the opportunities for more flexible learning promised by new hardware, plus its declining cost in relation to its increasing sophistication, often leads to it being introduced in ways which are sociologically naive. The sociology of Third World development is full of cases of technological items (hard or soft) introduced into societies without the cognitive or social support structures to ensure that they function successfully, with their consequent defeat by well established traditional ways of doing things. Higher education in the advanced societies often differs only in degree, not in kind. Small group teaching, for example, does not appear to be so radical a break with the lecturing past as replacing an ox-drawn plough with a tractor. Yet it is a just comparison: it presumes a new set of social skills, re-educated client expectations, and altered curricular and exam emphases – the absence of any one of which can devalue or destroy even this most basic of innovations.

The clean technological break is so appealing. In education it never happens. Sociological naivety here consists in believing that, simply by being introduced, new educational technology hardware can make all things new, remake the world in its own image. A bookless, teacherless, classroomless educational setting would still start life structured by mind-sets ('software') derived from the traditional school or college. In education there is no such thing as a fresh start; a green field site soon looks much like the world it was supposed to replace. The reason for this has been touched on above: educational technology is a *socio*technology. Hence in any innovation there is more going on than the mere replacement of devices by other devices: a whole social and intellectual structure linked to the established devices is also at stake – and such structures are much more resistant than mere machines.

Whereas in technical development machines replace each other with ever-accelerating rapidity, in sociotechnologies there is massive inertia. In a country like

Britain – materially poor, with a continuous political and social history – this inertia is cumulative: many of our yesterdays, hard and soft, live on beside us. Each generation's innovation becomes an inert form to the next, its ghostly guardians barring the way to the 'state of the technology' institution. In its full and proper sense, the educational technology of a modern British institution resembles a structure which has been continuously rebuilt, but with no demolition between the successive eras. What we can now do at the top of the building is conditioned by artefacts and architecture, ideas and practices inherited from previous eras. Innovators labour unnecessarily, or fail completely, when they remain blind to this conditioning.

The really massive inertia is predominantly located in the invisible, 'software' parts of the subsystems, and especially in the informal parts of software systems. In the real world, what can be done or should not be done is a political judgement, whatever the formal role structure may suggest. The successful innovator is often a skilled mobilizer of support from affected colleagues, appreciating that, since the innovation will impact on them, that impact needs to be managed. But there is always a limit to how far any one person's influence can reach, and in a complex system that may not be far enough.

That the informal parts of educational technology software have such inertia is due to a number of reasons, but principally to two:

a) the crucial parts are often impossible to get at, in either or both of two senses:– one may not actually *know* which part it is that should be worked on, eg through inadequate or defective conceptualization of the system; or one may *lack the resources* (material, political) to work on them even when identified.

b) complex systems that have evolved over lengths of time tend to have a high degree of interlock and mutual reinforcement among the parts of the subsystems. These accordingly reinforce not only each other but the system as a whole. Each item in a sociotechnology exerts its own constraints on changes possible to the system as a whole. There may be telling reasons why any single item should be altered, but change will be obstructed by the linkages already existing among the interdependent subsystems.

Let me give an (as yet hypothetical) example. An educational authority may be prepared to buy computers (ie hardware) for every school, eventually for every child. The achievement of their manifest objective, universal computer literacy, requires also that they finance the appropriate in-service education of teachers (formal software development), which they may be less willing to do. Exploitation of computers by children might be most effective if the children had them, and used them, at home, with schools becoming (in computing) a resource centre for occasional reference. This logical development will run up against public expectations concerning the nature and functions (manifest and latent) of a school. Over these informal aspects of the sociotechnology's software the authority has no control at all. In cases like these, public expectations condition the use of sociotechnology, eg the firm belief in Scotland that education means going to school or college to be taught by a qualified teacher. Social expectations are often linked more closely to the latent than to the manifest functions of schooling, eg to their screening or their baby-sitting function. In this way the home-based learning apocalypse of microchip millenarians comes to grief, not on deficiencies of the hardware, but on the widely accepted understanding that one of the functions of schools is to support the multi-income household. The net result of a lot of loudly spent money is not a new kind of education, but a familiar kind of education with a lot of unfamiliar computers in it.

Illustrative Case Studies

The case studies which follow have been chosen for what they illuminate of the relationship between innovation and educational technology. They are presented under the same set of headings to enable comparison. While all of them overcame inertia sufficiently to achieve their immediate objective, some impacted on the existing sociotechnology in a more problematic way than others. In the two more problematic cases, it was the informal rather than the formal software aspects of the prevailing sociotechnologies which made their lasting success more doubtful.

1. Textbooks with Holes in Agricultural Botany

The precipitating problem behind this innovation was the lack of reasonably priced textbooks in agricultural botany for Ordinary National Diploma level students. The original innovator produced, with an electronic stencil machine, cyclostyled notes in his field (plant anatomy), and was soon followed by colleagues in other subjects, eg crop botany, flowering structures, etc. The novel features of the notes were that all the technical words were underlined and explained in an accompanying glossary; there were questions with spaces (the 'holes') for students' answers and illustrative diagrams; and they could be easily modified by changing a page or a paragraph at a time. Not only could staff be sure that students had more accurate notes, they were also able to correct the answers to questions, diagrammatic material, and so on. There were some unanticipated benefits, listed below.

   a) *Problem/objective*
      □ to provide textbooks at appropriate level
      □ to improve students' notes
   b) *Resources/opportunities*
      □ staff were able to find time for preparing notes
      □ co-operative colleagues allowed system to become general
      □ electronic stencil machine facilitated corrections, updates, etc
   c) *Benefits*
      □ students' notes were complete and accurate
      □ with self-prepared diagrams and answers to questions
      □ easily modifiable over time
      □ easily extendable to other subjects
      □ the whole also usable as an assessment system
      □ less time was needed for information-giving lectures
      □ student laboratory performance improved
      □ with more self-directed student work
   d) *Constraints*
      □ none mentioned

2. A Videotape Illustrating Therapeutic Interventions in Cleft Palate Children from Birth to Six Years

The precipitating problem behind this innovation was an increase in the number of first year speech therapy students from 8 to 27. This made it impossible to give them all exposure to the 'combined clinic' for cleft palate children, so, to achieve the same purpose, staff decided to make a video programme. However, the other professionals involved in the combined clinics (plastic surgeons, orthodontists, ENT consultants, community nurses, etc) were so keen to have it for *their* students that the programme grew from 'just sticking a camera up in the corner and filming what happened' at the combined clinic to a filmed record of all the specialist interventions in cleft palate from birth to six. Again, there were some unanticipated benefits.

   a) *Problem/objective*
      □ student numbers too big for combined clinic
   b) *Resources/opportunities*
      □ one colour TV camera
      □ experienced and co-operative educational technologist

- colleague with TV experience
- multi-professional contacts in city health system
- high level college support

c) *Benefits*
- video of combined clinic AND of therapeutic intervention 0-6 years
- economical and effective in teaching
- multi-discipline approach of therapeutic team demonstrated
- from speech therapy students to multiple publics – including (not foreseen) parents of newborn cleft palate babies

d) *Constraints*
- time required considerably underestimated
- multi-professional co-ordination led to 'communication difficulties'
- only one camera

3. The Syndicate Method in Chemistry Teaching

In this innovation the lecturer was seeking to achieve some higher-order learning objectives than just the knowledge of chemistry appropriate to a degree. In addition to having attended a course on small group teaching at a well-known staff development unit, the lecturer was a counsellor for a voluntary organization.

a) *Objectives*
- to foster independent learning
- to improve motivation
- to develop group working skills appropriate to industry

b) *Resources/opportunities*
- small group teaching course taken by lecturer
- counselling experience
- parallel general studies class where method very successful

c) *Benefits*
- unclear – some students more interested and independent, others very hostile

d) *Constraints*
- exam remains the same
- student concern that new method will be less effective in exams
- deliberate (partial) non-attendance threatens course status

4. Group Projects in Agricultural Biochemistry Lab Work

This innovator had redesigned a laboratory course in biochemistry around a specially written manual; students carried out their projects in groups under the supervision of the lecturer concerned, of the demonstrators and of the highly skilled and committed lab technician.

a) *Objectives*
- to improve student work in biochemistry
- to foster independence in lab work

b) *Resources/opportunities*
- support from all colleagues
- full support from lab technician
- lab technician skilled to demonstrator level

c) *Benefits*
- improved lab reports and overall quality of student work
- nutrition chemistry brought nearer to agricultural situation, a commonly cited prerequisite for motivation in agriculture
- group leaders emerged among the students

☐ students could work independently of the timetable, therefore more complex experiments possible
☐ students able to use advanced instruments (not feasible with classes of 30+)
d) *Constraints*
☐ more time needed from all staff
☐ class size of 35 could not be exceeded without extra staff
☐ some student 'misfits' would not collaborate
☐ manual-led lab programme vulnerable to instrument breakdowns
☐ fixed quantum of available demonstrator input
☐ exams required as near as possible uniformity of student experience on course

Discussion

Problem-solving teachers are for the most part not architects, painstakingly bringing into existence an original integrated vision à la Mies van der Rohe. Rather they resemble those medieval stonemasons who, jostled by competing patrons and ignorant of the first principles of mechanics, threw up piecemeal architectural happenings, some of which have still turned out in retrospect to be visionary.

Viewed in our sociotechnological perspective, in all of the above four cases we see an innovatory teacher reaching for a new medium as a means to solving a teaching/learning problem. In the first two cases, somewhat to their surprise, their local innovation grows into something which is not only effective locally, with the original student public, but is also welcomed and added to by colleagues. The 'textbook with holes' is a new medium but the aims and content are unchanged: the textbook replaces the lecturer's voice with joint teacher/student print, but with no implications for associated software. In the second case (a rare example of a 'total innovation') the cleft palate videotape is 'pulled' by a market need (which it constructs at the same time as meeting) into a field which is genuinely green, with no inert software to joust with. In producing a teaching aid which has become more than a teaching substitute, they accidentally uncover a potentially national-level market beyond speech therapy, beyond even education – in retrospect, one might say, a truly visionary use of the medium.

Whereas these first two innovations seem to have set off virtuous circles and their future seems assured, the last two are not so happily placed. The syndicate method is an old message in a new medium, and to that extent should be unexceptionable. But despite its proven success with parallel general studies classes, the method has run into fundamental opposition in chemistry teaching (notwithstanding the fact that this was a degree-level course in a prestigious institution) from a minority of the supposed beneficiaries, the students. With their eyes firmly set on the exams, they reply to the innovator's claim that this method gives them experience of methods of working that are looked for by those who recruit for industry:

> 'That's as may be. But in the two hours it's taken us to do the chemistry of half a metal, we could have done the chemistry of a whole metal. We'll worry about industry's working methods when we get out into industry.'

This is a software problem, a clash of definitions of the situation, with the lecturer working several points higher up the taxonomy of learning objectives than the students. The new medium may carry an old message (ie chemistry) BUT the lecturer has also worked in a new objective: to change the students themselves in fundamental ways. For some this is too threatening, and, despite his counselling skills and teaching authority (still significant in Scotland), he is unable to carry them with him. Why not? Because the final assessment still measures straightforward chemical knowledge. Unchallengeable in their certainty that real education is what is measured in exams, some of the students begin to miss classes, thereby calling into question the lecturer's standing by his terms of service (another level of software). At this point, any lecturer begins to question whether the educational gains are worth the political risks.

For the argument of this paper, this is an exemplary case, illustrating its basic principle: it is not wise to introduce a technological innovation solely on the grounds of its apparent superiority to the existing system, since that system may be better adapted to the informal software environment of roles, expectations and politics. The more complex the system, the more difficult it is to predict the rebound effects to be expected from threatened interests, even when abstract (eg exams, conditions of service) or at several removes in the environment.

A similar lesson emerges from the biochemistry lab innovation, which is basically a reformed social subsystem organized around a new medium, the manual. The evident quality and effectiveness of the manual and the increased flexibility and interest in doing biochemistry projects in small groups rather than in a whole class situation can not hide the fact that this very successful innovation is precarious. It is precarious just because the innovator has designed it so well: he has precision-built it on present parameters to ultra-fine tolerances. For example, where would he be with an average lab technician, rather than the demonstrator-equivalent he has at the moment? What if the successive rounds of cuts led to one of the two demonstrators not being replaced, or his own workload being substantially increased, or the degree and the diploma courses being combined for lab sessions, etc? A lot of people are working very hard to make sure this innovation succeeds; but its dependency ramifies in so many subsystems of the sociotechnology outside his control that it must be judged vulnerable to knock-on effects from them. And here, too, there is dangerous inertia right at the centre of the exercise, the students he classifies as 'misfits'.

Conclusion

It is often to educational technology (narrowly conceived) that people turn to increase flexibility in learning systems. However, present conditions of (at best) steady state financing will mean that educational system managers will be able to buy the hardware but will be unable to invest in the appropriate training – the 'tractor parachuted into the bush' syndrome. Such promoters, whatever they may consciously think, communicate two beliefs by their actions: first, that because new devices are being promoted, educational technology itself consists of no more than devices; second, since the devices which offer the solution to problems of rigidity and stagnation are themselves new, educational technology itself has no history. They have allowed themselves to be so hypnotized by the innovatory potential of the new forms that they remain blind to the constraining potential of the old.

The belief that this is not the way to promote an intelligent application of educational hardware to achieving educational ends has been the impulse behind this paper. Although the argument is simple, almost a caricature, the facts behind it are still not universally understood. A further impulse behind the paper is my belief that, until they are, the stress, frustration and conflict which accompany attempts to increase flexibility in learning by means of educational technology will remain at unnecessarily high levels. Since stress at a high level inhibits the key quality of the innovator – the ability to take risks to solve problems faced by students in their learning – a proper understanding of their own technology is indispensable if staff are not to be frozen into the role of unwilling hands of an uncomprehended and unmanageable machine, educational in name only.

Educational technology is like the iceberg: what you see is only a fraction of what is there. As with icebergs, the visible part is so impressive that the submerged part tends to be forgotten. But for the innocent educator as for the unwary sailor, it is the submerged part which causes the problems.

Note

The project 'Innovations in teaching methods and staff development in the Scottish Central Institutions' was funded by the Scottish Education Department (SED) and based at The Queen's College, Glasgow, from whom the final report may be obtained. The views expressed in this paper are entirely my own and do not necessarily reflect those of the SED or of any of the Central Institutions.

1.4 Involving Learners in Open Learning Materials

J Meed
National Extension College, Cambridge

Abstract: Although open learning has been able to offer learners greater control over the time, pace, and place of their learning, the actual materials produced for open learning do not always reflect this learner-centredness. In practice, many materials are subject-based and teacher-centred.

To reverse this trend, we should design objectives that relate directly to the benefits sought by learners. And we should use in-text questions much less for testing knowledge, and much more as ways of involving learners in the text.

To achieve these aims, we will need to give learners much more control over the materials they study, both by involving them in the setting of objectives, and by making the steps by which they can achieve these objectives explicit.

Introduction

Open learning can be defined as learning centred on the individual's needs. It is usually undertaken by learners who have many other pressures on their time, and so we as open learning providers have to design materials and systems that enable learners to achieve their objectives in the most efficient way.

Most current open learning schemes go a long way towards meeting the needs of individual learners for a more flexible pace, place and time. Learners can study when and where they like – whether at home or at work – and are not obliged to attend strict college hours. They often have the additional freedom of choosing how long they intend to spend on their chosen course of study.

However, when we look at the materials designed specially for these open learners, we find far too often that they are much less learner-centred – in all too many cases they have remained as conventionally subject-based and teacher-centred as much traditional face-to-face teaching.

In this paper I plan to address this problem, and to:

- show exactly what I mean by stating that open learning materials are subject-based
- look at what we can do to make them more learner-centred.

We could examine many aspects of open learning materials – objectives, structure, diagnostic devices, in-text questions, reading and tutor-marked assignments, to name but a few. But to keep this paper down to a reasonable length, I will concentrate on just two aspects:

- objectives
- in-text questions.

Let's look at each in turn.

Objectives

What are Objectives?

Let's begin with a definition – I would describe objectives as a description of what the learner can expect to get out of studying a particular piece of work.

They are important in open learning in a number of ways:

- for authors, they help in the planning and structuring of what we write
- for editors, they help us to check that the material does actually do what it is supposed to do
- for learners, they can act as signposts to show what is coming, and as checklists of what we have studied.

So far, so good.

What can go Wrong?

It's the very centrality of objectives to planning and structuring that's the problem. If we conceive of the objectives in the wrong way, it's highly likely that what we write will leave a lot to be desired.

And that's just what happens. Materials can be written to objectives which fulfil all the educational technologist's criteria – yet they are boring and often irrelevant to the learner's needs.

The reason is that the objectives are conceived in a subject-based or teacher-centred fashion. Here's how you might find objectives written for a marketing course for small businesses:

> 'By the end of this module, the learner will be able to:
> - list five methods of launching a new product
> - describe each method in detail
> - apply each method to a given case study.'

I don't think there's much wrong with the writing of these objectives – but you can see already how the unfortunate learners may have to work through unnecessary hours of study in order to find out how to launch their new products. And it's quite possible that, having slogged painfully through the case study, they may find it so different from their own business that it's difficult to really apply what they've learnt in practice.

What can We Do?

What we should be doing is identifying first what the learners want to get out of their study – not what the subject covers. In sales jargon, we should be 'selling the benefits' rather than 'listing the features'. Should we even change the word 'objective' to 'benefit', or at least 'outcome'?

What kinds of benefits are learners likely to be looking for?

Generally speaking, they're likely to be in terms of things like:

- work/career
- pay/profit
- personal/social development

and some are likely to be more positive (eg looking for promotion, becoming a better writer) than others (eg surviving at work, coping with numbers).

How can we identify the benefits?

Presumably we should ask the learners. Can we involve them in early planning workshops? Should we carry out some kind of initial market research? By doing this we could make sure that we concentrate on what the learners themselves have chosen – not on what we think they ought to need.

What will benefits look like?

If we go back to my marketing for small business example, the benefit might be:

> 'This module will enable you to choose the best method for launching your next new product;'

or even:

> 'This module will help you launch your next product successfully.'

It's then possible for the whole module to be structured around the learner's own situation, so that he or she can do work that is directly relevant to his or her needs.

What are the problems?

The example I've chosen from marketing works particularly easily. In many cases, learners are:

- ☐ studying for a qualification in a syllabus that makes them carry out irrelevant work, or
- ☐ placed on a course by their manager, rather than from their own choice.

In either case, they may well have to carry out work that has little direct benefit for them.

Nonetheless, I feel we should still try to apply the benefit approach as far as possible. For the exam student, we can find out exactly what they're hoping to get out of the exam (a particular grade, for example) and plan materials accordingly. For learners acting on managers' orders, we can identify which of their own personal objectives can be achieved at the same time. And in the long term, can we bring pressure to bear on exam boards and employers to adopt a more learner-centred approach?

In-Text Questions

What are In-Text Questions?

In-text questions – or self-assessment questions, self-checks, activities etc – use any question that is placed within a module, and which does not (generally) require tutor feedback.

They can fulfil a number of functions:

- ☐ to test the learner's understanding of a section
- ☐ to help learners apply what they've learnt
- ☐ to get learners to do things away from the materials.

Above all they should be *involving* the learners in the materials – making the process of learning itself explicit to them.

At their very best, in-text questions are what makes open learning materials different – and successful.

What can go Wrong?

I first became aware of the problems surrounding in-text questions at the author training workshops I run. During the session on writing questions, a number of queries started to crop up with increasing regularity:

> 'How many questions should we write in any section?'
> 'How frequently should they occur?'
> 'Don't these questions get in the way of learning?'
> 'How can we stop the learners cheating by looking at the answers?'

In some cases, I would even get work submitted to me after a workshop with the questions on completely separate sheets of paper with instructions as to where to insert them in the text.

I became increasingly aware that these workshops were failing in that, although we were training authors to write excellent questions (just as we trained them to write excellent objectives), we were not helping them become good open learning writers. The questions were just being tacked on to textbook-like materials.

The problem was that the questions were being restricted to testing the learners' recall of what they had read, with the occasional break to ask them to carry out some kind of practical work or observation. The very term 'self-assessment question' increased this tendency.

I'm afraid that this is true in all too many open learning materials. The questions are not used to help learning take place. Instead, we assume that the learners learn by reading, and so we just test that they've learnt the right thing.

But do we actually learn by reading? Surely open learning students – just as classroom students – learn best by doing and thinking?

Once again, we've become very teacher-centred. And the risk is that we replace the worst of face-to-face teaching – long, boring lectures – with the worst of publishing – long, boring books.

What can We Do?

We need to make this active process of learning explicit. In other words, at the planning stage, we need to identify the activities learners will need to carry out if they are to succeed in their learning, and use these as the basis of the questions we will ask. If we can do this, we should be able to:

- put learners in control of their learning
- keep them fully involved in the materials.

It may be worth calling questions like this self-involvement questions, to differentiate them from self-assessment questions.

What will self-involvement questions look like?

They're likely to involve learners in things like:

- deciding what they want to achieve and how to go about it (so linking closely with the benefits they are looking for)
- thinking about what they are about to read
- drawing on their own experience
- reflecting on what they have read
- trying things out
- talking to other people.

Figure 1 shows an example of self-involvement questions in action. It's drawn from the National Extension College's course *Preparing for Social Science* by Roger Lewis and Liz Maynard. This course has consistently produced the best results and higher completion rates of any of NEC's courses, which would suggest that the approach works in practice.

In the example you can see how:

- the entire passage is based around questions (as is the course as a whole)
- learners are encouraged to find out for themselves, rather than having the information forced on them
- the authors' feedback is there to provide support and guidance, rather than incontrovertible evidence.

The course is therefore able to promote an active learning experience in which the learner is in constant command.

CLASS

In your answer to SAQs 1 and 2 you may have used the word 'class' and said that the two people (GP and shop assistant) come from different 'classes'. The word 'class' is very frequently used but often in a rather general way. We hear such statements as 'Britain is a class-ridden society' on the one hand and on the other, 'There's no such thing as class.'

SAQ 3: If I said 'The GP and the shop assistant come from two different social classes' what would you think I meant?

You may have written something like:
- they have different amounts of money;
- they have different life-styles;
- they have different chances in life;
- their parents were from different backgrounds;
- they have different amounts of importance and prestige.

'Class' can have a variety of meanings. This can make reasoned argument difficult, particularly in everyday contexts where people rarely stop to make clear the way in which they are using the word. Hence one of the first jobs of the social scientist, or indeed of anyone who wishes both to make himself clear and to understand others, is to define the terms he is using, in this case the word 'class'.

SAQ 4: Turn to your set book, Halsey.
1. Does Halsey use the word 'class'?
2. If so, where might we find a definition of how he is using the word?

This SAQ was deliberately phrased to make you think about your reading strategy. You need here to use a mixture of contents page and index — and common sense. The way to find out quickly whether or not Halsey uses the word 'class' is to look at the contents page and at the index. We're lucky first time — inspecting the 'Contents' shows up that Chapter 2 has the word in its title. We might thus expect a definition of 'class' either early on in that chapter or (just possibly) at the end of the previous chapter.

SAQ 5: Is the index any further help?

The index is not helpful — not, at any rate, in my edition; later editions may have a more comprehensive index. The index is in fact surprisingly unhelpful. On closer inspection you'll see that it contains only proper nouns — people's names, names of organisations (e.g. Trades Union Congress) or acts of parliament. You can thus find a reference to the Tridentine Mass but not to class and that's slightly peculiar, to say the least, in a book about social science. More useful indexes include concepts, like 'class' and 'status', as well as proper names.

As we predicted, Halsey offers definitions at the beginning of Chapter 2 — in the first five pages (in my edition pages 20-24 inclusive). Now it's important to say once again that Halsey's writing is far from easy to understand and the difficulty is likely to be most acute to someone who hasn't read much social science before. So don't be too alarmed if you find the following SAQ hard going. Be prepared to spend some time on it, say about 30 minutes.

SAQ 6: Read through pages 20-24 from the beginning of the chapter down to 'At the beginning of the century . . . .') and underline (or write out) those phrases or sentences which define most exactly how Halsey is using the word 'class' in this book. Don't pause for too long over passages which you simply cannot understand after, say, two close readings of these pages. Mark as many as seem to you to make sense and to be relevant to the SAQ.

continued

I marked the following:

1. 'Classes — for example, professional people or factory workers — are formed socially out of the division of labour. They make up more or less cohesive and socially conscious groups from those occupational groups and their families which share similar work and market situations.'
(page 21)
2. '... classes belong to the economic ... structure of society'.
(page 22)
3. '... the essential point is that in industrial society the anatomy of class is displayed in the occupational structure. Groups and individuals differ first according to the terms on which they can sell their skills and their labour on the market, and second according to the actual conditions of their work — its autonomy, or lack of it, its intrinsic satisfactions, and its attendant amenities.'
(page 23)
4. 'Class ... its foundation is in the market, not the law.'
(page 23)
5. '... classes emerge out of occupational structure, and power and advantage are unequally distributed between them'.
(page 23)
6. 'It is this definition of class in terms of occupation ... that I shall be using in this book.'
(page 23)
7. 'The number of classes that may be identified ... is partly a matter of convenience.... For our purposes ... it will suffice to distinguish three classes.'
(page 24)
8. The definition of
   (i) middle class (professional, managerial, administrative, higher technicians — the 'service class')
   (ii) lower middle class
       (non-manual employees, small proprietors, self-employed artisans, lower-grade technicians, supervisors of manual workers)
   (iii) working class (industrial manual workers, agricultural workers)
(page 24)
9. The last sentence of the section makes clear that *other* class groupings are possible and indeed necessary for purposes other than those Halsey is pursuing in this particular chapter.
(page 24)

(You may have selected slightly different passages. Spend a minute or two comparing my section with yours.)

SAQ 7: Stand back from these nine extracts. What, put simply, decides the 'class' of an individual given the terms Halsey is using?

His job. *See* (6) (the clearest, shortest statement) and (1) — 'for example, professional people or factory workers'. A man's job gives him an identity and indicates to society the extent of his 'power and advantage'. In (3) Halsey makes the point that a man's job (his position in the 'occupational structure') gives him both a 'market value' (his skills will be more or less valuable in money terms) and also a particular work experience ('autonomy, or lack of it ... satisfactions ... amenities'). We have made some comparisons along these lines with the doctor and the shop assistant.

Figure 1. *Example of text involving learner fully*

Conclusion

What are the general implications of all this for managers, writers and editors of open learning materials?

I would suggest that we need to do the following things:

- [ ] we need to involve learners more at the planning stage so that we can ask them what they want to get out of their learning
- [ ] we need to stop seeing ourselves as information providers, and to become instead facilitators of learning, working on behalf of the learners.

Both these changes of approach may be disconcerting. It's reassuring to feel that we are the experts in the subject, and it's tempting to hide ourselves away behind our expertise. Handing over any degree of control to our learners may leave us feeling insecure.

But if we want to put the learner at the centre of the materials, do we have any choice? As long as we keep firm hold of the reins, learners can only be passengers travelling down the road we choose for them. But if we do hand over the reins, and continue to sit beside them as guides or map readers, we will be valued just as greatly, if not more – and the learners will finish up at their chosen destination.

1.5 Training Authors to Write Open Learning Materials

T Burton
National Extension College, Cambridge

Abstract: The paper addresses itself to the problem of recruiting and training personnel to write open learning materials. Specifically, it examines: (a) what key existing competencies should be sought when recruiting an open learning author? (b) what form of training is most appropriate for this person?

The emphasis in (a) is that the writer of open learning materials is primarily a translator and facilitator, and that recruitment should therefore pay close attention to an individual's existing teaching style.

Specific features of this style will suggest aptness for training as an open learning author.

Discussion of (b) includes a brief overview of existing training possibilities, and their strengths and weaknesses, and argues strongly for a carefully-planned combination of initial and continuing briefing. However, the main emphasis of the discussion is that briefing should itself be an open activity, both in face-to-face and distance settings, and a major aim of this briefing should be to facilitate a change of perspective from topic-centredness to learner-centredness.

The discussion will conclude by relating author training to recent developments in the concept of competency-based education.

Introduction

I want to make two points by way of introduction to this paper: first on the nature of the topic, and second on its treatment. Taking the topic first, by training I mean the complete range of induction and support facilities needed by authors as they write for open learners. Having said that, I will concentrate on the area of training with which I am most familiar, that of the one- and two-day workshop, bringing in other methods as adjuncts of this. I hope that this paper will provide reasoned support for this approach to training and not simply be a rationalization, after the event, of 'the way we have always done it'.

The other half of the title uses the term 'open learning materials'. Again, a brief explanation. I will resist any temptation at this stage to define 'open learning' at length. Intead, let me simply offer a compressed, single sentence definition in standard lexicographic style: it may be tempting to debate this definition, but there is no space to do so here. By open learning I am referring to *any form of learning that is adapted to the varying needs of individual learners, especially in terms of their time, place, pace and topic of study.* And to round off my definitions, by 'materials' I mean primarily text-based self-study materials; again, this is the area in which I have had most experience, as a courses editor at the National Extension College. However, I hope that what I have to say will have direct bearing on training authors to prepare materials in other media, especially audio tapes and computer-based learning.

Second, a brief word about treatment. Anyone looking for pedagogic theory in this paper will, I am afraid, be disappointed. My involvement in open learning has been as a practitioner rather than a theorist, and although I have no wish to belittle the role of theory, my concern over three years of author training has been with what works in practice. Obviously training theory is useful to the extent that it informs practice, but my approach throughout has tended to be pragmatic and personal rather than theoretical. This paper is therefore a summary of my own experience. I am not attempting to construct a complex model, simply to offer some insights and pointers, and to pass on what has seemed to me to provide the training authors need.

I begin by stating the case against training workshops, and suggest that this reflects a misconception about open learning itself. I then go on to justify the use of workshops and consider what the key aim of any workshops should be. Finally I return to the earlier criticisms and suggest how we can draw from them a scheme for pre- and post-workshop training.

Criticisms of the Workshop Model

The mode of training that the National Extension College, and several other open learning bodies, has used most frequently in recent years, and particularly in connection with Open Tech sponsored projects, has been the two-day training workshop. There have been some criticisms of the appropriateness of this model for training authors of open learning materials, and I think these criticisms, though generally misplaced, are instructive, since they point to a pervasive misunderstanding of open learning itself – of what I shall call its 'centre of gravity'.

Critics of workshops suggest that there is a contradiction between this approach and the 'open' mode of the materials authors are being trained to produce. The point is often made by the authors themselves, especially those whose experience of open learning has been primarily of its 'distance' mode. 'If you are training us to write open learning materials', they say, 'shouldn't you be practising what you preach and training us at a distance?'. There is something to be said for this argument – in fact, I'll say it later in the paper. However, it seems to me to reflect two misconceptions.

What is the Role of Open Learning?

The first misconception is that open learning is a superior form of learning designed to supplant traditional face-to-face methods. Of course, neither point in this dual assumption is any more than partially true. Certainly open learning is superior for certain sorts of learner and in specific learning situations, and certainly there has been a tendency for institutions to seize on it as an answer to short-term financial and staffing problems – with the accompanying tendency to play down the potential of conventional methods. However, open learning is essentially a complement to traditional learning, and at best its philosophy is precisely that of the National Extension College: to extend educational and training opportunities rather than contain them, but to change their form.

The second assumption is that open learning, at its most open, implies learning using entirely self-contained materials, with no recourse to face-to-face contact or any of the methods of the old, institutionalized model. Authors approaching open learning with this belief see a workshop as diluting the perfection of a truly open approach, and suppose that materials that still depend to some extent on personal support are in some sense compromised. Yet nothing could be further from the truth. Paradoxically, once open learning becomes so open that it excludes the facilities of traditional learning its openness diminishes. There is much to be said for a package that enables learners to choose to study entirely alone, and provides within itself all the learner needs in order to do this, but once the possibility of for example telephone, face-to-face, or workshop-style tuition is removed we are tending towards the old closed models again.

In contrast to the assumptions I have just been challenging, I would suggest that a better defining feature of open learning is not its 'distant' or 'self-contained' character but its learner-centredness. The centre of gravity of open learning materials is the learner. This means, first and foremost, that a successful open learning package is responsive, as far as possible, to the evolving needs of the learner as he, or she works through it. As such it will provide regular opportunities for learners to check their progress and assess the continuing relevance of the materials to their situation. Learner-centredness also implies an emphasis on learning rather than teaching. The aim of an open learning package should be both to stimulate learners to make discoveries for themselves, by encouraging hypothesizing and deduction, and to apply their learning in the real world. Finally, the emphasis on the learner implies an awareness of the learner's context on the part of those who write the open learning materials: the learner's assumptions and expectations about learning, his responsiveness to varied styles of writing and self-assessment, and his opportunities to apply his learning in the real world. Each of these consequences of learner-centredness points to the workshop as a key form of author training.

Support for the Workshop Model

Writing text components designed to prompt self-assessment rarely comes easily to authors. Many of us have learnt to produce competent discursive essays; few of us can spontaneously build coherent discursive text around a scaffolding of assessment aids. In training authors to do this it is not enough to formulate a materials-based instructional sequence, even if such a sequence stimulates the author to match his or her assessment aids to the specific demands of the target audience. What the trainee author needs is the opportunity to experiment with a variety of approaches to writing in an environment that is flexible, supportive and able to provide rapid feedback on his or her attempts. Each of these features should be present in open learning, including where possible an opportunity for group discussion of work. But the timescale of an open learning package incorporating all these facilities is necessarily long and its costs high. Few authors can realistically be trained using such methods. The workshop salvages the interactive, learner-centred features of open learning in a much shorter timescale, and effectively at a lower cost.

The non-didactic approach of open learning is realized equally well in a workshop. The role of the workshop leader should always be to facilitate rather than to lecture. Educational – specifically open learning – theory may be invoked in response to queries or particular issues, but the focus should always be on the developing awareness and creative thought of the participants. And rightly so. To write fluently for open learners entails not the mastery of abstract technique (however compelling discussions about the FOG Index may be) but the development of a sensitivity towards the target audience that comes only through a process of individual discovery and deduction. I do not tell authors how to write; I try to not even show them. My aim is always to encourage them to show themselves.

Awareness of the learners' overall learning context is not easily raised by methods other than workshops. Again, the problem is one of providing input into, and feedback on, an evaluative process that is individual to each project and to each author writing for that project. The group discussion that takes place in a well-administered workshop is a powerful tool for raising awareness of the needs of learners; I cannot think of a more potent method of shifting authors' preoccupations away from their academic discipline and towards the specific needs of the target open learner. This consideration leads on to equally important points about the *content* of author training as opposed to its form.

The Starting Point for a Training Workshop

It is not the purpose of this paper to set out a training programme in detail. However, the question of the content of training needs to be addressed. Let me approach the topic obliquely. The key to successful writing seems to me not to be mastery of a range of interactive techniques – self-assessment, objectives, activities, and so on. These techniques are certainly important, but they follow from something else: a clear awareness of the learner as an individual, with whom the writer is communicating.

This awareness does not come easily. We identify writing too readily with communication, when it seems to me, at least, to be better characterized as self-clarification. As I write this paper I am only vaguely aware of you, the reader; and I can excuse myself by saying that I am not writing an open learning text. My main preoccupation is with clarifying and structuring my own insights into the subject matter: training authors of open learning materials. But this approach simply will not do when writing for open learners. Subject-centred writing tends not to be sensitive to the open learner's needs for directness, warmth, enthusiasm, inventiveness, question-raising, sympathy, all of which arise from the context in which the learner is placed.

I would therefore strongly argue for a workshop programme that begins with an activity in which authors draw out profiles of their 'target' learners (see Figure 1).

The results of this profile have a dual function. Within the workshop they form the basis from which all the other components of author training can be derived. Consideration of the learner's context makes clear the need – or lack of it – for self-assessment, objectives, activities and a distinctive writing style, and ensures that these components are used to answer real needs rather than as a standard recipe for 'correct' open learning practice. (Subject-centredness can invade writing for open learners by the back door, in the ill-considered use of accepted interactive aids.) Beyond the workshop, as writing begins, the profile reminds authors that they are writing *for someone* and acts as a further check against retreat into a subject-centred style. In this connection I have often added the advice that authors should write as if they are preparing an audio tape script or writing a letter to the learner. Significantly, in both of these cases the emphasis is on communication; neither medium is likely to encourage the detached self-clarification of conventional textbook writing.

What I have said in this section, which is the core of my paper, is not offered as a startling new insight. It is, however, offered as a solution to the greatest obstacle to the successful training of authors of open learning material: a lack of awareness of the learner. Once the penny has dropped, once this awareness has been raised, the techniques of preparing interactive components can be mastered more readily. Without such awareness authors lapse into the formal, detached teaching style that has been instilled through school and college essay writing and which still bedevils so many conventional textbooks.

YOUR TYPICAL OPEN LEARNER

- How old are they?
- How long is it since they left school/college/formal training?
- What qualifications did they have when they left?
- What was their attitude to school/college?
- What is their main reason for studying?
- What assumptions could you make about the attitudes of
  - family/friends
  - employers
  - learner
  to the course of study?
- How many books do they read annually
  - because they have to?
  - for pleasure?

Figure 1. *Profiles of 'target' learners*

Towards a Complete Training Programme

I said above that there is, nonetheless, something to be said for criticisms of the workshop approach. This 'something' is most substantial when the criticism is levelled at workshops as an *exclusive* form of training. First of all, the author of open learning materials has only limited time at his or her disposal. For many people a day away from the training centre or classroom is difficult and costly to arrange. The workshops should, therefore, be used to provide for the sort of training for writers for which it is uniquely adapted – primarily participative training in writing skills. Yet there is, inevitably, a need to inform as well as simply to train. Certain basic facts can only be evinced in a participative workshop in the most roundabout way, and this can be a frustrating experience for authors, conscious of the steady accumulation of work in their vacated offices and classrooms. The 'basic facts' seem to me to fall into three categories, each of which suggests its own mode of training.

First, facts about the open learning phenomenon. For a long time I began workshops with a session entitled 'What is open learning?'. It worked as a warming-up activity; authors might be encouraged to write down their own views on index cards and then compare and contrast them in a session similar to a Brains Trust. But, as this paper has emphasized, the point of departure for a workshop is consideration of the learner. Explanation of the nature of open learning and a general context of current developments can best be confined to pre-workshop briefing materials. The workshop leader can then concentrate, if he or she wishes, on matters arising at the start of the workshop or during the first coffee break.

Second, factual data in the form of examples of open learning materials. Again, my practice used to be to hand round copious quantities of xeroxed open learning materials during workshops. Introducing self-assessment questions, I would saturate authors with page after page of exemplars. Few participants had the chance to fully assimilate and ask questions about these; an opportunity to examine them before the workshop would be of value. Better still, since such an examination out of context might allow misconceptions to develop unchecked, a very limited range of examples distributed on the spot might be combined with a follow-up package, distributed to authors at the end of the workshop.

Third, facts about the author's own open learning package. What I am suggesting here only works adequately where the workshop is held in the context of a specific project. The workshop itself may or may not be used to evince these facts; much depends on the organization of the overall open learning project, the experience and responsibilities of the authors and – as I remarked earlier – the inevitably limited time available. Whatever approach is taken it seems to me essential that as they write, authors have access to a document that sets out clearly the structure of their materials, and that the workshop leader stresses the usefulness and importance of this document. This is especially vital in multi-author projects where consistency between individual authors is essential in order to make the package as transparent as possible to learners. The precise form of the briefing document can vary from project to project, but should ideally detail:

- target frequency of interactive components
- structure of the units and sub-units of the course
- target word lengths for these units
- terminology – including use of unit labels such as module, unit, section, terms for interactive components such as SAQ, activity, self-test and review
- the approximate relationship between word length and projected duration of study.

Figure 2 shows a briefing document that I have used with some success on a recent NEC project run for the Pharmaceutical Society of Great Britain. The use of such 'archaeological layers' is of course one of many approaches, and I offer it here as a stimulus to further invention.

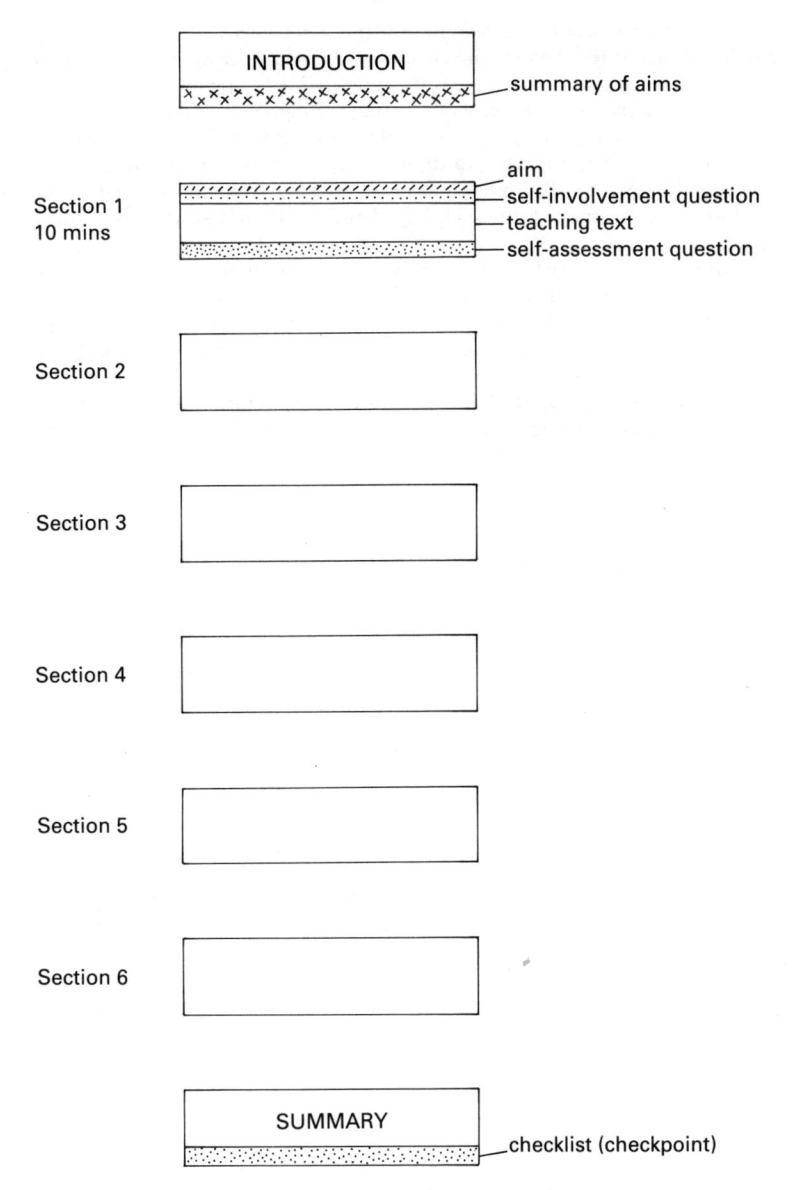

```
                    ┌─────────────────────┐
                    │    INTRODUCTION     │
                    ├─────────────────────┤──summary of aims
                    │xxxxxxxxxxxxxxxxxxxxx│

                                             ── aim
                    ┌─────────────────────┐
    Section 1       ├─────────────────────┤── self-involvement question
    10 mins         │                     │── teaching text
                    ├─────────────────────┤── self-assessment question
                    │:::::::::::::::::::::│

    Section 2       ┌─────────────────────┐
                    │                     │
                    └─────────────────────┘

    Section 3       ┌─────────────────────┐
                    │                     │
                    └─────────────────────┘

    Section 4       ┌─────────────────────┐
                    │                     │
                    └─────────────────────┘

    Section 5       ┌─────────────────────┐
                    │                     │
                    └─────────────────────┘

    Section 6       ┌─────────────────────┐
                    │                     │
                    └─────────────────────┘

                    ┌─────────────────────┐
                    │       SUMMARY       │
                    ├─────────────────────┤── checklist (checkpoint)
                    │:::::::::::::::::::::│
```

N.B. This plan allows for the amalgamation of sections where necessary

Figure 2. *Unit plan (one hour's learning time)*

I would also suggest, to accompany this document, a contact sheet of authors' and project officers' names, addresses and telephone numbers. I am aware that this may appear obvious, but it needs to be said. It is difficult to maintain cohesion in a multi-author project and nothing that can aid this should be ignored.

I have suggested that workshops must usually be complemented by other 'distant' forms of training because of time constraints, and have suggested three sorts of basic fact that might be conveyed by other means. I also feel strongly that, though the participative nature of workshops is ideal for training in writing skills, there is a further form of participation that is especially appropriate to open learning authors. This is, simply, participative experience of working through well constructed open learning materials. I have rejected this as an exclusive approach. As a complementary one it has two strengths. First, it can give authors direct experience of the model towards which they should aim – for example, in forms of interactivity and informality. Second, it reinforces the message of the workshop that the author's awareness of the learner's context is paramount. By working through an open learning package on open learning the author is placed fairly and squarely in the position of a learner and can experience at first hand some of the problems learners encounter. Of course, this experience is inevitably qualified and equivocal, but it still argues strongly for a package – particularly a pre-workshop package – aimed at introducing authors to open learning itself. Notable in this area has been the material generated by Celia Hall for the Open Tech project run by Capel Manor Institute of Horticulture: there is a continuing need for other, similar, packages that take equally seriously the training needs of authors.

1.6 MARIS-NET: The Development of an Online Information Service for Open Learning

M Dunnett and K Fraser
Scottish Council for Educational Technology (SCET), Glasgow

Abstract: In the development and operation of any flexible learning system, there is a continuing need for information concerning materials and resources. MARIS (Material and Resources Information Service) was set up under the UK Manpower Services Commission Open Tech programme to provide a comprehensive information service to open learning practitioners in industry and education throughout the United Kingdom.

The paper describes the development of the service from the early days as an offline service run on microcomputers to the present online interactive viewdata 'gateway'-type service.

Various aspects of the service are highlighted:

- experience of running a micro-based information service
- the development and integration of an online thesaurus
- the integration of viewdata and a database management system
- questions of quality and evaluation
- use of electronic mail as a tool to encourage networking of problems and experiences.

Introduction

MARIS (The Materials and Resources Information Service) was set up by the Open Tech Unit of the Manpower Services Commission to provide open learning practitioners with a source of information on learning materials. The service was originally operated as an offline, mediated service run on microcomputers, but as the database expanded, the requirements of the service outgrew the existing micros and an online minicomputer-based system was installed. This paper describes the development of the system and some of the problems and issues that were encountered on the way.

The Micro-Based System

The original contract for MARIS was awarded to the National Extension College in March 1983 with a contract to provide the service in Scotland being awarded to the Scottish Council for Educational Technology (SCET) the following December.

After analysis and investigation, a record format was agreed which described each piece of open learning material in terms of its content, subject area, skills to be developed, open learning features (self-assessment questions (SAQs), objectives etc), qualification to be gained (if any), a description of the actual materials, target group and contact details.

In view of the large amount of information to be stored for each record, some coding of the data would be necessary. A database management system which would allow this would be required. Our computer dealers, Professional Computer Services of Oldham, identified a product called RESCUE which would allow the coding to take place.

RESCUE uses a series of dictionaries to allow large amounts of data to be stored efficiently. For example, in the MARIS database the subject information was stored as a 3 digit number. When retrieving the record from the database, RESCUE automatically extracted the subject description associated with the number from the dictionary and displayed or printed it. This technique allowed us to keep the stored data below the maximum allowed record length of 1024 characters while displaying and printing over 3000 characters.

RESCUE also allowed us to create a number of report formats, enabling us to tailor the information sent out to suit the needs of the enquirer.

Although we were reasonably satisfied with the facilities that RESCUE offered, we began to become aware of problems as the database expanded and demand for the service grew.

As the number of records stored grew we found that search times lengthened, even on the faster dictionary field searches. This was compounded by the fact that some searches had to be refined due to the imprecise language used by our enquirers. The size of the database also forced us to split the database between two hard disk units. RESCUE was not able to link the two parts of the database, and so in effect each search had to be run twice.

In an effort to overcome some of these problems a new suite of programs to manage and search the database were written. These programs made use of some specialized hardware, including a 500k RAM disk which enabled us to hold indices to the data in memory and thus allowing faster searching. The new software also allowed us to move up to a multi-user operating system so that up to three terminals could access the database concurrently.

These developments increased the speed of searching considerably on the indexed fields, but free text searching was still painfully slow.

The development of the MARIS thesaurus was beginning to help with the specification of searches and with the classification of the information, but we were still unable to offer what the users really wanted – direct online access to the database.

The Mini-Based System

It was not until the beginning of 1985 that funds became available through Open Tech to enable us to move the database from our ICL micros to a larger system. A team of consultants from Wootton Jeffreys PLC of Manchester were appointed to carry out a study of the computing needs of MARIS and recommend a system which would fulfil those needs. After consulting with both arms of MARIS and with some of our major users they proposed the following system:

> a PRIME 9650 minicomputer with 2Mb RAM and 300 Mb disk storage;
> INFORMATION – a PRIME database management system;
> VIEWBASE – viewdata system which would provide access to the information for online users, including ENVOY – an electronic mail system;
> Multistream VPAD – part of a British Telecom PSS network providing local call access for the majority of users.

The computer was to be sited in Cambridge at the offices of the National Extension College, with access for the Scottish operation via a multiplexed leased line.

The proposal was accepted and the work to implement the system began. Wooton Jeffreys had three main tasks:

1. to build a suite of programs allowing the database and the various indices to be updated easily;
2. to build a viewdata system which would allow online users to search the database efficiently and easily;
3. to integrate the thesaurus with the main database and provide a management system for the thesaurus to allow updating to take place.

It is important to realize that we are using viewdata as a means of communicating information and not as a storage medium. The programs which allow the database to be searched extract the information from the database and format it to suit the viewdata pages. The viewdata pages are being used as a template to hold changing information.

The system was developed during 1985, with the thesaurus being installed in the database in February 1986. In parallel with the development of the materials database we have been developing other services on the system, including a database holding details of organizations and services useful to trainers, eg conference centres, media production facilities, etc. We also have a database called Window-Box which holds general news and information, adverts and our Noticeboard for general messages and queries.

With the development of any system of this size there are bound to be problems. Our main problems were concerned with the Multistream PSS service and with the standardization of the data.

Multistream is a fairly new development from British Telecom. The original equipment installed at the various access nodes would not allow some viewdata terminals to connect to the network. This meant that some users who were already using their equipment to access other viewdata services such as PRESTEL found that they could not access MARIS-NET. British Telecom have carried out an equipment replacement programme now nearly complete, which will eliminate that particular problem. The software which actually runs the Multistream network has had some problems resulting in users being disconnected from the system for no apparent reason. Again, British Telecom have undertaken a programme of software replacement which is gradually eliminating this problem.

Running an online service has forced us to be a lot more rigorous in our validation and standardization procedures for inputting and updating the data held. A lot of hard work had to be done to make sure that the data was in the format expected by the programs. Our micro-based system was less rigorous in this area and allowed data to be entered which did not exactly conform to the prescribed format. Again, the thesaurus has imposed a standardization of vocabulary and terms which was not available on the micro system.

The thesaurus has been under development since 1984 and has now become an integral part of the system.

Development and Integration of an Online Thesaurus

At the beginning of 1985 it was decided that the then MARIS database should be transferred onto a minicomputer so that an online service could be provided and so that the speed and efficiency of searching could be improved.

This move away from mediated searching highlighted a problem which had been obvious from the earliest days of MARIS – that of ensuring a consistent method of indexing and retrieving packages.

Our first attempts to solve this problem had been to produce a printed thesaurus of terms – the MARIS thesaurus, first published in May 1984. Comprising some 4,000 terms (2,500 indexing terms and 1,500 entry non-preferred terms) the thesaurus had been constructed using terms which providers of information and users of the database had used. Some of these terms were synonyms used almost interchangeably and once the most commonly used term had been chosen as the indexing term, the rest became entry vocabulary terms.

When the design of the new system was being discussed, it was decided that the thesaurus should become an integral part of the materials database and that all searches should be conducted through it.

The transfer of the thesaurus file onto the minicomputer gave us the opportunity to correct various inconsistencies in the data which had been an inevitable result of building a thesaurus manually. With the help of error checking, delete, input and amend programs developed by our computer consultants, Wootton Jeffreys, the data file was gradually corrected to its current state. These new programs enable the thesaurus to be speedily updated and amended.

Once the data file was correct we were then faced with two problems:

1. the need to reclassify 7,000 records
2. how the thesaurus should be presented to the user.

The first of these problems, although time-consuming, was soon overcome and bit by bit the new classification terms were assigned and input. This then left the presentation of the thesaurus.

The presentation of the thesaurus was solved mainly by Wootton Jeffreys, who decided that the viewdata presentation medium should be exploited to its full. What this meant in essence, was careful colour coding of the information. Combinations of blue, white, magenta and cyan have been used to differentiate between the subject, broader term (BT), narrower term (NT) and related term (RT). Thus the user's chosen subject always appears in white bordered by magenta at the top of the page, BT appear as blue on white, NT as white on blue and RT as blue on cyan. If there are too many BTs, NTs and RTs to fit in one page, then categories are given in the same colour banding with an indication of the number of *terms* pertaining to each. Beside each term (except BT) the number of packages linked to the term are given from any point in the thesaurus. Users may key # and will be taken to the HELP page which reminds them of the significance of the colour bands and the numbers. Movement up and down the trees is thus unlimited until such time as users opt to use a subject.

There are also built-in aids for users who key both non-indexing terms or terms which the thesaurus does not recognize. In the first instance, the user is informed by means of a screen that he has chosen a non-indexing term and what the indexing term is. He can then continue his search. In the second instance he is given the option to perform either a keyword or 'sounds-like' search which will present him with possible terms to try.

The thesaurus has been installed on the MARIS system since the end of February 1986 and already it seems to be doing what was intended, ie allowing users to find the precise information they are looking for. Its development is, however, continuing with new terms being added as and when necessary.

Quality

A question which MARIS is continually being asked to address is the question of quality; quality not only of the information we provide, but also of the materials themselves.

MARIS is obviously accountable for the quality of information with which users are provided. Every effort is made to ensure that all information about materials is as up to date and accurate as possible.

While we are prepared to vouch for the quality of the information we provide about materials, we have always been unwilling to commit ourselves to providing information about the quality of materials themselves. This is because of the difficulties involved in doing this satisfactorily. MARIS would have to be able to rate the technical, open learning and presentational quality of all items *and* also say how effective the packages are.

In most cases, MARIS staff are in no position to judge the technical and open learning quality of the packages accurately. This requires experts in their fields. The task of organizing a panel of such experts is immense and at present looks unlikely to be undertaken.

Presentational quality is potentially much easier to rate, although to some extent presentation is a matter of personal preference and in many cases reflects the budget available. In any case, while presentation may encourage users to buy a package, the effectiveness of the package must still be the chief consideration for any serious user. The effectiveness, good or bad, of any given package depends on the way in which it is used and the kind of support provided for the user.

For these reasons, MARIS is unwilling to provide a quality rating for materials listed on the database. We are, however, doing two things which we hope may help our users in their search for effective training packages.

Firstly, we have set up a resource bank of materials which users may come and examine and judge for themselves. This is being gradually built up with various samples of material.

Secondly, we are asking trainers who have used packages to indicate their willingness to discuss their views of packages they have used with other potential users. We will then keep their names on file and release them to any one who requires such information.

We hope that by providing these two services, users will be able to find a package which is suitable for their training needs and environment.

Use of Electronic Mail

One of the primary aims of Open Tech in setting up the MARIS-NET system was to provide a framework which would allow the sharing of information, news and problems among open learning practitioners.

ENVOY, our electronic mail system, has allowed our users to pass messages between individuals, organizations or groups of users. ENVOY has proved particularly useful to delivery systems where one main centre may have several satellite access points located in the area. ENVOY has enabled information to be passed between the headquarters and the satellites easily and efficiently.

We have also set up a noticeboard on the system which allows users to post a message for general consumption: asking for help with a particular problem or passing on a news item which would be of general interest, for example. Replies or comments can be posted on the noticeboard or sent to the individual privately by means of ENVOY.

Conclusions

Over the past two years we have watched MARIS develop from the offline system run on micros to a major nationwide online network system. We would hope that others might learn from our experiences. To anyone setting up a computerized information system we would offer the following thoughts:

1. Make sure your computing resources are adequate to meet your immediate and future needs.
2. Make sure you have some form of standardized classification and retrieval scheme with full data validation procedures in place.
3. Support your users as fully as possible. Encourage communication between the users and the operating centre.
4. Do not underestimate the amount of work needed to make a system friendly and easy to use.

1.7 OTTSU – The Development of a National Open Learning Consultancy Service 1983-86

J Coffey and J Simms
Open Tech Training Support Unit (OTTSU)

Abstract: OTTSU (Open Tech Training Support Unit) was an Open Tech Support Project specializing in the planning, development and implementation of open learning systems. It was funded by the Manpower Services Commission (MSC) for three years from April 1983 until the end of March 1986, receiving £270,000 in funding over that period. The project has now come to an end but a new company, OTTSU Ltd, has been formed by some of the consultants involved in the project and other staff concerned with its administration to carry on the work on a fully commercial basis. This paper traces the roots of the project in the Council for Education Technology (CET) Open Learning Programme, describes the services which OTTSU provided, describes the formation and training of the consultant base, reports on the achievements of OTTSU, and discusses issues concerned with management at a distance and the conflict between aiming at development work and aiming at a commercially viable business.

Origins of OTTSU

The CET Open Learning Programme, discussed fully at the Educational Technology International Conference in 1983 (Coffey, 1984) provided the background for the OTTSU development. The CET Open Learning Systems Programme had developed good working relationships with a wide range of individuals who had experience relevant to open learning. John Coffey in particular had worked closely with the Manpower Services Commission officers responsible for the development of Open Tech from 1980 onwards, providing advice on quality issues and on models for projects. A Quality Prompt List by John Coffey was in fact included in the Open Tech Task Group report in 1982 (Coffey, 1982).

Because CET had been so closely involved in working with others concerned with development of open learning systems, we knew that there was a great shortage of expertise available in the system which would be relevant to a novel programme such as the Open Tech. CET therefore held a seminar in January 1982 for 40 people who had been involved in various ways in the development of open learning systems in order to prepare for the expected needs of Open Tech projects when funding began in 1982. The introduction to the seminar programme spelt out the purpose quite clearly.

'The recent growth of open learning systems has made it clear that expertise in design of learning materials for use in open learning systems is in short supply.

The prospect of an 'Open Tech' programme without ready access to such expertise is worrying. It may be that a national register of consultants could be formed to overcome the problem. Before doing this there are many areas to be discussed concerning the contexts for consultancy work, skills for consultancy and how an informal register might be organized.

The Seminar has been structured to allow full discussion of these points. CET hope that positive proposals will emerge which can be acted on if and when an 'Open Tech' programme or other national open learning development programme begins.' (from the Seminar Programme, January 1982)

This was a most important event in the development of the thinking which underpinned the OTTSU operation. Later that year, and based on outcomes from the seminar, CET put forward a proposal to the Manpower Services Commission for an Open Tech Service Co-ordinating Agency. While this proposal was in fact turned down, it is important to note some of its features, because they had an effect on the development later of the OTTSU service. The introduction to the proposal, quoted in full below, sets out the argument.

'1. *Introduction*
  1.1 The 'Open Tech' programme has developed round the notions of problem-solving and collaboration. It is to be built on existing institutions and existing expertise. Nonetheless, its outputs are to be novel and will challenge many current habits of thought and associated working practices.
  1.2 OT development projects will be staffed largely by personnel familiar with conventional instructional systems. These personnel are unlikely to have any practical experience in the development and operation of open learning systems. Projects will vary greatly in the extent of their inexperience, but all are likely to need access to advice, consultancy, and training in some form. The OT task group recognized this in its concern for quality and staff development.
  1.3 While there are many who have expertise in one or more skills relevant to the development of OT offerings and the management of projects, there are probably few with expertise across the whole field. Such expertise as there is is located in a large number of institutions and individuals throughout the UK. The success of OT will depend to a considerable extent on identifying the sources of such expertise and deploying it at the right time.
  1.4 This paper proposes the establishment of an OT service co-ordinating agency (OTSCA) based on CET which will . . .
    (a) help project organizers identify their needs for advice, consultancy and training,
    (b) create links with institutions and individuals who have relevant expertise to offer,
    (c) deploy consultants and advisers as appropriate,
    (d) set up training arrangements for project personnel, consultants and advisers,
    (e) disseminate relevant independent and commissioned research findings,
    (f) report to OTU [Open Tech Unit] on a regular basis, submit a final report evaluating the work done, and make appropriate proposals for further work based on this evaluation.'

(from a proposal to MSC, 1982)

OTTSU Objectives

After discussion with Open Tech Unit (OTU) officers it was eventually agreed that CET should operate a more passive 'Open Tech Training Support Unit' to meet the following objectives . . .

'CET shall after consultation and in agreement with the Commission's Open Tech Unit establish appropriate organisational, managerial, administrative and financial arrangements to achieve the following objectives:
  i   assist Open Tech Unit staff in identifying needs for training and advice for Open Tech projects;
  ii   assist staff in Open Tech projects to plan and implement appropriate responses to such needs;
  iii provide workshops and consultancy for staff involved in Open Tech projects or Open Tech developments;
  iv   maintain and use a CET register of advisers and consultants with special expertise in the development and operation of open learning delivery systems, tutoring and counselling in open learning, and learning material design techniques to organize such workshops.'

(from the OTTSU contract, 1983)

It is important to emphasize that CET was asked to run the service in a passive manner, responding to requests which would emanate from the Open Tech Unit itself or from projects prodded by the Open Tech Unit to consult the service. No budget was set aside for marketing and the service was to be free, serving 12 to 20 projects in each year with workshops and consultancies.

The Development of a Service

It is not appropriate in a short paper of this kind to engage in very detailed analysis of the development of a service. However, four distinct phases can easily be identified, each with their attendant problems. These phases are:

(a) An initial scramble simultaneously to carry out work with projects, develop the service, find and appoint staff (April – October 1983): this period was complicated by the doubling of the Open Tech programme budget and consequent doubling in the potential number of projects OTTSU would have to service. Needless to say there was no corresponding doubling in OTTSU's budget!

(b) A very rapid growth in free services to projects developed from October 1983 to September 1984. Because of the massive increase in the numbers of projects OTTSU had to deal with, it soon became clear that there was insufficient money to provide a free service to all. However it was not until OTTSU ran out of money in September 1984 and started turning down projects that pleas to the MSC for some kind of reorganization were heard. It was agreed at that time that OTTSU would be able to begin charging for its services from the beginning of October 1984.

(c) The third phase started at the outset of this more commercial approach to provision of OTTSU services. Enabled to charge for services and accrue income, it became possible to consider prospects for continuation of the service beyond the formal end of the project in March 1986. The first work with projects outside the Open Tech ambit was undertaken during this period.

(d) From September 1985 until March 1986 there was a great deal of emphasis given to business planning and the transition from an Open Tech project to a fully commercial self-sustaining enterprise, OTSU Ltd, in April 1986.

The Services

It would have been possible to make OTTSU a very simple consultancy service concentrating entirely on providing training in learning materials design and tutorial support. However, the director of OTTSU had been closely involved in development of open learning systems since 1976 and saw many opportunities for other kinds of work. This, in a perhaps unfortunate throwback to the failed OTSCA proposal, encouraged him to provide a very wide range of services as well as providing opportunities for project managers to meet and discuss problems. Consultants were recruited to provide help in planning for open learning, specification and design of learning material, training of open learning tutors, marketing open learning, training in training needs analysis skills, business planning, costing and pricing, visual design techniques and many others.

The services were provided through individual consultancies, attachments of consultants to projects to help them through development periods, and 'tailor made' workshops. The process usually involved the following stages:

(a) an initial visit to discuss training needs with project staff and to devise jointly a programme to meet those needs;
(b) one or more workshops to train groups of staff in specific skills;
(c) consultancies to provide advice and guidance on specific aspects of a system. This occasionally involved some troubleshooting.

In addition to these 'tailor made' training programmes, OTTSU provided a number of other services. These included

(a) A series of 'open' workshops in conjunction with the Scottish Council for Educational Technology (SCET), the Materials Advice Resource Information Service (MARIS), the National Extension College (NEC), the Scottish Open Tech Training and Support Unit (SCOTTSU) and Marketing Solutions Ltd. The workshops were open in that they were not 'tailor made' and open to anyone who wanted to come along whether or not they were part of Open Tech.
(b) The seminars on specific topics were organized for project managers and others involved in projects. These gave project managers the opportunity to air many of the issues which they would not normally want to talk about to the Open Tech officers themselves.
(c) A set of *Project Development Papers* covering management of open learning, editing, commissioning video material, applications of technologies to open learning, development of delivery systems, marketing open learning, and making open learning responsive to learners, was also produced and made widely available. (OTTSU, 1984)
(d) A consultant referral service was developed from the register of consultants. A number of consultants obtained permanent jobs or other kinds of assignments through this service.

The Main Achievements

The measurable achievements are the numbers of consultancies and workshops carried out. Less tangible are quality issues: Figure 1 below gives a very clear indication of the amount of work covered.

It is worth noting the extraordinary variability in the number of workshops in different quarters of the project. These reached a peak of 61 workshops during January to March 1985. This was a period in which a large number of feasibility studies were conducted by the Open Tech into development of delivery systems. OTTSU provided

Quarter to	Workshops (1-4 Days)	Consultancies (Days)	Attachments (Days)
June 83	4	13	–
September 83	4	8	2
December 83	4	18	6
March 84	25	17	8
June 84	35	33	8
September 84	27	22	6
December 84	29	38	4
March 85	61	30	10
June 85	20	13	2
September 85	2	10	–
December 85	31	16	5
March 86	12	21	5
TOTAL:	254	239	56
OTTSU CONTRACT:	63	125	100

Figure 1. *OTTSU workload by quarter 1983 – 1986*

considerable training and other advice for these projects at that time. The following two quarters show significant drops in services. This was nothing to do with the quality of the services provided, but rather the cutback in funding available to projects because of a projected overspend on the Open Tech programme as a whole for the financial year 1985/86. This gave OTTSU an opportunity to initiate services to open learning activities outside the Open Tech, and develop its base for a commercial operation after March 1986. This variability made it extremely difficult to plan ahead and created periods of severe overwork for the administrative staff.

Quality of Service

The quality of service had been a concern from the outset. There was the problem of looking for high-quality consultants and monitoring their progress with individual projects. There was the problem of distinguishing between rave reports from one project and less complimentary reports from other projects after using the same consultant on similar kinds of assignments. There was the problem of trying to find ways of collecting information which could be useful in improving the service. After much thought we decided on the following:

(a) Consultants would write reports on all activities they undertook, whether they were for visits or workshops. Wherever possible these reports would also be made available to the projects concerned and opportunity would be provided for projects to give us independent feedback on their perceptions of what took place.

(b) For workshop activities an evaluation form would be used which would both measure participant satisfaction against a number of criteria and give participants an opportunity for free response.

(c) The Open Tech Unit staff themselves would be asked to fill in a questionnaire on their perceptions of the development of the service and wherever possible would be interviewed to develop the ideas expressed in the questionnaire form further.

(d) An independent evaluator would be appointed to review the data collected from these procedures and carry out further interviewing with clients to corroborate or refute the evidence gathered elsewhere.

(a) and (b) above were carried out throughout the whole three years of the project. (c) and (d) were concentrated on in the period September 1985 to March 1986. The evaluation (Dunn, 1986) pointed to a generally acceptable service. For example, Figure 2 below gives some indication of the views of participants on the value of workshops they attended. The figures are a compilation from data collected over three years.

Feedback from the Open Tech Unit too was, with one notable and inexplicable exception, generally complimentary about services that had been provided to projects.

	%	%	%	%	%	
Stimulating	48	42	7	3	0	Boring
Useless	2	4	13	35	46	Useful
Relevant	45	43	10	1	1	Irrelevant
Rigid	1	3	11	54	31	Flexible
Demanding	11	28	36	18	7	Undemanding
Coherent	35	42	18	4	1	Fragmented
Worth the time	57	26	11	6	0	Not worth the time

Figure 2. *Summary of feedback sheets from OTTSU workshops 1983–1986*

Where there were difficulties they tended to be over problems of information exchange and maintaining personal contacts, because of the very heavy workloads on the parts both of OTU and OTTSU staff.

However, the independent evaluator was also asked to look at specific projects in detail, and to examine in particular projects where there had been difficulties. This unearthed failings in the OTTSU operation (since rectified) which would be unacceptable in a fully commercial enterprise. For example, the follow-up by OTTSU after events or contacts was not good. This was shown with particular force by disparity of results between participant views expressed on feedback forms and the views of the project leader on the services which OTTSU had provided at the same two workshops. Figure 3 below is a summary of the responses given on feedback forms to OTTSU immediately after the events. The indication is general satisfaction.

Despite this general satisfaction, OTTSU did no further work with this client and, when questioned by the evaluator, the project leader reported that feedback to him from participants had indicated that they had had 'mainly bad' experiences at the two OTTSU events. The project leader went on to say that participants had reported finding OTTSU consultants naive, lacking in knowledge, poor presenters, and added that he would not use OTTSU again.

At least three issues emerged from this. Firstly, it points up the need to undertake careful follow-up of events and to monitor the expectations of all parties involved and the degree to which those expectations are met. Secondly, it shows with particular force the importance of identifying who the client is. For OTTSU this was always complex. The client could be the Open Tech Unit itself, the Open Tech project manager, the line manager of the Open Tech project manager, or the participants at workshops or other events. The needs of all groups could be quite different and meeting them simultaneously distinctly problematic. Thirdly, it points to a need to review regularly the feedback mechanisms which are employed to monitor quality of work and to evaluate their effectiveness.

It is important to emphasize, however, that the majority of OTTSU clients were happy with what they had received and came back for more. We are still left wondering why these rather odd disparities in perception occurred. It may perhaps be something to do with the need to find scapegoats when things are not going well. Certainly consultants recognize the 'scapegoat function' as an important benefit they can provide to their clients (as long as no one else hears about it, that is!).

	%	%	%	%	%	
Interesting	61	39	0	0	0	Boring
Useless	0	0	0	39	61	Useful
Relevant	78	22	0	0	0	Irrelevant
Too long	0	0	85	5	10	Too short
Inflexible	0	5	5	49	41	Flexible
Full	38	40	22	0	0	Empty
Easy	0	16	78	6	0	Difficult
Coherent	48	42	10	0	0	Incoherent
Unsatisfying	0	0	0	52	48	Satisfying
Well administered	58	42	0	0	0	Poorly administered
Confusing	0	0	15	32	53	Clear
Worth the time	74	22	4	0	0	Not worth the time

Figure 3. *Feedback from participants at two OTTSU workshops for one Open Tech project*

OTTSU consultants, in exactly the same way as other consultants, frequently found themselves in the midst of unresolved local difficulties which were nothing to do with the original assignment on which they had been sent. Some of these difficulties were political, such as power struggles within institutions. Some were problems of participant briefing, where the expectations of the manager of the project were quite different from those he or she had sent to attend workshops or other events.

However, we as project managers have to recognize that no one likes failure. It is far too easy to blame someone else for problems which have occurred and thus fail to see what can be learned from mistakes. Much more important is the point brought up by the independent evaluator.

'Whatever system of evaluation is used, data is its lifeblood and the manner in which information is maintained (eg recording all items on the customer file) and stored plays a crucial part in what information is available for decision making.'

Pressures of work and attempting to resolve problems wider than those included in our initial brief perhaps tempted us to pay too little attention to making intelligent use of the information which was readily available to us. One is tempted to say 'physician, heal thyself'.

The Consultants

During the course of the project OTTSU evolved a country-wide consultant network which in recent activities gained it considerable respect. The network comprised

(a) a team of nine lead consultants, who undertook initial contacts with clients and managed subsequent consultancy work with a client;
(b) 25 panel consultants, who became well known to the lead consultants and OTTSU administration. In addition to a very varied set of expertise and skills, they had essential consultancy abilities to deal with the difficult political and personal problems which emerge in all consultancy work;
(c) an informal register, which at one time contained 180 consultants with an extremely diverse range of skills. Clearly it was not possible for the administrative team to know all of these consultants well.

Creating and maintaining an informal register was one of the project objectives set at the outset. While an impressive list of individuals representing a very wide range of skills was put together on the register, it had a number of attendant problems which would have needed more resources to resolve. The principal problem lurking on all open registers is the dependence on secondhand information for quality assurance. If someone tells you that he or she is a good consultant and work records and references appear to back this up, there is very little more which can be done to check out quality. Where possible we attempted to use unknown consultants in controlled situations with other well-known consultants to test out their suitability for particular kinds of work. This became very difficult to do once the decision was taken to establish a commercial operation. The whole process would have been too experimental and too risky. Training could have contributed to a partial resolution of the problem, but OTTSU did not have the financial resources to provide free training to so many.

Since OTTSU's main task was to provide a good service to OTU and to Open Tech projects, the decision was taken to focus the main training effort on the lead and panel consultants who were providing the bulk of the service. The focus of training was on style and process rather than knowledge about open learning. It remains our belief that, while there are technical aspects of open learning development which are important background knowledge, the real problems are concerned with getting individuals to recognize the stage they are at in their process of development and obtaining agreement on realistic objectives for proceeding forward. The training provided for our consultants, therefore, promulgated beliefs and values intended to sustain a client-centred and open approach. The focus was on client needs, not just on expressed wishes. Consultants were encouraged to recognize their value to the client as outsiders. They were asked to recognize the tendency most of us have to resort to our expertise at times of stress, to learn to resist this, and to value more analytic approaches and process skills. Consultants were asked to avoid a 'solutions-looking-for-problems' approach, to be prepared to learn from clients, to give value for money, to stay flexible within their own range of styles, and to hold on to their own beliefs and values.

Issues

The project has been challenging and interesting. Because we believe it has been successful, we have been prepared to air some of the difficulties which the project faced and overcame. There are some final issues which we feel it is worth highlighting.

The project grew out of an innovative activity based in CET and the interest of the Council in open learning developments. As the need for commercial viability began to become pre-eminent, conflicts occurred between a desire to innovate and facing up to commercial considerations. In order to give OTSU Ltd a reasonable chance of survival, the commercial aspects had to take first place.

This conflict between commerce and innovation was sharply expressed in the OTU-OTTSU relationship. OTU certainly wanted a continuing innovative activity in the OTTSU project. This became increasingly difficult to give, and we question the wisdom of simultaneously trying to bring about a substantial national innovation in open learning and making self-sustainment a major objective for the constituent parts within such a short period as three years. This is not in any way intended to undermine the extraordinary achievements of the Open Tech programme in bringing about change in the education and training system, but to point out that the achievements might have been even greater without this particular constraint.

The question 'who is the client?' was a very important unresolved problem for OTTSU. The initial funding came from the Open Tech Unit and to that extent OTTSU had to treat OTU as a client. Later on, the projects were paying for aspects of the service and they too became clients. Within any one contract the client might be the individual learner, or might be a project manager or someone more senior. Sorting out the client relationship was not made any easier by the change in funding arrangements halfway through the project. The 'moving goalpost' syndrome which seems to attend some aspects of MSC work can be most damaging to quality.

In attempting to deal with projects it has to be recognized that OTTSU and other support agencies were almost always brought in too late to help projects. Everyone is an open learning 'expert' until they've tried. There also seems to be a feeling that to ask for help is a sign of weakness. This problem was evident from the outset of the programme and we wonder whether OTTSU might have had more effect if it had been given the freedom to be proactive in the early stages. OTSCA might have been better. We will never know.

References

Coffey, J (1982) A quality prompt-list for open tech projects. In *Open Tech Task Group Report: June 1982*. Manpower Services Commission, Sheffield.
Coffey, J (1984) The CET Open Learning Systems Programme: A contribution to career updating. In Shaw, K E (ed) *Aspects of Educational Technology XVII*. Kogan Page, London.
Dunn, W (1986) *An Evaluation of OTTSU's Customer Services*. (Unpublished).
Open Tech Training and Support Unit (1984) *Project Development Papers*. OTTSU.

1.8 Successful Development of Flexible Learning Systems – The Selection and Training of Personnel

C Stoane
Scottish Training and Support Unit (SCOTTSU), Dundee

Abstract: Flexible learning systems emphasize the needs and convenience of the learner. Their aim is to reduce or remove barriers which might prevent or hinder learners from having access to education and training.

The successful development of flexible learning involves the balancing of a number of factors which are largely within the control of the developers. Getting the right balance for particular circumstances depends on choosing the best of a series of options for each part of the system.

This paper considers the implications of a number of the factors which can affect the development of flexible learning. In particular, it looks at the personnel required to implement an effective flexible system, the roles they will adopt and the training that will be necessary to enable them to adapt to new roles.

Introduction

Education and training are going through a period of considerable change. In schools and colleges, in industry and commerce, there is a move away from traditional courses and teaching modes towards flexible programmes which allow open access to learning and training. Flexible or open learning enables education or training to be expanded beyond the confines of the traditional classroom and taken to the place most convenient to the learner or the employer, to be used when and how it is needed.

Effective continuing education and training is vital if the employees of today and tomorrow are to be kept up to date in order to compete in world markets; organizations must train and retrain their employees to keep them abreast of the latest technology.

Such an ongoing programme of training could be costly in terms of time and travel expenditure. But these training needs, generated by current changes, can, in many cases, be met effectively by open learning. Open learning widens access to training and makes possible learning systems which are more flexible and therefore accessible to users (Manpower Services Commission, 1985).

Implications of Flexible Learning

For many people traditional education or training is inconvenient or inappropriate because of barriers to access. Who are these people? They may be shift workers, employees who cannot be released from work, people housebound because of home commitments or disability, those unable, because of distance, to attend a course or those for whom a suitable course does not exist. An effective flexible learning system reduces or even removes the barriers which prevent the learner from obtaining training to suit his requirements. Figure 1 sets out the characteristics of learning schemes as continua, thus demonstrating on the left a totally closed, traditional system and on the right a totally open, flexible system.

No scheme would ever be totally open in every respect. Indeed it might he harmful if it was. Open access need only be provided where identified barriers prevent accessibility to the individual.

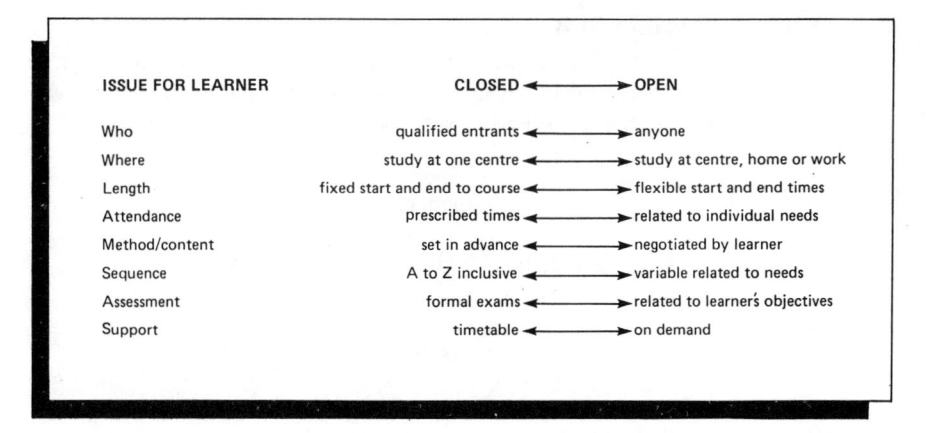

ISSUE FOR LEARNER	CLOSED ←――――→ OPEN
Who	qualified entrants ←――――→ anyone
Where	study at one centre ←――――→ study at centre, home or work
Length	fixed start and end to course ←――――→ flexible start and end times
Attendance	prescribed times ←――――→ related to individual needs
Method/content	set in advance ←――――→ negotiated by learner
Sequence	A to Z inclusive ←――――→ variable related to needs
Assessment	formal exams ←――――→ related to learner's objectives
Support	timetable ←――――→ on demand

Figure 1. *Dimensions of openness*

Flexible learning systems, however, by removing barriers to access in this way can in fact introduce other significant barriers for the learner. Isolation from tutors, teachers or trainers and from other learners, from a learning environment and the stimulation that all of these provide, can prevent learning from being effective. Anxiety about returning to formal study or taking it up for the first time can be a formidable barrier, particularly for mature learners. It is important that designers and those who implement flexible learning systems give consideration to such factors.

Need for Training

Flexible learning differs from other teaching modes in the elements and delivery of its systems (Davies, 1978, 1980). In the traditional setting the teacher or trainer is in control of the learning situation (Figure 2).

The teacher imparts knowledge to learners, usually at a predetermined time and place, and with most of the decisions about objectives, content and help being made by the teacher. Flexible learning systems, on the other hand, are learner-centred, or consumer-orientated (Twining, 1980) with the needs and convenience of learners determining the openness or accessibility of the system. The successful development of flexible learning involves the balancing of a number of factors within the control of the developers. One of these factors is the training of personnel for the new roles they will adopt.

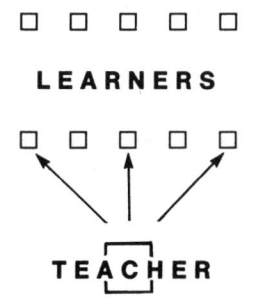

Figure 2. *Traditional teaching situation*

Roles Within Flexible Systems

In order to consider the new roles required to implement a flexible learning system, it is helpful to consider the elements which support learners within the system and which together provide the opportunity for flexible learning to take place (Figure 3).

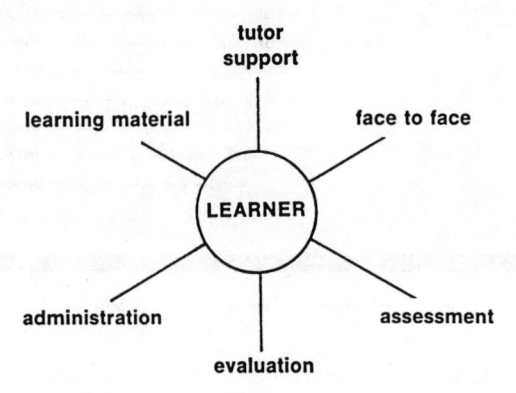

Figure 3. *Elements of the system*

Tutor Support

There is a very important role within flexible learning for tutors or trainers, and in some cases for coaches, mentors and proctors, but these are roles of guidance and support rather than imparters of knowledge. Learning materials provide the teaching element of the system.

Assessment

Without the regular contact of a tutor or trainer, materials must be designed so that learners can check their own progress and the tutor (trainer) can assess their progress. Using techniques of self-assessment questions (SAQs) with immediate feedback, and tutor-assessed assignments with formative feedback, the materials become interactive and the learning assessable.

Face-to-face Meetings

Some flexible learning systems will operate with no face-to-face meetings of tutors and students, students and fellows. Others will have meetings at times and places which are mutually convenient. Practical training and 'hands-on' experience of hardware often necessitate face-to-face meetings.

Evaluation

Any system must undergo evaluation to investigate its effectiveness, to develop and improve its implementation (Stoane, 1986). The evaluation of flexible learning is of vital importance because of its innovativeness, but because of its very flexibility it is perhaps more difficult to implement than traditional systems.

Administration

There is a much greater emphasis on the administration of flexible learning modes than of traditional systems. Distribution of materials, organization of tutorial support and maintenance of records must be efficiently organized if the system is to be effective.

Learning Materials

Structured packages, very different from textbooks, are used to enable learners to study at the time and place and often by the method which best suits them. Whether the choice of place is the learner's home or place of work, or by self study within the tutorial organization, the learner is frequently separate from the direct support of a tutor or trainer. Materials therefore must be helpful, supportive and motivational in their presentation.

In order to implement a successful flexible learning system, appropriate personnel will be required to carry out the roles involved in each of the elements of the system (Figure 4).

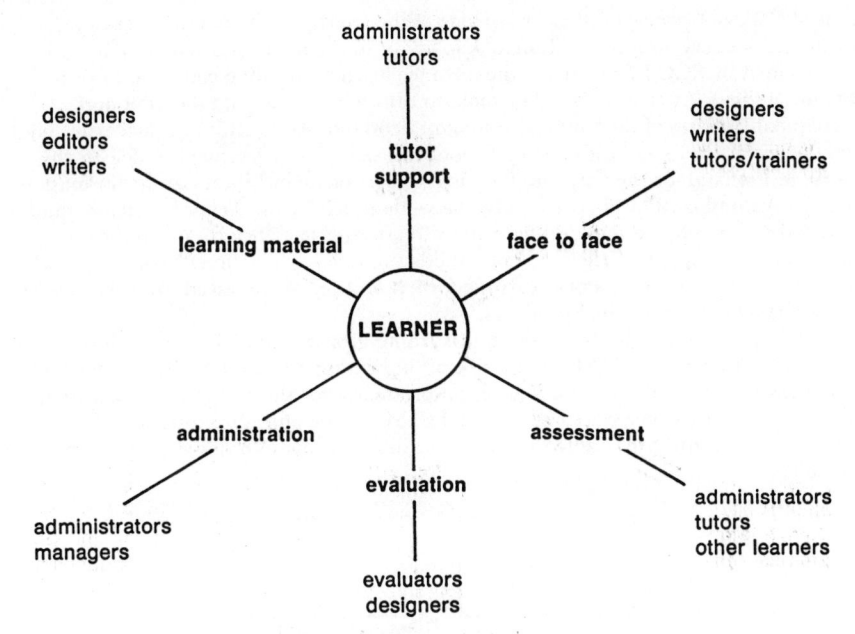

Figure 4. *Roles within the system*

Many of these personnel will directly perform the tasks associated with the role (eg tutors); others will be facilitators within the role (eg administrators).

Training and Support

Teachers and trainers accustomed to traditional modes of learning need to change their approach and attitudes in order to adapt to the roles required to implement flexible learning. The techniques necessary to implement successful systems could however be within the armoury of every teacher or trainer, given appropriate training (Twining, 1982).

The Scottish Training and Support Unit (SCOTTSU) has been set up by the Manpower Services Commission (MSC) under the Open Tech Programme, to train those involved in or about to become involved in flexible learning. Training is provided in the techniques required to develop the elements of flexible learning into an effective system successfully.

SCOTTSU Training Programmes themselves use flexible learning techniques, including a range of courses offered by distance learning. The following case studies illustrate some of the programmes in action.

Case Study 1: Training in Tutoring

Telford College in Edinburgh offers the SCOTVEC Certificate in Library and Information Science by distance learning. SCOTTSU has had a long-term training consultancy with this project. The course is open to all library assistants throughout Scotland; many enrol from the highlands and islands, often from geographically isolated locations. Materials sent to students are all print-based and the course contains a strong tutorial element, with two-way communication by telephone and letter between students and tutors. Initially potential tutors were identified from within Telford College because of their knowledge of the course, their commitment to the method of delivery and their willingness to adapt to the mode of delivery. These tutors were trained by SCOTTSU, using the distance learning training course in tutoring (Stoane, 1986a). After training, they took up tutoring roles during the pilot and subsequent running of the course throughout Scotland. As a result of a successful pilot and further marketing of the course, Telford has signed an agreement to deliver the course in England for the City and Guilds 737 Certificate in Library and Information Science. A number of local centres have been identified by the Telford manager, and potential tutors selected for training using similar criteria as before. A significant difference however is that the City and Guilds tutors have less direct knowledge and experience of the course in open learning format and are far removed from the delivery and management centre in Edinburgh.

Two important standards are set in this training programme. Firstly, trainee tutors must complete the SCOTTSU course of training within a fixed time, before the first intake of students, and secondly their appropriateness for the role as tutors is carefully monitored. Topics covered within the SCOTTSU course introduce tutors to the requirements of tutoring (Figure 5) within flexible learning in order to prepare them for this role.

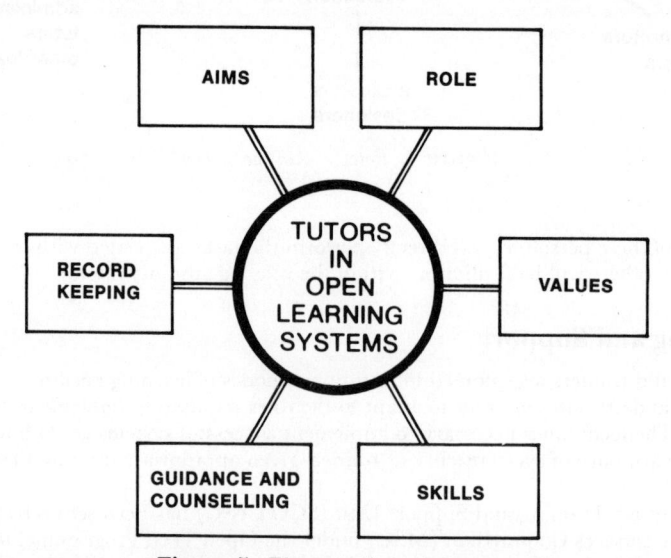

Figure 5. *Elements of tutoring course*

In this training programme with Telford particular emphasis has been placed on telephone tutoring, both for training and for use when trainees tutor in their own right. Because of the scattered student population this method of communication will be used frequently. This is supported by the fact that the telephone is a medium preferred and used with ease by most library staff.

Case Study 2: Training in Writing

The SCOTVEC course on open learning for small businesses in the tourist industry has worked with SCOTTSU from its early stages. At an initial workshop, writers identified for training were introduced to SCOTTSU tutors. Writers had been selected because of experience in teaching the subject face-to-face, interest in developing a more flexible approach and willingness to learn new techniques. Writing teams were set up, consisting of an editor and a group of writers for each topic area. A housestyle was established. The writers were trained at a distance in the techniques required to produce well-structured and interactive material. The structure of the SCOTTSU training course (Stoane and Stoane, 1986) is such that writers produce and send a first draft of material to their tutors for initial editing and assessment. Subsequent drafts are produced and assessed as necessary before the material is piloted (Figure 6).

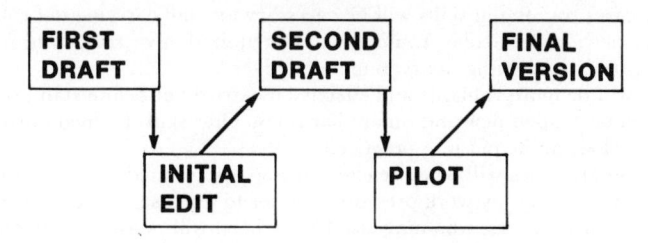

Figure 6. *Stages of production of learning material*

After piloting and revision, the materials were launched and met with a favourable response from clients both within and beyond the tourist trade.

Case Study 3: Evaluation Consultancy

A feature of the SCOTVEC course is its modular approach. Over 60 short units have been designed so that students can select the required number of units for their needs and study these in the sequence which suits them best. However identification of training needs in order to select appropriate units could present a problem. The project commissioned the design of a diagnostic tool or study selector (Shatz, 1985). During the first pilot of the study selector, SCOTTSU carried out a consultancy to evaluate its effectiveness. The work was carried out by telephone interviewing whilst the selector was in use by clients. Results of the detailed feedback collected during the interviews led to a major revision of the selector. Effectiveness of the revised form will again be evaluated by telephone interviewing. This technique is cost-effective, reasonably easy to conduct and enables useful data to be collected.

Case Study 4: Training in Administration

The role of the administrator is an important one within the delivery of open learning. The administrator is often the first line of contact for students and has therefore to be familiar not only with courses and materials on offer, but also with how the system operates.

TAYTEC Limited has, as a major delivery project for open learning, support centres in Tayside's three further education colleges. Tutors in each of the colleges provide support to students on TAYTEC courses. SCOTTSU ran a training workshop for the administrators appointed to the colleges and TAYTEC headquarters administrators. At the workshop, organized before the college administrators commenced in post, the roles and tasks they would perform were explored. At all stages of an open learning course, from pre-entry to post-course, an administrator can offer either direct support to a learner or can facilitate others, such as tutors or trainers, in supporting the learner (Stoane, 1985, 1986b).

Criteria for Effective Development

It can be seen that within each of the elements of a flexible learning system there are a number of key roles, and personnel appointed to carry out these roles will require a number of skills and attitudes if the system is to develop effectively.

Results of training programmes such as those described have made possible the listing of criteria for successful development of flexible learning.

Training

1. In many cases training in skills will be necessary for staff carrying out roles which are new. In particular, training will be required in writing, tutoring, administration, evaluating, marketing and delivery.
2. Training will be more valuable and effective if carried out before staff take up posts or embark upon new and unfamiliar roles. Thus skills learned during the training period can be put into practice.
3. Training programmes will be more effective and appreciated by staff if they are released from day-to-day work pressure in order to practise the skills. For example, trainee writers, who may also be teachers, will produce more efficiently if given time off work to do so.

Suitability of Personnel

1. Training and ultimate implementation of flexible learning systems will be more successful if the following criteria for staff selection are used. Staff should have
   ☐ knowledge of the flexible learning course or courses in which they will operate;
   ☐ commitment to flexible learning;
   ☐ willingness to adapt to new techniques.
2. It is helpful if the personnel selected have knowledge of the principles of flexible learning. If not, an induction period covering *Learning about Open Learning* (Marshall, 1985) could be useful.
3. For many of the roles previous teaching or training experience is not essential. Indeed, in many institutions engaging in production of learning materials there will be a need for a range of non-teaching staff, including editors, graphic designers and technicians. These staff should have 'appropriate qualifications and . . . relevant experience in either the public or the private sector'. (FEU/MSC, 1986).
4. Monitoring during training and implementation is essential for effective development.

Types of Training

1. Short relevant courses are what is required by clients engaged in busy working lives.
2. Training by open learning techniques is particularly favoured by clients. In this

way those who are training in the techniques required for flexible learning can not only train as and when convenient but also can experience this type of learning at first hand.
3. If training is by open learning, it is helpful if where possible an element of workshop or face-to-face approach can be built in.

Conclusion and Recommendations

There is little doubt that if we are to compete in future industrial markets there must be increased emphasis on, and new approaches to, education and training. Clearly, one way in which education and training can be made more widely available is by flexible or open learning. The use of open learning entails a change in the role of both management and the staff employed. The part played by non-teaching staff takes on an added significance. Such changes require training in the additional skills required for development work. The successful implementation of flexible or open learning schemes on any significant scale requires 'that institutions (companies and organizations) formulate staff development policies . . . for both tutorial and other staff . . . and that these policies be accorded priority.' (FEU/MSC, 1986)

Acknowledgements

The author is grateful to the following for permission to use case study material for this paper: Sheila McCullough, Manager of Telford Open Tech Project in Library Science; Aileen Pilidas, Administrator of SCOTVEC Open Learning Project for Small Businesses; Rick Crawley, Executive Director of TAYTEC Limited.

References

Davies, W J K (1978) *Implementing Individualised Learning: CET Guidelines 4*. Council for Educational Technology, London.
Davies, W J K (1980) *Alternatives to Class Teaching in Schools and Colleges: CET Guidelines 9*. Council for Educational Technology, London.
FEU/MSC (1986) *Implementing Open Learning in Local Authority Institutions: A Guide for Institution Managers and Local Authority Officers*. Further Education Unit and the Open Tech Unit of the Manpower Services Commission, Sheffield.
Marshall, I (1985) *Learning About Open Learning: A Self Study Course*. SCOTTSU, Dundee.
Manpower Services Commission (MSC) (1985) *Open Learning: It Gets Results*. Manpower Services Commission, Sheffield.
Shatz, H (1985) *Study Selector*. SCOTVEC Open Learning, Glasgow.
Stoane, C (1985) Study skills for home learners. *Programmed Learning and Educational Technology*, 22, p 347.
Stoane, C (1986a) *Training Course in Tutoring Open Learning Schemes*. SCOTTSU, Dundee.
Stoane, C (1986b) *Making Open Learning Work. A Guide for Administrators*. Council for Educational Technology, London (in press).
Stoane, C and Stoane, J (1986) *Training Course in Writing Open Learning Material*. SCOTTSU, Dundee.
Stoane, J (1986) *Training Course in Evaluating Open Learning Schemes*. SCOTTSU, Dundee.
Twining, J (1980) Factors influencing demand. *Coombe Lodge Report*, **13**, 6.
Twining, J (ed) (1982) *Open Learning for Technicians*. Stanley Thornes, Cheltenham.

1.9 Tutoring in Flexible Learning Systems (Workshop Report)

C Stoane
Scottish Training and Support Unit (SCOTTSU), Dundee

The workshop followed on from the previous paper 'Successful Development of Flexible Learning Systems – The Selection and Training of Personnel' and looked at tutoring, one of the elements of flexible learning system identified in the paper.

The workshop aimed to:

- identify the key aspects of the role of tutoring within flexible systems, and
- provide activities which would enable delegates to consider some of the techniques required to carry out such a role and to practise some of the necessary skills.

In a brief introductory presentation comparison was made between a conventional student and an open (flexible) learner, and the roles that teachers/tutors would carry out in each case. It became clear that in flexible learning there would be a shift from the role of imparter of knowledge, able to gauge the needs of learners and respond immediately, to one of support and guidance for learners much more in control of their own learning and requiring response tutoring to meet their needs.

In syndicate groups delegates explored potential problem areas which might be encountered in adapting to such a role. These were:

- building an appropriate and working relationship with each individual
- communication
- understanding learners and their problems
- avoiding delays in keeping contact
- assessment of learners' work
- record keeping.

The first three of these were developed in some detail, with activities to enable skills to be practised and discussed.

Building an Individual Relationship

An introductory letter sent to students by a tutor to welcome them to a distance learning course was the subject of debate. The letter demonstrated a number of pitfalls and was far from friendly. It enabled the groups to list criteria for tutors to use in making a first contact with students.

- Sound interested in students
- Do not sound threatening
- Do not overload students with information and demands
- Do not presume
- Be encouraging
- Be personal and friendly.

Communication

It is important that there should be a two-way communication: tutor to student and student to tutor, and indeed whenever possible student to student. Contact can be made in a number of ways including face-to-face encounters, by telephone, by writing and by use of audio cassettes.

A simulated telephone conversation between a tutor and a student was set up in order to demonstrate that certain subjects or concepts are difficult to put across by telephone because of the lack of visual contact. There are, however, ways to make a telephone session successful in spite of this lack, and some of these were explored.

- ☐ Arrange beforehand the questions to be discussed
- ☐ Send extra material in advance prepared for easy reference
- ☐ Structure discussion clearly
- ☐ Involve student actively.

Understanding Learners and their Problems

Counselling and guidance is an important part of a tutor's role in flexible learning. A tape recorded example of a conversation between a tutor and a student was played (George, 1985). In the example the student was indignantly complaining about an assessment of her work. Rather than a helpful and constructive conversation between the two, a fight ensued. Following the recording the group discussed how the situation could have been better handled with sensitivity, sympathy and understanding.

Reference

George, J (1985) *On The Line – A Telephone Tutoring Pack*. Open University Press, Milton Keynes.

1.10 Thinking: Can It Improve the Quality of Student Learning?

D Fordyce
Heriot-Watt University, Edinburgh

Abstract: The intellectual skills required to achieve meaningful learning have been defined as analytical thinking, imaginative thinking and purposeful reflection. This paper outlines the research work on meaningful learning which describes learning at two levels: macro-level, relating to an intent to learn, and micro-level, relating to a quality of learning outcome. The paper goes on to outline two approaches to teaching which address themselves to the intellectual skills inherent in meaningful learning, and from which an assessment can be made of the question in the title of this paper.

Background Statements

- This paper relates to a view of education which encourages *meaningful learning*. Meaningful learning relates to situations where there is active intercourse between the material a learner is working with and the cognitive structure of the learner.
- This paper discusses learning which is facilitated through structured learning experiences. To be effective, such experiences must take account of the fact that learners are individuals whose cognitive structures are unique. Cognitive structures are developed through experiences and the interpretation of these experiences.

Meaningful Learning

What do you do when you are reading an article such as this?
When a colleague was asked what he did, his response was,

'it depends on what (time) pressure I am under. When I am reading with a view to try to learn from the material, I need to create a (time) space to accommodate my style. My style is one of reading the material in blocks. The blocks may vary in length and relate to one idea or a group of associated ideas. My intention is to define my interpretation of those ideas based on my understanding, knowledge and experience. It may often happen that the terminology is specialized and idiosyncratic, consequently I may only have partial success in feeling confident about my interpretation. Once the blocks of an article have been explored, I then attempt to understand the article as an integrated piece of work, but now looking for the author's argument. This can often provide me with a new context from which to (re-)interpret my blocks. This process can often repeat itself, almost in a spiral, moving towards an understanding of the article but also a reshaping of my understanding of ideas contained within the article. I say a "moving towards an understanding" because often when returning to the article some time later different ideas can come to mind as a result of thinking over the article and possibly other reading.'

This long anecdote is provided to illustrate *one* style and approach to meaningful learning. 'To understand the psychology of religion observe the most religious man at his most religious moment' (Laurillard, 1979); by asking a university staff member involved in research how he tackled the reading of a research article, this would be most likely to bring out the main features inherent in someone trying to achieve meaningful learning.

The features inherent in meaningful learning which are documented in the research literature are:

1. Individuals hold concepts in some form of cognitive structure.
2. Cognitive structures are used to interpret events.
3. Cognitive structures may be reshaped as a result of interpretation of meaningful events.
4. Meaningful learning involves intellectual skills described by analytic and imaginative thinking.
5. Meaningful learning employs the powerful tool of retrospection.
6. Meaningful learning is time-dependent.

Research into the Nature of Learning

- The paradox about understanding the nature of learning is that the best way to learn about learning is to learn about learning.
- Donald Norman (Norman, 1978) described meaningful learning as 'complex learning'. The inclusiveness, generalizability and level of abstractness of the concepts we hold has been described by the phrase 'cognitive complexity' (Bieri et al, 1966). The key feature about the nature of learning *is* its complexity.
- Much of the literature relating to thinking and learning overlaps; this is shown clearly in Noel Entwistle's book (Entwistle, 1981) *Styles of Learning and Teaching*.

Learning can be perceived at two levels: a macro-level (broad canvas) and a micro-level (fine detail). Macro-level relates to intent (to learn), micro-level relates to qualities of learning outcomes.

The Broad Canvas: an Intent to Learn

Meaningful learning is only *one* outcome of a learning experience. For an undergraduate in a formal learning environment, where learning material is structured by a teacher, meaningful learning is the outcome of a deep approach taken with the provided learning material. The approach taken with learning material has been shown in several research programmes (Hodgson et al, 1980; Marton, 1982; Taylor 1980) to depend on learners':

- perception of relevance of material;
- conception of learning;
- orientation to studying; and
- the nature of assessment.

In short, a learner's approach depends on the learning context. Of the factors defined as influencing the level of approach adopted with learning material, the nature of assessment has been identified as having the greatest influence.

The level of approach taken with material has a direct bearing on how the structure of the material is coped with. This has, in turn, a direct bearing on the *quality* of a learning outcome.

A deep approach to learning material is an *intent*.

- it represents an *internalizing* of material;
- it relates to an *intrinsic* orientation to studying; and
- it is likely to result in the *vertical* structure of learning material being identified.

Such an approach consequently encourages the development of abstract and dynamic concepts and the reshaping of cognitive structures.

The Fine Detail: Learning Outcomes

Concepts held by groups of learners have been categorized into hierarchies (Gibbs, 1982; Gilbert, 1982), the categories being qualitatively different. In the sciences the different qualitative categories have been shown to be applicable over several continents (Champagne et al, 1983). Many basic concepts are formed in our early lives through our interpretation of our environment; they are often therefore associated with feelings. As many of these concepts are formed in unstructured learning experiences they are more likely to be what is described as 'naive'. But feelings form part of episodic memory and early memories form the bases of our cognitive structures, and naive early concepts are therefore deep rooted.

In terms of cognitive structure Figure 1 illustrates, for an area in engineering mechanics, the idealized nature of cognitive structure. Although it is shown there as a vertical linear system, it can be seen from the definition of the elements presented in Figure 2 that macroschema also become, or can also be described as, concepts. The ability of a learner to move from *fundamental* concepts to abstract ideas which form *higher level* concepts depends not only on 'intent', through deep processing (approach), but it also depends on the quality of the held and inherent concepts.

Much of the literature relating to categories of concept relates to what might be described as fundamental concepts. With the development of 'higher level' concepts processing may include backward development, deep processing involving:

- *analytic thinking*, defining what is not clearly differentiated in the existing cognitive structure;
- *imaginative thinking* from the new contextual situation, which can provide for 'intuitive leaps' as Bruner describes this process (Bruner, 1974); and
- *retrospection*, purposeful reflection on past and associative events (from episodic memory) and consequently other meanings (from semantic memory).

These three elements – analytic thinking, imaginative thinking and retrospection – make up the intellectual skills which are essential elements of deep processing and which Entwistle (Entwistle, 1981) suggests are likely to be lacking in many school pupils and are possibly in varying stages of development among students in further and higher education. Inference to such intellectual skills was also made by Osborne (Osborne, 1983) in relation to concept development – again an overlap with two sections of the literature.

So What Does This Say about Teaching Strategies?

Svensson (Svensson and Hogfors, 1984) has described teaching as being about

> 'the development of a way of thinking that is applicable to some class of phenomena. This way of thinking should be in some sense better than the thinking made possible by the preconcepts, ie be more efficient, have a greater productive power or encompass a larger part of reality.'

This statement again, albeit in different words, relates to the development of cognitive structures which in Ausubel's terms (Ausubel, 1978) are more 'inclusive, general and abstract' than they were prior to the learning experience.

> *But how do we ensure learners not only develop, but more importantly are capable of developing their thinking (about a particular class of phenomena)?*

There are two aspects here:

Concept	An abstract idea derived from or based upon a phenomenon or an assemblage of phenomena in the physical world.
Proposition	A rule, principle, or empirical law that asserts a generalization or relationship. A proposition may be an assertion about a certain phenomenon, or it may assert a specific relationship, between two or more concepts.
Microschemata	A mental structure that guides the analysis and interpretation of an identifiable class of phenomena. A microschema generally incorporates concepts, propositions, and more-or-less integrated networks of these two elements.
Macroschema	A mental structure which encompasses several microschemata.

Figure 1. *Components of knowledge in memory*

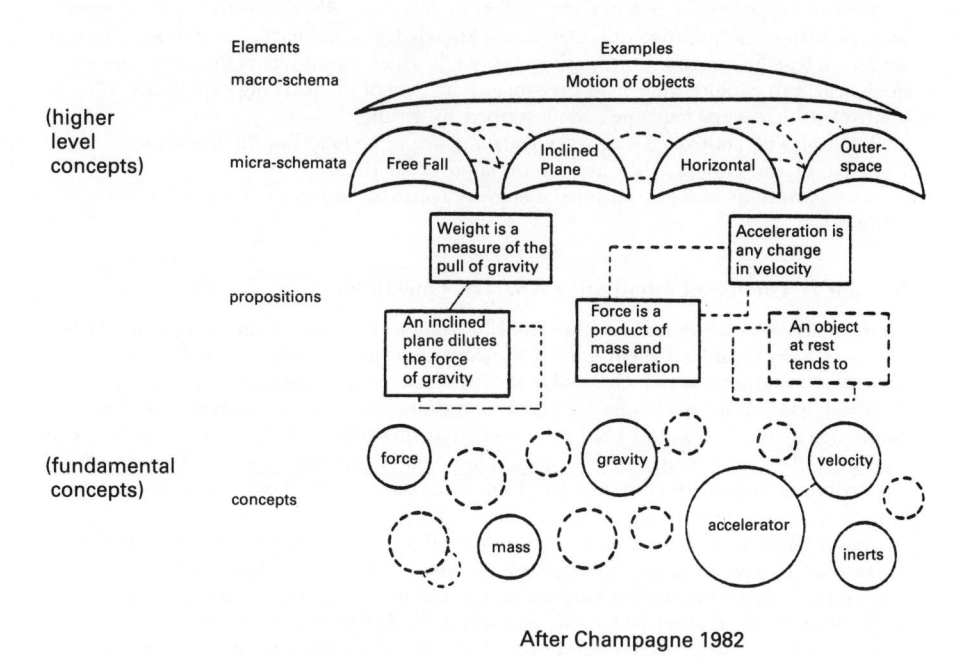

Figure 2. *Knowledge in memory*

After Champagne 1982

- □ the *doing*, by having a structure to the learning experience which allows learning to occur in a purposeful manner;
- □ the *ability*, which relates to the idea of study skills; the ability to handle content or data.

These two aspects will be considered separately: examples of structured activities to assist 'the doing'; and examples of skills development, to develop 'the ability'. Examples of activities will be drawn from the author's experiences in his university department.

Structured Activities: the Doing

Ausubel defines structured learning as one of working on (idiosyncratic) *anchoring ideas*; ideas already established in a learner's cognitive structure. A structured learning experience is the provision of:

- an *advance organizer*, which introduces the main principles of a new subject; and
- *comparative organizers* which indicate the main similarities and differences between the new ideas and the existing 'anchoring ideas'.

For skilled learners, listening to a structured argument can involve active learning; Ausubel argues that (quoting from Entwistle)

> 'the dictatic method which leads to receptive learning is effective and does not imply passivity on the part of the learner'.

Adult learners who choose to learn may come into this category and the design of complex learning experiences to ensure active linking may be inappropriate.

For less skilled learners, one major problem in designing effective learning experiences incorporating 'comparative organizers' is a knowledge of the nature of the preconcepts held by a learning group. One 'active' approach which circumvents this problem is to get learners to explore their held preconcepts as part of the learning experience – controlled 'discovery learning', as described by Bruner.

Examples of 'controlled discovery learning' are to be found in the literature (Nussbaum and Novick, 1981 and Champagne et al, 1983).

Two variations of the 'controlled discovery learning' approach are used by the author.

Variant 1: The use of Qualitative Analysis Questions

At the start of 'new' topics it is important to bring to the front of the mind of learners *their* preconcepts and get them to *check* these preconcepts against *their comprehension* of presented argument(s) (which involve these preconcepts). This is achieved using 'qualitative analysis' questions. These are questions requiring a graphical solution; numerical examples have not been introduced at this stage. The questions are designed to bring out specific 'naive' preconcepts. These 'naive' preconcepts have been identified through interviews with students, and from discussions with students in tutorial activities teasing out the exact nature of difficulties.

Two typical areas of misconcept within the subject of fluid mechanics relate to the Aristotelian–Newtonian view of mechanics as identified by Champagne. This is a concrete – abstract problem in Piagean terms. The areas relate to the use of feelings imposed on analogous systems (analogies where fluid elements are 'seen' as being discrete particles, which is not inappropriate on the microscale, versus a continuous medium on a macroscale). Two typical questions and typical answers based on 'naive' preconcepts are shown in Figure 3.

Using a bank of such 'qualitative analysis' questions students work initially as individuals, then they explore differences in their answers in groups. Group solutions are taken by the teacher/facilitator and recorded on a chalk board with no alteration. The reasoning behind solutions is explored when all solution variants are identified. The exploration is *facilitated* by the teacher.

Variant 2: Linking Questions

A similar approach is taken to questions which are designed to link related sections of a syllabus: *after* 'consolidation' tutorials have been tackled in one section, and *before* the next section is tackled. The questions are tackled initially by individuals and then by groups, with the linking questions going beyond what has been formally explained at

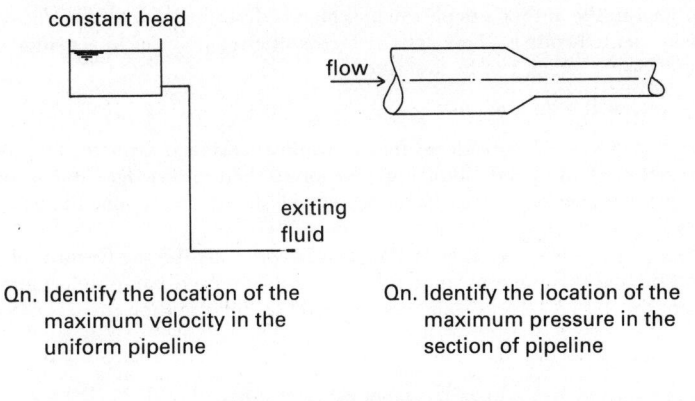

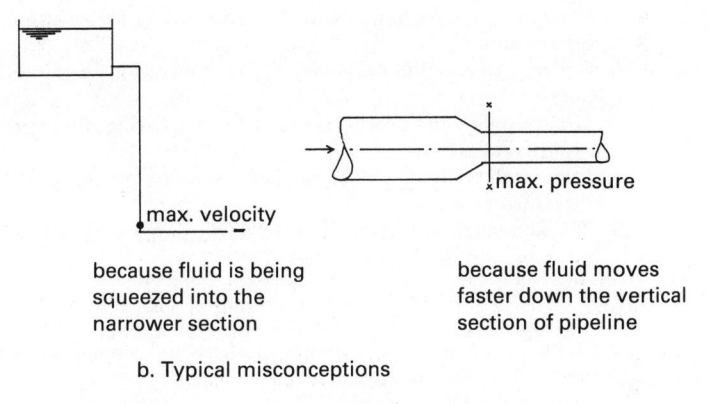

Figure 3. *Two examples of qualitative analysis questions*

any stage. This provides for 'cognitive dissonance', as described by Neisser (Neisser, 1976). Again solution variants (or part solution variants) are taken on a (wide) chalk board and then the reasoning behind variants is explored.

The success of such activities does depend on the learning environment created within a department. The author is fortunate that in his department the encouragement of a learning community is fostered.

Skills Training: the Ability

Although the structured learning experiences described do provide a mechanism whereby learners face difficulties in their thinking and possibly develop it, what has been described does not tackle directly the skills inherent in learning: tackling analytic thinking, imaginative thinking and retrospection in a purposeful manner.

Deficiencies in the skills of analytic thinking and imaginative thinking are particularly apparent in the 'linking question' approach described above. Many first year students come to a halt in their solutions to 'new' questions and feel they have no other way forward other than to want to be shown where to go. Such skills are not restricted to learning in engineering, such skills are an inherent element of creative design. In the arts, creative writing employs the same skills.

Such 'common' skills, and other personal and cognitive skills, are considered in a first year subject in the author's department which is described as *interdisciplinary studies*. This is a task-oriented course where activities are designed in order to consider specific skills within a format which can be described as

> do it – review it – do it again.

The process is that a skill is considered first in a non-specialized context; the processes inherent are reflected on by individuals, in relation to their knowledge, ability and experiences *and in relation to future similar situations*; the skill is then applied in a technically specialized, but not necessarily new, situation.

The skill of analysis is relevant here. Analysis is about identifying features of a situation and linking them in a meaningful manner. Data are pieces of information and the analysis of the data produces some meaning; this is the common process of any research.

A typical activity structure is:

Introduction 1. Introduce analysis, its relationship in a hierarchy, such as defined by Bloom (Bloom et al, 1956) and identify the possible alternative forms of analysis.
Do it 2. Students generate data about student learning habits using a prepared questionnaire.
3. Groups are asked to draw meaningful conclusions using other groups' data.
4. Groups define the processes they were employing, these processes are explored in plenary.
Review it 5. Individual students prepare a checklist of the process(es) of analysis in their own terms.
Do it again 6. The first stage of a design is tackled, the data being analysed for meaning and implication only.

As an exercise by itself what is described does ask students to focus on process and work from a familiar context, but what it lacks as it stands is purposeful reflection of analysis as a concept. This is built in by getting students to keep a diary where they record for activities such as the one outlined above:

☐ what they have learnt about (analysis) which they didn't know before
☐ what they can do better than they could before
☐ where (precisely) there is scope for enlightenment or improvement.

Assessment has been shown to have a major influence on how students approach learning material. With the skill programme outlined above, the diaries kept by students, which are submitted each week for tutor *comment* (not assessment), form the basis of assessment. With this subject, assessment is based on *quality of thinking* as expressed through diary entries.

So What of the Title of This Paper: Does it Work?

Three questions have been asked about the approaches to learning in the author's department. These are:

1. What evidence is there to justify such an approach?
2. What are the implications of such an approach?
3. Can it be shown that such an approach works?

The answers, in the order of the questions are:

1. There is justification from the literature as described in this paper.
2. The implications for individual teachers depends on their teaching style, which reflects their perspective of teaching.

John Gilbert and his colleagues (Gilbert et al, 1982) describe three concepts of the act of teaching based on interviews with teachers.
  (a) Blank mind assumption.
      Learners have blank minds which can be 'filled' with the teacher's knowledge.
  (b) Teacher dominance assumption.
      What the learner understands has little real significance for learning and can be easily replaced.
  (c) Student dominance assumption.
      Students views are strong and persistent and they are likely to persist or at least react with teaching in a significant way.

In the author's department a team teaching approach is adopted to year teaching. The skills awareness programme in the subject of interdisciplinary studies is facilitated by the year team members. This approach in the author's experience does develop a learning community spirit. Content, even in primary subject areas, is used as a vehicle to develop thinking.

3. (a) There are two provisos to this answer. It depends on how you as a reader place yourself in John Gilbert's list of concepts of teaching.
   (b) Whether you view quality of learning as more important than quantity of learning (syllabus coverage).

Hopefully this paper shows that there is a link between what is in the literature and the style of 'teaching' described by the author. Quality of thinking or 'education for capability' is the theme of the approach.

Within these 'limitations', the answer is yes.

The answer is not just based on the theory – practice link, but also on the comments made by visiting teachers and educationalists to the author's department *after they have talked to the students*.

Closing Comments

Two statements are appropriate to close this paper, the first by Galileo, the second used by Lewis, but its origins appear lost in time.

> Galileo: 'You cannot teach a man anything – you can only help him to learn.'
> Lewis (paraphrased): 'The genius and successful members of society do not do anything different from the rest of society other than they are aware of inherent processes and through practice are faster at applying these processes.'

References

Ausubel, D P, Novak, J S and Hanesian, H (1978) *Educational Psychology: A Cognitive View* (2nd edition). Holt, Rinehart and Winston, New York.
Bieri, J, Atkins, A L, Briar, J S, Leaman, R L, Miller, H and Tripodi, T (1966) *Clinical and Social Judgement: The Discrimination of Behavioural Information*. Wiley, New York.
Bloom, B S, Englehart, M B, Forst, E J, Hill, W H and Krathwohl, D R (1956) *Taxonomy of Educational Objectives. The Classification of Educational Goals Handbook 1 – Cognitive Domain*. Longman S Green, New York.
Bruner, J S (1974) *Beyond the Information Given*. George Allen and Unwin, London.
Champagne, A B, Gunstone, R F and Klopfer, L E (1983) Naive knowledge and science learning. *Research in Science and Technological Education*, **1**, 2, pp 173-83.
Entwistle, N J (1981) *Styles of Learning and Teaching*. Wiley, New York.
Gibbs, G, Morgan, A and Taylor, E (1982) A review of Ference Marton and the Gotenborg Group: a phenomenological research perspective in learning. *Higher Education*, **11**, pp 123-45.
Gilbert, J K, Watts, D M and Osborne, R J (1982) Students' conception of ideas in mechanics. *Physics Education*, **17**, 2, pp 62-66.
Hodgson, V E (1980) *Lecturing and Learning: A Study of Students' Experience*. Unpublished Ph.D. Thesis, University of Surrey.

Laurillard, D (1979) The process of student learning. *Higher Education*, 8, pp 395-409.
Marton, F and Svensson, L (1982) Orientations to studies, approaches to texts: a relational view of study skills applied to distance learning. *12th World Conference of Learning at a Distance*, Vancouver.
Neisser, U (1976) *Cognition and Reality*. W H Freeman, San Fransisco.
Norman, D A (1978) Notes towards a complex theory of learning. In Lesgold, A M (eds) *Cognitive Psychology and Instruction*. Plenum, New York.
Nussbaum, H and Novick, J (1981) Brainstorming in the classroom to invent a model: a case study. *School Science Review*, 62, pp 771-78.
Osborne, R J, Bell, B F and Gilberg, J K (1983) Science teaching and children's views of the world. *European Journal of Science Education*, 5, pp 11-14.
Svensson, L and Hogfors, C (1984) On science learning. Paper presented at the Sixth International Conference on Higher Education, University of Lancaster.
Taylor, E, Gibbs, G and Morgan, A R (1980) The orientations of students studying the social science formation course. *Study Methods Group Report No 7*. Institute of Educational Technology, Open University, Milton Keynes.

1.11 Cognitive Considerations in Developing Courseware Reflective of Adult Learning Needs in Computer-based Training

R D Spillman
Radford University, Virginia, USA

Abstract: Cognitive considerations in the development of courseware, reflecting adult learning needs in computer-based training, are an important element in the task of employee training. This paper describes and presents some cognitive considerations which can be used in developing courseware which reflects adult learning needs in computer-based training.

Introduction

Companies prefer successful participants in their computer-based training (CBT) programmes. CBT can be operationally defined as the application of computer-aided instructional programs in occupational or industrial contexts (Kamouri, 1983-4). Computer assisted instruction (CAI) software, also called courseware, comes in various levels of sophistication (Pressman and Rosenbloom, 1983-84) and can vary widely in form and application.

Purpose

In CBT avenues of communication exist in two directions: one avenue exists between the instructional software and the user, and the other between the instructional software and the computer. Taken together, these provide an important communication link contributing to retention of information, learner performance, and progress.

Meaningful learner interaction is a blend composed of implementing instructional strategies consistent with learner informational processing factors and learner needs. The purpose of this paper is to describe and present how the information processing factors of (1) memory and attention, (2) text characteristics, (3) graphics and visual processing, (4) cognitive characteristics of the user, and (5) feedback (Jay, 1983) in developing courseware relate to the adult learning needs of (1) having a positive learning environment, (2) personalizing learner needs, (3) considering individual learning differences, (4) using experiences, and (5) repetition (Lanese, 1983) in CBT.

Instructional Design

Systematic instructional design methods are needed to blend knowledge and technology productively. The result is deliberately planned instruction (Gagné, 1982) with intentional rather than incidental learning (Gagné, 1980) which teaches skills efficiently and effectively.

Gagné's nine events of learning (1977) can be used to organize an instructional lesson. According to Gagné, they support the internal cognitive processes necessary for learning. The events usually included in CAI development are: (1) gaining attention, (2) informing the learner of the objective, (3) stimulating recall of prerequisite skills, (4) presenting the stimulus material, (5) providing learning guidance, (6) eliciting performance, (7) providing feedback, (8) asssessing performance, and (9) enhancing retention and transfer. In some instances trainees are expected to provide part of the conditions for learning, or certain events may already exist in the environment outside the instructional programme.

Memory and Attention

Short- and long-term memory are fundamental considerations in developing instructional materials. Short-term memory involves recall over a short period of time. It is the system by which incoming information is handled. Long-term memory, on the other hand, involves recall over a long time period.

Adding to the information in long-term memory in such a way that it can be retrieved and applied is a primary concern of trainers. This is also of concern to learners as they want to succeed in meeting organizational and personal goals. Accordingly, a prerequisite is to develop courseware through instructional practices in which the system design is consistent with human information processing abilities. Violating cognitive principles in developing courseware reduces the overall effectiveness of CBT. Specifically, adults want to add to the information in their long-term memory in an environment which supports human information processing abilities. Pressman and Rosenbloom (1983-84) indicate that properly used CAI can accelerate learning and improve retention.

An environment conducive to learning includes interactive courseware which is flexible and adaptive. Interactivity is the degree of computer-learner dialogue present, and the amount, quality, and personalization of feedback (Kamouri, 1983-84). Generally, elaborate semantic processing produces better long-term memory (Jay, 1983).

Flexibility allows for user control by permitting learners to determine the sequence of information presented. Flexibility and user control are virtually synonymous; albeit, just as with interactivity, user control varies greatly in amount, quality, and personalization. Degrees of variation contribute to important relationships between user control and personalizing learning, considering individual learning differences, user experiences, and repetition.

Instruction reflective of learner goals has greater relevance for the learner as needs are personalized. Goal definitions form from a combination of two environments; the learner's personal life and on-the-job requirements (Lanese, 1982). Understanding relationships between these two environments aids learners in formulating goals as they relate to the work environment.

Individual differences reflect learners' backgrounds, experiences, skills, and knowledge (Forman, 1982). For example, two individuals may have the same goal but be at different levels of sophistication. User control allows learners to enter or continue instruction without repeating instructional sequences they already know. Consequently, numerous entry and exit points address the varying training needs of adults.

Control allows adults to adjust instructional presentation suited to their various learning rates and styles. Material broken into small segments allows learners to achieve a level of competence, absorb the information, become comfortable with it, and move on to the next level of learning. Adults then have the flexibility to self-pace learning.

Learners seek opportunities for repetition, which includes practising a new skill or acquired knowledge. Practice can provide learners with the opportunity to progress without the threat of classroom competitiveness, to chart their individual progress, and to be reinforced by the self-gratification involved in doing well (Yates, 1983). Reinforced repetition leads to mastery.

Adaptability is applying instructional decision rules to trainee's responses (Hillelsohn, 1984). It measures how information flow is controlled. It accommodates learner differences in displaying information by having the computer choose an instructional sequence reflective of learners' proficiencies and abilities (Kamouri, 1983-84). Consequently, branching allows learners to choose their sequence and follow a different path on each pass through the content (Cohen, 1983). Branching allows for individual differences among learners.

Just as needs of adults differ, they also have varying attention spans. User-controlled entry and exit at various points in courseware provides instruction according to an adult's attention span. Practice distributed over intervals increases long-term memory, but if intervals are too long the information may be forgotten (Hillelsohn, 1984).

Text Characteristics

Properly developed text characteristics increase retention, provide for individual learning differences, provide repetition, and add to the creation of a positive learning environment. Text assists in bridging the gap between the user and the instruction. Therefore, it should be consistent in format and address adults, the specific user group.

For novice computer users, menus provide the consistency needed by adults. This type of format reflects the 'keystroke model' developed by Card, Moran, and Newell (1980). They suggest that a more nearly error-free performance is promoted by fewer required keystrokes. This in turn facilitates user – computer communication and assists in the creation of a positive learning environment. Menu-driven programs load repetitive functions onto the computer, thus reducing human memory demands. The result is a reduction in the demands on the user's short-term user memory.

Menu-driven courseware increases material retention by providing a conceptual hierarchy. This approach organizes materials into a hierarchy allowing user choice. For example, an adult training in operational information systems may see a menu having several selections from which to choose. Selections might include (1) Data Entry, (2) Records Management, (3) Payroll Processing, (4) Processing Business Forms, and (5) Inventory Management. A user selecting item 2, Records Management, would then typically have a choice of several subtasks which could be performed. At this level, these choices might include (1) Address and Phone, (2) Personnel, (3) Credit Customers, (4) Inventory, and (5) Return to Main Menu.

A consistent display format provides repetition and contributes to an understanding of data hierarchy. Eggen, Kauchak, and Kirk (1978), in examining conceptual hierarchies as supplemental aids to textual materials, found that user retention increased if users could recall the hierarchical relationships. Presentations compatible with user perceptions assist in personalizing user needs.

Although menus are suitable for novice users, they do not adapt well to the changing sophistication of users. As users gain experience and familiarity with the

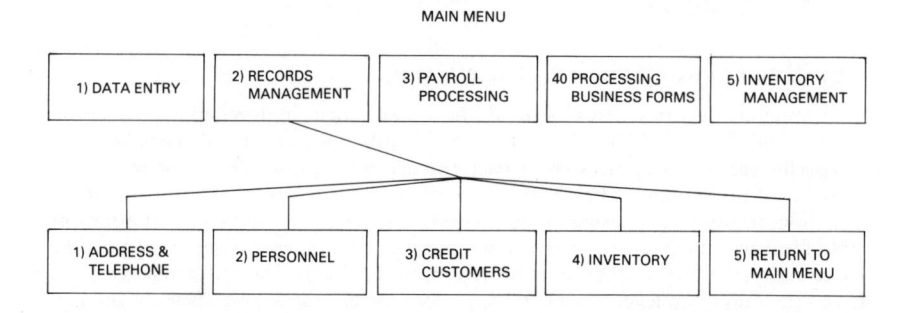

Figure 1. *An example of organizational hierarchy in a menu-driven program*

system and courseware, the menus tend to obstruct instructional presentation. If the only path to accessing a unit of instruction is through several intermediate menus, then those displays diminish the concept of user control.

Wise (1981) indicates that advance organizers aid users in combining and correlating pertinent information. An advance organizer is a visual display which provides a cue as to the type of desired input. The overhead associated with advance organizers is low enough to allow users to enter data at their own pace, supporting the concept of user control. Figure 2 is an example of an advance organizer.

LAST NAME:	SMITH
FIRST NAME:	MARY
STREET NUMBER:	5439 HYLAND AVENUE
CITY:	STOKESVILLE
STATE:	OH
ZIP:	43211-1234

Figure 2. *An example of an address file using advance organizers*

Furthermore, courseware should be user-friendly at any level of sophistication and should require a series of inputs from users through multiple presentation formats. Redundant presentation of material enhances human performance and supports the adult need of repetition.

Graphics and Visual Processing

Learning can be enhanced through graphics in several ways, such as inversing the display around specific text, changing text characters, boxing, or flashing. However they are used, graphics should relate to the unit of instruction and to the overall instructional objectives. For example, in Figure 2 boxes may appear at each cue indicating when input is desired from the user. This can also support the concept of advance organizers.

Simulation is a viable alternative when acts or events take a long time to occur; when special, rare, or expensive equipment is used; when users are susceptible to error; or the events themselves are dangerous (Hillelsohn, 1984). Properly implemented simulations recreate the essential elements of real world events with users participating interactively. Personalized simulation allows user control over cause-and-effect variables while supplying repetition and practice. Thus, simulations should provide learners with opportunities to demonstrate acquired skills and knowledge in lieu of formal examination. This provides a productive learning experience rather than a means for determining failure.

Cognitive Characteristics of the User

Cognitive characteristics of adults should be a major focus in developing courseware. Hannum and Briggs (1982) indicate that the identification of general characteristics and specific capabilities possessed by each learner occur prior to entering an instructional programme. They further indicate using learners' characteristics and capabilities in the actual design of instruction and for designating the most appropriate point of learner entry into an instructional program. Experience assessment provides a clearer understanding of what must be accomplished for the learner to achieve or surpass the minimum level of acceptable performance. Assessment assists in linking newly acquired skills and old ones, thus tailoring instruction to the learner's unique needs.

The training director should be a driving force in the creation of a positive learning environment by functioning more in the role of a learning manager of the learning process rather than as a pedagogue. Serving as a learning manager, the trainer can engage in dialogue, with the learner providing the trainer with greater understanding of learner fears and expectations. The learner has the opportunity to verbalize feelings and the trainer has the opportunity to acknowledge and use those feelings in planning instruction.

Feedback

The purpose of feedback is to inform learners about the accuracy of their performance after an instructional event (Smith and Boyce, 1984). Locating errors and providing information allows the learner to make mental corrections (Cohen, 1983). Properly designed, friendly feedback assists in creating a positive learning environment.

Feedback can be given after correct or incorrect responses and can easily be personalized by using the learner's name. Feedback is not necessary after every correct response. An intermittent reinforcement schedule maintains the highest rate of retention (Cohen, 1983). Extended feedback should provide information about why a response is correct or incorrect (Waldrop, 1984). Making mental corrections does not include the user terminating instruction in frustration.

Remediation should provide some means for learners to match an incorrect answer to the correct response (Cohen, 1983). Remediation could include varying presentations of material which guides learners to correct responses. Errors are made at the terminal instead of on the job without the fear of consequences. This in turn supports the need for repetition.

Feedback should also be diagnostic, and prescriptions can be generated based on instructional objectives which have not been mastered (Reynolds, 1983). For example, after completing a unit of instruction a post-test reveals that 16 out of 20 questions were answered correctly. Feedback can then indicate specific remedial instruction reflecting the number and relationships of questions missed. Diagnostic information presented in this fashion is personalized and considers the cognitive characteristics of the user.

Summary

Courseware which supports human information processing abilities and reflects adult learning needs can enhance employee support and willingness to participate in training programmes. Adults want to be successful employees and are very conscious of failing to learn and the consequences. However, courseware which cognitively supports adults and reflect their needs can be a very positive experience. Adults soon realize from participating in properly implemented CBT that training with a computer is not a means of determining failure, but a method of instruction to successfully meet both industrial and individualized needs.

References

Card, S K, Moran, T A and Newell A (1980) The keystroke-level model for user performance time with interactive systems. *Communications of the Association of Computing Machines*, **23**, 7, pp 396-406.

Cohen, V B (1983) Criteria for the evaluation of miocrocomputer courseware. *Educational Technology*, **23**, 1, pp 9-15.

Eggen, P D, Kauchak, D P, and Kirk S (1978) The effect of hierarchical cues on the learning of concepts from prose materials. *Journal of Experimental Education*, **46**, 2, pp. 7-11.

Forman, D C (1982) Self-paced training materials. *Educational Technology*, **22**, 5, pp 33-36.

Gagné, R M (1982) An interview with Robert M Gagné. *Educational Technology*. **22**, 6 pp 11-15.

Gagné, R M (1980) Is educational technology in phase? *Educational Technology*, **20**, 2, pp 7-14.

Gagné, R M (1977) *The Conditions of Learning* (3rd edition). Holt, Rinehart and Winston, New York.

Hannum, W H and Briggs, L J (1982) How does instructional systems design differ from traditional instruction? *Educational Technology*, **22**, 1 pp 9-14.

Hillelsohn, M J (1984) How to think about CBT. *Training and Development Journal*, **38**, 12, pp 42–44.

Jay, T B (1983) The cognitive approach to computer courseware design and evaluation. *Educational Technology*, **23**, 1, pp 22-26.

Kamouri, A L (1983-84) Computer-based training: A cognitive framework for evaluating systems design. *Journal of Educational Technology Systems*, **12**, 3, pp 287-309.

Lanese, L D (1983) Applying principles of learning to adult training programs. *Educational Technology*, **23**, 3, pp 15-17.

Pressman, I and Rosenbloom, B (1983-84) CAI: its cost and its role. *Journal of Educational Technology Systems*, **12**, 3, pp 183-208.

Reynolds, A (1983) An introduction to computer-based learning. *Training and Development Journal*, **37**, 5, pp 34-38.

Smith, P L and Boyce, B A (1984) Instructional design considerations in the development of computer-assisted instruction. *Educational Technology*, **24**, 7, pp 5-11.

Waldrop, P B (1984) Behavior reinforcement strategies for computer-assisted instruction: programming for success. *Educational Technology*, 24, 9, pp 38-41.

Wise, W S (1981) Improving the user/machine interaction. *Association for Education Data Systems Journal*, 15, 1, pp 23-30.

Yates, D S (1983) In defense of CAI: is drill-and-practice a dirty word? *Curriculum Review*, **22**, 12, pp 55-57.

1.12 Open Learning: The Student's Perspective (Workshop Report)

C Togneri and N E Paine
Scottish Council for Educational Technology (SCET), Glasgow

Abstract: In Scotland, little research has been undertaken which takes account of the large number of developments in open learning in recent years. The numbers of students studying by open learning will continue to increase. Students will have a wider than ever range of courses to choose from, with Open Tech and 16+ Action Plan modular programmes available. The aim of the survey was to provide information on the students' attitudes to working in particular open learning systems.

In November and December of 1984, students from different open learning systems in Scotland were interviewed. The institutions were chosen to reflect the variety of different models of open learning systems in Scotland. Students from a distance course, a resource-based learning unit, a community education course, a flexistudy scheme and an Open Tech programme were all interviewed. Students were asked general questions about their motivation, reasons for choosing open learning and the availability of information about open learning courses. The students' attitudes to key aspects of the open learning systems were investigated. In particular, the support system, the suitability and effectiveness of learning materials, and the appropriateness and efficiency of the administrative procedures were examined.

Background

This workshop was structured round two main components: the Scottish Council for Educational Technology (SCET) report *Open Learning: The Student's Perspective* which participants had the opportunity to read before the workshop, and a case study, 'Supporting Open Learners'.

Open Learning: The Student's Perspective is the result of a survey commissioned by the Scottish Committee on Open Learning and was undertaken by Carl Togneri of the Open Learning Unit at SCET in 1984. In Scotland, there has been little research which takes account of the large number of developments in open learning in recent years. This investigation provides information on Scottish students' attitudes to the important aspects of open learning: reasons for choosing open learning; pre-enrolment guidance and counselling; the learning materials; the support available, and the effectiveness and efficiency of the administration. 34 students from open learning systems covering postgraduate studies, flexistudy, Open Tech and learning by appointment were interviewed.

Discussion on what the students perceived as their needs, especially the support they received or would have liked, provided the background to the next stage of the workshop, the case study.

The Case Study

Participants were presented with a case study based round open learning in an industrial context. An open learning co-ordinator has been appointed in a large service company which offers a range of courses introducing staff to new technology. The company has a fairly large expenditure on learning packages, but has no provision for supporting the learners.

Participants had to make suggestions on the following points.

1. Devise a support strategy for your learners, given that the centre is open access and you would therefore be dealing with people from manual through to junior management level. The pilot suggested, however, that it will be mostly technical and supervisory staff who come in.
2. Also draw attention to the implications of this centre for the company, and the kind of structural change which has to be incorporated if it is to succeed.
3. Suggest any necessary internal staff development for the implementation of your plans.

Response to the Case Study

The first group set up a whole string of tasks that had to be fulfilled before the Open Learning Centre could be successful. These included:

(a) convincing the training manager that this was a worthwhile training initiative;
(b) seeking support from senior management and an idea of where they wanted the centre to go;
(c) mounting an awareness campaign within the company, explaining why the centre had been set up and who had access to it;
(d) seeking trade union support for the development of the centre;
(e) making sure that middle management would support learners coming through the centre and try to build on the training skills learned there.

It was also felt that if the centre was to be a success then there would have to be some kind of focus on conditions of service for staff going through it, which could involve financial remuneration, and that supervisors and first line trainers who would be working with trainees would need special attention.

The whole of the briefing task group would be organized through a series of explanatory workshops which started off covering policy with senior management, down to middle management and first line trainers and supervisors.

Before the target group would be able to use the centre, they would be given briefing sessions so that they were aware of its scope and capabilities.

Finally, it was felt that outside consultants might be brought in if essential, and that where subject expertise was required, outside tutors could be brought in, but only on a temporary basis until the expertise was located within the company.

The second group developed their strategy almost at the point where the first group left off, and it therefore forms quite an interesting and stimulating whole. The second group made two assumptions: that the company had a number of local service units (eg a chain store) and that the centre would be used for both compulsory training and self-referral.

The strategy outlined by the group included provision of *local* training facilities which need not necessarily be high tech. There would be a system of local mentors from personnel or training departments who would be available to help staff work through the materials. This would be supplemented by specialist contact at the training centre or head office of the company. This could be either by phone or by visit.

The central group would also handle all assessment, marking and monitoring of performance.

In order that the centre be as accessible as possible, it would be open longer than the hours of employment.

Any materials provided in the centre would be edited or amended centrally to ensure that they had direct company relevance. There would therefore be one central co-ordinating unit which trained and looked after mentors and specialist staff and materials, plus a network of local units which would handle the day-to-day training operation. The flexibility of provision and support would have to be very firmly based at local level and the success or failure of the scheme would depend on the sympathy, availability and sensitivity of the local mentors, who would need specific training to undertake their tasks.

In order that user motivation would be high, there would be a system of rewards built into using the materials. This would include certificates of completion and achievement and a financial bonus for success at the centre. Staff would also have the right to take home materials to follow up or further develop or extend their training.

In order to embed this kind of structure within the company, there would have to be a general monitoring of the staff development needs that emerged from the unit, and a deliberate attempt to implement career and course counselling for those obtaining new skills within the company.

The status of the centre would have to be clarified, and clear guidance given to mentors in terms of their supporting and counselling role.

Support Functions

In the workshop, the distinction between the hard kinds of support which cover areas such as marking, assessment and administration and the soft areas of support such as counselling, guidance, setting up strong motivation and support for the learner during the learning process was discussed.

The kinds of areas that participants felt support should cover include:

(a) putting a human face on the learning situation
(b) assessing the performance of the learner
(c) improving and sustaining the learner and creating a positive self-image for him or her
(d) covering the learning skills and techniques of study for the learner
(e) administering the learning process
(f) directing the learner to pre-courses
(g) offering counselling both pre-, post- and during learning
(h) setting standards and imposing parameters for the learner, or helping the learner establish his or her own parameters
(i) adapting the materials for the particular target group
(j) organizing and supporting learners wishing to set up self-help or group development sessions
(k) building in the learning to the lifestyle of the learner, or helping the learner build in learning to his or her own lifestyle
(l) feedback on content and supplementing content where necessary.

Finally, it was felt that any support strategy ought to have built into it a degree of support for the supporters and a degree of development for the supporters.

Conclusion

The discussion returned to the conclusion of *Open Learning: The Student's Perspective*, and to the issues around support in particular. The majority of Scottish students interviewed felt there were positive benefits to be gained from studying by open learning. Although students showed wide variations in their personal studying patterns and styles, the majority agreed that the flexibility of open learning and being able to study in a convenient place and at a suitable pace were the strongest advantages.

Isolation was the main disadvantage students commented on, and they felt that support was of crucial importance in cutting down isolation and helping them through the learning experience.

The workshop concluded with discussion round the following recommendations of the report.

Recommendations

Research
- More research in open learning should be undertaken: for example, there is little Scottish research into why students drop out of programmes of study

Pre-enrolment
- Publicity and information about opportunities to learn by the open learning method should be made more widely available. Materials and systems should be marketed to reach untapped markets
- Personal pre-enrolment counselling should include information, advice and guidance. Pre-testing would help to ensure the suitability and level of provision

Learning Materials
- Course designers should adopt a more rigorous approach to the design and production of learning materials
- Learning packages, including a range of media, with attractive layout, graphics and short units, will help to stimulate and motivate students
- Objectives to guide the students through the package and self-assessment questions (SAQs) to help the students assess their own learning should be built into the material
- New technology should be used in the production of material to facilitate updating and modifying

Support
- When courses are supported by one college and the materials provided by another, the supporting college should do everything possible to maintain exclusive contact with students
- Each student should be appointed a tutor who can provide personal and academic support
- The support system should build in face-to-face situations in individual or on a group basis
- More efficient use should be made of the telephone for individual tuition, teleconferencing and for routine student contact
- Assignment marking should encourage and aid the learning process
- Tutors may have to be actively involved in setting up self-help groups.

1.13 The Manchester Open Learning Delivery Scheme

S Rowlands
South Manchester Community College

Abstract: There is at the present time a very wide range of open learning provision in Manchester. The reasons that this development has taken place are: the local authority is supportive, in open learning terms; the geography of the city is advantageous; it is a city which is accustomed to educational change; the human expertise is there; there have been large amounts of funding brought in. An all-embracing interpretation of open learning has evolved in Manchester, largely concerned with responding to the needs of people in all circumstances. The Open Tech Delivery Scheme is a matched funded enterprise which has facilitated this. Its infrastructure is based on a central clearing house, three major workshop supermarkets and a number of outreach satellite centres. The management structure is a fairly traditional one, but operates on a day-to-day basis through democratic procedures. The achievements have been: 5,000 students; responsiveness to industry; streamlining of material to allow for customizing; introduction of common costing procedures; solutions to the problems of practical components; a response to training needs; computer back-up; institutional collaboration and accreditation. Where do we go from here? Hopefully access to learning within an individual's own living room.

Introduction

If you were to visit Manchester at the present time to look at its open learning provision, we would first of all need to ask you what aspects of open learning you were interested in: workshop, flexistudy, directed private study, distance learning or Open Tech, and in which specialism you would like to see it operated: special needs, craft, DIY, managerial and supervisory, CAD and CAM, and so on. I believe that the range of provision which you will see functioning in this single city at the present time is something unique in the whole of the British Isles.

Why Manchester?

There are a number of reasons why open learning has mushroomed so rapidly in the Manchester area and is able to operate so successfully.

Manchester is blessed with an educational authority which, although it is not able in the present economic climate to put large sums of money into fostering development and change, is not antipathetic towards innovation. The development and concentration of open learning systems fits in with the kind of facelift which the city is seeking to give itself generally.

A second favourable factor is the geographical location of the city. In size and structure Manchester is a 'manageable' city from a travel point of view. Sausage-shaped, it is possible to travel on a north–south route between major institutions in no more than 20 – 30 minutes, with most routes between institutions taking no more than 15 minutes. There is also a precedent for this, since most institutions work on a multi-site basis anyway. This means that cross-city links and structures are reasonably acceptable to those working within the system and reasonably practicable in a working day. Manchester is also fortunate in that it has an intercity motorway network which makes for ease of communications within, and easy access from without. In addition to this, its rail and air links provide an efficient means of access for those coming to Manchester. The geographical siting of Manchester in terms of the North West also means that there are major conurbations on our doorstep, and all within easy distance.

This would be nothing of course without the will for change in those working 'at the sharp end'. Change, although not necessarily always wise nor always acceptable to everyone, has become a fact of life to every Mancunian. Fortunately in Manchester we seem to have been well endowed with both enthusiasts and creative innovators which has enabled us to push ahead. A key to the remarkable development that has taken place is the fact that many of the people involved in open learning in Manchester have national standing and are situated in important managerial positions across the city and are thus able both to respond to change as it takes place and to influence it.

All this would have been nothing without the money to implement change, and the North West is an economically depressed area. Again it has been lucky for Manchester that within its confines we have people who have become expert at financial procurement – discovering where there is funding available and having the necessary keys to unlock the doors to release some of it – in Manchester's case, substantial amounts of it. Large amounts of money have come into the city, quite justifiably in terms of its high unemployment ratios, from both the European Social Fund and the Manpower Services Commission (MSC). These funds have enabled changes to be introduced and implemented much more rapidly than would otherwise have been the case. In Manchester over the last five or six years we have developed such a comprehensive range of provision in open learning that it is virtually possible to offer anything to anyone anywhere using open learning methodology.

The Manchester Dimension on Open Learning

An interpretation of open learning has evolved which is no longer flexistudy, Open Tech, workshop or directed private study, but a mixture of all these things and more. Put simply, it is concerned with setting up the systems and mechanisms across the city to enable us to do what, ethically speaking, we should always have been about in education (had the straitjacket of the current system not prevented us) – responding to the needs of people. And in my book it doesn't really matter whether the person concerned is the manager of a large multinational carrying a pot of gold or an unemployed youth bearing a UB40 – both will do nicely. If the system is large enough, flexible enough and professional enough it should be able to accommodate the needs of both.

The implications of this interpretation are that the institutions must become flexible enough both to respond to industrial needs on the clients' terms (and perhaps on their premises) and equally must have systems available which the individual can 'drop into' or which can meet him on his terms on his home base. This in turn has far-ranging implications for both the consultative and negotiative procedures which need to be made available, and also for the manner in which such opportunities are promoted both to industry and to the community.

The Infrastructure

The infrastructure for delivering open learning in Manchester has been set up by the Manchester Open Tech Delivery team. It is not an entirely new structure; much of it was already in existence before receiving Open Tech funding. What the Open Tech funding has facilitated is the setting up of certain new ventures and the drawing together of both new and old under the single umbrella of cross-city delivery. The venture is a matched funded one, being partly local authority funded and partly MSC funded, with the contractual brief therefore of delivery both to industry and to the citizens of Manchester: hence its all-inclusive structure.

The scheme operates through a central clearing house based in an annexe of one of the major institutions and three major 'workshop supermarkets' in further education institutions situated in the north, centre and south of the city. The bulk of enquiries netted via promotion in industry, supermarkets, television, radio and newspapers are disseminated via the clearing house system to the major workshops and their satellites. The clearing house system can, if appropriate, tap into institutionally-based workshops or other flexible areas of work within the institutions themselves as well. It also deals with enquiries for traditional areas of work, although this is not its major function.

Each workshop supermarket has a number of outreach centres attached to it to facilitate delivery to the 'far reaches' of the community of Manchester and the smaller locally-based industries. Referrals also travel through the system via cross-city agencies such as the Manchester advisory network. Walk-in enquiries of any kind are dealt with on the spot by tutor-counsellors based at each centre. The infrastructure is summarized in Figure 1.

How is it Managed?

Management of a single scheme of this magnitude now seems to be very simple and straightforward indeed, but it belies the amount of discussion it took to arrive at this stage and it also in some senses gives a false sense of security and certainty, for none of us know exactly what will happen after the funding period comes to an end in March 1987.

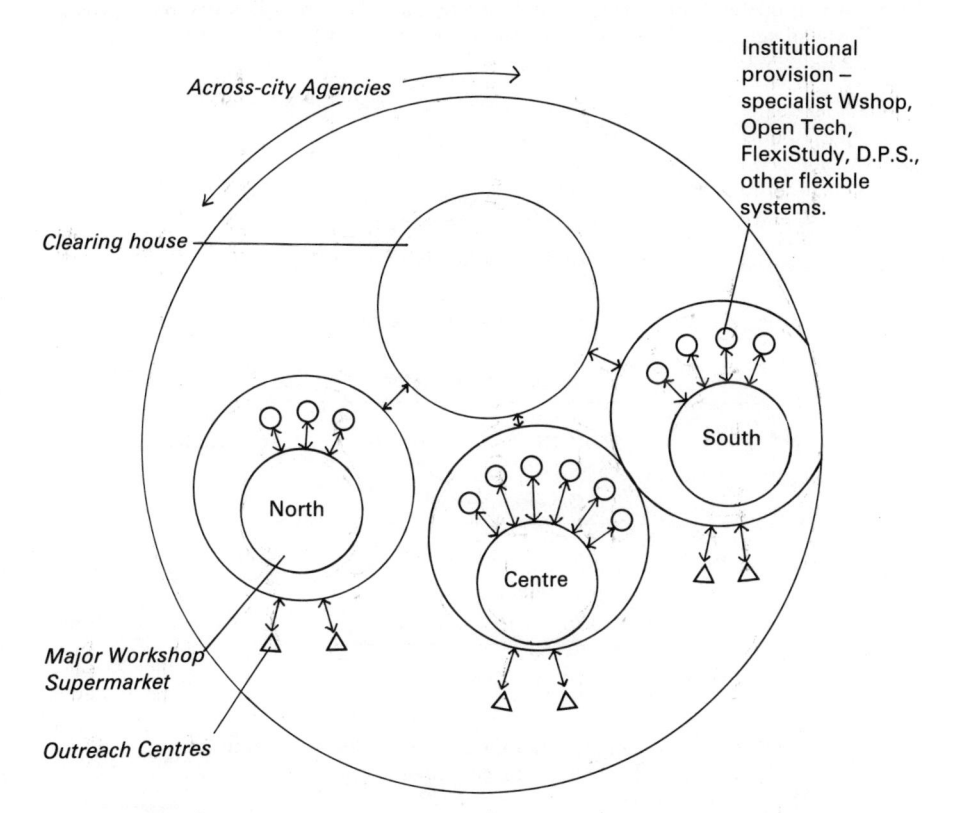

Figure 1. *Infrastructure of the Manchester Open Learning delivery Scheme*

At the present time, the whole scheme is guided by a steering committee with representatives from the Manpower Services Commission, local industry, the Manchester Open College Federation, under whose auspices the scheme was set up, the local authority and the major institutions. The project director (Principal of Central Manchester College) is answerable to the steering committee for decisions made on the day-to-day running of the project and also to his fellow principals. Recently appointed to assist him in doing this is an assistant project director. The steering committee meets on a quarterly basis to receive detailed reports on the progress of the scheme, and from time to time the emphasis has been changed according to the directions given.

Originally there were five senior co-ordinators appointed to the scheme, there being also a co-ordinator in the area of materials. This co-ordinator left to take up a permanent appointment. Three development officers were subsequently appointed last September to assist with the work of the co-ordinators.

On a day-to-day basis the scheme operates through the senior co-ordinators' close liaison with each other and with the development officers through regular meetings, as well as with the workshop co-ordinators, tutor-counsellors and key people within the institutions. The management structure shown in Figure 2 does not necessarily operate on the basis of seniority, for people who are institutionally-based such as workshop co-ordinators may well be senior to, for instance, the development officers.

Generally speaking the scheme works democratically, with senior co-ordinators being able to influence and take part in the decision-making procedure via regular meetings with the project director; for example, the development officer posts came into existence in this way, upon recommendation by the senior co-ordinators to the project director and subsequent agreement by the steering committee (Figure 2).

```
                         Steering Committee
                                 ↓
                 Project Director (and other Principals)
                                 ↓
                       Assistant Project Director
                                 ↓
                          Senior Co-ordinators
         ↓              ↓              ↓              ↓
     Marketing       Outreach       Support      Accreditation
                         ↘          ↙
                       Development Officers
              ↓                  ↓                  ↓
            North             Centre             South
                     ↘           ↓           ↙
                       Workshop Co-ordinators
              ↓                  ↓                  ↓
            North             Centre             South
              ↓                  ↓                  ↓
        80/90 Tutor-counsellors +full time tutors within the institutions +
                           4 outreach workers.
```

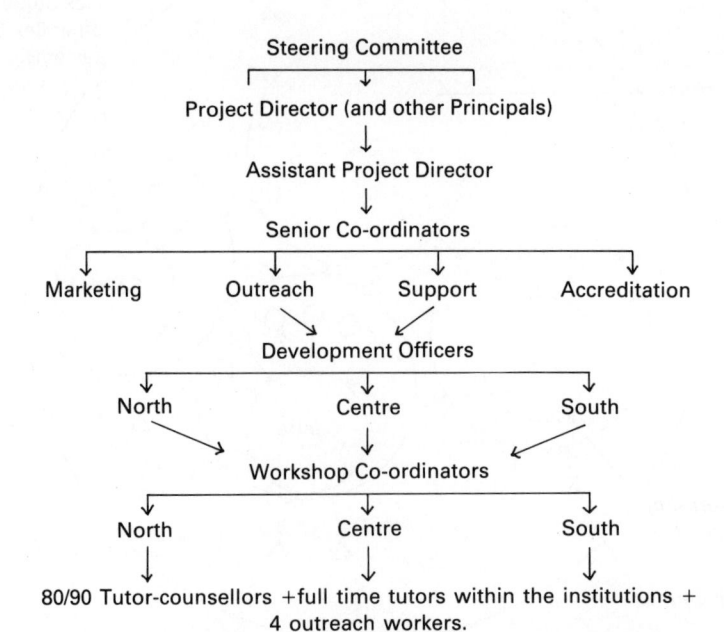

Figure 2. *Management structure*

Resulting Developments to Date

1. Something in excess of 5,000 students study on open learning systems in Manchester.
2. Greater awareness exists now within the institutions of the need to be able to make a flexible response to industry. This has resulted in the setting up of an industrial unit in one case, introducing specialist provisions which can be used internally but which can also be linked out to industry and better consultative procedures in general. There is however something like an 18-month to 2-year time gap between an industrial promotion and signing the contract.
3. Greater flexibility in both materials provision and in the handling of materials has resulted. The need to be able to customize existing materials to individual and company requirements has led to a streamlining of both editing and production procedures with provision for constant updating. Inability of Open Tech production schemes to deliver on time, or to deliver at all, has resulted in a heavy reliance on Manchester-produced materials and a diversification of writing expertise.
4. There has been a need for common costing procedures to be introduced across the city and a committee initiated by the local authority to look at this in terms of open learning has recently been established.
5. Attempts have been made to solve the problems of providing specialist practical facilities by the introduction of a cross-city practical grid which can tie the individual into studying in the communities specialist facilities within the institution.
6. Initiation of a comprehensive training programme in open learning in response to identified needs has taken place.
7. Computer record systems and an administrative backup system have been set up, and it is hoped that these will be completed by the end of the project.
8. The breaking down of institutional barriers and competitiveness to a great extent and the fostering of collaboration in a common purpose has been a worthwhile aspect of the scheme, although there are still pockets of suspicion in some areas. Cross-city representation for open learning on key institution bodies demonstrates this.
9. A comprehensive accreditation system is now being introduced to include open learning systems in Manchester via the Manchester Open College Federation, leading to a leaving passport.

Where do We Go from Here?

In terms of the Manchester Open Learning Scheme, the immediate future after March 1987 is perhaps less certain than long-term developments. In the long term, too much has been achieved for development to cease. A great deal has been learnt about taking learning to the learner and promoting it both in the community and industry. We are but a short step away from turning our institutions into major resource centres in the true sense of the word, both from the point of view of the hardware and the human resources. All that we need now is technology to keep pace to enable us to customize this and to give access to individually tailored programmes to the individual in his own home.

1.14 Theory into Practice

A Henderson
Leith Nautical College, Edinburgh

Abstract: This paper complements the paper based on Leith Nautical College's Open Tech project (Paper 2.7). The project is essentially distance learning, so in this paper I explain the models used for producing the materials and the delivery system. An analysis of the costs involved and how to arrive at a price for open learning courses is given. I have also included both student and company perspectives on distance learning.

Finally I report on an experiment to introduce open learning to the everyday lecturing situation, which gives rise to the need to examine whether or not we need traditional timetables for either the student or the lecturer.

Introduction

Leith Nautical College was approached by a major oil company in 1982 to write a distance learning course on digital electronics. The aim of the course was to update the knowledge of technicians who were originally trained on transistor-based equipment.

There were two constraints: firstly the course was to be studied at a distance – there would be no opportunity for the trainees to come to the college – and secondly the course had to have a practical content of 50 per cent.

The knowledge required by the trainees was similar to that of an already existing SCOTEC course which formed part of the Higher Certificate in Industrial Measurement and Process Control, and so this course was used as a base to work from.

The practical aspect of the course was carried out on an off-the-shelf logic kit.

The finished course was based on text: eight four-hour modules, each of which contained the learning material, two self-tests, a module test and a number of practical experiments. A video programme of 15 to 30 minutes duration was also produced for most of the modules.

Originally it was estimated that 15-20 trainees would take the course but in fact 50 trainees took the first course and 25 were put on a waiting list because of the availability or otherwise of the logic kits.

The initial work led to two further courses for the original client, by which time other companies were interested and a successful application was made to the Manpower Services Commission (MSC) for funding in excess of half a million pounds over three years.

This enabled the setting up of a proper resource production unit and a suitable delivery system.

Material Production

Courses were produced along roughly the following lines:

1. discussion took place with the client to ascertain the type of course and content;
2. subject specialists were contracted to write the 'content';
3. the company agreed the content;

4. the educational technologists decided how the content would be delivered to the trainee;
5. the text was typed, checked, had graphics inserted and was sent for approval;
6. the video programmes were produced, along with any other remaining materials;
7. the whole was packaged and sent out.

The main consideration here is that the authors need only produce the course content. There is no real need to train them to write distance learning materials because the production team handle everything, thus ensuring that the style of writing and format is the same throughout, resulting in a particular house style.

Delivery System

Physically, materials were sent to the company who passed them on through their internal mail a module at a time. If this did not suit them then the college would send direct. This is a lot more complex than it sounds, because the trainees involved worked two weeks on, two weeks off, so that if they were in transit and missed the post it would be a further fortnight before they received their materials. On top of that, some preferred to study offshore while others studied at home. Consideration was given to using senior people out in the field as the first line of help, with the trainees getting together to help each other. However, 50 trainees spread over 3 installations amounts to 17 per installation. Half are on leave, leaving 8 per installation, 2 or 3 of which are either working, sleeping or eating. So although it was possible for small groups to meet there was nothing like the possibility for, say, a factory-based project.

It was also intended that a trainee on leave could go along to a local college and have access to any necessary equipment. Funding was set aside for this, and it was additionally proposed to set up a small centre in Aberdeen. However it was soon realized that most of the trainees only pass through Aberdeen airport on their way home.

Each trainee was issued with a student guide which gave advice on how to study, who to contact with problems, explained the assessment and evaluation procedures, and contained checkout procedures for the logic kit and sheets of logic elements.

Evaluation consisted of a questionnaire, an attitude inventory, some interviews and self-marked tests. Each module contained at least two of these self-tests; the student attempted the test, then detached a copy to send to the college before marking it himself from model solutions given in the back of the module; these could be anonymous if the student so preferred.

The assessment consisted mainly of larger module tests. Each module had a test at the back, not self-assessment but intended to be externally marked, which was sent to the college for marking. Pre- and post-testing of the course was also carried out.

Each trainee was also assigned a tutor with whom he was encouraged to keep in contact. The tutor was responsible for keeping in touch with the trainee and keeping track of his work.

Video was used in three different ways:

(i) as a talking head to supplement the student guide
(ii) as used conventionally
(iii) to show the experiments on the logic kit.

Costing

This was the area which gave rise to much debate in the early stages, because no one could decide what to pay authors for their work and copyright. Other projects had managed to coax people to write for very small sums and/or a share of royalties but we felt that in the long term it would be best to pay a decent price for a good job done.

The following arose from careful consideration of previous work:

> material production would take 20 hours to produce 1 hour of student material. This would be reduced to 15 hours as expertise was gained, so a typical course would take 900 hours to develop and would cost between £15,000 and £20,000.

If the potential number of trainees cannot justify this expenditure, can the non-text resources be cut back or should distance learning be dropped?

Trainee Perspectives

The trainees had a number of incentives to take part in this project:
- the company was paying for it
- the company thought it a good idea
- knowledge would be updated
- the course was 'recognized' in the industry
- hands-on experience would be gained
- the materials could be studied at work or at home at a suitable time
- work is at the trainee's own pace.

With pre- and post-testing, individualized learning was possible so that the trainee only studied what he needed to. The course was recognized in that it was possible to take a SCOTEC exam and/or the OPITB was willing to give it recognition. Each trainee would no doubt perceive the above in different ways but no attempt was made to take this any further.

A trainee studying the course receives a module at a time from the company (or direct from the college). This will take the average trainee four hours to study and to complete the experiment. The experiments are of the type in which various chips are wired together to give a particular outcome. If this is completed successfully the circuit 'works' so feedback is immediate. If the circuit fails there is a checklist of possible faults, a wiring diagram and a video programme showing how to complete the wiring.

Exercises are included in the text where appropriate and these are marked by the trainee. Two tests are also included in the module, and as I have mentioned these are marked by the trainee and a copy is sent to the college for comment (carbonless copy paper is used). Once again feedback is immediate. Finally there is also the main module test, which is similar to the previous tests except that the answers are not available so it is returned to the tutor for marking.

Company Perspectives

The main consideration from the company's point of view is that the workforce's knowledge is being updated. Just as important is the cost; a 40- to 60-hour course based on text and a logic kit with video backup costs from £250. The company also supply a playback facility for the video and a quiet area for the trainee to work in. An alternative would be to send the trainee to college for two to three weeks, in which case the company would pay for
- transport to and from a rig (helicopter)
- travel to and from college
- tuition fees
- trainees' salary or paid leave
- trainees' replacement on the rig.

In addition to these points, there was tight manning with no provision to relieve technicians for training, and training offshore during rest periods was not encouraged.

It has been estimated that this could easily cost in excess of £1,000, in which case only key workers would get the opportunity. With distance learning at least four employees could be trained for the same price. The cost can be brought down dramatically if the course need only be text-based or if the trainees share non-text materials.

Use is made of a word processor to store the text, which introduces a number of advantages:
- ☐ words are easily interchanged for, say, the American market, where spelling is different
- ☐ trainee tests can be individualized
- ☐ material is easily inserted or deleted.

This last advantage means that all companies receive the same core of a course, but additional material can be tailored for one particular company. Two companies may for example require a course in digital electronics, but one wants a module in modern optics and the other a module in fluidics. The modules can be added, and at a later date another client could take both. Although these extra segments are originally written for one particular client, they become part of what is available to others, so the course is being continually developed and any material which is not used over a period of time would be removed.

Application to Everyday Lecturing

If a trainee can be successfully taught at a distance, then surely there is room for the same materials in the everyday teaching situation. Why should open learning students get all of the cake?

I was interested in the application of open learning and educational technology in the everyday lecturing situation. To apply the knowledge I had gained in open learning I set up a resource base for the teaching of maths. This consisted essentially of a single room which was capable of seating 30+ students, some filing cabinets, lateral files, microcomputers and access to video playback.

A copy of all maths teaching material was kept in the room so that resources would be available to tackle any problem which arose. About 60 per cent of the material was in a form which could easily be converted for individualized learning, but as the 16+ modules were being written from scratch with student-centred learning in mind it was decided to start in this area.

Material was produced in appropriate form and some video programmes were made.

Students were made fully aware of the system. Each piece of work was self-contained and had a number of problems and exercises to be completed. When the students had completed pieces of work they were left in a box to be marked. These are picked up from the box each day and marked for the following day. Attendance is variable: either the student attends each period, or is allocated attendance on the strength of work completed. The student who stays ahead and completes all necessary work does not need to attend. The tutor is always available at certain times, and other arrangements can be made through normal channels.

The lecturer does not waste time conversing with students who don't need help. Provided that counselling is good enough the average students need not get involved in the 'class'. This results in a much smaller class of those who need help.

In practice two classes each of approximately 15 students were timetabled together. The resulting class of 30 were timetabled for 3 hours' contact and 1 hour of self-study. After the initial pieces of work the class was reduced to about 10 students at each session, of which about 5 were in need of help. Each student could therefore be given 10 minutes, and in practice they could often be grouped so that they were getting even more time. In a normal class of 15 the lecturer would talk and chalk first, which would leave say 30 minutes for the class – 2 minutes each.

Future Perspectives

If we are to make best use of educational technology and open learning then there are a number of traditional areas which need to be looked at. In particular we should turn our attention to timetabling, class contact and counselling.

16+ modules are criterion-referenced, so there is no such thing as a bare pass, or a very good pass. How, therefore, do you tell the difference between a good student and a better student? The answer is supposed to be that the better student has more modules to his credit.

However, students following these courses are restricted by timetables of so many periods a week for so many weeks, to give a total of 40 hours, when a new phase of modules starts.

A very good student may finish a module early but he can't go on to the next one until the next phase except where open learning is operating. If this is taken to its logical conclusion then we must abandon traditional timetables and leave the student free to make up his own.

The whole class no longer needs to meet as a group, so smaller rooms can be utilized or, as students tend to work individually, it is possible to have a number of classes in one room along with a number of lecturers.

As previously mentioned, I carried out an experiment with two classes timetabled together. Although these classes were small by some standards I was entitled to four hours' contact time per week for each class giving eight hours' contact. I met with the students three hours a week, the fourth hour being self-study for the student, so I had five hours a week in which to twiddle my thumbs. In practice though this time was used to counsel students, mark worksheets and prepare materials.

It seems obvious that class contact can come down but that it must be offset by an increase in counselling time. There are advantages for both the lecturers and management: the time it takes to produce a piece of learning material is the same no matter how many students use it, so there is a saving in preparation time where large classes are involved; and where large classes are involved the counselling time needs to be increased. The total number of hours worked therefore doesn't really change, but the lecturer becomes more a practitioner of learning.

The main conclusion I have come to is that it is vitally important to know where the student is in his work, and just as important that the student knows where he is. This can only be achieved by good counselling.

1.15 Open Learning and Modular Vocational Education: Some Problems in Practice

C Togneri
Scottish Council for Educational Technology (SCET), Glasgow

Abstract: In Scotland, the Action Plan has transformed vocational opportunities in post-compulsory education. The Action Plan aims for open access for students. Access to learning opportunities is however limited for many learners by family commitments, work patterns, geographical distance and physical handicap. Open learning in the Action Plan can overcome some of these barriers to learning by creating a more flexible learning system.

This paper discusses the work of a SCET project which has been funded by the Scottish Education Department (SED) to promote and develop Open Learning in the Action Plan. The SCET project, in collaboration with five regions in Scotland, is developing a number of modules in a variety of vocational subjects for open learning delivery. Evaluation of the key stages of developing and piloting of new programmes of study is a major task of the project.

In implementing innovation in education, a number of practical problems will be encountered. This paper addresses the following key problems: (a) developing effective self-study packages from a module descriptor, (b) evolving analogues of formative and summary assessment suitable for open learning when there is a shift from norm-referenced exams to internal, continuous, criterion-referenced assessment, (c) the multiple role of the tutor in open learning in a modular system, and (d) evolving delivery systems in a number of contexts appropriate for a range of students, eg adults, YTS and TVEI students, disabled learners and senior pupils in rural schools.

Background

The 16+ Action Plan has dramatically transformed post-compulsory education in Scotland. Following the publication of *16-18s in Scotland – An Action Plan* in January 1983, implementation followed in August 1984. This was a time of tremendous activity and an unprecedented time for such dramatic changes in vocational education.

Modular Programmes

Existing courses in the non-advanced further education sector were replaced by modular programmes of study. The majority of modules are of 40 hours' duration, though there is provision for half, double or treble modules. Each module descriptor contains a statement of the learning outcomes, which state what the student is able to do by the end of the programme of study. Assessment has changed also. There has been a shift from norm-referenced exams to criterion-referenced assessment, which is internal and continuous though externally moderated. Each module descriptor includes the performance criteria for each learning outcome. Essentially, the Action Plan is a student-centred approach to learning, with the emphasis on students learning rather than teachers teaching.

Since August 1984, the uptake of the Action Plan has been dramatic. Approximately 430 centres are delivering modular programmes. This includes every further education college (61) in Scotland, 60 per cent of schools (300) and to a lesser extent, community education centres. Over 800,000 modules are being studied by 69,500 students.

Open Learning and the Action Plan

Access to learning opportunities is a key aim of the Action Plan. For many learners, however, access to these opportunities is limited. Module availability is inevitably unequally distributed throughout Scotland. Students in smaller further education colleges and schools, particularly in rural and island areas, do not have the same choice of modular provision. It is increasingly recognized that the Action Plan has relevance for adult learners, who may wish to pursue a programme of vocational training or to opt in on a limited basis. The Action Plan offers enhanced opportunities for adult learners. But how accessible are these opportunities? For many adults, there are barriers to learning which prevent them from taking advantage of the present opportunities. Irregular work patterns, family commitments, distance from colleges, disability and inflexible provision can prevent students having access to learning opportunities. Open learning, by creating flexible learning opportunities, can open up access to the Action Plan. Students have the choice of studying in a way which fits in with their lifestyle.

It was against this background that the 'Open Learning in the 16+ Action Plan' project at the Scottish Council for Educational Technology (SCET) was funded in August 1984 for three years. The focus of the project is to promote and develop open learning in the Action Plan. The overall aims of the project are to: identify a number of modules suitable for open learning; support the development of modular packages; evolve appropriate delivery and support systems, and to evaluate the total experience.

Regional Co-operation

The project is a co-operative one, between SCET and five Scottish regions – Fife, Highland, Lothian, Tayside and Strathclyde. This is a significant feature of the project, as the regions are widely different in the geographical spread of their populations. Some rural regions are relatively thinly populated with few institutions. Others have large urban populations. Both need extended open access to learning opportunities.

In response to these different demands, the regions already have expertise in a range of flexible learning patterns, including distance and flexistudy schemes and learning by appointment centres.

Selection of Modules

The early stages of the project concentrated on the selection of a group of modules for open learning development. Each region is developing two modules. The modules being developed are:
- communication 1/2
- communication 3/4
- maths G2
- introduction to computers
- computer software
- office organization and information processing
- starting and running a small business
- financial record keeping 1
- marketing 1
- consumer studies.

This group reflects a greatly varying range of skills from 'hands-on' experience of computing, conducting surveys and interviews, as well as attaining competence in basic skills in literacy and numeracy.

The Learning Packages

Each learning package has been designed to cover the learning outcomes of the modules with an individualized learning package. It is important that a student-centred approach which allows for choice in the route through the package and also in the range of activities which the student can choose to do is adopted. In this way students can choose a project or topic which is appropriate to their vocational needs.

The packages have been designed to cover the learning needs of a diverse range of learners from senior school pupils studying on their own, to adult learners working at home or in their workplace. It is important that the materials are motivating and attractive. A range of media has been developed and includes video, computer software, tapes, slides and resource packs of information. Print-based material is, however, the most popular medium. Of particular interest is the marketing module link with broadcasting. In Scotland, viewers of the new Yorkshire Television series for Channel 4, *The Marketing Mix* have the opportunity to link this with an open learning package. NETWORK Scotland will handle all referrals for the series. Formative assessment in an important aspect of the Action Plan. This is incorporated into the packages with self-assessment questions (SAQs) and activities which provide feedback to the student on his own progress. Tutor-marked assignments and folios of work allow the tutor to provide this crucial feedback to students and provide equivalents to the feedback offered to learners in a conventional situation.

Piloting

The ten module packages are being piloted to assess the effectiveness of the learning materials and to explore different types of delivery and support systems.

Piloting is in two phases: regional piloting on a limited basis, and inter-regional piloting on a full-scale basis.

Regional Pilot

At present each region is piloting the two modules developed in its own institutions. The aim of the regional pilots is to gain fast feedback from a limited number of students, support staff and administrators. Close monitoring of the pilot will reveal any problems in the material and enable the packages to be amended before large-scale piloting. It will also highlight areas of good practice and reveal any weaknesses in the delivery and support systems.

A limited target audience of approximately 25 students are piloting each module. The regions vary in their needs for flexible approaches in learning and this is reflected in the target audiences for the regional pilots. In Highland the students are a fairly homogeneous group. They are predominantly adults studying at a geographical distance from the colleges. By contrast in Tayside there is greater heterogeneity in the group, which includes senior pupils in rural schools, deaf and severely physically handicapped students and home-based adult learners.

Inter-Regional Piloting

In the second phase, the ten modules will be piloted by the five participating regions. The aim of this large-scale piloting is to gain feedback from a diverse range of institutions. This will involve a heterogeneous target audience working within different systems. It is specifically planned to analyse the adaptability of the packages for those outside the region which developed the package and to assess the appropriateness and effectiveness of different delivery and support systems.

Evaluation

Evaluation of all the aspects of the open learning systems involved – material, support and management – is an essential activity of the project. In the earlier stages, the focus of evaluation was on the learning packages. The factors which influenced the selection of modules for open learning development were examined. Following this, the writing and production process was closely monitored. The colleges involved are providing valuable information about their experience of producing packages, including the writing process and the resources costs involved. The methodology used for the technical production was of interest, particularly in assessing how far modern technology had been employed. Many of the colleges were developing open learning materials for the first time. The information collected has relevance for any organization moving into materials production. The writers are sharing their experience of writing, including eliciting the factors which facilitated the development of packages and the problems they faced.

The next phase of the evaluation was piloting of the packages. As the open learning modules are applicable to a diverse range of students, profiles of the target audience are being drawn up. An important consideration is looking at the open learning system from the student's point of view and judging how responsive the systems are to their needs.

The students are being asked about all aspects of their open learning experience, including:
- their motivation for studying by open learning
- how they found out about the provision
- their feelings about the effectiveness of the learning packages
- the management and administration
- the guidance and support they were offered.

Students' comments are of crucial importance in amending and improving systems.

Tutors, administrators and other support staff are keeping records of the amount of time and the duties involved in supporting open learning. There has been a positive response to this, as staff feel this is an opportunity to highlight the many and varied tasks involved in offering support.

Methodology

The evaluation of the project is essentially an ongoing process and as such much of the feedback is informal. Structured interviews and questionnaires are the main methods of collecting information. In the first phase of piloting, approximately 90 per cent of students are being interviewed. As there will eventually be a large number of students, some in geographically remote areas, a postal questionnaire will be used to investigate students' attitudes. This questionnaire is itself being piloted. In the light of students' responses, it is being restructured to make it more stimulating and easy to complete. Follow-up interviews, either face-to-face or by telephone, will be conducted with a sample of students.

Issues

In implementing innovation in education, there are inevitably practical problems which will be encountered.

When this innovation is across a range of institutions working within different contexts and working through common problems, mutual problems can be shared and solutions explored.

Although the issues which follow are the problems highlighted in the development and piloting of the ten modules in the SCET project, they are doubtless shared by many institutions developing open learning systems in a modular context.

Support

Support for students is a vital factor in the success of open learning. In successful implementation of the Action Plan, the role of support staff is expanding. The subject tutor has multiple responsibilities which are different from those of a classroom teacher. These include pre-enrolment guidance and negotiation of modular programmes. Many students, particularly adults returning to study, are unfamiliar with modular provision and studying by open learning, and need guidance and counselling. The tutor has increased responsibility for formative and summative assessment, diagnosing learning difficulties at a distance, and supplying remediation or extension work. Although tutor support will often be available on a direct basis, much of this essential contact will be non-contiguous, by letter or telephone.

Often extra support is needed at the place of study. Particularly where 'hands-on' is essential or students have special learning needs, a mentor or local support worker can provide useful and in some instances essential mediation. Deaf students and students with severe physical handicaps are learning from standard open learning packages, but with the mediation of a specialist tutor. In such a system, tutor and mentor roles need to be clearly defined so that the student is clear about the nature of the support offered by each.

Peer contact is another valuable source of support. It is useful in overcoming some of the loneliness experienced by a number of learners by providing mutual support as well as helping learners to gain feedback on their progress. Tutors can underestimate the importance of peer support and may have to build this deliberately into the system by organizing group tutorials and self-help groups.

Delivery Systems

If centres are to provide a range of flexible learning opportunities, innovative responses are called for. Delivery systems appropriate to the requirements of specific modules need to be evolved. But of greater importance is that the systems should be responsive to the needs of the learners. Open access is available in the range of open learning systems which already exist, particularly flexistudy and resource-based systems. But if open access to modular provision is to meet the needs of a heterogeneous group of learners which will include young people in schools as well as TVEI, Youth Training Scheme (YTS), adult learners, other models of open learning need to be devised. This may include links with schools, colleges and community education as well as work-based learning and mixed mode learning.

Assessment

The shift from norm-referenced exams to internal, continuous criterion-referenced assessment has obvious implications for open learning systems. Effective analogues of formative and summative assessment need to be evolved. The key factor is to evolve assessment mechanisms which maintain national standards but do not necessarily constrain the openness of the system.

There is no standard solution to this. Formative assessment can be successfully integrated into the package by a range of methods; activities, projects, and so on. Summative assessment can be more problematic. In flexistudy or learning by appointment schemes, this does not present such a problem as the students are in regular contact with their colleges and tutors. However, when the student is working at a considerable distance or is housebound through disabililty, other responses are called for. On the one hand, presenting centres need to be innovative in their interpretation of assessment procedures, and SCOTVEC needs to be flexible in what it demands of presenting centres.

Staff Development

Many lecturers and teachers are adopting new roles and responsibilities as writers, tutors and managers. Training in developing effective open learning material is a priority when developments are in a new curricular area. When materials being developed are in-house college productions, training is not only needed in the skills of writing, but also in the production skills of editing, graphics and layout.

Organizers and tutors in colleges, schools and community education are taking on new responsibilities in administering and supporting open learning. Often this involves a fundamental change of attitude from being the sole provider of learning to becoming a facilitator.

The role of the open learning tutor is expanding as the tutor gains multiple responsibilities for the negotiation of modular programmes, for pre-enrolment guidance, and for supporting and assessing the students through their modular programmes.

Staff development is needed to familiarize staff with their new roles and to create an awareness of the different demands of an open learning system.

At best, staff development is organized flexibly, on a regional basis. Staff are given the opportunity to identify their own training needs and are provided with the opportunities to develop new skills on a negotiated basis. Often this involves staff using open learning methods themselves. Unfortunately, this is the exception. In many cases, staff development is a low priority.

Conclusion

The full impact of open learning in the Action Plan is still to be realized. The signs are that the range of flexible learning opportunities will increase significantly. Colleges and schools are moving towards greater access to the Action Plan. Distance schemes and flexistudy programmes are expanding their provision to incorporate a wide range of open learning opportunities. Two Open Tech projects are adopting totally modular programmes. TVEI and YTS schemes are moving towards open access to opportunities. The SCET project, with the focus on developmental research, is in a unique position. It can identify and suggest solutions to problems of implementing open learning in the Action Plan.

1.16 The Concept of Open Tech and the Reality of Implementation within a Local Education Authority

A S Donald
Rochdale Open Tech

Abstract:
'The citadel of established practice seldom falls to the polite knock of a good idea. It may however yield to a long siege, a pre-emptive strike, a wooden horse or a cunning alliance.'
Barry MacDonald (1975)

It could be legitimately argued that sooner or later anyone involved in education must come face to face with that wide gulf, that great divide, which so often separates educational policy from its implementation.

For that reason it is the author's intention to examine the Open Tech initiative from two different approaches, that is the concept of Open Tech and the reality of implementation.

The Concept

If one was forced to acknowledge any one figure who could be credited with pointing the way towards the concept of Open Tech, then James Prior could perhaps qualify more than most. Support for the notion of Open Tech was voiced by him while in opposition to the Labour Government in the 1970s.

Recognition of such a need appeared to stem from the lack of training opportunities at managerial, supervisory and technician level in this country when compared to many of our overseas competitors. This point has been substantiated by a recent comparative study of education and training provision in Japan, Germany and the United States. Such concern has consistently been voiced in the past, and certainly throughout the last 100 years, but this particular innovation is better understood in the context of initiatives taken in the 1960s in the recognition by both Labour and Conservative governments of a need to improve the quality of the nation's workforce.

It is necessary to acknowledge that any initiative or curriculum innovation cannot be viewed arbitrarily in isolation from the historical, social and economic environment at any given time. In the United States in the 1960s there was growing evidence of the 'back to basics' movement characterized by the publicity given to the speeches of Admiral Rickover. In addition there was an increasing demand for accountability in education, made manifest in the increasing emphasis on behavioural objectives. Further evidence of this mood was demonstrated in the mandatory inclusion of evaluation within the Elementary and Secondary Education Act, Title 1 of 1965.

These factors in the United States were to some extent reflected in the United Kingdom by the strong emphasis on behavioural objectives adopted by the Industrial Training Boards following the 1964 Industrial Training Act. This Act was also significant in that it led to a further education curriculum which often reflected an artificial distinction between education and training. The increasing need for a greater emphasis on technical education also resulted in the inception of the Technician Education Council and the Business Education Council following the 1969 Hazlegrave Report.

Of particular significance also was the success achieved by the Open University and, therefore, the growing demand for some vocationally-based provision along similar lines to the Open University seems hardly surprising.

At this point it is important to record the significance of the 1973 Employment Training Act, which was directly responsible for the birth of the Manpower Services Commission (MSC). It was to this body that the present government turned in 1979 and requested that a framework for the provision of an Open Tech be drawn up. This was duly done, and by 1982 an Open Tech task group report had been completed.

As the result of the task group report the Open Tech programme was launched by the MSC in August 1982 with a budget of some £50m for projects up to March 1987. This budget is currently catering for some 150 projects:

Material Developments Projects	105
Delivery Projects	18
Practical Training Facilities	17

Who is Open Tech Aimed At?

The target population to whom the Open Tech initiative is directed is a combination of supervisors, technicians and management personnel. The intention is to focus on the education, training, retraining and updating of skills required by this client group in order to meet identified industrial needs and to assist in the achievement of job enhancement and personal aspirations.

The attainment of such an aim may be reduced to two primary objectives which form the basis of most Open Tech projects:

- to produce or adapt open learning materials in identified markets reflecting specific needs;
- to develop delivery systems designed to provide tutorial support and practical facilities, in addition to distributive arrangements to assist training through open learning methods.

The achievement of these aims falls within the objectives of the new training initiative and is further reinforced by the emphasis given to the Open Tech as an integral part of the adult training strategy.

It is interesting to note that the Open Tech task group report is purposely imprecise in dealing with definitions relating to 'technician', 'supervisor', or 'adult'. It is clear, nevertheless, that the initiative is not intended for school leavers for whom adequate provision already exists under the Youth Training Scheme.

What is Different about Open Tech?

In order to refer to a difference one must acknowledge a comparison of some sort. To do this it is necessary to identify traditional education and training provision and the constraints within which it functions.

These constraints or barriers may be seen as:
(a) geographic problems arising from distance, transport and cost
(b) administrative: entry qualifications, formal assessment procedures
(c) modes of attendance and teaching methodology
(d) psychological fears associated with a return to formal learning
(e) constraints arising from employment and the needs of production, shift work and the difficulties of unsocial hours.

One must be careful, however, to avoid the dangers of seeing further education provision only in terms of such constraints or relying too much on unsubstantiated reports of some negative aspects of such a diverse educational sector. Nevertheless constraints do exist, and it is the function of Open Tech projects to assist in their removal.

Who Bears the Cost?

The ability to pay for education and training through Open Tech initiatives is, to a large extent, determined by the nature of the target population. Many open learning initiatives will be employer-led and the employer will pay all or some of the fee involved. Alternatively, open learning opportunities may be seen by many employed staff as a means of improving promotion prospects and updating skills for which they are prepared to pay. The redundant and unemployed may see such opportunities as job enhancement and as a form of investment.

The unemployed do, nevertheless, present a need for special consideration where open learning costs are concerned and this is an area of concern which both local and national government will need to address.

The Reality

While the foregoing is intended to reflect the concept of the Open Tech Programme, the reality may be seen in reviewing the practicalities of its implementation.

In this respect Rochdale is relatively singular because of the unambiguity of its commitment in appointing permanent staff, the relative size of the borough, and the fact that the Open Tech unit is independent of local further education colleges.

This unit is staffed by:

1 Manager
2 Trainer/designers
2 Co-ordinators
1 Counsellor
1 Clerical Assistant.

Within the borough there are three FE Colleges: a technical college, a college of art, and a college of adult education. The Open Tech unit will be based within a converted cotton mill and share the premises with a variety of education and training agencies.

In keeping with the notion of 'openness' it is intended to use the premises as an administrative base but organize and co-ordinate practical and support provision throughout the borough according to individual needs.

Problems of Implementation

The gap between policy and implementation is nowhere more evident than in the arena of Open Tech delivery projects. Indeed the Further Education Unit (1985) has recognized that an adequate range of solutions and procedures necessary for the implementation of open learning systems has yet to be devised.

However, many of the practical problems associated with the implementation of the Open Tech initiative may be broken down into the following areas:

(a) organizational
(b) administrative
(c) professional.

(a) Organizational

Any innovative project arising from the Open Tech initiative invariably results in the need for the staff involved to be flexible in responding to both the identified needs of the learner and the interests of the delivery project.

In theory the function of a delivery project is to assist and encourage industry and commerce to analyse identified problems and to resolve such problems, where possible, by means of training through open learning methods.

This presupposes that industry

- is aware of its problems
- is prepared to discuss problem areas
- will admit that training of any description is needed
- is prepared to spend money on training
- is prepared to accept the validity of the cost-effectiveness of open learning.

Identification and analysis of training needs is an extremely complex task which can only commence by invitation from an employer. Such skills and expertise have to be acquired and even staff armed with the necessary skills to carry out the analysis of training needs can be pre-empted by a failure to 'sell' the benefits of open learning as a training solution. No less important is the need to recognize that the need to acquire and apply marketing techniques, in particular sales skills, becomes a priority in Open Tech staff development programmes.

This, in turn, requires local authorities to overcome the dysfunctions which exist between the inherent bureaucracy within an authority and the flexibility required of a delivery project within such a bureaucracy.

Open learning with a vocational bias on a scale envisaged by the Open Tech initiative represents relatively uncharted waters for those involved in local authority delivery projects. New skills are required with an urgency underlined by the need to be self-sustaining by March 1987.

In the selection of existing open learning materials for any given training situation, there exists an organizational procedure involving decisions concerned with

- obtaining reliable information from suppliers regarding availability of materials
- acquiring sample or specimen copies
- negotiating price
- ordering materials
- reconciling a supplier's insistence on payment before delivery with LEA policy of payment on delivery
- ability to respond rapidly to customer needs in supplying materials at short notice
- ensuring availability of supporting hardware.

(b) Administrative

However vital the organization procedures may be, their importance can only be appreciated when viewed in parallel with the administration of an open learning delivery service.

Such administration takes account of the fundamental needs of registration and recruitment of both students and tutors and the recording of a wide variety of information. The importance of accurate records cannot be overemphasized and may be seen as a prerequisite to both internal and external evaluation. For this reason data requires to be stored on such items as student and tutor assessments, extent of student support provided, details of each student including starting date, course particulars, progress, evidence of monitoring, and counselling support provided. In addition to this databases are required on stock control, description of available resources and a breakdown of learning packages which also reflects the costings involved.

(c) Professionalism

A further dimension which must be addressed is what I would refer to as professionalism. By this I mean the need to clarify to some extent subjective areas such as the distinction between tutorial support and counselling; a need to critically assess the professional worth of suppliers' learning materials and reject if necessary; and to exercise a measure of trust regarding information returned by students and tutors in order to avoid drowning in interminable cross-checks and paperwork. There is also the need to ensure a constant interplay of feedback and reinforcement between project staff, tutors and students and an integral desire to continually acknowledge that the activity is student-centred.

The issues referred to represent only a token reflection of the multitude of temporary difficulties encountered in the implementation of such a major initiative. The suggestion that these issues, and those alluded to, are of a temporary nature is quite deliberate. The principle of open learning and the enormous benefits to be accrued by its widespread implementation must surely ensure that problems are seen as short-term obstacles and not excuses for delay by the apathetic.

References

Further Education Unit *Implementing Open Learning in Local Authority Institutions* (RP274). 1985.
Kelly, A V (1980). *Curriculum Context*. Harper and Row, London.
MacDonald, B (1975) *The Programme at Two (Mimeo)*. Centre for Applied Research in Education, University of East Anglia.
MacDonald, B and Walker, R (1976) *Changing the Curriculum*. Open Books, London.
National Economic Development Council/Manpower Service Commission (1984) *Competence and Competition*. NEDO, London.
Nisbet, J (1984) Curriculum evaluation at the national level in *Evaluating the Curriculum in the Eighties*. Hodder and Stoughton, London.
MSC (1981) *An 'Open Tech' Programme. A Consultative Document*. Manpower Services Commission, Sheffield.
MSC (1984) *Open Tech Newsletter* (September issue). Manpower Services Commission, Sheffield.
MSC (1982) *Open Tech Task Group Report*. Manpower Services Commission; Sheffield.
(1969) *Report of the Committee on Technician Courses and Examinations*. HMSO, London.
White Paper (1981) *A New Training Initiative: A Programme for Action*. HMSO, London.

1.17 Resistance to Innovation in Traditional Organizations and Institutions: Bleak Prospects for the Implementation of Open Learning Systems

J W Gritton
Northern Regional Management Centre

A Jackson
Teesside Polytechnic, Middlesbrough

Abstract: The origins of this paper are to be found in the Northern Regional Management Centre (NRMC)'s experience of developing and establishing open learning methods and in the authors' beliefs formulated on the basis of this experience. That the experience has been gained solely in the field of management education, largely in the northern polytechnics and industries and only in those aspects of open learning where the NRMC has chosen to work, places limitations on the paper. The NRMC's place and role in regional public sector education – as a self-funding developmental organization – and the undeniable readiness with which management education adapts to open learning methods strengthens the arguments put forward.

The paper falls into two parts:

☐ a detailed review of the literature of resistance to innovation with particular reference to the world of education;
☐ a review of resistance and obstacles specific to open learning and an outline strategy upon which development might be based.

Literature Review

Many aspects of British life, not least further and higher education, are currently experiencing the most rapid and far-reaching period of change in their history. Its powertrain is the technological revolution, whose principal educational consequence, parallelled as it is both by increased understanding of how and why adults learn and by changes in attitude towards the individual person, will increasingly be liberation of the individual learner from institutional and organization space-time-material resources constraints, via more individually-focused learning approaches. The descriptors of those approaches – self-managed learning, self-driven learning, open learning, distance learning, action learning, contract learning – have already become current educational 'buzz words'. The process of change and innovation is already in flood; an urgent process of institutional adaptation must reflect and further facilitate that reality.

There is, however, an abundant British and American literature on change, innovation, and consequent organizational resistance. The general conclusions to be drawn are highly pessimistic – that, though 'innovation' has become a key concept to the modern world, and especially to education (Whiteside, 1978) and an increasing rate of change is a major feature of our society (Steiner, 1971; Schon, 1971; Hall and Kevles, 1982) nevertheless the characteristics of individuals and groups within organizations and the characteristics of organizations themselves, repeatedly combine together to promote resistance. Klein (1976) has observed that

'the literature of change recognizes the tendencies of individuals, groups, organizations and entire societies to act so as to ward off change... The dynamic interplay of forces in social systems is such that any stable equilibrium must represent at least a partial accommodation to the varying needs and demands of those involved.'

Like the mycelium of fungi, resistance is there – invisible from the surface, but there nonetheless.

Published studies of institutional structures (Griffin and Lieberman, 1974; Kelly, 1975; Hartley, 1980; Gritton, 1985) repeatedly suggest a tendency towards reaction rather than proaction, and an outlook which favours innovation less than successful operation of traditional activities. Scissons (1980) concluded, for instance, that redundant executives were more aware of the need for change, less tolerant of routine, and more independent and critical in thought; argued that 'individuals who function in the area of personal deviance are most vulnerable', while least vulnerable were those 'important for maintenance of the status quo'; and advised that managers wishing to avoid redundancy should place themselves 'in the position of maintenance of one or more solidly profitable aspects of the organization', avoid critical analyses of the need for change, and instead attempt 'a positive and well thought-out "we can make it work" image'.

Moreover, resistance is reinforced by the fact that it represents a living and an ongoing process whose human components are constantly adapting to environmental necessities and learning from experience. In short, resistance to change must itself be considered an essential component of all change situations. Klein (1976) and others (Sarason, 1971; Zaltman et al, 1977) have seen its desirability especially in education – to protect individual, group and community integrity against 'the various changes which are being proposed and funded before they are adequately tested'; and against 'the frequent alienation of the planners of change from the world of those for whom they are planning'. Klein continues:

'A necessary prerequisite of successful change involves the mobilization of forces against it . . . The defender . . . usually has something of great value to communicate about the nature of the system which the change agent is seeking to influence.'

Thus not only is even more research on the subject essential (Klein, 1976) but also, just as 'management of change' is thought to be an essential aspect of the managerial function, so also should 'management of resistance to change'.

The various details of the resistance process have been closely scrutinized. The recurrent conclusion is that the extent and intensity both of individual and of organizational resistance must not be underrated, and that resistance to change is much more than just reaction to the complexity of the change proposed, or simple inertia on the part of individuals or organizations. Rather, argues Giacquinta (1975), receptivity or lack of receptivity to change must be seen to be 'due primarily to structural forces'.

First, several characteristics commonly displayed by traditional organizations and institutions appear clearly to obstruct change and innovation (Frohman and Havelock, 1969; Pincus, 1974; Gray, 1975; Pennington, 1975). They include lack of structural clarity; lack of decentralized decision-making; lack of free communication and planning involvement; lack of appropriate reward patterns; training which stresses in-group procedures and values; outdated leadership conceptions; need for stability and equilibrium; processes for ordering the environment in ways relevant to the existing interests and identity of groups within the organization; enduring patterns of social behaviour; a tendency to suspect the motives and goodwill of outsiders; an emphasis on organizational pride; a demand for commitment and identification; giving strongly-drawn roles and thus encouraging conformity to existing patterns and known routines; and lack of appropriate linking roles in the organizational structure.

Looking at one factor in more detail, namely internal communications and involvement in planning, we see that the importance of the problem has been repeatedly stressed since the 1950s. Coch and French (1952) demonstrated that industrial workers merely informed of management plans to change work procedures resisted the change more than those involved in discussions, and there was lower productivity, higher absenteeism and more rapid manpower turnover as a result. Chesler and Barakat (1967) showed that teachers' lack of involvement in school policy-making reinforced unwillingness to accept change. Schein (1970) insisted 'one of the commonest problems of present day large-scale organizations is that staff units within them obtain information which they are unable to impart to their management'. Gross (1971) argued the effect (in promoting resistance) of proposals for which practitioners lacked appropriate knowledge or skills which were unclear, and for which necessary re-education was unavailable. Griffin and Lieberman (1974) concluded that the innovator was 'faced with a potential, if not actual, dysfunctional decision-making apparatus with built-in communication and articulation difficulties'. Goodridge (1976) stressed that failure to give correct information, at the right time, and in appropriate form, to those most affected by change would stimulate both initial and longer-term resistance. Klein (1976) stressed that 'the motives of innovators are especially apt to be suspect when the planning process has been kept secret up until the time of unveiling the plans and action recommendations'. Zaltman et al (1977) underlined the importance of 'the gatekeeper' – 'a person who has sufficient control over a channel of communication so as to be able to control what information flows through'. That position could be crucial, since poor upward communication could result in practitioners having 'little opportunity to show senior administration personnel innovative or at least alternative solutions'. Similar emphasis has been made by Pellegrin (1966a, 1966b); Dalton (1974) and Nagi (1974).

In short, as Schein (1970) has demonstrated, *resistance* to change is without doubt 'one of the most ubiquitous organizational phenomena . . . Many of the procedures which organizations develop to maximize their day-to-day effectiveness lead to a psychological climate in which innovation and creativity may actually be punished'. The point is well supported by Frohman and Havelock's extensive study of the field literature at that time (1969). Survival is 'probably the first commandment for organizations', whilst stability is a 'defining property' of all. That argument was reinforced by Schon's important monographs (1967, 1971) which portrayed all organizations as essentially conservative because of risks implicit in innovation and change. Schon (1971) argued that 'change threatens disruption of the stable state whose achievement and maintenance has been central to the existence of the organization'; and that all social organizations are 'self-reinforcing systems which strive to remain in something like equilibrium'. Similarly, Griffiths (1975) insisted that 'organizations are *not* characterized by change', whilst Gray (1975) reiterated that the ways an institution resists change represent the most significant feature of its dynamics.

Moreover, whether or not a traditional institution has recently been successful does not seem to improve the gloomy prognosis. If successful, then a 'slack' change-producing situation is likely to prevail (Cyert and March, 1963; Klein, 1976) in which change will be seen as merely a supplement to existing structures and operations, which are not to be disturbed. If unsuccessful, when a 'distress' change-producing situation prevails, the change likely to be necessary will be felt by some to be a threat which must be opposed, because of personal feelings of uncertainty or even anxiety.

This can produce what Schon (1971) has termed 'dynamic conservatism . . . a tendency to fight to remain the same'. Schon insisted:

> 'Belief in the stable state is strong and deep in us. We institutionalize it in every social domain. The more radical the prospective change, the more vigorous the defence – the more urgent the commitment to the stable state . . . change in organizations has its impact on the person, because beliefs, values and the sense of self have their being in social systems.'

Following similarly pessimistic lines, scholars (Graziano, 1969; Schon, 1971; Klein, 1976) have detailed methods through which individuals within organizations use traditional procedures and structures to deal with a perceived innovatory threat. Schon (1971) has portrayed the process as 'an active and more or less systematic resistance which employs a variety of strategies', which 'often takes the form of hostile resistance, overt or underground', and represented variously by 'selective inattention', 'counter-attack', 'containment', 'isolation', 'co-option', or acceptance of 'the *least change* capable of neutralizing or meeting the intrusive process'. Resistance policies thus include permitting the innovation but then diffusing it within existing or strengthened structural patterns so that nothing actually happens, or happens only symbolically, as in changes of name or title – Gray (1975) sees this as 'bending while the pressure is on' – denial of appropriate resources so the innovation is starved; or failing to utilize the innovation so that it merely 'withers on the vine'.

The critical role of *individuals* in facilitating or obstructing innovation – their conservatism, preference for the familiar, and need for certainty and security in situations of change, seen by Appley (1982) as 'the resistance imposed by an attachment to both an habitual value system and a fear of rapid change' has likewise been spotlighted by a succession of scholars since the 1950s. For instance, the obstructive influence of self-distrust, feeling of weakness or impotence, fear of failure, dependence on others, need for approval, and generally low self-esteem attracted considerable research attention in the USA during the 1950s and 1960s (Lippit, 1958; Janis, 1963; Michael, 1965; Chesler and Barakat, 1967; Watson, 1971; Klein, 1976; Appley, 1966, 1982).

Such phenomena may have particular significance in relation to authoritarian personality types, whose willingness to accept direction from dictatorial leaders and aggressive rejection of changes arising from other forces or bodies, was demonstrated by Adorno's major study (1950/1969). That argument was reinforced in respect of education by Rokeach (1960) and Lin (1966). The authoritarian syndrome may be one determinant of the almost inevitable conservatism of the leadership in traditional organizations spotlighted by such writers as Griffiths (1964/1975), Gray (1975) and Boyer (1983).

Other characteristics of individuals which scholars have shown likely to affect attitudes to change adversely include a poor level of education (Corwin, 1975); low professionalism (Daft and Becker, 1978); poor experience; inadequate personal value systems; low group and interpersonal esteem; feelings of fear, insecurity, or unsatisfied needs; low self-perception and lack of confidence (Guskin, 1969a; Coleman, 1966); and even female sex.

Such institutional and personal resistance to change and innovation has been shown by Stewart (1972) to be particularly prevalent in *public* institutions; progressive and radical change is almost always found in the private sector.

Of that public sector, one major component is education, and numerous scholars (Mort, 1964; Bourdieu, 1967; Drucker, 1970; Griffin and Lieberman, 1974; Hoyle, 1974; Zaltman et al, 1977; Muscatine, 1982; Boyer, 1983) have specifically pointed to educational institutions' resistance to change and high esteem of traditional activities, as against the practice of some scientific, engineering and industrial organizations. This is particularly so since, as Klein (1976) has pointed out, they are 'especially vulnerable' to threat from innovation, whilst, as Zaltman et al (1977) have stressed, they are 'in a unique position with regard to ignoring forces for change [since] they enjoy the protected status of a public agency with a conscripted client and are less subject to the immediate pressures of the marketplace'. Mort (1964) using American high schools as his example, averred that change 'comes about through a surprisingly slow process and follows a predictable pattern. Between insight into a need . . . and the introduction of a way of meeting the need . . . there is typically a lapse of a half-century'. These findings in respect of American schools have been underlined by Goodlad, Klein et al (1970), Griffin and Liebermann (1974), Berman and Pauley (1975), Berman and McLaughlin (1977), Muscatine (1982) and Boyer (1983).

Mort also cited evidence suggesting that the phenomenon applied no less to other parts of the public education sector. Similarly, and in the specific case of British institutions of higher education, Locke's illuminating article on polytechnic government

(1975) clearly hints at the virtual impossibility of developing innovative attitudes, structures and practices in polytechnics, and especially innovations likely to reflect or command that degree of staff support considered vital by so many scholars (eg Gray, 1975; Klein, 1976; Hewton, 1982; Boyer, 1983).

An even bleaker picture emerges from Hewton's important study (1982) of five rigorously thought out and carefully set up innovations in polytechnics and universities, three of which failed through no intrinsic demerit, but simply through failure to recognize political and/or cultural obstacles within the respective institutions. Small wonder that Raymond Williams (1984) has felt justified in asserting that 'in universities even now, even those most open to innovation, the curriculum is one which, by and large, was defined in the late 19th century'.

The likelihood, therefore, of our existing educational institutions voluntarily responding and adjusting to the curricular and learning implications of both the educational technology revolution and the social revolution – in particular, to the urgent need for a root-and-branch dismantling of traditional curricular, methodological, resourcing and structure assumptions in order to facilitate a radical shift of emphasis towards technologically based student autonomy and self-management of learning – appears minimal.

Tactics for – and against – Innovation

It is easy to argue that educational establishments are under such economic and competitive pressures that they must, and therefore will, change. All the evidence cited above indicates that change will be resisted, probably successfully. Threat – the ultimate threat of redundancy – does not encourage the threatened to take risks; rather they seem to hope that safety will lie in their being inconspicuous. Examples are not hard to find; few of those college departments with unduly high ratios of staff to students have produced a flood of applicants for redeployment.

The reasons for lecturer resistance to change are not hard to hypothesize. Any accepted definition of open learning (eg Coffey, 1977) makes it clear that changes in learning methods and materials, in methods of assessment, and shifts in the power to make academic decisions have major implications for the role of the lecturer. Sapiential authority may count for less, the carefully prepared lecture become redundant, and the security and order conditioned by curriculum and timetable disappear. Traditional career patterns will almost certainly be threatened. Should the lecturer not resist? The role of 'defender' of valued institutions and proven practices will be easy enough to sustain. The sanctity of academic discipline and the complexities of educational administration will make the task of the innovator much more difficult than that of his counterpart in industry.

Nor are all current national policies for educational development wise, despite the major impetus given by Open Tech and the Adult Training Strategy. The National Advisory Body's low full-time-equivalent (FTE) rating for an open learning student does not encourage a change of attitude in the colleges. And the now widely-held assumption that open learning must be self-funding must be questioned both on social and economic grounds. Socially it is unjustifiable that an open learning student should bear the full cost of his education – perhaps five times greater than the cost to the student of a conventional course. 'No student should be disadvantaged by the learning mode he chooses' (Chitty, 1985). Economically it makes poor sense to penalize from birth learning methods which hold so much promise and which, we are told, are so vital to national economic wellbeing.

In tactical terms the implementation of open learning, its implanting in the educational system, is a matter of timing; any venture which fails to establish itself during the next two years will lose the impetus of current government pressures for change. Yet the next few years will be times of continuing financial stringency for education, in the face of which the traditional establishment is likely to close ranks and focus its economics more closely on the fringe areas which will include most innovation.

There can be no single 'best strategy' for development, nor can any strategy be validated except by experience. However, basic concomitants suggest themselves as essential for a sound foundation to be achieved whilst the going is reasonably good.

Financial Self-Sufficiency

There can be no greater safeguard against organizational threat, despite the comments above on financing and pricing. Implicit in this object are three main tactical achievements.

- ☐ financial autonomy, even though this cannot be achieved without organizational, even personal, risk
- ☐ control of learning design, for reasons of financial viability and practicality of delivery
- ☐ an adequate range of learning and associated activities so as to be able to capitalize on all possible sources of income.

Academic Independence

The procedures adopted by many colleges to cope with the demands of the validating bodies or to co-operate with them are likely to be both a source of delay and a rallying point for the defenders. Successful innovation will have to establish its own approaches to validation.

Close Links with the Existing Establishment

Although apparently contradictory with independence, it would be foolish for any new enterprise to come into direct conflict with existing providers or to fail to make use of existing further education, higher education or community resources.

Critical Mass

Early achievment of a critical mass of activity is essential for

- ☐ financial viability
- ☐ viability of resourcing the breadth of academic disciplines involved
- ☐ (most important) providing a career structure for staff involved.

It might be reasonable to recommend scientific study of the conditions favourable to innovation. This is not the authors' view. For one thing, research itself is a common delaying tactic. For another, the tide of events is such that there is not time. Plans need to be made now on the basis of such experience as we have; decisions must be based on such observations as are possible and supported by personal belief and commitment.

References

Adorno, T W et al (1950/1969) *The Authoritarian Personality*. Norton, New York.
Appley, D G (1966) Anxiety and the human condition. *J of Canadian Association of University Student Services*. **1**, 1 pp 23-31.
Appley, D G (1982) Human development and curricular design. In Hall, J W and Kevles, B L, (eds) *In Opposition to Core Curriculum*. Greenwood Press, Westport, Conn.
Bennis, W G et al (1976) *The Planning of Change* (3rd edition). Holt Rinehart, New York.
Berman, P and Pauley, E W (1975) *Federal Programs Supporting Educational Change, Vol 2: Factors Affecting Change Agent Projects*. Rand, Santa Monica.
Berman, P and McLaughlin, M W (1977) *Federal Programs Supporting Educational Change, Vol 7: Factors Affecting Implementation and Continuing*. Rand, Santa Monica.

Bourdieu, P (1967) Systems of education and systems of thought. In Hopper, E (1971) *Readings in the Theory of Educational Systems*. Hutchinson, London.
Boyer, E L (1983) *High School: A Report on Secondary Education in America*. Harper & Row, New York.
Bradley, J (1983) *Inside Staff Development*. National Foundation for Educational Research (NFER), Guildford.
Chesler, M A and Barakat, H M (1967) *The Innovation and Sharing of Teaching Practice*. University of Michigan, Ann Arbor.
Chitty, A (1985) Open learning or closed? *Education* 20/27 December 1985.
Coch, L and French, J R P (1952) Overcoming resistance to change. In Swanson, G E *et al* (eds) *Readings in Social Psychology*. Holt, New York.
Coffey, J (1977) Open learning opportunities for mature students. In Davies, T C (ed) *Open Learning Systems for Mature Students*. Council for Educational Technology (CET) Working Paper 14.
Coleman, J S (1973) Conflicting theories of social change. In Zaltman, G (ed) *Processes and Phenomena of Social Change*. Wiley, New York.
Corwin, R G (1975) Innovation in organisations. The case of schools. *Sociology of Education* **48**, 1, pp 1-37.
Cyert, R M and March, J G (1963) *A Behavioural Theory of the Firm*. Prentice-Hall, New York.
Daft, R L and Becker, S W (1978) *The Innovative Organizations Adoptions in School Organizations*. Elsevier, New York.
Dalin, P (1978) *Limits to Educational Change*. Macmillan, London.
Dalton, G W (1974) Influence and organizational change. In Kolb, D A and Rubin, I M *Organizational Psychology*, Prentice Hall, New York.
Drucker, P F (1970) *Technology, Management and Society*, Harper and Row, New York.
Frohman, M A and Havelock, R G (1969) The organizational context of dissemination and utilization. In Havelock, R G *et al*, (ed) *Planning for Innovation*. University of Michigan, Ann Arbor.
Giacquinta, J B (1975) Status, risk and receptivity to innovation in complex organizations. *Sociology of Education* **48**, 1 pp 38-58.
Goodlad, J I, Klein, M *et al* (1970) *Behind the Classroom Door*. Jones, Worthington.
Goodridge, C G (1976) *Factors that Influence the Decision to Adopt an Educational Innovation*. Unpublished PhD thesis, University of Wisconsin.
Gray, H L (1975) Exchange and conflict in the school. In Houghton, V, *et al*. *The Management of Organisations and Individuals*, Ward Lock/OU, London.
Graziano, A M (1969) Clinical innovation and the mental health power structure. In Zaltman, G (1973) *Innovations and Organizations*. Wiley, New York.
Griffin, G A and Lieberman, A (1974) *Behaviour of Innovative Personnel*. Eric Clearinghouse on Teacher Education, Palo Alto.
Griffiths, D E (1964) Administrative theory and change in organizations. In Miles, M (1964) *Innovation in Education*, Teachers College Press, Columbia University, New York, and in Houghton, V *et al*. (eds) (1975) *The Management of Organisations and Individuals*. Ward Lock/OU, London.
Gritton, J W (1985) Managing open learning – if we can! In Jackson, A (ed) *Open Learning and the Training of Managers: A Look at the Way Ahead*, NRMC/AMEC, Washington.
Guskin, A E (1969a) The individual. In Havelock, R G, *et al Planning for Innovation*. University of Michigan, Ann Arbor.
Guskin, A E (1969b) Interpersonal linkage. In Havelock, R G *et al* (ed) *Planning for Innovation*. University of Michigan, Ann Arbor.
Hall, J W and Kevles, B L (1982) Social imperatives for another curricular change. In Hall, J W and Kevles, B L (eds) *In Opposition to Core Curriculum*. Greenwood Press, Westport.
Hartley, J F (1980) The personality of unemployed managers: myths and measurement. *Personal Review*, 9, 3 Summer, pp 13-18.
Havelock, R G et al (1969a) *Planning for Innovation Through Dissemination and Utilization of Knowledge*. University of Michigan, Ann Arbor.
Havelock, R G (1969b) Specialized knowledge linking roles. In Ibid.
Havelock, R G (1969c) The message: types of knowledge and information and their characteristics. In Ibid.
Havelock, R G (1973) *The Change Agent's Guide to Innovation*. Educational Technology Publications, New York.

Hewton, E (1982) *Rethinking Educational Change: a Case for Diplomacy*. Society for Research into Higher Education (SRHE), Guildford.
Hoyle, E (1974) Professionality, professionalism and control in teaching. *London Education Review*, **3**, 2.
Janis, I L (1963) Personality as a factor in susceptibility to persuasion. In Schramm, W (ed) *The Science of Human Communication*. Basic Books, New York.
Kelly, H (1975) You're brilliant, bored and fired. *Canadian Business*, **48**, 4, pp 36-39.
Klein, D (1976) Some notes on the dynamics of resistance to change: the defender role. In Bennis, W G et al, *The Planning of Change* (3rd edition). Holt, Rinehart & Winston, New York.
Kogan, M (1978) *The Politics of Educational Change*. Fontana, London.
Lin, N et al (1966) *The Diffusion of an Innovation in Three Michigan High Schools*. Michigan State University, Chicago.
Lippitt, R et al (1958) *The Dynamics of Planned Change*. Harcourt Brace, New York.
Locke, M (1975) Government of polytechnics. In Dobson, L et al (eds) (1975) *Management in Education: some techniques and systems*. Ward Lock/OU, Milton Keynes.
Michael, D N (1965) *Factors Inhibiting and Facilitating the Acceptance of Educational Innovations*. Institute for Policy Studies, Washington DC.
Morrish, I (1976) *Aspects of Educational Change*. Unwin, London.
Mort, P R (1964) Studies in educational innovation from the Institute of Administrative Research. In Miles, M (ed) *Innovation in Education*. Teachers College Press.
Nagi, S Z (1974) Gatekeeping decisions in service organisations: when validity fails. *Human Organization*, **33**, 1, Spring, pp 47-58.
Pellegrin, R J (1966a) The place of research in planned change. In Carlson, R O (ed) *Change Processes in the Public Schools*. University of Oregon.
Pellegrin, R J (1966b) *An Analysis of Sources and Processes of Innovation in Education*. Center for the Advanced Study of Educational Administration, Eugene.
Pennington, R C (1975) *A Critical Examination of the Nature of Resistance to Change and of those Characteristics of Individuals and Organisations which Appear to Encourage it*. Unpublished MA essay, Sheffield University.
Pincus, J (1974) Incentives for innovation in the public schools. *Review of Educational Research*, **44**, 1, pp 113-19.
Rokeach, M (1960) *Open and Closed Mind*. Basic Books, New York.
Rosenblum, S and Louis, K S (1981) *Stability and Change: Innovation in an Educational Context*. Plenum, New York.
Sarason, S B (1971) *The Culture of the School and the Problem of Change*. Allyn and Bacon, Boston.
Schein, E (1970) *Organisational Psychology*. Prentice Hall, New York.
Schon, D A (1967) *Technology and Change*. Delacorte Press, New York.
Schon D A (1971) *Beyond the Stable State: Public and Private Learning in a Changing Society*. Temple Smith, London.
Scissons, E H (1980) For whom the axe falls: the profile of the outplaced executive. *Personnel Review*, **9**, 3, Summer, pp 19-21.
Shaw, K E (1975) Negotiating curriculum change in a college of education. In Reid, W A and Walker, D F (eds) *Case Studies in Curriculum Change: Great Britain and United States*. Routledge, London.
Steiner, G (1971) *In Bluebeard's Castle. Some Notes towards the Redefinition of Culture*. Faber, London.
Stewart, W A C (1972) *Progressives and Radicals in English Education*. Macmillan, London.
Watson, G (1971) Resistance to change. *American Behavioural Scientist*. 14.
Whiteside, T (1978) *The Sociology of Educational Innovation*. Methuen, London.
Williams, R (1984) Talk on Channel 4 TV, 2 May 1984.
Wright, W H et al (1986) *Implementing Open Learning in Local Authority Institutions*. FEU/OTU, London.
Zaltman, G et al (1973) Resistance to innovation. In Zaltman, G et al (eds) *Innovations and Organisations*. Wiley, New York.
Zaltman, G et al (1977) *Dynamic Educational Change: Models, Strategies, Tactics and Management*. Free Press, New York.

1.18 Promoting Independent and Informal Learning for Adults (Workshop Report)

D Hall and V Smith
Council for Educational Technology (CET), London

Abstract: This paper reports on workshop activities which focused on two recently completed CET projects (Spring 1986).

The paper presents a rationale for the approach to the workshop. This provided participants with opportunities to learn about the thinking and practice of promoting learner-centred strategies and asked them to take on the role of potential adult learners. The separate facets of the session are outlined and feedback from participative exercises has been included.

The workshop explored some contexts, processes and resources for independent and informal adult learning, including applications of the new technology. These two related, but nevertheless distinct, learner-directed systems for adults offer flexible and often individualized modes of learning, which can meet a wide range of learning needs and aspirations.

Introduction

This workshop aimed to introduce participants to two forms of learning which can offer adults flexible ways of meeting their learning needs.

The two Council for Educational Technology (CET) projects, namely PLAILS (Public Libraries and Adult Independent Learners) and the CET Information Centres' Project (Learning Links), shared a common focus, that of learner-centredness, but the strategies and contexts for each project were quite different. The workshop therefore explored both the contexts and some of the processes for each project by presenting the educational philosophy of the work to participants and by involving them in some practical tasks.

Overview of Workshop Session

The workshop consisted of five distinct sections:

1. adult learners
2. some contexts for adult learning with special reference to informal and independent learning
3. starting points for learners, with particular reference to the role of public libraries
4. using computers to stimulate and support informal adult learning
5. open forum.

1. Adult Learners

After a brief general introduction participants were asked to identify for themselves possible contexts and reasons for learning by looking at their life roles (parents, citizens, employees, managers, etc) and at their personal interests (hobbies, Third World issues, trade union activities, etc).

No feedback was requested from this exercise but delegates were asked to bear in mind their personal learning needs when considering the relevance of independent and informal learning.

2. Some Contexts for Adult Learning with Special Reference to Informal and Independent Learning

A range of possible contexts as learning options for adults were considered before focusing on the specific contexts for informal and independent adult learning. The following spectrum of options provided a basic map for locating the contextual framework of the two CET projects.

Face-to-face education/ training courses	Supported open learning	Community-based informal learning	Self-directed independent learning

Specific contexts for informal adult learning activities, the main concern of the Learning Links project, were presented (self-help learning groups, clubs, societies, learning exchanges and media-based learning groups) as were the client groups for which public libraries might be of particular relevance (community groups, people engaged in self-directed research or training, people pursuing independent study, leisure interests, and short-term learning projects). In each context the full range of learners, from those who are 'sampling' to those who pursue serious long-term learning programmes, can be found.

3. Starting Points for Learners, with Particular Reference to the Role of the Public Library

Adult learners, especially those who have not engaged in any form of planned learning for some time, may return to learning by a number of different routes. These can be separated into direct and indirect starting points. The former would include direct contact with education and training providers as well as an approach to resource centres. The latter might come about through visits to such agencies as Jobcentres, careers services, and other information or advice centres. The public library also comes within this category.

In order to identify for themselves the positive and negative experiences potential learners might encounter when using the public library as a starting point, participants were asked to carry out the following task in small groups:

> Assume that you are going to use the local public library system to try to:
> ☐ obtain information and learning materials
> ☐ obtain help and guidance in planning your learning project, and
> ☐ find out about other sources of information and help
>
> *on one of the topics listed below*:
> ☐ management in small business
> ☐ word processing
> ☐ holistic medicine
> ☐ the world's forests (conservation vs. economic development)
> ☐ the role of school governor
> ☐ French
> ☐ traditional jazz
> ☐ the feminist movement in the 20th century
> ☐ Salvador Dali.

Identify:
(a) The most useful things the library is likely to provide for you.
(b) The greatest difficulty you are likely to encounter in pursuing your learning via the library.
(c) The most useful source(s) of additional help to which the library might refer you.

This exercise resulted in the following feedback from participants:

(a) Participants thought that the most useful services a library is likely to provide would include:
- ☐ specialist help ⎱
- ☐ books and booklists ⎰ resources
- ☐ rooms and meetings/lectures
- ☐ access to an information network } information

(b) The greatest difficulties learners might encounter were thought to be:
- ☐ the quality of reception for enquirers ⎱ guidance
- ☐ level of perception about an enquiry ⎰
- ☐ availability and cost of good quality non-print materials ⎱ resources
- ☐ range of materials ⎰
- ☐ timelag in obtaining materials ⎱ access
- ☐ opening hours ⎰

(c) Additional help which would be desirable:
- ☐ specialist searches ⎱ information
- ☐ named contacts of key persons in other agencies ⎰
- ☐ tutor resources ⎱ resources
- ☐ resources for the community ⎰

The above grouping of the main points illustrates the key elements of *information, access, guidance* and *resources* for adult learners which are necessary to overcome external and internal barriers to learning. Such barriers relate to time, place, cost and organizational requirements as well as personal circumstances (external barriers). Others exist because of adults' poor self-image, fear of assessment and role conflicts (internal barriers), to name but a few examples.

4. Using Computers to Stimulate and Support Informal Adult Learning

The workshop session took up two of the key elements listed above. Guidance and information had been central to the Learning Links project which developed two software packages to assist adult returners to learning.

Participants were introduced to one section of the Learning Links interactive self-assessment program (past learning experiences). The relevance of the other parts of the program (reasons for learning, modes of learning, interests for learning and practical matters) was pointed out, and some sample results were presented to illustrate how adults might identify their learning goals by working through the program.

These sample results provided the basis for searching the various databanks which have been set up by the four information centres developed by the Learning Links project. Searches were carried out by using the keywords identified in the self-assessment process, eg someone interested in birdwatching might find useful information by searching options 1, 2, 3 and 4 from the following top menu of the Learning Links database:

1. Informal learning
2. Home-based learning
3. Learning exchanges

4. Non-examination courses
5. Examination courses

The search revealed possible learning activities on the informal and home-based databanks. This request (for activities associated with birdwatching) could also have provided the basis for a potential learning exchange and could have been added as a record to this databank.

5. Open Forum

A brief discussion on the problems associated with direct client access to databanks was followed by considering a question raised earlier by a delegate: to what extent is the work of the two CET projects relevant to YTS (Youth Training Scheme)? While the relevance of the ideas and the practical outcomes was acknowledged, no direct experience could be offered, since the projects had not focused on the age group involved in YTS schemes.

Summary

The workshop demonstrated what is involved in promoting independent and informal learning for adults by drawing on the experience of two recent CET projects. Since these forms of learning are still very much in their infancy, requiring consistent effort and good support from those responsible for facilitating adult learning, this session focused as much on the factors contributing to or hindering these flexible systems for adult learners as on strategies for facilitating independent and informal learning for adults.

1.19 Structure and Organization in Instructional Text

A M Stewart
Dundee College of Technology

Abstract: It has been argued that the content and structure of passages of text are inextricably linked and that students will learn from text better if they can follow the organization of the material and later use that organization. It has also been argued that authors can help readers to comprehend text information by making sure that the design of their text supports the comprehension processes that readers must perform, including, *inter alia*, identifying the important ideas in the text, organizing those ideas, and integrating those ideas with prior knowledge.

The purpose of this paper is to consider ways in which the organization of text can be made explicit and the ways in which this organization can be related to the cognitive processes of the reader, through either verbal or typographical cueing. Verbal cueing strategies explored include linguistic devices such as cohesion, but concentrate on instructional design aspects, including advance organizers, graphic organizers, adjunct questions, and learning objectives. Typographical cueing examined includes the use of space, headings, and layout.

Introduction

Despite the onset of electronic communications, printed materials will continue to be a fundamental part of the teaching/learning system for a considerable period of time. Although research into printed materials has not been conducted for as long as printed materials have been available, it has been suggested by Britton and Black (1985) that the study of discourse structures seems to have begun in the Western world before 600 BC. Research relating to instructional text has been carried out from three different perspectives – that associated with the physical characteristics of text and typified by the research on legibility and readability; that associated with ways of improving instructional text and exemplified by the research on illustrations, adjunct aids, and typographical cueing; and that associated with the way people learn from text and characterized by the research on the psychology of human memory and learning.

In the field of instructional text design there exists, at present, research findings from various perspectives, the theoretical foundations of which are not equally defensible. Psychological study of human learning was previously dominated by associationism but, as Voss (1984) has noted, with the emergence of cognitive psychology there is now a concern with *what* is assumed to be learned and *how* something is learned. Earlier research findings need to be re-examined in the context of current cognitively-oriented research, and the purpose of this paper is to describe a theoretical framework for the reading comprehension process within which the means by which the structure and organization of text can be designed to facilitate comprehension can be examined.

Reading Comprehension

Chall and Stahl (1982) have observed that large-scale studies of reading comprehension were undertaken during the 1970s, influenced by a variety of disciplines including linguistics, psycholinguistics, and cognitive psychology. From an analysis of that substantial body of research, Stewart (1985) derived the following principles for the design of instructional text:

> 'If the ideas in discourse are emphasized and indicated in the organization of the text, the reader is likely to form representations and networks of representations in keeping with the organizational plan.'

> 'If the design of text takes into consideration the process of comprehension involved in reading to learn with respect to text-based and reader-based variables, comprehension will be optimized.'

These principles reflect key contributions to an understanding of the reading comprehension process from psycholinguistics and from cognitive psychology. Psycholinguistics research makes it clear that comprehension is concerned not so much with recall as with transformations, inferences, and integrations (Lachman and Lachman, 1979) and with the notion of levels where the highest level demands 'thinking' or at least some construction of ideas (Perfetti, 1977). A significant contribution to reading comprehension can be attributed to Kintsch (1979) who argued that reading comprehension is a constructive process involving not just the text but the reader's prior knowledge of the topic. His concept of 'text representation' as propositions is consistent with the now widely held view of the propositional representation of knowledge in which, as Gagné (1985) has pointed out, the proposition corresponds roughly to an idea and 'words, phrases and sentences represent ways of communicating ideas, whereas propositions represent the ideas themselves'. The concept of propositional representation is an integral part of a cognitive view of psychology, but the important issue is really the extent to which the reader constructs meaning through interaction with the text (Kintsch, 1982; Goodman, 1984).

The reader's purpose and goals can influence the construction of meaning (Saljo, 1984), so variables can arise from both the reader and from the text. Different cognitive representations can be stimulated by the use of different structures and emphasis plans in text (Meyer, 1984), and this could have important implications for the designer of instructional text. Meaning is formed as a result of the dynamic interaction between the reader's existing abstract knowledge structures and the clues available in the text (Schallert, 1982), an assumption which is fundamental to the schema-theoretic view of comprehension and which provides an important foundation for the development of text-based ways of activating relevant schema and making the organization of text more obvious.

It is reasonable to conclude from the research on reading comprehension that the way text is comprehended and remembered is a function of both the structure of the text and the knowledge utilized by the individual (Voss and Bisanz, 1985). Reading comprehension is a complex issue with, as Spiro and Myers (1984) have noted, individual differences in reading performance arising from factors on bottom-up (or text-based) processing, top-down (or knowledge-based) processing, the interaction of top-down and bottom-up processing, and the metacognitive control processes that manage the whole system.

It is within the theoretical framework for reading comprehension outlined above that the issue of structure and organization in text is explored.

Highlighting Structure and Organization

Winne (1985) has pointed out that information in permanent memory is highly organized and can be pictured as a complex network or hierarchical array, with three basic forms of information being theorized – concepts, propositions, and schema – where a concept is a basic unit of information that represents a category, a proposition is like a sentence that relates two or more concepts, and a scheme is a collection of propositions organized to describe prototypes of phenomena or events. Not only are the forms of information organized, they achieve meaning by their relationships to one another.

Brandt (1978) has argued that the content and structure of passages of text are inextricably linked and that students will learn from the text better if they can follow the organization of the material and later use that organization. Glynn and Britton (1984) have argued that, since comprehension of text can be a cognitively demanding task, authors can help readers to comprehend and recall text information by making sure that the design of their text supports each of the component comprehension processes that the readers must perform, including, *inter alia*, identifying the important ideas in the text, organizing those ideas, and integrating those ideas with prior knowledge. The organization of text can be made explicit through both verbal and typographical cueing systems (Glynn et al, 1985) and it is within that framework that the issue of structure and organization is examined.

(a) The Role of Verbal Cueing

Verbal cueing can be either of a linguistic nature (ie concerned with the semantic and syntactic structure of the text), or of an instructional design nature (ie verbal support such as advance organizers and adjunct questions which, although an integral part of the text, are not really part of the content).

Linguistic aspects of structure and organization are not the focus of this paper, but it is worth noting in passing that Singer (1985) has identified three organizational features of text: cohesion, content, and staging. These features, if recognized and used by students, can lead to better processing of information. Similarly, Meyer (1984; 1985) has argued that a text follows a hierarchy of content and that a writing plan must explicitly or implicitly suggest to the reader the type of overall structure or scheme to use in interpreting the topic. Various features of the text including its structure, coherence, and content can influence learning from reading, but the main concern here is for other textual factors supplementary to the main content (ie instructional design factors) which play an important part in the comprehension of text and are, thus, important elements in the design of text.

In a recent review of instructional psychology, Resnick (1985) acknowledges that the current view of reading comprehension is too recent to have generated many instructional applications yet, but that (a) a few efforts to teach reading strategies have been made, and (b) older lines of work on advance organizers, questions, and other adjuncts to text may eventually be reinterpreted in light of the constructive view of the reading process.

Anderson (1984) has claimed that schema theory supports the practice of providing advance organizers along the lines proposed by Ausubel (1968), and Jonassen (1985) has argued that advance organizers function, according to Ausubelian cognitive theory, as conceptual anchors in the reader's knowledge structure for subsuming new information presented in text. There is certainly convincing evidence that advance organizers can be effective (Meyer, 1979; Luiten et al, 1980) and equally convincing evidence that the activation of prior knowledge can be effective (Adams and Bruce, 1980; Peeck et al, 1982). Is the role of the advance organizer in the activation of prior knowledge really the facilitating of a 'set-to-learn' disposition toward the text? If so, if verbal material provided prior to the main text is able to activate schema and prior knowledge in the reader, and is able through this and through its own structure to set the framework and organization of the main text, then it is creating a set-to-learn context and is, in a real sense, an advance organizer. On this basis, Stewart (1985) derived the following principle:

> 'If the reader is oriented by a brief verbal organizer toward the application of existing knowledge to the assimilation of the main features of new knowledge in text, then comprehension of that new knowledge will be facilitated.'

It is possible for an advance organizer to be other than verbal. Following upon the work of Weisberg (1970) with visual advance organizers, there have been attempts by a number of workers to assess the value of advance organizers being presented in a nonverbal form (Snowman and Cunningham, 1975; Koran and Koran, 1980; Bernard et al, 1981) or as a graphic representation of words (Moore and Readance, 1980, 1983); Alvermann (1981), investigating the relationship between graphic organizers and text structure, has argued that the organizer may influence the learner's encoding process by providing anchoring ideas which help to 'hold' incoming information from text that is less than optimal in its organization. There is a case for graphic organizers being particularly effective when the intention is to relate to structure because there is the potential not only to activate schema and indicate emphasis but – because of the possibility of dual coding or whatever other explanation there is for imagery – a higher level of cognitive operation, viz. relationship between ideas, can be presented as a starting point. Stewart (1984) observed that the availability of a teacher-provided graphic organizer based on the topic analysis helped students to identify the hierarchical structure of a text, and concluded that 'If a graphic organizer is used to convey isomorphically the structure of ideas in text, then comprehension of the structure will be facilitated' (Stewart, 1985). Rothkopf (1965) is credited with the creation of what has become the highly active area of educational research known as 'adjunct questions', but it has been acknowledged that he began his investigations under the theoretical banner of neo-behaviourism, although subsequent research in the area has assumed a cognitive perspective which emphasizes the active and constructive role of the learner (Lindner and Rickards, 1985). Research into the effectiveness of adjunct questions has been concerned mainly with position (before or after), type (factual or meaningful), and frequency of inserted questions. It leaves little doubt as to the effectiveness of adjunct questions (Anderson and Biddle, 1975; Duchastel and Whitehead, 1980), with verbatim adjunct questions producing robust positive effects irrespective of position while semantic post-questions tend to produce larger increases (Hamilton, 1985), an outcome which suggests the inducing of a deeper level of processing and attention being focused on relevant prose material. Resnick (1985) asserts that there has not emerged an integrative account capable of linking questioning effects either to schema theories of reading or to general propositional models of reading. However, it may be that the context in which this research could more appropriately be considered is that of 'qualitative outcomes of learning' (Marton and Saljo, 1984; Entwistle and Ramsden, 1983; Saljo, 1984) since, if the reader can be induced through the adjunct questions to adopt a 'deep approach' to learning from that particular reading experience, then not only a deep semantic processing, but a more meaningful processing is likely to occur. Setting the work on adjunct questions in that context led Stewart (1985) to derive the following principle:

> 'If higher-level questions are inserted in text they are likely to induce a deeper level of processing on the part of the reader.'

Singer (1985) notes that teacher-provided activities that initiate or stimulate learning (ie mathemagenic activities) include, in addition to questions embedded in text, the establishment of purposes and goals. However, in a recent evaluation of the effectiveness of stating learning objectives, Hamilton (1985) notes that objectives have consistently produced positive effects only for the retention of verbatim verbal information. In the majority of investigations, most of the objectives have been low-level recall of information. It remains to be seen what would be the effect of a high-level objective. While an advance organizer may activate a particular schema or set of schemata, it is unlikely that the statement of an objective would have the same effect. What is much more likely is that the statement of a high-level objective (ie high-level in the Bloom or Gagné sense) would induce a set-to-learn from which deep processing would ensue. There does not appear to be any research which examines the effectiveness not only of high-level objectives but of high-level inserted questions which measure achievement of the high-level objectives. It could be hypothesized that such an interaction would lead to the desired deep processing and, consequently, comprehension of the text. On this basis, Stewart (1985) proposed the following principle:

> 'If a high-level learning outcome is stated as an objective in advance of reading, the learner is likely to adopt a deep approach to reading of the passage.'

(b) The Role of Typographical Cueing

Hartley (1982) has argued that the clarity of instructional text can be improved by manipulating its layout. He has also argued that the use of space aids the reader's perception of the structure of the document as a whole, helping the reader to comprehend the document's organization (Hartley, 1980). Waller (1980) has argued, however, that there is no consistent set of rules on which to base the kind of effective-reading instruction that advises students to make sensible use of visually signalled text structure, and has proposed that typographic signals and the use of space need to be seen as an organizational system operating at the macro-text level in much the same way as punctuation operates at the micro-text level. He has also pointed out (Waller, 1982) that, within the notion of 'text as diagram', layout can serve as part of the writer's repertoire of syntactic cues for giving a discourse direction and coherence and as an aid to selective reading, making accessible the structure of the content of a text. It is important to note, however, that, as Hartley (1985) has pointed out, spatial and typographic cues need to be used consistently. Unfortunately, it is relatively rare for spatial or typographical cues to be used in this way, yet their potential lies in their being used not only consistently, but in concert.

Hartley (1984) has pointed out that the structure of complex text can be demonstrated more clearly to the reader by the consistent and planned use of spacing in both its vertical and horizontal dimensions, and he has argued that space can be manipulated, in particular, to group and separate functionally related parts of a text, a view that has also been expressed by Stewart (1978; 1984) who argued for the integration of typographical and spatial cueing, particularly with regard to headings. Waller (1985) has argued that the concept of text as diagram requires that typographically structured pages must be seen in their wholeness and must operate within the artifactual limitations of the print medium in a way that contrasts with the normal view of prose. He claims that typographical and spatial factors can be used to clarify the larger structural relationships in a text, thus easing the cognitive burden.

Rennie, Neilson, and Braun (1981) claim that the theoretical framework and rationale for typographical cueing studies related to the superordinate structures of discourse are drawn from schema theory, metacognition, and typographical cueing: schema-theoretic research demonstrates the psychological reality of macro-structures in the reading of expository text and the influence of prior knowledge on comprehension; metacognitive research, in exploring reader's introspective judgements about text processing, has shown that successful identification of top-level structures is a developmental skill; and research related to the effect of typographical cueing has shown that cues provide an isolation effect by visually setting apart the cued words, resulting in a higher probability of recall of cued information.

Glynn et al (1985) set the effect of typographical cues firmly within a cognitive framework, but they see the role of typographical cues in relation to management of the reader's attention by helping him/her to identify, organize, and interpret the most important content in a text. In their view, the comprehension of instructional text is a formidable cognitive task, since it requires the reader to call upon large bodies of relevant prior knowledge and concurrently carry out 'component comprehension processes' which include recognizing the words in the text and retrieving their meanings, identifying the important ideas in the text, organizing these ideas, and integrating them with prior knowledge. Spatial and typographical cueing can therefore contribute to the identification of important ideas in text and, potentially, to the organization of those ideas, and help to bring about the cognitive structures associated with text comprehension.

From the available research in relation to typographical cueing, Stewart (1985) derived the following principle:

> 'If headings in text are chosen and arranged spatially and typographically to reflect the structural relationships in the text, comprehension of both the structure and the content of the text is likely to be enhanced.'

Conclusion

The organized and structured nature of knowledge in memory has implications for the way in which instructional text is designed. The ways in which verbal and typographical cueing are employed should be determined not so much by intuition or aesthetics as by the potential contribution which the resulting organization and structure can make to the ready assimilation of the material to the existing knowledge structures of the reader. Such contribution can be achieved through the application of the identified design principles.

References

Adams, M and Bruce, B (1980) *Background Knowledge and Reading Comprehension*. Reading Education Report No 13, Centre for the Study of Reading, University of Illinois at Urbana-Champaigne.

Alvermann, D E (1981) *The Compensatory Effect of Graphic Organizer Instruction on Text Structure*, Paper presented at the annual meeting of the American Educational Research Association, Los Angeles, April 1981.

Anderson, R C (1984) Role of the reader's schema in comprehension, learning and memory. In R C Anderson, J Osborn and R J Tierney (eds) *Learning to Read in American Schools*. Lawrence Erlbaum Associates.

Anderson, R C and Biddle, W B (1975) 'On asking people questions about what they are reading. In G Bower (ed) *The Psychology of Learning and Motivation, Vol 9*. Academic Press.

Ausubel, D P (1968) *Educational Psychology: A Cognitive View*. Holt, Rinehart, and Winston.

Bernard, R M, Peterson, C H and Ally, M (1981) Can images provide contextual support for prose? *Educational Communication and Technology Journal (ECTJ)*, 29, pp 101-108.

Brandt, D M (1978) *Prior Knowledge and the Author's Schema and the Comprehension of Prose*. Unpublished doctoral dissertation, Arizona State University.

Britton, B K and Black, J B (1985) Understanding expository text: from structure to process and world knowledge. In B K Britton and J B Black (eds) *Understanding Expository Text*. Lawrence Erlbaum Associates.

Chall, J S and Stahl, S A (1982) Reading. In *Encyclopedia of Educational Research Vol 3*. The Free Press.

Duchastel, P C and Whitehead, D (1980) Exploring student reactions to inserted questions in text. *Programmed Learning and Educational Technology*, **17**, 1, pp 41-47.

Entwistle, N J and Ramsden, P (1983) *Understanding Student Learning*. Croom Helm.

Gagné, E D (1985) *The Cognitive Psychology of Learning*. Little, Brown & Co.

Glynn, S M and Britton, B K (1984) Supporting readers' comprehension through effective text design. *Educational Technology*, 24, 10, pp 40-43.

Glynn, S M, Britton, B K and Tillman, M H (1985) Tyographical cues in text: management of readers' attention. In D H Jonassen (ed) *The Technology of Text Vol 2*. Educational Technology Publications.

Goodman, K S (1985) Unity in reading. In A C Purves and O Niles (eds) *Becoming Readers in a Complex Society*. Eighty-Third Yearbook of the National Society for the Study of Education, National Society for the Study of Education.

Hamilton, R J (1985) A framework for the evaluation of the effectiveness of adjunct questions and objectives. *Review of Educational Research*, **55**, 1, pp 47-85.

Hartley, J (1980) Space and structure in instructional text. In J Hartley (ed) *The Psychology of Written Communication*. Kogan Page, London.
Hartley, J (1982) Designing instructional text. In D H Jonassen (ed) *The Technology of Text*. Educational Technology Publications.
Hartley, J (1984) Space and structure in instructional text. In R Easterby and H Zwaga (eds) *Information Design*, John Wiley & Sons.
Hartley, J (1985) Typographic design. In T Husen and T N Postlethwaite (eds) *International Encyclopedia of Education Vol 9*. Pergamon Press.
Jonassen, D H (1985) Controlling the processing of text. In D H Jonassen (ed) *The Technology of Text Vol 2*. Educational Technology Publications.
Kintsch, W (1979) Levels of processing language material. In L S Cermak and F I M Craik (eds) *Levels of Processing in Human Memory*. Lawrence Erlbaum Associates.
Kintsch, W (1982) Text representations in W Otto and S White (eds) *Reading Expository Material*. Academic Press.
Koran, M L and Koran, J J (1980) Interaction of learner characteristics with pictorial adjuncts in learning from science text. *Journal of Research in Science Teaching*, **17**, 5, pp 477-483.
Lachman, J L and Lachman, R (1979) Comprehension and cognition: a state of the art inquiry. In L S Cermak and F I Craik (eds) *Levels of Processing in Human Memory*. Lawrence Erlbaum Associates.
Lindner, R W and Rickards, J P (1985) Questions inserted in text: issue and implications. In D H Jonassen (ed) *The Technology of Text Vol 2*. Educational Technology Publications.
Luiten, J, Ames, A, and Ackerson, G (1980) A meta-analysis of the effects of advance organizers on learning and retention. *American Educational Research Journal*, **17**, 2, pp 211-218.
Marton, F and Saljo, R (1984) Approaches to learning. In F Marton, D Hounsell, and N Entwistle (eds) *The Experience of Learning*, Scottish Academic Press.
Mayer, R E (1979) Twenty years of research on advance organizers: assimilation theory is still the best predictor of results. *Instructional Science*, **8**, pp 133-167.
Meyer, B J F (1984) Text dimensions and cognitive processing. In H Mandl, N L Stein, and T Trabasso (eds) *Learning and Comprehension of Text*. Lawrence Erlbaum Associates.
Meyer, B J F (1985) Signalling the structure of text. In D H Jonassen (ed) *The Technology of Text Vol 2*, Educational Technology Publications.
Moore D N and Readence, J E (1980) A meta-analysis of the effect of graphic organizers on learning from text. In M J Kamil and A J Moe (eds) *Perspectives on Reading Research and Instruction*. Twenty-ninth yearbook of the National Reading Conference.
Moore, D N and Readence, J E (1983) *A Quantitative and Qualitative Review of Graphic Organizer Research*. Paper presented at the annual meeting of the American Educational Research Association, Montreal, April 1983.
Peeck, J, van den Bosch, A B, and Kreupeling, W J (1982) Effect of mobilizing prior knowledge on learning from text. *Journal of Educational Psychology*, **74**, 5, pp 771-777.
Perfetti, C A (1977) Language Comprehension and fast decoding: some psycholinguistic prerequisites for skilled reading comprehension. In J T Guthrie (ed) *Cognition, Curriculum, and Comprehension*. International Reading Association.
Rennie, B J, Neilsen, A R and Braun C (1981) The effects of typographical cueing on memory for superordinate structures in connected discourse. In M L Kamil (ed) *Directions in Reading: Rresearch and Instruction*. National Reading Conference.
Resnick, L B (1985) Instructional psychology. In T Husen and T N Postlethwaite (eds) *The International Encyclopedia of Education Vol 5*. Pergamon Press.
Rothkopf, E Z (1965) Some theoretical and experimental approaches to problems in written instruction. In J D Krumboltz (ed) *Learning and the Educational Process*. Rand McNally.
Saljo, R (1984) Learning from reading. In F Marton, D Hounsell, and N Entwistle (eds) *The Experience of Learning*. Scottish Academic Press.
Schallert, D L (1982) The significance of knowledge: A synthesis of research related to schema theory. In W Otto and S White (eds) *Reading Expository Material*. Academic Press.
Singer, H (1985) Comprehension instruction. In T Husen and T N Postlethwaite (eds) *The International Encyclopedia of Education Vol 2*. Pergamon Press.
Snowman, J and Cunningham, D J L (1975) A comparison of pictorial and written adjunct aids in learning from text. *Journal of Educational Psychology*, **67**, 2, pp 307-311.
Spiro, R J and Myers, A (1984) Individual differences and underlying cognitive processes in reading. In P D Pearson (ed) *Handbook of Reading Research*. Longman.
Stewart, A M (1978) *Redesigning the 'Primary Health Worker' guide*. Internal report NUR/HMD, World Health Organization, Geneva.

Stewart, A M (1984) *Relationship between topic analysis, graphic organizer and typographical structure of text.* Internal report NUR/HMD, World Health Organization, Geneva.
Stewart, A M (1985) *The Design of Print as a Medium of Instruction.* Unpublished paper, Dundee College of Technology, Dundee.
Voss, J F (1984) On learning and learning from text. In H Mandle, N L Stein, and T Trabasso (ed) *Learning and Comprehension of Text.* Lawrence Erlbaum Associates.
Voss, J F and Bisanz, G L (1985) Knowledge and the processing of narrative and expository texts. In B K Britton and J B Black (eds) *Understanding Expository Text.* Lawrence Erlbaum Associates.
Waller, R H (1980) Graphic aspects of complex texts: typography as macro-punctuation. In P A Kolers, M E Wrolstad, and H Bouma (eds) *Processing of Visible Language 2.* Plenum Press.
Waller, R H (1982) Text as diagram: using typography to improve access and understanding. In D H Jonassen (ed) *The Technology of Text.* Educational Technology Publications.
Waller, R H (1985) Using typography to structure arguments: a critical analysis of some examples. In D H Jonassen (ed) *The Technology of Text Vol 2.* Educational Technology Publications.
Weisberg, J S (1970) The use of visual advance organizers for learning earth science concepts. *Journal of Research in Science Teaching*, 7, pp 161-165.
Winne, P H (1985) Cognitive processing in the classroom. In T Husen and T N Postlethwaite (eds) *The International Encyclopedia of Education Vol 2.* Pergamon Press.

1.20 Multimedia Learning Packages

K L Kumar
Staff Development Centre, Baghdad, Iraq

Abstract: Packages of learning materials offer a high degree of flexibility in time and pace of learning as well as in the selection of media. Modular systems of teaching, learning and computerization have evoked renewed interest in the design, evolution and usage of multimedia resources.

The paper outlines a methodology of preparing alternative media-mixes for a given set of terminal objectives. A matrix procedure of assigning points and decision-making on the basis of cumulative scores for alternative combinations is recommended. It is demonstrated how the overall learning effectiveness may be maximized through a judicious synthesis of different audiovisual materials. The three hierarchical principles proposed for pragmatic syntheses are those of appropriateness, variety and cost-effectiveness. A selection algorithm together with a flowchart is proposed to identify the most appropriate audiovisual materials for the achievement of a desired learning outcome. It proceeds through a series of decision points, ie key questions posed to the designer. Some useful guidance on the same has also been included. The principles of variety and cost effectiveness have also been discussed.

An action study on the use of a multimedia package has revealed that the flexibility offered by it is in part offset by the inadequate interest and slower progress of 30 per cent of the learners. Overall benefits of self-learning and flexibility are, however, difficult to quantify.

Introduction

Recent advances in student-centred methods of teaching, learning and evaluation stem from the belief that the essence of all teaching activities is to facilitate learning by the student. Researchers on the mechanics of learning (Brown and Brown, 1984) and on other topics such as motivation, self-paced learning, retention, recall, application and creativity have revealed that learning is most effective when the learning resources are mutually complementary and they offer flexibility of selection and use. Development in modular systems of instruction, manuals for students and teachers, and open door laboratories have taken place in the light of such realizations. Learning packages promise to offer the desired flexibility and the mutual complementing of learning resources.

Need for Different Media

Different media are characterized by such factors as accessibility, the building up of information, unmasking and overlaying of information, movement, sound accompaniment, presentation of pictures, and so on. The objectives which govern the selection of one or other of such media are discussed in the following section.

The effectiveness of a medium otherwise appropriate for an objective varies with the passage of time; it may reach a high value and may remain high for a short interval of time, but it must drop down thereafter. This fact is attributed to the relatively short attention span of a learner brought about by a given stimulus. In order to sustain the interest of the learner, it is necessary to identify the alternative media and switch over from one to another at times (Percival and Ellington, 1984). The progress of a teaching-learning session may also need a change of medium in other cases to meet the objectives. A conceptual framework of temporal effectiveness of some media is presented in Figure 1. Further research is necessary to determine the relative effectiveness of different media for different target populations. Such qualification would assist the process of selection and optimization of media used over a given period of time.

Media Selection Algorithm

A pragmatic approach to selecting the most appropriate medium for the desired instructional objective is to establish the mechanics of the thought process which should take place in the mind. It consists of posing a series of questions to oneself, seeking responses and proceeding to identify a suitable medium. The first question is to ensure that there is indeed a need to look for an audiovisual medium. The subsequent questions enable one to narrow down the choice for the required characteristics, ie projection, motion picture, and so on.

A complete flowchart for such a procedure is shown in Figure 2.

Principles of Selection

Media selected by the principal of appropriateness as above, may not always be the most suitable or the most practicable. Two more principles, those of variety and cost-effectiveness, enter into the selection process in strict order. According to the former principle, media must be changed in order to vary the nature of the stimulus. Sometimes more than one medium may be appropriate. In such cases variety poses no problem. In others, variety may sometimes be introduced at the cost of appropriateness. Similarly, if alternative media are available or manageable, one may start with the cheapest; otherwise cost-effectiveness may demand some sacrifice in appropriateness and variety (Brown and Brown, 1984).

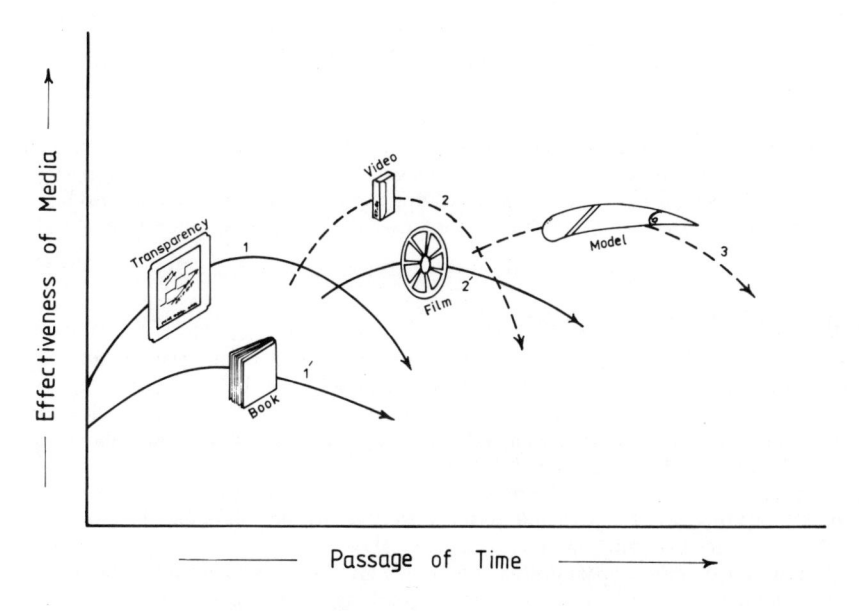

Figure 1. *Temporal effectiveness of some media*

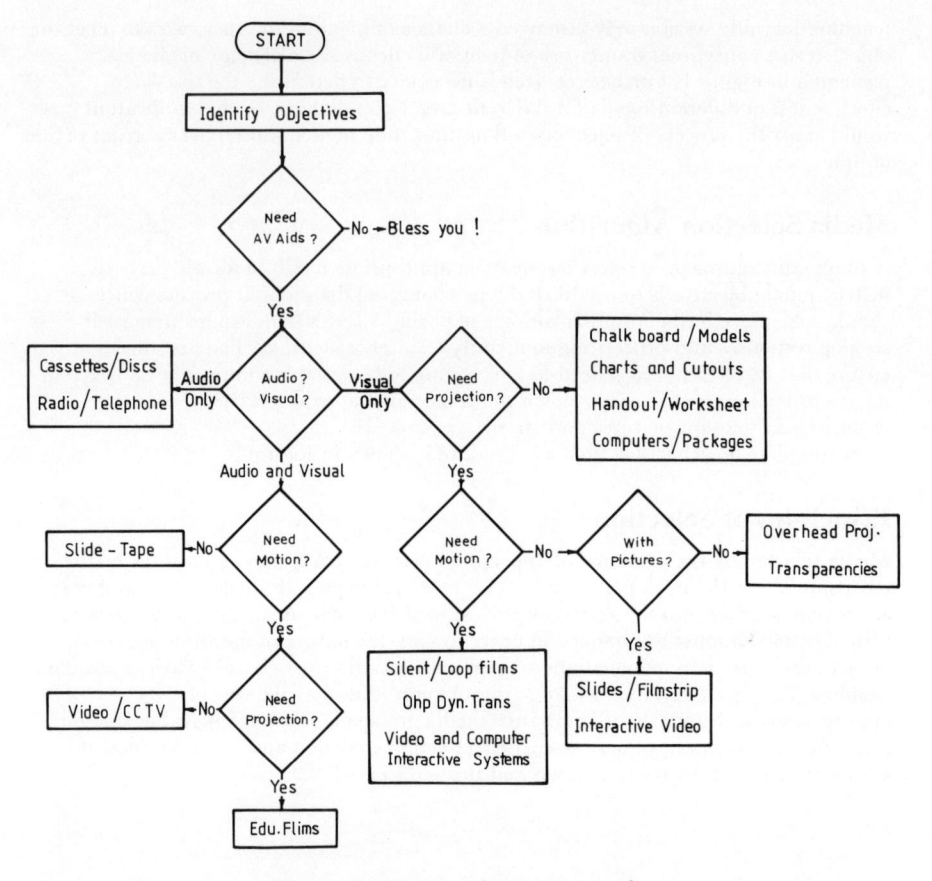

Figure 2. *Selection of appropriate media*

Developing countries such as Iraq which have an abundance of high-technology media procured several years ago may find it more cost-effective to utilize such media, even if simpler media would have been adequate. On the other hand, one may have to be content with using simple contrivances and straw models in some other developing countries.

Optimal Matching of Aids

Having determined the appropriate aid for each objective in a unit of instruction, one is faced with the problem of optimal matching. A technique for doing this has been developed by identifying more than one aid for each objective, by rating the aids, say from one to three, and by generating a decision matrix. A typical decision matrix for a unit is shown here. It may be noted that the media options which are either not available or which are not considered cost-effective are simply scored out. For example, educational films were not available in the author's institute and hence the film medium was deleted from the matrix (Figure 3).

Ratings for different media options are totalled and those which rank high are selected for the media mix. For example, four options, ie, textbook, workbook, slide/tape and models were identified to constitute this media mix.

S.N.	Media Options	\multicolumn{6}{c	}{Objectives in Unit 'n'}	Totals
		1	2	3	4	5	6	
1	Textbook	2	1	3	1	2	3	12
2	Handout	1	2	1	3	1	2	10
3	Workbook	1	2	2	3	2	3	13
4	Overhead projector transparencies	2	1	2	1	3	1	10
5	Slides/filmstrip	1	3	2	1	1	1	9
6	Slide/tape	3	3	1	2	3	1	13
7	Videocassette	1	1	1	2	2	2	9
8	Educational film (deleted)	1	2	3	1	2	2	11
9	Model	2	1	3	2	1	2	11
10	Computers	1	2	2	2	1	1	9

Figure 3. *A decision matrix for media selection*

Computer-Controlled Media

The advent of computers has opened up a new avenue in the implementation of learning media. The dimension of interaction which is either missing or slow in other audiovisual aids is provided almost instantly by computers. Interactive video has already demonstrated this capability (Rushby, 1984).

A computer may control the learning experiences of a student through a strategy previously programmed by the software designer. The computer thus directs the student to learn by using its input/output system, to study the audiovisual aids arranged separately, to conduct some experiments in a laboratory, and so on. Each time, the student returns to the computer for further guidance and evaluation. Furthermore, certain decisions are also built in to enable a student to proceed at the maximum pace, sometimes by skipping certain steps and branches of activities which may be required by other students. Computers are, therefore, emerging as potential interface devices between students and media packages for effective learning (Grubbs et al, 1986).

Effectiveness of Packages

Multimedia packages for teaching are teacher-powered; their effectiveness depends upon the degree of enthusiasm and strategy adopted by the teacher. Learners are, however, compelled to participate. On the other hand, once a learning package is prepared, the teacher's role is minimal. The learner is instructed, motivated, assisted, and finally evaluated, through the media. Mechanization of the process of education may itself act as a barrier. Key punches and computer coding of messages may also inhibit progress in the initial stage.

An action study to assess the effectiveness of learning packages was undertaken by dividing a class in mechanics into two random groups, one being considered as the control group and the other the experimental group. The former was taught by a teacher in a conventional style, mainly by chalk and talk technique with some student-teacher interaction and with the use of some audiovisual aids. The second group was provided with packages for self-learning together with flexibility of usage, for example variability in the times of day when they could study, and alternative media. It was observed that the strongest plus point for the package was its round-the-clock availability. In fact, the same point also proved to be its weakest for 30 per cent of the students who did not complete the study. They postponed self-learning indefinitely and were taken by surprise by the test. Subsequent investigation revealed that such students give high priority to the scheduled tasks like classroom lectures and tutorials and low priority to others. The comparison also showed that 50 per cent of the students learnt more thoroughly and performed better with learning packages than otherwise. The packages also encouraged guided learning.

Acknowledgements

The author wishes to acknowledge his gratitude to the Unesco Headquarters and to the Foundation of Technical Institutes, Iraq, which facilitated this contribution.

References

Brown, J and Brown, S (1984) *Educational Media Yearbook*. Libraries Unlimited, Littleton, Colorado.
Grubbs, J H, Sheridan, L and Charles, W E (1986) Integrating the computer into engineering at West Point. *Engineering Education*, 76, 4, pp 219-222.
Percival, F and Ellington, H (1984) *A Handbook of Education Technology*. Kogan Page, London.
Rushby, N J (1984). In Hills, P J (ed) *An Introduction to Educational Computing*. Croom Helm, Kent.

1.21 Flexible Learning in a Multimedia Environment

P Barker, J Lees and D Docherty
Teesside Polytechnic, Middlesbrough

Abstract: The creation of computer-based teaching systems can often necessitate the use of a variety of different learning strategies. Of these, the most popular are those that employ the computer for basic information provision, exploration of a learning domain, and/or pre-programmed guided instruction. Implementation guidelines for each of these approaches are often derived from a simple keyboard/display model of student interaction. In this paper we illustrate how didactic dialogue can be made more exciting and flexible by the provision of a multimedia learning environment based upon a work station model of interaction.

Introduction

Over the last decade there has been an almost explosive growth of interest in applications of the computer as a training and learning resource. Consequently, the production of effective courseware has become a major factor influencing the successful uptake of this approach to teaching.

Three fundamental philosophies are commonly employed as a basis for the provision of computer assisted learning (CAL) and computer based training (CBT) experiences for students. The methodologies inherent in these philosophies are often referred to as 'the informatory', 'the exploratory', and 'the instructional' realizations of CAL. Each requires a different approach. The first simply presents information to students; perhaps just to satisfy their curiosity, to facilitate some research-oriented task, or to aid a decision-making process. The second approach involves the provision of both a computer-based learning environment and a set of tools that will enable this environment to be explored by the student; essentially, this CAL methodology is based upon the 'microworld' approach advocated in the early work of Papert (1980). The third approach to CAL uses the computer as a delivery vehicle for previously planned, prepared, and tested courseware material: although reminiscent of programmed instruction, it is far more sophisticated. By combining the methodologies embedded in these three approaches, very flexible learning systems can be developed.

In the past, conventional approaches to CAL have been based primarily upon the sole use of a keyboard and a screen, or a cathode ray tube (CRT). The advent of powerful and versatile microcomputers has made it feasible to replace this basic peripheral combination by a sophisticated CAL work station. The construction of work stations is made possible because of the local storage, processing power, and interfacing ports that microcomputers make available. Interfacing ports enable a wide range of teaching aids and peripheral devices to be contained within the student's local interaction environment. Because the environment provided by a CAL work station can contain a wide variety of add-on devices it allows sophisticated instructional strategies involving several different media to be developed.

This paper describes three applications of multimedia CAL. Two of these involve primary school children. The first (involving informatory CAL) illustrates the use of an interactive video system as a provider of information. The second is based upon the exploratory approach to CAL, in which children of one age group prepare courseware to aid the integrated multi-activity learning of younger children. The third application deals with instructional CAL. It uses a number of different media and an 'adventure game' simulation in order to produce courseware which is interesting, effective and motivating. The advantages of and problems encountered in using each of these approaches are outlined and discussed.

The Multimedia Method

The basic model that most people have of CAL/CBT is one in which instructional information is presented to a student by means of some form of TV display; student responses (or, at least, a subset of them) are then monitored by means of either a conventional or special purpose keyboard. The TV display and keyboard are interlinked by a 'black box' (the computer) containing instructional software (often called courseware). Through the latter, an attempt is made to fulfil some of the pedagogic requirements of its user population. This is a very simplistic (although, admittedly, often low-cost) approach to CAL.

An alternative model of CAL is that involving the use of a work station to which a cluster of peripherals is attached. Each of these is selected to meet the particular requirements of the instructional tasks that are to be fulfilled. Underlying this approach is the basic concept of multichannel or multimedia instruction (MMI). It is this approach which we discuss in this part of our paper. The following section then illustrates some practical applications of our methodology.

When discussing the use of computers as an instructional resource, it is important to consider the 'interface' requirements of two broad categories of computer user. First, the needs of the authors and instructors who specify, design, construct, and administer learning resources must be considered. Second, consideration must be given to the trainees and students who use the resources to increase their knowledge of, or adeptness in, some skill-oriented activity. Each of these categories of user will require an appropriate interface to support information exchange (or dialogue) with the computer. In the case of students, this will usually be a learning dialogue, whereas in the case of courseware authors this will involve a fabrication dialogue. The basic nature of the interfaces that can exist between authors and computers has been discussed extensively elsewhere (Barker and Yeates, 1985; Barker, 1986a). Therefore, in this paper our major concern is with the interfaces that exist between computer-based instructional technology and its student users.

The basic ideas underlying our approach to multimedia CAL are embodied in Figures 1 and 2.

In Figure 1 we illustrate the concept of a multimedia interaction environment. It shows how a number of different peripheral devices (of differing information bandwidth and directionality) may be utilized to facilitate student-computer dialogue. This figure depicts only the online aspect of the MMI learning process. Of course, this will normally be augmented by many off-computer activities. These may perhaps involve the use of a special workbook, playing a game, reading a passage from a textbook, using an instrument of some sort, and so on. An important aspect of the MMI approach will therefore be the provision of a multimedia resource pack containing all the materials needed for use within the global environment in which the work station is sited (Barker, 1986). Each of the case studies described in the following section of this paper has an appropriately designed resource pack.

Figure 2 is used to emphasize an important point which might not be obvious from Figure 1. This concerns the multiple roles of the computer itself. That is, within a MMI environment the computer is not only used as a medium of instruction in its own right, it is also used to control the activity of the other instructional media as well.

The Case Studies

In order to appreciate the potential of the multimedia approach to CAL, it is important

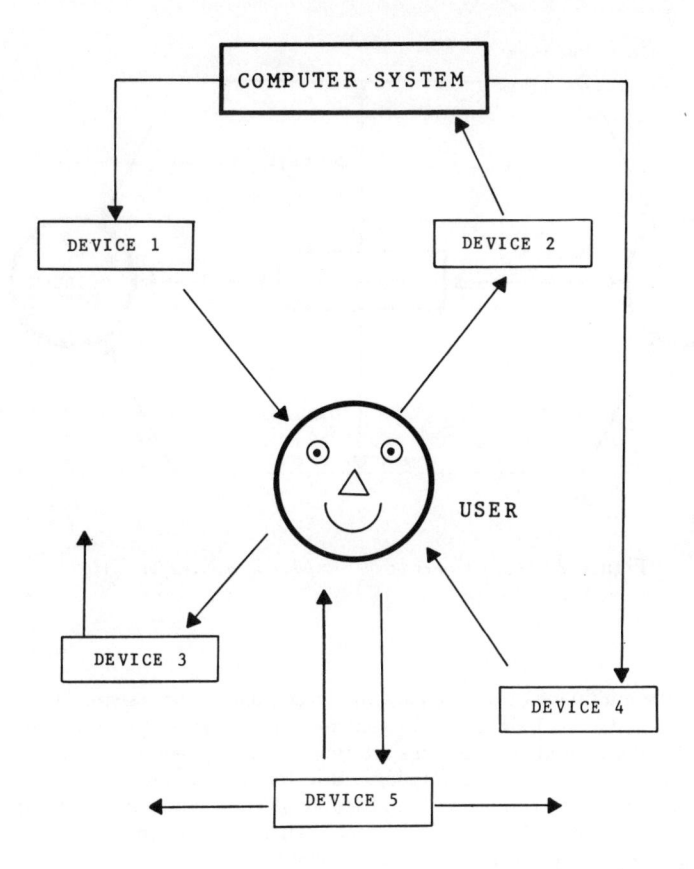

Figure 1. *Multimedia interaction environment for CAL*

to realize the many different ways in which this method of computer-based teaching can be employed. Therefore, in this section of the paper we outline three different case studies in which we have utilized this methodology. Individually, these involve the use of the informatory, exploratory, and instructional approaches to CAL.

Informatory CAL

One of the work station projects upon which we are currently working involves the production of a learning centre that is able to realize two important design considerations. The first is the ability to function without the need for a conventional QWERTY keyboard. The second is the ability to provide easy access to material contained in an audiovisual knowledge base (Barker and Skipper, 1986). Within the student interaction environment a variety of devices are used. Amongst these are an electronic book, a touch-sensitive keypad, a TV monitor, a video disc and an audio unit. The electronic book (Tandy, 1985) is used to facilitate student input to the system by means of touch operations made on the surface of graphic paper-based overlays; a collection of these (each of which can be uniquely identified by the computer) is

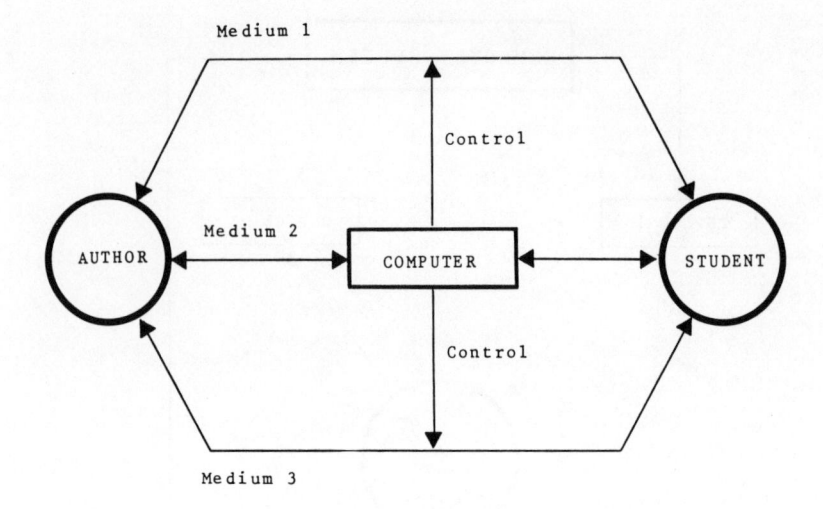

Figure 2. *Multiple roles of the computer in multimedia CAL*

contained in the multimedia resource pack that accompanies the system. The touch-sensitive keypad (Barker, 1981) gives the student control over the presentation of the instructional material. Only four options are allowed: recap, continue, stop, and finish. The TV monitor is used to show animation, static graphics, and teletext overlays; it is also used to present audio commentary and sound effects obtained from the video disc. Other prerecorded sound effects (and narration) can also be presented via the audio unit – a rapid access tape recorder (Barker, 1986b).

The workstation described above can be used for a variety of applications; one of those which we are implementing involves providing the learner with access to information about birds.

Within this domain the student can choose the specific topic of instruction by means of selection operations made via the electronic book. This is accomplished by selecting an appropriate page from the MMI resource pack and entering it into the electronic book. Each of these pages contains ten high quality bird pictures, a 'start' box, and a 'next page' box. On any given page individual coloured pictures provide close-up views of specific birds. Once the required overlay page has been selected from the resource pack, the student can get information about the bird of interest by simply touching its picture. This causes pre-stored information from the video disc and audio tapes to be retrieved and presented to the student. The video disc material may involve animation (showing the bird in flight) and static images (particular views of the bird showing its markings). The audio unit is used to present recordings of the bird's call or song. The resource pack also includes a workbook containing further instructional information about the birds, exercises and other activities for the student to undertake.

Exploratory CAL

This case study outlines a novel approach to exploratory CAL that involves two groups of children, a multimedia learning environment, and a story, *Billy's Blue Balloon*, that has been programmed into an electronic work station.

Early learning within children requires the development of a wide range of basic skills. A typical curriculum is therefore likely to include reading, numeracy, craft, organization, communication, social awareness, and so on. Learning activities relating to the development of these skills can be presented to a pupil in two ways: either as discrete compartmentalized activities or as a set of interrelated tasks that form the basis for the full integration of cognitive, creative, and motor skills. In this case study we describe how exploratory CAL within a multimedia environment can be used to develop integrated learning experiences for middle infant children (aged 6-7 years).

The work station used to provide the exploratory CAL facilities was based upon a BBC microcomputer running the MICROTEXT author language. Use of the workstation was combined with a number of other activities involving a workbook, Language Master cards, conventional audio tape, group discussion, contact with a mentor group, and so on. The instructional vehicle used to integrate student use of these resources was a story that had been previously programmed into the computer by a group of top junior children (age 10-11 years) who thus acted as a courseware development team for the software project. This group used MICROTEXT to create a series of highly coloured CRT frames that together embodied the story of Billy's blue balloon.

The program scenario that was developed involves a small boy, Billy, and the blue balloon which he buys at the fair. Whilst walking home the balloon escapes from the string and flies up into the sky and begins to be blown around by the wind. At the mercy of the wind the balloon is blown to all the places of interest around Billy's home town.

Through the concept of an escaped balloon blown by the wind, the children explore the environment created within the program structure. The children decide the direction of the wind and are thus able to investigate the variety of 'CRT frame locations' that have been programmed into the work station. The input requirements throughout the program are kept to single key responses: N (north), S (south), W (west), and E (east). These indicate the direction of the wind moving the balloon within the environment. After the children have 'played out' the electronic story they are given workbooks to complete: this will generally involve numerous sessions at the work station replaying parts of the story in order to gather the information needed to complete the exploratory assignments and exercises contained within the workbook.

The courseware development methodology used in this case study is quite novel since it involves a group of top juniors (the development group) working alongside a group of middle infants (the learning group). We believe that this approach could prove an extremely useful and cost effective way of introducing CAL workstations into the primary classroom.

Instructional CAL

An important feature of instructional CAL is its ability to facilitate the teaching of particular skills; then, by means of appropriate assessment metrics, it is possible to determine how well the student is able to perform various tasks which require the use of the acquired skills. We have been producing a multimedia package that can be used to develop map reading and navigational skills. Two major tasks were identified as being important. First, understanding grid references and being able to use these to specify locations on a map. Second, being able to operate a compass and use it (in conjunction with the map) to move from one geographic location to another. The maps used in this system were large-scale (1:50000) Ordinance Survey (OS) sheets of the UK.

In order to develop a system that could be used for the realization for the first of the above tasks we used a work station that could provide inexpensive colour graphics of relatively high resolution (a BBC microcomputer) to which was attached a high resolution (X,Y) digitizer/stylus. The computer CRT was used for displaying control menus, presenting informatory CAL frames, and for generating test frames. The purpose of the latter was to assess students' abilities to specify (and/or interpret) an OS grid reference. The test frames involved displaying a simulated grid system on the CRT, randomly placing an object(s) within it, and then asking the student to key in either its six-figure grid reference or the identity of an object at a particular location. The CRT was also used in conjunction with the other interaction device – the digitizer. In this context, its function was to provide directives and feedback about interaction activities being performed on the surface of the various sets of paper-based pictorial interface documents that could be mounted on the surface of the digitizer.

Two sets of documents are provided in the MMI resource pack for this system: training cards and actual map sections. The former are used to develop the student's skills both with respect to using the stylus (the minor skill) and understanding OS grid references (the major skill). The map sections (obtained by cutting up actual OS sheets) are used as part of a simple computer-based 'adventure game' simulation that we are producing. At present this involves taking the student for a randomly generated 'walk' around a particular geographic area. During the walk the student may be asked: to go to particular points (as specified by a computer-generated grid reference): to walk in a particular direction at a specified speed for a given length of time; or to perform a variety of other tasks related to map usage. The computer monitors what the student is doing by means of his/her stylus activity, map section changes, and the various answers that are keyed in through the keyboard. The student's adeptness at performing simple manipulations with real maps can therefore be assessed.

Conclusion

Approaches to CAL and CBT that are based purely upon the keyboard/display model of interaction suffer from a number of serious inadequacies and limitations. In order to overcome some of these limitations we advocate the use of a work station model that acts as a basis for the creation of sophisticated and stimulating application-oriented multimedia interaction environments. We have demonstrated the utility of this approach through a series of case studies that indicate how it facilitates the design of highly flexible learning systems.

References

Barker, P G (1981) Experiments with a touch sensitive keypad. *Electronics and Computing Monthly*, 1, 7, pp 20-24.
Barker, P G (1986a, in press) *Author Languages for CAL*, Macmillan, Basingstoke.
Barker, P G (1986b, in press) A practical introduction to authoring for computer assisted instruction. Part 6: Interactive Audio. *British Journal of Educational Technology*.
Barker P G and Skipper, T (1986) A practical introduction to authoring for computer assisted instruction. Part 7: graphic support. Submitted to *British Journal of Educational Technology*.
Barker, P G and Yeates, H (1985) *Introducing CAL*. Prentice-Hall International, Hemel Hempstead.
Papert, S (1980) *Mindstorms: Children, Computers, and Powerful Ideas*. Harvester Press, Brighton.
Tandy (1985) The Electronic Book, page 125, Tandy Electronics Store Catalogue.

1.22 The Ubiquitous Trigger: A Flexible Resource

N J Rushby, S Weil, A Schofield and G Delf
Centre for Staff Development in Higher Education, University of London

Abstract: This paper examines the development of the 'trigger' video technique and its use as a flexible component within various training materials. Unlike the more usual kind of training video, the trigger technique uses very short, subjective video camera sequences to stimulate – trigger – group discussion. The trainees are intimately involved in the incident they see on the screen and, in the ensuing discussion, are encouraged to examine their attitudes and beliefs. The paper introduces the trigger technique and traces its development at the Centre for Staff Development in Higher Education, University of London, through a series of case studies, showing how each application has contributed to a better understanding of its strengths and weaknesses. Although much of the material is on video cassette, it can be regarded and used as a simple form of interactive video: its use with computer-controlled videodisc is a natural progression which enables the material to be used at a distance from the trainer. What is now becoming clear is that triggers can be used as components within linear video case studies, blurring the distinction between linear and interactive video, and increasing the flexibility of the technique.

Introduction

There are two common perceptions of interactive video. Those who come from film or video see it as a way of resequencing linear material to make it more interesting or effective; while those whose background is in computer-based learning or training see it as a way of enhancing the computer-based courseware with audio and high-quality animated colour graphics. The reality is that interactive video is a new medium whose potential we are only just starting to appreciate. Some of the characteristics of interactive video have been available to us in linear video, although we have rarely made use of them. Videocassette players have controls which can be operated by the learner to stop or freeze the action, to restart it, to fast forward or to rewind. Yet with one or two exceptions (some of the self-study material produced by the Open University, for example) these facilities are seldom used. This paper examines a technique called 'trigger video', which uses linear videocassette in a semi-interactive form, and traces its development into a videodisc-based technique used for training in interpersonal skills.

Trigger Video

It was a combination of enthusiasm for the potential advantages of video and dissatisfaction for existing material that provided the stimulus for the first series of 'trigger' videos produced by the Centre for Staff Development (*Call Yourself a Manager?*).

The approach introduced two innovations to the use of video in management training.

First, unlike most materials, the programmes are not recorded in a documentary or fictional form but as a series of very short scenes, each depicting a different type of organizational problem. Typically, some 50 such scenes will be included in a single (linear) video tape. Appropriate scenes are selected by trainers to meet particular training objectives, and are then shown singly to trainees, who are asked to respond in a number of ways. Typically, one scene may lead to one or two hours of discussion and analysis, and so the materials are extremely cost effective.

The second innovation is that the viewer is placed on the spot: dropped into a problem to which he or she has to respond immediately – just as in real life. In all the episodes, what is said is aimed directly at the viewer who, imagining himself or herself as the person addressed, has to respond to the issues presented. In developing such programmes considerable emphasis is placed on the need for immediate responses, bringing a reality to the material and allowing users to identify readily with what they see on the screen. Research undertaken on the effectiveness of previous programmes emphasizes that it is this perceived reality by users which leads to the high surface validity of the material.

By using such material, participants readily discover significant differences in the way they perceive the behaviour they see on the screen. These differences permit the further exploration of strategies to manage the problems that they face, and to come to terms with the influence of their own interpersonal behaviour on the required decision. The method shares much in common with management simulations but, because of the richness of the visual medium, becomes a more powerful force for learning than many such traditional methods.

The Role of the Trainer

Many existing training methods do not bring out the importance of interpersonal behaviour and relationships. Conversely, some methods which attempt to do just that may be unpopular with trainees who will sometimes strongly resist taking part. Many people do not like to discuss openly their feelings about other people or difficult situations. The short video episodes can trigger a response in the viewer which can be taken and discussed in relatively supportive surroundings, but even so the trainer should be aware that there will still be problems in getting people to identify their real feelings. Different episodes affect different emotional levels. In most cases the initial feelings will be exposed and discussed without too much difficulty. However, the process becomes more difficult the further one tries to dig down into peoples' emotions. For that reason, feelings should be discussed only to the extent which is legitimate for the particular training purposes and which the trainer can manage. The use of the episodes in this context should provide a basis on which individuals can identify and understand feelings which are relevant to their role, and also develop an adequate vocabulary, which is frequently lacking, to express emotional reactions.

Some questions for trainees that apply particularly to using the triggers for focusing on interpersonal issues are:

- ☐ how did I feel?
- ☐ what did I think?
- ☐ what would I probably do?
- ☐ what would I really want to do?
- ☐ what did I think the person was thinking about me?
- ☐ what did I think the person wanted from me?
- ☐ what did I feel about him or her?
- ☐ has a similar thing ever happened to me and what did I do then?

By use of these episodes, and with appropriate interventions from the trainer, individuals can come to appreciate the important distinctions between how they feel and what they think, and also to expend their often limited vocabulary to identify feelings. They can distinguish between what action they would take and what they would really want to do, and so on. For example, a particular incident may make them feel very angry but expression of that anger may be inappropriate in the situation: the need to identify those personal feelings, to understand both the reasons for them and their effects on the other people involved is an important learning point.

The triggers can also be used as miniature case studies. Here the emphasis is different: as well as asking individuals for their feelings about what they saw, they may also be asked about more cognitive issues in the situations. The group might describe the main points arising in an episode and identify the organizational issues, analyse the communications between manager and employee, or determine and examine the behaviours identified, and so on. The subject groupings on the tape may often form the basis of the use of the episodes as miniature case studies. The main advantages of using the episodes for general management training in this way is that they do bring reality to issues: participants can see the behaviours exhibited. The episodes are deliberately 'short' on information, and the trainer may wish to supplement this, depending on the group concerned.

The successful series of seven sets of triggers for management training was followed by three sets focusing on adolescence in order to meet staff development and training needs in the teaching and caring professions and, more recently, by a programme on racism in organizations. This line of development is now being extended into the area of cultural awareness with materials for training teachers working with overseas students.

Towards Interactive Video

As we have seen, the trigger video technique can be a powerful tool for the trainer experienced in its use, but is incomplete as a resource for self-study. It relies on the trainer to lead the discussion, to elicit feelings, and to challenge attitudes. This led to the intriguing question of whether interactive video could be used to mediate trigger video and to act as a surrogate for the live trainer. Technology-based training is perceived to be unsatisfactory for learning interpersonal skills, but if the trigger technique could be packaged in some way, then this perception might be shown to be false.

Towards a Sustained Conversation

We can think of the single trigger, to which the trainee (or trainees) respond, as being the first half of a dialogue as shown in Figure 1b. As such, it is an advance on the more traditional cameo-style video, shown in Figure 1a, which does not prompt a response. Our aim in using interactive video was to move towards a more sustained conversation between the trainee and the learning materials. *Who Do You Think You're Talking To?* is a trigger-based interactive video programme commissioned by the Local Government Training Board to train bus crews to handle difficult situations in their dealings with passengers. It consists of eight episodes, each based on a typical incident (an indignant passenger who has been waiting for too long, a passenger who is lost and does not speak English, a rowdy group of young people annoying other passengers, two 'punks' looking for trouble, a drunk, etc). The driver is asked how he or she would respond if the incident actually happened to him or her, and then a follow-up scene is shown, to illustrate the likely consequences of their action. In this way the interactive dialogue is extended, from two steps in the 'linear' triggers, to three 'interactive' steps which may be repeated as shown in Figure 1c.

The package was designed on the assumption that an extension of the trigger video technique could be used to illustrate typical problems faced by the drivers of the one-man buses, and to help the drivers explore a range of possible responses. Although the trigger technique had been proven in many other applications, its success rested on presenting a series of typical incidents with credible outcomes, in such a way that the driver felt they were (or could be) real. The perceived validity of the incidents is one of

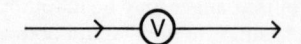

Figure 1a. *The single step cameo video*

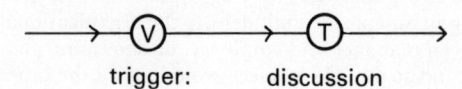

trigger: discussion

Figure 1b. *The two step dialogue of trigger video*

Trigger: Discussion: Consequence

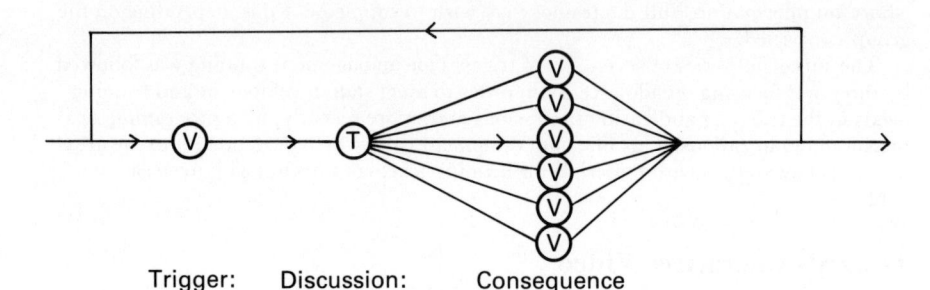

Figure 1c. *Three step dialogue on video disc*

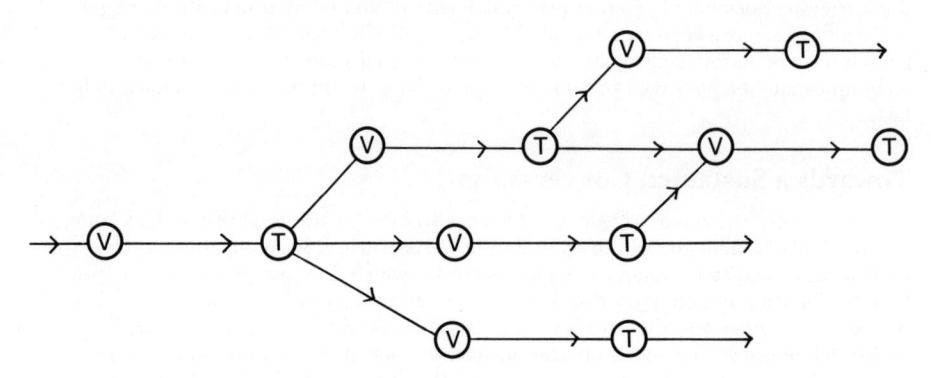

Figure 1d. *A sustained dialogue through interactive video*

the keys to using trigger video, whether on linear cassette or disc. The scenarios and a draft script of the incidents were developed by talking to bus inspectors and drivers and it soon became clear (somewhat to our relief!) that most of the problems could be covered by about eight incidents and that for each of these there were only about six likely outcomes: other problems and outcomes could be considered to be variants of these.

The programme is built on an underlying model of transaction analysis, and at its end the pattern of responses is used to give a commentary on the trainees' actions and on the different actions they might take in order to calm difficult situations instead of inflaming them. With different software (the computer program that controls the video disc) it would be possible to build up multi-stage case studies as described earlier, or change the focus of the material from customer care training to an aid in the recruitment and selection process.

The Interview Simulator

It is a natural progression from the three-step dialogue of the bus crews disc to the sustained dialogue that is being developed for the interview simulator. This project involves collaboration between the Centre for Staff Development, Lucas CAV, Kodak and the Trustee Savings Bank, and will explore the problems of simulating a 30-minute dialogue. The trainee will 'interview' a simulated applicant, initially selecting questions from a menu, but in later phases, using a voice recognition system with a subset of natural language. The applicant will be simulated by some 300-400 short subjective video sequences held on disc, selected and sequenced to provide realistic responses to the interviewer's questions.

The project has two main aims. Firstly, to deliver a series of increasingly sophisticated interview training packages, and secondly, to explore the limits of our ability to use interactive trigger video as a flexible learning resource.

1.23 Interactive Learning Systems and the Learner

D J Morrison
Royal Air Force School of Education and Training Support, Nottingham

Abstract: The concept of the interactivity of computer-based tutoring systems is examined in order to identify the critical aspects of interactivity in learning. The measure of interactivity apparently used most often by program designers is seen to focus on physical interactivity at the expense of the more crucial mental interactivity induced in the learner. Most commercial interactive programs are found to be based predominantly on behavioural learning models, and the claims that such programs are adaptive to the needs and knowledge of the learner are questioned. Two main lines of research and development concerning interactive tutorial systems are identified, and the issue of machine control of learning versus user control is raised.

Introduction

The word 'interactive' currently appears to be in vogue in the education and training worlds. Usually applied to computer-based learning systems, the term 'interactive' seems to lend a certain prestige to the systems so labelled, the implication being that systems not carrying the label are in some way inferior. But what is meant by an interactive learning system? The purpose of this paper is to examine the concept of interactivity in relation to learning. In the process of the discussion I hope to convince the reader (if he or she is not already convinced) that the term 'interactive', in its current usage in association with computer-based tutoring systems, is very often a red herring. Attention will be focused on the crucial interaction in learning – that between the learner's thoughts and the material to be learned. Subsequently, two main lines of research on and development of interactive learning programs are distinguished: that based on artificial intelligence (AI) principles, using machine control of the learning situation, and that based on user control of the learning situation. The relative strengths and weaknesses of the two approaches are discussed.

The Nature of Interactivity

Interactivity is usually defined in terms of user involvement in system operation. For example, Parsloe (1983) defines interactive video as follows:

> 'Quite simply, a video programme which can be controlled by the person who is using it. Usually, this means a video programme and a computer program running in tandem. The computer program controls the video programme – and the person in front of the screen controls them both.'

Manufacturers of interactive video systems also favour emphasis on the responsiveness of the system to user input. Interactivity is not seen as an all or none process, but rather as a continuum of levels of involvement. For convenience of classification of interactive video systems, the Nebraska Videodisc Design/Production Group (Parsloe, 1983) devised a scale of levels of interactivity for videodisc players which has since been used extensively for both tape and disc-based systems. The scale distinguishes five levels of interactivity from a zero level, in which 'interactivity' extends only to 'play', 'stop' and 'rewind' functions, to level 4, which envisages a complex work station, linking many information sources and co-ordinated by the user.

The Crucial Interactivity

While the above perspectives on interactivity are of some practical value, they have served to focus attention on the *physical* aspects of interactivity. The message seems to me to be that the more buttons the user has to press, the better and more interactive is the system. This preoccupation with physical interactivity has been at the expense of concern for the really crucial interactivity – that between the users' thoughts and the material to be learned. It is the level and indeed the quality of thought stimulated in the learner which is of central importance in effective learning.

Current Interactive Program Design

There are those who may argue that a great deal of attention is paid to the mental aspects of interactivity in program design. There are numerous instances in the literature in which the Socratic principle of questioning the learner is propounded as the sound basis on which programs have been designed. However, on closer examination it is found that the vast majority of this questioning is either of the multiple choice form or of the constructed response type. It is my firm belief that the degree of mental interactivity permitted by these forms of questioning, as they are used in most interactive programs, is inadequate for many of the learning tasks set. This is particularly true for those tasks demanding higher levels of cognition. I suspect that Socrates would feel much maligned to be associated with such restrictive practices as multiple choice or constructed response questions.

The poor quality of much of today's educational software (which includes much of that designed for 'interactive' systems) is an acknowledged problem (Nicolson and Scott, 1986). There may be a number of political and economic reasons for poor standards of software in this country, but, from the educational point of view, the programs fail to have a significant impact on learning because they induce paltry levels of mental interactivity in the learners. In the main, the programs are boring, often achieve less than could be achieved through the use of another medium (such as books), and do so at enormous expense.

The Learner

It would appear that the behavioural models of the learner on which programmed learning was based continue to be the predominant influence in instructional design for computer-based learning materials.

Despite the fact that the computer will accommodate almost any instructional design model, the majority of program designers assume that the behaviourally-based format is the most appropriate for computer-based learning (Clark, 1984). This practice is apparently continuing into interactive video program design (Council for Educational Technology, 1985; Laurillard, 1984; Gayeski and Williams in Zuber-Skerritt, 1984). The principal characteristics of behaviourally-based programs are, firstly, that they dictate the content sequence so that the extent of learner control amounts to his or her initiation of a branching sequence at various points in the program and, secondly, that programs control the learning strategy by determining the mode of delivery for any given sequence (Laurillard, 1984). Thus, the additional claims made for many commercial interactive programs that they can adapt to the needs and knowledge of the individual learner seem to be overstated. The 'needs and knowledge' of the learner are in fact assumed by the program designer(s).

In order to determine a learner's needs it is necessary to understand how he or she learns. Limitations of space preclude any detailed review of current learning theory here, but I shall attempt to summarize some of the main ideas. The limited view of learning afforded by behavioural models has given way in recent years to cognitive, information processing models of learning. The learner is now seen as a highly complex information processor who adopts individualistic strategies for learning. The range and kind of learning strategies used by an individual constitute his or her learning style. The learning outcome in any situation depends on whether the learner adopts a deep or surface approach to processing the information (Marton and Säljö, 1976a, 1976b), whether either of these approaches is made in an active or passive mode (Entwistle, 1981) and whether the style adopted is holistic or serialistic in nature (Pask, 1976a). Pask (1969, 1976b) has identified the importance of conversational techniques in learning and in this conversation theory I believe that he has discovered the foundation on which *all* instructional systems ought to be based. The ultimate interactivity at which learning/tutoring systems should be aimed is that of the learner in conversation with himself over the material to be learned. The depth and elaborateness of such conversations will determine the extent of learning achieved. The final arbiter in determining conversational effort is the learner, not the responses demanded by the system.

Increasing emphasis is being placed on the capacity of people to learn how to learn (Novak and Gowin, 1984). This too must be taken into account in the design of tutorial systems.

The Future of Interactive Programs

The present shortcomings of current interactive computer-based system software are well known in academic circles and, in some quarters, a great deal of research and development work is going on in order to make interactive systems more effective in enhancing learning. Two main lines of work can be discerned which adopt very different approaches to the problem. These two solutions to interactive systems design are described below.

Adaptive Instructional Programs

The artificial intelligence movement is in pursuit of 'expert' tutorial systems which will provide students with optimum instructional strategies. The development of 'intelligent' systems demands the incorporation of a comprehensive description of the learner in association with complex decision heuristics which permit the computer to 'judge' what is the best strategy to deliver following each student response.

Some impressive programs such as SOPHIE (Brown et al, in Sleeman and Brown, 1982) have been developed which permit a higher level of conversation between user and computer than has hitherto been possible.

One of the advantages of giving complete control of the learning situation to the computer is that assessment records can be accumulated for each students as he/she progresses through the learning material and this information can be used to aid the computer in 'judging' which strategy to deliver next. Thus, the computer can 'learn' about the student as the latter works his or her way through the program. O'Shea (1982) has developed just such a 'self-improving' tutorial program. The computer is, therefore, not only an aid to learning but is a manager of learning.

Notwithstanding the advances made in AI, the extent to which AI programs are adaptive to the needs and knowledge of the user is questioned here. The term 'adaptive' has as many shades of meaning as does 'interactive'. Certainly programs like SOPHIE are adaptive insofar as the instructional strategy delivered is a function of user input. However, to claim that the computer's response is wholly appropriate to the individual sitting in front of the screen is, I believe, to claim too much. The claim is excessive simply because there is no such thing as a comprehensive description of the learner. It may be possible to design a program which will accommodate a learner's preferred learning style, but to what extent can this be assumed to be stable? The research is unable to provide a definitive answer to this question. It may also be possible in a program to account for the learner's personality type, but how is this to be defined and diagnosed? Furthermore, how is motivation to be monitored and controlled?

Apart from the pragmatic difficulties of designing adaptive interactive video programs, the ethos of the AI movement has to be questioned. The idea of an adaptive instructional system may be appealing to many people, but do we really want to give computers full control over learning situations? Do we want machines to get to 'know' us well enough to adapt to our 'needs and knowledge'?

Adaptable Programs

The alternative to adaptive systems is to give control back to the learner and provide him/her with a wide range of interactive video programs which deal with the subject matter in a variety of ways, ie an adaptable system which permits the learner to find his or her own way through the material according to his or her own needs and knowledge.

While an adaptable system removes the difficulty of having to model the learner in the way required by AI systems, a number of other problems arise. The principal difficulty is in deciding how much control over the learning situation any individual is capable of exercising effectively. Laurillard (1984) investigated the feasibility of giving a group of learners absolute control over a short IV program. The results indicated that the students chose very individual pathways through the material to good effect. However, a revised version of the program incorporated some guidance to the students on what each of the various instructional strategies offered and this was found to be helpful. It was also noted that, left to their own devices, students tended to watch the video programme all the way through rather than deliberately interrupt it in order to work through the various activities initiated by the control program. Thus, students seem unable to make full use of the control of the mode of learning: that is, they are uncertain when to watch and listen and when to do.

The use of adaptable interactive video programs forces the educational or training establishment concerned to exert more effort in encouraging students to learn how to learn. Although there is considerable controversy in the research literature over the relative efficacy of program control and student control over learning, the more recent evidence favours student control (Laurillard, 1984). The recent upsurge in literature on learning to learn is testimony to this shift towards student-controlled learning which is seen to induce high levels of self-motivation (Papert, 1980).

In conclusion, I have argued that the conventional view of interactivity focuses too much attention on physical aspects of interaction and too little on the crucial, mental interactions which affect learning. The behaviourist tradition continues to restrict the development of effective programs, despite the existence of more expansive and complex theories of learning. Whether future interactive learning systems will take the form of adaptive expert tutorial systems or adaptable, learner-driver systems (or, indeed, both of these) will be determined by the practitioners at the front line of education and training. It is my personal hope that we choose the latter, for

> 'Power is nothing if it is not power to choose. Instrumental reason can make decisions, but there is all the difference between deciding and choosing.'
>
> (Weizenbaum, 1976)

References

Clark R E (1984) Research on student thought processes during computer-based instruction. *Journal of Instructional Development*, **7**, 3, pp 2-5.

Council for Educational Technology (1985) *An Introduction to Interactive Video*. Booklet of the National Interactive Video Centre. CET, London.
Entwistle, N J (1981) *Styles of Learning and Teaching*. John Wiley and Sons, Chichester.
Laurillard, D M (1984) Interactive video and the control of learning. *Educational Technology*, **14**, 6, pp 7-15.
Marton, F and Säljö, R (1976a) On qualitative differences in learning. I – outcome and process. *British Journal of Educational Psychology*, 46, pp 4-11.
Marton, F and Säljö R (1976b) On qualitative differences in learning. II – Outcome as a function of the learner's conception of the task. *British Journal of Educational Psychology*, **46**, pp 115-127.
Nicolson, R I and Scott, P J (1986) Computers and educational: software production problem. *British Journal of Educational Technology*, **17**, 1, pp 26-35.
Novak, J D and Gowin, D G (1984) *Learning How to Learn*. Cambridge University Press, Cambridge.
Papert, S (1980) *Mindstorms. Children, Computers and Powerful Ideas*. Harvester Press, Brighton.
Parsloe, E (ed) (1983) *Interactive Video*. Sigma Technical Press, Wilmslow.
Pask, G (1969) Strategy, competence and conversation as determinants of learning. *Programmed Learning and Educational Technology*, 6, pp 250-266.
Pask, G (1976a) Styles and strategies of learning. *British Journal of Educational Psychology*, 46, pp 128-148.
Pask, G (1976b) Conversational techniques in the study and practice of education. *British Journal of Educational Psychology*, 46, pp 12-25.
Sleeman, D and Brown, J S (eds) (1982) *Intelligent Tutoring Systems*. Academic Press, London.
Weizenbaum, J (1976) *Computer Power and Human Reason. From Judgement to Calculation*. Penguin Books, Harmondsworth.
Zuber-Skerritt, O (ed) (1984) *Video in Higher Education*. Kogan Page, London.

1.24 Interactive Open Learning – Is it on Line for Branching Out?

C L G Sangster
Training Resource Services, Richmond

Abstract: The desire for structured self-study, as in programmed learning, has progressed towards the current interest in open learning. In this, the important extra element of interactivity is now considered necessary to maintain motivation and test understanding. Open learning can thus present carefully analysed material at a level and pace suited to the individual learner, monitoring performance as it progresses.

It is considered important that any open learning programme is both specific to company or departmental needs and structured to give continuity, logical development and feedback. It must be related to active training and on-job mentoring and reinforcement.

Interactive open learning will be presented using a variety of media options, including text, interactive tape-slide, computer-based training (with slide option) and interactive video. Any programme will tend to have a basic link medium, probably text, with special media sections selected for their ability to achieve stated objectives. As well as basic criteria for deciding to apply open learning to areas of training, there will be presentation, cost and degree of interactivity criteria to apply to the media options. This should result in a unified whole, with the information presented and tested by applying the best methods and media. It can succeed in the long term, given the appropriate level of funding and high level support.

Introduction

Self-study has been with us ever since stylus inscribed on clay or brush on papyrus. There has always been the instructional necessity and the psychological need to receive feedback on this learning – to assist the learner to clear the various hurdles which stand in his way. This assistance has traditionally been met by some form of tutorial response, written or verbal. We see this functioning effectively in advanced higher education, correspondence courses, and of course in the Open University.

Parallel with these developments, we have had an increasing desire in education and training to structure this information and feedback in a more integrated fashion – pre-empting some of the potential hurdles, monitoring progress and thereby leading the learner through a sequence of information and events towards specified goals or objectives. So self-instructional materials and programmed learning were developed, where potential learning needs were identified and linear or branched solutions presented to satisfy specified objectives.

Doubts were inevitably felt, however, as to the effectiveness of these methods, especially when considered in relation to the production time involved. Were we relying on too high a level of learner motivation? Could we really pre-empt all major questions, allowing the learner to progress to the end with no queries or misconceptions? A greater degree of feedback was seen as necessary – some interactivity to compensate for this lack of tutor availability.

Interactivity

What is meant by this new buzz word in further education and training?
The Oxford dictionary has: 'to interact, v.i. – to act reciprocally or on each other.'

Webster's dictionary has: 'to interact, v.i. – to act upon one another.'

So, with our branched programme learning and multiple choice questioning, we already had an element of interactivity. This has been lifted to a more advanced level with the advent of computer-based techniques. Depending on the authoring system employed, we can have a choice of branches; feedback loops for remedial study; student and/or program analysis during operation; questioning using a variety of answer completion techniques, and the facility to 'fast track' through sections if required. When compared with human interaction, however, the level of the reciprocal action between computer and learner is at a very basic level in many programs. For example, programs may give only one 'wrong' response frame although, with four question options, there will be three separate error explanations required. This can be caused as much by scarcity of memory, small disc capacity, or limited design time as by weak programming. Remedial loops are often simply repetition of previous sections, whereas in face-to-face training, a tutor would be more likely to explain the problem using a different approach or method.

Some degree of interactivity can be achieved using synchronized, random-access tape-slide, as well as the more flexible interactive video medium. We must not of course forget or underestimate the value of the text medium, used on its own as question pages or completion sections in manuals, or in association with another linear medium to check understanding. Increasingly, we are seeing the need for a broader approach – not considering any one medium as the 'total training solution', but looking to a multimedia delivery for the best satisfaction of any particular set of learning objectives. This approach, which has of course been in existence in a loosely-structured way in education for many years, is currently experiencing development in the open learning approach in business training.

Open Learning

In open learning, we are attempting to 'package' training so that relevant techniques and detail, designed to be company-specific, can be learned by personnel in as flexible a way as possible. The programmes will normally be delivered in some form of learning centre close to the learner's working environment. Depending on the media used, it could be possible for the individual to study the material at his own desk. Much of the admittedly high development cost can thus be justified on the grounds that course delegate expenses (hotels, travel, course fees, etc) are reduced or negated and that the learner is absent from his work place for only limited periods of time.

To be effective, open learning must be both structured and work-specific. It is not enough to present a loose collection of commercially available materials on a subject, in the hope that the student can glean the appropriate information from them. Commercially available materials can of course be incorporated – there is little point in attempting an in-house video if sections of professionally produced programmes can be used (with attention to copyright restrictions). However, the relevant sections would have to be built into the total programme structure, with

- ☐ preamble identifying relevant teaching points to note;
- ☐ viewing of identified video section;
- ☐ summary and question section.

On many occasions, text or materials will have to be specially written and produced to establish specific company procedures or operations. The particular media combination selected for each will depend on the availability of hardware for delivery, the content and the long-term reference value to the learner, as well as the particular learning objectives. Any open learning programme will thus finish up as a structured, specific, multimedia exercise, aiding the learner to progressively achieve a sequence of established objectives. Interactivity will be built into the total programme with periodic tests, potential branches and optional study sections to allow the learner as much flexibility as possible. Some tutorial assistance might even be incorporated, with at the least encouragement to discuss queries with a superior.

Relationship and Priorities

What is the relationship between open learning and the total training programme within an organization? Could training ultimately be totally satisfied by open learning techniques? We have already established that some of the more open-ended question sections will depend on debriefing with a tutor or superior to evaluate the response. Because some areas of training – interpersonal skills, for example – rely on human interaction, open learning must be seen as one of a variety of training methods available. However intelligent artificial intelligence becomes in the foreseeable future, the 'what if' approach to human interaction problem-solving will be very restrictive. Structured, self-paced learning is best suited to factual areas of study, allowing ground rules and basic detail to be established and practised in a controlled, safe environment, prior to real application. When dealing with areas of management development, for example, there is an obvious experiential gap between the self-learning level and the application in day-to-day management. How do we assess the effectiveness of this total training and monitor its implementation in the work environment?

The Assessment of Effectiveness

In assessment, we find a positive application of interactivity. But what are we attempting to achieve in assessing performance in the course of training? At the simple level, we are checking on basic recall but, in cognitive level training, we will want to progress to the higher levels – of analysis, synthesis and even evaluation – as quickly as possible. There is only a limited amount of assessment of these higher levels which can be carried out by the normal self-assessment, multiple choice type of interactive questioning. This is where additional interactivity through the tutorial – simulated exercise and mentoring and discussions both in and out of the direct training experience – is very necessary. In business training, a trainee's effectiveness will tend to be gauged by the level of performance rather than raw scores. Unfortunately, many managers do not appreciate the learning progression implicit in the taxonomy of objectives, often having too high an initial expectation of trainees who apply the results of short intensive training. This lack of understanding could be improved if managers had a closer involvement in all stages of the design, presentation and on-site reinforcement of training. In this way open learning interactivity can assess the effectiveness of the training programme, identifying weak areas requiring amendment. It can assess the learner's ability to respond to the requirements of the material, within the control limits of the programme. The total assessment of the effectiveness of the training will require additional human involvement to monitor the application of learning, given increasingly complex situations.

Implementation

As has been implied above, implementation will be a progressional exercise, with trainees gradually practising the higher levels of application within their work environment. It will come about positively through a combination of self-paced open learning and practical, monitored application. It is therefore necessary in the majority of developmental training areas to have interactivity at different levels. Some objectives will be achieved using mechanical, self-study levels; others will require human involvement. Some of this current human involvement might in time be superseded by fifth generation, artificial intelligence, applying the 'what if' symptom/treatment approach. The need for the tutor and mentor will however always remain at the reinforcement and application levels. Open learning techniques applied at the more factual, theoretical levels could release the personnel necessary for this practical, experience-based assistance.

The Benefits of Open Learning

So, how does interactive open learning stand at this stage of our examination? It is a positive means of reinforcing analysed needs. It allows self-paced learning with minimum disruption to the learner's work schedules. By applying a variety of media in the total delivery, it projects each message in the clearest, most appropriate way. Within the potentially flexible routes through any programme, it maintains quality and standards of delivery, however often it is applied. Interactivity will help to maintain learner interest and motivation, while at the same time monitoring performance and the effectiveness of the programme. If carefully designed, it will also help to carry out remedial training through response branches, although there is still the requirement for supplementary human interaction to reinforce initial training. Open learning programmes could represent a major percentage of the structured input in a department-centred approach to training. In this, the training function is seen as one of support, aiding the development of personnel within the department by the department. A combination of open learning, some active training and on-job mentoring, applied to the analysed specific needs of the department, will bring the most positive results.

The Selection of Media Options

As has been stated throughout this paper so far, the open learning philosophy will normally encompass a multimedia approach, incorporating some permutation of text, audiovisual, interactive video and computer-based training (CBT) materials. We have already established that one of the prime objectives of open learning is to permit flexible learning, both in content and pace, with interactivity to maintain and monitor levels of understanding. Interactivity can be applied in the variety of media options identified above, using appropriate techniques. Detailed analysis will initially establish learning needs and objectives, followed by decisions about content and the best means of delivery for particular sections. We must not approach the open learning design exercise with closed ideas about delivery methods. This is a simple educational technology concept. One gets the impression on occasion that open learning is synonymous with computer-based training. This is not so. CBT is a valuable training medium for some subject areas and totally inappropriate for others. One could say the same for any single medium. Open learning is a multimedia experience. The Lucas open learning project, for example, is based on text modules (complete with interactive sections throughout) with tape-slide, interactive tape-slide and CBT elements applied where appropriate to reinforce units. Post-test sections are carried out by CBT or self-corrected tests, with discussions with superiors recommended where written answers are too evaluative to be compared with sample responses.

Interactivity in the Different Media

Let us look briefly at the forms of interactivity possible with the different media mentioned above.

1 Text

Interactivity will be interspersed throughout the content of manuals, taking a variety of forms. These will include multiple choice questions, sentence completion, responding (in writing) to a given situation, describing an example which illustrates a given theory and progressive exercises or model building to illustrate a theory. It can also be incorporated in checksheet, response exercises presented at stages throughout a linear audiovisual programme.

2.1 Basic Interactive Tape-Slide Video

A tape–slide programme can incorporate stop pulses, allowing the learner to be given information with pauses for testing, carried out by means of a test paper or practical exercise. Solutions can be presented when the programme is restarted. Similar techniques can be incorporated in specifically-produced video programmes.

2.2 Interactive Tape-Slide

At a more complex level, using random access equipment, we can incorporate question/answer sections, with the audio track on hold. The learner will be presented with a multiple choice question slide, similar to a CBT frame. Using the random access facility, the learner accesses a selected answer number which calls up a related slide. This either confirms correctness or presents remedial teaching. Question and remedial slide branches continue until the programme is restarted for another information section.

3 Computer-based Training (CBT)

Here, information is presented in written form on screen, with the potential for graphics. The quality of graphics will depend on the system, with some degree of basic animation possible. Interactive sections allow the learner to be questioned, again at a variety of levels depending on the system used. We examined some of the options earlier, in the interactivity section. The major benefit of computer-linked interactivity is the degree of branching and programme flexibililty which is possible for the creative author, within the limitations of any particular system.

4 CBT Linked with Slide

This compensates for some of the graphic limitations of 3 above, where slide display commands can be incorporated into the CBT program, permitting videotext page and slide to be presented on parallel screens simultaneously for cross-reference.

5 Interactive Video

This can be used at the basic level of inserting question sections into existing video materials, with breaks in the video programme where question/answer videotext frames are presented.

At the higher, integrated level, video, audio and videotext elements are scripted to produce a unified whole, with interactivity possible throughout. The video component can be either tape- or disc-based. Disc gives faster access times and single frame capability, although a relatively expensive master must be produced, restricting subsequent alterations to the programme.

Relative Production Costs

When planning and designing a total open learning programme, there are various considerations relating to potential media use. As well as considering the medium most suited to the particular message, we must also consider availability of delivery hardware, relative costs and production timescales. The long-term success of open learning techniques will depend on there being a wide availability of structured, specific programmes. This takes time as well as being expensive, and we will on occasion have to apply cheaper techniques to allow for the breadth of material required within an available budget. Costs will vary between large and small commercial companies and between such companies and internal production agencies, where manpower and plant costs are often hidden. As a rough guide, commercial costs would currently vary, for 40–60 minutes of interactive learning material, between approximately £2,000 for printed texts and around £15,000 for an interactive video, with interactive tape–slide costing approximately £3,500 and CBT approximately £5,000. These are 'ball-park' figures, but give some indication of the overall costs involved when considering open learning.

Selection Criteria

Open learning is therefore an effective means of presenting information in a structured though flexible way, with interactivity allowing some degree of remedial teaching and evaluation. It is expensive and time-consuming to produce and will be a component element of the total training programme, which must always include some element of human interaction and reinforcement. In order to establish the viability of the open learning approach for any given subject area, several selection criteria might be considered:

(a) Are there specific company procedures, priorities and techniques which must be learned by all personnel within a specified group?
(b) Is there a sufficient number of personnel who must be trained on-site to justify the programme development costs?
(c) Will the subject material and detail remain accurate for an acceptable and cost-effective period of time?
(d) Can commercially available materials (which satisfy company procedures and objectives) be incorporated into the total programme, thereby reducing costs and production time elements?
(e) Are there adequate budget and development resources available to establish a viable learning programme within a reasonably short timeframe?
(f) Can senior management support be relied upon to assist in the design, learning motivation and post-learning reinforcement necessary to make any learning programme effective?

1.25 Open Learning and Information Technology

J Whiting
University of Ulster, Newtonabbey

Abstract: Open learning may be defined as learning undertaken by persons at places and times of their own choosing, at rates determined by them and their abilities and interests, and the availability of materials outside more traditional means of education. Distance learning is virtually synonymous with this definition but lays more stress upon the remoteness of the student from educational institutions and teachers. Information technology is here taken to mean the fusion of modern computer and communications technology with the domains of knowledge and information. The areas of open learning and information technology are therefore entirely complementary to one another. Implicit in this view for the educational technologist is the realization that the most important facet of the complementarity is the design of the interaction between them to facilitate learning. On the one hand there are groups of learners exhibiting a much wider range of abilities, ages, learning styles and real-world experiences than is usually encountered in any other area of post-school education, including most of the field of continuing education. On the other there is a diverse and rather poorly organized collection of methods and techniques for the dissemination, presentation and evaluation of educational materials, which are in any case in a continuous state of rapid and dissimilar development. Whatever one's ideological position, the discussion of the interface between open learners and the technology of information provision must be related to and evaluated in terms of its educative efficiency. Here, efficiency refers not only to economic provision but also to factors such as the educational impact of multi-media learning packages, the assessable outcomes of the learning and the close monitoring of the entire experiment. For experiment it is, as evidenced by the available reports of the Open University and the numerous projects sponsored by the Manpower Services Commission, training authorities and Open Tech. The issues raised by this view of the relationships between open learning and information technology are discussed.

Introduction

Both 'open learning' and 'information technology' are modern terms which describe new syntheses of older ideas. Two definitions are given to assist in what follows:

1. Open Learning

Volitional learning undertaken by persons with motives of self-improvement or interest, characterized by learner-centred perceptions and carried out at places, times and rates largely determined by the learner.

2. Information Technology

A fusion between the technologies of computing and communication and the domains of information and knowledge.

These attempts at definition, like most other attempts at definition in this field, might be disagreed with by almost everyone. However, they are those which are used in the context of this presentation. What is important to the title, however is the joining of both to do four things:

1. to make *rational* use of information technology in education;
2. to *enhance* the speed and quality of learning;
3. to *apply* information technology to open learning;
4. to *lessen* the isolation of the open learner.

Each of these four aims contributes to this discussion of the relationships between open learning and information technology.

Rational Use

There are many laudable and some successful attempts to make use of information technology. The commonest emphasis appears to be toward teaching people about the technology of computers and electronic communications. Increasingly, emphasis is being placed upon the use of the technologies to produce, and in a small way to distribute, teaching software and documents. Few people as yet regard information technology as a complex and versatile educational medium through which the teacher and the learner can attain high-quality results in shorter times than have so far been demonstrated. Information technology presents the possibility of denser and richer means of expression, contact and learning than any other educational technology. This is because, for one example, electronic means of communication are now sophisticated enough to be used by anyone with the cheap equipment now available, such as home computers and modems. One large experiment of this nature is the Times Network for Schools (TTNS), which is hosted by British Telecom's Telecom Gold network and therefore available to all the UK population through a local telephone call. Prestel is another example, though one more biased toward provision of information, and (because it is Viewdata) much less flexible than TTNS. The Open University DEC 20 computer is also regularly accessed by registered students, again mostly via local calls.

On TTNS the telephone is used for information retrieval and transmission (electronic mail) and for word processing and keyword searches through defined documents. The system is flexible enough to be configured by any user group to provide more sophisticated types of databases and search strategies. It can also be used to distribute text files and computer programs. It also supports the viewdata format alongside its more usual 80 column ASCII mode, and can host high resolution graphics as well.

The key insight about such a system is that, like the computers upon which they are implemented, they become fully interactive channels of communication. Teaching is by and large founded upon humans communicating with each other face to face. Educational technology is concerned with improving this communication. Information technology, rationally applied, extends interactive and virtually face-to-face communication beyond the necessity for human contact in the flesh via the all-pervasive telephone network. Soon the telephone will have the bandwidth to communicate real-time vision (via fibre optics) and sooner than that, satellite receiver/transmitters will be available to fulfil ideas first proposed by Arthur C Clarke many years ago.

Enhancement of Learning

Research in psychology (cognitive or otherwise), education and training resembles the state of knowledge of botany and zoology at the start of the 19th century: many contrasting theories, some pragmatic knowledge and a great deal of argument. Not enough is currently known to specify a method or even a typology of methods of teaching which will result in optimal learning by anyone who makes use of them. Methods of assessment are controversial in any case, and are likely to remain so for a long time yet. The nature of learning is itself a contentious and poorly defined concept. Without starting all the arguments over again, it is possible to assert some rules of thumb.

The first is that when well-motivated, people prefer to learn at their own speed, in their own way. Secondly, human-to-human contact, whereby the teacher conveys enthusiasm as well as information and knowledge to individuals and groups of students is essential to promote interest, motivation and learning. Thirdly, both learning and motivation are increased by sympathetic and helpful assessment and comment given at frequent intervals. Fourthly, contacts between students studying the same or similar areas or topics leads to increased learning through synergistic peer-group discussion. Fifthly, diversity of teaching methodologies applied to students is better than single strategies, since no two individuals are the same in their appreciation of, or learning from, one particular method or medium. Sixth, seeking of attitudinal data from teachers and students is essential so that teaching materials and methods can be optimized. Seventh, and last, remedial tuition has to be allowed for throughout the teaching and learning process.

Given such rules of thumb, it ought to be obvious that open learners will benefit from sophisticated teaching software and communications as part of their learning via a reasonably proficient and flexible computer work station. The need for cross-links between students, as well as student-to-teacher links, can make conditions right for a 'community of endeavour' to form among a geographically scattered group of people. The use of computer-mediated tuition, user modelling and software-driven formative assessment goes a long way towards overcoming the lack of human contact, though such contact, as the Open University summer school and local tutoring arrangements demonstrate for example, is still essential.

Here also electronic mail of the sophistication provided by TTNS can help a great deal; it is a much quicker, easier and more free system of information exchange than a man carrying a piece of paper with marks scratched on it up the garden path. Ask any business user of Telecom Gold. Provision of a variety of teaching methodologies not only encompasses books, television or radio, but also teaching software. There are no reasons why a topic cannot be taught by drill and practice, simulation, machine tutorial or discovery-learning methods, all though educational software. When intelligence is added to software, either in the form of domain-specific expert systems or intelligent tutoring systems (or preferably both) then the idea of the software generating a user model of the individual and making use of it to adjust the speed and nature of the tuition given by the software will begin to become real. If performance records are also kept centrally and compiled, as well as data deriving from attitudinal surveys, then the software can be rapidly improved and optimized.

Application

Both the communication and computer aspects of information technology apply to open learners. The need for open learning by increasing numbers of people is recognized by government in the form of the MSC Open Tech programme and the Open University. Many universities and polytechnics are also beginning to establish open learning centres. Applying information technology to open learning will, I hope, come to mean two things.

First, full use of the interactive communications provided by TTNS, Prestel and other national networks, both amateur and professional. Second, the production, distribution and use of intelligent teaching and training software. The second aspect will require sophisticated computer work stations as cheap as today's home computers, but far more versatile. Many centres in the UK, USA and elsewhere are actively developing such pieces of equipment. However, the problems do not lie in the hardware at all. Hardware is now so cheap and versatile that virtually any competent dealer can make one for less than £200. The problems lie in the software for the communications and, more importantly, for the teaching roles.

Teaching software has to be easy to use. Today, that means WIMP (Windows, Icons, Mice and Pointers) front ends like Digital Research Gem and Epson Taxi, not forgetting the Apple Mackintosh which started it all. With such interfaces, the keyboard returns to its typewriting role. In five or ten years time, speech recognition will have advanced enough to dispense with this also. It is already possible for computers to read printed documents directly. The teaching software will have to be equally sophisticated. However, software of such a level is very hard and time-consuming to produce, for several reasons.

First, programming at the level of sophistication required is a skill which few teachers possess, despite the existence of a variety of authoring systems to make the task easier. Second, style, presentation and other aesthetic considerations demand a level of talent and appreciation that is rare, and mostly unteachable to those who lack it. Last, since teaching software ought to be as interactive as possible and ought to develop some sort of internal model of its user in order to bias its tuition strategy more closely to what it sees that the user will require for optimal learning, artificial intelligence techniques will be needed and not explicit programming. Progress on such software, via expert systems and intelligent tutors, is slow and uncertain at present. Current intelligent tutors like GUIDON and TUTOR are nowhere near the degree of sophistication needed. They cannot yet do what any teacher does instinctively, adjusting tuition toward optimization of individual's learning in a flexible and sympathetic way. Developments in educational software programming must be directed toward the development of intelligent knowledge-based systems and away from explicit programming.

Lessening Isolation

An open learner is most often a distance learner too. Even if he or she attends classes or tutorials, the amount of face-to-face contact is smaller than in full-time school, college or tertiary education. The open learner is therefore more isolated both geographically and intellectually. The issues so far discussed show their most important manifestations here. The open learners must be made to feel that they are part of a well-motivated community of people who share common objectives, and who can assist each other. They must therefore be in frequent contact with their tutors and each other through electronic communication methods. Teaching material and programs should be distributed in the same way. Hence *rational* use of interactive communication facilities and hardware, *enhancement* of learning via pragmatic and intelligent approaches to multimedia teaching, and *application* of information technology in terms of both software and hardware all contribute to the *lessening* of isolation and promotion of learning.

Implications

If the propositions above can be accepted, then they raise issues of great importance for all teachers and trainers. These issues are best approached, to my way of thinking at least, from an 'ideal model' of an open learner.

So what is a picture of an ideal open learner? I suggest that there are three dimensions by which to describe him or her:

1. motivation;
2. equipment;
3. support.

Any open learner and his or her environment can be assessed in each dimension. The ideal will be a very well-motivated learner; will possess (or be loaned) a sophisticated computer work station, and be in full interactive communication with his or her tutor and peers at any time via cheap and versatile electronic communication facilities. The three dimensions are interdependent and, when properly integrated, synergistic. For example, if a poorly-motivated student is provided with good electronic communications and sophisticated teaching software sympathetic to his strengths and weaknesses, then it is quite probable that his motivation to learn will increase. If he encounters difficulties, his tutor and his peers are only a short time and distance away through electronic mail and document exchange facilities. The tutor may send documents, advice or remedial software to help. Other students who have encountered the same or similar problems can provide advice. Who knows what may happen?

Issues Needing Discussion

In a brief paper like this, the full implications cannot be explored in the detail they warrant. However, the issues raised are quite clearly:

1. financial;
2. technological;
3. attitudinal.

Financial

'Where does the money come from?' The answers I see are from the student who wants to learn, from government and local funding bodies such as the LEAs who should have the same objectives (though this is dubious at present) and of course from private industry, both manufacturing and service.

Technological

'Does the technology exist, and can it be used for open learning?' In terms of computer hardware, of course it does, and it will rapidly improve. This is also true in terms of electronic communication, since TTNS and other networks are already being used to peck at the edges of this area. In terms of information, intelligent software and research, the answer is unfortunately no.

Attitudinal

There are two questions to be asked here. First, 'Are there people who want to be open learners?' The answer is certainly yes; ask the colleges, universities and polytechnics how many students they have to turn away each year. Second, 'Are there people who are capable of producing the teaching materials and software?' The answer here is yes, after a fashion, but few have the time or money to devote to the task. There is certainly little current encouragement for anyone who wishes to take the time to do so.

Conclusion

Those are the issues which seem important to me. There are no doubt others. Society is undergoing rapid change. Employment is no longer a right. What work there is is mostly in new service industries which require better educated applicants. At the same time as the facilities to produce these are being reduced at all levels of the educational systems, that system itself sticks to the last it knows and produces, by traditional and labour-intensive means, the persons with 10 O-levels, 3 A-levels and a degree to fill these vacancies. Hence, three million unemployed; a less well-educated 'lump' which ought to be encouraged toward less formal and traditional methods of tuition in order that they might compete on more level terms with the more fortunate minority who benefit from the current educational system. And hence, of course, open learning and information technology, which is where I came in.

1.26 Flexible Learning through Computer-Mediated Communications: Opportunities and Limitations

G McI Boyd
Concordia University, Montreal, Canada

Abstract: Three main kinds of flexibility are offered by personal computer telecommunications in conjunction with mainframe computers running conferencing software: physical flexibility (choice of place and times of study), affiliative flexibility (choice of fellow students and tutors with whom to work) and epistemological flexibility (choice of paths of learning, and of learning goals within an area of study). Some current projects are briefly discussed.

The opportunity for holding nearly ideal non-dominative discourse of the type advocated by Jürgen Habermas is pointed out, together with the opportunities for developing new learning that this implies. Four classes of limitations inherent in personal computer-mediated communications today are discussed: technical (audio and graphics, etc), economic, sociocybernetic, and subject domain. Despite these limitations and the sparsity of research on effectiveness, experimental use of PC-mediated communications can be reasonably recommended for scattered populations of adult learners in advanced subject areas ranging from philosophy to accounting.

Introduction

By personal computer-mediated communications (PCMC) is meant the use of student-owned computers to exchange messages, preferably via the main computer of some educational or training organization, and via public telecommunications. The messages may be 'asynchronously' exchanged like ordinary postal mail. Alternatively a number of people may be online together participating in 'synchronous' discourse.

Whatever is communicated is usually recorded (if only temporarily) at both ends, and may therefore be edited and re-transmitted quite easily. Archiving of contributions is both possible and inexpensive.

The public telecommunications may simply be a direct telephone call from a student's PC to a nearby school, or it may involve a Prestel/Micronet call through Pandora messaging centres to other parts of the country. In North America packet switched data services such as Datapac or Telenet are the preferred long-distance modes.

New Educational Opportunities

The new opportunities for flexible learning provided by PCMC are mainly of three kinds:

1. epistemological – new opportunities for flexibly structuring discursive learning
2. affiliative – new opportunities for peer tutoring and for establishing long-term affiliations between students and their school or university, and among students
3. physical flexibility – new opportunities for students to study in more convenient places and at more convenient times.

Let us consider each of these at greater length.

Epistemological – Discursive Flexibility

In many respects what is new here is very old: small group and personal tutorials have always, at least potentially, offered this kind of evolutionary flexibility. It disappeared with the introduction of large classes and with mass media (print, radio, TV) used for education at a distance, and for reducing educational costs.

What is really new is the possibility of a rapid exchange of ideas where all communication is public and recorded. Non-verbal dominative language is not possible. Verbal promises, threats, and rank-pulling appear in hard print with names and dates and times attached. This is no hazard for the legitimate authority of the teacher or tutor, but it does impose a check on the abuse of that authority, and upon student abuses of the discourse space.

The relevant theoretical framework for this sort of situation is Jürgen Habermas's theory of discursive rationality (1973) and Gordon Pask's conversation theory (1980), which are complementary. What is particularly relevant from Habermas is his ideal of discourse where all that counts is the relative merits of the arguments advanced: '... that no force except that of the better argument be exercised; and that as a result all motives except that of co-operative search for truth are excluded'. This is an ideal situation for such education as respects the mind, as well as for the development of new scientific knowledge, etc. In his educational conversation theory Gordon Pask assumes that such motives and such non-dominative discourse prevail at the outset. He then establishes a framework relating possible aims to paths of knowledge and understanding–attainment, with proximate goals and topics appropriate to each learner's knowledge and learning style.

If our educational aims include learning how to learn and learning how to co-operate rationally, then the learning activities that we prescribe need to possess great flexibility, and a minimum of constraint which has not rationally been agreed upon. Instructional objectives need to be negotiated, not imposed by an expert's task analysis. PC-mediated teleconferencing provides a forum in which such negotiative activities can readily be accommodated. It provides an option for more democratic adult learning.

Who pays attention to whom and in which ways does constitute the basis for a 'relevant credibility status game' (Boyd, 1975), but a very public one. The relationship between status and quality of ideas can be assessed by everyone equally.

Opportunities for Affiliative Flexibility

PC-mediated communications offer new opportunities for flexible association among students and tutors, and for long-term affiliation with educational institutions. At the managerial and developmental level there are also opportunities for more and more convenient communications among tutors and course team or professorial staff, as Tony Kaye has pointed out recently (1986).

Although many students choose distance education options because they do not want to be encumbered with social interaction obligations but merely want to get on with the job of learning particular skills and knowledge, there remains an appreciable number who would like to make personal contacts and friends. Among students studying for the professions there is a need to create and develop 'old boy networks'. Computer-mediated conferencing readily supports and helps maintain such contact networks (Boyd, 1985).

Coalitions of less certain value can also be formed and mobilized. I know of one teachers' strike which was partly mobilized through a computer network set up to teach mathematics teachers new skills.

In a society such as that of North America where competitive opportunism is part of the ideology propagated by the commercial entertainment media, it is very important for educational institutions to promote and teach co-operation and team spirit. The learner-to-learner messaging capability of PCMCs can make this possible even when the individuals would have great difficulty arranging regular face-to-face meetings. Peer tutoring is an obvious example of what is possible. It is also possible to run educational simulation games with *teams* of players, rather than just individuals.

Physical Flexibility

Both times and places may be arranged flexibly to suit learners' and teachers' individual needs. Of course, this is also possible when learners work with books and audiocassettes. In many countries postal turnaround time is in the order of weeks rather than days so that conventional media do not provide for quick diagnostic feedback when the learner needs it. Computer conferencing and electronic mail can be as rapid as is convenient for the people involved, like the telephone. But unlike the telephone it does not have to be simultaneous, and it can transmit diagrams and print out text.

Even where face-to-face study meetings are practical they may be a wasteful use of time if many students are ill-prepared or if the learning tasks which really need to be carried out require only a small amount of time compared to the travel or queueing time involved in getting the class meeting together. In such circumstances computer-mediated conferencing can complement face-to-face meetings which need occur only when all concerned are ready.

Limitations of PCMC for Education and Training

Five kinds of limitations need to be considered: economic, technical, sociocybernetic, knowledge and skills-domain related, and, as it were, 'conceptual'. By conceptual limitations is meant the slowness of teachers and administrators to make the imaginative leaps necessary to find appropriate uses for personal computer-mediated communications. This paper is addressed to leaders in the field to help alleviate such 'conceptual' limitations.

Economic Limitations

Computer hardware and telecommunications are steadily becoming cheaper, and more nearly universally accessible. Costs of PCs with modems (personal computers with couplers to connect to ordinary telephone lines) are still appreciable in comparison to other study aids. The threshold for a usable arrangement is several hundred pounds per student initial capital cost. Computer conferencing central host system costs can vary upward from a few thousand pounds to many tens or even hundreds of thousands depending on system scale. Telecommunication costs vary greatly. In Canada there are no time charges for local (same city) telephone calls no matter how long they are so that communications costs are negligible within a given urban area. DATAPAC packet switched services are available by local call, and they provide extremely cheap long-distance communications (about five cents to send a thousand words of text from Montreal to Vancouver – $2.50 per Kilopac). In the United Kingdom, Tony Kaye (1985) estimates that evening and weekend access would cost Open University students about 40p per hour.

The cost of the teacher's or tutor's time to read, comment upon, mark, edit, and restructure course material is consequently the major central operating cost of PCMC teaching – like an ordinary school class.

Unlike television, or CAI-type CAL, 'front end' instructional design and course production costs need not be much higher than for an ordinary face-to-face course. There will however be an appreciable capital investment of a one-time nature in the computer-mediated conferencing software and the standardized rules of play for all users. This investment serves all courses given, like a school building.

Current costs make advanced technical and professional course teaching by PCMC feasible, particularly if student/trainee time is costed, and the students are geographically dispersed.

Technical Limitations

Probably the most serious limitations are partly technical and partly commercial or 'political'. Many areas of study and training require fairly complex and detailed graphics. These certainly can be produced and exchanged with particular and rather expensive types of personal computers (usually glorified with the appellation: 'engineering work station'), but affordable machines lack quality, and there is very little standardization. Prestel does provide standards for low-resolution graphics, or medium-resolution photographic (picture-Prestel) transmission which go some way toward meeting the need. In North America very few PCs have NAPLPS (the equivalent of Prestel) decoders and diagram transmission is consequently difficult unless all students have the same model of PC (Aguilar, 1968). For language teaching and music studies the recording and transmission of sounds is necessary and for many other studies it can be helpful.

At the computer conferencing system software level there are still many technical limitations, partly because this is a new field, and partly because natural language processing is still a research area. Features which make a system easy for newcomers and casual users, such as menus arranged in tree structures, prove awkward and tedious to practised and proficient users. Some systems provide both tree menus and command-line relational database facilities at an additional overhead cost.

Options such as 'voting', useful for simulation gaming, and for collecting readers' ratings of the value or timeliness of contributions are available on only a few of the most sophisticated systems, like EIES at New Jersey Institute of Technology (Turoff, 1983).

Natural language parsing adequate to the task of, for instance, automatically eliminating redundant contributions, is far beyond the present state of the art. Consequently the editing and rearranging facilities available to the course tutor or teacher are very important.

Some software systems and protocols allow for anonymous or pseudonymous communication which can result in some nasty 'lets you and him fight' games according to Karl Zinn (1986) one of the developers of the CONFER system at the University of Michigan.

Sociocybernetic Limitations

Any many-person learning activity requires rules of order. These may be only implicit, such as good manners, or they may be spelt out. In addition to general rules about turn-taking and such like, a teacher also needs to intervene to alter the direction of discourse when it strays too far from the lesson. This is steersmanship or cybernetic prescription.

With PCMC the students have a great deal of control over what they look at and for how long, and of course over what they do or don't contribute. Our work with the Canadian Higher Education Research Network (CHERN) on the CoSy conferencing system at Guelph University indicates that initially the main difficulty is to encourage people to alter their daily habits to include checking their electronic mailboxes. Where credit courses are involved, and especially in corporate training ventures, the fact that every access and contribution can be tabulated introduces a control loop to maintain participation.

Even when people make a habit of reading and contributing it seems that they start mainly by dealing with technical problems and exchanging social information. Definite guidance is usually needed to keep the proportion of substantive work high. Mutual appraisal as to the timeliness and value of each others' contributions may easily be carried out using 'voting' facilities. Some polite conventions and a nice balancing of social and task concerns have to be fostered by the course leaders. Trust is essential.

Subject Domain Limitations

Both the types of subject matter, and the level of the learners are somewhat constrained. This constraint is partly technical: the letters of English and numbers of accounting are easily handled, as is computer programming (or computer science). Music and art make more difficult demands which are best met with other media.

Advanced courses where people are expected to take a good deal of responsibility for their own learning and where they have a lot of good examples to share with each other are favoured.

The learning of principles and problem-solving techniques, and perhaps also the development of a sophisticated sensibility (towards literature, for example) are at least theoretically what such a conversational medium ought to teach best. Romiszowski (1981) makes a strong distinction between learning 'reproductive skills' for which 'expositive' teaching methods are best, and the learning of 'productive' skills which is best served by guide 'discovery strategies'. The latter appear more appropriate for mediation with computer conferencing, conventional CAL perhaps being better for the former.

Conclusion

The opportunities and limitations of personal computer-mediated communications have been discussed, based on observations of existing situations with courses given using EIES, CoSy, CONFER, and so on, and theoretical considerations.

This paper is in a sense a continuation of a series of papers which have been given at ETIC and published in *Aspects of Educational Technology*, where the central concern is the formation of networks of knowledgeable people who appreciate each others' knowledge and teaching and research skills. Among others, I have contributed to the series *Toward the Transparent University* (Boyd, 1975) and *Networking as an Educational Technology* (Boyd, 1977).

The underlying theme is a concern for improving the strength, size and effective durability of educational coalitions as collective factors in society. For us to have a saner and perhaps happier world there needs to be a different balance between the cultural and the merely economic (pluralistic) factor groups of society. It is possible that existing coalitions of educators may be strengthened by PCMC and in turn may shape this new and very plastic medium better to meet important educational needs.

References

Aguilar, L (1968) A format for a graphical communications protocol. *IEEE Computer Graphics*, **6**, 2 pp 52-62.

Boyd, G. M (1975) The importance and feasibility of transparent universities. In Evans, L and Leedham J (eds) *Aspects of Educational Technology IX*. Kogan Page, London.

Boyd, G M (1977) Contribution and appraisal networking as an educational technology. In Hills, P J (ed) *Aspects of Educational Technology XI*. Kogan Page, London.

Boyd, G M (1985) The importance of providing for life-long affiliation with distance education institutions, with personal computer communications. *Canadian Journal of Educational Communication*, **14**, 1, pp 8-27.

Habermas, J (1973) *Legitimation Crisis*. Beacon Press, Boston.

Kaye, T (1985) Computer mediated communications systems for distance education. *Project Report CCET/2*. The Open University, Milton Keynes.

Pask, G (1980) *Developments in Conversation Theory*. Academic Press, London.

Romiszowski, A J (1981) Strategies for the teaching of knowledge and skills. In Percival, F and

Ellington H (eds) *Aspects of Educational Technology XV*. Kogan Page, London.
Turoff, M and Hiltz, S R (1983) Exploring the future of human communication via computer. *Computer Compacts*, **1**, 2, pp 78-83.
Zinn, K (1977) Computer facilitation of communication within professional communities. *Behavior Research Methods and Instrumentation*, **9**, 2, pp 96-107.
Zinn, K (1986) Personal communication.

1.27 Presenting Computer Aided Design (CAD) to the Distance Learner

K J Adderley and P J Lucas
Warley College of Technology

Abstract: This case study typifies a new concept in distance learning. Students use a remote work station linked to a central computer via the national telephone network to access the kind of computer software used by medium and large industries.

A course, designed at the Warley Open Tech Unit in Sandwell, focuses on the education and training of technicians and supervisors in computer aided engineering. It presents topics in modular form requiring a total study time of approximately 300 hours.

In focusing on one typical module (Two-Dimensional Computer Aided Design) the authors highlight the many practical issues arising during the process of curriculum development and the challenge to develop in the remote learner the basic skills for selecting and using CAD packages.

The eventual behavioural outcome of the learner is achieved by applying distance learning techniques, tempered by specific constraints and industrial collaboration, to a challenging and novel concept. This concept, exemplified by the working model for the delivery of practical CAD/CAM training on a flexible learning basis throughout the UK, has been developing through an Open Tech project dependent for its success on the close collaboration of industry, government agencies, and education.

Introduction

This case study, which reviews a wide range of decision points in our course, aims to stimulate your interest in taking a fresh look at curriculum development issues in your own field, and to inspect the rationale of our style of presentation, particularly for those who may use our materials in the future.

The Computer-Aided Engineering (CAE) Course

Background

It is well known that between 1981 and 1987 the Manpower Services Commission (MSC) is funding a number of Open Tech Projects that are intended to provide a flexible means of training, retraining and updating technicians and others in industry and commerce. Four of these projects are directed towards computer aided engineering (CAE), ie those aspects of design, production and testing which make substantial use of computers.

Between them, these four projects provide training over a wide range of industrial and commercial activities, from operating 'high-tech' equipment to decision-making at levels ranging from general awareness to accomplished skill.

Course Aims

The Warley open learning course, in close collaboration with Delta CAE Ltd, provides practical experience at the learner's own terminal to develop the skills needed to use modern sophisticated industrial software.

The course is structured in modular form and embraces computer aided design (CAD), computer aided manufacture (CAM), computer aided testing and robotics to a target audience comprising designers, draughtsmen, production engineers, workshop supervisors and skilled operatives. Their ages may range from 21 to 55 years.

Most modules represent 30 hours of study time, including 20 hours of computer interaction. Three shorter modules, with no practical component, are rated at 20 hours each. Each module stands alone but in combination with the ten others constitutes a 300-hour course, eventually to be validated by the Business Technician Education Council (BTEC) either for a post-experience certificate or for half of a Higher National Certificate (HNC).

Flexibility

Given that the learner has access to a graphics computer terminal which may be purchased or hired from the college (Figure 1), the practical work may be carried out at home, in an office, in a factory or in a college.

Figure 1. *Using the Hektor work station*

In Module 2, which is the subject of this case study, learners develop practical skills by being guided through graduated exercises in the application of a typical two-dimensional draughting and design software package. These exercises enable them to create drawings of manufactured articles (or parts) at their own work station. Figure 2 provides an example.

The software available to them is the Drawing Office Graphics System (DOGS), a package costing about £30,000 from PAFEC Ltd in Nottingham. Traditional training for draughtsmen using this package is through two full-time short courses of four to five days' duration, spaced several months apart.

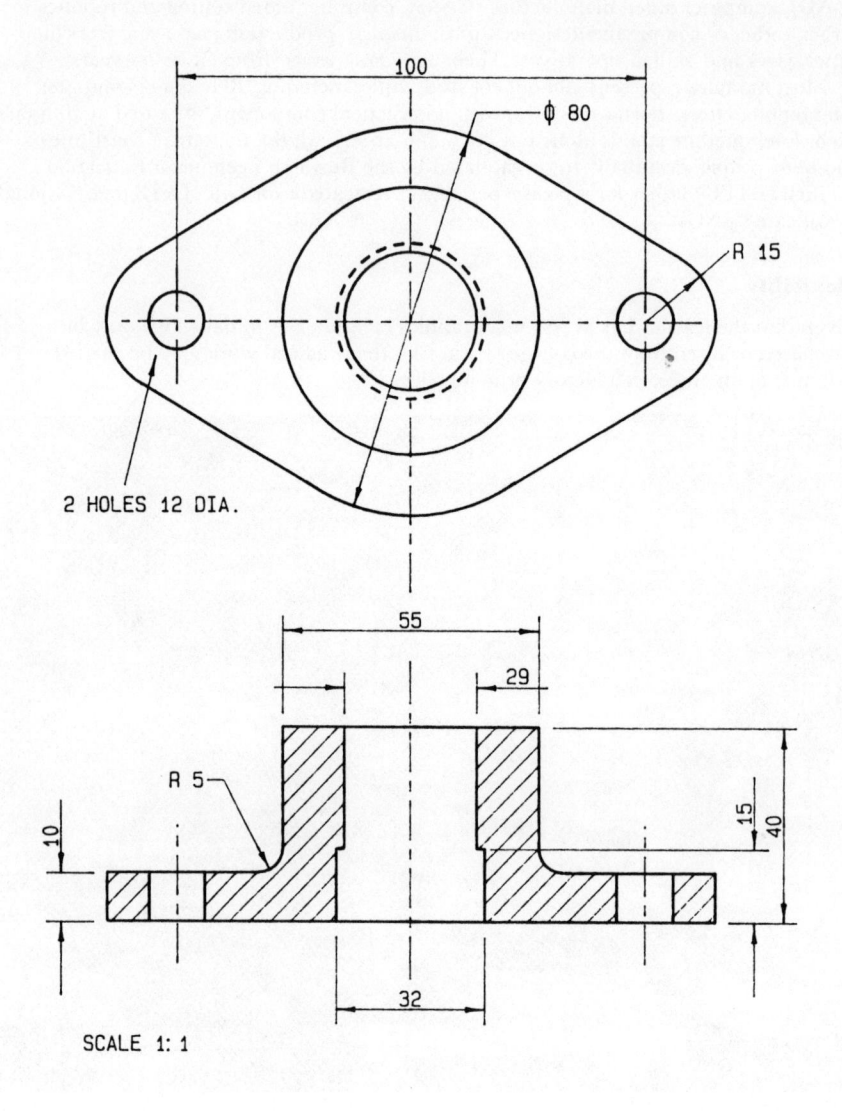

Figure 2. *Foot bracket details*

Using the Warley material, the learners may study at a time, place and pace to suit their individual needs. Apart from periods required for routine maintenance and backup procedures, access to the computer is very flexible, ie 24 hours per day, 7 days per week. Currently, access is completely open throughout the period of study – about eight weeks per module. However, should the system show signs of strain at peak periods a negotiated rota arrangement would become necessary.

Whilst learners may register with Warley, we encourage those living outside the West Midlands to register with their nearest local centre in order to minimize telephone charges. There will soon be at least 12 centres in the United Kingdom running our software.

The computer system is the *host-peripheral* type, typical of a computer bureau service. All the computer packages, the working memory, the files, etc are housed in a central computer and disc store. The learner accesses these packages by linking the terminal to the host computer via the national telephone network using a modem to *mo*dulate and *dem*odulate the transmitted signals.

At Warley we have a PRIME 550 computer (2 megabytes of memory) backed up by 300 Mbyte (300,000 Kbyte) of disc storage. 15 of our 120 outlet ports have direct connection to the national telephone network.

Staffing

The course team is comparatively small, comprising a project director and two author/editors. These three are backed up by a computer technician, an administrator, a typist and part-time tutors/trainers from Warley College of Technology and Deltacam Systems Ltd.

Constraints on Curriculum Development

Once the kind of learning system is decided, the central purpose of any course is to achieve the course aims by using the most effective teaching/learning techniques. 'So what's new?' you may ask. Whilst this principle may not be novel, its application to our CAD module witnessed the evolution of many ideas which were new to us, despite our breadth of experience in teaching conventional courses in higher education and our involvement with other Open University or Open Tech programmes.

Unlike distance learning texts for degree subjects or O and A levels, our CAD module explains sophisticated practical techniques to people whose spatial and manual skills may exceed their literary ability. This presents a challenging problem of motivation and presentation style. The established motivating techniques, ie video recordings, audio cassettes, tape–slide packs or tape–photograph packs, so characteristic of modern open learning systems, were barred to us by financial and resource limitations.

At least our learners would have access to a computer. How could we make the best use of that? A golden opportunity, you may think, to incorporate interaction by following established computer aided learning (CAL) practice. But there were restraints here too. Once students had called up the draughting package, the opportunity for instruction via the screen was extremely limited.

Although the draughting package offered a built-in help facility for resolving very specific queries, it was not designed for interactive learning. It was therefore impossible to devise interactive teaching frames or to adopt an author language to guide learners or to monitor their progress within the package.

For the transmission of information over long distances the computer system is a much more expensive medium than print. Furthermore there would be no gain in efficiency by the instant transmission of didactic exposition. So the printed word constituted the primary expository medium.

In reviewing the decisions made as the module evolved we can identify four major categories: organization, context, format and style.

On the *organizational* front we constituted a newly formulated course team with organizational and general authoring skills. We had no firm design for a reasonably priced graphics work station, and very limited detailed knowledge of the skills required. Hence the main issues to be resolved were:

- How can the authors improve subject knowledge quickly?
- How can we utilize existing source materials efficiently?
- How can the authors sharpen their interactive writing skills?
- Which hardware supplier will best meet our needs for a comparatively cheap graphics terminal?
- Who will pilot the learning materials?
- How can we guarantee the accuracy of the final product in both its technical and educational aspects?

Some of these issues presented no great difficulty. The authors attended appropriate training courses and capitalized on experience gained in working in the Open University and the Southtek Open Tech project at Brighton. Technical literature was scanned for suitable case studies. Technical validation was placed in the hands of Delta CAE Ltd and Warley College with significant input from two nationally respected experts, one in CAD and the other in technical editing. The hardware problem was eventually resolved by placing a contract with the Open University to develop a graphics version of their HEKTOR III microprocessor, which when put together with a modem, a monitor and a mouse provided us with a suitable computer graphics work station at very low cost (just under £600).

Once in reasonable draft form, the modules were piloted by a dozen learners from both industry and education with backgrounds ranging from technicians with ONC awards to engineers with higher degrees. Resolving the organizational and presentation issues naturally coloured the broad canvas on which all 11 modules would ultimately be painted. Since issues concerning content are germane to the individual modules, let us now turn to one of these: Module 2.

Case Study of Individual Module

The content was deemed to embrace both a general awareness of current trends in CAD and an in-depth training in selected practical skills.

- How might we best *sequence* the content to accommodate these diverse requirements?

We identified three possible approaches. Should we:

Model 1: Progress from the particular to the general?
Model 2: Progress from the general to the particular?
Model 3: Devise a multilayered sandwich of 1 and 2?

Each model has certain advantages and disadvantages. Model 3, which was ultimately adopted, breaks up the content into manageable slices (Figure 3). By introducing the 'hands-on' component as early as possible and returning to it at intervals throughout, this structure capitalizes on the intrinsic motivation built into all interactive computer-based systems. Figure 2 typifies the level of skill we would expect the average learner to achieve during the course.

The *style* and *format* of presentation must be understandable to learners whose reading may be limited to the more popular newspapers and practical hobby magazines. It must also motivate them or *entice them into the pages of print*. We anticipated no motivational problems in their being drawn in to the work station, once they had overcome any initial fear of the unknown – a common problem with those

Theme	Awareness, A or Practical Interaction, P
How to Study this Module	A
How to Use the Workstation	P
Available Hardware	A
Basic Features of CAD	A
Basic Features of DOGS	P
Typical Features of CAD	A
Central Features of DOGS	P
Low Cost CAD	A
System Selection	A
What Next?	A
Optional Exercises	P
Glossary	A
Help/Manual Extracts	P

Figure 3. *Module structure*

generations of learners whose formal training ended before the microelectronics revolution started. So we got them to play a couple of games to start with – just to persuade them to feel friendly towards the work station.

Some Issues Raised

The above aims and constraints evoke many questions:

- In what parts of the UK will the central computer(s) be situated?
- Which parts of the DOGS package should we cover? ie should we have a broad superficial coverage or an in-depth narrow coverage?
- How can we recover from situations where learners accidentally alter pre-set variables which are not in the syllabus?
- Can we possibly introduce any elements of computer assisted learning?
- To what extent could we extend the limited help facility already built into the DOGS package?
- How might learners be motivated to read lists of objectives?
- How can we present typescript in ways that draw the reader into the page?

From Constraints to Opportunities

Defining the boundaries of a problem is a well-known first step in devising a solution. The restrictions discussed above provide not only a welcome constraint to our learning system but also a fascinating challenge to the curriculum developer. The particular ways we responded to this challenge are stated briefly in the remainder of this paper.

The printed text:

- breaks down into 15 study sessions;
- talks the learner easily and clearly through the technicalities;
- carries case studies reprinted from engineering journals and press releases;
- fully exploits the word processor's capabilities;
- emphasizes key sections by adding logos in the margin;

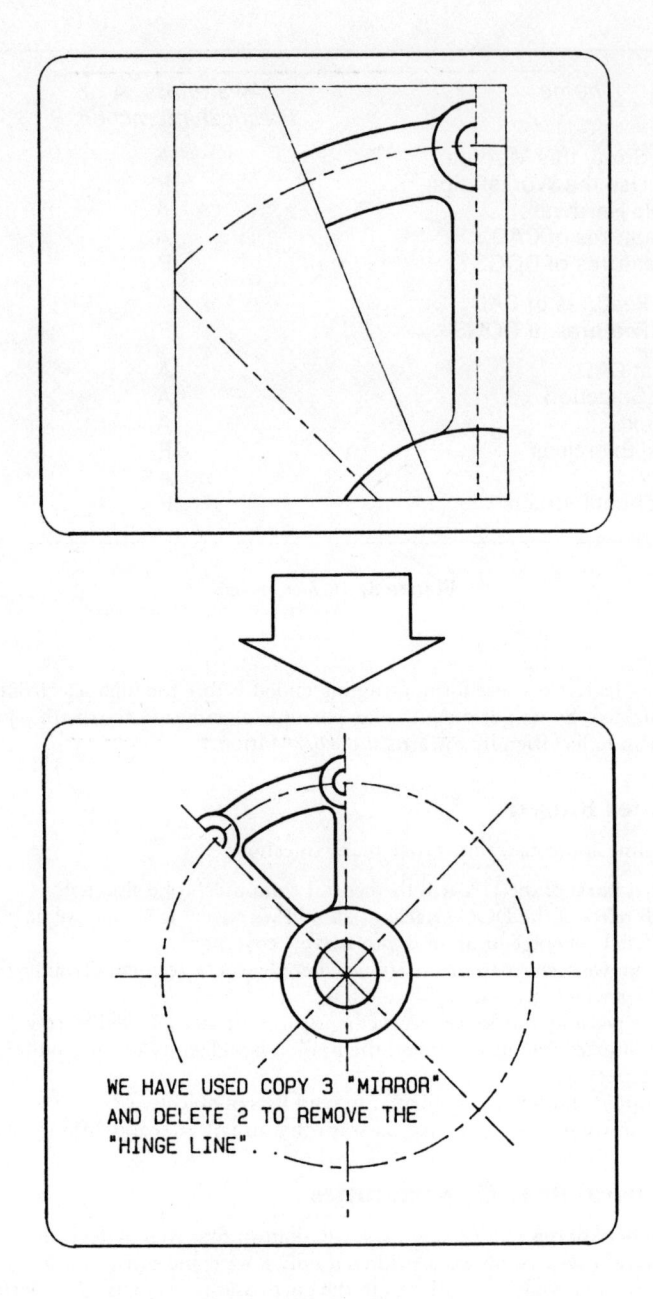

Figure 4. *Wheel construction*

- varies the stimulus through questions, activities, worked examples and optional exercises;
- carries a 100-page reference section detailing each command introduced;
- contains an extensive HELP section.

The software:

- carries custom-designed demonstration drawings which are sent downline to be built up frame by frame at the remote work stations;
- can be delivered worldwide on magnetic tape;
- carried an inbuilt (but minimal) HELP facility.

Perhaps we should emphasize that the final style of presentation did not mysteriously appear overnight but evolved instead through discussion primed by the literature (eg Lewis, 1984 and Adderley, 1983) and by workshops sponsored by the Open Tech Training and Support Unit.

We have designed our own stencils and logos; consciously placed an *aims* box at the head and an *objective* box at the end of each study session and divided the self-assessment questions (SAQs) into two distinct categories. One tests what has gone before, the other anticipates what is yet to come. We also vary the stimulus within each SAQ category by a wide range of question types.

Deciding on the best place to locate answers can provoke extensive debate. We have placed category 1 answers at the end of the module and comments on the anticipatory questions, wherever possible, on the page following the activity.

The whole module is highly interactive, two key features being the step-by-step format for the 'worked examples', and the frame-by-frame demonstration of 'drawing creation' together with transmitted text explaining the commands used. Eight such demonstrations are sent downline to the learner using the DOGS software. Figure 4 shows a frame from one of them.

Conclusion

Developing and publishing the first two modules in this CAE course has been an excellent learning experience for the whole course team. We are very confident that our own learners will feel equally well rewarded when they tackle the course. Present indications from the pilot trials and the subsequent uptake confirm this prediction. The ongoing evaluation provides not only invaluable feedback for the course team as we prepare the remaining modules, but also useful data from which to update Module 2 when the time comes.

References

Adderley, K J (1983) *A Training Scheme for Authors of Distance Learning Materials*. MA thesis, University of Sussex.
Lewis, R (1984) *How to Help Learners Assess Their Progress*. Council for Educational Technology.
RAF *A Guide to the Design of Learning Packages*. Resources Development Unit of the RAF School of Education.

Acknowledgements

The authors gratefully acknowledge the extensive support of Delta CAE Ltd, Warley College of Technology and the MSC Open Tech Unit.

1.28 Videotex – Interactivity is Flexibility: The Canadian Experience

D J Gillies
Ryerson Polytechnical Institute, Toronto, Canada

Abstract: Telidon/NAPLPS, the Canadian videotex system, has been designed for flexibility through terminal independence and interactivity. Flexibility is evident also in the relationship of videotex to various facets of the teaching/learning process: technology, time, content, format and pedagogy. A summary review of 20 educational videotex applications in Canada describes and demonstrates the potential use of videotex as a component of flexible learning systems.

Introduction

This article treats the notion of flexibility in learning systems in generic terms rather than as a formal description or specific category. It deals with videotex in general as a flexible learning system *per se*, points out that interactivity is essential to videotex, and equates the system articulation of interactivity in its several facets to flexibility.

Background in Videotex

As a teacher in the instructional media programme at Ryerson Polytechnical Institute (RPI), I am interested in technological innovations which appear to have instructional applications. The waves of informatics and telematics innovation continuously washing over teachers and learners today may produce the King Canute syndrome in many of them, but much useful flotsam is left when the tide goes out. It seems to me that videotex is one of the best of these, with a great deal of teaching/learning potential, as I hope to make clear. My interest in videotex arises from several bases. I am writing a technological history of the origins of videotex (and teletext). I was a member of the team which, working through the Distance Education Department of RPI, designed and taught Canada's first videotex page creation training course for the 1979-82 field trial of Telidon[1] carried out by Infomart[2] and Bell Canada.[3] I was the first Director of a Telidon Public Initiatives Programme project in which the RPI Nutrition Information Service produced a 2,500-page *Food and Nutrition Information Directory*, which became part of the public sector database in the aforementioned Telidon field trial. Most recently I have written the Telidon section of a Canadian sourcebook on telecommunications and distance education (Stahmer, in press). These divergent but cognate streams flow together to inform this article.

Videotex Technology

Videotex (sometimes still referred to by its original British name, 'Viewdata') presents visual information to a user on a television screen. It is silent[4] and the images are still frames[5], called 'pages'. These pages are stored in central computer data banks. The information in these databases is produced, stored and made available for retrieval by 'information providers'. The information in the data banks travels primarily in the switched telephone network. Prestel is the British videotex service, France has Télétel,

Germany Bildschirmtext, and in Canada and the United States the original Telidon has been replaced by North American Presentation Level Protocol Syntax (NAPLPS) a more advanced system.

Videotex Interactivity

Videotex is 'interactive', ie the user of the service chooses what he wishes to appear on his television screen by means of a keypad or keyboard. The notion of interactivity is the best starting point to explore the flexibility of videotex systems.

Flexibility: Interactivity

At present, with very few exceptions, the videotex user is significantly restricted in an important realm: he can only access information from data banks; he cannot input it. It was the intention of the originator of videotex, Sam Fedida, that videotex users also be information providers, resulting in a full interchange of information among a community or within society at large (Fedida, 1975, 1983). Douglas F Parkhill, a Canadian informatics pioneer, wrote of the 'computer utility' in the sense of a public utility such as telephones, electricity, gas or water (Parkhill, 1966), and later of the 'electronic highway' (Parkhill, 1985): a public informatics utility. While interactivity is not (yet) complete, a longer-term view of an emerging technology suggests that we at least keep full interactivity as a goal. Even the present kind and level of interactivity offers a great deal of choice, and, with it, flexibility. How does videotex, particularly Canadian videotex, achieve this flexibility?

Flexibility: Technology

From the earliest days of videotex research in Canada a user terminal was planned which would contain its own intelligence, ie a microprocessor and a display processor. The picture coding scheme would be independent of the user terminal hardware configuration and the system used for carrying the information (Bown and Sawchuck, 1981). The originators of Telidon built in flexibility by future-proofing. Unlike the British and French alpha-mosaic approaches with their low-resolution graphics which were terminal-dependent, the Canadian system produced alpha-geometric or alpha-photographic images by a coding scheme – Picture Description Instructions (PDIs) – which was terminal-independent. The main facets of technological flexibility are:

- ☐ Terminal independence: from the outset videotex was flexible enough to be adaptable to technological innovation whenever it might occur (Bown *et al*, 1978). The effect of videotex terminal independence is that the user may call up pages on many makes of computer, including business and industrial work stations of varying format, resolution or software configuration, eg using videotex boards. The main benefit is to the personal computer user.
- ☐ Technologically basic: a combination of the telephone, the television receiver and the computer, all readily available or easily acquired.
- ☐ Varied delivery modes: the signal may be carried by telephone line, whether wire or optical fibre, or by coaxial television cable, 'piggybacked' onto television as teletext, broadcast by satellite, or narrowcast by microwave.
- ☐ User-friendly: videotex is transparent to the user and menu-driven, so no computing or programming training is required. Its hierarchical tree structure simplifies user choices and decisions (if correctly designed). All these features invite use.
- ☐ Updating: pages may be changed in seconds, allowing time-sensitive information to be kept current.
- ☐ Combinable: videotex may be used in combination with videotape, videodisc or

optical disk, eg to provide both static and moving images or titles on the screen. When the user's videotex terminal is suitably equipped, videotex telesoftware may be downloaded to his computer.
- ☐ Gateways: gateways in a videotex system provide access through the main computer(s) to external computerized databases like libraries, airline reservation systems and banks. For teaching/learning activities gateways enhance both the opportunity to browse and to conduct very specific research, and to remove locational barriers.
- ☐ Graphics: the high-resolution NAPLPS graphics provide illustrative support for many purposes: maps, diagrams, charts and spatial relationships, for example.

Flexibility: Time

- ☐ Constant availability: videotex material is always online, available when the learner has time to study, and in off-peak hours down loading of telesoftware can take advantage of cheaper telecommunications costs.
- ☐ Duration: because the learner can control the rate of acquisition of learning materials, individualized pacing and focusing of attention, inquiry and feedback can take place.
- ☐ Age: anyone over the age of five or six can use appropriately designed pages.

Flexibility: Scale

- ☐ Database size: from one page to hundreds of thousands; hypothetically limitless.
- ☐ Complexity: videotex data can vary between a single concept and a lengthy narrative, all with illustrations.

Flexibility: Content

- ☐ Type: videotex pages are useful for all types of visual content, unless constant motion and sound are required.
- ☐ Information providers: information is provided by individuals, organizations, governments, universities, education authorities, schools, libraries, banks, the mass media, private and public bodies, profit and non-profit groups, all at the local, regional or national level; almost anyone can be an information provider.
- ☐ Users: there is as much variety among videotex users as among information providers.
- ☐ Privacy: confidential material such as legal, political, financial, insurance or personal documents may have limited accessibility to 'closed user groups' by means of private codes.

Flexibility: Format

The standard format for videotex pages is the television screen. In addition, pages may be converted into

- ☐ offline stored data on disc or tape
- ☐ transparencies
- ☐ photographic prints
- ☐ posters
- ☐ projected television
- ☐ black-and-white or colour print-outs on paper
- ☐ overhead projectuals.

Flexibility: Pedagogy

In addition to the teaching/learning potential of videotex derived from the flexibility of technology, time, scale, content and format, additional benefits are available.

- ☐ Formality: as formal learning gives way to an increasing extent to non-formal learning, there is a concordance with the development of open systems, including videotex, within the information society.
- ☐ Programmed learning: the tree structure of the videotex database permits the programmatic structuring of instructional materials with a very large choice of learning routes.

Videotex: Teaching and Learning in Canada

There have been several studies dealing with aspects of videotex in teaching and learning in Canada (Gillies, 1984; Wilson, 1984; Stahmer, in press). I have chosen several applications which exemplify some or all of the flexibility discussed above. All used Telidon or NAPLPS technology. Any additional technology is mentioned in each citation. The listing is by province from west to east.

British Columbia

Institution: Adaptive Testing Network, Victoria
Application: automobile driving test
Institution: Arts, Sciences and Technology Centre, Vancouver
Application: primary school education; the Centre's displays
Institution: Open Learning Institute, Vancouver
Application: distance education materials
Institution: University of Victoria, Department of Creative Writing
Application: electronic journalism and publishing
Additional technology: microcomputer page creation

Alberta

Institution: Alberta Education Correspondence Schools, Edmonton
Application: ☐ access to public, university and college libraries
☐ correspondence courses
☐ in co-operation with the Alberta Educational Communications Authority (ACCESS), a grade 12 'Mechanics of Machines' course
Institution: Athabasca University
Application: distance education
Institution: University of Calgary
Application: 'Teaching Grammar in an Integrated Language Arts Programme'
Additional technology: telephone teleconferencing system

Manitoba

Institution: Manitoba Educational Telidon Association, Winnipeg
Application: primary and secondary school courses
Institution: Manitoba Telephone System, Infomart and Cybershare, Winnipeg
Application: for non-formal home learners:
☐ community college CAI
☐ secondary schools: BASIC programming
electricity
mathematics of finance
technology mathematics

□ business library: calculation and simulation programs
□ information library: nutrition, agriculture

Ontario

Institution: University of Guelph, Department of Rural Extension and Office of Educational Practice
Application: □ education, information to rural/remote students
□ courses in biology, neural anatomy, zoology
□ VET-TEL: veterinarian continuing education
□ enhancement of university's instructional function
Additional technology: □ on-campus: microcomputers, campus computer network, telephone
□ off-campus: local and packet switched telephone system
Institution: Lurentian University, Sudbury
Application: extension courses: computer literacy, physical education, health, local economy
Additional technology: distribution by cable television
Institution: Ryerson Polytechnical Institute, Nutrition Information Service, Toronto
Application: food and nutrition information directory
Institution: TV Ontario, Ontario Educational Communications Authority, Toronto
Application: EDUTEX: □ student guidance information service
□ Canadian press news service
□ general primary, secondary and tertiary curriculum-related information
□ provincial and municipal government information
□ Living (general interest)
□ national arts and culture review
Institution: University of Waterloo
Application: □ on-campus course and programme information
□ correspondence course supplementation
Institution: University of Western Ontario, London
Application: □ educational, research, service and general information for the university community
□ WESTEX news service from the Graduate School of Journalism

Quebec

Institution: Edemedia Ltd, Montreal
Application: university level □ CAL biology
□ programme and course information
Institution: University of Quebec in Montreal, Telematics Laboratory
Application: 'Image-2' informatics, mediatics and telematics
Additional technology: 'Plato' CBE
Institution: Téléuniversité, University of Quebec in Quebec
Application: □ course administration and management
□ electronic editing
□ adult education courseware
Additional technology: 'Plato' videotex software

New Brunswick

Institution: University of Moncton, Faculty of Arts
Application: provincial cultural history
Additional technology: microcomputers

Prince Edward Island

Institution: University of Prince Edward Island, Charlottetown
Application: Red Cross educational materials
Additional technology: videotex-adapted microcomputer

Some of these videotex applications to teaching and learning are current, others have ended (*see* Stahmer, in press). They are cited as examples of the range of Canadian activities in this important realm of education.

Conclusion

The Canadian videotex system – Telidon and NAPLPS – were designed and developed for optimal flexibility of production, implementation and operation. As the educational applications demonstrate, Telidon and NAPLPS have great potential as components of learning systems. It remains to be seen if imaginative educators exploit them to the full.

Notes

1. Telidon was the original Canadian alpha-geometric protocols and videotex/teletext systems developed at the Communications Research Centre (CRC) of the Canadian Department of Communications (DOC) and made public in August 1978.
2. Infomart Ltd is a company established by Torstar Corporation and Southam Incorporated to design and operate videotex services.
3. Bell Canada is the private telephone company which operates a regulated monopoly in Ontario, Quebec and parts of the Northwest Territories.
4. Audiotex and audiovideotex, ie videotex with sound, are under development.
5. On some videotex systems a simple animation effect may be produced by using the 'blink' on/off function.

References

Bown, H G, O'Brien, C D, Sawchuck, W and Storey, J R (1978) *A General Description of Telidon: A Canadian Proposal for Videotex Systems*.
Bown, H G and Sawchuck, W (1981) Telidon – a review. *IEEE Communications Magazine*, pp 22-28.
Fedida, S (1975) VIEWDATA: an interactive information service for the general public. *Proceedings of European Computing Conference on Communications Network*.
Fedida, S Interview with the author. London, April 1983.
Gillies, D J (1984) Videotex and teletext: teaching and learning – an international survey. In National Research Council of Canada, *Proceedings of the Fourth Canadian Symposium on Instructional Technology*. Ottawa.
Parkhill, D F (1966) *The Challenge of the Computer Utility*. Addison-Wesley, Reading, Massachusetts.
Parkhill, D F (1985) The necessary structure. In Godfrey, D and Parkhill, D F (eds) *Gutenberg Two: the New Electronics and Social Change* (4th edition). Press Procépic, Toronto and Victoria, British Columbia.
Stahmer, A (in press) *A Sourcebook in Distance Education and Telecommunications* (working title). Department of Communications, Ottawa.
Wilson, J (1984) Educational applications of videotex/Telidon in Canada. *New Technologies in Canadian Education paper II*. Office of Development Research, TV Ontario, Ontario Educational Communications Authority, Toronto.

1.29 Clear, Foggy and Black Boxes: Towards an Adaptable Environment for Novice Programmers

P M Goodyear
University of Lancaster

Abstract: This paper describes an experimental approach to the acquisition of programming skills by students following a course for non-specialist computer users. A major problem on such courses is matching the complexity of the programming task to the needs and abilities of the learner. Projects which are complex enough to interest the student can also be cognitively overwhelming. Simple tasks within the capacity of the novice programmer often fail to provide adequate motivation for the non-specialist. The course concerned was a two-year programme in environmental studies. The central problem was to construct a learning situation rich enough in environmental studies content and methodology to engage the students, while controlling the surface complexity of the programming task. The solution adopted was for tutors to construct a 'toolkit' of ecological modelling procedures in the programming language LOGO. LOGO's particular virtue of having an extendable vocabulary enables teaching staff to provide novice programmers with procedures that make working in the task domain concerned much more straightforward. The procedures concerned have different degrees of 'opacity'. Students treat some as 'black boxes', where external function is more important than internal structure. Other procedures need to be understood in detail – usually because they are at the heart of the modelling/programming task. Learning to program in this environment is closely bound up with moving from a 'black box' to a 'clear box' understanding of the procedures involved.

Introduction

Teachers concerned with scientific subjects in higher education have for many years argued that computer programming skills are of great value to their students' learning. In several areas they are viewed as essential (Pierce, 1967; Computer Board, 1983; Harding, 1984). The standard response to this perceived need is to provide students with service courses in computer programming. This task is often subcontracted to the computing centre or computer science department. Such an arrangement can be unsatisfactory – it can be difficult to find adequate time within the students' main subject of study to allow an adequate course on programming; computing departments may be overwhelmed with requests for service courses; computing specialists rarely have sufficient subject knowledge to provide motivating example problems with which students may work. This paper describes an experimental programming course component developed collaboratively between educational computing and subject specialist tutors in a Polytechnic CNAA DipHE Environmental Studies programme. A central problem addressed was that of providing a programming environment rich enough in environmental studies content and method to engage students fully in the tasks, yet not so complex that they were overwhelmed by the scale of the learning problems. Given that students bring very diverse levels of programming knowledge and aptitude to such courses as this, task difficulty levels needed to be flexible in order to match learner needs. It is easy to design projects which are rich enough to interest the novice programmer but which he finds cognitively intractable. Conversely, sequences of simple tasks within the capacity of the novice programmer often fail to provide adequate motivation for the non-specialist whose principal interest is not the acquisition of programming skills.

Programming and Modelling

The second year of the DipHE programme contained a component on ecosystem modelling, based on local research by the environmental studies course team (eg McPhee, 1985). In 1984–5 the practical computer-based work associated with this component was undertaken by a year group who had followed a relatively conventional one-term course in BASIC programming. The programming skills brought to the ecosystem modelling task were extremely diverse. A small group of programming enthusiasts were capable of developing fairly sophisticated programs for calculating system parameters and graphing results. Others could recall fundamental program control structures and elements of syntax but were overwhelmed by the task of converting a graphical representation of a simple ecosystem model into executable code (cf Kreitsberg and Swanson, 1974). The tutors leading the course attempted to meet the problem by writing a number of modelling programs which the students then ran. After examining results from the programs they modified sections of the BASIC code (mainly assignment statements representing equations in the model) and re-ran the programs. By this iterative process of comparing computed results with real-world data, and modifying the equations, they moved towards a satisfactory model of nitrate flows in the ecosystem under investigation.

An interesting feature of the practical sessions was the pattern of social interaction in the lab. The working teams which formed, in this usually convivial year group, brought together students with similar levels of programming ability. The more competent and enthusiastic programmers kept to themselves and there was an unusually poor level of inter-team collaboration. In addition, the kind of interaction taking place between student and computer was similar to that characterized by the term 'revelatory learning' (MacDonald et al, 1977). Most of the students were running the tutors' simulation – they were not making and testing conjectures about the ecosystem through constructing their own model.

For the 1985–6 year group, it was decided to tackle this problem by providing students with the tools and skills to construct their own (programmed) ecosystem models. In attempting this, it was recognized that:

(a) the programming course in BASIC was an inadequate preparation for the complex task of transforming a graphical, mathematical, or word model into computer-executable form;

(b) most students were unable to separate the programming tasks central to the representation of a model from peripheral tasks concerned with the user-interface – indeed, the 'presence' of the screen often left students fixated with superficial aspects of the project such as the design of graphical displays;

(c) while the process of model specification lent itself to 'top-down' design methods, the same was not true of programming the model in BASIC (even structured BBC BASIC). This is partly a perceptual problem. While language dialects like BBC BASIC do allow the use of procedures and user-defined functions, which aid the modular construction of a program, these procedures are not first-class programming objects. That is, procedure headings are not much more than annotations to the main text of the program. Procedures cannot, for example, be called up by name by a screen-editor, for display or modification. In consequence, students do not so easily perceive them as distinctive functional 'figures' clearly separate from the 'ground' of the main body of a program, or from each other. This can be contrasted with languages such as LISP, LOGO or BOXER (Papert, 1980; Di Sessa, 1985).

A Toolkit Approach

Recognition of the fact that students' modelling programs tended to conflate what should be separate functions suggested that the course team should distinguish between those programming tasks which were central to the modelling exercise and those which were associated with peripheral activities, such as data input or graphical display. Those programming tasks identified as intrinsic to the students' learning should continue to be carried out by them, while the peripheral tasks could be undertaken by the course team. The actual solution adopted was to construct a 'toolkit' of useful modelling procedures in a dialect of LOGO running on the Research Machines 16-bit Nimbus microcomputer (Goodyear, 1986). These procedures covered tasks such as:

- initialization of parameter values in the model
- time-series data input
- saving data or the current model on disc; retrieving from disc
- graphing model outputs; tabulating results
- performing transformations of data lists (eg logarithmic transformations).

In most cases the procedures were complex, containing several levels of sub-procedures. A particular virtue of the first-class status of procedures in LOGO is that this complexity can be hidden from novice programmer/learners. Indeed all of the toolkit procedures were written so that they could be used by the students as 'black boxes'. That is, they needed to know only *what* the procedure did, and how to use it. They did not need to 'look inside' the black box in order to understand the details of its construction. For example, to plot two data lists called 'fish.numbers' and 'nitrate.level' against one another, the student need only type

> graph :fish.numbers :nitrate.level

He would not need to know that the 'graph' procedure automatically rescaled the data to fit appropriately on the VDU. Transforming a list of data (into logarithmic form, for example) is a similar frequently needed and intuitively simple task which, nevertheless, needs some fairly complex programming to accomplish. Unlike LISP, LOGO has no provision for applying a function (such as 'log') to each of the individual numbers making up the elements of a data list (Touretsky, 1984). Therefore the toolkit needs to contain a procedure which enables any function to be applied to each of the elements in any data list of any length. The toolkit procedure which does this is called 'transform' and looks like this:

> **transform func list**
> **if emptyq :list [result []]**
> **result pf (first eval se :func first :list)**
>   **(transform :func bf :list)**

It is not recommended that nervous novice programmers even see this, let alone be led to believe they need to understand *how* it does what it does. It is an ideal candidate for black box treatment.

Other procedures – those which are at the heart of the modelling exercise – need to be written by the learners themselves. These will include relatively low-level procedures as well as a master procedure whose internal structure determines the overall shape of the model. These procedures will be planned and written through a process of top-down stepwise refinement, in which each successive layer or level in the modelling and programming task contains more detail and less abstraction than its predecessor. This approach to complex problem-solving should be familiar from top-down approaches to international design (Romiszowski, 1981). It is a cornerstone of current thinking in commercial software production (Sommerville, 1982) and is central to Papert's (1980) ideas on learning through building and debugging computer programs (Goodyear, 1984). Having a good methodology for controlling complexity is vital, since students need to understand not only the inner workings of the procedures they write, but also the ways in which these procedures relate to each other.

There are two helpful representational symmetries at work here. The first, as we have seen, is that both the *specification* (in written text, mathematical or graphical form) of the ecological model and its *implementation* as a set of LOGO procedures can be represented at several levels of abstraction or specificity. The second is that each of the processes active in an ecosystem can be represented as taking some input, transforming it in some way, and producing an output. For example, a 'predation' process may take as its input the number of organisms in each of the predator and prey populations and produce as its output the number of prey consumed. Similarly, this process may be represented as a LOGO procedure, written as an information transforming function, which takes one or more data inputs and produces an output. Recognition of these symmetries, and of the cognitive value of having multiple representations of a problem (eg Stevens, Collins and Goldin, 1982) suggested that the students be given, or be encouraged to develop, a number of different representations of ecosystem models. These included free text descriptions, text descriptions structured as hierarchically numbered sentences, ecosystem structure diagrams and ecosystem flowcharts. Each proved a valuable aid in program specification.

Foggy Boxes

By definition, all of the student-written LOGO modelling procedures were 'clear' or 'glass' boxes, with no internal mysteries. Almost all of the teacher-provided toolkit procedures were black boxes to almost all of the students. However, the clear box/black box division is not a sharp one, for it depends on the understanding of the internal structure of a procedure and this understanding varies between students and will vary for any one student with the passage of time. While some procedures were deemed to be too complex for even the ablest students to come to grips with (eg 'transform', described above), with the result that their internal definitions were buried from students' sight, others were seen as 'foggy' boxes, which a number of students might attempt to understand in detail. An example of the motivation behind this might be to adjust the display of results generated by the model, perhaps to build up several years' data on screen.

Most programming courses, and especially those for novices, concentrate on *writing* programs. There is rarely much time given to *reading* other peoples' programs, unless they are over-simple 'toy' examples. This is usually due to a tutor's belief that non-trivial programs will be all but incomprehensible to the novice programmer (eg Schneiderman, 1977; du Boulay and O'Shea, 1981). The 'foggy box' approach suggests a new environment in which learning to program might take place – one which mixes the learner's own LOGO procedures with those provided by the tutor, and where the tutor's procedures are understood first in terms of their external behaviour and only later in their inner workings. The ease with which LOGO procedures can be displayed, modified or otherwise manipulated facilitates the learning-by-tinkering implicit in Papert's (1980) notion of 'bricolage'. The addition of tutor-written toolkit procedures enriches the programming environment with content and thereby offers a motivating context for the non-specialist learner acquiring programming skills.

Peer Collaboration

A final advantage observed in the 1985–6 ecosystem modelling exercise using the LOGO toolkit was the substantially greater level of collaboration occurring within and between programming groups in the practical lab. Where the previous year's BASIC programming work had seen a gulf between the adept programmers and the rest, expertise in the LOGO workshop seemed more evenly distributed. This may be due, in part, to a filtering out of programming expertise brought in by home-computer enthusiasts. But an additional factor is the way in which the different components of the LOGO toolkit, and different learner-written modelling procedures, came to be understood and adopted by the various programming groups. None of the groups had time to achieve a thorough understanding of the whole set of procedures created, while even the least able groups knew more about some procedures than did their colleagues. The high level of social interaction and peer-teaching characteristic of LOGO use in early education (Goodyear, 1984) was readily observable.

References

Computer Board (1983) *Computer Facilities for Teaching in Universities*. Computer Board for Universities and Research Councils, London.

Di Sessa, A (1985) A principled design for an integrated computational environment. *Human-Computer Interaction*, 1, pp 1-47.

Du Boulay, B and O'Shea, T (1981) Teaching novices programming. In Coombs, M and Alty, J (eds) *Computing Skills and the User Interface*. Academic Press, London.

Goodyear, P M (1984) *LOGO: A Guide to Learning through Programming*. Ellis Horwood, London.

Goodyear, P M (1986, in press) A toolkit approach to computer aided systems modelling. *Proceedings of the 6th Computers in Higher Education Conference*. Lancaster University.

Harding, R (1984) Everyone is a programmer now. *Computers and Education*. **8**, 1, pp 51-58.

Kreitsberg, C and Swanson, L (1974) A cognitive model for structuring an introductory programming curriculum. *Proceedings of the AFIPS National Computer Conference*, 43, pp 307-311.

MacDonald, B et al (1977) Computer assisted learning: its educational potential. In Hooper, R (ed) *NDPCAL Final Report*. Council for Educational Technology, London.

McPhee, E (1985) The movement of nitrates in the Darent Valley. *Darent Valley Research Report 3*. Thames Polytechnic, London.

Papert, S (1980) *Mindstorms: Children, Computers and Powerful Ideas*. Harvester Press, Brighton.

Pierce, J R (1967) *Computers in Higher Education: Report of the President's Science Advisory Committee*. US Government Printing Office, Washington D.C.

Romiszowski, A J (1981) *Designing Instructional Systems*. Kogan Page, London.

Schneidermann, B (1977) Teaching programming: a spiral approach to syntax and semantics. *Computers and Education*, 1, pp 193-197.

Somerville, I (1982) *Software Engineering*, Addison-Wesley, London.

Stevens, A, Collins, A and Goldin, S (1982) Misconceptions in students' understanding. In Sleeman, D and Brown, J S (eds) *Intelligent Tutoring Systems*. Academic Press, London.

Touretzky, D S (1984) *LISP: A Gentle Introduction to Symbolic Computation*. Harper and Row, New York.

1.30 Electronic Banking and Home Banking Services

I Graham *Bank of Scotland, Edinburgh*
J Stewart *Computer Education, Scottish Education Department*

Abstract: The first part of this paper describes the electronic banking service operated by the Bank of Scotland which incorporates 'Home and Office Banking Services' (HOBS). The second part of the paper describes the educational application of a 'Home Banking Services' module. The paper therefore brings together a commercial use and an educational application of computer technology.

PART 1: Home and Office Banking Services (HOBS) (I Graham)

Introduction and Background

The banks have long been leaders in introducing and applying technology. It is now 25 years since the Bank of Scotland set up its first centralized computer accounting system, so the use of computers is nothing new in banking. Everyone who has a bank account is affected by computers in numerous ways. In the early stages it was by computer-printed statements. Nowadays practically all payments, such as salaries, standing order and direct debit payments are paid by one computer 'speaking' to another, with no paper involved. Technology has brought about another important change – we now allow our customers to 'talk' directly to our computers, something which was unthinkable not too long ago. This is achieved through the use of automated cash dispensers outside our branch offices, as well as the most recent technological advance into home banking.

The idea of banking at home is nothing new – the mattress, the loose floorboards and the piggy bank have been with us for some considerable time, but using this latest service our customers can carry out, from their homes or offices, seven days a week, a whole range of banking transactions which previously required a trip to the bank.

For some years now, a prime objective of most of the British clearing banks has been to expand the volume of their business without having their costs increase by the same proportion. Our main cost is, of course, the setting up and maintenance of our 'bricks and mortar' branch network. Setting up a new branch is not cheap and involves capital expenditure of somewhere in the region of £600,000 to £750,000. It is fairly obvious therefore that you do not open up hundreds of new branches overnight; that must be viewed as a long-term project. However, it was always felt that a large network of branches was needed to give a proper service to customers. The possibility of home banking as an alternative to opening new offices was born. It could provide a service to customers and at the same time meet our objective in terms of cost. Naturally, the decision to proceed was not quite as straightforward as that. For a start, where were these new customers to come from? Other events in the banking world provided the answer to that.

As recently as 15 to 20 years ago the Scottish banks regarded their market as Scotland alone. A gentleman's agreement existed between the banks by which the Scottish banks operated north of the border (apart for the small presence in London which was essential to our operations) and the English banks remained south of the border. Our problem was that Scotland was already considered 'fully banked'. The situation changed around the time that oil was discovered off the shore of Scotland. The international banks appeared in Scotland for the first time. First to arrive and set up in our main centres (Edinburgh, Glasgow and Aberdeen) were the foreign banks, followed closely by the English clearers. We had no option but to reciprocate. So for the first time we saw the market from which we could draw customers as being the whole of the United Kingdom and not just Scotland.

We set about establishing a series of regional offices in the main commercial centres in England. As I mentioned earlier, the cost of each is high so we could not open hundreds of new offices. These offices are primarily to seek and maintain corporate business and are not capable of supporting large volumes of personal customers. So how could we provide a high level of service without a 'blanket' network of branches? Some other way would need to be found to look after them. Home banking looked like a possible solution.

There were however a further three factors emerging which pushed us towards the decision to proceed:

(a) the public's demand for, and acceptance of, other bank services such as cheque books, cheque guarantee cards and credit cards;
(b) the enthusiasm of the public for cash dispensers (ATMs). Evidence of this can be seen in the queues which form at these machines outside the banks even on rainy days, while the tellers stand inside with no-one to serve. The result of these two trends is that the average personal customer now has little or no need to visit a branch. Accounts can therefore be controlled by the bank from a central unit, irrespective of how close or far away from the customer it may be sited. Our research backs this up. It shows that first accounts are opened at a particular bank for a particular reason – the branch may be close to home, close to work, parents already bank there and so on. But what is also clearly shown is that once that connection is established it will probably remain there even if the customer moves house or job. It generally takes a service which is not available elsewhere, like home banking, to cause a move. In these circumstances we felt confident that we could attract and hold centrally a large number of new customers who did not have one of our branches in the immediate vicinity.

The third factor had nothing to do with banking at all. It was
(c) the boom in home computer ownership. We estimated that this would run out of steam unless real continuing uses were found to supplement or replace the craze in video games. Why not appeal to home computer owners by offering a service which would put their equipment to practical use?

The arguments all seemed to point one way: home banking.

The first home banking service was introduced to the United Kingdom in November 1982 by the Nottingham Building Society's Homelink service, with Nottingham Building Society providing the savings account and Bank of Scotland providing the current account with cheque book and credit card facilities. We built on the experience gained on Homelink and in January 1985 launched our own Home and Office Banking Service (HOBS) throughout the United Kingdom. The Bank's commitment to Homelink is unaffected by the introduction of our own service and we shall continue to support Homelink.

How Does it Work?

Home banking is operated by the customer telephoning our computer and keying instructions on a keyboard. All that is needed for this is a screen (a normal domestic television will do), a telephone jack socket and a viewdata adaptor. Alternatively, a computer may be used with the appropriate modem attached. Using the keyboard, instructions are sent down the telephone line to the bank's computer and the information requested is sent back up the telephone line and displayed on the screen.

The Choice of Carrier

Communications costs are critical to the acceptability of any online service both from the point of view of the service provider and the consumer. The availability of low-cost communications was a key requirement in developing home banking. It will be readily appreciated that the Bank of Scotland, while having a natural network in Scotland to support almost 500 branches and its other business activities, has no corresponding network in England and Wales where the bulk of this new market is to be found. Operating a private network under these conditions is quite uneconomic and was rejected as an option at an early stage. It was also clear that the most cost-effective technology through which to deliver the service is viewdata, which demands minimum sophistication – and therefore minimal cost – in customers' terminal equipment.

The requirement was therefore for a publicly accessible viewdata service, and the decision was taken to use Prestel on the grounds that we can use the Gateway facility to retain all data on our customers' accounts within our own computer systems while the availability of local nodes gave access at local telephone rates to practically the whole of the United Kingdom.

It has recently been announced that home banking will soon be available to ICI's AGVISER customers through the Istel network.

Security

Access to the system is granted by entering the customer's unique security codes. These are, of course, in addition to the carrier's security which forms part of the Bank of Scotland's checking and identification procedures. Customers are asked to enter their Keycard number, that is, the number of their ATM card, followed by a self-chosen password of up to eight alpha or numeric characters. Provided these are entered correctly the customer is allowed to pass through the 'gate'. Only three wrong attempts per day are allowed, after which all access is barred until the bank is satisfied that no unauthorized use is being made of the service.

What Functions are Available?

Home and Office Banking is available 17 hours per day, Monday to Friday, and 15 hours per day at weekends.

The functions available range from perusing information on balances and statements through cash management information for business customers; ordering cheque books and printed statements; paying regular bills to switching money between accounts.

Information

Comprehensive information is provided on all the customer's accounts, whether current, savings, loan or mortgage, provided only that these accounts are operated and marketed entirely by the Bank of Scotland.

As well as balances, the customer is provided with a detailed 'snapshot' of the account including items in course of processing, accrued interest and charges and details of any electronic transfers pending.

Through the statement option, details of up to 250 past transactions – or three months' activity – are available online to the customer on all his or her accounts.

There are comprehensive tabulations of standing orders and other regular payments showing the beneficiary, amount, next payment date and frequency of payment.

Businesses are provided with special facilities within the cash management module to identify the value of cleared funds and to project overall cleared balances forward for three working days. These details have only been available before to major corporations via more sophisticated and expensive corporate cash management systems.

Service Requests

Customers may request other services or facilities through home banking. The initial implementation has been for requests for cheque books and printed statements on any of the customer's accounts. This facility lends itself to handling requests for a whole range of services from loan facilities to enabling customers to take up special offers. The opportunities are wide and new facilities will be added as appropriate.

Bill Payments

Most of us make payments to regular suppliers, but where the amount of each payment is indeterminate or the payment dates are not fixed, a standing order is not appropriate. Examples of these payments are utility bills (gas, electricity and telephone) with, in addition, the settlement of credit cards and retailers' charge accounts.

A bill payment facility has been included in home banking whereby customers can make payments to predefined beneficiaries. The bank will take a written mandate from the customer for each payee, whose details will be recorded in the computer system by our own bank staff. From then on the customer instructs each individual payment simply by entering the amount and the payment date. The payment date can be up to 30 days forward to allow our customer to instruct payment on the day the bill arrives but still take full advantage of any free credit period.

Inter-Account Transfers

Improved money management is a key feature of the service. Customers can transfer funds between their accounts both to maximize interest earnings and to minimize borrowings.

We have introduced the HOBS Investment Account, which is only available to home banking subscribers, both personal and business. Interest rates are paid on a structured basis. That is, for amounts deposited over £2,500 we pay 1 per cent below Bank of Scotland base rate; for amounts between £1,000 and £2,500 we pay 2 per cent below Bank of Scotland base rate; and for amounts up to £1,000 we pay 3 per cent below Bank of Scotland base rate. However, interest accrues on a daily basis, which enables customers to make use of every last penny of spare funds effectively. The home banking day runs from 5pm to 5pm: therefore, any fund transfers instructed prior to this time will start to earn interest that night.

Where Does Banking Technology Go From Here?

It is hard to see how home banking as a single product could be enhanced to any great degree, as the facilities offered cover everything that the customer could wish for, but we do still have a few more ideas to implement.

Taking an overall view, the traditional role and monopolistic position of the banks is threatened by a range of powerful and ambitious adversaries – building societies, insurance houses, large retail stores and many more are all contenders for delivering loan and financial management services. Some of them will achieve penetration by use of sophisticated technology. We must respond by using all the technological tools at our disposal. Current activities include plastic card developments, electronic funds transfer at point of sale (EFTPOS) and ATM reciprocity. It will take a particularly wise soothsayer on a good day to predict what technology will allow us to do in ten years from now.

Part 2: HOBS (Education) – Learn to Bank on Modern Technology (J Stewart)

There have been several initiatives in Scottish education suggesting that computers have a place in the curriculum. One of the best known of the earlier ones is the Bellis report. This followed the conventional path recommending the study of computers and programming as end products. Later, in 1978, the Education for the Industrial Society Project (EISP) set up a small group of microcomputer users in Scottish schools. This group, who were teachers and not computer experts, produced the first widely available course for computer awareness. The Microelectronics and Computing in the Curriculum Project was the next Consultative Committee on the Curriculum (CCC) scheme. Its S1/S2 course guidelines put strong emphasis on the theoretical study of computers, but the implementation was effected by practising teachers, and this factor moved the final course towards participation by the pupils, with study of uses of computers rather than the computers themselves. In both of these initiatives, programming was given a back seat, and the emphasis was on implications and applications. The earlier maths-based course content was left behind, which is appropriate, since the vast majority of applications today are not concerned with the manipulation of statistics.

This change in the attitude towards computing did not occur in an academic vacuum. It is merely one manifestation of the general move to make education reflect the reality of society. Ten years ago, when the Consultative Committee on the Curriculum (CCC) set up the Education for the Industrial Society Project, it started to weave links with industry and commerce. This project was directed to study the needs which an industrial society should realistically place on its education system. It produced a series of courses which were aimed at preparing today's pupils for today's society, and these were distributed across Scotland. At a local level, many authorities have appointed schools/industry liaison officers, and modern studies has been very active in embracing relevant courses. The EISP recommended that the computing work should be carried forward, and the Microelectronics and Computing in the Curriculum project was founded. Today, some of this work is carried forward by the Joint Working Party on Technological Studies, and now, in industry year, the links are stronger than ever.

It is not to be thought that this is a local issue: most areas in Scotland have appointed advisory personnel and principal teachers to further the advancement of learning in the fields of computing and communications. In most cases the remit is directed to include schools/industry liaison. Although the earlier emphasis was on courses promoting awareness of the potential of computers, this is not to be seen as differing significantly in outlook from the more intensive study of computing as evinced by the new S-grade computing course. This new discipline puts strong emphasis on the appraisal of case studies, and the use of the computer as a tool, and it is envisaged that there will be considerable takeup of the HOBS (Education) package in this course.

It was in this area that the Scottish Education Department first became interested in the educational possibilities of the HOBS package. The Bank of Scotland had produced a short 'demonstration' version of the program on a BBC micro. The bank allowed this version to be developed by an educational team to meet the needs of an ongoing course, so that the schools version would allow 20 pupils to run their 'own' bank accounts. Here the package allows the pupil to see the computer at work, and how it does the job, but even more innovative is the idea of showing the pupil how the computer can change the way in which a job is tackled. Up to now, we have looked at the way the computer does a human job. Now we are looking at a new style of business made possible by a computer. Particularly important is that the program is a very close simulation of a real application. We think Scottish education will benefit immensely from the Bank of Scotland's generous support for the development of this package.

It is our hope that more packages will be developed to show the way real firms use real programs to do jobs. This represents a break from the tradition of a teacher, in his spare time, dreaming up an idea and developing it personally so that if he or she is lucky, someone may notice it and take it further. That model allows democracy and individualism but encourages piecemeal development, duplication of effort and rapid improvement of under-resourced and amateurishly presented materials. We hope that HOBS (Education) will show how central development can keep Scotland to the fore.

1.31 Working with Copyright

C W Osborne
Middlesex Polytechnic, London

Abstract: Copyright is commonly seen by educational interests as a major obstacle to the use of potentially valuable resource materials. And when the materials in question have a strong audio or visual component, the prospects for their use are not good unless the materials fall within the fairly limited scope of various licences. But printed materials, both UK and foreign, offer a more promising outcome, provided that institutions are prepared to pay and staff are able and willing to commit some time. The paper looks at copyright as it relates to printed materials: what copyright is and does (including some popular misconceptions); the illegality of unauthorized multiple copying; the procedure whereby permission can be sought; and possible means of making the best use of copyright texts within available resource limits.

Introduction

> *'The copyright laws seem to have been formed to prevent the sensible use of resources in teaching.'*

There can be few teachers who, at one time or another, have not found themselves echoing the sentiments expressed above. And indeed, for non-print media, it is difficult to argue against the contention that, by effect if not by intention, the copyright laws virtually preclude any use of material other than that within the fairly limited scope of licence schemes offered by the BBC, the IBA (Channel 4), the Open University, the Performing Right Society, the Mechanical Copyright Protection Society, et al. In recognition of the difficulties (some would say virtual impossibilities) in these areas, this paper will focus on printed textual materials where the prospect of a satisfactory outcome is real.

The copyright laws exist; and however much education may see itself as a special case, it must comply – or face the consequences, as some recent legal actions have more than adequately demonstrated. It is unfortunate that these laws are not noted for their simplicity, even when concentrating solely on printed materials, and this paper cannot hope to address the full range of legal niceties (those interested in copyright as it affects education should consult the articles and other publications by Geoff Crabb of the Council for Educational Technology); rather, it starts from the basic premise that

> although an idea itself cannot claim copyright, an idea worked on and translated into a permanent and communicable form (as a complete text, an individual poem, a translation, a design, a diagram, an illustration, or whatever) is *automatically protected*.

Note that there is *no* onus on the author or publisher to claim or assert copyright – and that the too-prevalent opinion among academics (themselves often authors, ironically) that non-assertion is tacit permission is ill-informed. This is one of the major problems in dealing with copyright: namely, disabusing intelligent people of popular misconceptions. Only too frequently one comes across arguments like: 'I used it before so why can't I use it again?'; or 'This was a handout at a conference, so the author won't object'; or 'I know the author and it's OK'; or 'I'm not making any money out of it so copyright doesn't apply'; or 'What's the difference between making a single copy for myself and making copies for my students?'. These seem not unreasonable questions, but the response to all of them must be that, unless there is definite (documentary) proof to the contrary, all these circumstances and usages are likely to be illegal. The argument that 'I broke the law once, why can't I do it again?' clearly merits no serious response; the misconceptions inherent in the others will be explored below.

What Does Copyright Do?

There are many would-be users of copyright material who have the simple answer to this question: it's to make publishers (and authors) rich. Sadly, there are numerous authors (and publishers) who would respond to this contention with derisive hilarity. Undoubtedly some authors do profit from their writing, and have benefited their publishers accordingly, but they are few and they tend to obscure the more important function of copyright: it offers authors and publishers *protection* against, and *control* over, the uses that others may seek to make of their work.

It is important to realize at this point that there are two types of copyright: authors have the copyright in their *text* (although they often assign this to their publishers as agents); and publishers have a separate *typographical* copyright in their published edition. The former applies for the life of the author/editor/translator plus 50 years (or 50 years from posthumous publication); the latter for 25 years from the date of first publication of each edition – but *both* permissions are needed for copying to be legal. Accordingly:

1. the publisher has a right to reimbursement for his work and interests – and the author cannot usually dispose publisher's rights;
2. the author may, or may not, feel justified in asking for payment. It is one matter to distribute a text amongst professional colleagues at a conference, but another to see it widely disseminated, particularly when this might erode sales of a potential or actual book;
3. the author has a right to protect his/her *reputation*. Copyright allows an author to prevent use of material in a place, manner or publication with which he/she does not wish to be associated, or to prevent others using it for their own profit; it allows control over the spread of material and ideas to which the author no longer adheres; and it offers protection against material being used in a manner likely to be injurious to the author's reputation, whether by selective quotation and editing or by calculated juxtaposition with texts by other authors.

Where Misunderstandings Arise

To explore all the possible roots of misunderstandings of copyright would be too daunting – even if some statements seem so naive that the challenge seems almost surreal! But undoubtedly the commonest delusions are:

1. 'Copyright is not involved because no money changes hands' – simply not true (see above).
2. 'Copyright does not apply to out-of-print materials' – again, not true (unless all applicable copyrights have lapsed, as outlined above).
3. 'The copyright law allows copying for educational use' – a partial truth, but *not* relevant to large-scale use of material. Briefly, there is certain provision in the Copyright Act (1956) under the so-called 'fair dealing' clauses whereby use can be made of copyright material for purposes of 'criticism or review' and for 'research or private study' (which, some argue, precludes placement in a library). The Act itself does not define 'fair', however; and, although guidelines issued (and now withdrawn) by the British Copyright Council proffered some suggestion (based on word-count and/or on a maximum ten per cent of any

complete copyright work), it is recognized that the real worth of an extract may need to be measured other than by length. So the onus is on the user to be cautious. And in any case, there is *no provision for making multiple copies* for student use. This is the area to which attention can now be directed.

Obtaining Copyright Clearance – Procedural Considerations

From the foregoing text, it should be apparent that any large-scale educational use of copyright material must carry the appropriate permission(s), whether this use comprises a single but substantial copy (presumably for a member of staff and/or a library) or multiple copies for students. Stages in the permission-seeking process are likely to be as below:

1. Recognize that permission may be charged for. Does money exist to meet such costs, and those of the actual copying? How much is the use of the material really worth? It was noticed at Middlesex Polytechnic that virtually half the 'required material' on one course was found to be dispensable when it was to be charged for.
2. Check that the required material actually *is*, or *need be*, under copyright (it's permissible to live in hope!). For example, copies from a Molière play taken from a new edition will involve publisher's rights (and maybe editor or translator rights also), whereas use of a suitably old edition could avoid all such costs.
3. Verify bibliographical details of the required extract *as they relate to the true holder of copyright*; ie a paperback edition or an anthology may carry its own typographic copyright but the textual copyright, if still extant, is likely to rest with the original publication. And it is to this publisher that application should be made, to this edition that bibliographic details should refer, and from this publication that copies should be made.
4. Compose a suitable letter/application form. Alongside bibliographic information, the letter should draw attention to the following:
   □ duplication to be strictly for *educational* use (the commercial rates between publishers themselves are higher)
   □ a *specified* number of copies to be made
   □ a stated period of use (an annual need – or stocking up for the next ten years? The former is preferable usually)
   □ distribution to be *free* and *solely* to students registered on a *named* course at the institution. (Distribution 'at cost' risks being seen by some publishers as too closely approaching commercial publication; it is imperative to make clear that there is *no* intention of profit)
   □ text will *not* be edited or abbreviated in any way, and no supplementary text or comment will be appended
   □ a full credit statement will appear on each copy produced, stating author, title and source/copyright holder of the item (and, ideally, the institution's name and a reference number identifying the relevant permission)
   □ a notice will appear on all copies forbidding reduplication (it is a nice touch if this notice is in colour – any 'pirates' are then revealed by their lack of true colours!).
5. Make necessary application to the publisher. It is possible to make an initial phone contact, but this is not normally the best procedure. In any case it is essential that permission is put in writing (and safely filed). Publishers' addresses can be found in cumulative annual editions of the *British National Bibliography* or in *British Books in Print*; applications should be directed to the Permissions Department.
6. Await reply, and then pay – or reflect again on the educational worth of the material.

7. Prepare the permitted copies in the light of the undertakings given and/or publisher conditions specified (some publishers ask to see copies of what is produced).

Organizational Considerations

It should now be apparent that although individual teachers can negotiate clearance, there is great scope for some formal institutional provision. Advantages of a central unit could include:

- if the unit works as a processing centre for all multiple copying, it will be easier for the institution to identify, and eliminate, copying that is illegal;
- the unit can act as a filter to catch requests that carry inadequate or patently incorrect bibliographic data; it can ensure that all legitimate copying carries appropriate notices, and can act as a central point of contact and of records both for publishers and teachers;
- it can advise courses and staff on copyright matters – not least, the need for advance planning and early application (a minimum of six weeks would be advised to cover all the likeliest legitimate delays);
- the unit can build up a database of known publisher rates and attitudes – and can thereby advise courses at the planning stages, either regarding likely outcome of applications or likely costs;
- the unit could collate information from all its sources and thereby identify means of minimizing cost. There are important, and potentially rewarding, distinctions between: *public information* (eg some government publications, company reports, etc); *professional journals* or *house publications* (which are perhaps likely to value public relations above considerations of income); *strictly commercial* materials which, if not solely motivated by profit, nevertheless depend on income for their survival; and *others*, such as newspapers, current affairs journals and the like, where response would depend very much on the nature and authorship of the specific item involved;
- lastly, the unit would be demonstrable proof of the institution's acknowledgement of copyright, both in bringing the use of copyright material under control and in seeking to make such use purposive and efficient.

Other Possible Developments

A logical extension of *ad hoc* copying is the packaging of copyright materials into a coursebook of collected texts, ideas, exercises and questions, perhaps with linking text or comments by the teacher. Such a 'package' may well engender in students a higher value rating on its contents, while the course may find some economic advantages in (limited) mass production of enough copies for a couple of years' supply. Unfortunately, this good idea may involve additional problems:

- convincing publishers that this is not a move into a more 'commercial' operation – and higher rates of fee;
- reassuring publishers as to how, and where, material would be used; publishers might ask to see a draft of the total work, including any notes to accompany the text (notes that a publisher felt were uncomplimentary or prejudicial to his author or material might have to be rewritten). The publisher would also check for editing or amendment of the text and for any unfortunate sequencing of material (unintentional or intentional) through which an item might be seen in a false or prejudicial context;
- more preparation work over a longer time, with the whole package waiting upon the last item being cleared. The coursebook may pass through several draft editions, and thereby involve some renegotiation of items already cleared;

- [ ] items in a package may date or be superseded, so care is needed in deciding on production levels (and hence the terms of the approach to publishers), weighing economies of scale against likely life of the package.

Another potential development is a licence authorizing educational institutions to make copies at need, to periodically submit a record of all materials used, and to pay at a pre-specified rate per page/copy. Such an agreement has now been reached in the UK between the Copyright Licensing Agency and the local authorities (schools interests); more difficulty is being encountered with higher education and a date for a settlement cannot yet be guessed at. But a licence, certainly for the first few years, is not likely to bring all the advantages that might be wished for. The two likeliest areas of disappointment would be: the absence of certain publishers, publications and categories of material; and the irrelevance of the licence to overseas publishers (notably those from the USA) for whom normal clearance procedures would remain necessary.

Conclusion

In the limited space available, this paper can do little more than identify key considerations in the relationship between copyright and education. It is acknowledged that much has not been mentioned, and that some statements are gross simplifications of a complex reality. But the key issues are touched on; and the advice for action is known to produce results. The message is that, for print materials at least, copyright is not as insuperable an obstacle as it might first seem. True, it does demand extra planning by courses and staff, and it may well impose a new (and unwelcome) yardstick against which to evaluate desirable teaching materials – but are either of these necessarily bad outcomes? When the need is real, permission can usually be negotiated; there may well be a cost, but perhaps this too can be managed through perceptive and informed selection of sources and materials. Copyright is not just about money, any more than good ideas and good materials are truly produced at no cost – maybe we just don't like paying for something which has been taken for granted for too long?

Section 2:
Flexible Learning and Training

2.1 Keynote Address
Flexible Learning: Developments and Implications in Training

D Tinsley
Director, Open Tech Unit, Manpower Services Commission, Sheffield

It is a privilege to be asked to give this keynote address at the start of a day devoted to the development of learning systems in training. My task is to set the scene before the practitioners play their roles in describing the revolution in training practice which has been brought about by the application of flexible learning techniques.

Based on the work of your association over the past two decades and on the practical experience of the Open University, the use of learner-centred systems for training has received a massive boost through the work of the Open Tech programme. During this day of presentations and workshops, you will witness a quiet revolution just on the brink of becoming a very loud one indeed!

By the end of April, at the Spring Open Conference and Exhibition in London, over 100 organizations will be demonstrating their new training products to directors of companies, senior managers and trainers. Some 15,000 hours of training materials will be available for sale from Open Tech projects alone, representing about half of the expected outcome from the programme at the end of the current funding period in March 1987.

Spring Open is the first major national conference and exhibition devoted to the marketing of open learning systems in training. Alongside Open Tech projects will be the National Extension College (NEC), the Open University (OU), the Skillcentre Training Centre Agency and many other organizations who have created learner-centred systems and are now ready to enter this new training market.

Certainly, we cannot ignore the major input that the Open Tech programme is having on the vocational education and training systems. But it would be unwise for me not to rehearse the key reasons for the investment by government of £45 million on new training materials and methods, or to record the main events which have led to the present situation when so many key projects can report to this conference on significant progress.

Open Tech was started as a fundamental component of the government's new training initiative, which was announced in 1981. The initiative has three main objectives:

to modernize training in occupational skills by replacing age limits and time serving by *training to standards*;
to provide better preparation in schools and colleges for the *transition* from full time education to work;
to *widen opportunities* for *adults* to acquire and update their skills.

Delegates will recognize that much has already been achieved in meeting the first objectives through the development of the Youth Training Scheme (YTS) and the Technical and Vocational Education Initiative (TVEI). Widening opportunities for adults has not been so well publicized, but much is being done through the MSC's job training programme to provide occupational courses, short courses in new technology, training for enterprise, and job preparation courses for the unemployed.

Alongside these programmes, the Department of Education and Science (DES) has promoted the PICKUP and REPLAN initiatives, which have done much to bring the forces of the further and higher education systems to bear on the training and retraining needs of adults. But by far the most significant contribution to meeting the initial objective has been the Open Tech programme, with its 140 projects devoted to the creation of new training systems for technicians and supervisory managers using the methodology of open learning.

At the outset of the programme, the methodology of open learning had not been applied to the training of technicians and supervisors to any great extent. But the demand for updating and continuous training in new technologies and management methods could not have been met through traditional courses. There were too many barriers to access:

local courses were often not available;
times of attendance were unsuitable;
starting dates were inappropriate;
travel and subsistence costs were too high.

At the same time, many traditional courses were unsuitable for adult trainees because they had course structures, content and methods designed with younger age groups in mind.

Finally, the entry requirements and accreditation systems were too formal to appeal to the adult learner or to gain favour with the employer who wished to pay only for a skill to be acquired, not a paper qualification obtained.

Open Learning has provided the answer to these constraints through the development of training systems which enable the learner to learn at a time, a place and a pace which suits his or her own circumstances. All of the Open Tech projects apply open learning methods to their work, whether in materials creation, support systems development or delivery arrangements. Several Open Tech projects are reporting today on the application of open learning to their own sector. My task is to draw out the key lessons they have learnt and their prospects for the future.

I do not need to remind this audience that the creation of open learning materials is not a trivial activity. From the outset, the Open Tech projects have found the writing, editing and production of training materials a hard and demanding task, often beyond the skills of the original project team. To help solve this problem, the Open Tech Training and Support Unit (OTTSU) was created to provide external consultancy from a team of experienced training systems designers and managers. I would like to take this opportunity to pay tribute to John Coffey, John Sims and their team of consultants for their invaluable work in helping Open Tech projects get into action.

OTTSU is now working alongside another Open Tech project, the Training and Support Service (TSS) of the Institute of Training and Development to provide a series of workshops and consultancy services for trainers and developers of open learning systems. As with all other Open Tech projects, OTTSU and TSS have to become self-sustaining at the end of the MSC pump-priming period. I am pleased to report that the demand for support services and consultancy is growing to the point where these projects will be able to continue their work after March 1987. The key message for today is that most of us can benefit from calling on consultant services to help bring the best available practice to bear on our training enterprises.

But our projects were also unsure about the existence of other open learning materials before embarking on new writing. To help them avoid reinventing wheels, the Materials and Resources Information System (MARIS) was established to record any published training materials for technicians and supervisory managers. Based at Ely, Cambridgeshire, MARIS now holds over 7,000 records of open learning materials, as well as files on resources for open learning and an open learning bibliography.

By checking with MARIS whether existing materials were available, Open Tech projects have avoided costly duplication. But MARIS has now become MARIS-NET, and an online service is available to interrogate MARIS or to create your own databases for training alongside MARIS within the Cambridge computer. A new thesaurus has been installed to simplify searches so that users can obtain the records they require with the minimum of delay.

MARIS-NET is now being used within Open Tech delivery projects to help create a retail market for flexible training systems. Feasibility studies are testing the use of viewdata systems to sell training products direct to the customer, to give advice on training products and to refer potential customers to a local training agent who can help select the most appropriate training system for the learner.

Through MARIS-NET we can explore the ways in which learners can not only take responsibility for their own learning but can also make their own choices of what to learn and what learning system to buy.

The delivery projects are a fundamental part of the whole Open Tech system. Eventually it is expected that everyone in England, Wales and Scotland will have easy access to a delivery project. Many local education authorities have shown an interest in delivering open learning and so this may soon happen. Delivery projects help the learner to obtain open learning materials and they also support the learner while studying. They provide:

> advice on choosing material appropriate to his or her existing experience and future needs;
> advice on study skills and planning study time;
> tutorial guidance and assessment of progress;
> access to practical training facilities for 'hands-on' experience;
> individual and self-help group discussions.

Most delivery projects act as a central co-ordinating agency for a given geographical area. The centres may be colleges, adult education institutes, company training centres or practical training facilities. Tutoring can be organized on a face-to-face basis or by telephone, correspondence, a computer network, audio cassette or by outreach facilities in local centres.

Delivery projects are also able to identify individual and company training needs and provide a suitable tailor-made training programme using open learning materials and resources. The key point for today, however, is that open learning systems need a sophisticated delivery service to ensure that learners are provided with all of the necessary resources for learning at times and in places appropriate to their needs.

It was inevitable that the Open Tech approach would have a far-reaching impact on the organization and financing of local authority institutions. For many further education colleges, open learning for adult clients was a totally new operation, requiring major changes in the management of resources. With help from the main bodies concerned with these issues, the Further Education Unit (FEU) has prepared a report on implementing open learning in local authority institutions. This report is a guide for institution managers and local authority officers on the key points of importance to those engaged in forming policy on the provision of open learning including management policy, resourcing, tutorial staff, support services, and costing and pricing.

The guide is essential reading for local authority administrative and tutorial staff, and highlights the basic flexibility which is required if open learning is to flourish both as a method for full-time study or as a service to external clients. Whilst most of the potential constraints focus on management attitude rather than formal regulation, significant national issues have still to be resolved: among them the calculation of tutorial case loads and Burnham grading systems, and the recognition of open learning in inter-authority payments and rate support calculations.

But the industrial and commercial clients for open learning will not wait for ever whilst the further education systems are putting their houses in order. New styles of operation are required now and Open Tech projects are showing the way.

Practical training facilities have been established in several parts of the UK to enable open learners to gain access to the machinery, computers and other equipment they need for 'hands-on' experience. The key points which make the practical training facility different from traditional further education provision are that the client can make an appointment for practical training and can purchase training by the hour.

This means the practical training facility must have a reception system which can reserve machines or computers at times to suit adult clients, both during the week and at weekends. There is no reason why similar centres should not be established in all local technical colleges.

We are proving within Open Tech projects that if further education colleges are flexible and responsive to adult training needs there is much new business to be won. The key word must be *flexibility* backed up by a *proactive marketing system*.

Eastek is a good example of a delivery project which is taking the marketing of open learning very seriously. Based on its main Ipswich centre, Eastek serves the three counties of Suffolk, Norfolk and Essex. Freephone Eastek brings you into contact with a sales person, who can arrange an Open Tech training programme for you with tutorial support from your local college of further education, adult education centre, skillcentre or industry training centre. If tutorial support is needed from a local college, Eastek organizes the contact and administers the payment under a special arrangement with the local authorities.

At this point I must stress that the prime aim of the Open Tech programme is to help to update the skills of the employed adult population and those who are seeking to change jobs. While we are anxious to help unemployed individuals wherever possible, the target for our promotion is the company director and the trainer.

A recent survey conducted by PA Management Systems Limited dealt with 17 large companies who have been involved in testing Open Tech materials. In every case, those companies are now engaged in the process of conducting an intensive review of the way in which open learning could be embodied in future training programmes. In the case of the British Steel Corporation, the process has gone still further, and the corporation has already approved a major two-year programme of involvement in open learning.

Comments by some of the other companies are equally pertinent. The Boots company said that:

'open learning is an idea whose time has come.'

British Caledonian considered that open learning:

'should be developed and expanded broadly across the company.'

British Rail reported that:

'in particular, trainees recognize the wider range of opportunities available under Open Tech learning'.

The survey report has a stream of similar quotes, all of them from companies whose recognition of the need for a commitment to training has been long-standing. One phrase which occurs with marked frequency throughout the comments is 'cost effective', and some companies have identified subsidiary benefits which they had not, perhaps, expected; Rolls Royce Aero, for example, describes open learning as 'a powerful motivational as well as teaching tool.'

The PA survey helped us to understand the value of open learning to large companies. We are now looking at the value of open and flexible learning systems for small companies who find that the constraints of time, opportunity and expense have until now made training a difficult option.

Many of our 92 materials-generating projects have developed modules which are of interest to the small firm. One project, based on the North East Wales Institute, has designed training packs specifically with the small firm in mind. The programme is now exploring ways in which these training products can be marketed to the small firm and how appropriate support can be given when required.

A key question for this conference is how much external tutorial support is required by learners in small firms, especially when budgets are tight and time is precious. In the project run by the British Institute of Innkeepers, the main learning activity is supported by the package materials, which can be bought on their own. The materials are designed for self-study with support from a 'mentor' within the company. If necessary, tutorial support can be paid for separately as required from a local college. The accreditation system is also costed on a separate basis and is provided as an option by the Institute. Early evidence shows that learners do not need to call on much external support. Time will tell what the right balance should be for effective learning.

By March 1987, all of the current Open Tech projects will have completed their contracts and moved towards self-sufficiency. This last year is crucial for projects which are new to the business of publishing and marketing. Of particular concern is the viability of each new training business after pump-priming comes to an end. We have used a major financial services company, Deloitte, Haskins and Sells, to advise projects on the preparation of business plans and the conduct of future financial operations. This is quite new work for some of our projects, which started as an idea within a college and have now developed into fully operational businesses.

The Manpower Services Commission has just received a paper on the future of Open Tech after the end of the current programme. I thought that you would be interested to hear what we expect will happen after March 1987.

The main focus of MSC's work will be the 'embedding' of open learning techniques in the vocational education and training structures of the UK. The name Open Tech will stay with the projects currently funded, but it is not intended to be used for future pump-priming activities.

Working in close partnership with the Department of Education and Science, any new development funding will be focused on clearly identified gaps in current provision or on training needs of a specialist nature which cannot be financed through the normal workings of the training system.

A crucial activity will be influencing of local authority further education systems to adopt open learning techniques with parallel activity taking place in the statutory and non-statutory training organizations. Within MSC a flexible learning systems group meets regularly under the chairmanship of the chief executive to review the extent to which MSC's own programmes are adopting open learning approaches in funding mechanisms and training methodology. This work will continue under the new programme.

Finally, it is intended that codes of practice will be developed to ensure that open and flexible learning systems are of good quality and that claims made for open learning are properly accountable.

Underpinning this work will be continued support for infrastructures of databases and evaluation services to ensure that the future of open learning is secure and cost-effective.

Matters of immediate concern are the development of flexible accreditation systems which allow for the use of open learning as an agreed form of study, and the accreditation of prior learning (or experiential learning) which enables the learner to purchase the minimum further training required to reach the next skill target. The review of vocational qualifications forms, of course, a background to these concerns.

I have said enough to set a major agenda for your consideration during the day. Whilst we will never have all the answers, I am sure you will find today's illustrations of flexible training practice of value in your own work.

Open Tech has caused a major revolution in training practice. It has caused a significant reappraisal of further education systems and has been warmly welcomed by its main customer, British industry.

What I hope is that the momentum gained will not be lost and that trainers will unite in adopting flexible, learner-centred training as a key route to improving the nation's profitability.

2.2 Identifying Training Needs – An Iterative Answer

R Matheson and A Garry
Heriot-Watt University, Edinburgh

Abstract: This paper describes a local collaborative project to identify the training needs of a particular group of engineers. The purpose of the project is to identify and analyse patterns of needs – not to set up educational provision to meet them. In continuing professional development (CPD) programmes, the needs of the participants are usually assumed or presumed. Therefore we suggest that any attempt to identify less accessible needs must be through meticulous enquiry after scrupulous iteration. This has led us to devise a detailed scheme for needs identification which emerges partly from research and partly from iterative design and validation of pilot activities.

The challenge we are faced with when identifying training needs is how to motivate learners to express their needs. What mechanism can we use to change unformulated needs into declared needs?

In order to identify training needs we designed educational activities in which learning was not the goal. Through constant iteration we designed workshops purely to identify relevant needs.

Introduction

In September 1985 we set up a local collaborative project to identify training needs in the construction industry. We felt this would provide an important link between training needs in industry and educational provision in colleges and universities.

This was because in our search we found that many providers either subjectively declared the needs of the learners or directly asked the employers to voice the needs of their employees. The methods used to identify needs often took the form of interview or questionnaire with little or no learner participation. We therefore felt it was vital to use some kind of activity that allowed and even stimulated learners to express their needs. We decided to use workshops to identify such needs. Although not specifically educational, the workshop process we designed would enable participants to identify relevant needs and prompt them to consider such needs in total.

In order to get participants to express them, we had to consider what total needs there were. We felt there were four different categories of requirement (Garry and Cowan, 1986):

1. An *expressed* need – which has been identified and which the learner is quite willing to explain to others.
2. A *felt* need – which has been identified reasonably accurately as a deficiency or as a scope for improvement – but the learner does not wish to make it public, for one reason or another.
3. An *unformulated* need – which is concealed amidst vague or unformed feelings of disquiet on the part of the learner about certain aspects of competence. The learner knows there is something wrong, something is missing or something which (s)he wants to gain – but cannot quite put a finger on it.

4. An *unperceived* need – of which the learner is totally unaware, although others, looking from a detached standpoint, may see it clearly.

In order to identify the needs of the participants we had to use some device to transform felt and unformulated needs into expressed needs. We believed that by putting learners through various activities we could help them to consider and formulate their own relevant needs.

In the case of unperceived needs, we would have to ask the employers and senior members of the firms to identify them.

What Do We Mean By A 'Training Need'?

Having defined the types of need, we had to define what we meant specifically by a training need. We believe a training need exists when it is impossible to exploit possible potential without further learning. A training need is therefore the difference between work performance and work aspiration. In other words:

(a) The disparity between an individual's competence and what he/she hopes to achieve.
(b) The contrast between the way employees execute his or her job and how their employer expects them to carry it out.

We realized that this definition of needs and training needs would shape the methods we used for their identification, because we would now have to consult employee and employer, and we further believed that there would be differences between what the employees regarded as their needs and what the employer perceived them to be.

Methodology

In designing the activities to identify training needs we felt it was imperative that each procedure was thoroughly evaluated and altered accordingly. This would ensure that there was a sound foundation for successive activities and that each iteration would be progressively refined. Thus every iteration would come from the objective analysis of the outcome of the previous activity.

Every activity, be it research or interview, has to be analysed. This in turn will suggest a plan for the next activity. When that activity has run, the outcome has to be analysed with its implications. This iterative format is illustrated in Figure 1.

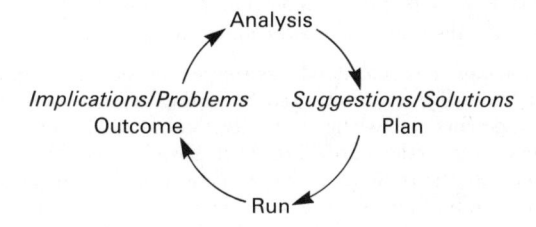

Figure 1. *Iterative format for activity analysis*

We thus began the workshop design process by researching the area of needs identification. Having done this we analysed the data we had collected and used this as the basis for subsequent activities.

Analysis

After initial research in this area, we decided to conduct individual interviews to find out how we could induce learners to express their needs (Figure 2). How could we

```
1.  Research
       ↓
2.  Interviews
       ↓
3.  Pilot I
       ↓
4.  Pilot II
```

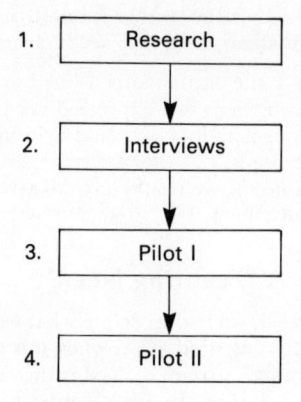

Figure 2. *Developing the methodology*

transform an unformulated need into a felt need, and a felt need in turn into an expressed need? In order to get people to express their needs, we had to ask ourselves what environment would make people more prepared to express themselves. Here are some of the conditions which motivate learners to express their needs.

1. If the subject under discussion is not directly threatening.
2. If there is time and motivation to consider and express subject area.
3. If there is a comfortable and supportive atmosphere – good design of room, proper facilities, consideration of participants as individuals.
4. If the participants believe their information will be confidential.
5. If general needs are discussed in group situations.
6. If specific needs are addressed in individual sessions.

At this point, we felt we were ready to begin to plan a workshop.

Planning a Workshop

In planning a workshop we had to consider the implications of our lists of criteria for workshop design to get the optimum expression of needs.

1. The first problem we encountered was that needs identification proved to be a very threatening subject area. If needs exist then it suggests that there are gaps in either competence, knowledge or understanding. This implicit criticism means that learners are generally unwilling to declare their needs.
   In order to combat participants' fear of being seen to be incompetent we felt it was important to build up a sense of self-worth amongst them. Therefore we decided to try to approach training needs in a positive manner. Training needs would now be seen as points upon which development could take place, rather than deficiencies.
2. We realized that consideration and expression of needs would take a considerable length of time. Thus we decided on a two-stage process. We would run two successive workshops which would give participants enough time and encouragement to express their needs.
3. We hoped to achieve a comfortable atmosphere by explaining the project and asking the participants directly for advice. We emphasized that in many cases providers set up courses without consulting the learners and therefore we looked to them to inform us of their needs.

4. We planned to assure the participants of the confidentiality of their information.
   5. We decided to run group workshops to discuss general needs so that:
      (a) Participants could generate ideas amongst themselves.
      (b) We could use time more effectively.
   6. We felt it was also important to conduct individual interviews so that participants could express specific and private training needs.

Having considered the points above, we began to plan a pilot workshop. We therefore drew up a list of objectives. These objectives would help us gauge our progress and record our ideas. The objectives for the pilot workshop were:

   1. To identify total needs within a workshop situation.
   2. To test out the structure of the workshop and evaluate the process.

Running the Pilot Workshop

Having planned the workshop carefully we were now ready to run it.

The group of engineers we chose was made up of graduates, technician engineers and even associate members of various firms. We had worked with these engineers before on previous occasions and therefore could rely on them to be co-operative and give us feedback on the procedure.

Outline of Workshop

   A. Introduction
   B. Skills and qualities necessary to be a competent civil engineer
   C. Goals, expectations and problems
   D. Plenary session
   E. Questionnaire

Outcome of the Pilot Workshop

In this exercise we identified a long list of common expressed needs. However, we did not unearth felt or unformulated needs. This was because we had tried to squeeze too many activities into one session. This exercise suggested that our formula for identification of needs was acceptable, but that we would have to modify it.

Analysis of the Pilot Workshop

In order to improve the format for needs identification, we had to carry out rigorous evaluation. We did this by asking ourselves the following questions directed at improving presentation and results:

Format of the Evaluation of the Pilot Workshop

   1. What was the general aim of the pilot workshop?
   2. And what were the specific aims?
      A. To see how the structure succeeded in terms of:
         i) how much information we got and how much was relevant for our purposes;
            which questions worked;
            which questions did not;
         ii) the way the participants responded to the workshop situation;
         iii) the kind of environment that was created.

B. To examine how we succeeded:
   i) in our presentation;
   ii) in the clarity of explanations;
   iii) in the facilitation of the workshop –
       how we worked as a team;
       what our roles were.
3. Did we succeed?
4. What lessons were learnt?
5. Questions/points raised by the workshop.

Having analysed the results from our research, interviews and pilot workshop we began to plan another workshop. This in turn was eventually piloted and we planned the next workshop. It was tempting to call each new workshop the final one. However, as each design was constantly refined we could at best call each iteration the penultimate workshop format (Figure 3).

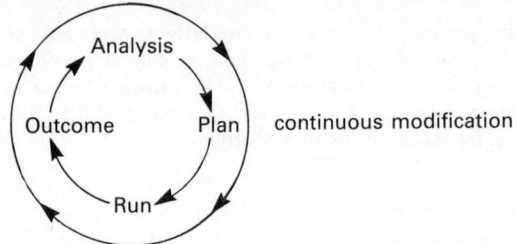

Figure 3. *Workshop modification*

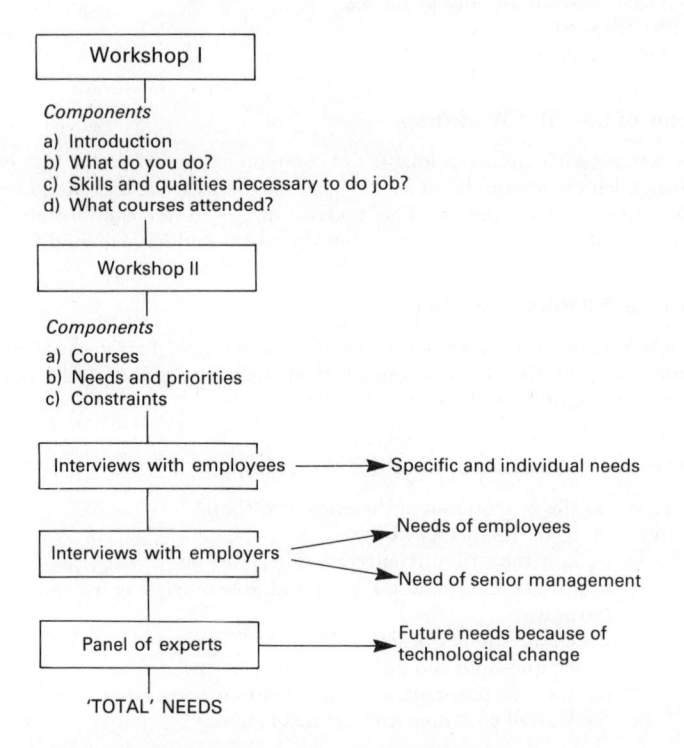

Figure 4. *Methodology for identifying needs*

It is true to say that improvements are less drastic after every iteration if thorough and objective analysis has been carried out. But even if there are not specific alterations within the format, there are always bound to be other modifications. For instance, the facilitator's presentation can be improved, workshops can be tailored for certain firms, and interviews can be adapted for specific individuals. Figure 4 summarizes the methodology for identifying needs.

Conclusion

This methodology has proved more searching than using questionnaires and interviews alone, since these do not provide sufficient time and motivation to consider deeper needs. They can only identify immediately expressible needs and these are often not the most important ones.

Identification of needs can only be a workshop activity. It may never be totally perfect, but can be developed rigorously and iteratively to produce an appropriate answer. After all as Josiah Gilbert Holland said:

> 'Heaven is not reached at a single bound;
> But we built the ladder by which we rise
> From the lowly earth to the vaulted skies,
> And we mount to its summit round by round.'

Identification of needs – an iterative answer.

References

Garry, A and Cowan, J (1986) To each according to his needs? In Percival, F, Craig, D, Buglass, D (eds) *Aspects of Educational Technology XX*, Kogan Page, London.

2.3 The Business Analyst – A Client-Centred Approach to Training Needs Analysis

J Coffey and L Wilcock
Council for Educational Technology (CET), London

Abstract: The need for training is treated with complacency by the majority of small business managers, despite the fact that many small business failures can be directly attributed to a lack of training in key areas such as marketing, financial control and management techniques. The Business Analyst project attempted to tackle this problem by developing a tool which would allow small business managers to identify the strengths and weaknesses of their firm for themselves and plan appropriate courses of action.

If as a result of this analysis a need for training was perceived, it would be seen by the small business manager as a solution to real problems within the firm and not as an avoidable extra.

This paper outlines the client-centred approach to training needs analysis within small firms adopted by the Business Analyst project, and traces the development of the package.

Background

Small businesses have recently become a major concern for the UK economy and of particular interest to training establishments. In 1983 when the Council for Educational Technology (CET) began to explore ways in which open learning could be applied to the small business sector, we were aware of the very rapid growth in the numbers of small businesses, up by 110,000 to a total of 1.4 million between 1978 and 1983. Since then this rise has continued, with business startups outstripping closures. In the six months to June 1985 there were 54,000 companies registered. This represented an increase of ten per cent over the same period in the previous year. However we also had to take into account the very large numbers of liquidations, which had also shown an increase. In 1985 there were 13,647 liquidations against 8,227 in 1981. 60 per cent of all failures occur during the first three years and it is quite clear that many of these result from a lack of expertise in finance and financial control, in general management, and in marketing techniques. Despite these facts the small business sector appears complacent about training and, since the growth of small businesses is of increasing importance to the UK economy, it is vital for us to find ways to overcome this apparent reluctance to increase skills and expertise.

In preliminary surveys and interviews which CET carried out with staff from colleges, from small firms and in centres concerned with advising small firms, it became clear that

(a) colleges were concerned by their inability to provide adequately for small firms and recognized that some of the reasons behind this failure were linked to organizational and administrative constraints
(b) colleges did however perceive that small firms were an important and untapped sector of the training market
(c) small firms viewed colleges as inflexible, unresponsive and unaware of their needs

(d) small firms saw training as an unimportant and therefore avoidable cost
(e) small firms have great difficulty in identifying their own training needs, and are likely to be unable to identify material of use to them.

Since the CET Open Learning programme had a particular interest in finding ways to help users of education and training services become more sophisticated in their selection of learning opportunities, there was obviously a prime case for CET to make an initiative in this area. We saw our role as twofold. Firstly we wanted to find ways to help small firms develop strategies for improving their businesses and we recognized early on that these strategies might or might not have implications for training. Secondly, we wanted to try and develop a way of marketing training in a sector which appeared to need it, but appeared to be particularly resistant to it.

The Target Group

Our initial surveys of the literature highlighted the difficulties that organizations had had in adequately defining a small firm. Definitions vary a great deal and usually describe firms in terms of turnover or in numbers of employees. There are other systems employed. In the case of road transport, for example, the measure can be the number of vehicles used in the firm. For our purpose, the focus was primarily on management issues and we therefore defined small firms as those having

(a) the management functions largely undifferentiated and concentrated in one or a very few people
(b) less than five recognizable managers.

We also had a particular interest in the stage which a firm was at in its development. We noticed in our preliminary surveys that small firms in the process of growth experienced a large number of problems associated with the management of growth, and the stresses and role changes which this imposed on owner-managers and people close to them.

There are a number of internal and external factors involved in determining the growth potential of a small firm.

The key internal factors are outlined in Figure 1.

Leadership
- Ambitions of owner/manager
- Determination
- Capable of delegation
- Ability to motivate the staff

Resources
- Skilled labour
- Availability of resources

What Makes a Good Growth Company?

Experience
- Willingness to accept outside equity capital
- Willingness to buy in management
- Good contacts
- Market skills
- Negotiating skills

Idea
- Good idea for development
- Market potential
- Ability to spot market gap
- Ability to compete

Control
- Effective management control
- Control of debtors
- Stock control
- Targeting
- Exploiting technology

Figure 1. *Key internal factors for growth potential of a small firm*

External factors which will influence the growth potential of the firm include

- ☐ the state of the economy; demand generally, interest rates, the availability of money;
- ☐ the availability of advice and assistance;
- ☐ the impact of social change on the community, individual and group attitudes and the workforce;
- ☐ the market – demand for product, level of competition;
- ☐ the attitude of local and central government and the level of taxation.

The internal and external factors impinging on the small firm will together determine the degree to which the business is able to develop and grow from its current state into a larger and more profitable enterprise (Figure 2).

WHERE THE BUSINESS COULD GO

The Outcome (Targets)

Key Internal Factors ▶ **The Process of Development** ◀ **Key External Factors**

The Base Potential for Development
WHERE WE ARE NOW (Performance)

Figure 2. *A model for growth in the small firm*

Typically, a small business manager in beginning a business specializes in technical work (which in any case will probably be one of the major interests in encouraging him or her to enter small business in the first place), organizes around personalities, centralizes decision-making, uses intuitive action to solve problems, communicates by telling (that is, in a one-way communication system) and controls by personal inspection. By contrast the professional manager, a person who is able to manage a business in growth, needs to have very different attributes. There has to be much more emphasis on work done through others. In achieving effective delegation the manager organizes to achieve objectives, decentralizes decision-making, adopts a systematic approach to problem-solving, encourages two-way communication and controls by exception. Making the transition from the typical small business manager to the professional manager is traumatic and not achieved by everyone.

The Business Analyst

The Business Analyst is a self-assessment package developed by CET to help small business managers manage growth effectively. The Business Analyst enables such managers to identify the strengths and weaknesses of their firms and plan appropriate courses of action. The package comprises information and checklists covering the most important topic areas in management, marketing and finance, action sheets, planning sheets and a user guide.

The Development Process

The stages in the development process were many, but the key ones were

(a) the production of pilot material which concentrated on management questions
(b) pilot workshops in two very different areas of the country, an industrial textile closure area in the North West and a rural area in the South West, to obtain a wide cross section of size and types of firm
(c) follow-up visits to the firms concerned after three months to interview the managers and obtain comments on the use of the pack within the firm.

The feedback obtained in this way enabled us to further refine the package and add features to meet the needs expressed.

The Business Analyst was published through McGraw Hill in January 1986 (CET, 1986).

Key factors in the success of the development were

(a) the involvement of an *ad hoc* group representing diverse interests including public, private and small firm interests;
(b) the involvement of a graphic designer from the earliest stages of the development process;
(c) a strong focus from the earliest stages on marketing the product. This was more sharply felt because of the virtual absence of funding for the project.

Marketing

The *ad hoc* group and the publisher both recognized the value of the Business Analyst. However they pointed out most forcefully that without a marketing strategy the package would be of little value. We therefore put considerable effort into solving this particular problem. The potential market was large, disparate, volatile, inaccessible by direct means, and sceptical. Clearly the group would be a very difficult one to approach. The method we chose was to find potential multipliers who had direct contact with small firms. The list of potential multipliers was large and included banks, accountants, chambers of commerce, enterprise agencies, small firms services, small business clubs, COSIRA, management schools, group training agencies, colleges, and franchises from large companies. Workshops are now being planned for these groups. The purposes of the workshop will be to encourage both a more flexible and client-centred approach to training, building on the work of the Business Analyst project, and to provide a 'cascade' pack of support materials to enable agencies involved in the initial workshops to provide workshops for the small firms constituency itself. The cascade materials will include models for identifying business training needs, an overview of business training needs, ways of thinking about establishing performance priorities, the relationships between such priorities and training, and – perhaps most important of all – considerations of the benefits which can accrue from investigating business training needs.

The workshops, which will begin summer 1986, have attracted interest and financial support from the Department of Employment Small Firms Service, the Manpower Services Commission's Adult Training Campaign and the Department of Education and Science PICKUP programme.

The Next Step

The Business Analyst helps a small firm manager find out what kinds of problem face the firm, and indicates directions which can be taken. The manager is, however, still left looking for sources of advice and training. This is one area where a computerized system could have considerable benefit and which CET would have examined in detail had funds been available. The approach would have been analogous to that adopted in another aspect of the CET's Open Learning Systems programme, the Learning Links Project, which looked at computer applications in informal adult learning. In the course of this work software was designed to help individual adult learners identify their learning needs and interests. Further programs were planned to link the outputs from such an analysis to databases of available local learning opportunities, learning exchanges, and self-help groups which CET had also developed.

Clearly, a similar approach could be adopted in the business training field. Databases are emerging which contain a great deal of information about the learning opportunities appropriate to small businesses. The Educational Counselling and Credit Transfer Information Service (ECCTIS) and the recently launched Materials and Resources Information Service Network (MARIS-NET) are examples. The challenge will be to develop an expert system sensitive enough to cater for the diverse needs of large numbers of small firms in a flexible way, devise the protocols needed to link with the many electronic databases (current and planned) of business and training information, and create efficient electronic means to deliver appropriate training where and when it is needed.

References

Council for Educational Technology (1986) *Business Analyst: a Self-Assessment Package*. McGraw-Hill, Maidenhead, Berks.

2.4 Open Learning and Training within Small Businesses: A Case for Study

T Moffatt and R Laidler
Durham Small Business Club
E Polden
North East Open Learning Network
B A Gillham
Newcastle-upon-Tyne Polytechnic

Abstract: A recent research exercise conducted in the areas around Durham has shown very clearly that small firms do little or no training. Indeed, many such firms questioned whether they *should* incur the extra expense involved.

The sponsors of the project detailed in this paper took the view that training ought to be seen as an essential investment rather than an unnecessary cost burden, contending in essence that training is less expensive than ignorance. The same study also revealed that small firms were interested in training which could be pursued flexibly and individually in terms of pace, place and time.

A useful open learning package on marketing management was identified as meeting an established need of many small businesses.

This paper provides details of an open learning training model, which *initiates* open learning in the small firm, *monitors* its development, *motivates* its users, *evaluates* systematically its progress and outcomes, and *reveals* just how powerful the innovation might be in the hands of key personnel in small firms.

The paper reports on the progress made by the development to date and tentatively explores some of the lessons to be learnt from it.

Introduction

In April 1984, Durham Small Business Club Ltd (DSBC) started a Local Collaborative Project aimed at training within small business. It was the first of its kind in the United Kingdom. The results of this project were published in November 1984, in a report entitled *Education and Training in the Small Business Sector for Owner/Managers and their Key Staff* (DSBC, 1984).

The research revealed a number of significant findings. The main findings relevant to this paper were as follows:

- ☐ small firms do very little planned training
- ☐ except for a tiny minority of highly motivated firms, very small businesses employing between 1 and 50 employees do almost none at all
- ☐ many firms expressed a strong interest in training but were, for a variety of reasons, unable to organize a planned programme
- ☐ a number of firms expressed an interest in training which could be done at a place, pace, and time suitable to the individual or firm. In fact, without really knowing what open learning was, they were pinpointing some of its key characteristics
- ☐ the main reasons for low takeup of training cited were the total cost of training, time off the job, and a dislike or even fear of college-based courses.

Much evidence is available to support the thesis that there is a positive correlation between training undertaken and improved performance. The evidence from performers in many fields, including sport, singing, and acting – whether professional or amateur – strongly supports this view. Sadly, the same people who will train avidly for leisure pursuits are able to ignore the case for training in their business life, and fail to recognize that training is an investment, not a cost.

In 1983 DSBC became managing agents for a Youth Training Scheme (YTS) programme catering for the training of young people. The work was aimed specifically at eight different small business areas.

Since that time, the Club has been actively promoting training, seeing it as one of the principal ways of helping small firms towards expansion and job creation. The evidence clearly indicates the success of the training for young people based within small firms.

Clearly, both the need and the will are there already.

So in January 1986, Durham Small Business Club, in co-operation with the North East Open Learning Network (NEOLN), organized a pilot programme to introduce 15 small firms to training using an open learning package. The package selected was the *AnCo Marketing Management* programme. The venture has been financially supported by the MSC, and this paper seeks to provide some early discussion of the pilot study.

The Development of the Training Model

The main factors which seem to inhibit the development of training in small firms identified in the local collaborative project were:

- the cost of time lost from the job
- the direct financial cost of attending traditional courses
- the inconvenient timing of existing provision
- a generalized suspicion of academics, classrooms, and bureaucratic organizations and
- a lack of motivation to undertake it.

By its very nature, open learning is able to overcome many of these inhibiting factors, and the local collaborative project provided evidence that small firms were likely to be responsive to an open learning approach to training. The current pilot project, which has been developed by the Durham Small Business Club in collaboration with the North East Open Learning Network, was specifically designed to address these problems. It was anticipated that such a scheme would provide encouragement for small enterprises to become involved in systematic training. In effect, the scheme was to function as a possible model for the further extension of training in the small business sector through open learning methods and materials.

The broad objectives of the scheme were therefore:

- to introduce training into part of the small business sector
- to introduce the firms to the concept of open learning, and encourage them to explore it for the provision of further training
- to enable firms to carry out their own in-house training, using open learning materials
- to provide a support structure which would maximize the benefits and likely success of the training
- to make the programme flexible, in order to meet the specific requirements of individual businesses.

From the outset, the scheme was built around the creation of a substantial support little or no previous training experience, and no knowledge of open learning materials, would require a substantial support system.

Accordingly, a model was designed which was capable of providing support for the learners and trainers from two sources:

- internal support, relying upon the resources available within the firms and
- external support, provided through the supporting agencies – in this case the Durham Small Business Club, and the North East Open Learning Network.

The internal support would be provided from within the firm principally by a key member of staff, who would take on special responsibility for implementing the firm's training programme. This person would be called the *training co-ordinator*.

Each firm participating in the scheme was asked to identify a responsible person as its training co-ordinator, and to give a commitment that a minimum of one hour per week would be set aside for staff training.

The external support was provided on two fronts: *firstly*, support designed to facilitate the operation of the training procedures themselves, and *secondly*, support in the form of a parallel business consultancy which related to the subject of the training.

To provide this second element in an economical way, it was decided to use a 'return-a-tape' system rather than the traditional form of consultancy. This in fact meant that each firm was provided with two blank audio cassettes, on which business problems relating to the area of training could be recorded. These were posted to DSBC, which then arranged for an appropriate consultant to reply. Any one firm could avail themselves of up to three 'consultations' of this type.

From the outset, the scheme was built around the creation of a substantial support structure:

- the identification of a training need, and the selection of suitable open learning materials to match it
- the designation of the training co-ordinator by each of the firms involved
- the provision of a workshop for the training co-ordinators, which would assist them in using the training materials within their firms
- the provision of a simple guidance booklet on the nature of open learning materials, and containing suggestions about how they might be used for 'in-house' training. This booklet was intended specifically for the owner/managers, and training co-ordinators
- the provision of a follow-up workshop for the training co-ordinators to share experiences and explore problems
- the provision of at least one visit to each firm by workshop tutors in order to provide help with the practical implementation of the training
- the general availability of advice by telephone on specific training problems
- the opportunity to make use of business consultancy related to marketing management via the return-a-tape system.

This pilot scheme has been fully supported by the Manpower Services Commission through its Employer Training Grants. These grants have met the major part of the costs. As a result, the necessary developmental costs have not acted as a deterrent.

15 companies have been involved in the initial scheme. These have had workforces ranging from 100 up to 200 employees. This wide variation was a deliberate policy during recruitment, since one objective of the pilot study was to assess the appropriateness of this model for firms of varying size.

The subject of the training in this case was *marketing management*, an area identified in the early research as one of concern to most small firms.

The open learning package selected was an anglicized version of the Irish Industrial Training Authority's *Marketing Management* package.

The material provided a nominal 40 hours of training, and comprises:

- eight booklets
- two audio cassettes and
- one videocassette.

This marketing management programme may be worked through in any order, and does not assume any previous knowledge of marketing. It is aimed specifically at owner/managers or managers of small companies and their staff.

The pilot scheme commenced in January 1986. During the workshop for the training co-ordinators, the members asked that the scheme outlined above be amended to allow one further workshop. This subsequently involved the addition of an informal feedback workshop after about six weeks.

Flexibility of operation, being an important principle upon which this scheme was mounted, necessitates that this and other changes should be made.

The Progress of the Scheme and some Tentative Conclusions

Following the recruitment of the 15 firms, the programme involved the following elements:

The Initial Training Workshop

This four-hour workshop was designed to ensure that the participants:

- had an opportunity to see, handle, use, and discuss the AnCo materials
- were aware of the nature of the existing AnCo package and its components, its structure and organization
- were made aware of elements of structure 'added on' by the organizers of the scheme to support company efforts to use the materials
- were fully aware of the likely problems involved in implementing an open learning training programme
- had an opportunity to rehearse a possible set of answers to these problems, and to design a 'start-up' action plan
- had considered a variety of ways in which to enhance and customize the materials for use in their own company's interests.

The workshop was perceived very positively by the 12 participants who completed the evaluation forms. Overwhelmingly, they found it stimulating, useful, relevant, flexible, full of discussion, well conducted, demanding, challenging, coherent, active, and well worth the time spent on it. On the other hand, they considered it rather too condensed, and were not totally convinced that it was geared to their specific needs.

The workshop tutors had reservations, particularly about the shortage of time available, the rather superficial experience gained of the package, and the minimal use made of the Open Learning Guide which had been created to accompany the scheme.

Nevertheless, an enthusiastic group of proto-trainers left the first workshop having already decided that they would value an *interim reaction meeting* after a period of about six weeks. The organizers were able to agree quickly to the provision of this extra element of support.

The Four-Week 'Phoneout'

It had been assumed that participants would avail themselves easily and comfortably of the telephone and consultant support system available to them.

This did not happen, and the organizers therefore decided to contact all 15 firms. The object of the contact was really threefold:

- to find out precisely what was happening
- to key into any problems for which help and support could be provided and
- to remind participants of the proposed future meetings, and to spur on any activity and development.

The overall impression from these contacts was of training co-ordinators still in a stage of preparing themselves, and sorting out their ideas, with direct training activity still in the offing.

Business pressures and time pressures were frequently mentioned. One or two people had begun to pick up real weaknesses, like the assumptions the organizers had made about the participants' general awareness of open learning and training, and the training scene in general.

Clearly the proactive phoneout was a necessary component of support, and later evidence showed that it did spur participants on to more purposeful activity.

The Interim Discussion Meeting

This occurred about six weeks after the initial workshop, and a fortnight after the phoneout.

It was organized on a part-formal, part-social basis in the evening. Initially, it was envisaged that an hour of formal feedback would be followed by an hour of less formal talk between participants.

In fact, nearly three hours of powerful, critical discussion ensued.

Three questions were posed:

1. what were the participants' experience of and feeling about the programme?
2. were the participants meeting any special problems?
   and
3. what did the participants want from the organizers for the next part of the scheme?

There was a great deal of criticism of the mode of training which had been advocated for this pack, and considerable doubt about its suitability for more than a small number of staff in the participant firms. This criticism often stemmed from what appeared to be a relatively poor understanding of what open learning involved, and of how customization and adaptation might be achieved.

It was observed that the guide – which advocated flexibility – seemed itself to become inflexible and prescriptive in its later parts.

The main problems noted were associated with the:

- availability of time for the training co-ordinator *and* the trainees
- low priority given to training work when faced with other work demands, plainly a problem of commitment
- unsuitability of the materials for some of the specific target groups selected for training
- lack of entertainment value in the materials
- over-zealous adherence to the open learning guide
- inaccessibility of equipment – particularly video recorders.

The next step that participants felt to be most urgent was the arrangement of individual visits to each of the participant firms. The purpose of this visit was to permit detailed discussions and suggestions about how to proceed before the final workshop.

The Final Workshop

This has yet to take place, but will centre around the individual experiences of those who have participated.

It is expected that this will prove to be a learning experience for both the training co-ordinators *and* the organizers of the scheme.

The key questions addressed by the training co-ordinators before this workshop will be:

- [ ] assessing the value of the initial workshop in retrospect
- [ ] indicating matters that this workshop failed to prepare them for
- [ ] judging what benefits the work on the open learning materials has conferred on those involved
- [ ] reflecting on their own feelings about this new style of company-based training
- [ ] assessing the feelings of the others who participated
- [ ] suggesting other areas which might be approached in a similar way
- [ ] providing a detailed critique on the AnCo marketing management package
- [ ] judging the intent, effectiveness, and convenience of the various elements of the support structure
- [ ] indicating the ways in which the materials and procedures were adapted to fit the specific circumstances within an individual firm
- [ ] rating the outcomes of the training provided by this procedure
- [ ] making suggestions and comments on any aspect of the development.

The final meeting is likely to prove productive in terms of discussion, raising of awareness, and perhaps in the ultimate extension of training into firms hitherto on the periphery of the training scene.

Some Tentative Conclusions and Reflections

Our findings so far indicate the need for a much more elaborate preliminary preparation if open learning training procedures are going to become part of the day-to-day operation of small businesses.

1. The initial selection of the package – which was good of its type – is unlikely to lead to success if it is taken too far beyond its announced target group.

    Perhaps we went too far beyond the owner/manager group in our anxiety to get maximal payoff. On the other hand, customization was clearly a way to modify the target group, but it overestimated the capacity of our training co-ordinator group. Of course, we now know much more precisely the kinds of firms likely to find these materials effective.

2. Participants needed a firmer grasp of the basic notions of open learning, flexibility of operation, and customization. This suggests that a more substantial series of training co-ordinator workshops would be desirable.

    On the other hand, quite small changes, like the opportunity to inspect the materials and the open learning guide *before* the workshop, would have eased things considerably. In any case, additional time was most often what the co-ordinators did not have available!

3. Any rigidity in the system seems likely to reduce the level of success achieved.

    For example, the fact that the separate components of the package were not available for purchase individually led to nearly insuperable problems of management. For future use of this package, it will clearly be necessary to negotiate with the publishers the right to purchase the components separately.

4. There were clear indications that the support structure is essential to the success of ventures like this. Support of the passive or reactive sort seems less valuable than proactive support, which impels interaction and activity. It seems that it is a necessary part of raising the activity's priority level and generating the time, energy, and knowledge base necessary to sustain it. It is also essential to avoid the worst effects of feeling isolated. Feeling isolated appeared to be a more extreme problem amongst training co-ordinators than amongst open learners in general.

In summary, all 15 firms seem to have embraced the idea of open learning, and getting involved in training, even where this particular package proved relatively unsuitable. This willingness to be involved is often not well matched by the capacities necessary in order to do so. The AnCo package clearly worked best with highly motivated owner/managers, and most problems were experienced in trying to extend the material down the staff ladder.

Considerable energy will have to be devoted to training the trainers.

It is likely that open learning will prove an excellent vehicle for small firm training, but an appropriate support structure must be designed for every programme. It is essential that this support structure involves a high degree of monitoring by the programme organizers in the interests of systematic improvement.

And that, after all, *is* what we are after – systematic improvement in the interests of small businesses, and of the wider community.

References

Anco Industrial Training Authority (1985) *Marketing Management.* CASDEC Ltd in association with Anco.

Durham Small Business Club (1984) *Education and Training in the Small Business Sector for Owner/Managers and their Key Staff.* Durham Small Business Club Ltd.

Durham Small Business Club and the North East Open Learning Network (1986) *Training and the Small Firm: a Guide to Open Learning.* DSBC/NEOLN, Durham.

North East Open Learning Network (1986) *Training Models Fact Sheet No 1: Marketing Management.* North East Open Learning Network 5.

2.5 Industrial Dimensions of Open Learning: A Comparison of Approaches Adopted by Lucas Industries plc and the Austin Rover Group

S Perryman and M Freshwater
Open Tech Unit, Manpower Services Commission, Sheffield

Abstract: This paper describes some characteristics of company-based open learning systems including Lucas Industries plc and the Austin Rover Group. Areas particularly emphasized include learning objectives, materials quality and format, management of the learning environment and measurement of the effectiveness of open learning systems.

Introduction

Companies facing rapid changes in technology and organization have begun an involvement with open learning. They believe that it will provide cost-effective provision which is both more flexible and suited to the needs of adult employees who are seeking technological updating and management skills training. As a result of the encouraging progress made by the industrial pioneers and the exhortation of government to commit greater resources to adult training, an increasing number of companies are adopting models of industrial open learning. We should therefore examine and understand the major features of industrial open learning systems and the similarities and differences between different industrial models.

As a first step in this direction, this paper compares and contrasts open learning at Lucas and the Austin Rover Group, who have two different but broadly complementary systems. It offers additional ideas and options for company staff who are considering the adoption of open learning methods, and illustrates and explains industry's expectations about open learning so that learning material producers in the further and higher education sector can tailor their products more easily to meet the needs of industry.

The paper begins by outlining the main features of each industrial model. Similarities and differences of each are compared for four key issues: company objectives; learning materials development; delivery and support; and cost and the measurement of effectiveness. The final section summarizes points and highlights lessons which each organization's experience can offer.

Main Features

Both Lucas and Austin Rover are large multi-site organizations in the engineering sector.

Lucas' open learning development unit is based at Lucas Research Centre. The unit is responsible for courseware development and provides consultancy and advice to help develop open learning delivery systems in Lucas Group companies. Five learning centres have now been established, one at each group company.

The Austin Rover Group open learning unit is based at the company's residential training centre. Austin Rover now has open learning centres at ten separate sites across the group. As at Lucas, each centre is responsible to the site training manager, with a functional link to the open learning development unit.

The companies have developed their own multimedia courseware including computer based training (CBT), video, audio, text and practical kits to meet their specific in-company needs. (Austin Rover currently has over 30 programmes totalling 300 training hours, Lucas 8 programmes, divided into 23 units totalling approximately 254 hours.) In addition, both companies purchase externally produced materials to meet more general needs (Austin Rover currently have approximately 20 programmes, and Lucas 29). In each company the use of open learning methods has been met with continuing enthusiasm by learners and, as a result, trainee throughput has been high. Austin Rover has had more than 7,000 trainees in 2 years and Lucas over 800 trainees in the first 6 months. Both companies have developed strong senior management commitment to these new methods, and see the role of open learning increasing as part of their training response to new technology and organizational change.

Company Objectives

The following table summarizes the objectives set by each company for their open learning initiative.

Austin Rover	Lucas
– Reduce the unit cost of training. – Provide training close to the place of work (ie make it more accessible). – Make training available at the right time. – Provide flexibility and individualized learning. – Allow individual development outside narrow job confines. – Focus on technical and clerical staff.	– Improve training availability. – Improve the impact of training. – Use open learning to stimulate change in the company. – Evaluate the effectiveness of open learning in a manufacturing environment. – Focus on improving current job competence. – Focus on engineers and managers.

Figure 1. *Objectives of each company*

The table shows a number of common objectives and highlights differences in the philosophy behind each company's approach. Lucas's focus is improving and developing the current job competence of specific groups of engineers and managers, in order to stimulate structural changes within the company and as part of a major training for competitiveness campaign. Austin Rover have a broader target audience and a concern for developing the individual potential of their workforce outside the normal confines of their job. This emphasis on opening up access to training has led to the substitution of open learning in place of conventional training where it is cost-effective to do so and by additional open learning provision to meet new needs as they arise.

Learning Materials Development

The process of learning materials development, from needs analysis through to design, writing, editing, piloting and production, is too complex to cover in any depth in this short paper, but we wish to consider major differences of approach which underlie apparently similar development methods. Both companies produce multimedia packages with a strong computer-based element; both have learning materials covering manufacturing, information technology, engineering and management skills, and a growing interest in new training technologies such as interactive video and intelligent knowledge-based systems. In addition they buy learning materials from external providers whenever appropriate in order to avoid high development costs.

Needs analysis and learning design methods are similar. In each case broad needs are determined in three ways: through regular meetings of company training managers; by responding to requests from senior management; and through analysis of data resulting from formal training audits. Subsequently, the learning programme designer or training adviser will discuss detailed proposals with the company department concerned. As part of this process, Austin Rover have developed a nine-stage analysis method which assists the training adviser to ensure that the need is real and that open learning is an appropriate and cost-effective solution.

It is at the learning design and writing stage that major differences between the two companies' approaches occur.

Austin Rover favour an in-house development process. This involves using outside consultants only to cope with overload or to assist on specific technical aspects (eg interactive videodisc technology). The functional structure of their team (see Figure 2) reflects their approach, and every effort is made to retain writing capability in-house and to use trainer training to develop open learning writing expertise with a view to partly (and gradually) transferring responsibility from the central unit to plant level.

```
1 Manager            – Research and Development
5 Training Advisers  – Interactive Video
                     – Video
                     – Courseware Development Manager
                     – Marketing and Sales
3 Training Officers  – Courseware Development
1 Training Officer   – Plant Co-ordinator of Open Learning Centres
```

Figure 2. *Structure of the open learning team at Austin Rover*

Lucas prefer to sub-contract the writing phase and see their role as offering clear management and direction to a wide range of outside professionals who offer expertise in computer-based training (CBT) authoring, video production, graphic design etc. The stronger emphasis which they place on developing the learning system and environment is also reflected in their organizational structure (see Figure 3) which is systems- rather than function-based.

Use of CBT

We turn now to the more specific matter of computer-based training, used by both companies. Lucas opted to buy an expensive high-quality and sophisticated CBT hardware and authoring system (WICAT WISE) from the outset and in addition now convert courseware for lower-cost delivery on IBM PC at some centres. Austin Rover initially experimented with low cost Apple-based equipment (using the Superpilot authoring language) and later developed their own authoring language, Artplan, to enable them to write CBT for their company office automation system, the DEC Rainbow, and for the IBM PC. This development allowed them to produce higher quality graphics and layouts in their courseware. The DEC Rainbow also offered them

```
┌─────────────────────────────────────────────────────────────────────┐
│ Operations manager                                                  │
│ 1 Courseware design manager                                         │
│ 2 Learning programme designers  – planning and analysis.            │
│                                 – course design.                    │
│                                 – management of subcontractors for  │
│                                   materials production.             │
│                                 – pilot testing and rework.         │
│                                 – maintenance and validation.       │
│ 1 Learning systems manager      – development of the open learning  │
│             and                   computer management system (on    │
│ 1 Assistant systems engineer      WICAT)                            │
│                                 – technical/computer developments.  │
│                                 – training and support for learning │
│                                   centre managers.                  │
│                                 – learning centre co-ordination.    │
│                                 – establishing new centres.         │
└─────────────────────────────────────────────────────────────────────┘
```

Figure 3. *Structure of the open learning team at Lucas*

the potential of wider access by networking training across the company and the IBM PC format allowed easier marketing of products outside the company.

Text Production

Lucas places more emphasis than Austin Rover on the *appearance* of the texts from which learners will be working. Material is laid out by a professional graphics designer and is professionally printed to a high standard. Austin Rover adopted a lower cost text-production method using photocopied typescript. More recently they have purchased an Apple Mackintosh to enhance the design and quality of their text to meet the growing sophistication of learners within the company.

Validation of Materials

In both cases the technical content is checked by the subject matter expert and appropriate line management are consulted throughout the development phase to ensure the product will be what they want. Lucas pilot the materials on a small selected group and then rework before full release, whereas Austin Rover prefer to release the materials in full and field test them in the learning centres, recalling those elements which are found to be unsatisfactory. Prior to release for field test, detailed proofreading and technical checking is conducted by the subject matter expert, the client, and the open learning unit.

Bought-in Material

Both are increasingly interested in purchasing learning materials from other providers and share common views on desirable features for these packages as summarized in Figure 4.

> Learning materials should:
> - stand alone (ie no external tutor support necessary)
> - have computer-based assessment and management
> - be purpose written – not an adapted text book
> - have the correct technical content, level and style for the target population
> - make the learner feel comfortable
> - be accurate and error-free
> - be available for multiple use (ie re-usable and with additional learner workbooks available for sale)
> - have adequate internal feedback – interactive and with self-assessment

Figure 4. *External materials – desirable features*

Delivery and Support

While both organizations began with similar delivery and support methods – essentially a tutor-free learning centre with computers for learning management and assessment – experience has led to a number of refinements in each model.

Austin Rover

Austin Rover has widened access to open learning facilities by extending the open learning centre opening hours to allow casual users seeking personal development access outside normal hours of work (this has been a notable success). In addition, new developments will link the CBT system into the local area networks (which are being developed across the company) permitting direct delivery of training via computer and telephone system to senior employees in their own offices.

Quality of delivery has been improved in a number of ways by:

(a) transferring CBT to the DEC Rainbow system which offers colour, high resolution graphics and improved response times;
(b) developing a register of tutors available in each plant who will answer queries and give help when learners experience difficulties;
(c) forming links between conventional and open learning provision to provide hybrid courses. These have the dual benefit of time savings in relation to conventional provision and improved learner support through an opportunity to share experiences and receive formal tutorials.

Lucas

Lucas have preferred to limit access to their open learning centres to key groups of employees with opening hours at first restricted to normal office hours. Recently however opening hours have been extended in two centres to help managers who wish to use the centre, but who cannot afford time during the day. The success of the first five learning centres has also led to interest in developing more outlets across the group.

For cost reasons, Lucas initially delivered WICAT CBT material through IBM PC XT machines in a limited number of cases. The number of WICAT terminals in the learning centres is to be increased in order to take full advantage of the system's graphics capability. It has been recognized that the additional hardware cost is small in comparison with courseware development costs and is justified by the increased quality of learning materials. Lucas now places strong emphasis on student support.

Experience has shown the need from day one for *all* students to be comfortable with the learning arrangements, to feel in control of their learning and to be able to succeed with their learning package. A tutorless system without learner support is not the answer for them.

Support is given through an unobtrusive but comprehensive system which manages the learning environment. The system relies on two elements: personal contact and computer management. Personal contact has two functions, to provide pre-counselling for every learner so that no one receives the wrong level of training, and to be on hand to help learners overcome minor problems and confusions. Computer management, using the highly sophisticated WICAT SMART system, provides the learning centre manager with comprehensive information on the progress of each learner, including the time taken for each course element, the quality of learner responses, the learning route and the point reached by the learner at the end of each learning session. The information is used by the centre manager as a prompt to indicate if additional support is needed and as a record from which centre utilization can be planned and measured. The information is retained as long as necessary to ensure successful learning takes place, but permanent records of this complexity are not held. SMART also helps learners. The use of their time is optimized and their interest enhanced by individualizing the path taken through the material and skipping those areas already known by the learner.

In summary, therefore, Austin Rover places emphasis on developing the openness of their system and uses computers to assist the learning of the individual student.

Lucas, on the other hand, prefer a system involving less open access with a strong emphasis on the supportive control of the learner through personal contact and the computer management of the learning system.

Cost and the Measurement of Effectiveness

This section will briefly describe the criteria Austin Rover use to analyse the cost-effectiveness of their system. Their approach may provide a useful model for others to follow and will help to illustrate the difficulties inherent in setting cost-effectiveness criteria for open learning. Lucas, who have been operating for a shorter period of time, have developed a broadly similar approach, although less emphasis is placed on demonstrating a reduced unit cost of training than at Austin Rover.

Austin Rover have developed a four-stage method of analysis. Plant utilization figures from each learning centre are used to establish the throughput of trainees in the system. Detailed analysis is undertaken of fixed and variable costs, learning hours available for study, and trainee throughput, for each in-house developed and bought-in learning package. Summaries of this information are then used to develop two important ratios:

(1) total cost *vs* total learning hours;
(2) total cost per learning hour *vs* trainee throughput.

Finally, in order to demonstrate that unit costs of training can be reduced using open learning, a break-even analysis has been developed for certain key subject areas.

Figure 5 shows the model which Austin Rover use to determine this break-even point. They have found that while the initial fixed costs of developing open learning are high (approximately £800 per hour), subsequent variable (or running) costs per student are approximately half those of conventional learning. In one recent example, where it was anticipated that 300 people would undertake basic electronics training, the break-even point was 113 trainees, and the estimated cost saving for 300 people was approximately £20,000.

Both companies recognize that analysis of this type is problematic due to difficulties in defining terms. Learning hours are perhaps the most difficult to define since by the very nature of open learning, trainees are able to study at their own pace. As a result,

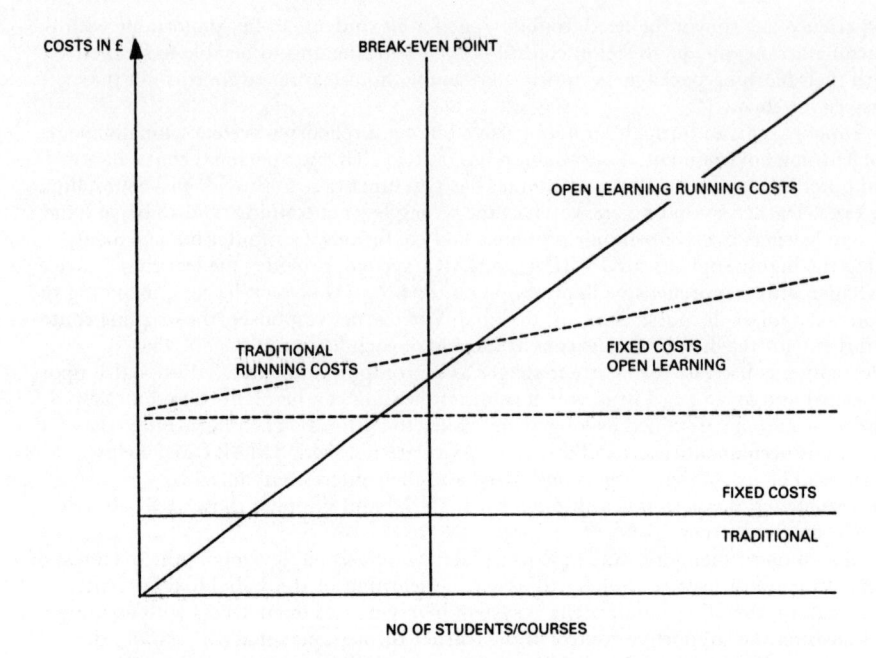

```
                    COSTS IN £ ▲           BREAK-EVEN POINT




                                                              OPEN LEARNING RUNNING COSTS




                                                                          FIXED COSTS
                              TRADITIONAL                                 OPEN LEARNING
                              RUNNING COSTS




                                                                          FIXED COSTS
                                                                          TRADITIONAL



                                         NO OF STUDENTS/COURSES
```

Figure 5. *Cost comparison between open learning and traditional training*

both Austin Rover and Lucas have found that learners can take between half and twice the expected time for a package. In order to overcome this problem, both companies have monitored longest, shortest and average 'run times' for each package and have adjusted their expected times accordingly.

Learning centre utilization is also a difficult issue to handle because learner throughput is hard to measure (do you count learners when they start a package, or when they complete it? How do you cope with large variations in the lengths of packages?). From a cost point of view high utilization of the capital equipment may also be more important than a simple count of trainee output. Lucas and Austin Rover cope with this problem in different ways, Lucas by measuring the number of two-hour learning periods available at the learning centre which are actually used, Austin Rover by measuring computer utilization for trainees commencing CBT packages.

Problems occur when deciding what elements to include in running costs (travel and subsistence? the opportunity cost of being away from work? depreciation? heat and light? notional rent?), and when agreeing a basis of comparison between the development costs of open learning in relation to conventional training.

On the issue of running costs, Austin Rover tends to make a worse than realistic case for open learning against conventional training by counting depreciation costs for the substantial volume of computer equipment employed in open learning centres but by not counting travel and subsistence and opportunity costs which are substantially less with open learning.

On the issue of development cost, development hour to learning hour ratios have been established, through experience, for use in calculating comparative courseware development costs between open learning and conventional learning (100:1 for open learning, 15:1 for conventional course development).

In summary, therefore, measuring the cost and cost-effectiveness of open learning is an important part of both companies' work, but particularly for Austin Rover who are attempting to use open learning to reduce the unit cost of their training. Both companies experience similar difficulties in defining terms and developing effective measures. Despite these difficulties, Austin Rover have been able to demonstrate that in appropriate circumstances (ie when trainee numbers are likely to be above 100) reductions in training cost can be made by using open learning instead of conventional training methods. Lucas, who are more concerned with improving training effectiveness than with making direct cost savings, would point out that open learning methods may also be the most appropriate solution for smaller volumes of training due to open learning's other inherent advantages (eg impact, flexibility, convenience). Cost is important, but it is only one factor in the effectiveness equation.

Lessons Learned

What then are the lessons learned by each company as their open learning systems have developed?

For Austin Rover, the most important lesson is that open learning offers advantages for technological and manufacturing training. They believe that costs and training time savings are possible if the learning development process is managed properly and if the subject of the learning material is chosen with care. However, the high cost of in-house courseware development has led them increasingly towards purchasing materials developed outside the company for their more general needs, preferring to develop their own materials only for company specific needs when externally sourced materials are not available or do not meet their quality standards.

Austin Rover originally experienced some difficulty in helping their training staff to adjust to open learning. More recently, however, staff retention problems have arisen among the open learning team due to their enhanced skills and to the growth of open learning opportunities outside the company.

The future of open learning in Austin Rover looks very encouraging. The company has plans to develop networking arrangements for courseware delivery, to explore a developing interest in interactive video and intelligent knowledge-based systems, and to develop programmes to meet growing training needs at operator level. Further lessons can be learned from Lucas' experience of open learning. The company is particularly concerned with getting the process of management right in three main areas:

(a) management of the company climate (ie ensuring both top management and union support);
(b) management of the learning development process (not underestimating the problems, giving clear direction and not trying to plan in detail too far ahead.;
(c) smooth unobtrusive management of the learning environment (making all learners feel comfortable and in charge of their learning while ensuring adequate support to enable them to succeed).

The future for Lucas is also most encouraging, with a rapidly growing number of learners, opportunities to develop new learning centres across the Lucas Group, and plans to implement technological innovations in the learning process.

Conclusions

I hope that the differences in approach highlighted in this paper may help to provide some options for the development of industrial open learning systems.

Both models described offer valuable examples of open learning in action, and we hope that the details given here may prompt discussions with further and higher education circles about the fit between college provision for open learning development and the requirements of industrial companies; and within industry about the most effective way to establish in-company open learning arrangements.

Austin Rover and Lucas have been pathfinders in the development of industry-based open learning. We want to encourage other organizations to learn from these successful ideas and methods as they build their own open learning systems.

2.6 The Development of a Large County-Wide Open Learning Service: Devon Open Tech

C Greenwood
Devon Open Tech

Abstract: Devon is the third largest English county, covering about 2,500 square miles with a population of almost a million. Devon Open Tech is one of the 17 local education authority Open Tech projects in the UK. It has pump-priming funding from the Manpower Services Commission over two years to develop and extend open and flexible opportunities for education and training in over 200 subjects.

This paper explains the context for Devon Open Tech, the needs which it is meeting and the development of systems to respond to a wide variety of educational and training demands. Key features of the development are explained, including: planning, organizational structure, administrative systems, marketing, staff development, resourcing, costing and pricing, tutoring, roles of institutions, the LEA policy developments and options for long-term viability. Devon Open Tech is widely regarded as providing a successful model for an authority-wide open and flexible education and training service.

Introduction

Devon is the third largest English county, covering about 2,600 square miles of the south-west peninsula. It has a population of almost 1 million, of whom roughly three-quarters are over 16. The existing further education service makes a very important contribution to the economy and social life of the area, but many people need to travel long distances to reach their nearest college.

Problems of access have also been aggravated by real reductions in expenditure on education and public transport over the last decade or more. Consequently, the further education service as a whole (see the map of Further Education Colleges and Community Colleges, Figure 1) is less able to offer a full range of subjects and levels of study at all places. Some courses are only available at one or two centres and people have to travel to these if they can.

Devon Open Tech is one of 17 local education authority-based Open Tech projects and is the only one in England south of Birmingham and west of London. It began in April 1985 and has two-year developmental funding from the Manpower Services Commission (MSC), after which it must be sustained from other sources. During the period of MSC funding there is no contribution from the LEA and one aim of the project is to investigate ways in which the project can be sustained after this period.

The Context of Open Learning

The further education statistics for the county show that 98 per cent of the half million people in the 25 to 64 age group are not attending the colleges. The skills and knowledge in this group could be considered as vital to the county's economy and it is therefore important that there are continuing education and training opportunities available which meet their needs (both vocational and non-vocational). The great majority of adults are unable to attend courses run at colleges during the working day on a conventional attendance basis.

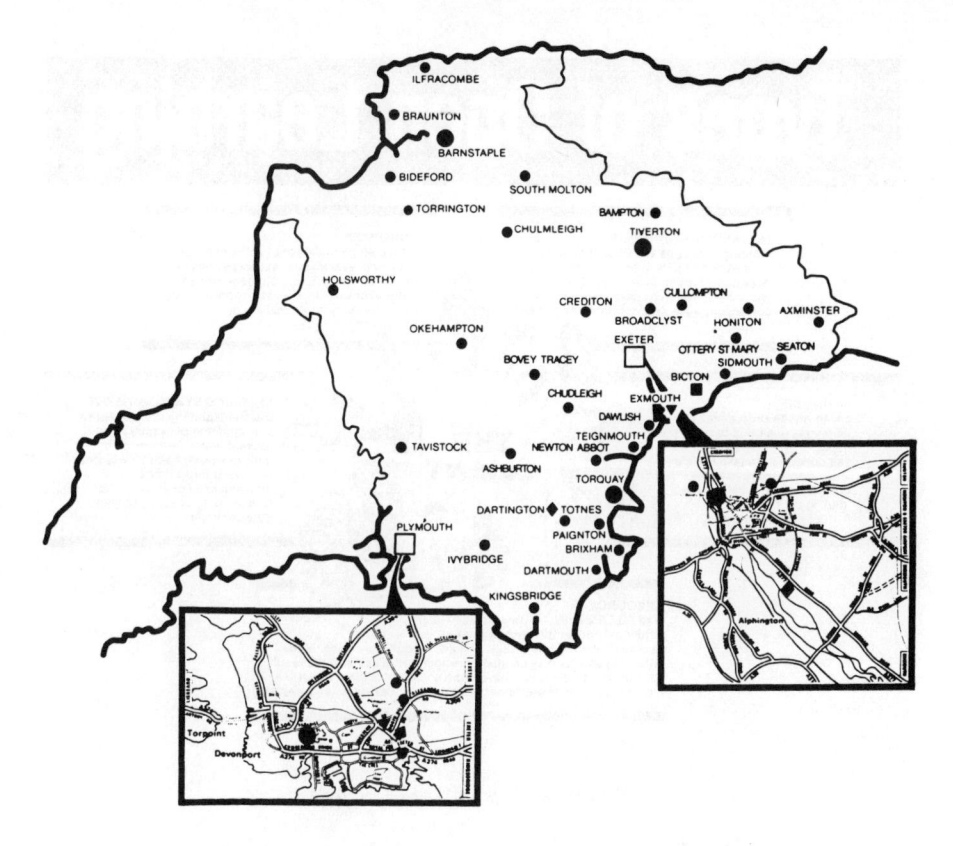

Figure 1. *Further education and community colleges in Devon*

Many mature people are also reluctant, for a number of reasons, to become part of a 'class' in what they think will be an academic atmosphere – one in which they feel at a disadvantage. Devon Open Tech is adding a new dimension to the existing service as a whole so that it can reach more people in ways which are convenient *to them*. It is helping all parts of the service to adopt more open and flexible types of courses which are more client-centred, eg those types shown in Figure 2.

Apart from the further education colleges in the county, there are 21 rural secondary schools which also provide an education service for adults and are designated as community colleges. There is also a strong network of centres within the community education service and an ethos of client-centredness which is in harmony with the expansion of open learning opportunities.

Work began two months before the official start of the project in order to prepare the detailed submission and agree the plans within the LEA and with the MSC. The main requirement of the MSC was that the project should develop a network of open learning support centres which could 'deliver' open learning and provide support to local learners. Since there are already about 100 other Open Tech projects producing open learning materials (and many other organizations also providing materials), Devon Open Tech does not have a brief to produce learning packages.

The main aim is to embed open learning principles and practices throughout the adult and further education service. In essence, many people know of and identify with their local 'Tech', and in Devon we are seeking to create a network of all the local

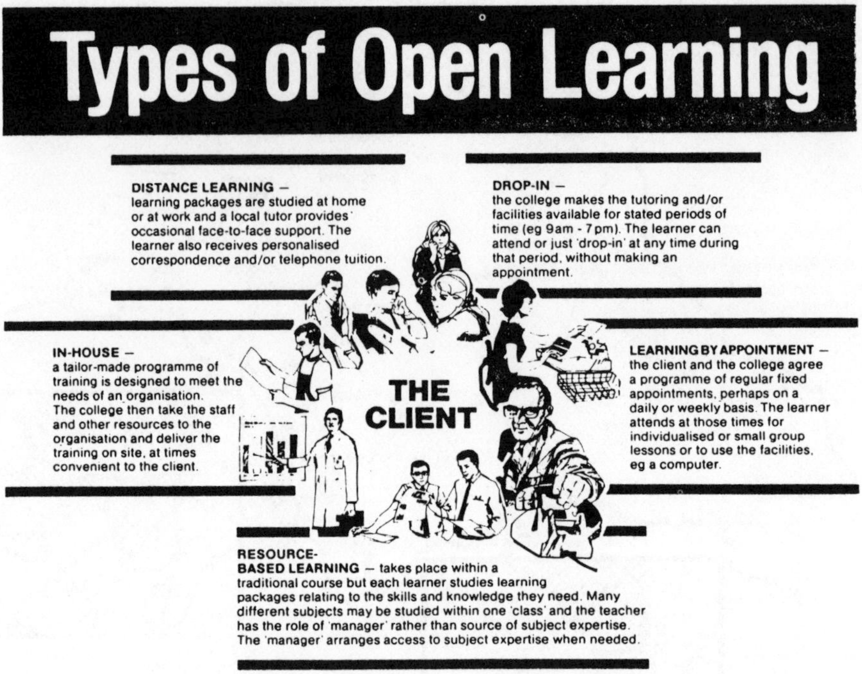

Types of Open Learning

DISTANCE LEARNING — learning packages are studied at home or at work and a local tutor provides occasional face-to-face support. The learner also receives personalised correspondence and/or telephone tuition.

DROP-IN — the college makes the tutoring and/or facilities available for stated periods of time (eg 9am - 7pm). The learner can attend or just 'drop-in' at any time during that period, without making an appointment.

IN-HOUSE — a tailor-made programme of training is designed to meet the needs of an organisation. The college then take the staff and other resources to the organisation and deliver the training on site, at times convenient to the client.

THE CLIENT

LEARNING BY APPOINTMENT — the client and the college agree a programme of regular fixed appointments, perhaps on a daily or weekly basis. The learner attends at those times for individualised or small group lessons or to use the facilities, eg a computer.

RESOURCE-BASED LEARNING — takes place within a traditional course but each learner studies learning packages relating to the skills and knowledge they need. Many different subjects may be studied within one 'class' and the teacher has the role of 'manager' rather than source of subject expertise. The 'manager' arranges access to subject expertise when needed.

Figure 2. *Types of open learning*

centres as a county-wide Open Tech, which gives people access to open learning opportunities at any point on the network. In setting up the project a degree of strategic independence from colleges has been adopted in terms of organization, in creating an appropriate identity and in locating the project base.

The actual service for any individual or employer may be assembled from several different elements and locations, eg learning materials from one source, tutorial support from another, and practical facilities at a third. One basic feature of our approach is to reflect the broad provision of the existing adult and further education service. Hence Devon Open Tech offers open learning in both vocational and non-vocational subjects. Over 200 subjects are now offered.

Planning and Developments So Far

The proposal included setting up a 'core' team of four, based in commercial office space in Exeter, comprising the project director, a deputy director, a financial administrator and secretary. At the Exeter base there is an administrative centre and a meeting/display/demonstration area. There is also a team of seven field officers (six full-time posts) responsible to the project director but working closely with further education and other colleges around the county and responding to client's needs. The core team was established in June 1985 and the field officers joined between July and September. The full team was therefore together for the first time at the beginning of the current academic year.

Staff Development

During the autumn, the team of field officers received training in some key areas of their roles, eg marketing, 'selling' the benefits of open learning, consultancy skills and supporting and tutoring open learners. The latter has been important because, even though the field officers do not normally act as tutors, they need to have a good knowledge of what is involved in order to enrol, guide and monitor tutors.

The county-wide register of tutors was started in October 1985 and there are now over 400 tutors registered. 70 have taken part in fortnightly workshops on supporting open learners as part of a continuing programme of staff development. All of the training and staff development aspects of the project have been carried out extremely well by the Open Tech Training and Support Unit (OTTSU), which has recently made the transition successfully from being an Open Tech project to a private consultancy company, OTSU Ltd.

Information Systems

During the early stages the information systems needed for the effective development and management of the project had also been planned and have been progressively introduced, almost all on computer, to assist in each of the following areas of work:

(a) marketing, research and intelligence;
(b) logging and analysis of enquiries;
(c) locating available learning resources (there is an online link from the Exeter office and from each field officer's base to the computer database of the Materials and Resources Information Service – MARIS – in Cambridge;
(d) matching client's needs to available learning resources or services;
(e) county-wide tutor register and records;
(f) student records;
(g) employer records;
(h) external organizations;
(i) budgetary planning and control;
(j) project management, evaluation and monitoring.

These information systems are already proving to be essential and will provide a firm organizational basis for the longer-term expansion and development of the project. Additional systems are being implemented to help with purchasing, stock control and sales of learning materials.

Marketing Strategy

Early publicity in the autumn of 1985 to test the market indicated much greater interest than the project was at that time able to cope with. The marketing strategy is therefore being developed very gradually so that the rate of enquiries grows as the capacity of the staff and systems to respond is increased. The amount of individualized guidance, counselling and advice needed by clients and the work involved in arranging suitable learning materials, tutorial support and other facilities was underestimated in the first instance. This difficulty arises out of the individualized nature of most open learning and the range of options which, in theory, are available to the client. It also arises partly from the absence of an educational guidance service for adults in the county – so that field officers' time has often been spent carrying out that function, which would not ideally be such a major part of their brief.

Apart from direct press advertising, there has been editorial coverage in local and regional newspapers, a two-page special supplement in one weekly free newspaper which went into 92,000 homes and businesses, and several interviews broadcast on local radio stations. The project has also published a leaflet for employers, one for individuals, a detailed booklet explaining Devon Open Tech to over 2,000 members of college staff and an occasional newsletter, aimed at the general public as well as people in the education service. A joint promotional exercise with the Council for Small Industries in Rural Areas (CoSIRA) is currently being targeted at about 400 firms. The Devon Open Tech exhibition stand has been used on about 15 occasions and is on show somewhere for about 60 per cent of the time.

It seems that there is a very large market for open learning if our small amount of early advertising is a reliable indication. The emphasis since then has been on finding ways of improving the speed and effectiveness of response to enquirers, on targeting the marketing activities more accurately and on communications directly to industry.

Official Launch

An important stage in the setting up of the project was reached in mid-October 1985, when the official launch conference and exhibition was held in Exeter. About 270 people packed the venue to hear the Rt Hon Dr David Owen, MP for Devonport, launch the project at what was regarded as a very successful event.

Growing Number of Learners

Since the start of the scheme in September 1985, the number of open learning students has now reached 200. Because the management and information systems and staff expertise are much better developed now than they were six months ago when the first learners were enrolled, the rate of increase in numbers of clients is likely to be greater during the next six months. There is now about one year of MSC funding left before the project will need to be sustained from its income and from other sources, and the clear objective is to increase the number of learners as quickly as possible, while remaining consistent with the proper development of systems of response, management and quality control.

Open learning may be a potential solution to the problem of maintaining a good range of subject options in the smaller school sixth forms if introduced in a carefully managed and monitored way. Nearly all of the county's 21 community colleges and some secondary schools have therefore approached Devon Open Tech for advice and some small-scale pilot exercises may be explored.

Conclusion

If Devon Open Tech can be successfully developed as part of the permanent continuing education and training scheme, it will enrich the county's service to the economy and to the community. If the principles and practices of open learning can be embedded into the mainstream of adult and further education, then education and training may begin to make an even more significant contribution to the lives of the half a million mature adults in Devon to whom it presently appears to be largely irrelevant or impossible.

The development of Devon Open Tech is part of the general drive to make the further education service more responsive. The experience so far suggests that the 'drive' will need to be sustained for at least a few years if it is to be successful. The total budget for the Devon Open Tech project is about half of one per cent of the county's further education budget. The total budget for the whole of the MSC's Open Tech programme is less than that, as a proportion of the national further education budget. In order to move open learning into the mainstream of further education and training, we shall probably need to convince policymakers that part of the existing budgets should be devoted to the longer-term process of helping the system to 'open up' and become more accessible to all.

2.7 Distance Learning Programmes for the Offshore Industry

A Watson, J A Ford and J T J Orr
Leith Nautical College, Edinburgh

Abstract: The Open Tech Programme is now becoming established as an effective means of developing and extending opportunities through open and distance learning for updating, upgrading and retraining adults at technician and supervisory levels of skill, in order to meet identified training needs and to assist personal development and aspirations.

The programme as a whole is targeted at a wide range of industries and Leith Nautical College has undertaken to design and develop a range of distance learning material aimed specifically at the offshore oil and maritime industries in subject areas such as rig stability and process control.

The college embarked upon the preparation of distance learning material for specific and individual company requirements some time ago. The effectiveness of that initial development work led to the award of the Open Tech Project in 1984, which serves the offshore and maritime industries on a much broader and altogether larger scale.

The aim of the paper is to present the design and operation of such a distance learning scheme and its related delivery strategy drawing on experience to date with schemes currently operating in the North Sea, and in particular to examine the potential benefits and cost-effectiveness of such a programme.

Introduction

This presentation opens by describing a particular training need in a particular industry at a particular time. How that need was satisfied, and how the result was developed into a major Open Tech project serving the offshore industry, forms the remainder of the presentation.

The Background

In the early 1980s, Britoil was operating two production platforms in the North Sea. The newer platform 'Beatrice' contained production processing and associated facilities controlled and monitored by a computer-based system. The older platform, 'Thistle', had been in production since 1978 and the more traditional pneumatic and analogue electronic equipment was being upgraded gradually to include computer-based systems.

The result of this upgrading was that technicians, skilled in the maintenance of the traditional equipment, found that they were being called upon to maintain the new computerized equipment without having the necessary background or training.

The Training Requirement

It was realized within the company that they had here a dual training requirement, namely:

1. Technicians who had recently become involved in new technology had to have the opportunity to develop this knowledge and skills.

2. In the longer term, all technicians would require to be updated in new technology as part of their career development.

Having identified the need the problem was how to satisfy it. The facts were as follows:

- all offshore personnel worked on a shift system with tight manning
- there were no personnel members to relieve technicians for training
- since the workload offshore was very heavy it was deemed essential that the personnel involved have uninterrupted rest periods in order to be at peak efficiency. For this reason, training during offshore rest periods was not encouraged by the company
- only when training was urgent or particularly important were arrangements made to release personnel
- with relatively large numbers to be trained, conventional training could be expensive and very difficult to implement.

The Possible Solution

The company approached Leith Nautical College late in 1982 to discuss the possibility of producing a custom-built training programme which could be operated on a distance learning basis to satisfy the requirements of the technicians.

In January 1983, at a meeting between Britoil training department and Leith Nautical College representatives, a structure of three courses to fulfil the requirements was agreed, each course to be approximately equivalent to a one week full-time residential course. It was decided that the first course be used as a pilot and a detailed content was discussed and approved.

The Pilot Course

The pilot course was entitled 'An Introduction to Digital Logic', and consisted of:

Written Material

The written material was divided up into modules of approximately 4 hours' study time each to give students recognizable targets.

Practical Material

So that students could get hands-on experience, a practical kit was chosen. This was an off-the-shelf battery- or mains-operated logic kit which had the capability of providing the opportunity to carry out experiments beyond the needs of the pilot course. It also therefore met the needs of succeeding courses.

Video Material

Due to the extent of the target audience, video material was produced. It was used to complement a booklet introducing the students to the course to develop mathematical points more easily than in the text; to introduce the student to the operation of the logic kit; and to demonstrate practical experiments which could not be carried out on the kit.

The course was intended for electrical and instrument technicians but was offered by the company on a voluntary basis to all technicians. The target response was approximately 25. This was easily reached and the final takeup was nearer 70.

The Delivery System

Leith Nautical College despatched all course material to Britoil training headquarters. Britoil staff delivered the material to the students, one module at a time. The first issue consisted of:

- student guide
- pre-course questionnaires
- module 1 materials
- practical kit
- pre-printed envelopes to return material
- videotapes.

As each module was completed, the necessary tests were returned to Leith Nautical College via Britoil training headquarters and the corrected materials returned to the student by the same route. Records were kept of student progress both with the company and with Leith Nautical College. Each student could, if he so desired, have direct contact with his college tutor either by post or 'phone.

Towards the end of the pilot course a sample number of participating students were interviewed in order to assess student reaction to the course and, as a result of the interviews, a questionnaire was sent to all participating students.

Finally students were required to attend the college for one day in order to complete final assessment and to carry out experiments which were not possible on the practical kit.

Initial Lessons Learned

1. The course had, in general, met the expectation of the students.
2. The video material and practical work was well received.
3. One to three hours seemed to be the normal study period used by the students.
4. The majority were definitely interested in further courses using similar distance learning techniques.
5. Due to the fact that the students were living and working in a closed environment, they were able to discuss and solve their problems together. The result of this was that there was no great demand for direct tutor contact.
6. The final one-day attendance at the college was abandoned as being unnecessary since it was found that the students had reached a level of ability satisfactory to the company without the additional cost and inconvenience which this involved.

Due to the success of the pilot course, a second course entitled 'Digital Electronics' was prepared and most students, having successfully completed the pilot course, then commenced the second course. The system operated with this course was similar to that used for the pilot course.

The experience gained from these two courses encouraged the college team to prepare a submission to the Manpower Services Commission to request funding through the Open Tech scheme for a project to produce a series of courses for the offshore and maritime industries in the distance learning format, the first of these being the third course in the series produced to the requirements of Britoil.

The proposal was considered and approved by the Manpower Services Commission for a three-year funding, commencing in April 1984.

The Open Tech Project

The award of this Open Tech project by the Manpower Services Commission (MSC) on 6 April 1984 was to be a milestone in moving from a relatively small-scale experimental distance learning scheme specific to Britoil into a major project, with a significant level of funding for the further design, development and testing of open access learning materials for technicians in the offshore oil and maritime industries. This was the beginning of a commercial enterprise with the aim of being self-financing by April 1987.

The agreed objectives of the project included:

1. the design, development and delivery of open learning materials to meet the identified training needs of the industry and to include the subject areas of instrumentation and control, microprocessor/microcomputer applications, digital systems, stability for semi-submersible rigs and hazardous cargo operations
2. the establishment of an active and effective collaboration with the industries and associated bodies
3. the establishment of an effective delivery network
4. the identification of staff development needs and the formulation and implementation of ways of meeting those needs
5. provision of the appropriate facilities for student support, counselling and registration
6. the systematic evaluation of materials and methods used in their preparation and delivery
7. the establishment of the appropriate organizational, managerial, administrative and financial arrangements to achieve the objectives.

Like most Open Tech projects, the MSC funding is intended to serve as 'pump-priming' to promote the development of a level of business activity and commercial expertise to ensure financial self-sufficiency beyond 1987.

Overall funding of the project is of the order of £200,000 per year for the three-year period, and is allocated to six major budget categories:

1. project management;
2. production;
3. delivery systems;
4. staff development;
5. marketing;
6. capital equipment.

Allocation of funding within the total budget is in line with the projected spending profiles of each category (Figure 1).

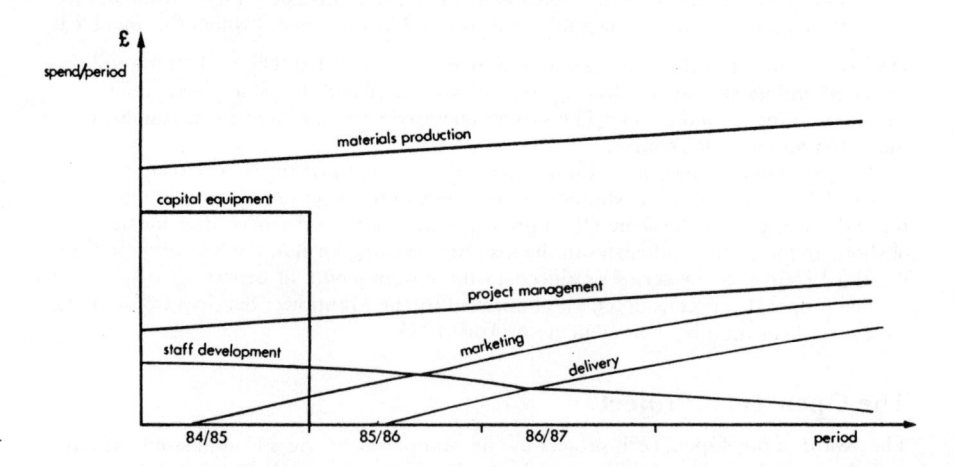

Figure 1. *Allocation of funding within the total budget*

An important feature of the Leith project is the support of open learning material by video. The MSC grant for capital equipment included finance for upgrading the existing video production facility already in the college to a modern, fully equipped production unit, producing on low-band U-matic and incorporating a range of electronic and digital effects units, allowing a high production quality of professional standard to be achieved.

Wider Activities

As the project staff have gained experience and developed their own expertise in the techniques of video production, the project has begun a deliberate move into the commercial production of video programmes for training and has already undertaken a small number of productions, the most important of which to date is a pilot project with the South of Scotland Electricity Board (SSEB) at the Torness nuclear power station, covering the operation of gas circulators in the nuclear reactor. This is an area of the project's business activity which it is intended to develop fully.

Project Structure

The project is guided on policy by a steering committee made up of representatives from the target industries, advisors from associated institutions and other interested bodies. Project staffing includes seven full-time, short contract staff, as well as part-time college staff. A number of external contributors, who are subject specialists, are also employed on a contract basis to write and evaluate materials (Figure 2).

Materials Development

From the college's earlier work with Britoil it was known that the target students would be working on a shift system in remote inaccessible locations and would live in areas scattered throughout the UK, or even abroad.

The design of good distance learning material, as well as an effective delivery system and support network, was seen to be crucial to achieving good 'first shot' delivery and to cope with the geographical spread of students.

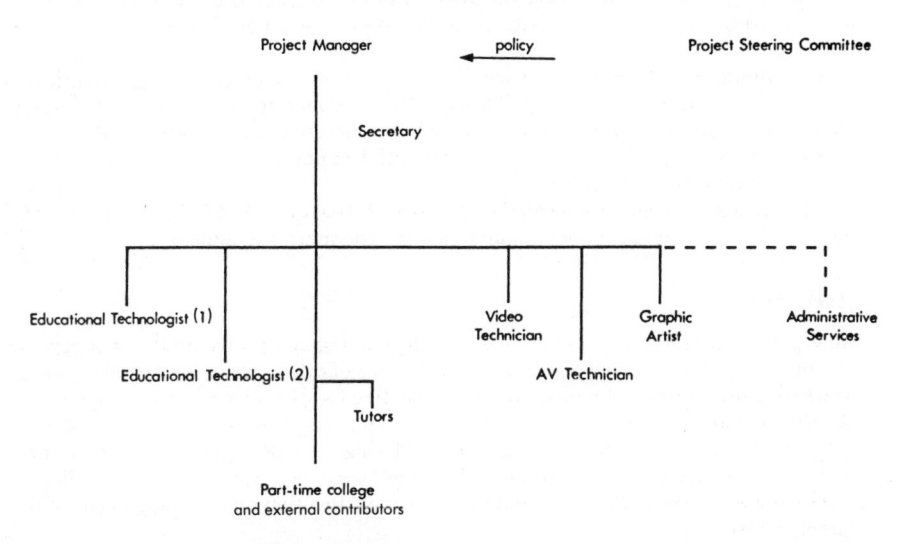

Figure 2. *Project staffing structure*

Each course is developed as a series of text study modules of approximately four hours' study, and is structured to be as active as possible. Self-assessments, worked examples and tutor-marked assignments are built in, with key topics covered by video, and practical work carried out where appropriate using a practical kit.

The project staff at the outset set about developing a house style which would satisfy the various design requirements of the learning materials and prepared a 'house style guide' in the form of a short publication which is now used by all authors as a firm guideline in preparing script. Further structuring of the text is subsequently carried out by the educational technologists, who then work closely with the author or editor to produce a final draft. They also advise on the use of supporting resources, including scripting for video.

Delivery Systems

Two delivery systems account for the majority of our work to date. The first of these operates in the same way as the original pilot scheme with Britoil. The company retains control of the administration of the scheme, and all materials are sent to the student through the company's training officer, who enrols the student, maintains records of progress, and directs all communications between the student and his tutor. In this way the company can directly monitor the operation of the scheme.

In the second system, the company plays no part in the administration of the scheme and the learning material is sent direct to the student's home address. The college is required to submit a monthly progress report to the training officer for his information. This system gives the college tighter control on the delivery mechanism.

Where appropriate, arrangements can be made for a student to gain access to practical facilities in his own home area through the MSC regional delivery networks and practical training facilities set up under the Open Tech Programme.

Open access is also offered to students who live or work in the local area and who are able to attend the college for face-to-face tutoring sessions or for access to practical facilities.

A third delivery system, used less frequently, directly involves other MSC delivery centres. They buy in the learning package and sell it on to the student in his own local area, with the support centre adding value to the package in the form of tuition and support. In this way, control over the delivery of the package is given to the centre, which must be able to demonstrate the ability to provide all of the necessary support to the student.

In addition, the 'Maritime Network', an association of colleges having a nautical or maritime interest, has been set up. These colleges co-operate in the delivery of a range of open and distance learning material which is either produced by the member colleges themselves or is bought into the network from other producers such as the National Extension College (NEC).

The member colleges are located on the British coastline. Individually they serve their local areas and as a national network serve the maritime industry.

Marketing

All Open Tech projects are concerned with developing acceptable products or services, without which they will fail to survive, irrespective of other strengths they may possess. Marketing objectives and policies have to be defined at the outset and must identify clearly the markets in which the products or services are appropriate in terms of geography and types of customer, as well as offering a credible plan for reaching the market which is consistent with other business objectives, such as pricing policy.

Good market research is essential to assess the education and training needs of the target industries.

In the case of the Leith project, the market research was directed at the offshore industry. It aimed to assess their understanding of and commitment to open learning as a training technique, and to identify subject areas for future development.

A target group of company training managers in the offshore and maritime industries was identified and surveyed through postal questionnaires and personal interviews.

The response rate was low, but the survey did serve to inform the target audience about the activities of the project and provided the basis for the development of an overall marketing strategy. The project has since been officially launched and is following a prepared marketing plan in order to promote its products and services to the industry further. This plan aims at promoting the activities of the project to the market through advertising and trade exhibitions as well as direct mail and personal selling.

It is hoped to continue to influence the training policies of the target industries towards an increasing commitment to open and distance learning as an effective means of meeting their training needs.

Conclusions

1. The student feedback so far is very encouraging and indicates that open learning is being well received.
2. The three delivery systems are proving to be effective in providing tutor support and practical facilities to the remote student.
3. The companies involved in the programme have reported significant cost savings by training through open learning.
4. The use of video provides an important means of communication and support to the remote student.
5. The student drop-out rate is low. This may be due, at least in part, to the fact that the company, having paid for the course, expects the student to complete it.
6. This project is demonstrating to the offshore industry that open learning can be successfully applied to meet their training needs.

Acknowledgements

The Open Learning Unit of Leith Nautical College wishes to acknowledge the advice and assistance given by the offshore industry in the development of this programme.

2.8 Considerations on the Co-ordination of Flexible Learning Initiatives in the Agricultural Industries

A R G Tallis and J St J Groome
Consultative Group for Training and Education in Agriculture

Abstract: During the 1970s the advisory, education and training services formed the Consultative Group for Training and Education in Agriculture (CGTEA) to make recommendations on issues of common interest. An issue which quickly emerged was open (flexible) learning, and the Open Learning group was therefore set up to investigate and make recommendations.

Due partly to the funding of curriculum development – mainly through PICKUP, Open Tech and local collaborative projects (LCPs) – there has been a considerable amount of interest in the subject. This has resulted in several areas of disconnected development activity with dangers of duplication, unnecessary competition and inefficient use of resources. Even LCPs are only collaborative locally, and selectively at that. This, together with the move towards more entrepreneurial extension services, resulted in the Open Tech funding a support project steered by the open learning group to encourage effective collaboration and efficient use of all the services available.

The paper outlines the reason for the project, how it was set up, in what activities it has been and intends to be engaged, problems encountered and solutions tried. The agricultural industry has its own advisory service, training board and mono-techs and can be regarded as a microcosm of a national system. Therefore the lessons learned can be applied in a wide context and are of general interest.

The Agricultural Extension and Development Services

The importance for Britain of approaching self-sufficiency in food was recognized many years ago by Government, which provided and financed an Agricultural Development and Advisory Service (ADAS) together with a number of agricultural research stations co-ordinated by the Agricultural and Food Research Council (AFRC). Their aim was to ensure British agriculture remained highly productive. A network of agricultural education establishments evolved providing further and higher education for existing and potential farmers and allied industries. 20 years ago the Agricultural Training Board (ATB) was set up with the objective of maximizing the effectiveness of all the services by actively encouraging skills training in the industry's workforce, so that new techniques and technology could be adopted (Figure 1).

Consultative Group for Training and Education in Agriculture (CGTEA)

Ten years ago, probably because funds were showing signs of drying up, the extension services decided to work together, trying to integrate their output and to avoid duplication and role conflict. Out of this the Consultative Group for Training and Education in Agriculture (CGTEA) was formed.

The CGTEA's role is to discuss issues of common interest and make recommendations, with which all members of the group agree. Initially, the group dealt with relatively unimportant matters, mainly connected with members' interrelationships, such as charges for courses and instruction provided by one member

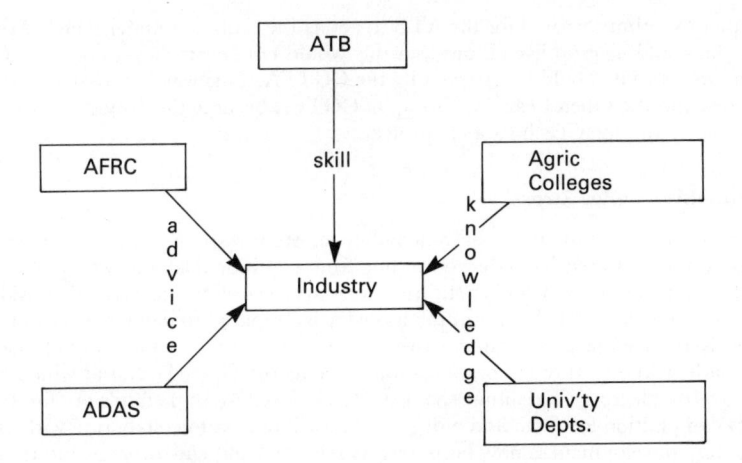

Figure 1. *Agricultural extension services*

for another. The first major issue tackled was the development of a preferred national youth training scheme for the industry. This is now in its third year, with an enrollment of five to six thousand trainees each year. The scheme is used as a model for schemes in other industries and is regarded as an exemplar by the Manpower Services Commission (MSC), who provide some of the finance.

Establishment of the Open Learning Group

Shortly after establishing the YTS working party, the group realized that there was rising interest in open learning and established the open learning group. The aims of this group were to:

- ☐ encourage open learning development for the industry;
- ☐ make recommendations on open learning development and delivery;
- ☐ co-ordinate initiatives and developments;
- ☐ encourage collaboration between developers;
- ☐ assist and advise on marketing and evaluation of open learning.

Shortly before the open learning group was set up, a committee operating in East Anglia and based at Essex College of Agriculture in Writtle published a report on open learning (Writtle Agricultural College, 1983). This identified the need for a structure to support open learning initiatives. The structure would have similar aims to the open learning group. Additionally, it pointed to the need for a small national material and course development unit. In order to investigate the extension services' opinion on these issues and open learning in general, an invitation seminar was held in 1983. The seminar report (CGTEA, 1983) included recommendations that the Open Learning Group should take on an executive function, particularly to co-ordinate initiatives in open learning funded by the recently established Open Tech unit of the MSC.

The CGTEA Open Tech Project

Following the seminar the Open Tech unit invited the ATB to develop a proposal for a scheme to co-ordinate Open Tech projects in the industry. The ATB believed that, if it was to do so on its own, there was unlikely to be any degree of co-operation and collaboration from and with other organizations. Therefore the proposal that was subsequently submitted was for the ATB to act as the umbrella under which a small secretariat could be established, but that this would not become a part of the ATB and that the secretariat should be directed by the CGTEA. This was eventually agreed by all parties and the Open Learning Group of CGTEA became the project steering committee of an Open Tech support project.

Relationships under Stress

During the last few years it has become policy for organizations funded by central and local government to receive reduced funding from traditional sources and to recover the fund shortfall from those who benefit from their services. This has created considerable competition for the limited amount the industry is prepared to pay for services it had previously received largely for free. At the same time a significant amount of finance is being made available through organizations such as the Open Tech unit which are charged with effecting curriculum changes. Again, because these funds are limited, there is competition for them and a degree of unwillingness to collaborate with others. Curriculum development is now becoming as secretive and cut-throat as industrial development. Flexible learning by its very nature leads organizations into extending their roles and responsibilities. This in turn leads to traditional role-boundary erosion and inevitably to role conflict. It has been stated that the promotion of open learning concepts has totally destabilized the whole extension service.

CGTEA Open Tech Support Project Objectives

The agreement with the MSC is based on the following objectives:

- to establish effective collaboration with other organizations;
- to advise providers of the Open Tech initiatives in agriculture and support the marketing process;
- to act as an enquiry centre for open learning in agriculture;
- to develop a framework for open learning initiatives and a model for open learning package dissemination;
- to find a means of financial support for open learning after Open Tech funds are exhausted;
- to assist those wishing to become involved in open learning delivery.

One of the project's first initiatives in 1985 was to produce a written 'framework' of open learning recommendations, activities, support availability and issues, which required clarification and determination, before open learning could be effectively integrated with the existing extension provision (Tallis and Watson, 1985). In order to attempt to gain support for the framework, concerned organizations were invited to a workshop to discuss and hopefully determine some of the issues. The report of the workshop and the recommendations arrived at were included as essential parts of the framework. 'Collaboration' was considered the key to ensuring successful adoption, though the usual list of organizational constraints were also identified. Full collaborative development was seldom likely to be the answer. There was a place for individual organizations winning and keeping their own share of funds and of the market, and for small groups of organizations sharing funds and forming partnerships. Immediately after the workshop the project was able to employ the services of Jeremy Groome. So at last there was a project co-ordinator, practically full-time, without existing loyalties to any of the factions engaged in open learning, who was able to give the project the concentrated attention that was required.

Providers and their Problems

The allocation of MSC Open Tech funding to the agricultural and horticultural industries for the three years from 1984–5 to 1986–7 totalled about £1,300,000, which was divided between the following projects:

Topic (1)	Authoring Organization (2)	Budget (3)
Arable	Lincolnshire College	194,500
Grassland	Welsh Agricultural College	171,500
Mushrooms	ATB	120,000
Engineering	West Suffolk College of FE	134,100
Microelectronics	East Devon College of FE	310,950
Land based leisure	Capel Manor Institute	393,000

(1) This list does not include sub-contracted topics of fish farming and forestry.
(2) Contract holder is listed, but not the various collaborating partners.
(3) £85,000 from MSC and £35,000 from ATB.

Figure 2. *Allocation of MSC funds for the promotion of open learning materials in horticulture and agriculture*

No funding was made available for large sectors of the industry, such as field and glasshouse horticulture, non-ruminant livestock or any of the allied industries. The funding allocated to Writtle College as pump-priming to prepare material on farm accounts and business management was never utilized and, unfortunately, the monies were not re-allocated within the industry.

On a geographical basis, the allocation was haphazard with no allocation in Scotland and, with the exception of a small collaborative contribution from Seale Hayne College in Devon, no experience in writing open learning material has been gained by any agricultural college south of Bedfordshire. Such a polarized distribution quickly lost open learning friends in all the deprived sectors.

As mentioned above, the requirements forced on institutions to bid for Open Tech funds created competition between educationalists and trainers. This has subsequently limited co-operation in other areas. The lack of institutional experience in subcontracting writers has also led to a wide range of financial and copyright agreements. These are likely to contribute to restricting access to material when it does eventually become available.

This isolation of the writing groups has reduced the potential usefulness of the initiative as a series of pilot projects investigating package formats. The utilization of any central body as a monitoring organization has, so far, been rejected as too sensitive and the likelihood of any short-term evaluation being implemented is ruled out because of the limited timescale of the current funding. All the projects are indeed running in parallel due to Open Tech funding policy. The opportunity to run one or two pilot projects to identify the range of pedagogical, technical and administrative/marketing needs was not taken. Projects are therefore individually discovering new techniques and making similar or the same mistakes – a highly costly experience!

Open Learning and the Market

All the MSC projects have been developed by county-based, or at best regional, organizations. The delivery network established by the Open Tech unit leaves many large rural areas uncatered for, and the national organizations of ADAS and ATB are likely to be overlooked or may decide not to be involved in the marketing of the new learning materials. As these nationally-based organizations have achieved only a shallow penetration of the market over the last decade, there must be concern that the Open Tech deliverers, with a much broader market to service, will not be able to attain any better results. The major concern is that the open learning deliverers will end up competing with the current established provision, rather than identifying their own market niche.

To be entirely honest no one knows if growers/farmers will respond to open learning – the market has not yet been tested comprehensively. Small-scale individual surveys conducted through PICKUP in the West Midlands by the TUFF (Training and Updating For Farmers) Project based at Harper Adams College and by EARAC (East Anglian Regional Advisory Committee) at Shuttleworth Agricultural College have indicated the reverse. Farmers like contact with their contemporaries, have well-established communication networks and like training to be locally oriented.

CGTEA Support Project

The support project, with MSC funding of £105,000, was the last in the sector to be manned, which immediately created problems in trying to contribute to the servicing of the material production projects. The major tasks, developed from the contractual objectives listed above, were:

- to develop an awareness campaign throughout the industry;
- to establish a communications network between the various materials producers;
- to develop a corporate reputation for open learning with the potential intermediaries and users;
- to supply specialist services to materials producers either on an individual or group basis.

The first task had been addressed before the project was manned through the collaborative workshop held in 1985. This attracted 76 participants who formed a useful core of contacts. It is a healthy feature of the scheme that the support project contract with the MSC requires it to liaise with all institutions involved in open learning and not just the Open Tech projects. Contact has been maintained through a series of more or less regular newsletters, newsflashes and information updates. In addition, the support project has taken on the role of promoting the packages through various educational databases and course directories. These include the PICKUP short course directory, ECCTIS, TTNS and MARIS. A contract has also been taken out with Farmlink to develop a new register of open learning programme availability.

One of the major problems requiring ongoing attention is the integration of open learning with the current provision. Group discussion with college staff goes some way towards allaying employment fears but there is a general feeling that this is not winning any battles. Therefore a new approach has been adopted whereby college-based, non-residential, adult-oriented courses are being promoted alongside the open learning provision. This will allow learners to make their own decisions. Plans are in hand with MARIS-NET to develop such a database, which will come online by the middle of the year.

The Open Learning Group steering committee was expanded to include representation from all the materials-producing projects and thus at a superficial level it was quite easy to establish a project network. However, if anything more intellectual was going to develop, there was a need to gain the confidence of the individual project managers. This has not been easy because of the close association of the secretariat with the ATB which is seen as a major competitor in the open learning stakes.

The development of a corporate reputation has perhaps been the easiest task to achieve, through the production and distribution of leaflets and information packs on

OPEN LEARNING OPPORTUNITIES IN

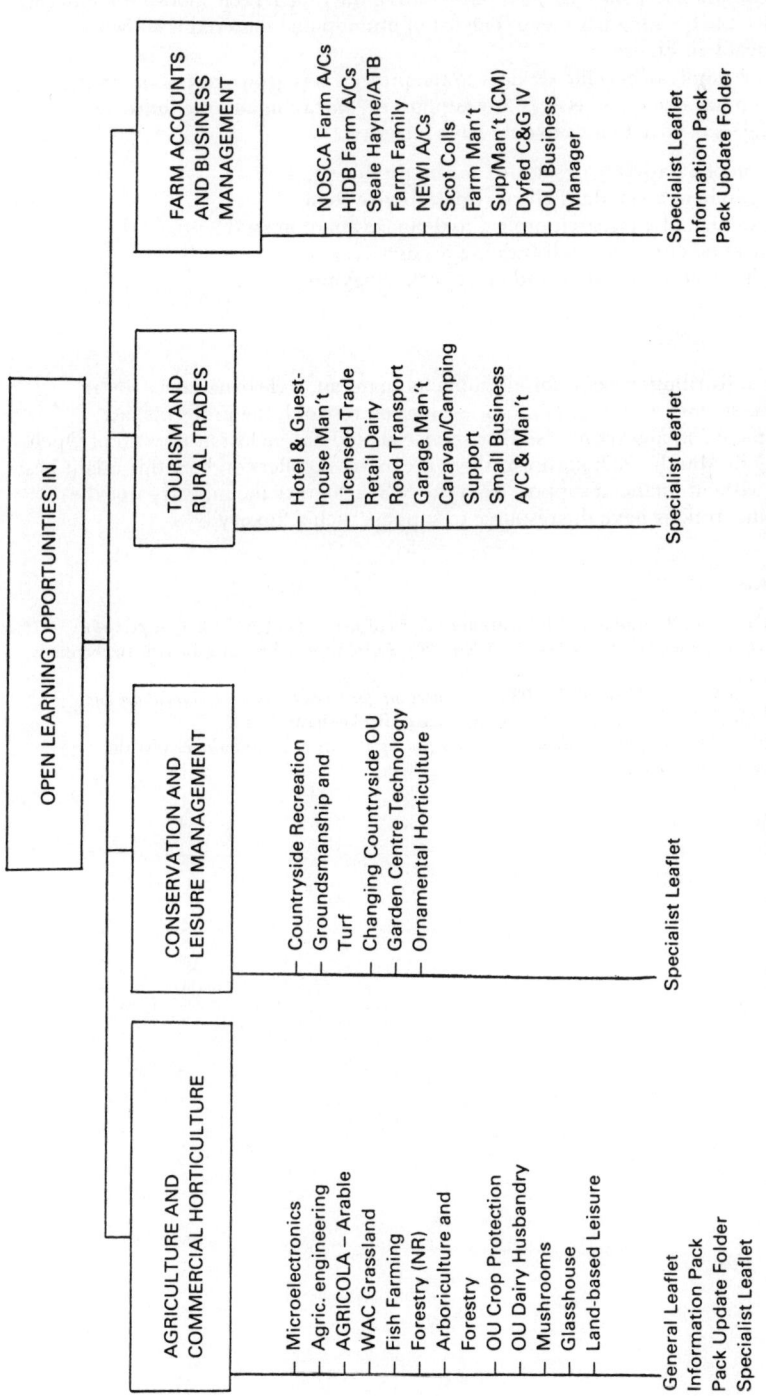

AGRICULTURE AND COMMERCIAL HORTICULTURE
- Microelectronics
- Agric. engineering
- AGRICOLA – Arable
- WAC Grassland
- Fish Farming
- Forestry (NR)
- Arboriculture and Forestry
- OU Crop Protection
- OU Dairy Husbandry
- Mushrooms
- Glasshouse
- Land-based Leisure

General Leaflet
Information Pack
Pack Update Folder
Specialist Leaflet

CONSERVATION AND LEISURE MANAGEMENT
- Countryside Recreation
- Groundsmanship and Turf
- Changing Countryside OU
- Garden Centre Technology
- Ornamental Horticulture

Specialist Leaflet

TOURISM AND RURAL TRADES
- Hotel & Guesthouse Man't
- Licensed Trade
- Retail Dairy
- Road Transport
- Garage Man't
- Caravan/Camping Support
- Small Business
- A/C & Man't

Specialist Leaflet

FARM ACCOUNTS AND BUSINESS MANAGEMENT
- NOSCA Farm A/Cs
- HIDB Farm A/Cs
- Seale Hayne/ATB
- Farm Family
- NEWI A/Cs
- Scot Colls
- Farm Man't
- Sup/Man't (CM)
- Dyfed C&G IV
- OU Business Manager

Specialist Leaflet
Information Pack
Pack Update Folder

Figure 3. *CGTEA – Open Learning Group materials promotion profile*

the various courses and packages, again integrating the Open Tech sponsored material with other flexible learning packages. The list of promotional material is shown diagrammatically in Figure 3.

Finally, the supply of specific services to the projects has grown out of the improving confidence that has emerged between the support organization and the individual project managers. The activities to date have included:

- provision of a database of selected media producers;
- investigation of a standard client registration system;
- establishment of a research project to define evaluation strategy;
- identification of project staff training needs;
- fire-fighting administrative and office technology problems.

Future Opportunities

By acting as a distribution point for all publicity material, a clearing house for all database accesses and as a focal point for evaluation research the project is fast becoming sensitive to market needs. This service should not be lost at the end of Open Tech funding in March 1987; however, there are as yet no offers on how this might best be achieved without financial support from the MSC. Neither the industry nor the educational institutions have the resource to support such a 'luxury'!

References

Consultative Group for Training and Education in Agriculture (CGTEA) (1983) *Report of a Seminar on Open Learning in Agriculture 19/20 July 1983*. Agricultural Training Board, Beckenham, Kent.

Tallis, A R G and Watson, N R (eds) (1985) *A Framework for Open Learning in Agriculture and Commercial Horticulture*. Agricultural Training Board, Beckenham, Kent.

Writtle Agricultural College (1983) *Distance Learning in Agriculture and Horticulture*. Writtle Agricultural College, Essex.

2.9 Flexible Learning Systems: Process Technology – Glass

A Hirst and A Hearsum
Glass Training Ltd, Sheffield
M Cross
Wakefield District College

Abstract: Glass Training Ltd is a non-statutory training organization covering approximately 40,000 employees. As part of its role in pioneering new training activities to meet the changing needs of industrial personnel, it has taken the initiative to develop flexible learning schemes, in particular two open learning ventures.

One such venture, aiming to update and develop a more competent workforce, has been developed jointly by the industry, Wakefield District College and Glass Training Ltd. This development has already demonstrated clearly that changes in learning methodology can produce remarkable results and benefits, when the commitment is there from all parties, co-operating to achieve agreed aims.

The choice of tuition, employer support and quality learning materials are paramount to ensure success when abandoning traditional teaching methods in favour of a flexible adult learning strategy. Here the shift is towards the student, and his/her own management of learning and development.

Introduction

Glass Training Ltd (GTL) is a non-statutory training organization covering approximately 40,000 employees in the glass industry. It was formed three and a half years ago at the demise of the statutory training board. It operates very differently from its predecessor, and far more successfully, in that it helps to provide objective training enabling companies to improve their performance.

GTL has taken many initiatives and pioneered new training activities. Flexible learning systems is one of our fields of interest.

We do receive some funds from the Manpower Services Commission (MSC) but this exercise has so far been solely funded by ourselves. It has proved to be a first-rate investment, not just because of the outstanding BTEC results or the new methodology of development of individual students, but for wider reasons.

The Glass Container Industry

Bottle-making used to be achieved by traditional manual skills with employees working in small self-contained teams. With the advent of mechanization, organizations developed into functional structures with rigid job definitions. The structure was mechanistic, not built for change – in fact, it resisted any forces for change. It has not entered the integration phase, where the requirement is for an integrated system with human and organizational goals combined – employees take initiatives, set objectives, have some freedom to operate and are acknowledged as an important resource. A flexible and responsive workforce is needed.

Could we find a flexible learning system to help us? It has to be flexible, for container manufacture is a continuous process – 24 hours a day, 360 days a year. The four days off are at Christmas, not Hogmanay. Employees work a continental shift system which means their hours of work vary from week to week. We knew Wakefield College were active in the field of flexible learning, so contact was made and they responded. Malcolm Cross was our contact, and he has led the development of the scheme described here.

Flexible Learning in the Glass Industry

How was this exciting co-operative venture started two years ago?

Wakefield District College has for many years been involved in developing flexible learning and readily joined forces with GTL and the industry it represents to develop a flexible programme of study. The programme aims to overcome the difficulties already outlined and suits the needs of the craft and operator levels of employee who hitherto have had very little opportunity to participate in any further education and training.

After much discussion, the decision was made to have a scheme that would give a nationally recognized qualification, be technologically relevant to the industry and also consciously aim to develop the student in the wider sense.

The final programme met the criteria of the Business and Technician Education Council (BTEC), the validating and certification body, in both content and mode of delivery but more importantly it meets the needs of industry as perceived today.

At least 20 meetings were held with all the interested parties and by this very close co-operation and liaison, particularly with the industrial representation, we not only made sure that we were getting the content right and sorting out the broader aims, but we were also ensuring a better understanding on the part of all the participants.

Aims of Scheme

The aims of the scheme are to give workers in the glass industry, particularly those at craft and operator level, the opportunity to participate in a programme of study with the primary aim of improving business performance which:

1. develops more effective communication and study skills;
2. is industrially relevant;
3. updates technical knowledge and introduces new technologies;
4. broadens his/her horizons and improves educational standards;
5. gives an awareness and an appreciation of the roles of others in his/her company organization;
6. develops a positive attitude to problem-solving and teaches techniques that enable a critical evaluation of the work situation;
7. develops personal effectiveness, is part of career development and when suitable assists in staff identification for future needs;
8. provides acknowledgement of the student's efforts, commitment and standard of achievement by a nationally recognized qualification;
9. contributes to the development of a more flexible, responsive and competent workforce;
10. has a system of learning and personal development which is positive, supportive and which demonstrates empathy with the student.

Units of study that make up the programme are a mixture of national standard units and college/industry devised units. Also, some of the standard units were amended to be more relevant to the glass industry.

The units and sequence of study are as follows, although they may well be amended as our experience grows and a fuller understanding of industrial needs develops.

Programme of Study – April 1986

mathematics
physical science
general and communication studies
glass technology A

plant technology
glass technology B
instrumentation systems
general and communication studies
mathematics (1)

fault-finding
glass technology C
plant maintenance processes
process measurement
use of computers

mathematics
computer assignment
safety in process industry
plant and process control

glass technology D
plant and process control (glass)
project

Learning material has come from various sources, bought in or written by Wakefield District College and other agencies under the auspices of the Manpower Services Commission (MSC) Open Tech in Glass Manufacture project.

The specialist glass technology units use learning packages developed for a programme of study in glass manufacture developed by GTL, again under the auspices of the MSC.

The Modules

The seven modules studied (equivalent to three units of study) are as follows:

1. the nature of glass
2. raw materials and batch mixing
3. the glass preparation process
4. glass melting furnaces
5. glass forming processes
6. glass faults and glass annealing
7. secondary processes for glass.

Selection and counselling of students is obviously critical when embarking on such a system of learning, particularly in respect to the time commitment. We are confident that we will improve with these procedures and are looking to develop further schemes to match the need.

Currently students are basically in two main areas, South Yorkshire and Lancashire. Marked differences already exist between the two areas in many facets of the scheme. For example, in Yorkshire there has been only 1 withdrawal out of 37 to date, whereas in Lancashire there is more than a 50 per cent dropout. The involvement of company personnel differs and, to some extent so does the mode of delivery, but one thing is common: the very high standard of achievement by everyone studying on the programme.

In Yorkshire, of the 69 units assessed, 44 were of distinction level (80 per cent), a figure confirmed by the BTEC moderator who, like the tutors and students involved, is highly delighted.

The significance of such high standards and the all-round commitment that is being made has yet to be fully appreciated by all the sponsors.

The motivation of the students in making the best of this new opportunity is exciting and the organizers look forward to more participants on the scheme.

A feature of the development process is to regularly review the successes of the scheme and use these experiences to improve the process and validation aspects.

Sample Student Profiles

The profiles given below indicate the type of students attracted by the scheme:

Kenneth R. married 1 child
Redfearn National Glass (Barnsley)
Engineering fitter and union convenor
City & Guilds Full Tech. in Engineering
    (part-time day and evening)
Left school at 15 years
Age: 31

Vince C. married family
Redfearn National Glass (Barnsley)
Trainer sorter (previously self-employed salesman)
No previous qualifications
Left school at 14/15 years
Age: 42

Donald L.* married 2 children
Beatson Clark (Rotherham)
Sorter (previously paper mill worker)
No previous qualifications
Left school at 16 years
Age: 39
* most outstanding student on this course, with distinctions in all unit assessments

Sharon P. married
Redfearn National Glass (Barnsley)
Laboratory technician
HTC physical chemistry (part-time day study)
Left school at 16 years
Age: 29

The essential tutoring is arranged in-house. For example, at Redfearn National Glass, Barnsley, two Wakefield District College staff are in attendance from 12.00 hours to 18.00 hours to accommodate various shift patterns. There is a similar arrangement at Beatson Clark (Rotherham), Rockware Glass (Doncaster) and Pilkington Bros (St Helens). The companies provide excellent facilities and resource backup. At Readfearn National Glass, when specialist glass technology expertise is required, the tutors are able to call upon the company's glass technologist. At St Helens it is the college tutor who provides the glass technology expertise, which helps to illustrate how the scheme can accommodate any particular situation and company or individual interpretation.

We do not know all the answers, nor the difficulties yet to be appreciated in this complex and sophisticated adult learning strategy, but we face the future with confidence.

The programme is not cheap for the industrial sponsors, but very much cheaper than the traditional provision which depends on the release of the student from his place of work, which is becoming increasingly difficult, if not impossible.

Currently the cost in Yorkshire is approximately £2,500 for a full study programme leading to a BTEC Ordinary National Certificate in Engineering (Process Technology – Glass).

The scheme organizers and industrial partners do plan to carry out specific evaluation and a more positive marketing strategy to sell the benefits of such an innovative approach, which is attempting so much more than the traditional off-the-job training courses.

Summary

Glass Training Ltd has welcomed the effort from the further education sector on this project, particularly the enthusiasm of Malcolm Cross of Wakefield District College, to make the project succeed. The primary role of Glass Training Ltd is to help our companies discover and manage successful training initiatives which improve business performance. BTEC in process technology is only one of many achievements developed on a collaborative basis with other training providers.

Glass Training Ltd will work with anyone who has something to offer which makes learning easier and more flexible. The main benefit of using Glass Training Ltd is to help companies select the most economic quality training provision related to any programme of change.

2.10 The Application of Flexible Learning to Training in Craft Courses

J G Taylor
Skills Training Agency, Manpower Services Commission, Sheffield

Abstract: The Skills Training Agency (STA) has, over the last 18 months, researched and developed schemes to make its training more flexible and therefore more attractive to customers and learners. One approach has been the development and use of open learning materials within a number of courses. Several learning packages have been piloted in skill centres. Some packages have been purchased from open learning material producers; others have been produced in-house.

This report describes the production and piloting of an open learning package on bonding knowledge in bricklaying. 'Bonding' is the arrangement of bricks within a structure to achieve maximum strength. The package was produced by STA staff. It was piloted in ten skill centres to measure its benefits for learning effectiveness. A total of 40 learners took part in the pilot. Results showed an average saving of 18 hours of instructor time per learner by using the package. More than 80 per cent of the learners preferred this method of learning to classroom teaching for coverage of the knowledge concepts in the course. They asked that more learning material be presented in this form.

Introduction

The Skills Training Agency (STA) was established as a separate agency within the Manpower Services Commission (MSC) on 1 April 1983. Its task is to provide an efficient, up-to-date range of training services that are responsive to changing training needs. The services are provided through its network of 60 skill centres and the newly formed Mobile Training Service.

The agency provides training services on a fee-paying basis to the Commission's training division and to employers. About 95 per cent of the income earned during 1984/85 was from the training division. Most of this was for training of unemployed adults on Job Training Schemes (JTS). The income earned from these services must cover expenditure so that the books are balanced each year.

Training offered by skill centres had traditionally been associated with construction, engineering, motor vehicle maintenance, welding and fabrication practices. There is a change in the range of services now being offered. The move is towards training in skills relevant to present-day needs, including the application of new technologies and more local, flexible and modular delivery. Access to skill centres for training is being increased through evening and weekend working. In the last 18 months, the STA has researched and developed the application of open learning as a way of increasing the flexibility of training delivery in many of its courses. Results obtained from this approach are presented in the report.

The Open Tech programme has focused on funding schemes for material production and delivery systems applicable to adult training in technician, supervisory and management skills. The initial materials produced had limited application in STA courses run at the time. It was therefore decided that the STA would produce a number of open learning materials for trial. Materials have been produced in the areas of bricklaying, carpentry/joinery, vehicle electronics, CNC machining and trainer training. Since that decision was made, a wide range of materials have become available from other producers. Several have been bought to cover the areas of electronics, computer application, industrial measurement, pneumatics, handling hazardous materials and safe lifting practices. All have been validated in skill centres to assess their value and potential application.

This report focuses on the STA production of an open learning package and its validation in bricklaying courses run for unemployed adults. It includes results of that validation and its implementation for cost-effective flexible learning.

Production of an Open Learning Package

The first open learning package produced in the STA was developed for use in bricklaying courses. There were several reasons for this choice and these were:

- (a) the annual intake of learners to this type of course averages 2,000;
- (b) this intake represents a significant portion of total throughput of learners in skill centres;
- (c) a new national training syllabus has been established by the construction industry which necessitates inclusion of additional related knowledge;
- (d) coverage of the new syllabus demands additional course attendance time and hence extra costs;
- (e) the principal customer for the course preferred not to fund additional costs;
- (f) there was no existing learning material of immediate value for ensuring that the new syllabus was covered in the standard duration.

The open learning pack was designed to cover sufficient knowledge items in the new syllabus to avoid increasing the course duration. Factors for consideration in pack design were:

- (a) learner group and their reading age;
- (b) motivation of learner group to study partly in their own time;
- (c) cost of pack should be acceptable to training organization;
- (d) pack should incorporate elements of learning to develop practical skills;
- (e) pack use by learner should minimize support of instructors;
- (f) outcome of pack use by learners should be credible, ie acceptable by examining body.

A member of staff was delegated for design and production of the pack. He had worked in the agency for several years, partly as a bricklaying instructor and subsequently as a general tutor for instructor training. A programme was organized so that both he and other staff could be acquainted with open learning methodology. The programme was led by consultants from the Open Tech Training and Support Unit (OTTSU). The programme consisted of consultant-led workshops and guided practice over a period of four months. At the end of this, the pack design was begun.

The starting point for design of the pack content was the City and Guilds Certificate Syllabus in Brickwork and Masonry (588) and the work of the Construction Industry Training Board (CITB) in meeting objectives established in the New Training Initiative. From analysis of information gained from the above bodies, the decision was made to produce a pack on 'principles of bonding'. Learning bonding knowledge and skills is begun at the start of any bricklaying course and continues through to advanced stages. It is an underlying and continuous part of the course.

The finished pack consists of nine modules, each of which demand about two hours' study time. Each module is free-standing and deals with a particular aspect of bonding. For example, module 1 covers principles of bonding, whereas module 9 deals with bonding squint corners in half a quarter lap. The pack comprises of a set of plastic miniature bricks and ceramic blocks. These are for use in experiments described in the modules. The learner must carry through a series of experiments where dry bonding is practised. These experiments replace those normally done by bricklayer trainees on a building site. They provide opportunities for the learner to practise and consolidate the principles of bonding. Since the pack is self-contained, it gives the learners flexibility to learn at their own pace and when it suits them.

Validation of the Bonding Pack

Once completed, arrangements were made to try out the pack in a number of skill centres. Objectives of the trial were to determine

(a) if learners can achieve their learning objectives through use of the pack;
(b) acceptance of this mode of flexible learning by various groups of learners;
(c) the development needs of instructors involved in managing flexible learning systems;
(d) if course duration can be reduced without detriment to performance standards;
(e) the cost-effectiveness of flexible learning systems in comparison with traditional training methods;
(f) the skill centre administration requirements for effective delivery of this form of flexible learning.

The trial was planned in conjunction with a senior psychologist. Ten skill centres participated in the trial, and each nominated one bricklayer instructor to use the package in classes. A two-day workshop was attended by all instructors in order to familiarize them with the package and method of validation. Some time was also given to open learning methodology, since none of the instructors had been involved in this mode of learning delivery. The workshop was very valuable. Instructors were motivated by the package and worked through it during the workshop. Agreement was reached to carry out the trial in the following ways:

(a) four learners were selected by each instructor to work with the package;
(b) instructor support was made available to those learners, but only on request;
(c) learner response was monitored at a distance;
(d) learners were tested on completion of the pack;
(e) instructors and learners were interviewed using a structured format on completion of the pack.

Validation Results

A total of 40 learners participated over a 3-month period. On completion, all the modules were inspected and then returned for the learners to keep. All instructors and learners involved were interviewed by the psychologist at the end of the validation programme. Results obtained are discussed in the following sections.

	% of Learners
Have done some bricklaying in college course	5
Have done labouring with bricklayers	30
Have done labouring but not with bricklayers	25
No work experience but some DIY	20
No experience since leaving school	30

Figure 1. *Pre-entry experience of learners participating in validation trial*

Learner response

Learner response to the package was good. Most had no prior experience of bricklaying, as can be seen in Figure 1. In most cases, learners quickly gained confidence in use of the pack and worked through it independently. The need for instructor intervention and guidance during related practical work was less with those who had studied the pack than those who had not. Results from the test, carried out on completion of the syllabus content in the pack, showed that learners had absorbed and retained the principal concepts. Figure 2 shows that 80 per cent of the learners preferred this method of learning to conventional methods used in skill centres (ie classroom sessions). Most asked that more material be presented in this way, because

(a) it could be easily understood;
(b) mistakes made in private saved embarrassment in front of others;
(c) major points were covered.

	% of Learners
Prefer traditional learning modes	12
Unable to decide	8
Prefer learning by the open learning method as exemplified by bricklaying pack	80

Figure 2. *Learner preference for learning mode*

Instructor Response

Some instructors delivered the whole pack at once so that learners could proceed from start to finish; others delivered it in stages, usually one module at a time. In the second mode, instructor and learner interaction was encouraged at the end of each stage. Instructors using the latter mode did so to improve monitoring of the learning process and measure learner time spent on each module. Both methods produced similar end results and no clear preference was established by instructors or learners.

Demand on instructor time was reduced by those learners involved. On average, the pack saved about 18 hours of instructor time per learner. Some instructors considered the figure was as high as 24 hours. This enabled more time to be spent with learners not involved with the pack. Use of the pack generated much interest in the learner group. Those learners involved appeared very enthusiastic and the others asked to be involved in part of the programme. In some cases, instructors drew in more learners to participate.

The two-day workshop for instructors involved was sufficient to give the necessary backup information. The role of instructors in an open delivery system was however still important. Some learners would still need help and reassurance whilst learning in this mode.

Discussion

Validation trials have shown that this mode of open learning delivery is acceptable to adult learners in STA bricklaying courses. Acceptance of this flexible learning approach depends on meeting specific criteria of quality, which include:

(a) learning material relevant to the course of study;
(b) language appropriate to the level of the learner's understanding;
(c) material which incorporates facilities for learner to assess progress;
(d) material which is not too patronizing to the learner.

Further trials are proceeding to validate open learning material in other craft courses. Results so far support the findings made for the bricklaying package.

Experiences gained during validation indicate that not all learners respond to this method of learning. Selection of the learner group was determined by instructor expectations of those considered able enough to learn this way. It is considered though that with some development, most learners would quickly adapt to a self-study procedure, which is crucially important in an open learning delivery system. More attention should therefore be given to the development of individuals in learning to learn.

Not all instructors readily adapt to managing a flexible learning delivery system. In the validation programme described, support was obtained from managers of all the skill centres involved. This support proved vital in the early stages where a small number of instructors had some misgivings about the likely benefits. Despite the two-day workshop, further development was needed for that small number and some coaching was carried out. Production and validation costs were monitored throughout the programme. In-house production of the bricklaying package has been financially attractive and helped to develop staff in open learning methodology. Unit costs of production have been analysed to determine the price per hour of learning covered. This is the yardstick used by other producers of open learning material. The following have been included in the analysis:

(a) all costs for development of staff associated with the package production;
(b) costs of validation programme;
(c) staff resources used in producing pack;
(d) costs of producing 1,000 finished learning packs.

Assuming that the package has covered 18 hours of learning, the unit price per hour is approximately £3.00. This is much less than prices quoted for other open learning producers. Furthermore, use of the package makes no extra demands on skill centre resources other than the need for instructors to be capable of administering this delivery method. Present-day charges for skill centre courses in bricklaying show the package cost to be just acceptable. However, additional advantages of flexibility in use of the pack make it an attractive means of training delivery. Furthermore, the unit price quoted would decrease if the market copes with a larger production than 1,000. Subsequent in-house production of open learning packs is expected to further decrease costs as a result of the increase of expertise.

Summary

Production of the first open learning package on bricklaying and its validation has proved to be a very useful development exercise for STA staff in open learning methodology. Both learners and instructors have responded favourably to this form of learning delivery. Use of the package has reduced the amount of time instructors need to spend in contact with learners. The average saving amounts to 18 hours per trainee but is higher in some cases. The saving and acceptance by learners increases the flexibility of learning delivery by enabling the instructor to:

(a) control the delivery rate of learning of knowledge elements to suit the learner's ability;
(b) adjust the balance of knowledge and practical training to suit the learner's needs;
(c) have more time to give to supervision of practical training;
(d) accept the intake of learners to the course at different stages.

Use of the package by learners assists in reducing the course duration without detriment to performance standards. Production costs of the package and its validation have been justified in the savings brought about in raising flexibility. Savings are likely to become more favourable as more experience is gained in producing open learning material.

The STA is validating other material in its skill centres. Experience is being gained in maintaining adequate administration systems to support learners in flexible delivery of learning. The economies of open learning material production are also being analysed to determine whether the STA can justify production of material. The STA wishes to share its experience with others in order to assist in the development of flexible learning throughout UK education and training providers.

2.11 A Flexible Learning Scheme for the Training of Non-Craft Industrial Job Evaluators within the UKAEA

H I Ellington, E Addinall
Robert Gordon's Institute of Technology (RGIT), Aberdeen
J G McBeath
Dounreay Nuclear Power Development Establishment, Caithness

Abstract: The United Kingdom Atomic Energy Authority (UKAEA) employs several thousand non-craft industrial workers, all of whom are graded according to a standard system. This involves each non-craft industrial job being appraised by a team of experienced job evaluators and awarded an overall mark that determines into which of six pay bands the job should be allocated. This paper describes how the three authors have developed a systematic scheme for helping trainee job evaluators to develop the wide range of skills needed to carry out this work fairly and effectively. It shows how the scheme is based on the use of three key components: a self-instructional package on the non-craft industrial job evaluation system and the set of standard jobs on which it is based, a four-stage algorithm that enables any non-standard job to be evaluated by using a series of scales to compare it with the standard jobs, and a suite of 12 case studies that provide practice in the use of the algorithm, which is available in both manual and computerized versions. These three components can be used in a variety of training situations ranging from self-instruction by individuals working at their own pace to formal courses run to meet the specific needs of particular UKAEA establishments. The scheme is currently being implemented at the UKAEA's Dounreay nuclear power development establishment in Caithness (where the scheme was developed) and is also being made available to other UKAEA establishments.

Introduction

Since 1976, the two Robert Gordon's Institute of Technology (RGIT) authors, H I Ellington and E Addinall, have been heavily involved in the development of educational, training and publicity materials for the United Kingdom Atomic Energy Authority (UKAEA) working in collaboration with staff at the UKAEA's Dounreay nuclear power development establishment and London headquarters (see Ellington and Addinall 1981, 1983, 1985). This paper describes the latest collaborative project of this type – development of a flexible learning scheme for use in the training of job evaluators – the people who are responsible for grading non-craft industrial jobs within the UKAEA.

The UKAEA's Non-Craft Industrial Job Evaluation System

In its various establishments throughout Britain, the UKAEA employs several thousand non-craft industrial workers (formerly known as general workers), all of whom are graded according to a standard, centrally-administered system. This involves appraising each job under four broad areas or 'mainheads': 'acquired skill and knowledge', 'mental requirements', 'physical requirements' and 'working conditions', by comparing them to a range of 'standard jobs'. To quote the official UKAEA memorandum on the non-craft industrial job evaluation system, these 'have been selected by the National Joint Industrial Council so as to cover a wide range of different types of work throughout the Authority and to provide a balanced distribution of standard jobs between establishments, thus making standards readily available for reference by both central and local assessment teams'. The assessment produces a set of four marks, which, after weighting to allow for the different relative importance of the four mainheads, are added to produce an 'aggregate weighted mark'. This is the mark that determines into which of the six non-craft industrial pay bands the job is deemed to belong, the range of marks that correspond to each of the six pay bands shown in Figure 2.

In practice, job evaluations are normally carried out locally by teams of at least four experienced assessors, all of whom are members of the 'management side' of the establishment concerned (scientists, engineers, administrators, labour officers, etc), with the final mark awarded under each of the four mainheads being obtained by taking the average of the individual assessments. If such a local evaluation is disputed, arrangements are made for the job to be re-evaluated by a team of highly experienced assessors drawn from other UKAEA establishments. If this central team assessment is itself disputed, an independent appeal body containing representatives of both the management and trade union sides is brought in as final arbiter.

Why a More Effective Training Scheme for Job Evaluators was Needed at Dounreay

The main weakness of the above system is that it is totally dependent on the ability of the members of an evaluation team to decide what is an appropriate mark for the job being considered under each mainhead. This is a highly subjective process in which they have to rely entirely on their own judgment and experience, since the system makes no use of absolute or objective criteria for the allocation of these marks, and (up to now at least) has been based on the formation of an 'overall impression' rather than on an analytical approach. Thus it is not uncommon for the members of an evaluation team to vary considerably in their estimated worth of a job under one or more mainheads, or even to disagree over the pay band into which they think the job should be allocated – particularly if it is a borderline case. As would be expected, such disagreements tend to decrease as the experience of the job evaluators involved increases, but the fact that there is no effective substitute for such experience has always posed considerable problems about how to bring new job evaluators to the required level of competence in a reasonable time. Indeed, the traditional method of producing new job evaluators has simply been to give them an introductory one-day course on the system and then put them through a lengthy 'apprenticeship' in which they gradually pick up the required skills by observing experienced job evaluators in action.

The above problems about the training of new job evaluators were recently compounded at the UKAEA's Dounreay establishment by the realization that an alarming proportion of their most experienced job evaluators were approaching retirement age. The Dounreay management were therefore faced with the imminent prospect of having to train a whole batch of new job evaluators in order to replace these highly skilled 'old hands', and, if they were not to suffer an unacceptable temporary reduction in the overall effectiveness of their job evaluation team, of bringing them to an acceptable level of competence rather more quickly than had proved possible in the past. It was because of this that the two RGIT authors were approached by Dounreay's labour manager, Mr James McBeath, late in 1984, and asked if they could help him to develop a scheme whereby this could be done.

How the Overall Plan for the Scheme was Developed

Following preliminary discussions with Mr McBeath in Aberdeen, the two RGIT authors visited Dounreay in order to discuss the matter further. In the course of this two-day visit, which took place in December 1984, they held wide-ranging discussions with Mr McBeath and his colleagues in the Labour Department and met representatives of senior management and the trade union side. They also toured Dounreay's process plant division (the division responsible for the reprocessing of spent fuel from Dounreay's prototype fast reactor) in order to see at first hand the range of jobs that non-craft industrial workers carry out there. As a result of this extremely useful visit, and subsequent study of all the various documents relating to the job evaluation scheme that they had been given, the RGIT authors were able to formulate a possible strategy for providing the sort of 'accelerated training' that Mr McBeath and his colleagues wanted.

The scheme that they subsequently proposed to Mr McBeath was based on three key elements, each of which would be designed to help achieve a particular set of objectives relating to the production of a competent job evaluator. The first would be designed to give the trainees a thorough knowledge of the job evaluation system and the 36 standard jobs on which it is based, and would take the form of a self-instructional manual incorporating self-assessment. The second would be an algorithm designed to make the actual process of evaluating a job easier to carry out by a non-experienced person; this would entail the use of a series of scales by which the job under consideration could be compared with the various standard jobs, and would involve a much more systematic, analytical approach than had been used by most job evaluators up till then. The third would be a suite of carefully-chosen, highly-structured case studies, designed to provide a vehicle whereby the trainee job evaluators could attain the required level of competence – and confidence – in the use of the algorithm in the shortest possible time.

It was proposed that the actual training process should take place in three stages, namely:

Stage 1: study of the self-instructional manual by the selected trainees, working at their own pace at their normal places of work

Stage 2: attendance by the trainees at a 2 – 3 day course, at which they would be introduced to the job evaluation algorithm and given practice in using it by carrying out some of the case studies

Stage 3: follow-up work in which the trainees would first complete the remaining case studies and then be given experience of working with experienced teams of assessors on actual job evaluations.

The above scheme was proposed to Mr McBeath in a detailed feasibility report delivered in January 1985, and a decision to go ahead with its development and implementation was made shortly afterwards.

The Preparatory Work

Once it had been decided to proceed with the development of the scheme, the two RGIT authors made a further one-week visit to Dounreay during the Easter vacation in order to carry out the extensive preparatory work that they had indicated would be necessary before work on the actual training materials could begin. Specifically, this involved two tasks:

1. carrying out a detailed examination of all 36 standard jobs used in the job evaluation scheme in collaboration with Dounreay's labour department and members of their job evaluation team, in order to agree on how the marks awarded under each of the four mainheads should be broken down under the various 'subheads' into which each is divided (see Figure 1) – something that had never been attempted up till then.
2. holding further discussions with Dounreay's labour department and job evaluation team in order to decide which standard jobs should be used in the

various scales that would form the basis of the job evaluation algorithm round which the training course was to be built.

Work on both of these tasks was duly completed by the end of the week, thus providing the two RGIT authors with all the basic data that they needed in order to enable them to start work on the training package. The importance of this preparatory work (without which the package simply could not have been produced) cannot be overstressed.

Development of the Actual Training Package

Work on the development of the three elements of the training package was completed between April and September 1985. During this time, Drs Addinall and Ellington made three further visits to Dounreay for discussions with all of the people who had become involved in the project (these now included staff of Dounreay's education and training centre, who would be responsible for administering the training scheme, as well as several other members of Dounreay's job evaluation team). The work on each of the three elements is described below.

The Self-Instructional Manual

As was explained above, it had been decided that the most effective way of giving trainee job evaluators a thorough knowledge of the UKAEA's non-craft industrial job evaluation scheme and the 36 standard jobs on which it is based was to have them study a suitably designed self-instructional manual *before* attending any formal training course.

It was decided to write the first part of this manual (the part dealing with the actual job evaluation system) in three sections, each of which would be followed by a battery of self-assessment questions designed to show the trainee whether he had mastered the material and identify any remedial work required. The three sections were:

Section 1: General description of the non-craft industrial job evaluation system.
Section 2: Detailed description of the four mainheads used in the system.
Section 3: How the system is implemented within the UKAEA.

This first part of the manual covered all the material included in the official UKAEA Memorandum on the job evaluation system (LAB/W/227, dated 1979) together with explanatory information where it was felt that this was necessary. It eventually turned out to be 32 pages in length.

When it came to the second part of the manual (the part dealing with the 36 standard jobs) it was decided to adopt a somewhat different structure, namely:

1. a short introductory section instructing the trainees to study the standard jobs one at a time and providing a standard set of questions to be answered on each;
2. a complete list of the 36 standard jobs, given in order of their 'aggregate weighted marks' within each of the six pay bands;
3. the complete job description for each job, together with a detailed breakdown of the marks awarded to the job under the various mainheads and subheads used in the job evaluation scheme (the breakdowns that had been produced during the RGIT authors' Easter visit to Dounreay).

Production of (3) involved editing the official job descriptions for the 36 standard jobs into a standard format and having them all retyped – a not inconsiderable task, taking into account that they ran to a total of 126 pages. In all, the second part of the manual turned out to be 172 pages long – over five times the size of the first.

The Job Evaluation Algorithm

The main reason why it had previously taken so long to produce fully competent new job evaluators was the highly subjective nature of the job evaluation process, which meant that it normally took a new man or woman many years to develop the necessary skills. The authors had concluded that it might well be possible to shorten this training time considerably by adopting a more analytical approach to the evaluation process.

The algorithm that was eventually developed consisted of the following four stages:

Stage 1: Carrying out a preliminary 'overall appraisal' of the job by comparing it with all standard jobs of similar type, the 36 standard jobs being divided into two groups – 'scientific, laboratory and process' jobs and 'service' jobs – for this purpose. The first appraisal involves looking at the job 'as a whole', without taking account of the separate mainheads or subheads, and deciding where it falls within a ranked list of standard jobs of the type in question.

Stage 2: Carrying out similar comparative appraisals with standard jobs of the same type under each of the four mainheads used in the job evaluation scheme, without making any attempt to break down each mainhead under subheads. This second appraisal involves deciding where the job falls within four separate lists of standard jobs, each of which is ranked in terms of the marks awarded in respect of the mainhead in question.

Stage 3: Carrying out an even more detailed appraisal of the job, this time under each separate subhead of the four mainheads. This involves determining the position of the job on 20 separate scales, each consisting of a series of carefully selected standard jobs ranked in terms of the marks awarded in respect of the subhead in question (the marks that were determined during the preparatory work described above). The different subheads into which each mainhead is divided are shown in Figure 1.

Stage 4: Carrying out a final evaluation of the job involving
   (a) comparing the total marks awarded to the job under stages 1 – 3;
   (b) repeating any stage or section(s) thereof necessary to make these marks agree to within ten per cent;
   (c) finding the average of the final three marks and using this to assign the job to the appropriate pay band using the table shown in Figure 2.

Each stage of the evaluation process entails completing a pro forma, those used in Stages 3 and 4 being given in Figures 1 and 2 respectively.

The algorithm has been produced both in manual and in computerized forms, the latter being modelled for a BBC B microcomputer and being contained in six menu-driven programs. It is intended that the manual version of the algorithm (which enables the job evaluator to award marks between the points on the various scales) should be used for all 'serious' job evaluation work, while the computerized version (where only the scale point marks can be awarded) should be used for 'user familiarization' and 'demonstration' purposes, and also for 'drill and practice' work.

The Suite of Case Studies

The suite of case studies that constitutes the third and final element of the training package is essentially a vehicle for enactive learning, designed as it is to help trainee job evaluators to gain experience of (and confidence in) job evaluation by using the algorithm in realistic situations. It consists of 12 separate case studies, all based on actual jobs at Dounreay – jobs that were carefully chosen so as to cover the full spectrum of non-craft industrial jobs carried out on the site. For obvious reasons all the jobs are non-standard jobs, and, in order to increase the effectiveness of the case studies, an attempt was also made to choose jobs that do not correspond too closely to

PRO-FORMA 3

- for use in Stage 3 of the job evaluation process - appraisal under the Subheads of the four Mainheads

NAME OF JOB

MAINHEAD	SUBHEADS	UNWEIGHTED MARK ASSIGNED TO JOB UNDER SUBHEAD	WEIGHTING FACTOR	OVERALL WEIGHTED MARK FOR MAINHEAD (rounded up or down to nearest whole number)
A - Acquired Skill and Knowledge	(a) Education			
	(b) Training			
	(c) Experience			
	TOTAL		1.0	
B - Mental Requirements	(a) Good Memory			
	(b) Ability to Reason			
	(c) Speed of Reaction			
	(d) Even Temperament			
	(e) Co-operation			
	(f) Perseverance			
	(g) Mechanical Sense			
	(h) Initiative			
	(i) Disparate Attention			
	(j) Ability to Visualise			
	(k) Sense of Responsibility			
	TOTAL		0.9	
C - Physical Requirements	(a) Muscular Strength			
	(b) Stamina			
	(c) Agility			
	(d) Sensory Accuracy			
	TOTAL		0.5	
D - Working Conditions	(a) Phys. Disagreeableness			
	(b) Ment. Disagreeableness			
	TOTAL		0.5	
	Aggregate weighted mark awarded to job Under Stage 3			

Figure 1. *The pro forma used in stage 3 of the job evaluation process*

PRO-FORMA 4

- for use in Stage 4 of the job evaluation process - the final evaluation of the job

NAME OF JOB

Aggregate weighted mark awarded to job in Stage 1
Aggregate weighted mark awarded to job in Stage 2
Aggregate weighted mark awarded to job in Stage 3

Average aggregate weighted mark

Aggregate weighted mark	Pay Band
0 - 65	1
66 - 105	2
106 - 145	3
146 - 185	4
186 - 225	5
226 - 285	6

Pay Band to which job is allocated

Figure 2. *The pro forma used in stage 4 of the job evaluation process*

INSTRUCTIONS ON HOW TO CARRY OUT CASE STUDY

INTRODUCTION

This is one of a series of Case Studies that have been developed for use in the training of job evaluators within the United Kingdom Atomic Energy Authority. All members of the series are based on non-standard jobs at Dounreay Nuclear Power Development Establishment, where the training scheme was developed. The Case Study should be carried out in the three stages described below.

STAGE 1 - QUALITATIVE APPRAISAL OF JOB

Study the JOB DESCRIPTION given in Section 2 thoroughly, reading it at least three times. If possible, combine this study with observation of the job actually being carried out and interviews with the person carrying out the job and his/her immediate supervisor. As you carry out this work, fill in the QUALITATIVE APPRAISAL PRO-FORMA that is provided in Section 3, making sure that you complete every section.

STAGE 2 - QUANTITATIVE APPRAISAL OF JOB

Use the ALGORITHM FOR EVALUATION OF NON-CRAFT INDUSTRIAL JOBS WITHIN THE UKAEA to carry out a systematic quantitative evaluation of the job and complete PRO-FORMA'S 1-4 provided in Section 3 (these are copies of the four pro-formas that are used in the algorithm). Detailed instructions on how to carry out this evaluation are given in the algorithm.

STAGE 3 - COMPARISON WITH MODEL EVALUATION

Once you have completed both STAGE 1 and STAGE 2, compare your evaluation of the job with the model evaluation given in Section 4. This contains completed versions of the QUALITATIVE APPRAISAL PRO-FORMA and PRO-FORMA'S 1-4, together with explanatory notes on the latter. If there are serious discrepancies between your evaluation and the model evaluation, discuss these with an experienced job evaluator.

Figure 3. *The standard 'instruction sheet' used in the case studies*

standard jobs (the authors did not want to make the case studies too easy).

All 12 case studies were produced in exactly the same format, the resource materials for each comprising:

1. a set of instructions on how to carry out the case study (see Figure 3);
2. a detailed job description for the job being evaluated;
3. a set of five pro formas for use in the various stages of the evaluation process (see Figure 3 for details);
4. a model set of completed pro formas together with explanatory notes (again see Figure 3 for details).

How the Training Scheme is being Implemented

At the time of writing (October 1985), plans for the implementation of the job evaluation training scheme are still at a early stage, since work on the development of the package of materials that will form its basis has only just been completed. It is, however, intended that these will be roughly as follows.

(a) Demonstration of the materials to the staff in the UKAEA's main London office, who are responsible for administering the non-craft industrial job evaluation system.
(b) Demonstration of the materials to labour officers and job evaluators from other establishments within the UKAEA at a two-day seminar to be held at Dounreay in April 1986.
(c) Running a series of three-day courses for new job evaluators at Dounreay, the first being provisionally scheduled for September, 1986.

It is expected that the materials will also be used in a variety of other ways. A number of experienced job evaluators at Dounreay, for example, have indicated that they would like copies of the self-instructional manual and job evaluation algorithm, since they feel that these could well be of considerable assistance to them in their everyday job evaluation work. Indeed, it is expected that the two documents will eventually be made available to all job evaluators at Dounreay, and possibly also to job evaluators at other UKAEA establishments if they achieve general acceptance throughout the authority. It also seems likely that the various documents will be used in a range of instructional roles throughout the UKAEA, so that they can genuinely be described as 'flexible learning materials'.

Conclusion

At ETIC 82, the two RGIT authors presented a general case for increased collaboration between education and industry, arguing that educational technologists working in the higher education sector are particularly well placed to play a significant role in forming such links (Ellington and Addinall, 1983). At the following three ETIC conferences, they presented papers describing specific examples of such collaboration (Ellington, Addinall and Blood, 1984; Ellington and Addinall, 1985; Ellington, Addinall and Caudill, 1986). This latest ETIC paper continues the series, and also presents what the authors hope is an interesting case study on (a) the application of an educational technology-based systems approach to the solution of a very real industrial training problem, and (b) the use of flexible learning materials in industrial training. Thus they again hope that their work will be of interest to colleagues on both sides of the education/industry 'divide'.

References

Ellington, H I and Addinall, E (1981) 'The nuclear debate' – a new educational package for teachers. *Simulation/Games for Learning*, **13**, 3, pp 120–125.

Ellington, H I and Addinall, E (1983) Forming links between education and industry – how educational technologists can help. In Trott, A, Strongman, G and Giddon, L (eds) *Aspects of Educational Technology XVI*. Kogan Page, London.

Ellington, H I, Addinall, E and Blood, J (1984). Providing extension training for offshore personnel – an educational technology-based approach. In Shaw, K (ed) *Aspects of Educational Technology XVII*. Kogan Page, London.

Ellington, H I and Addinall, E (1985) Building experiential learning into an in-service course for middle managers. In Alloway, B S and Mills, G (eds) *Aspects of Educational Technology XVIII*. Kogan Page, London.

Ellington, H I, Addinall, E and Caudill, P (1986) 'Licensed to drill!' – a new multi-media educational library incorporating computer-based learning. In Howe, A and Rushby, N J (eds) *Aspects of Educational Technology XIX*. Kogan Page, London.

Acknowledgements

The authors would like to acknowledge the contributions made by those at Dounreay who helped them: David Anderson from the labour department, and Cyril Davison, Wilson McPherson, Derek Redford and John Sinclair from the job evaluation team.

2.12 Industrial Updating in Software Engineering via Distance Learning

J Chapman
Open University, Milton Keynes
D Saunders
BBC/OU Production Centre, Milton Keynes

Abstract: Distance learning at postgraduate level has been part of the Alvey strategy for its perceived training needs. A course on software engineering is one module in the *Industrial Applications of Computers* programmes offered by the Open University and supported by Alvey and the Science and Engineering Research Council (SERC). Techniques for effective distance teaching for these courses are new and problems in producing the courses and in student learning differ from those experienced with undergraduate courses at the Open University.

This paper considers the home experiment facility, which provides computing resources, and the videocassette which gives a 'real world' context for the subject matter. Problems associated with providing these components and with their use by the students form the basis of this paper.

Introduction

The Scientific and Technical Updating Programme (SATUP) at the Open University is a large-scale operation directed at industrial updating courses using distance learning so that participants' normal work suffers minimal disruption while new methods and techniques are being learnt. Techniques for effective distance teaching for these courses are new and problems in producing the courses and in learning from them differ from those experienced with undergraduate courses at the Open University.

Distance learning at postgraduate level has been part of the Alvey strategy for its perceived training needs. The *Industrial Applications of Computers* programme of courses has been supported by them and by the Science and Engineering Research Council (SERC). This programme consists of a series of modules, each of which takes approximately 100 hours of study. No formal entry requirements are needed, but some previous experience or knowledge is essential. A student completing eight modules and a project is eligible for the award of a Masters degree or, without the project, for a Postgraduate diploma. These modules have a rolling intake throughout the year and there are two examination dates each year, so that students are not restricted to studying in conventional term times; they can fit this work into any time slots convenient to them.

One of the foundation modules is software engineering (Open University, 1984). This module is aimed at electronic engineers whose work involves designing hardware and the associated software for embedded real-time systems. These systems can have components supplied as hardware or software, but the practitioners usually have a hardware background supported by some programming skills at assembly code or machine code level. Software engineering encompasses methods and techniques for specifying, designing and implementing large, complex systems with regard being taken of quality, cost and development time. The case studies in the course focus on systems which have the task of monitoring and controlling other equipment and processes.

The module is composed of eight teaching texts, a home experiment facility (HEF), a videocassette showing the techniques being applied in industry and a set of assignment questions. The student is directed through these by a study guide. Typically, after reading one of the unit texts a student will do the related practical work and view a band on the video cassette, guided by the video notes, before attempting any assignment questions based on that part of the course. The assignments are graded and commented on by a tutor, but the mark does not contribute to the course assessment.

This paper looks at two components of the study materials: the home experiment facility and the videocassette.

The Home Experiment Facility

Although programming forms a small part of the software life cycle, it was considered vital that students should support their theoretical work with practical computer experience. It was decided that all modules in the industrial application of computers programme would make use of a specially designed microcomputer that could be used at home; this would remove problems of the continuity of production and maintenance of any commercially supplied machine and would enable additional interfaces to be provided to which a number of unusual peripherals could be connected. For example, the robotics course involves practical work with a robot arm, and the module on real-time monitoring also requires special processes which have to be controlled. The home experiment facility consists of the microcomputer Hektor III, a modem for linking with the Academic Computing Service (ACS) computing network over a standard dial-up telephone line and a suitable video monitor or a television set, which the student provides. Also provided are a set of experimental exercises and an HEF user manual. The latter describes how to use the HEF in stand-alone mode for assembler level work and on-line to a remote mainframe to run UCSD Pascal. The ability to use (and produce) documentation of this sort is another skill required in software engineering which students are therefore putting into practice while gaining familiarity with the computer system.

The first part of the experimental work enables a student to become sufficiently familiar with the kit to use it as a computing tool kit. The work involves using the HEF in stand-alone and online modes. Using this tool kit and the theoretical knowledge gained from the appropriate unit texts, a student can tackle part II which contains exercises related to software engineering. Part III contains additional exercises which are not so highly structured. These extend the use of techniques taught in the course and expect the student to use information from the HEF manual to be able to carry out the tasks.

This approach to providing appropriate experience in the new techniques has not been free of problems. The problems can be divided into those experienced by the students which are associated with using the computing kit itself, and those problems met by the course team whilst trying to provide exercises of sufficient complexity, based in realistic contexts, that students gain valuable software engineering experience from doing them.

Problems of Using the Home Experiment Facility (HEF)

An underlying problem is that of resistance to using a special microcomputer when many of the students have their own computer, or at least easy access to one. This is a difficult argument to counter, particularly when the student does not plan to take any of the other courses in the programme and is paying for the course and the kit. The assembly code programs can be written on any 8085A-based micro but there are some built-in programs which can be used in stand-alone mode and these are not available on other machines. When the HEF is used online to the ACS computer network students can use UCSD Pascal and a number of Pascal programs provided in the course library.

Although different versions of Pascal could be used, the course makes use of the separate compilation facilities and the semaphores provided by UCSD Pascal. Units save students from having to type in standard pieces of code themselves and semaphores enable the coding of concurrent processes. These concurrent processes are the basis of real-time computing systems, which is the application area of most concern to this course. Consequently it is important that students can access the ACS computer. Other equipment could be used for this but the stand-alone capabilities are also needed.

The course software could be distributed, rather than students accessing it via an online link. However problems of reliability and maintenance would still be the responsibility of ACS. Where a company has enrolled staff on this course and purchased a home experiment facility for use by a series of staff it becomes difficult to locate the current student user of the system. Any software provided in the library can be updated without reference to an individual. This means that errors in programs can be rectified and the new version issued relatively quickly.

If the distribution and maintenance of course library programs cannot be solved for stand-alone computers, a compromise solution may be to use more powerful micros which will support UCSD Pascal themselves but use a network to down-line load any course programs and modules required.

Problems of Exercise Complexity

Software engineering, like other Open University courses, states prerequisites for studying the course but these are recommendations and are not enforced. They can be satisfied by previous qualifications or by experience in the field. Students may misinterpret the amount and level of knowledge implied by the prerequisites. Some students therefore start the course with inadequate background, and possibly a biased view of what the course will entail. This obviously creates problems when they start reading the texts, since these were written with the assumption that students would be able to follow designs written in a top-down way using Pascal as the program development language. Consequently students are distracted from the main objectives by their inability to follow the notation used. We hope to improve this situation by offering a simple diagnostic test of the essential concepts.

Software engineering addresses problems of scale and the control of that complexity, but students employed in implementing particular aspects of a solution may not be aware of how their component fits in with all the others, since they are not concerned about the control aspects. The practical work has to teach students where each stage in the life cycle interfaces and this requires a realistically large piece of software which must also not take up excessive amounts of time. Part II of the experimental work involves working from a requirements document through all the stages up to implementation and testing, to give a taste of what the subject is about. To students with little previous experience at this level the task is perhaps a bit daunting, and it also fails to live up to their expectations as there is a relatively small amount of programming. Other students who are more familiar with the scale find the exercises too simple and therefore not worth the effort.

Ideally students should be involved in all the stages of system development on a project in their company and guided by a tutor. This obviously has problems of organization and possibly of industrial security. An alternative is some form of residential school where the exercises can be tailored more easily to the needs of each student. Since the rolling intake allows students great flexibility of study pattern it would be very difficult to time any residential schools, and they would probably involve students being away from work.

The Videocassettes

The reason for having a videocassette was to illustrate that the practical aspect of the subject covered not only the details of good design techniques and the like, but also to give an awareness of the industrial or commercial environment in which these techniques would have to be applied – what a colleague at the Open University has called 'a smell of the oil'. We therefore wanted to make a video recording of a particular software engineering project which we could use as a case study, preferably including the problems as well as the successes, so that we could provide an authentic view of how the academic material is used out in the 'real world'.

The world of software production is well-known for the fact that its products are often late or inadequate. Consequently we anticipated that an organization working in this field would be wary of allowing video cameras to view their operations and that we would have a difficult time finding a willing participant. In fact, we were allowed to follow the development of a computerized message-switching system for the Meteorological Office by Systems Designers International (SDI). They had been awarded the contract for this project by the Ministry of Defence in October 1982, and we followed their progress with our cameras from June 1983 (when they had just finished their system design) through to July 1983 (the completion of factory acceptance tests for the system). Although there were obviously some worries about the risks involved in exposing themselves to the media, SDI had sufficient confidence in their project team (and also in our intentions to show what happened without sensationalism) to allow us an almost free rein in what we wanted to record. In all, we were present with our cameras for a total of two weeks, spread over the twelve-month period.

The final edited version of the videocassette is structured into six bands, each of about 15 minutes' duration; the student is expected to watch each band at a single sitting. The first band is an introduction which sets the scene of the project, shows the organization and people involved, and outlines the strategy which is used in the analysis of the software production process. The remaining bands concentrate on particular topics: specification, program design, data design, concurrent processes and quality control.

A variety of different video techniques were used at different places in the cassette. Perhaps most important for students were the times when our cameras could play their fly-on-the-wall role, albeit with several bright lights and rather more people than would normally be present. We were fortunate that there were times – for example, during system testing – when neither we nor the participants knew just what would happen, and we were able to convey some of the tension of those moments in our recording. Of course we weren't present all the time throughout the project, and so we decided to recreate some of the incidents which occurred. For example, there was an occasion when the entire test system became completely unresponsive, and subsequent investigation showed that this was due to a software error called a 'deadly embrace'. As this was a concept which we wanted to include in our teaching, we asked the programmer involved to pretend that he was about to find this error again, and followed this in the cassette by an explanation of the cause of the problem.

We also used a substantial number of animated graphics to explain the dynamic concepts involved. An example of this was when we wanted to explain the data structures used to store the meteorological messages within the system. These messages were stored in queues, the basic principle being first in, first out. However, there were 128 different possible output routes, and four different priorities of message for each route, so rather than employing 512 different queues a more complex technique had to be evolved. In order to explain this technique we used animations to show messages arriving and departing, and how pointers within the system kept track of which message was next to be despatched on any given route.

The final video technique used in the cassette was the most straightforward: the inclusion of interviews with some of the more senior staff involved in the project. Although plain and undemanding, these interviews nevertheless could still offer students something valuable: the chance to hear people who had just worked on a real project and could look back on the high (and low) points of their involvement, could say why they did things one way rather than another and could give just a hint of the enthusiasm which they brought to their work.

The use of videocassette rather than television was essential, as students needed to be able to view one band on a particular technique and after one viewing to be able to review the material. This use has analogies with the way many Open University courses use audio cassettes, but we have much less experience with videos.

Summary

This course has involved us in a number of new problems. The responses to our use of the videocassette and home-based computing is influencing our approach to these media in courses we are currently preparing. We have learnt something about the problem of providing home computing for industrial updating courses. So we can now use the experience in the provision of home computing for undergraduates.

References

PMIT600 Software engineering (1984) The Open University, Milton Keynes.

2.13 Professional Training by Distance Learning: The YMCA/NELP Certificate Course for Youth and Community Workers

L D Richardson
Freelance Educational Technologist, London

Abstract: Youth and community work, with its high proportion of face-to-face contact and its need for 'people' skills, might seem an unlikely candidate for a professional training course taught by distance learning. But the experimental certificate course prepared by the YMCA National College – based on their experience of running a full-time initial training course – provides a good example of a flexible learning system.

The course combines three distinct elements: distance learning materials in the form of study packs and audio tapes; face-to-face meetings: group tutorials, residentials, and individual sessions with a fieldwork supervisor recruited and trained by the college; and finally, the students' experiences 'on the job'.

A modular structure, 'word processed' and xeroxed study packs designed for easy revision, and the introduction of computer-marked assignments are other 'flexible' design features.

These elements of the course, and the learning process undergone by the course team, together with future plans for extending this approach to other areas of professional training, will be described in a brief informal paper.

The Youth and Community Service: A Profession with Flexible Training Needs

The youth and community service is a remarkably varied profession. Qualified workers may find jobs in youth work, community work, youth social work, play organization, church work, advice work, community relations or probation. Their employers might include local authorities, voluntary organizations such as the Scouts, and central government departments and agencies such as the Manpower Services Commission (MSC).

It is a young profession, with most training courses dating from the early 1970s onwards. The standard pattern of initial qualification is a two-year full-time certificate course, at a polytechnic or college of higher education. There is no nationally prescribed curriculum, but courses cover roughly similar ground: basic sociology and psychology; counselling skills; group work; community work or community development; and management skills. It is also a profession with a very large group of part-time and voluntary workers: some half a million, supervized by approximately 4,000 full-time workers. Local authorities provide short in-service training courses for both groups, but in 1978 the Consultative Group on Youth and Community Work Training became concerned that approximately one in seven full-time youth and community workers were unqualified. The available two-year courses were not appropriate for this group: mature students and experienced workers, many with family commitments. Instead

> 'it might be possible to plan a qualifying course which would essentially take training to the unqualified and endeavour to exploit the learnings possible within their existing job. Such a project would reflect developments in distance teaching' (Consultative Group, 1978).

A parallel concern also suggested the need for flexible training: the fear that

> 'conventional training may only distance the indigenous workers from their roots, [and] separate the professional from the community.' (Hoggart, 1983)

'Indigenous' in this case meant black and Asian youth leaders. But all experienced youth workers who left their posts to attend college equally cut themselves off from their home communities, and deprived those communities of leaders for two years. So there were three good reasons for considering flexible training:

(1) The youth service could improve its effectiveness by training a large pool of unqualified staff.
(2) A significant number of workers were unable to attend full-time courses. Among these were a high proportion of women and members of minority groups.
(3) Black, Asian and white working-class communities would benefit especially, if training could be delivered to workers in their own neighbourhoods.

A Flexible Solution: the YMCA National College

During the 1970s a similar problem existed in the YMCA: about 20 senior workers lacked a professional qualification, yet their responsibilities as managers of local associations meant that it was impossible for them to attend the two-year qualifying course based at the YMCA's own national college. The college had been established in 1970, and was responsible for both initial and in-service training within the YMCA, as well as offering initial training to youth workers generally.

Already in 1976 it had put forward staff training proposals which included a distance learning element; and following on from this in 1979 the college responded to the Consultative Group's suggestions with new proposals for 'a part-time certificate course in youth and community work by distance teaching', to be validated by North East London Polytechnic.

Its aim was

> 'to make professional training in Youth and Community Work available and readily accessible to those unqualified workers . . . who are not able to utilize existing training provision.'

Intake was to be as open as possible. Students had to be 21 or over, with a minimum of two years' full-time experience in youth work; but academic qualifications were less important than 'the ability to make full use of the course'. Of the 36 students accepted for the pilot course, 19 had no formal academic qualifications and another seven had less than the five 'O' Levels required by most of the two-year courses.

It would be firmly based in day-to-day practice:

> 'The main emphasis of the course would be to enable the "student" to utilise the full potential of his/her daily work situation in developing professional attitudes, understanding, knowledge and skills. . .' (YMCA, 1979)

All of these aims derived from the philosophy of the YMCA national college, on whose two-year course the syllabus of the new course was also to be based.

Figure 1 summarizes the history of the project from 1978 to 1986.

I now want to turn to the course as it is today: to describe its features and their functions within the total scheme; and finally, to sketch out where we think this experiment in flexible professional training may lead us.

The Elements of the Course

The course has three major elements:

1. Study packs and tapes for distance learning, posted at approximately monthly intervals;
2. face-to-face sessions;

May 1978	Consultative Group on Youth and Community Work Training suggests the need to 'take training to the unqualified'
1979	YMCA College proposal to DES for certificate course jointly validated by NELP
1980	DES grant allows appointment of full-time tutor – organizer
March 1971	Feasibility study shows a need: 458 unqualified workers unable to take up full-time training
December 1981	First module written Second full-time tutor appointed College staff member seconded half-time
February 1982	Pilot course begins with 36 students
1984	Fourth tutor seconded from College
May 1985	DES approves funding for permanent course with annual intake Freelance writer/editor appointed
July 1985	30 students graduate from the pilot course: one failed, three withdrew, two referred
September 1985	First intake of permanent course

Figure 1. *Chronology of the course*

3. the student's own professional practice, which serves both as the subject matter for learning and an important learning method.

Major features of these three elements are summarized in Figure 2.

The Role of the Distance Learning Element

The study pack is the core of the distance learning element of the course. Study packs are produced simply, using word processed text in a simple layout, which is xeroxed and bound into card covers using treasury tags. Turnaround time is rapid, and changes and corrections can be made up until the last moment.

The structure of the study pack is shown in Figure 3. Coloured paper is used to identify the different sections, a simple technique which helps students find their way around the contents.

Audio tapes were used extensively in the pilot course, and the most successful of these are being retained.

CMAs are a new feature. They are used to check learning, and to give the student reassurance that material has been understood correctly. They are time-consuming to produce, but seem to be effective.

The Role of the Face-to-Face Element

Face-to-face sessions are designed to teach the bits that cannot be easily taught by distance learning methods, such as the skills of working with a group, and to provide contact between students, and between the student and the college.

Group tutorials and residentials are similar in their aims to their Open University equivalents. The week-long residentials include 'intervention workshops' in which students bring forward samples of their practice for analysis, and a formal course meeting of the entire group.

Supervision owes little to distance learning methods, but is probably the most important aspect of face-to-face contact, as well as the most frequent. The role of the supervisor is to help the student focus on his or her practice and the learning to be drawn out of it. Non-managerial supervision is relatively common in youth work and

1. Distance learning materials
   - a study pack containing items, readings and course information;
   - sometimes, an accompanying audio cassette;
   - computer-marked assignments, using NEC's MAIL program.

2. Face-to-face provision:
   - supervision sessions with a professional worker recruited and trained by the college, once a fortnight;
   - group tutorial sessions (regional study days) with other students in the region, led by a regional tutor;
   - Residentials: one week in each year, plus an introductory three-day residential at the beginning of the course.

3. Professional practice:
   - field experience placements (two weeks a year) in another agency;
   - recording: one and a half hours a week, based on events in the workplace;
   - activities;
   - assignments and project reports;
   - self-assessment: the student's evaluation of his/her own learning.

Figure 2. *The elements of the course*

Inside the study pack:

NOTICES
Course information: due dates, assignments, project reports

ACTIVITIES
based on the student's work

COURSE PLANNER

ITEMS
the meat in the sandwich: knowledge, skills and attitudes

READINGS
Extracts from books, articles, plays; photographs; case histories (bound separately)

BRIEFINGS
Current articles in the youth work field, with an introduction

CMA QUESTIONS
to test understanding of material in the items

FEEDBACK SHEET

Figure 3. *The study pack dissected*

related professions such as social work (Dobey, 1984; Hope, 1984) and is an important element of the two-year course.

Figure 4 shows the theoretical balance between distant and face-to-face elements, in terms of study time.

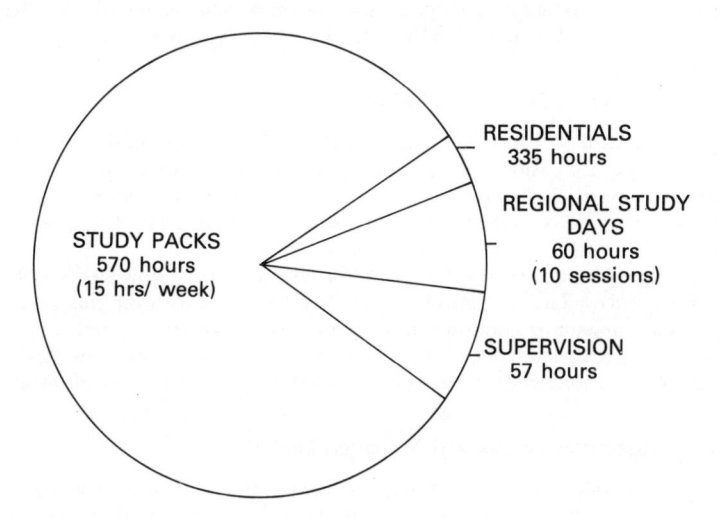

Figure 4. *The balance between distance learning and face-to-face*

STUDY PACKS — 570 hours (15 hrs/ week)
RESIDENTIALS — 335 hours
REGIONAL STUDY DAYS — 60 hours (10 sessions)
SUPERVISION — 57 hours

The Role of Practice

The elements listed in Figure 2 under 'professional practice' are all based on material in the study packs. How then does the course manage to teach professional skills of dealing with people by distance learning?

The answer to this question lies in the course philosophy, which is to base learning on the student's work experience, with the study packs as a guide to help make that learning more effective.

The course is organized topically into modules on working with individuals, with groups, and within organizations and communities; and functionally into four major phases of the professional task: appraising, planning, intervening, evaluating.

Experience from incidents happening at work is captured by the student using recording techniques, which are taught in the early study packs; time is allocated for this in each study period. But the student's own job will not provide the full range of experiences useful for learning. This experience is therefore supplemented by assignments and activities, and by a placement in another agency. These course requirements are designed to give students experiences which they would not get in the normal course of their work: planning a visit to another agency, interviewing a manager, or surveying their neighbourhood, for instance. Guidelines on tackling the tasks are in the study packs.

The self-assessment – which is the student's own evaluation of what has been learned – is another important feature. The college believes that ability to evaluate one's own practice – or in this case one's learning – is a fundamental professional skill. By giving the student responsibility for this, and making it a major part of the assessment, the course also underlines the value of autonomy: a value which it is hoped trainee workers will apply to their relations with the young people with whom they work.

In these days, the course materials act as a model and a guide to the knowledge, skills and attitudes seen as important for professional youth workers.

Issues Raised by the Course

The major issue which a course of this type raises is 'what is different about teaching a professional course, especially one based on practice, at a distance – and what are the problems in doing so?' Our experience suggests some conclusions which differ from those of the distance learning models with which we began the pilot.

The Red Herring of Student Isolation

One of our major fears was of student isolation; the experience of the Open University and the National Extension College had suggested this as a major problem. But unlike students on conventional courses, our students were not separated from their workplace or their families, and these networks gave them important areas of support, as well of course as adding to the pressures on their time.

They were isolated from the college, and from each other, however, and this did have consequences. The absence of informal student links with the college led to some confusions and misunderstandings in the pilot period. We are currently exploring the possibilities of giving students an 'electronic grapevine' using online methods; but relatively few of our current students have access to computers at home or at work.

Learning Objectives versus Self-Managed Learning

In planning the pilot course, the course team chose the method of learning objectives. As with student isolation, this was received distance learning wisdom, and the project's first full-time tutor-organizer spent much time converting his colleagues.

Attempts to fit the course materials into the learning objectives mould have now been virtually abandoned, except to provide signposts to the contents of a particular item. There seems to be several reasons why learning objectives did not work well for us:

- ☐ the practical basis of the course makes it very difficult to predict what learning will take place in a particular case;
- ☐ assessment is continuous, and based partly on the student's own analysis of what he or she had learned. If a major portion of assessment is the ability to state what you have learned, there can be no requirement that this corresponds to present learning objectives.

These perceptions will undoubtedly guide our strategies as we develop further distance learning materials; like our students, we are seeking to learn from our experience!

Where Do We Go From Here?

Flexible learning can contribute to professional training, even in as 'soft' an area of knowledge as youth and community work. The course has successfully combined distance learning methods in the study packs with established elements of youth work training and support, such as supervision. There are surely lessons here for the future.

When the Department of Education and Science (DES) approved funding for the pilot course in June 1981, one of their aims was to use it as a testbed for training in related professional fields, such as teaching or social work. The Open University has long taken the lead in in-service training courses for teachers by distance learning, and the courses produced by their new Department of Health and Social Welfare are extending their interest to the 'caring professions', such as nursing and social work.

But there are still gaps which we think the YMCA College can fill. At present we are working on two new projects, apart from the revision – often substantial – of the pilot certificate course. Both they and the revision itself indicate the course's flexibility in a different sense: that of being adaptable to different ends.

One project is a modular course for managers in the YMCA, which can be adapted to fit the needs of other voluntary agencies. There is a possibility of linking this into more general management training as a specialist module.

The second area of interest is the diploma in youth and community work: a higher qualification which could be achieved by a combination of validating short in-service courses and a modular course similar to the certificate one, but at a higher level.

The success of the YMCA course has led other educators in the youth and community field to consider a part-time route to initial qualification. This has caused some concern from those who fear that part-time training offers a second-class education: cheaper, and therefore attractive to local authorities scrabbling for savings, but one which marks a 'clear shift away from broad educational objectives based on leisure and time for reflection' (Gutfreund, 1984). We at the YMCA College, and incidentally our colleagues at the Open University (Wiggins, 1984; Kirwan, 1984b) believe that such fears are unfounded. Flexible learning is not only less expensive in terms of state support for individual students; it is if anything an enhancement of conventional learning rather than a poor copy of it. Reflection on one's learning, if learning is based on working practice, is easier if you are able to hold the yardstick up to day-to-day events; the full-time certificate course is 'distance learning' in the sense that its students are remote from this everyday source of experience and education.

The flexible learning route to professional training is different: the aims may be the same, in this case to produce qualified youth workers, as in full-time courses, but the course methods and the experience of the students will be different in important ways. These differences, as in any form of learning which responds more flexibly to student needs, may well be improvements. There is no need for flexible learning to take second place to the inflexible kind.

References

Consultative Group on Youth and Community Work Training (1978) *Training Provision for Unqualified Workers (by distance teaching)*. Unpublished report.
Dobey, S (1984) Much more than 'a shoulder to weep on'. *Youth in Society*, 87, pp 19-20.
Gutfreund, R (1984) Drift and development in the youth service. *Youth in Society*, 89, pp 13–14.
Hilgendorf, L and Abrahams, F (1985) *Evaluation of the YMCA Distance Learning Course for Youth and Community Workers*. Tavistock Institute, Unpublished report.
Hoggarth, L (1983) Against the odds: training youth and community workers. *Youth and Policy*, **2**, 2, pp 34-38.
Hope, B (1984) Managerial and non-managerial supervision. *Youth in Society*, 87, pp 19-20.
Kirwan, T (1984a) The YMCA distance learning course in youth and community work: a case study. In Lewis, R (ed) *Open Learning in Action*, Council for Educational Technology.
Kirwan, T (1984b) The part-time training debate (letter). *Youth in Society*, 91, p 9.
Kirwan, T and Kitto, J (1986). *Final report on the distance learning project, September 1980 – August 1985*. Draft unpublished report.
Wiggans, A (1984) The part-time training debate (letter). *Youth in Society*, 91, p 9.
YMCA National College, In-Service Training Group (1976) *Draft proposals both for initial training of new employees and for in-service training of existing personnel*. Unpublished report.
YMCA National College (1979) *Outline proposals for a YMCA/NELP part-time certificate course in youth and community work by distance teaching*. Unpublished report.
YMCA National College in association with North East London Polytechnic (1981) *Certificate in Youth and Community Work (Part-time by Distance Teaching)*. Submission documents.
YMCA National College (1981) *Feasibility study: report to the DES*. Unpublished report.
YMCA National College (1983) *A report to the Department of Education and Science on the first year of operation of the distance learning course*. Unpublished report.
YMCA National College (1984a) *Certificate Courses in Youth and Community Work*. Submission to CETYCW for endorsement of both courses.
YMCA National College (1984b) *Course Report on YMCA/NELP certificate course in youth and community work, part-time by distance learning*. Unpublished report.
YMCA National College (1984c) *Proposals to the Department of Education and Science for the establishment on a permanent basis of the certificate course in youth and community work part-time by distance learning*. Unpublished report.

2.14 Flexible Learning and Youth Training – A Case Study of Educational Development

R Houlton, J Hill and D Partington
Co-operative College, Loughborough

Abstract: Since 1983 the Co-operative College has been developing a discovery learning system called CUE! and based on audio tapes, associated workbooks, adviser guides and residential courses (Sharples, 1985). This paper provides an overview of the development process, with particular emphasis on the environmental conditions which made it possible.

Introduction

Creating a new learning system requires the interaction of three factors: an effective demand backed with hard cash; an agency capable of delivering a product to meet the demand; and a supplier capable of sustaining the process of research and development and producing the product. To understand the development process, it is necessary to examine each of these factors in some detail.

Demand

Demand for work-related education and training can usually be divided into three segments: public, institutional, and personal.

Public demand is manifested in the flow of funds through the Department of Education and Science (DES), the Manpower Services Commission (MSC), and a host of other public bodies and agencies. It is also associated with a variety of conflicting debates and signals about the long-term goals of the British economy and British society. The need for a new learning system for young school leavers has been a subject of public discussion since Jim Callaghan, then Prime Minister, delivered his 'great debate' speech at Ruskin College.

In 1982, faced with unprecedented levels of youth unemployment and large numbers of school leavers, the Manpower Services Commission launched the Youth Training Scheme (YTS). Every school leaver was guaranteed a place on the scheme for 12 months – which included 13 weeks' off-the-job training. Partially funded by the European Economic Community (EEC), the scheme is probably the most significant single training demand ever financed by the public sector.

Institutional demand is rooted in the current and future requirements of employers and modulated by budgetary constraints and alternative recruitment strategies. To give one example: an employer may decide not to have a training department and recruit, by offering higher levels of remuneration, personnel trained by others. The collective signals about employer training requirements are usually transmitted by trade associations, the Confederation of British Industry (CBI), chambers of commerce, and so on. However, there is often a credibility gap between the public pronouncements of employer bodies and the actual performance of their constituent members.

Personal demand relates to the training/education needs of individuals. At the micro-level of work-related learning it is important to distinguish between manifest and latent demand. The manifest demand in the office, on the shop floor, in the store, and in the management suite relates, firstly, to what is available in the market – which in many instances is very little – and secondly to people's expectations, which in many instances are low. For the majority of the population the experience of school-based learning has been one of limited choice. Children of seven who respond to questions about the future with the ambition to be an architect, an actress, to play for Scotland, can easily find themselves at 17 unemployed, filling shelves, on a production line, or in a routine clerical job. The latent demand for work-related training at the micro-level is often unknown and not necessarily supportive of an employer's business operations. People may dream as much of 'getting out' as 'getting on'.

Supply

The launch of YTS by the MSC in 1982 was the launch of a market without a product. New training systems and services, particularly for off-the-job training, had to be developed. Under normal conditions the delivery of the right product at the right time and at the right price is not a simple process. However, with the truncated timescale laid down by the MSC for the development of YTS the problems were complex.

The initiative which led to the development of the CUE! system came from a group of training officers in retail co-operative societies who knew from their previous involvement with MSC work experience schemes that the delivery of off-the-job training would be difficult.

The training officers were knowledgeable about the alternatives already in the market. In their view, traditional day release courses at colleges of further education (FE) would not be attractive to low achieving school leavers (LASLs) who would see it as a return to 'school'. Many of the FE tutors lacked experience in handling this 'difficult' group, and many colleges lacked staff with the necessary up-to-date working experience in the detail and distributive industries. Correspondence courses were not considered an option because of their dependence upon high levels of motivation, literacy, and numeracy.

Many training officers would have preferred to set up their own training system and hire instructors. But in 1983 it was difficult to make the case for expansion to senior managers. Many training departments had been cut back as a result of the winding up of the grant-giving Distributive Industry Training Board, which had provided them with financial support. Having just cut 'training empires down to size' as some of them put it, senior managers were not receptive to any suggestion that the empires be restored. The second difficulty was about the Youth Training Scheme itself. There was scepticism about its proposed operations, its funding, and the willingness of young people to participate in the scheme. Uncertainty is always a major constraint on development and forward planning.

The training officers wanted an off-the-job training package that would be attractive to the trainees, that they could manage and control themselves, and which would be developed without any impact on their budgets. The package should not cost more than a traditional 13-week day-release course at a college of further education. They also required the system to be flexible in the following respects:

☐ Operations
☐ Context.

The training officers wanted learning materials which would enable them to operate their off-the-job training programmes at the time most convenient to their business. And, as the learning programme developed, it needed to evolve around the context of retailing in the trainee's own community.

COMMUNITY completes a trilogy of tapes which deal with the relationship between modern retailing and its customers.

Melton Mowbray, a small market town famous for meat pies and Stilton cheese, is examined in depth by Louise Dennis. Many of the key people in the town talk about their job and relationship with the Community, including the MP, a Councillor, the Vicar, a Trade Union Official, and the Editor of the Melton Times.

Community

Commons, Food, fare, provisions.
Commonwealth, Republic, nation, state, people.
Commotion, turmoil, tumult, agitation, excitement, violence, perturbation, disorder, turbulence. *Calm*
Communicate, convey, speak, tell, respond.
Communicant, Participant, sharer, partaker.
Communicate, *v.n.*, Commune, converse, speak, talk, correspond.
Lead.
v.a., Confer, bestow, impart, give, grant, vouchsafe.
Declare, announce, reveal, divulge, disclose.
Touch, join, adjoin.
Communicative, Open, unreserved, sociable, affable, chatty, free. *Reserved*
Communion, Converse, intercourse, fellowship, participation.
Sacrament, Eucharist.
Community, Society, association, state, brotherhood, college, people, public, body.
Sameness, similarity, likeness.
Commute, change, alter, replace.
Exchange, barter.

What's the difference between a department store and a hypermarket, or a variety chain store and a Co-op?

Why did Coca-Cola's sales suddenly go sour?

Find the answers and many more — on this CUE tape.

This could be the start of something...
BIG
Cue!

BIG

Sir Hugh Fraser, formerly Chairman of the House of Fraser — David Sainsbury, Finance Director of J. Sainsbury Ltd. — Dennis Cassidy, Managing Director of British Home Stores — Françoise Baulier, of the French Retail Co-operative Movement, — all make a contribution to this introductory CUE tape.

What went wrong at Coca-Cola?

Who was that illegitimate baby?

Who's looking after the potatoes?

Find the answers and many more — on this unique tape.

Figure 1. *CUE! cassette covers*

The Producer

Fortuitously, these training officers had close connections with the Co-operative College, an international management and adult training centre, and approached it for help. With a history stretching back into the 19th century, including pioneering with work-related curriculum development for young people from the 1880s to the 1930s, the college was independent of public sector further education. In 1980 it had created a research and development department, the CLEAR unit, which was already providing training services and systems to developing countries, and promoting curriculum development projects in Britain (Hill, 1983). It had first-class residential facilities, a range of post-experience courses for adults, and unrivalled access to modern retailing through its trade association links. One major problem in designing a new training system is the range of options and permutations which are theoretically possible. But time and resource constraints usually dictate the key components (Houlton, 1978).

The first component of the new system was to hand – residential courses. It was also decided to attempt to make the second component pre-recorded audio cassettes. As the 'Walkman' personal stereo was the 'appropriate technology' of the youth culture of the 1980s, it seemed worthwhile to utilize it for learning and personal development.

	Generic Title	Marketing Title	Available	Duration
1	Introduction to retailing mark 1	This could be the start of something BIG	June – Oct. 1983	1 day
	'' mark 2	''	Nov. 1983 – Oct. 1985	2 days
	'' mark 3	''	Oct. 1985 –	15 days
2	Markets and marketing	People	June – Nov. 1983	5 days
3	Facing the public mark 1	Images	Nov. 1983 – June 1986	8 days
	'' mark 2	''	June 1986 –	10 days
4	Seasonal trade case study mark 1	Toys	Nov. 1983 – June 1986	12 days
	'' mark 2	''	June 1986	12 days
5	Food case study mark 1	Dairy	Jan. – Dec. 1984	11 days
	'' mark 2	''	Jan. 1987 –	12 days
6	Shopping centres	Shopping centres	Jan. 1984 –	5 days
7	Locations	Locations	Feb. 1984 –	18 days
8	Social and political framework	Community	Oct. 1984 –	10 days

Figure 2. *CUE! modules: generic and marketing titles availability and duration of training*

Research

The CLEAR unit knew from its previous research that many work-based capabilities are achieved through action, self-management, experience and reflection. This is a complex and flexible model of learning entirely different from that of traditional school-based learning. This 'action: discovery: capability' model had been successfully applied to short intensive management training courses by the college, and further tested in a long-term course for unemployed adults. But it was by no means certain that the model could be applied to youth trainees.

The initial research was carried out with young people between the ages of 15 and 20 from two large comprehensive schools in Nottinghamshire and at a large food and department store in Long Eaton. This provided an indication of the scale of the problem. With the changing nature of employment, many young people at school realized that they needed to acquire a range of capabilities to match the kaleidoscope of work situations. However, because of the inflexibility of school curricula and timetables, many of them, particularly those labelled as low achieving school leavers (LASLs), were alienated from formal learning. Yet they appeared to be unprepared for, and apprehensive of, learning through action.

In contrast, many young shop employees cited instances where they had learned through the 'discovery: action: capability' route, albeit informally. The research also established that a key catalyst in this process was an older, experienced working colleague who usually provided guidance, support, and positive criticism. The final component of the system came out of this research – a mature colleague at work would be designated adviser, guide and counsellor to the trainee.

Development – The Learning Package

In July 1983 the pilot CUE! package was launched on 13 suspicious young women and two reserved young men. They had every right to be wary. The first audio tapes were basic, the assignments sketchy, and the overall plan rudimentary. Group dynamics were also a major problem as some of the youngsters had been selected because they were 'difficult cases'.

Seasoned management tutors were employed to play the initial adviser/guide roles – and subsequently reported that it had been a particularly demanding assignment. All the trainees' parents were contacted and interviewed at home to establish the amount of family support that could realistically be expected.

Three findings came out of the development work which proved to be operationally important. First, the trainees did not want the audio tapes to be 'instructional': they did not want to be lectured to. All the tapes have since adopted a 'magazine' format and there has been no criticism from the trainees. Secondly, professional teachers, no matter how experienced, were found not to be an effective substitute for an experienced shop-floor adviser. Finally, most parents were anxious to support their children and saw it as a means of maintaining a relationship despite the inevitable tensions between parents and teenagers.

Once these important design considerations had been established, the production of tapes and workbooks was put in hand. Over 90 days of discovery learning assignments have been produced. Every trainee using CUE! in 1985 was interviewed and asked to assess and comment on the materials. Whilst numerous improvements were suggested, there were no comments which indicated any need for major restructuring of the approach.

The current range of discovery learning modules is shown in Figure 2, together with the number of days allocated to each. The generic titles of the modules are not used on the actual materials. 'Introduction to Retailing' is presented to the trainee and adviser as 'This could be the start of something BIG'. 'Facing the Public' becomes 'Images'. Figure 3 provides an outline of the assignments and time allocations of the introductory module.

Assignment	Duration
(1) Welcome and introduction	1 day
(2) Department stores	2 days
(3) Coca-Cola	2 days
(4) Co-operatives	2 days
(5) Variety stores	2 days
(6) Organizations	1 day
(7) Supermarkets/superstores	2 days
(8) Potatoes and chips	1 day

Figure 3. *Time allocation for module 1 assignments*

Development – Residential

In establishing the overall specification, the training officers had been insistent that any residential programme should be integrated with the rest of the learning materials. 'No climbing up mountains for the hell of it!' At the same time they accepted that a residential course would be beneficial in providing trainees with an opportunity to consolidate their learning, develop social skills, and meet their peers from around the country. A second residential course would allow for an evaluation of progress and develop a sense of continuity.

Experience with the pilot group at the Co-operative College provided valuable information about the needs and behaviour of young people in a residential setting. The determination of young people to explore the limits of acceptable behaviour had not been anticipated – and neither was the extent of smoking and under-age drinking. It was soon clear that youth trainees would need close and constant supervision. Another surprise was the discovery that single study bedrooms were not appreciated by the young women. Mattresses were dragged along corridors in the evening so that they could enjoy the security of sleeping five to a room. It was decided that bunked accommodation would be more appropriate – and there have been few complaints since.

The first residential course was developed to the point where it has become a well-rehearsed routine. The trainees make a study of retail practices and examine auctions, markets, small stores and shopping centres in Nottingham and Melton Mowbray. Their goal is to produce a promotional video programme using a closed circuit television studio. Following the course, the trainees have to design a supporting publicity booklet. On the second residential the trainees are given hands-on experience with computers with a practical application to marketing, stock and price controls, and bar codes.

For many trainees the residential courses are the highlights of the whole CUE! system. For some it is the first time they have been away from home. And, although they work very long hours while they are at the college, many of them regard the experience as an adventure and a holiday.

Subsequent Development

In 1984 the MSC released details of a set of general core skills which were to guide the design and development of YTS on-the-job training. The CLEAR unit made a systematic analysis of the coverage of each of the core skills in each of the modules

"BIG" INTRODUCTION TO RETAILING — Keywords	Welcome and Introduction	Assignment: Department stores	Assignment: Coca Cola	Assignment: Cooperatives	Assignment: Variety stores	Assignment: Organizations	Assignment: Supermarkets/superstores	Assignment: Potatoes and chips
Count / Work out / Check and correct / Compare		✓✓✓✓	✓✓✓✓	✓✓✓✓	✓ ✓	✓	✓	✓✓✓✓
Interpret			✓	✓				
Estimate			✓	✓	✓		✓	
Measure / Mark out	✓	✓✓	✓✓	✓✓	✓✓			✓
Compare / Recognize value		✓	✓	✓	✓		✓✓	✓
Find out / Interpret		✓✓	✓✓	✓✓	✓	✓✓	✓	✓✓
Provide information	✓	✓	✓	✓	✓	✓		✓
Notice / Ask for assistance / Offer assistance / React / Discuss / Converse		✓ ✓✓	✓ ✓ ✓✓	✓ ✓✓	✓ ✓	✓ ✓		✓ ✓✓
Plan / Diagnose		✓✓	✓✓	✓✓		✓	✓	✓
Decide	✓	✓	✓	✓	✓	✓	✓	✓
Check / Monitor / Notice		✓ ✓	✓✓✓	✓ ✓			✓✓	✓✓✓
Locate / Identify / Handle, lift or transport / Adjust / Arrange / Carry out procedures / Check	✓	✓✓ ✓✓	✓ ✓	✓	✓	✓ ✓	✓ ✓	✓ ✓ ✓
Adopt safe practices / Lift or transport / Manipulate / Operate / Set up / Assemble / Dismantle					✓✓			
Carry out procedures / Check / Restock								

Figure 4. 'Big' core skills analysis

RICC REVIEW SUMMARY	Introduction to Retailing	Seasonal Case Study	Facing the Public	Locations 1.	Locations 2.	Shopping Centres	Community	Residential 1.	Residential 2.
Keywords	15 days	12 days	10 days	7 days	11 days	6 days	15 days	5 days	5 days
Count	4	2	1	3	10	1	4	3	3
Work out	6	2	3	3	11	4	4	3	5
Check and correct	4	1	1	2	6	3	4	3	5
Compare	6	2	4	4	6	3	4		6
Interpret	2	3	5	4	12	3	7	5	10
Estimate	4		1	4	11	4	10	5	5
Measure	6		2	4	7	3	6		
Mark out	4		3	4	7	3	6	1	2
Compare	6	2		1		3	4	3	6
Recognize value	2	3		1		2	3	4	6
Find out	6	5	6	2	9	8	25	11	11
Interpret	6	5	7	4	10	6	26	12	15
Provide information	7	5	9	3		5	19	16	15
Notice	2	2		1			8	7	4
Ask for assistance	4	3	2				13	11	16
Offer assistance		1					1	4	2
React	2	1	1			1	6	3	2
Discuss	4	4	3	1	2	1	7	14	11
Converse	4	2	1				7	12	10
Plan	6	2		2	3	4	8	5	10
Diagnose	4	1	1	1	2	1	4	2	6
Decide	8	5	3	1	1	3	6	13	16
Check	5	4		1		2	5	3	7
Monitor	3	3		1		1	6	2	6
Notice	5	5		1		2	4	4	2
Locate	7	3	2	2	3	3	11	3	3
Identify	6	4	2	2	3	4	11	3	3
Handle, lift or transport								4	3
Adjust								1	
Arrange		2	1	1		1		4	2
Carry out procedures	2	1	1		1			6	6
Check	1	1		1	3			2	3
Adopt safe practices								8	1
Lift or transport								2	1
Manipulate								1	
Operate						1		4	3
Set up	1								
Assemble	1			1					
Dismantle								3	1
Carry out procedures								10	3
Check					2			8	2
Restock								2	1

Figure 5. *Core skill coverage of system*

(Figure 4). Remembering the limitations of discovery learning it was hoped that the CUE! system would at least cover 30 – 40 per cent of the core skills. Much to the researchers' surprise CUE! actually achieved 100 per cent cover (Figure 5).

After running the CUE! system for two years the CLEAR unit received a grant from the Distributive Industries Training Trust to develop a three-year certificated programme based on discovery learning. The first stage was launched in February 1986. However, there is no guarantee that the new Retail Capability Certificate will find favour with the industry. Since the introduction of the Youth Training Scheme many retailers have confronted the problems identified by the Midlands training officers in 1983. A number began YTS with a traditional day-release programme, only to be forced to organize the off-the-job training in-house when trainees absented themselves from college in large numbers. There are now a variety of schemes available to the market – which must be to the advantage of young people.

Review

The CUE! system has provided flexibility in the areas originally requested – *operations* and *context*. In addition to offering flexible scheduling, the system also allowed trainees to join YTS at any time of year – something that was almost impossible with traditional FE. As each trainee's programme unfolds, it examines local and regional retailers, thus creating a unique learning path. This means that CUE! reduces the competitive pressures which arise in homogeneous learning situations, and is therefore not only flexible in time and space but also provides a unique experience for each trainee.

Flexibility also extends to the *process* and *content* of CUE! Trainees are encouraged to manage the *process* of their own personal development and learning skills through assignments which take them out of their work environment. From this, trainees develop their potential in communication, initiative, decision-making, co-operation and problem-solving, gaining confidence in their own ability to learn by investigation. Trainees who require longer to complete an assignment, or who wish to complete to a very high standard, have the freedom to do so.

Finally, CUE! is varied in *content*. In this respect its design contrasts with recent trends in curriculum development which have tended to reduce the material to be learned to relatively small pre-specified units. The design and development of CUE! has been founded on the expansive concept of 'role' (customer, consumer, supplier, retailer, citizen) rather than the reductive concept of 'skill'. Nevertheless, as the core skill analysis revealed, the system does provide an opportunity to develop the skills that the MSC requires from youth training.

References

Greaves, S (1985) Training for retailing. *Employment Gazette*, **93**, 10, October, pp 415-416.
Hill, J R W (1983) Co-operation and co-operatives in the curriculum: a pilot project in schools liaison. In Trott, A, Strongman, L and Giddens, L (eds) *Aspects of Educational Technology XVI*. Kogan Page, London.
Houlton, R (1978) Management education and training: analysis and processes. *Bulletin of the Society for Co-operative Studies*, **33**, pp 42-54.

Acknowledgements

The authors thank Jim McCloskey and Andrew Christensen of the CLEAR Unit for their core skill analysis of the CUE! system.

2.15 Social Work Education and Open Learning

R Brewster
Social Work Education Adviser, Edinburgh
M Lever
Strathclyde Open Learning Project, Glasgow
D Fordyce
Heriot-Watt University, Edinburgh

Abstract: Open learning is an alternative educational philosophy in which material design and delivery is oriented towards the needs and constraints of the learner. There are implications for courses based on such a philosophy in terms of material and staff development costs.
  In Scotland, the Central Council for Education and Training in Social Work (CCETSW), as the advisory and validatory body for social work education and training, needed to evaluate the implications of such a philosophy. As a mechanism for such an evaluation, CCETSW designed an extended professional development programme for a volunteer group of its educators and trainers. The outcome of the programme is the production of open learning material relevant to social work. The development programme consists of an initial workshop focusing on the nature of open learning, and defining the needs of the potential material developers. Post-workshop support is provided to individuals and groups based on their defined needs. The feedback from the program will provide CCETSW with the evaluation they required.
  In terms of professional development this programme is innovative in its extended structure, which provides post-workshop support when participants have the major problem of implementing new skills and ideas.
  The paper outlines the design and current progress with this programme.

Background

Open learning is a philosophy of education where the provision is oriented towards the learner. There are two features of learner orientation:

- constraints in time and access to education (access relating to the ability of learners to take advantage of an educational provision and to prerequisite entrance qualifications); and
- variations in individuals' learning styles and strategies.

The first of the two features is the hallmark of open learning; the second of the two features relates to the quality of any learning experience. Overcoming the constraints of time available to study and of access to formal education create special challenges for, and demand particular skills of, the providers of open learning experiences.
  The Central Council for Education and Training in Social Work (CCETSW) is a body which advises on and validates the quality of education and training provision in social work. Evaluation of educational philosophies and innovations within philosophies is an ongoing commitment for such a body.

Introduction

Open learning has to some extent always existed alongside formal education provision, formal education being defined as timetabled classes within educational centres.

Open learning, as a philosophy, has developed over the past 10 – 15 years to become a recognized alternative to formal education provisions. This is the result of change in the education and training needs of industry and commerce. It has also been aided by advances in educational technology.

The more flexible nature of an open learning provision makes it expensive, as reflected in the pump-priming sums provided by the Manpower Services Commission (MSC) through the Open Tech programme, and has implications for the professional development of the providers. Because of these factors CCETSW, as an advisory and validating body, needed to consider the implications and potential of open learning.

CCETSW in Scotland initially published an internal discussion paper, 'Open Learning, Distance Learning and Educational Technology', which raised several issues which it would need to consider in relation to the implications of open learning. For example:

- how 'open' can qualifying courses be, especially in a professional context which implies restricted access?
- there would be a need to clearly define core competences in social work
- there would also be a need to consider the feasibility of presenting and assessing interpersonal skills in what could be a distance learning mode.

These and other issues raised were fully discussed by a group of people involved in aspects of open learning in Scotland called to advise CCETSW in March 1985. Because of the disparate nature of existing open learning provision, the suggestion from the meeting was to attempt to operate a professional development programme to evaluate open learning directly in the field of social work education and training. A working group was formed to plan a funded programme commencing in the autumn of 1985.

The Programme Structure

The aim of the programme was to allow CCETSW in Scotland to evaluate the implications and potential of open learning. This was to be achieved through social work educators and trainers developing open learning packages. CCETSW would part-fund, -support and -monitor the development of the packages; the programme would terminate in a workshop in which material producers and CCETSW would explore open learning from a position of experience. Figure 1 shows the programme structure in outline.

In the detailed planning much debate centred on how to organize such a professional development programme.

- In Scotland there already exist bodies, such as the Scottish Council for Educational Technology (SCET) and the Scottish Open Technology Training and Support Unit (SCOTTSU), which operate skills training workshops for

participants → professional development programme → development of open learning projects ↘
                                                                                                    workshop → evaluation of open learning as an alternative philosophy
C.C.E.T.S.W. (Scotland) → part funding, support, monitor ↗

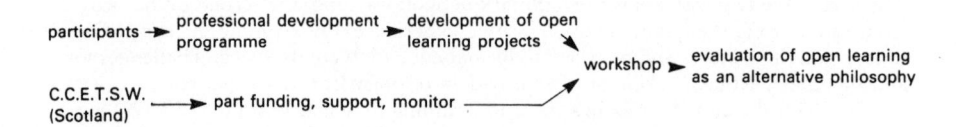

Figure 1. *Outline of programme structure*

open learning. They provide consultancy, seminars and workshops on demand and for different skills levels.
☐ But there is a stage before these workshops in which clear awareness of philosophy and consequently specific learner needs are the objectives.
☐ In addition, skills training workshops are a simulation exercise which may give an added awareness of the issues.
☐ But, what support is provided for individuals doing it for the first time, for real? How can these individuals use that experience to evaluate their efforts and subsequently improve?

The model of professional development finally adopted was a 12-month programme. The programme was to commence with a 30-hour residential 'awareness and needs identification' workshop, and terminate with a workshop which evaluated experiences. In the intervening period a support programme for individuals and groups would operate, based initially on the declared needs identified at the initial workshop. Although the principal objective was for participants to develop open learning packages, this was not to be a mandatory requirement of participation in the initial stage, the 'awareness and needs identification' workshop.

Figure 2 outlines the programme structure. There are three stages to the programme, a design which was described as open learning for open learning.

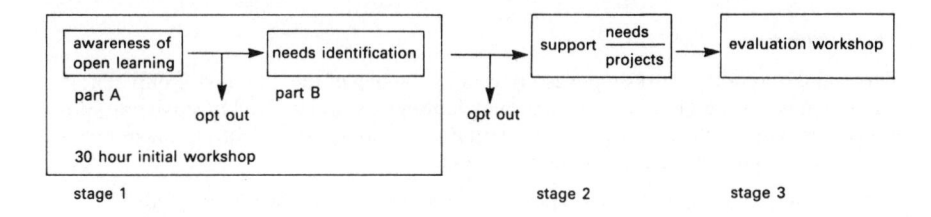

Figure 2. *Model of professional development programme*

As the programme is to enable CCETSW to assess open learning and as the structure of the programme is open learning for open learning, it was decided to evaluate each stage and, as a mechanism to ensure rigour, it was also decided to write up and publish papers about each stage at the end of each stage. The papers would describe the detailed plan before a stage and include the evaluation of that stage. Currently the programme is in stage two, the support stage. Stage one, the workshop, took place in October 1985 in Pitlochry.

Stage one and the plan for stage two are reported here.

Stage One: Awareness and Needs

The Workshop

The 30-hour residential workshop was planned to fulfil three functions:

Part A (Figure 2)
☐ to focus on the learner and the nature of learning, to encourage consideration of how learners learn, what constraints operate and how to try to overcome these;
☐ to focus on the nature of open learning systems in order that open learning as a philosophy might be more clearly defined;

Part B (Figure 2)
☐ to facilitate the consideration of the needs of individuals as a necessary pre-condition of stage two.

To provide a context for the workshop, participants were asked as a prerequisite for enrolment in the programme to identify a particular training project which they would wish to pursue for personnel in their agency (trainers), or a student group (educators).

For part A, participants were paired and asked to design an outline open learning programme on their partner's project. Inputs were provided on the nature of learning and examples of working open learning projects were described to allow the nature of open learning to be defined and clarified through group discussion. The examples of working open learning projects were selected to include a range of technology. Each participant also received a folio of background material on learning theory and the design of learning experiences.

The workshop commenced at 11.00 am on day 1 and part A terminated at 10.00 am on day 2 with the debriefing by pairs of programme designs.

Part B was a follow-on from part A. From the experience of part A individuals were asked to declare and prioritize through a facilitated exercise specific needs in relation to the development of an open learning project. Over lunch, declared needs of those who had continued with the programme were compared to identify common needs. The groupings were declared using Chinese wall posters for group response in the last session. The result of the afternoons discussion was an outline plan for stage two and participant support (for those who now had decided to stay with the project). This was not as 'clear' an exercise as originally planned as will be described in 'the outcome' below.

The Evaluation

The evaluation of the workshop was undertaken by one of the planning group. The evaluation consisted of interviews with the planning group involved in stage one and interviews with participants and observation of working groups during stage one.

The interviews with the planning group defined:

- feelings about the workshop just prior to the start of the workshop which identified the effect of last-minute adjustments in the detailed structure to stage one;
- their perspective of the roles they were taking in relation to each other;
- the detailed plans of events during the workshop prior to their execution. This defined the expectation of outcomes to specific events and how these were to be achieved from the facilitator's perspective.

The interviews with participants gave specific feedback on expectations which had been created and how these married or conflicted with actual events. This feedback was not given to event facilitators during the workshop.

The observations of working groups gave illuminative feedback on how specific events were interpreted. This was compared with expectations of outcomes defined by event facilitators, and supported the evidence from participant interviews.

The Outcome

- Of the 20 participants to enrol on the project, 18 carried on to part B, the definition and prioritization of needs.
- A late modification to the style of presenting open learning systems at work occurred which resulted in more focus being given to the technology rather than to the inherent philosophy; some diversion from the objectives of part A resulted, creating conflicts in expectation.
- There was perceived to be too abrupt a change in the workshop between part A and part B; that is, a focus on open learning and a focus on individual needs in relation to open learning. More time, it was felt, was needed to assimilate the meaning and implication(s) of open learning before individual needs were

focused on. This led to a difficulty in the discussion stage of part B. The difficulty arose in the clustering of needs and the presentation of a clear idea of what the next stage was and where it started. As a result the workshop was terminated with a commitment from the planning group to define clusters of needs and present a follow-up structure for stage two, based on the need of individuals as declared in part B, which was now able to include 'supplementary' needs which were the result of a reflection of part A.

'Supplementary' needs were requested within 14 days to avoid too great a delay and resultant loss of impetus.

Stage Two: Support

14 participants out of the original 20 remain in stage two. The principal objective for them is the development of an open learning project. This is being supported by consultancy arrangements between individual members of the planning group (six in number) and groups of participants. The planning group are in constant contact to share expertise and define the location of specific expertise in relation to individual project support.

As a general format this is going over, again, the criteria defined in the workshop in relation to open learning: define learner needs, styles, constraints; relate the features of specific media to the nature of the learning of the target group (their needs, styles and constraints); evaluate material.

This process has been a 'do it – review it – do it again (but now with support)' style of professional development.

Currently consultancies are in operation.

Alongside project consultancies the 'support' of declared (and supplementary) needs is being undertaken. Five categories of declared and supplementary needs were identified:

Category One

Identification of databases. A typical statement under this category was:
'Could I have a resource list of literature on open learning and where available?'
This 'need' was responded to by pointing individuals in the right direction.

Category Two

Liaison with others.
This category of need was declared by the general statement:
'use of groups to check out/share difficulties'.
The nature of difficulties defined were typified by the following paraphrased examples:
personal problems – working with colleagues not of the same mind;
to get ideas from other 'practitioners' not necessarily in same field.
This category of need is intended to be satisfied by linking with the Open Learning Federation in Scotland, who have regional practitioner groups. The initial 'session' will adopt the format of the BBC television programme *Question Time*. A panel of experienced practitioners will answer questions from the social work group.

Category Three

Particular needs (skills).
This was typified by the needs statements:
'practical skills with computer'; 'computer graphics'.
Specific courses are available on skills training through SCET and SCOTTSU.
Details of such courses are being made available to individuals.

Category Four

Particular needs (knowledge about general package design).
Typical questions here were:
How do you plan and implement an open learning programme?'
'How do you design/structure an open learning programme? – Do you have to gain knowledge and competence together as you go along or are they best gained in sequence, knowledge then competence?'
Literature is available relating to package design. A small workshop is to be offered as an introduction.

Category Five

Particular needs (knowledge about open learning theory).
This 'need' had the largest number of statements/questions under the general headings: theory of adult learning; assessment and evaluation; open learning – social skills *vs* cognitive skills; open learning – groups *vs* individual, albeit within groups.
These knowledge needs are to be tackled through a seminar as a first stage which answers specific questions relating to the specific headings. The seminar will be a discussion around specific examples of courses which have addressed themselves to areas defined by the social work educators and trainers.

Closing Summary

The first stage of this project has been successfully completed. That success has three elements (identified from the evaluation):

1. some people have decided to proceed no further either because open learning is inappropriate to their needs or because they have not enough time, but this is now an informed decision
2. some people have reinforced the knowledge that what they do already *is* open learning, and that they need no further help
3. some people have defined their needs within open learning and are proceeding to stage two.

This is not to imply that the workshop was successful for all participants. There is always a mismatch between some of the aims of a planning group and some of the expectations of participants; some participants will be disappointed and even angry. Their criticisms have been considered and some will be used to modify the event when it is run again.

The second, support, stage is in progress. At present the programme is dealing with the support of specific projects and of defined needs. The two forms of support, project support and defined needs, are different but not mutually exclusive. Some participants have specific projects for which they are being offered support *and* wish also to follow through defined needs.

The second stage of the development process will be more fully reported at a later stage.

2.16 A Flexible Learning System in Nurse Education

P I Pleasance and J Juett
Charles Frears School of Nursing, Leicester

Abstract: There can be little doubt that a library can appear a daunting place to a student new to the world of advanced study. Add to the library a full range of audiovisual aids and other learning resources and the problem can reach mammoth proportions. Just where do you start? This paper describes a pilot project being undertaken in a school of nursing. The project uses a microcomputer to co-ordinate the offerings in a multimedia learning resources centre so as to facilitate the most effective use of the student's private study time. It is envisaged that the skeleton program produced will have applications in a diverse range of educational fields.

Introduction

The preparation of the adult learner for professional competence makes special demands of teaching staff. The adult learner brings his personal baggage of prejudice, preconceptions and personal experience. Measured in years, or in experiences, some adult students will arrive at the start of a new educational journey weighed down with material which may enhance or inhibit the new learning.

Part of the role of the teacher is to assess this material and to build upon it until professional competence is reached. This building is done by providing an individual experience which takes previous learning into account. Entwined with this provision is the learner's current ability, his motivation and his self-imposed time allocation for the task, all of which may enhance or constrain his progress.

Certain factors within the individual – previous experience, ability and motivation – multiplied over a group of students present the teacher in adult education not only with an enormous range of learning potential but also an enormous range of individual need. One way to meet this need is the allocation of tutorial time. Usually this is unrealistic in terms of staff time, the number of learners involved, and possibly even the number of geographical sites at which students are located.

Nurse education contains all the rewards and difficulties associated with general adult education. The spectrum of learner ability may range from a previous higher degree in a related subject to a handful of 'O' levels. These previous learning experiences will be reflected in the learners' expectations of educational strategies within a school of nursing, namely, an approach close to student-centred learning.

Nurse education is moving towards meeting the different aspirations of today's nurse learner. The work of the curriculum planners and the educational psychologists has been applied from within nurse education (University of London, 1982; English National Board for Nursing, Midwifery and Health Visiting, 1983). The added impetus of two major investigations (Royal College of Nursing, 1985; United Kingdom Central Council for Nursing, Midwifery and Health Visiting, 1985/6) will be seen by some to move it even further. The essence of these changes is the shift from an apprentice learning style towards the attitudes and practices of advanced further and higher education in preparation for a physical move which has been widely recommended in the reports previously mentioned.

The final issue which needs to be considered in this context also arises from the statutory bodies controlling nursing and nurse education. It has been stated explicitly that the student should be able to take responsibility for his own learning and for his own professional development. The teacher of nursing is required to facilitate self-directedness within the students of the profession.

To summarize, there are certain problems inherent in the provision of education for nurses which demand attention. Not the least of these is the wide range of ability and previous experience present within any one group. Coupled with this is the rapidly changing climate in which the needs of the individual are to be met.

In Leicester's Charles Frears School of Nursing this problem is compounded by the number of students involved. There are approximately 1,000 learners following six basic courses and a number of post-basic courses.

It must be said that learning resources do exist to meet the needs of these students. What cannot be found so easily is the tutor time required to identify appropriate resources for each individual learner's requirements. Implicit within this is the difficulty of identifying with each learner the type of resource which most appeals as a learning medium. A modern multimedia learning resources centre is a bewildering place to start to identify not only learning needs, but also a pleasing and appropriate 'teacher' from the array of books, journals, charts, slides, tapes, videos, computer aided learning (CAL) programs, etc.

What follows is an attempt to find an educationally viable solution to the problem of assisting students to exploit the potential of a multimedia learning resources centre fully.

Historically, the nursing profession has been hesitant about the use of technology in the education of its members. This is perhaps in part due to the essentially vocational nature of the nurse and his or her attitudes towards training, but there is little doubt also that an important factor has been the scepticism on the part of nurse educators towards the quality of some of the software that has been produced (some programmed learning materials and, more recently, some computer assisted learning programs). Because of factors such as these, it is seen as essential that any educational implementations of the computer be of the very highest standard; otherwise uptake is unlikely to be substantial or long-lasting.

The members of the computer interest group of the Charles Frears School of Nursing, in recognizing these points, identified several other related themes:

- ☐ There is an increasing number of nurse teachers who are showing an interest in the potential value of the use of the computer as an adjunct in the preparation of nurses.
- ☐ It is generally felt that the most effective and beneficial implementation of CAL is in patient simulation (Pleasance, 1984) through which nurses can actually test out the implications that different nursing interventions will have for a patient. Conversely there seems little point in simply setting up very expensive hardware if all that it is going to do is 'turn pages' (Pleasance, 1984).
- ☐ It is acknowledged that the computers available in schools of nursing for student use are almost exclusively the small microcomputer variety (BBC model B, Commodore 64) (Pleasance, 1985) and machines such as these are not really suited to the requirements of programs of this type.
- ☐ There are not, as yet, the resources available within schools of nursing (including expertise, but mainly time) to realistically undertake a project based on patient simulation.

Thus it was decided to instigate a pilot project of a suggestion first mooted in 1984 (Pleasance, 1984): to use a small microcomputer (BBC model B) to direct the learners in a multimedia learning resources centre towards the most appropriate learning materials.

It was anticipated that such a project should form an effective marriage between computer technology and the realistic aims of nurse learners for self-directed education.

Following extensive discussions to decide an appropriate model, MICROTEXT from the National Physical Laboratory was used to produce a framework program. This would require the nurse teacher to 'fill in the spaces' in order to produce a complete package for the selected subject, with individual resources chosen from amongst the bank specific to that school of nursing. It is also envisaged that this framework could be used by teachers/learners of other academic specialities. The project was dubbed 'computer management of learning'.

Before proceeding, additional prerequisites were determined, ie that the program should be:

(a) 'user-friendly', which was interpreted as meaning that it should be fully documented on screen and should be 'menu-driven'
(b) not overpowering or confusing to the student, ie avoiding 'things' happening too suddenly
(c) flexible, ie able to be modified by the teacher without difficulty according to learner feedback; and should be capable of providing a student profile for the teacher to enable the learner's progress to be assessed and post-use guidance offered

and finally,

(d) that the student should always feel in control of the computer and should always be able to proceed how and when he or she wishes.

The finally agreed flow diagram for the structure of the package is shown in Figure 1.

It is important to identify certain specific features within the program.

1. The learner selects the main topic from a menu.
2. It was decided that the various grades of learners who would use the system would benefit from using different resources, although obviously there could be some overlap. Thus the user is asked to select his grade from a menu. As a result of this selection, the appropriate module is called from disc. This is carried out from within the program with no additional intervention required on the part of the learner.
3. It was considered that a page of text instantly appearing on the screen could seem somewhat threatening, especially to a user unfamiliar with computers. Thus text appears at a readable rate. The danger of this approach is recognized in that it can force a slow reader to read too fast to gain maximum comprehension. The rate of printing is simply altered by the teacher, after appropriate trials.
4. For the same reasons, it can be daunting if the instant the user touches a key, the screen changes. Thus a short delay (usually 0.8 seconds) is built in before anything 'happens' following a student interaction.
5. The learner selects from a second menu the specific area of his or her chosen subject, eg relevant anatomy and physiology. Thereafter he or she is directed to a set of multiple choice objective test questions which are designed to cover the area in the form of a pre-test of knowledge. Multiple choice questions are chosen because of their prevalence in nurse education. The teacher may replace these questions with any other single response type of question. The number of questions is variable. The program will keep a running score and also assess performance in blocks of three questions. Thus, with careful selection, the teacher can subdivide items to test different aspects of the subject and thus identify areas of satisfactory knowledge or particular weakness. The teacher has to insert those different aspects into vacant slots in the body of the program so that the results can be fed to the student. It is comparatively easy to alter any of the numbers or fields to suit individual requirements.
6. It is worthy of note that MICROTEXT is inherently 'user-friendly', eg it allows upper and lower case options. This has been enhanced by allowing, wherever practical,

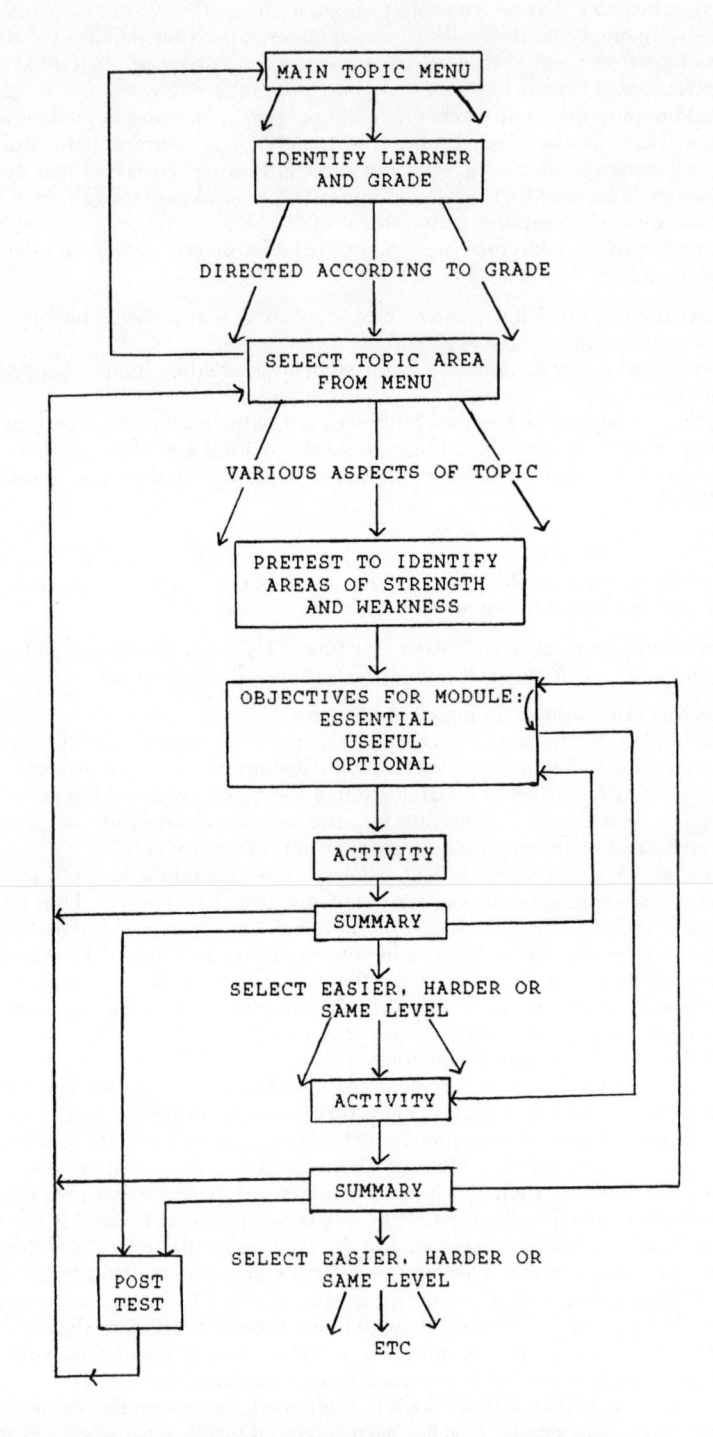

Figure 1. *Computer managed learning program flow diagram*

single-key entry. The student is always told where the RETURN key is required. Likewise the flexibility and self-directedness is built in by always giving the option to return to the menu, to reselect or quit, or to proceed.

7. As far as the objectives of the module being studied are concerned, these have once again to be 'edited in' previously by the teacher. They are colour-coded and identified as ESSENTIAL, USEFUL, or OPTIONAL. (The classification may well be influenced by the grade of learner for whom the module is being prepared.) The learner is advised that whilst he or she is able to move freely amongst activities designed to meet the different levels of objectives, he or she should endeavour to ensure that the essential ones can first be met.

8. The student is now presented with the first activity and told of its format, location, and given any specific information that he needs. He then would leave the computer, watch the video, read the article or whatever, before proceeding with the program.

```
                ACTIVITY                                    (E1)


FORMAT:
LOCATION:
DESCRIPTION:


DETAILS:


This activity will help towards meetin
the following objectives:


       ESSENTIAL    Yes
       USEFUL       Yes
       OPTIONAL     No




       COMPLETE THIS ACTIVITY BEFORE
                 CONTINUING



            Press RETURN to continue
```

Figure 2. *Example of blank activities display*

The activity page (Figure 2) also contains information about the level of objectives which the activity will help to meet. The first activity is geared towards the essential objectives, but following a summary page, the student is presented with a menu offering the following options:

(1) Return to previous activity
(2) Proceed to next activity
(3) Proceed to final test
(4) Change to easier level (if available)
(5) Change to harder level (if available)
(6) Review objectives
(7) Return to menu

An explanation of these options may be helpful.

Option (2) will take the learner sequentially through all the activities, starting with those geared towards meeting essential objectives, eventually reaching those geared to achieving the optional level objectives.

Option (3) permits early access to the post-test if he or she feels the learning needed has been achieved.

Option (4) would permit a student who is working on activities specializing in useful objectives to return to activities geared towards essential objectives.

Option (5) is the opposite of option (4).

Option (6) allows the student to see the objectives again, but the program automatically returns to the activity which has just been concluded.

Option (7) once again permits the learner to change direction completely, or to quit.

It is considered that this menu is important in the maintenance of the flexibility of the system and of the self-directed nature of the program.

At present the program has provision for nine separate activities (three for each level) although this, once again, may be amended by the teacher. On completion of the activities, or sooner if selected, the student is asked to undertake a post-test which at present re-uses the questions of the pre-test. Whilst this may serve the purpose of demonstrating that learning has taken place, it may ultimately be necessary to compose different questions to fulfil this function.

Finally, the student is encouraged to proceed to select a further module with which to continue his or her study.

In criticism of the program, the following points should be discussed.

First, whilst every effort has been made to foster 'user-friendliness', it must be acknowledged that considerable work will need to be undertaken by the teacher in order to implement the system. Whilst this is true of any framework program, in this example a working knowledge of MICROTEXT is a prerequisite. Of course, full documentation will be provided to assist in this area.

Second, there are dangers in a program that uses a predetermined format, and indeed, uses a variety of colours. Whilst an attempt has been made to be consistent, field trials are now required to monitor and evaluate the opinions of the users.

Third, it is recognized that using a teacher-selected bank of learning resources may itself restrict self-directedness. The limited number of resources identified could inhibit the use of other equally valuable ones. The learner should be instructed that they form a basis only and should be recommended to follow up any leads discovered during his study.

The computer must be seen as a signpost only and not as a definer of what is worthwhile. The educational process must always be seen as more important than the technology.

In conclusion, this project is at an early stage of development. What is eagerly awaited are student trials. Early feedback from teaching staff led to a complete rewrite of the algorithm resulting in the program which is presented.

References

English National Board for Nursing, Midwifery and Health Visiting (1983) *Syllabus for Mental Illness Nursing*. END, London.

Pleasance, P (1984) Computer assisted learning for nurses. *Library Association Nursing Interest Sub-group Newsletter*, **4**, 3, pp 6-10.

Pleasance, P (1985) NUMINE for nurses. In Alloway, B S and Mills, G M (eds) *Aspects of Educational Technology XVIII. New Directions in Education and Training Technology*. Kogan Page, London.

Royal College of Nursing (1985) Commission on Nurse Education. *The Education of Nurses: A New Dispensation*. Royal College of Nursing, London.

United Kingdom Central Council for Nursing, Midwifery and Health Visiting. (1985/6) *Project 2000*. UKCC, London.

University of London (1982) *Syllabus for the Diploma in Nursing*. University of London, London.

2.17 Flexible Learning in Hospitality Crafts

T Baum
Council for Education, Recruitment and Training (CERT), Dublin

Abstract: CERT, the state training agency for hotels, catering and tourism in Ireland, is responsible for the research, development, assessment and certification of national certificate courses at craft level. The main emphasis of CERT's work relates to traditional catering craft subject areas within the educational system, such as food production, food service, bartending and housekeeping.

However, in response to a researched need identified within the hotel and catering industry in Ireland, a new experimental full-time programme has been developed and piloted which lays particular emphasis on the combination of a number of basic skills with a strong hospitality and social skills dimension. Graduates of this experimental hospitality crafts course are now meeting a clear manpower deficiency within the small hotel/guesthouse sectors of the Irish industry.

Of considerable general interest to educational technologists are the approach to teaching, learning and assessment which features very strongly in the design and implementation of the hospitality crafts course. The programme emphasizes strategies which are flexible and learner-centred. This approach is seen as central to the course's prime objective of educating and training a multi-skilled, flexible workforce for the hospitality industry.

This paper describes the consultative, development, piloting and evaluation processes involved in translating a general research finding into a highly flexible educational and training package, which prepares young people for a hitherto undefined but much demanded role in the hotel and catering industry.

Introduction

Tourism, both foreign and domestic, is a key industry in Ireland. This relates both to employment, with upwards of 60,000 permanent jobs and approximately 30,000 seasonal positions linked to tourism, and to the contribution which this sector makes to the national economy. In 1985, tourism generated over IR£800 million or over seven per cent of the gross national product. Of this, almost IR£500 million relates to foreign tourism earning. Tourism is also geographically widely dispersed throughout the country and makes a significant contribution, locally, to the employment and economic wellbeing of most regions of the country. The tourism sector, however, is highly volatile and subject to very competitive and fickle market influences. Thus quality, in terms of product standards, particularly in relation to service, is of prime importance to the long-term wellbeing of the industry, and state investment in ensuring such quality is high.

Responsibility for ensuring the maintenance (and indeed improvement) of standards in this context is vested in two bodies. Bord Failte Eireann, the Irish Tourist Board, carries out a wide promotional and grading function, primarily related to product facilities. CERT, the state training agency for hotels, catering and tourism, is responsible for initial education and training for the industry at craft level within the college system; for the provision of career development opportunities for personnel working in industry; and for a wide range of diagnostic and advisory services in industry.

This paper focuses on the development and implementation of a new one-year full-time craft apprenticeship-type course for the hotel, catering and tourism industry, styled the 'hospitality crafts course', from its research and negotiation origins through to its operation as a national certificate programme of the National Craft Curricula and Certification Board for the hotel, catering and tourism industry in Ireland.

The National Craft Curricula and Certification Board was established in 1982 under the auspices of the Department of Education and CERT.

The Board's remit is primarily concerned with the research, development, implementation, assessment and certification of programmes offered at craft level within the educational system and leading to qualifications giving professional craft status to young people within the hotel, catering and tourism industry. The initial task for the board on its establishment was to develop and introduce replacement programmes for courses which have traditionally been followed in Ireland and lead to certification by the City & Guilds of London Institute. This is being undertaken on a phased basis, and currently three national certificate courses with direct equivalents within the City & Guilds range of courses are on offer. These are single or double skills craft training programmes designed for school leaver entrants. These skills-based courses and their attendant personal development dimensions have been described elsewhere (Baum and McLoughlin, 1984).

However, one of the main objectives in the establishment of the National Craft Curricula and Certification Board was to ensure that the needs of the Irish hotel, catering and tourism industry and those of young people seeking a career within the industry be met more fully and appropriately than hitherto by the City & Guilds system. A direct consequence of this has been the utilization of CERT's ongoing research programmes to identify new areas for curriculum development.

This information has provided a broad backcloth to the hotel, catering and tourism industry in Ireland and its manpower needs in relation to traditional employment areas, as well as identifying new and changing areas within the context of education and training requirements.

Preliminary unpublished findings from pilot studies undertaken in preparation for CERT's (1985c) comprehensive *Manpower Survey of the Hotel and Catering Industry* identified a distinct trend within the hotel industry in particular, towards what has subsequently been labelled 'multi-skilling'; workers at craft and operative level undertaking duties in more than one department of an establishment. This was particularly evident in relation to small and seasonal hotels. However, traditional training, both in college and within the industry, prepares workers for specialized departmental employment. This finding, which was consistent with non-empirical evidence obtained over a number of years through CERT's contact with the industry and its various associations, prompted investigation of the potential for a new educational programme to meet this need within the industry. While the general trend was established through the research investigations, the specific structure, content and educational approach suited to meet this identified training need for 'multi-skilled craft workers' was not so clear. In other words, the broad identification of the need for a new educational and training course or, alternatively, the instigation of significant changes within existing programmes was established. Identifying how this need should be met and how the requirements from the standpoints of industry, young people and education should be satisfied constituted the second stage of the research and development process.

A wide range of options existed in considering approaches to meet the need, options which all contained elements of validity in relation to some or all of the objectives for this new approach. These objectives emerged from deliberations within the National Craft Curricula and Certification Board and its committees, as well as through direct discussions with educational and industry contacts. Broad objectives which were identified include:

1. to provide a multi-skills vocational education and training programme for young people entering the hotel, catering and tourism industry;
2. to provide a trained workforce for a sector of the industry whose needs were not currently met through existing CERT-funded programmes;
3. to provide enhanced awareness in young people of the hospitality and social skills necessary for a successful career in the industry;
4. to investigate the implications for educational and training practices, within catering education, of objectives 1 – 3 above;
5. to investigate the implications for student assessment, within catering education, of objectives 1 – 4 above;
6. to monitor the new approaches adopted and to determine their implications for teaching and assessment within existing craft programmes;
7. to assess and meet the in-service staff development requirements of college teachers and work experience supervisors which may arise as a consequence of the objectives outlined above.

These objectives formed the basis for a series of consultative seminars with representatives of those sectors of the industry where the multi-skilling concept was most clearly in evidence, particularly small hotels and guesthouses; tourism attractions and locations; and industrial and institutional catering outlets. The common denominator which emerged very clearly from these seminars was the need for young people to enter the industry:

- with basic core skills developed in a number of departmental areas – dining room, kitchen, reception, bar and housekeeping;
- with an awareness and appreciation of the tourism industry and the broad context of work within it;
- with, above all, a 'hospitality' outlook in relating to customer needs and all aspects of service.

The Concept

These points became the cornerstone and prime curriculum design challenge in the development of the new programme and encapsulate the main departure which was sought from existing craft courses in catering. It was at this point in the development process that the original manpower and training impetus for the programme became subservient to the influence of educational processes. By this I mean that it became abundantly clear that the requirements identified by industry would be met not through a new approach to course content and skills training but through a teaching and learning philosophy derived from the need to develop the hospitality and customer orientation requirement. That is not to say that programmes of education and training of waitresses and bartenders, for example, do not require and include a distinct hospitality dimension. However, these courses are primarily concerned with the development of requisite technical skills and knowledge to enable young people to operate at a professional level within the industry. Teaching methodology, in college and industry, as well as the approach to the assessment of students, strongly reflect this skills-based priority. In this respect the influence of City & Guilds traditions and practices are evident and it is furthermore interesting to consider that the Institute's General Catering Course (705), the closest in conception to the new programme, likewise adopts a skills development emphasis within the range of traditional craft areas, which are encompassed in the course.

The development phase of the new hospitality crafts course therefore laid prime emphasis on the preparation of a curriculum which would concentrate on the 'hospitality approach, stressing customer needs and contact, rather than a traditional product and technical skills emphasis' (CERT, 1985a). This approach is evident within the main aims of the new course which are to:

1. give young people basic skills, experience and knowledge which have application throughout the hospitality industry;
2. develop an understanding of the hotel, catering and tourism industry in Ireland and to appreciate its social, economic and international dimension;
3. provide an integrated programme of training, education and work experience which can serve as a foundation for their working lives;
4. enable students to identify the links and similarities that exist within all sectors of the industry, so that they can understand and respond to the customer demands and expectations of each sector;
5. help students assess their potential, to think realistically about employment prospects and to make them more attractive to potential employers in the hotel and catering industry;
6. encourage students to become progressively responsible for their own personal development;
7. develop and maintain a more versatile, readily adaptable, highly motivated and productive workforce (CERT, 1985a).

These aims, therefore, especially by comparison with those of more traditional skills-based courses, were selected to place particular emphasis on a learner-centred course of study through which, it is hoped, the desired range of interpersonal and professionally adept social skills would be developed. Particular stress was placed on seeking to overcome some of the difficulties faced by students, which have been identified by CERT with respect to other courses in craft training education. These, essentially, relate to the area of student attitude, adaptability and independence, especially, in preparing for the world of work (Baum and McLoughlin, 1984).

The hospitality crafts course curriculum, syllabus and assessment documentation were all designed to meet these various educational and training objectives, placing particular stress on

- the interdisciplinary approach, utilizing the concepts of customer needs and hospitality as the strand common to all technical areas of work;
- ensuring that the context of service and hospitality is evident to students at all stages during the course;
- linking the personal development of the student directly to the world of work and leisure;
- developing career planning skills in students and encouraging enterprise and realistic ambition within the industry;
- developing independent learning and research skills in the student with particular emphasis on their transferability and value in helping to achieve personal and career goals;
- developing teamwork, so important within the industry, through a wide range of group and class activities, both of direct practical industry application and of more general social and citizenship value;
- utilizing techniques of assessment consistent with the overall course philosophy and thus relying heavily on coursework, project and competency skills assessment as a means of determining a student's suitability for a career in the hotel, catering and tourism industry;
- carefully selected and monitored periods of work experience in industry to reinforce and further develop college learning.

Piloting of the course in one college during 1984–85 allowed for a careful interventionist and illuminative evaluation of the new approach supported closely by a subcommittee of the board's Curricula Advisory Committee and regular monitoring by CERT personnel. Early on in the development process, teacher support materials were seen as critical to the success of the new course and the embryonic teacher's manual (CERT, 1985b), prepared prior to piloting, was substantially revised in content and presentation as a result of experience gained at this stage. Likewise, the sample weekly assignments, the cornerstone to the assessment of the course, were tested and evaluated by participating teachers and CERT and modified significantly as a consequence. The standardization of the marking of these very varied project activities, which focus on eclectic areas of study including learning, creating, skills development, work orientation, life preparation, communicating, leisure, sensing, feeling and thinking, has proved a challenge which has not been entirely resolved. It would have been tempting to reject the assignment-based approach to assessment on grounds of complexity and unreliability and, therefore, to have reverted to a more conventional approach. However, its validity in terms of assisting with the educational and personal development of the students and with the achievement of the course aims is clearly evident both to the teachers directly involved and to those assessing the course externally. Consequently, the approach has been modified and will continue to be monitored closely but will not, despite evident imperfections, be replaced by more conventional techniques of assessment. Indeed, the key challenge in this area relates to the development of a standardized national system of validation and assessment which, on the one hand, does not compromise the course's eclectic and individualized approach while, on the other, meeting the national board's concerns for uniform standards in the award of its national certificate.

Conclusion

The National Craft Curricula and Certification Board accepted the hospitality crafts course as qualifying students for the award of its national certificate for the 1985 – 86 academic year. Following an intensive in-service course for teachers in September 1985, the course is currently operating in three colleges with a total enrolment of 45 students. Subjective evaluation by those closely involved with the course – students, teachers and CERT personnel – suggests a successful approach, both with regard to training and educational criteria. In the long term, the main determinant of the success or otherwise of the course will be in the manner in which its graduates assimilate and progress within the hotel, catering and tourism industry. To date, information on this dimension is limited but positive. However, long-term follow-up research will closely monitor ex-student progress in industry and will, undoubtedly, influence the future of the new course, in terms of its content, structure and availability.

It is evident from the above description that a definitive verdict on the success or otherwise of the new hospitality craft course will not be forthcoming for some time. Whatever decisions are made with respect to the course – and criteria adopted in this decision-making may reflect issues far removed from the educational or training arena – the process of research, development, implementation and evaluation has itself broad implications for the work of the National Craft Curricula and Certification Board, the colleges operating its courses, the teachers and CERT as the responsible training agency, as well as ultimately for young people seeking craft training for the industry. The influence on this broad range of activity relates to the teaching of the intangible elements within hospitality education, the development of dimensions complementary to practical skills training in hotel, catering and tourism courses.

Thus, the development process involved in the establishment of this new course, and the implications which have been identified and responded to in relation to teaching and learning, are probably the most significant outcomes of CERT's work in this field and it is in this area that long-term influences can be anticipated.

References

Baum, T and McLoughlin, L (1984) Compensating for deficiencies in the second level system. *Irish Educational Studies*, 4th January.

Council for Education, Recruitment and Training (CERT) (1985a) *Hospitality Crafts Course*. CERT, Dublin.
Council for Education, Recruitment and Training (CERT) (1985b) *Hospitality Crafts Course Teacher's Manual*. CERT, Dublin.
Council for Education, Recruitment and Training (CERT) (1985c) *Manpower Survey of the Hotel and Catering Industry*. CERT, Dublin.

2.18 A Training Package in Support of a Training Aid

C I B Skellern
Royal Air Force, Germany

Abstract: The Royal Air Force has a requirement to develop air combat skills in the aircrew of its operational squadrons. The Air Combat Manoeuvring Instrumentation (ACMI) facility at Decimomannu in Sardinia is used to simulate engagements in a live flying environment. To prepare aircrew for this exacting task, a training package containing two videotapes and supporting documentation has been developed. The overall objective of the package is to enable each squadron to derive maximum training value from the allotted hours on the ACMI range. The package is reviewed, the approach appraised and more general issues concerning the place of simulation in training are discussed.

What is ACMI?

The Royal Air Force has, over the last 25 years, made an increasing use of simulation as a training method to develop the skills of its aircrew towards meeting the operational task. The Air Combat Manoeuvring Instrumentation (ACMI) is a sophisticated training aid which employs simulation in a live flying environment to develop aircrew skills in air combat. Our air defence squadrons use the ACMI facilities at Decimomannu in Sardinia alongside NATO aircrew from West Germany, Italy and the United States of America. The ACMI has the following four main components or subsystems:

Airborne Instrumentation Subsystem (AIS)

This component is a 'pod' fitted to each aircraft, which transmits data relating to the flight parameters and weapons activities of that aircraft. Examples of such data being constantly transmitted are: speed, heading, 'g', relative bearings between participants and missile launch.

Tracking Instrumentation System (TIS)

The data from each AIS is received by a network of ground stations, the TIS, which then communicates the information to a central master station.

Control and Computation Subsystem (CCS)

The CCS is the computing heart of the system. The data gathered from the master receiving station is recorded, translated in real time and then transmitted to the fourth subsystem for display.

Display and Debriefing Subsystem (DDS)

This fourth subsystem, the DDS, is the component where man and machine interface. The output from the computers is displayed on normal VDUs and on large projection system television screens. Here the controllers can watch the live combats, direct the actions of the crews involved and report the success and failures of all weapons firings. As well as relaying the combat sortie live, the information is stored for replay at a subsequent debrief.

A typical sortie profile will begin with all the participating crews attending a briefing in which the training objectives are outlined and then amplified. Each crew, or team of crews, will then hold separate briefings to determine their strategy and tactics for the airborne combat exercise. Once the mission has been flown the crews assemble in the DDS to debrief by replaying the sortie tape. Here the facility to 'freeze' the action enables critical events to be discussed at length. The feedback thus received enhances the learning already achieved and provides a platform on which to build future exercises.

The Training Problem

All commercial organizations demand that investments they make in training must produce benefits in efficiency which will normally be reflected in better output and profitability. The Royal Air Force is no exception in looking towards value for money from training. The cost of the ACMI to the RAF is high for two main reasons. First, the hire of the facility is necessarily expensive, as a large capital investment has been made in its development. Second, the site is remote and requires that a support detachment of personnel and equipment is maintained to service the aircraft and repair minor defects. With such a large outlay of capital, maximum benefit must be gained from the training with minimum wastage. The problem identified was that aircrew using the ACMI for the first time were not fully prepared for what to expect. Consequently, the development of meaningful individual skills and team techniques was not being achieved until late in the training period. Some of the more advanced skills that could be developed were not being attempted, as early sorties concentrated on familiarization. A most important ingredient in this unpreparedness was the essential requirement for each squadron of aircraft to have its own range training officers (RTOs) in the DDS to control the sorties from the ground. These RTOs had to learn the complexities of the controlling console, interpret the visual display of the air combat, and transmit information verbally to the pilots of the aircraft they were controlling. Mistakes made by the RTO could severely degrade the training value of a sortie. The training of these RTOs began only when they arrived at the ACMI. The time taken for the RTOs to develop complex procedural and conceptual skills determined, to some extent, the rate at which the whole squadron progressed.

Production of a Training Package

Once the training problem had been identified, the solution pointed towards the development of a training package which could be distributed to all future ACMI users and employed to provide familiarization training and to begin the note learning of the required console operating procedures by the designated RTOs. The following training and enabling objectives were formulated as a first step and are listed simply as behavioural statements with their associated conditions and standards removed.

Each aircrew member must be able to:

(a) describe the ACMI system and its four component parts
(b) state the capabilities of the ACMI system as a training aid
(c) describe the elements of a typical ACMI air combat sortie.

Each aircrew member designated as a range training officer (RTO) must be able to:

(d) list the functions of each of the RTO's console buttons and dials
(e) state the setting up procedure on the RTO's console for an air combat sortie

(f) state the RTO's responsibilities when controlling an air combat sortie
(g) state the safety parameters and rules of engagement to be observed.

The medium chosen to achieve the training objectives best was television. Although assembling the closed circuit television (CCTV) equipment at the ACMI was a relatively simple exercise, the determining of the professional/technical content was the largest and most difficult task to achieve before filming could begin. A detailed account of the production of the video is beyond the intention of this outline; however, the major difficulty encountered was when filming in the DDS, where light levels on the screens stretched our cameras to their limit. (A line signal transfer from the computer output to our video recorders was not available due to the incompatibility of the equipment.) The end product, the training package, contains two videos; the first is designed to meet the objectives (a) to (c) and lasts for 16 minutes. The second, a more specialized video, covers objectives (d) to (g) – the RTO's task – and lasts for 15 minutes. A booklet to support the videos is contained in the package and directs the learner towards a suggested approach to achieving the objectives. The visual picture and the written text must be used together if the procedures are to be learned in association with the appropriate concepts. The package obviously offers a flexible learning situation to the student in that he can progress at his own pace. Also the package is flexible in that it offers the learner a chance to manage his own learning by allowing him to use small and usually unanticipated periods during his primary operational flying programme. From a management stance, the package is flexible as the master videotapes and printed originals can be edited/amended to reflect any changes that might arise. However, one of the prime factors in choosing the package format was that the material contained in it was unlikely to change. It is estimated that the design ratio of time taken to make the package to time taken to complete the learning task is 200 hours to 4 hours, or 50 to 1. This is a significant calculation when deciding whether the investment in a training package will give a worthwhile return.

Evaluation of the Training Package

A number of references have already been made as to whether the outlay of effort is justified. An evaluative judgement should only be made on consistent feedback information. The ACMI package has been distributed to all RAF squadrons who require air combat training and visit Decimomannu. Feedback will be gathered primarily by the permanent RAF staff at the unit who will hear criticisms at first hand and who will be able to assess any improvement in initial skills exhibited by future visiting aircrew.

Workshop Discussion

After the formal presentation of the ACMI training package in which the two videotapes were viewed and the supporting documentation was examined the following topics were thrown open for discussion:

(a) Is this training package an effective approach?
(b) What improvements could be made to the package?
(c) Are there suitable alternative approaches to prepare aircrew for this exacting task?
(d) What value has simulation in training and what is the most suitable formula to manage it?
   (i) What problems does simulation cause the learner?
   (ii) What problems does simulation cause the instructor?

Conclusion

In the Royal Air Force, and indeed in most commercial environments, the technology 'in use' is becoming more sophisticated. Furthermore, in military flying the technology is being used to the limits of its capabilities (and sometimes beyond). The sophistication and complexity in techniques of use adds a double burden to the person who has to learn. The ACMI is a prime example of an advanced training aid which is a necessary expense to achieve a particular task. The cost of 'getting it wrong' is not easily calculable but is extremely high. Thus, the investment of resources in producing a training package to enhance success is a worthwhile venture. For this, and many other similar situations, it must *not* be a case of 'spoiling the ship for a ha'penny worth of tar'.

2.19 Open Learning in Further Education and Industry

G N Burrows and D Tyldesley
North Manchester College

Abstract: This paper focuses upon some issues involved with the training relationship between further education and industry insofar as it relates both to an emerging training dichotomy and developing open learning techniques. The need for a considerable adult retraining campaign, it is argued, implies a need for new training techniques and systems. The use of open learning techniques is seen as a possible solution to some training problems, and their use may imply the acquisition of changed skills and attitudes on the part of both colleges and companies. The situation may also require a change in the nature of the provision further education offers to support industrial training.

Introduction

The concern that delivery systems have been designed to fit the needs of the college and not the student may be illustrated by just two recent comments from within the further education sector:

> 'My principal would not allow me to enrol students who could not attend the college'.

> 'I'd love to teach on your open learning scheme.'

Such comments are all too prevalent within the further education system, and are symptomatic of the resistance to change which is ever present. Unfortunately colleges can no longer afford to resist the changes which have been identified as crucial by a number of bodies. Yet the further education system is still, largely

- □ uncaring about the changing needs of its students and their employers;
- □ unwilling to adopt learning strategies other than formal lecturing and teaching;
- □ unaware that the situation is moving towards a need for facilitators, and not teachers.

Resistance of this sort is founded upon the bedrock of traditional methods and practices; it is reinforced by an infrastructure of outdated and inappropriate regulations and administrative 'norms'. Finally, it is consolidated by the comfort of the 'selective negligence' inherent in statements like 'things will get better', and 'engineering must soon pick up again'.

The Ruskin College speech, which opened the 'great debate' on the place of education in the decline of the national industrial performance, also signalled the struggle to allocate blame between education and industry. Perhaps it truly belongs to both. But what is certain is that while allocation of blame is the major preoccupation important opportunities and initiatives may be missed. Sadly, open learning may be a potential casualty in this war, not because of any inherent characteristic, but rather because of a marred analysis of the present, changed problem for training.

Historically, industry has largely maintained its trained workforce by adolescent recruitment and training – usually in the form of apprenticeship. Further education supported this model, by providing a 'for-life' educational background. But now, as Manpower Services Commission (MSC) research has recently shown, there is a requirement to adjust to the need for adult retraining, partly a result of poor adolescent recruitment, but largely the consequence of the opposite side of that coin – the large percentage of adults already holding jobs. The latter do not satisfy the industrial demand for skilled craftsmen and technicians, but their retraining may be a better economic proposition than a new wave of apprenticeship. An apprentice may cost, with day or block release, £17,000 to train, and still need to acquire the experience that results in real productive competence. The on-the-job retraining of an experienced worker, in this situation, becomes a real economic alternative.

To quote from the MSC publication, *Planning for Change*:

> 'Survival and prosperity require a skilled and flexible workforce. We will only achieve this through a strategy of continuous training and retraining which enables people to develop and update their skills.'

Industrial and commercial organizations are increasingly recognizing the adult/adolescent dichotomy, together with the other training requirements – a need for twice as many technicians, multi-skilling, and for supervisory skills. But at the same time, financial constraints and the production requirements of a leaner workforce make this process more difficult. Though the MSC is helping with the Adult Training Strategy, a conscious further education service can do much to help industry in the resolution of these difficulties. The key words that constantly re-occur are 'flexibility' and 'cost-effectiveness', concepts reflected in the National Economic Development Council (NEDC)'s report, *Competence and Competition*. In this situation, many companies may find an answer to their training needs in open learning methods.

The further education system is fast approaching a critical situation, with falling student numbers and a badly outdated curriculum which does not meet the needs of students, industry or commerce. Industry is moving away from the traditional time-based training methods and now recognizes the necessity for skill-based training with identified levels of competence. The further education structure is still very much time-based, despite the fact that the majority of courses have criterion-based learning objectives. To make matters worse, this time-based structure is further restricted to the college working day and academic year. Access to the college resources therefore remains restricted.

Further education has always been a resource-based facility with high capital investment across many of its faculties, and a labour-intensive delivery system. Its nearest approach to cost-effectiveness was when classes were large and salaries and wages were low. The reverse is now the case and the traditional delivery system is fast becoming unaffordable. But such a system is far from indispensable, and when its various aspects, revolving around a tutor-centred delivery system, are considered, it can be seen that many of them can be replaced by a good student-centred system of learning.

Much of this can be achieved by using good student-centred open learning material as a core onto which the other aspects can be bolted. Most of the material that fails to establish itself in an open learning situation does so because it relies heavily, perhaps intentionally, on tutorial support. This simple factor of heavy tutor involvement renders it virtually useless in many open learning situations.

The failure of such material invariably stems from a lack of understanding and appreciation of the requirements of the open learning user. The originators of the material often produce it with the college environment very much in mind. The writer is probably chosen because of his lecturing capabilities and authoring skills. The material therefore may emerge as enhanced lecturing notes, which are perfect for the tutor, but unintelligible in many respects for the open learner. Such material is little better than an assembled package which comprises a textbook supported by a study guide.

The material must be structured to suit the open learner who, it should be assumed, is studying in total isolation. The text must therefore be:

1. informative about the learning objectives;
2. friendly without being patronizing;
3. comprehensive and thorough in its treatment of the subject;
4. clear in highlighting the 'must know' information;
5. succinct in its summary;
6. extensive in its provision for student self-assessment.

Advice and guidance in setting up open learning schemes, overcoming many of the apparent problems, and breaking down the traditional barriers to it is now very well documented. There is a great deal of information available on resourcing, resource deployment, pricing, staffing and staff development. A large number of producers of open learning material now market their products in virtually every discipline offered within the further education system. Many of these producers will soon have the capacity to apply their newly acquired skills to developing and producing material which is beyond their original areas.

The role of the tutor will change dramatically to one of counsellor, mentor and director of studies. The tutor's skills, knowledge and expertise will have to be channelled into the role of an educational adviser. If effective open learning material has been adopted, tutoring should become almost non-existent. In fact, the person appointed to this multi-faceted task will need to be very aware of the dangers of slipping back into the traditional mould. Such a retrograde step would do good quality open learning material a great disservice.

However it is not only changes in staff attitudes that are required. Change is also needed of the college system itself. Much closer liaison with industry is needed, extending to in-company operation where this is both desirable and beneficial.

The experience of the writers in introducing open learning into five medium-sized engineering companies in the north-west have highlighted many interesting and perhaps less obvious benefits for industry, and also suggests less conventional ways in which further education can assist industry in meeting its needs. In operating with these companies, various models were used for the delivery of an open learning training programme. These were:

(a) The use of company 'mentors' to conduct or support in-house training. A mentor might be the trainee's supervisor or line manager.
(b) The establishment of a company training centre, offering a drop-in facility for company personnel. Each centre should provide a library of relevant learning packages, audiovisual and computing facilities, and tutor-mentor support.
(c) The provision of a one-to-one training facility based upon learning materials, with appropriate tutor support which might be provided by the college.
(d) The use by the trainee of a college open learning centre to gain easy access to training facilities and tutorial support.
(e) The use of learning packages to accelerate and individualize conventional training operations, whether in company or in college.

Whatever the model used, several interesting points emerged:

1. The majority of the companies did not have sufficient knowledge of open learning to be able to design and resource an effective programme – they required outside expertise of further education to achieve this.
2. At the technician and supervisor level, the sophistication of training required was overestimated by the training manager. Many adults have high practical skills but a low academic base. Before embarking on such sophisticated programmes as CAD/CAM training, therefore, employees needed to establish their own confidence level, both in the learning situation and actual knowledge by studying basic subjects such as maths and physics.
3. Firms were able to demonstrate commitment to their employees by training them in-house, which resulted in a feeling of increased job security and productivity.

4. As the confidence level of the adult trainee increased, so did commitment to the introduction of new technology.

Of the five models of open learning used, the most interesting in terms of development for the company and further education was that in which the mentor and trainee were both company employees, such mentors being perhaps the trainee's supervisor or line manager. For both industry and further education the role is unconventional, for the mentor needs to acquire not only counselling and tutorial skills, but also the more difficult qualities of inspiring sound, communicative team-work and considerable empathy. But any member of the further education staff involved in such an industrial operation also needs to extend his/her range of skills, perhaps in these areas:

- ☐ identifying training needs
- ☐ removing initial apprehension *vis-à-vis* open learning
- ☐ designing training programmes
- ☐ identifying resource material
- ☐ identifying trainees/mentor
- ☐ training the trainer
- ☐ mentor training
- ☐ assisting with further planning.

Hence the further education lecturer may need to stand completely outside his traditional role in order to make his contribution to the training within industry effective.

Unfortunately, a large number of educationalists in the further education sector have been left behind, with the introduction of new approaches to education and training initiatives. Additionally these people have had increasing demands placed upon them, quite rightly, to liaise closely with industry, and to provide education and training programmes to meet the specific needs of industry. If this is to be done effectively, new attitudes and approaches will have to be developed. In-service training is essential to enable selected personnel to market and develop programmes professionally. Training is only effective if it is supported by senior management. Hence further education staff need to become confident and skilled in communicating with senior personnel within industry and to be trained in the identification of training needs.

Open learning concepts and methods do represent a new training technology, particularly when, in appropriate situations, they are allied to the advanced computer and video techniques that are becoming available, but both partners in the adult retraining relationship – further education and industry – must be prepared to play their part in converting potential into reality. For further education, the task is to:

1. understand thoroughly the implications and techniques of this new technology;
2. design training packages upon the specific basis of the company's identified needs;
3. conduct pilot schemes and establish continuing systems that successfully meet needs;
4. establish close and mutually beneficial relationships with client companies.

For industry, the task includes the need to:

1. analyse rigorously its training needs, including the frequent element of some 'educational' underpinning;
2. be prepared to experiment with new training methods;
3. demonstrate a commitment to the fullest co-operation with colleges;
4. seek quality training to the mutual benefit of company and workforce, and not merely conduct a cost-cutting exercise.

In short, both partners must co-operate fully in their own retraining process – the colleges to convince, and to establish new methods and systems, and the companies to be prepared to experiment, to co-operate, and to suspend judgement until results are known. Finally, in this learning process, the onus upon the further education system is to produce real, productive training quality; that upon industry is to provide proper support, and to pay an economic price.

2.20 Flexible Qualifications for Flexible Learning

P Ellis
Hotel and Catering Industry Training Board, London

Abstract: Ready access to suitable qualifications provides learners with recognition of the competences they achieve as their careers progress, employers with clear-cut evidence of existing skills and knowledge as a basis for recruitment, and educators and trainers with reference points to facilitate the building of progressive programmes which take existing achievements into account. In an environment where diversity and flexibility of learning opportunities is increasing and open access to these opportunities is being encouraged, it is necessary to ensure that this same flexibility is available within the qualification structure.

Based on the development of an occupational qualification within a particular industry, this paper identifies a number of general principles in enhancing flexibility within qualifications, including:

☐ avoiding unnecessary pre-entry requirements;
☐ separating the qualification from the method of achieving competence;
☐ avoiding assessment tied to particular locations or times;
☐ facilitating progression to and from related awards systems.

Modularization has special strengths in this context, but the precise consequences of modularization are dependent on the detailed design decision made, and a high degree of flexibility is not an inevitable consequence of adopting a modular format.

Introduction

The future for the hotel and catering industry in Britain is bright. Record numbers of tourists are visiting on holiday and on business, spending more than ever in hotels and restaurants, on entertainment and travel. The British are eating out more often, going to the pub, local wine bar or bistro.

The hotel and catering industry already employs 2.3 million people, ten per cent of Britain's workforce, and 40,000 new jobs are being created each year. The demands the industry makes on the skills and flexibility of its staff are high; the customer is immediately affected by the technical and interpersonal skills of employees.

Many young people prepare for a career in the industry by taking a college course leading to the award of City and Guilds, BTEC or SCOTVEC certificates and diplomas. The value of these awards is recognized and respected, but vocational preparation is not confined to the colleges. Many thousands of supervisors each year attend trainer skills courses to learn how to pass on their skills in the workplace. The industry commits substantial resources to training and for many individuals entering the industry training and experience gained at work, rather than in colleges, is the main route for advancing their careers.

What has been lacking up to now has been an award which would allow practical skills acquired in the workplace to be recognized by a qualification. An indication of the scale of the gap is that only 20,000 individuals each year receive qualifications through the existing system compared to around 700,000 who enter the industry 'fresh'; that is to say, they were not employed in hotel and catering immediately prior to their current jobs. Then there is the career progression of continuing staff to consider.

It is important to distinguish between unqualified and unskilled. Many individuals in the industry without qualifications have extensive skills, but these skills are not formally recognized. This situation is detrimental in a number of respects. Employees seeking to build a career in the industry do not have ready access to recognition of the skills they have developed. Recruitment cannot in the majority of cases be based on clear-cut evidence of possession of appropriate skills. Trainers and educators have no reference point of skills already mastered to facilitate building progressive training programmes which take account of existing achievements.

In an environment where diversity and flexibility of learning opportunities is increasing and open access to these opportunities is being encouraged, the gap between possession of skill and recognition can only grow. It was against this background that a project team at the Hotel and Catering Industry Training Board set out to develop CATERBASE.

CATERBASE

CATERBASE is an occupational qualification for people working in the hotel and catering industry, with the emphasis firmly on the word 'working'. It is an industry-based award which will allow people working in the industry to obtain a national qualification based on their normal activities at work. Assessment will be an informal and ongoing process, which will build on normal workplace organization and the supervisor's role within this, rather than artificially creating an assessment 'situation' on top of normal workplace activities. Assessment will, however, be based on tightly defined and carefully communicated standards of performance. These standards will be practical in emphasis rather than theoretical.

From its very inception, flexibility has been at the heart of the CATERBASE concept.

Devising a new occupational qualification is a complex undertaking. There are a multitude of considerations – technical, political, organizational and administrative – to be taken into account. It is the intention of this paper to approach only those aspects which directly affect the flexibility of the product on offer.

Flexibility = No Entry Requirement/No Set Delivery System

CATERBASE is an occupational qualification; it is not linked to any training or delivery system. CATERBASE recognition is based on the demonstration of specified standards of performance alone; on arrival at a target, not the route used to get there, the time taken along the way, or on any prerequisite before starting off. There may thus be any number of ways of achieving the competences defined by CATERBASE; trainer-centred and learner-centred approaches; highly structured or informal approaches; existing routes and ones still to be devised. Some training or learning approaches may be more effective than others and as such may justifiably be the subject of recommendations from other quarters. However, within CATERBASE, for the purposes of accrediting the competences achieved by individuals, no limitations will be placed on how these have been achieved.

Flexibility = Accessibility of Assessments

Assessments which are tied to specific locations or 'test centres' or particular times, as in formal 'tests', can create restrictions to the availability of the system to potential users. A decision was made, therefore, to build into normal work practices rather than create an artificial situation specially for the purposes of assessment.

It has been accepted that the supervisor in the workplace has responsibilities for the quality and smooth flow of work and, if given sufficiently unambiguous statements about performance standards required to make an award, should be able to match these against the observed performance of an individual to see if there is a match. Assessment thus becomes an ongoing process in the assessee's own workplace and competences can be readily and progressively credited as they are demonstrated.

This assessment approach obviously poses its own unique set of demands. It does, however, have substantial potential benefits, not only in cost and convenience terms, but also in moving away from small samples of behaviour as the basis for assessment, and in greater validity.

Flexibility = Modular Design

The modular basis of CATERBASE contributes much to its flexibility. There are, however, many ways of defining a modular framework, and the precise characteristics of the resulting system depend crucially on the detailed design decisions made.

Firstly, since CATERBASE is intended to accredit competences demonstrated in the workplace it must, if its full value is to be realized, readily fit in with workplace practices and organization. Modules thus represent operations or activities which are carried out in the workplace rather than having a more abstract or academic base. Each module represents an 'employable unit' of competences, a group of competences which typically occur together in the workplace, enabling assessment and accreditation to be completed without extensive reorganization.

Modules are independent, and capable of being credited alone or in combination. Because of this, even the most junior staff will be able to find a small number of modules which in combination represent their jobs. Having gained recognition in a number of relevant modules, they will be able to progressively build on existing achievements adding further modules as their careers develop.

Linked to the independence of modules is the decision that all necessary competences for acceptable performance of a module must be integrated within it. Efficient and safe working, maintenance of hygiene, utilization of interpersonal skills and so on appear as and when they are relevant within every module. There is thus no need for the addition of any supplementary modules to establish operational competence and the employer can identify an immediate function in the workplace which the holder of even a single module can perform.

From the employer's point of view the 'operational' basis of CATERBASE modules, and the facility to bring them together in any combination, makes them an extremely useful approach to specifying jobs within the organization.

A final very practical point concerns the size of modules. Many modular systems, especially those concerned with the delivery of learning, specify some uniform size for modules, even if only by reference to some relatively arbitrary or subjective criterion. After some thought it became evident that, given the workplace emphasis of CATERBASE, each module must bring together only those competences which occur together fairly universally across the industry, otherwise the openness of the system would be damaged through debarring a proportion of individuals from gaining appropriate accreditation (the module being the minimum unit of accreditation) by virtue of not having the opportunity to demonstrate all the competence defined by the module.

Some fairly small modules have therefore been created, giving priority to the ability of the system to fully represent the skills possessed by an individual in preference to preserving a standard module 'size'. The system thus emphasizes profiling of competences rather than awarding credits to which a summative numerical value can be given.

Flexibility = Links with Other Awards

Whatever the internal virtues of CATERBASE, it would be only partially effective in opening up paths to recognition and career progression if it did not link readily to other awards. CATERBASE is *not* being developed in isolation and it does not seek to displace existing qualifications, especially further education awards, but to complement and support them.

Links are being forged with the various further education schemes with a view to drawing together the requirements which are made for practical performance. Eventually it will be possible for the CATERBASE qualified individual to be accepted as having satisfied the practical requirements of a City & Guilds, SCOTVEC or BTEC catering award, thus shortening his or her route to these qualifications. Conversely, the full-time college student taking up employment will be able to readily meet industry's requirements as specified by CATERBASE because these will be the same as the standards encountered in college.

CATERBASE will thus meet several disparate needs:

- it will provide full-time college students with an opportunity to gain industrial recognition of the skills they were introduced to at college;
- it will stand in its own right as a qualification for those whose aspirations are primarily practical;
- it will provide a stepping stone for others to previously unattainable educational qualifications.

The last possibility is an exciting one. In our industry we now have an opportunity to make a dent in the total of 94 per cent of employees who possess no relevant occupational qualification and at the same time to facilitate progression and transfer to other systems. Pre-industrial links are not being ignored either; links with the Certificate of Pre-Vocational Education (CPVE) and the Technical and Vocational Education Initiative (TVEI) are being actively investigated.

Conclusion

From this study of the development of a new occupational qualification within a particular industry, a number of principles can be abstracted with general relevance to enhancing flexibility within qualifications:

- unnecessary pre-entry requirements should be avoided;
- the qualification should be separated from the method of achieving competences;
- assessment should not be tied to particular locations or times;
- modularization may enhance flexibility, but the precise consequences of modularization are dependent on detailed attention to the framework devised;
- progression to and from related awards systems should be facilitated.

References

Ellis, P (1986) The Macro technology of training. In Rushy, N and Howe, A (eds) *Aspects of Educational Technology XIX*. Kogan Page, London.

Ellis, P and Reeves, T (1983) *Manpower Changes in the Hotel and Catering Industry*. Hotel and Catering Industry Training Board, Wembley.

Hotel and Catering Industry Training Board (1983) *Hotel and Catering Skills – Now and in the Future*. Hotel and Catering Industry Training Board, Wembley.

2.21 Flexible Learning for Examination Purposes

J W James
Analytical Chemistry Open Tech (ACOT) Project, London

Abstract: The suitability of open, distant or flexible learning courses to meet the requirements of examining bodies must depend on how well the material and support provided for the learner meet the various criteria identified by the examining body for its examinations. Using the ACOT (Analytical Chemistry Open Tech) scheme as an example, a generic thesis is advanced whereby, using the headings, study guide, practical support and tutorial backup, an examining body may evaluate a flexible course in comparison with the objectives of its own examinations. Some advantages are arguably seen in favour of flexible learning.

I had in mind when I thought up the title of this paper the use of open, distance and flexible learning for the preparation of candidates for public examinations which may possibly lead to a professional qualification. Therefore the title may merely be a polite way of asking the rather pointed question 'should a student who has studied in an open or distance learning mode be eligible to sit an examination for a professional body's qualification?'

I hope that the question can be answered by the application of logic and common sense, and it is on that basis that I hope you will accept me as a protagonist for open learning and professional bodies' examinations.

Whilst I shall speak in a generic sense, I shall rely heavily on the ACOT project for exemplification. 'ACOT' stands for Analytical Chemistry Open Tech. The idea was that of Dr Brian Currell of Thames Polytechnic; it was fostered by the Committee of Heads of Polytechnic Chemistry Departments, funded by the Manpower Services Commission (MSC) to the tune of £275,000 and managed at Thames Polytechnic. I have been lucky enough to be the project manager, ably assisted by Dr Norma Chadwick.

Returning to the title of this paper – for those of you who still remember steam radio, Dr Joad and the 'Brains Trust', it has of course got to depend on what you mean by open, distance or flexible learning. I have seen many definitions of these terms. None of them are too helpful at the start of a logical approach, so I would like to start with the one thing which all definitions have in common: that is, that students do not attend a teaching institution regularly and at set times to receive the majority of the information that they need to study, in order to acquire the necessary knowledge for the achievement of the objectives set in the syllabus or study guide of any examining body (Figure 1).

"any student does **not attend regularly** or at set times, a teaching institution to **receive** the majority of the theoretical **information** that he/she needs to study, to **acquire** the **knowledge** to be able to **achieve** the **objectives** in the syllabus of the examining body".

Figure 1. *Distance, flexible or open learning*

Crudely put, the student does not go to lectures to acquire the knowledge that he needs. All open, distance or flexible learning systems therefore strive to replace the information offered in the lecture room by some other medium, whether it is text, audio, TV, videos or computer.

There are of course disadvantages to this approach. What does the flexible student miss? (Figure 2)

Misses his/her mentors

Facilities for practice of skills

Misses fellow students

Figure 2. *Disadvantages*

1. Firstly he misses the regular contact with his mentors, which we will call a tutorial.
2. Secondly he has no access to facilities to practise any practical skills he needs to develop.
3. The distance learner tends to be lonely; that is, he misses the company of and interaction with his fellow students.

The appropriateness of any distance, open, or flexible course to fit a candidate for one of our examinations must therefore depend on how well the learning material replaces the lectures in providing information and indeed how, or whether, the disadvantages and problems just identified are dealt with by the flexible system adopted.

I would like now therefore to address each of these areas individually.

Lecture Replacement

Lectures are a way of offering students information for their understanding and absorption so that it becomes knowledge for them to use in their future career. The lectures are offered against the requirements of a study guide or a syllabus, as defined in the specification for the qualification in question. Distance learning material must offer at least the equivalent to lectures to be satisfactory. We have come to think of distance learning material in terms of different media: television, audio tapes, videodiscs, text, diagrams and photographs – not to mention computer-based training systems. But the medium is not as important as the information it contains. Let me digress momentarily to describe how the ACOT Project has dealt with the preparation of text material (Figure 3).

In any given subject area we have brought together at least two, and often more, polytechnic lecturers who are expert in the subject area and involved in its teaching at the LRSC level. The LRSC is the licentiate grade of membership of the Royal Society of Chemistry (RSC). The lecturers, who have subsequently become authors, have identified the various topics which should be included in our material. Before preparation, a list of objectives is drawn up of what the student should be able to do when he has completed study of the material. Teaching text is then written which is sufficient of itself to provide the necessary information for the student to be able to tackle the objectives. The text will refer the student to alternative sources for the information, where it may be expressed in a different way or even amplified, but since

```
                                    ┌──────────┐
                         Identified→ │ Subject  │
                        ╱            │  area    │
                       ╱             │  topics  │
                      ╱              └──────────┘
                     ╱               ┌──────────┐
                    ╱    Formulated→ │ Student  │
┌─────────────┐    ╱                 │ learning │
│ Polytechnic │───╱                  │objectives│
│  Lecturers  │   ╲                  └──────────┘
└─────────────┘    ╲                 ┌──────────┐
                    ╲      Wrote→    │   Open   │
                     ╲               │ learning │
                      ╲              │   text   │
                       ╲             └──────────┘
                        ╲            ┌──────────┐
                         Set→        │   Self   │
                                     │assessment│
                                     │questions │
                                     └──────────┘
```

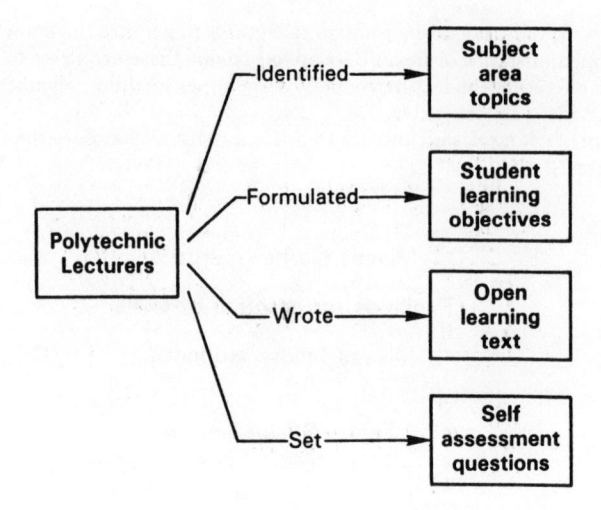

Figure 3. *Preparation of text material*

we have to remember that the distant learner may not have ready access to libraries and the like, the text must enable him to be self-sufficient.

The text material is not complete yet; at intervals the student is presented with self-assessment questions which are designed to test the objectives which were initially defined. The questions are often multiple choice, calculations or true/false identification, so that the student can compare his assessment with the various responses provided at the end of the text or book. The responses provide the opportunity for additional learning material to be given. The response accompanying the right answers often reinforces the main issue, but the responses given to the 'wrong answers' provide remedial help, often expressing a concept in different words or a different form to help the student. We tend to take the view that if the student has not got it right we didn't explain it very well in the first place. The self-assessment questions are interspersed regularly in the text so the student can gauge his progress and challenge his understanding.

There are other activities for the student besides the formal self-assessment questions which form part of the teaching text. He may be guided through a calculation, for instance, plot a graph and learn from it, and so on. The text also contains summaries at appropriate intervals. Whilst text is being prepared it has been interchanged between authors for comment and evaluation. Finally it has been through a peer review by our editorial board, who have taken their task extremely seriously and who have honed and polished the material towards perfection. In summary, therefore, ACOT text is defined by both contents list and learning objectives and has been subject to rigorous quality assurance. We have decided that for analytical chemistry – the theoretical aspects, that is – teaching text of the type I have described is the most appropriate medium. We see no advantages in video, TV or computer techniques for passing the mass of information we have. Text is the most convenient for the student and the cheapest to produce. Figure 4 offers a comparison of such text with that of a traditional lecture.

With regard to the content of information offered to the student, the examining board can see by studying the course contents, the objectives and indeed the entire teaching text, precisely how their study guide or syllabus has been interpreted for the student. In the lecture situation, such interpretation is up to the lecturer in question and is undisclosed to the examining board.

	Open Learning	Traditional Lecture
Syllabus	Course contents Objective Text	Syllabus
Challenge	1 : 1	1 : Many
Notes	Augmented text	?????

Figure 4. *Comparison of open learning and traditional lecture materials*

The self-assessment questions provide a constant challenge to every individual student so that he may assess his progress towards achieving the objectives of the course. Challenge in the lecture room is perhaps rare and in any event, a one-to-many situation is inefficient and meaningless to the biggest part of the audience. It is also a salutary lesson for most lecturers to view the incomplete and inaccurate notes that many students make of their lectures. In the distance mode the teaching texts are essentially lecture notes which the student augments with his own annotations, by worked examples, by answering the self-assessment questions, and so on.

All in all, therefore, I think that well-prepared textual material can provide an excellent substitute for the lecture and arguably has some advantages over the lecture system.

Practical Skills

The learning of practical skills of almost every technical subject and practising them needs the 'tools of the trade'. In the case of analytical chemistry, the tools are both expensive and must be used in an appropriate laboratory facility. There is no question of 'home kits' for use in the kitchen. There is therefore no distance learning substitute for attendance at a laboratory to learn and practise the manipulative skills of the analytical chemist. In our case, each theoretical unit gives a list of practical objectives in terms of what the student should achieve in the laboratory in order that his practical ability matches the theoretical knowledge he has acquired. ACOT students will therefore achieve their practical objectives by attending their nearest polytechnic, as they do today.

It is no secret that the project team in the early days of ACOT came under severe criticism because some people felt we were indeed going to try to deal with practical subjects in a distance mode. One of the most widely quoted statements was that analytical chemistry is a practical science. Clearly from what I have said I agree, but there is, apart from the fundamental principles, a great deal of theoretical knowledge and reasoning necessary to decide what to do in the laboratory to solve the problem set, before one can even think of entering the laboratory to do whatever needs to be done. This is an area that we believe has been neglected to date, and one that can be rectified at a distance from the live laboratory using one of the more modern techniques, ie computer-based training. The advent of the powerful high-resolution screen microcomputer and the availability of authoring language software provides exciting possibilities.

Thus ACOT is producing what we call computer aided learning material (CALM), which students will use in an Apricot or an IBM PC to teach them both how to set up and use a variety of analytical instruments to solve specific analytical problems, and indeed to test their ability to do this (Figure 5). In other words, our software packages

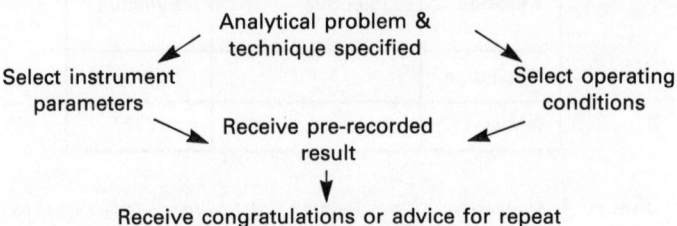

Figure 5. *Computer aided learning material (CALM)*

will mimic the setting up of a GC machine, asking the student to make decisions about samples, about the use of derivatives, about the support phase, about the temperature, about the carrier flow rate, and so on. He will be made to live with his decisions by being shown the chromatagram he would have obtained in the laboratory under the conditions he chose, but helped if necessary towards a satisfactory result.

We are very excited about this approach because we believe that the student will reach examination time with far more experience in making such decisions than he could possibly have had time to do in the conventional laboratory. This form of distance learning can therefore be seen as an improvement on the traditional courses.

Tutorials

As I indicated earlier, the distant student, in not attending an institute regularly, would miss interaction with his tutors. Tutorial advice, guidance and backup is perhaps of greater importance to the distant student than to the institute-based student because of the isolation factor. Arrangements can, of course, be made for distant tutoring by Open University-style tutoring, telephone tutoring and – in the case of analytical chemistry – tutoring at the time the student attends for practical sessions.

Summary

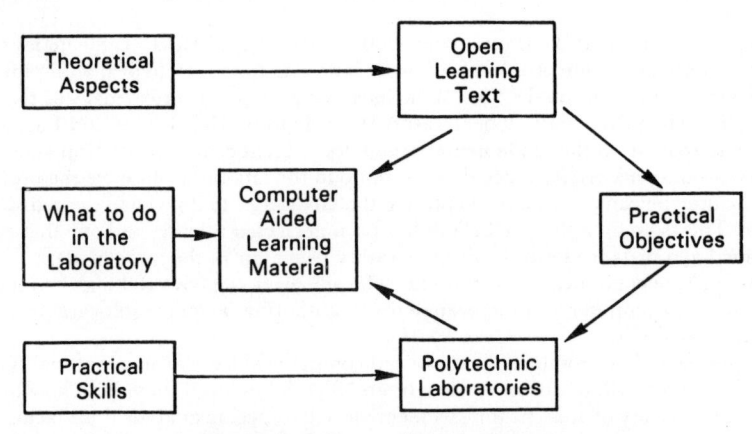

Figure 6. *Summary of course components*

By this time you will realize that in the particular case of the ACOT project we are not offering a full distance learning scheme, but a mixed distance and institute-based operation. It is therefore perhaps just as well that the words 'open' and 'distant' are being overtaken by the new word 'flexible' which is perhaps much more descriptive of what is actually happening, and is not open to interpretation in a way which would be contraindicated in the teaching of the subject.

Returning to the professional body and their examinations in the context of flexible learning, I believe we have virtually reached a generic type situation which is exemplified by ACOT. I would suggest that any such body will wish to satisfy itself that the provisions of any flexible scheme for one of its qualifications must satisfy the examining board under the headings shown in Figure 7.

TRADITIONAL	OPEN
Lecture	Course content Objectives Quality
Practical Classes	Practical classes CALM augmentation
Tutorial	Appointment Telephone At practical sessions

Figure 7. *Educational scheme provisions which must satisfy an examining board*

The content, objectives, and quality of any distance learning material must be compared with the examining boards syllabus and/or study guide.

Practical Arrangements

The practical objectives must be compared with the board's appropriate study guide and the facilities and supervision monitored as currently.

Tutorial

The arrangements for tutorials and the staff involved need to be identified and monitored as currently.

In the case of ACOT I am happy to tell you that the Examinations and Institutions Committee of the Royal Society of Chemistry has said 'the Committee approve the use of ACOT material for the theoretical sections of the approved CAC Syllabus where appropriate, provided such changes are approved by the Society in advance'. The syllabus in question is that approved for each specific institute. In fact, in coming to that decision, I feel the committee must really have accepted the logic presented to you today, and have confirmed that the ACOT scheme conforms to the RSC standards.

2.22 Trainer Training – A Changing Role

C R Thorpe
Training Support Services, Beaconsfield

Abstract:
    Who needs training – when?
    Responsibility for training
    The trainer's changing role
    New skills for the trainer
    Qualifications
    The work of training support services (TSS)

The paper covers all the above topics, looking at the changing face of training, the shift in responsibilities and the subsequent new role for the trainer. New skills are required not just in the trainer training field, but in business, and new qualifications schemes must meet the new generation of trainer skills.

Introduction

Training and development should not be regarded as a once-for-all investment confined to young people only, but should be seen as a lifelong process of personal development in or out of employment. Organizations and groups need training as much as individuals and the failure to recognize this may negate the effect of training provided for individuals. Responsibility for training lies with individuals, employers, government and professional bodies.

However, within the current economic climate the trainer or training manager finds himself very much in the position of needing to justify his role. There is a need to become more business-orientated, to produce a training business plan and to show in economic terms the effect on growth and development for the organization.

Role of the Training and Development Function

Main Role

It is very clear from the evidence available in the United Kingdom and elsewhere that the training and development function has a critical support role to play in helping the organization become successful. Both British and American studies of successful companies show that training and development are highly related to good organizational performance. Indeed, the evidence is sufficiently strong to be able to make the following statements:

- Training and development processes are among the key management tools available for quickly achieving outstanding performance.
- Not all organizations which have high levels of training and development investment and activities are successful.
- The major difference is that successful organizations ensure that training and development activities are part of a total performance improvement strategy – they are business-needs oriented.

Thus, training and development's role is concerned with helping the organization to be successful.

Main Focus

If the main role of the training and development function is to help the organization become successful, its main focus must be on those activities that will help this to come about. The key objectives of the organization *must* also be the key objectives for the training and development function. We can, therefore, state that the main focus of the training and development function is:

> identifying, assessing, and – through planned learning – helping to develop the key skills and abilities that enable individuals to perform current or future jobs as required to meet the key organizational objectives.

Main Emphasis

As market conditions, technology, economic policies and the like change, so must the organization's objectives (if it is to survive and be successful). The training and development function must also change in response to these new or modified objectives. It will then face a period of relative stability until further fundamental changes occur. The training and development function, if it is to make a successful contribution to organizational performance, must have its main emphasis on either activities designed to help the organization to maintain *current* levels of performance or to adapt and cope with *changing* circumstances.

In some cases an emphasis on *both* kinds of activity may be required: for example in a large organization in a relatively stable market which is diversifying into new markets (sales training, for example, would become change-oriented). It must be clear, however, which part of the training and development function has the main emphasis – change or maintenance. We can state that:

> the training and development function will help to maintain organizational systems, practices, and performance, or will help the organization to change – it must be clear as to which is the current emphasis.

The Trainer's Role

Role

Role refers to the collection of behaviours, attitudes and values that are expected of a person occupying a given position in an organization (or society). The expectations associated with some roles, such as that of a fire prevention officer for example, are clear. Others, like those associated with the role of the trainer, are more ambiguous.

It has been said that:

> '... there can be no single statement of what the role of a training specialist should be. It is conditioned by a combination of the objective necessities in his firm, subjective and personal elements brought out by the attitudes of managers, and his own conception of his role and personal skills – he and the job help to make each other.' (Nadler, 1969)

There have been a number of attempts at making sense of the many training roles. Figure 1 is a summary of the range of trainer roles referred to in the literature and identified in our research.

It is unlikely that any single trainer will undertake the full range of trainer roles. How do trainer roles translate into what trainers actually do?

Trainer activities appear to be determined by three factors:

Type of Role	Trainer Role
Giving direction	Training policy formulator
Goal determination	Training need identifier and diagnostician, generator of ideas for training initiatives, formulator of training objectives.
Preparing initiatives	Researcher and curriculum builder, materials designer and developer, training administrator and organizer, training marketeer.
Implementing initiatives	Direct trainer, OD agent, catalyst, facilitator, coach, mentor, training adviser, consultant, agent of learning transfer to the job.
Evaluation	Validator of training, assessor of training quality, evaluator of training contribution.
Associated activities	Manager of training resources, trainer and developer of trainers, liaison officer.

Figure 1. *Trainer roles and type roles*

- the type of organization;
- personal preferences;
- professional training trends.

The examples set out below illustrate some fairly typical and some less typical training jobs.

Examples of Fairly Typical Training Jobs

Tutor. Works in an 'executive training college' of a nationalized industry and has been seconded to training from another function for three years. He lists his major activities as the setting of course objectives, doing background work, course design, preparing course materials, tuition and evaluating the courses. He is not involved in the identification of organizational needs. This is the responsibility of the principal and senior tutor.

Training officer. Works for a large pharmaceutical/chemical industry. He has developed and run courses in a number of subject areas, including supervisory training. However, course work is only one part of the job. He arranges day release courses at local educational establishments, supervises three training administration assistants, and is involved in staff recruitment as well as the preparation of staff for redundancy. He also has an involvement in public relations exercises.

Company training manager. Works for a private airline. He lists his activities as (a) the management of training staff (five) – allocation of work, monitoring of job performance and giving advice; (b) receipt and perusal of information; (c) administrative paperwork – dealing with budgets, forward planning, reading and writing papers, feeding information upwards; (d) direct training, and (e) various *ad hoc* activities.

Senior training adviser. The training adviser works for one of the Industry Training Boards. His activities are numerous and diverse and include the following:

- running management workshops;
- sitting on college advisory committees;
- running careers days;
- acting as a consultant to companies;

- direct training, mainly at supervisory level;
- coaching individuals;
- holding ITB staff meetings;
- doing company need analyses;
- doing appeal work for colleagues;
- levy exemption work;
- marketing of own training activities;
- attending regional ITB management meetings;
- acting as a catalyst, mainly in small companies;
- administrative work.

Examples of Less Typical Training Jobs

Manager, training quality assurance. Works for a large organization that produces computer and other electronic equipment. This is a somewhat unusual job in that the trainer's main activity is to prepare training standards and then to monitor that these standards are achieved. Interestingly his status is similar to the other trainers in the department so he does not have any vested authority that he can use to achieve his objectives. He also:

- develops trainers;
- assists with programme development;
- makes recommendations to the head of training;
- arranges for consultants to give presentations;
- deals with administrative matters;
- does some direct training.

Management training executive. Works for a large organization that produces computers and other electronic equipment. This trainer's task is to identify potential sales managers in the organization and then to 'nurture' them. Most of his time is spent in establishing contact networks in the organization in order to identify the potential managers. He then runs management development workshops with select groups and acts as a mentor to the individuals. At the end of the day he is in a position to advise top management on the selection of the best people for the job.

With the current changing climate, there is a distinct trend for training activities to become much more diverse. This has serious implications for additional skills that trainers will need.

Additional Skills for Trainers

The range of skills will be diverse but is likely to include the following:

- working more closely with senior managers;
- understanding the needs of a changing business;
- effective use of outside training resources, eg making full use of open learning systems;
- understanding the *full* range of training/learning options.

If trainers are going to need these new skills, this has implications for the providers of trainer training. Figure 2 illustrates where the current emphasis lies and the need to become more organizationally oriented.

Most of the emphasis to date has been on the development of trainer core competencies.

We now need to take this to the next stage to ensure that trainers are responsive to the needs of the organization. However, there is still the requirement to provide training in the basic concepts which are common to the jobs of most trainers. There have already been some important initiatives in this direction.

'Traditional' Trainer Training	Organization-centred Trainer Training
Emphasis on:	Emphasis on:
Detailed needs analysis processes	Reacting to priority organizational needs
Course design and implementation	Design of a range of learning opportunities
Centralized training function mentality	Training embedded in the day-to-day running of the organization
Broad programmes of development from trainers (must cover everything)	Training for trainers available on specific topics
Syllabus-led	Client-led
Trainer-centred	Learner-centred

Figure 2. *Traditional VS organization-centred trainer training*

Alternative Approaches to Trainer Training

Any new approach must ensure flexibility in order to cope with the broad range of demands arising from the trainer's individual needs and responsibilities.

1. Open Learning for Trainers

Over the last few years, several developments have taken place to make available a wide range of open learning materials covering an extremely broad range of trainer training topics. Materials are now available in subject areas including:

- ☐ benefits of training
- ☐ identifying and analysing training needs
- ☐ setting objectives
- ☐ validation of training
- ☐ formulating training plans
- ☐ youth training
- ☐ information technology training
- ☐ supervisor development
- ☐ evaluation of training
- ☐ implementation of training
- ☐ trainer roles
- ☐ administration of the training function
- ☐ management of the training function.

These materials certainly provide a good grounding in the basic trainer skills and offer an extremely flexible approach. However, they do little to bridge the gap between traditional skills and the requirements of the operations of organizations in current climates.

Bridging the Theory – Practice Gap

The aim must be to help trainers to become more business oriented. This cannot be achieved by trainers attempting to develop themselves in isolation from what goes on in their organization. They need to relate theory to real business issues. One way to do this is to use managers in the organization as mentors. They can act as sounding boards for ideas, give feedback on trainer performance and help the trainer 'keep his feet on the ground'. This way the trainer's credibility in the organization will be increased because of contacts established and developed with those in influential positions.

Trainer Self-Help Groups

Trainer 'self-help groups' are also a useful mechanism for trainer development. These are simply groups of trainers who get together to discuss issues and problems that are of common concern. While the process is not usually a formal one, it does provide the opportunity for trainers to exchange information about successful training strategies, training methods that have been used and useful resources that are available, as well as any other topics of interest.

The Role of Trainer Support Services

In October 1984, the Institute of Training and Development (ITD) was commissioned by the Open Tech unit of the Manpower Services Commission (MSC) to study the needs and priorities for the *training of trainers* through an *open learning approach*. The aim was to identify what needed to be done to create an effective national system. It was completed in December 1984.

The study identified an urgent need to establish a unit to provide a national focus for the promotion and development of open learning for trainer training. It also identified a range of priorities, needs and opportunities to open up transfer training which could form the basis of a programme of action.

Subsequently, in March 1985, a two-year contract was awarded to the ITD to set up a unit to provide a nationwide support system.

The unit established at Beaconsfield to carry out this work is known as 'Trainer Support Services'. It is felt this name well described its aims: a range of services to support trainers in their development and day-to-day job functions.

The unit, which operates independently of ITD, acts on a commercial basis and offers:

1. An information service for individuals, organizations and trainer training providers on materials, programmes, resource centres and support services. The unit also offers evaluation and advice.
2. A materials development and production unit which provides a full development, consultancy and commissioning service. Current products under development include a programme aimed at directors and senior managers on the use of training to obtain improved business results, and a programme for training managers on coping with change.
3. A marketing agency for providers of trainer training open learning materials and associated materials. The intention is to create a focal point for the marketing and sale of materials for users in the UK and overseas.

The need for change in the role of trainers and training managers is highlighted with the development of the training managers programme, the objectives of which are outlined below.

Training managers must:

- ☐ develop their role and function with senior people in the organization;
- ☐ become more aware of the needs of their organization;
- ☐ recognize and cope with changing needs of their organization;
- ☐ manage and organize training to meet the real needs of the organization;
- ☐ convince senior managers of the critical value of training in achieving business excellence.

To support this programme and emphasize the last point, a separate development is near completion aimed at businessmen, senior managers and directors. Through the programme they learn how to direct and control specialist training resources to get business results.

They explore the key issues and business problems facing them, the changes they need to make to solve these problems, and which of their employees will be involved. They specify what will be new about the jobs that people involved will be doing, and what training they will need to acquire the skills necessary for the change to happen effectively and to get the required results.

There can be no doubt that trainers must be ready to adapt to changes in the business environment and ensure that training is an integral part of the company strategy and business plan.

Reference

Nadler, L (1969) The variety of training of roles. *Industrial and Commercial Training*, **1**, 1.

Section 3:
Flexible Learning and Education

3.1 Keynote Address
Flexible Learning: Developments and Implications in Education

M Roebuck
HM Inspector of Schools, Scottish Education Department, Edinburgh

Abstract: Recent and past developments in education which have promoted flexibility are considered as part of an analysis of mechanisms which might support flexible learning, and with a view to identifying the aspects which will need to change or be changed if flexible learning developments are to be made effective, sustained, evaluated and disseminated.

Flexible Learning

Having been asked to give this keynote presentation, it was clearly incumbent upon me to be clear what I thought flexible learning was. As it must have struck most speakers before me, the term has a variety of interpretations.

For example, was it the same as open learning? That seemed a popular line. Or was it individualized learning, or individual learning? Would it be self-directed learning, or self-study? And, looking from a different angle, did adaptive teaching promote flexible learning?

On the other hand, were all these differences merely semantic? A constant problem in education is the jargon; the semantic discontinuities, the gobbledegook, which separate the experts (or is it the inexperts) from the practitioners. Educational technology seems particularly prone. If the educational technologists are not redefining the concept of 'a technology of education', they are looking for a new name.

But to return to flexible learning. Do we already have it? What elements are flexible? Do we want it anyway? Or is 'flexibility' just another buzz word? (In a course submission it is not difficult to find a recommendation such as 'the actual operation of this unit of the course should remain flexible'. The thought immediately arises that this is the part of the submission that has not been thought through. A demand for 'flexibility' may turn out to be an inability to define precisely what the *expected* outcomes are, not only how *unexpected* outcomes will be accommodated.)

It was at about this point that I began a process of self-indulgence. I looked back at the proceedings of the 1966 Conference. I asked myself whether that conference 20 years ago, on a bleak campus in Loughborough, was about 'flexible learning'. The term did not seem to have been used. Some of the presentations were pretty inflexible, including my own, as Derick Unwin found when he moulded them into the first proceedings. But they were often about individual learning, or individuals learning, and sometimes even about individualized learning.

In my own case the emphasis was on the running of courses which were 'programmed'. They were highly structured and paced, and so to that extent were not flexible at all; but at the same time, within the structure there was a great degree of learner-dependent activity. The focus was on individualizing the experience within that structure; of providing *feedback* to individuals; of ensuring that what *they* experienced on the courses reflected the experiences they were to produce for students.

In the conference of ten years ago, held in Dundee, John Cowan talked about *freedom*. He expressed concern about the low-level nature of the objectives achieved (though maybe not those aimed at) in highly structured courses. In his view, courses attempted to be flexible in their pacing and routing but ended up being restrictive in the opportunities for self-directed learning.

Such situations are not restricted to higher education. In a report published in 1982, individual and individualized learning were distinguished in terms of what was found in classrooms where 'the amount of "individual work" observed was encouraging but virtually no "individualized" work was seen. Similarly "group work" tended to be individual pupils working *in* a group rather than pupils working *as* a group' (Scottish Education Department, 1982).

A Working Definition

For the purposes of this paper a working definition might be that flexible learning is characterized by flexible approaches to the provision and design of ways of meeting learners' needs. Thus flexible learning requires both flexible teaching and flexible learning approaches.

Clearly this could embrace open learning, self-study, individualization and the like, though it may not include flexible ways of meeting teachers' needs.

Prerequisites

In 1966 I was very keen on hierarchies of prerequisites (Gagné, 1965). Pursuing that line, what might be prerequisites for this 'flexible learning'? They are set out in Figure 1.

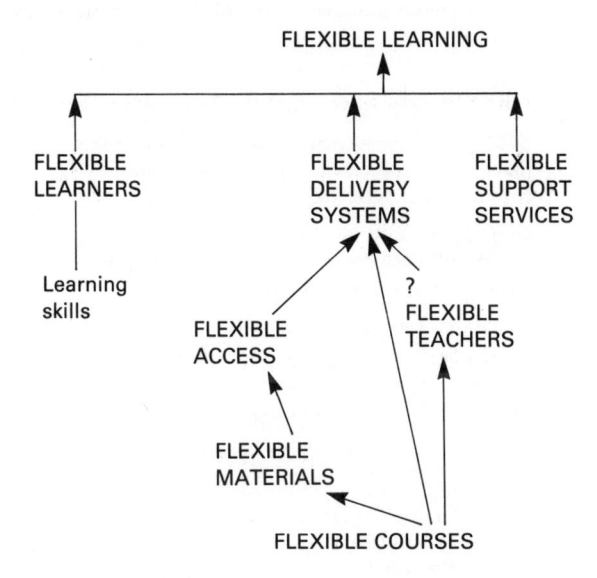

Figure 1. *Prerequisites for flexible learning*

For each of these prerequisites, in their turn, there will also be certain controlling necessary characteristics. For example, the *flexibility of the learners* may be determined by their skills, attitudes and motivations, by the numbers and their geographical location.

Similarly the flexibility of the *delivery system* will be determined by teachers' and lecturers' skills, attitudes and motivations; by the materials and devices available, and by the assessment procedures adopted.

The *organizational context* will influence the degree of flexibility attainable through course structures, management structures and timetabling, as well as examination and certification requirements.

Finally, *support services* also play a controlling role via accommodation, the forms of resources services, and the availability of staff development and retraining.

Clearly it would be possible to reorder these factors, or group them in different ways, redefine or add others; but the important question would seem to be not how they interact but how *flexible* each of them has to be to make a significant contribution? And how flexible *can* each be?

And if flexible approaches to meeting learners' needs are the aim, which of these elements are or is most crucial? The sort of questions which need to be considered include:

- ☐ Does flexibility derive from the design of materials? Is that the touchstone?
- ☐ Is it a matter of developing skills in the learners? Or of changing the attitudes of teachers?
- ☐ Can flexibility be developed with rigid teachers?

Or am I being too simplistic? Is the response always that it is too complicated, that education and training are multivariate, and a single aspect cannot alone provide that change agent?

Educational Developments and their Impact on Flexibility

Over the last two decades we have seen a variety of devices and approaches introduced with a view to changing classroom practice. Many of them have in their turn appeared to hold the key to flexibility.

What Characterized the Changes which had the Potential to Increase Flexibility?

Print	– published texts → teacher-produced materials – plain paper copiers (reduce, collate, enlarge) – copyright changes (licensing)
Audio	– language labs → portable group units – wired radio speaker systems → cassette players – off-air radio → replay units
AV	– blackout → daylight viewing – hand strip/slide projectors → automatic projectors
Video	– film → video – live TV → recorded TV/video – special projection needs → portable video
Computer	– batch mainframe → online micros – distant 'centre' → classroom terminal – service → hands-on – fixed commercial software → teacher generated/adapted software
Telecommunication	– for headteacher → for classes to use
Organization	– whole class → mixed modes/small groups – special AV rooms → own classroom – resources backup service
Curriculum	– more clearly linked to the needs of all students – modularized (and thereby inevitably 'flexible'?) – resources for courses

Have they Increased the Flexibility of Learning?

At one point it was clearly the view that providing a variety of resources would encourage the use of a range of approaches; or that providing devices with built-in flexibility would give the student freedom. These theories have not worked out, even though there have been changes in the learning and teaching environment which could have facilitated or even stimulated more flexible learning conditions.

Let us look at a few examples.

The *overhead projector*: Has it given more flexibility to the learner? In 1986 it is still being used as a kind of blackboard, even in the presence of a blackboard, and why? Because training films show it that way, and because the screen is over the blackboard. And where else might the projector be put? You have to look for the power point – that is usually between the blackboard and the door.

The *video recorder* is used extensively, but it is used essentially as a timeshift device, without interaction and in conditions which make discussion, or individual or group use near impossible.

There are examples of exceptionally good practice but at the same time we find school policies in 1986 which say:

> 'the technician must be present at all replays'

(because the headteacher did not trust the staff); or,

> 'recordings must be wiped one week after making'

(decided in 1976 when the school had only six cassettes, making nonsense of any moves towards planned integration or the use of cassettes which allow three hours of recording).

Such problems are not limited to schools. For example we find a similar policy in a college (1985):

> 'Video-recorders were to be put into college library for student use, but had to be kept in locked carrels to prevent "unauthorized" use. The tracking had to be altered so that only those tapes selected and specially dubbed by the senior technician, and held by the library, could be viewed.'

(The fear was that students would view illegal tapes. That the senior technician and the staff frequently used 'illegal' tapes was ignored. The outcome was an expensive, totally unused facility.)

The scene is nevertheless promising. What has happened is that much of this provision of resources at school and post-school level has put a greater control for the design of the 'conditions for learning' in the hands of the individual lecturer or teacher. At the same time much curriculum change has been aimed at producing the same effect. But the management of the context has not necessarily encouraged flexible use.

Frequently the practice that has resulted is characterized by increased flexibility accompanied by increased frustration, for both students and teachers.

Handling Skills

- ☐ wider range of equipment for the lecturer to master
- ☐ students are often more familiar with the equipment than teachers; this circumstance is not exploited

Organization

- ☐ falling school rolls – smaller numbers of support staff
- ☐ increase in equipment – no increase in support staff
- ☐ changing expectations for support staff – but unclear job definitions

- longer school periods – increased opportunity for integration of equipment use (or for longer boring sessions) but either pupils or equipment must move

Buildings

- classrooms which do not match the basic requirements to promote flexibility (limitations of power points, screens, blackout, furniture)

Support Services

- librarians' knowledge not properly utilized because few in teaching have been advised on how they can best be used

and so on . . . and there are exceptions.

Essential Factors in Promoting Flexibility

If devices cannot stimulate flexibility, what can?

Let us return to the list of elements in Figure 1 (learners, delivery system, organizational context, and support services). The current bandwagon is open learning. According to Lewis and Paine (1985), open learning requires flexible materials because

> 'no two learners are alike. Each learner is an individual and just as the good teacher caters for each individual so should a learning package. Learners differ in ability and experience; needs, wants and purposes; and learning styles. The package designer has to find ways of catering for these differences.'

To achieve this open learning has eliminated (or bypassed) some of the usual constraining factors associated with course structure, accommodation, teacher/lecturer skills and attitudes and support facilities, and replaced them with a new operating environment.

Rigidity is removed almost by definition.

At the same time, and in particular, the teacher as mediator is replaced by the teacher as tutor and supporter. The need for flexibility on the part of the teacher is achieved not by trying to obtain an attitude change within an existing job, but by a change of job.

But it has introduced new constraints, and while for example the Open Tech has developed on the 'Heineken principle' (reaching those parts the traditional training system does not reach), in the face of traditional economics it may end up being much less pervasive, if each provision is forced to be self-supporting. I hope it does not become reduced to an exclusive cocktail.

But open learning is still in the honeymoon period. Although clearly the Open University, the flagship of open learning in the UK, has had to forego educational principles in the face of economic pressures, most of the other open learning developments have yet to experience harsh competition. What open learning has already done is to take away from the lecture room door that piece of brown paper. Putting teaching materials on BBC2 exposed the quality. Open learning materials require and at the same time provide the opportunity to promote openness and accountability.

Tom Foggo in his paper at this conference identified a number of factors associated with changes, in particular with the introduction of open learning. These included the effect on the role and security of the training officer of going towards open learning. He or she may not be able to cope with this change, or the necessary retraining. And, at the same point in time, the management structure may also have difficulty in assimilating open learning and accommodating its traditional expectations.

As, for example, in Scotland we move towards an open learning network across the colleges of education to support in-service, we know that a big problem is that of updating the skills of those who are to support the network, even though we have had more than ten years of open learning teacher education in educational technology.

Is each flexibility matched by equal and opposite inflexibilities?

Flexibility and the Quality of Learning and Teaching

If we look back at the factors in Figure 1, while we have not considered all of them, one is crucial: the role and contribution of the teacher to supporting, sustaining and devising flexible approaches.

The evidence to date tends to lead us to believe that if by flexible learning we mean differentiating and individualizing then we have not been particularly successful. And if we are going to bring about a significant change in conditions for learning we have to address (a) the skills, attitudes and motivation of the teacher as mediator; and (b) the management structure which supports or destroys attempts to assist teachers in changing their role or perceptions of the role.

Remember that you are all enthusiasts and few of you are teachers *per se*. It is not you that we have to worry about supporting. It is the average teacher in the average classroom or lecture room, down the road, just now.

Let me illustrate this need by quotations from two publications. The first is an inspectorate report of 1982 which is still valid, and the second is from a 1985 publication reviewing classroom research.

> 'The approach widely adopted by Scottish teachers . . . was whole class teaching . . . a high degree of uniformity of method from one teacher to another, and from one school to another. . . Teachers described the objectives they hoped to achieve . . . as "imparting content" or, more explicitly, "covering the syllabus". . . Teachers justified the class-teaching approaches they had adopted on severely practical grounds. Syllabuses were crowded and demanding. In order to cover them, corners had to be cut by concentrating on what was to be learned. . . A wide range of approaches required similarly wide access to resources, and more time for preparation. The traditional attitudes of teachers to the role of teaching were reinforced by the widely held view, not least among parents, that teachers are there to control learning: "teachers should teach". The use of audiovisual items, notably television, has increased significantly. Teachers tended to use them on an opportunist basis or as regular (timetabled) events in their programmes, rather than as integrated aspects of their courses. Even when design had allowed for some teacher intervention, this was unlikely to take place. Parallel roles for teacher and technology continue to be reflected in the use of expressions such as "aids", "learning from television", "using slide-tape" and so on. . . All teachers are familiar with the normal range of approaches, methods, and techniques that the methodology of their specialism affords them. Much of what the survey revealed is by way of commentary on the quality of the selection made from that range, and its application, rather than a criticism of the methods themselves. . . The concept of a "subject methodology" carries with it connotations of a systematic approach to choice of methods, that the learning process may be facilitated and made more effective. It further suggests that their balance and appropriateness should be kept under review. . . But in the great majority of schools . . . there was little evidence of a positive policy for evaluating the effectiveness of teaching or resources.' (Scottish Education Department, 1982)

> 'The failure of many large-scale curriculum development projects of the 1970s to bring about systematically the desired changes in the school curriculum stimulated much empirical research into the processes of curriculum innovation and implementation . . . Research findings pointed towards teachers adapting rather than adopting the curriculum. New principles and recommendations were found to go unrecognized by teachers who at most translated them into procedures which more closely resembled their own familiar practice.' (Calderhead, 1985)

Why should this be? Certainly it seems clear that the principles underlying the approaches were not made explicit; and they were not exemplified in teacher education courses to a sufficient extent. Training in the 'subject' and training in the underlying psychology ('educational technology' in its widest sense) were too often unrelated.

The Challenge

The challenge is how we enable lecturers and teachers across the country, within the constraints of cash, time, working conditions and examination requirements, to be better equipped to promote flexible approaches.

It requires staff development which focuses on teaching and learning strategies.

It requires management of and flexibility in promoting that staff development.

It requires a review of policies and practices at authority, institution and department levels.

It requires evaluation and self-evaluation.

Summary

1. Flexibility may be only a buzz word.
2. It may be an objective which is unattainable.
3. There are several factors which impinge upon flexibility. None can operate in isolation.
4. Only a few are crucial. Some which have been the centre of attention in the past are dependent rather than determining factors.
5. Some apply more to further education and the training sector than to schools.
6. The key pervasive element is the need to provide support for the role change of the teacher, and for policy shifts to maintain that role change.
7. We need (a) a different focus for staff development and (b) a policy basis to implement that approach and allow its evaluation.
8. The policy shift at institution and at authority level has to be focused on
   (a) the need to emphasize differentiation in, and the quality of, learning and teaching approaches; and
   (b) the need to evaluate policies and practice, and to encourage self-evaluation on the part of teachers and those others managing and supporting the learning and teaching process.

References

Calderhead, H (1985) Teachers' decision making. In Bennet, N and Desforges, C (eds) *Recent Advances in Classroom Research*. Scottish Academic Press.

Gagné, R M (1965) *The Conditions of Learning* (1st edn). Holt, Rinehart and Winston, New York.

Lewis, R and Paine, N (1985) *How to Communicate with the Learner. Open Learning Guide 6*. Council for Educational Technology for the UK, London.

Scottish Education Department (1982) *Learning and Teaching in Scottish Secondary Schools: the Contribution of Educational Technology*. HMSO, Scottish Education Department, Edinburgh.

3.2 To Each According to His Needs?

A Garry and J Cowan
Heriot-Watt University, Edinburgh

Abstract: At the heart of this paper is a simple classification scheme in diagrammatic form. The writers use it to describe the various conditions in which needs are held by learners, and to concentrate attention of the transitions through which needs may move from one condition to the next. It is these transitions which are the real area of interest. They provide an opportunity for effective facilitation of learning, which can only take place with commitment on the part of the learner. That commitment is only ensured when needs are moved into the expressed state, and can be formulated as objectives with which the learner identifies intimately.

The model is illustrated by reference to two distinct educational situations – one in continuing professional development (CPD), the other in self-directed undergraduate learning. In each case the writers made a heavy commitment to facilitation of activities in which unperceived needs would be perceived, formulated needs would be defined and felt needs would be expressed. All of this effort was directed ultimately towards the generation of goals and objectives which would more comprehensively and fundamentally express the needs of the learners.

The writers report that they unearthed unfamiliar patterns of objectives when they followed this approach. And they argue, with illustrative examples, that this led to more purposeful development on the part of the learners concerned.

The experience led the writers to have second thoughts about the exercise of responsiblity for directing learning, in both continuing professional development and higher education. They now find it difficult to accept that objectives that are chosen for a learner are likely to be sufficiently fundamental; and they feel that there are implications with regard to the commitment of the learners to objectives which have been chosen for them. They do not see a solution in self-directed learning which is virtually autonomous or independent learning, since many significant needs may go undiscovered and unresolved without external facilitation.

Introduction

The needs of the learners, in continuing professional development (CPD) and elsewhere, are usually decided by almost anyone other than the people who are directly concerned. The learners take part in programmes which respond to patterns of needs which someone else has identified on their behalf, or programmes built up around a particular provider's expertise. In these circumstances it is hardly surprising that motivation is frequently superficial, immediate learning and development negligible – and participation only ensured by bribery or pressures of one form or another.

Classifying Needs

It is helpful to classify needs from the learner's standpoint:

1. *An expressed need* is one which has been identified and which the learner is quite willing to explain to others (for whatever reasons).
2. *A felt need* has been identified reasonably accurately as a deficiency or as scope for improvement – but the learner does not wish to make it public, for one reason or another.

3. *An unformulated need* is concealed amidst vague or unformed feelings of disquiet on the part of the learner about certain aspects of competence. The learner knows that there is something wrong, something missing or something which (s)he aspires to gain – but cannot quite put a finger on it.
4. *An unperceived need* is one of whose existence the learner is totally unaware, although others – looking from a detached standpoint – may see it clearly.

| UNPERCEIVED | UNFORMULATED | FELT | EXPRESSED |

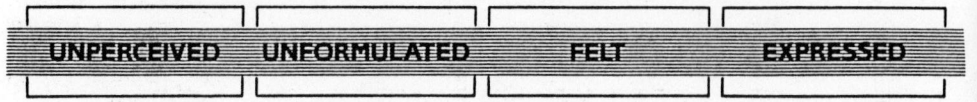

Figure 1. *Classification of needs*

We illustrate this simple classification scheme diagramatically in Figure 1. Each of our four groupings corresponds to a state of mind or to an attitude (Figure 2) on the part of the learner. (S)he is *oblivious* to unperceived needs; (s)he is *concerned* about unformulated needs – even when (s)he can't specify them; (s)he has *decided* what the felt needs are – even if (s)he is not prepared to declare them; and (s)he is committed to *expressed* needs, by declaring a diagnosis of them and aspiring for improvement.

| UNPERCEIVED | UNFORMULATED | FELT | EXPRESSED |
| OBLIVIOUS | CONCERNED | DECIDED | COMMITTED |

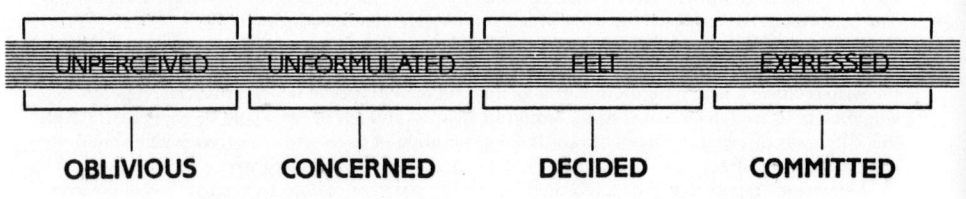

Figure 2. *Types of needs – and corresponding state of mind*

Needs can readily move from one of our categories to the next, through a transition stage – though the transition will not usually happen without prompting. Sometimes it will be initiated internally; more commonly the prompting is a consequence of external intervention which may be a deliberate facilitation of development.

In the case of *unperceived* needs, facilitation can present us with a challenge which prompts us to perceive a need.

When *unformulated* needs are systematically explored, we gradually find it easier to define them (in our own minds at least) – and so they become felt needs.

As soon as we regard it as safe and supportive to express a *felt* need, it will move through the transition into the final (expressed) category.

Once needs have been *expressed* they become potential objectives for an educational or development programme.

These points bring our diagram to the condition shown in Figure 3, where we have likened the movements of needs between relatively settled categories to the movement of salmon up a stream containing still pools and turbulent rapids. The turbulent rapids are the transition stages which are not traversed without struggle or prompting. The still pools are the relatively established categories. And the flow of the stream, if we push the analogy further, represents the natural tendency for ideas to drift off into obscurity if no effort is made to encourage them to move towards expression – and resolution.

The Implications of CPD

In our recent CPD project we examined the source of the goals around which CPD programmes have hitherto been formulated. We found an abundance of totally

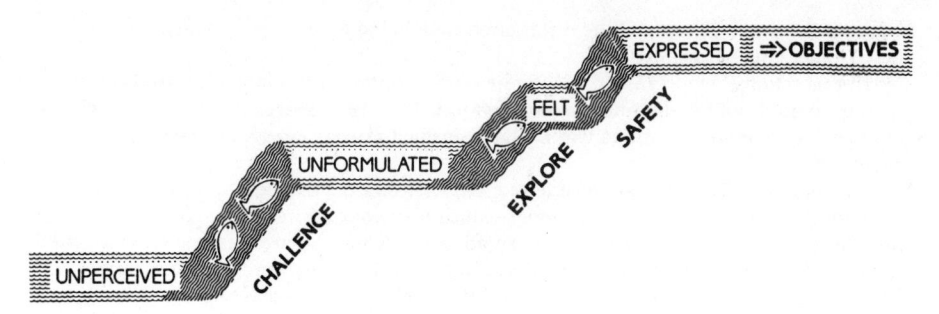

Figure 3. *Needs and transitions*

subjective and dogmatic statements, which were frequently based on no demonstrable evidence. Where enquiries had been undertaken, these were open to valid criticism because of poor research methodology, inadequate or incomplete data, or unsound analysis. As a result we concluded that there are grounds for believing that the programmes were coping with superficially considered or even incorrectly stated needs.

We went on to investigate the potential of self-help groups striving to identify and respond to total patterns of needs. We then devoted almost half our effort to the facilitation of the transition of needs into the expressed condition.

We were only involved with a relatively small number of professional civil engineers, so we cannot make sweeping claims about our efforts. We only groped our way towards strategies which appeared to facilitate meaningful development; yet we never unearthed all the needs of our participants.

We facilitated transitions in various ways. We designed activities which would bring unperceived needs to the attention of our participants and invite their appraisal of them. We allocated time to allow exploration of unformulated needs in areas of disquiet or concern. It was then relatively simple to create the supportive environment in which needs (which were now felt with conviction) could be expressed for a purpose.

The remainder of our time (often less than 50 per cent of the total) was devoted to facilitating professional development with regard to fundamental needs which are not common primary goals in the conventional forms of continuing professional development.

An Intermediate Review

We felt justified in asserting that most CPD provision (in our discipline, at least) caters only for a fragment of the total needs of the individuals, is directed towards objectives which have not been thoroughly identified by participants or providers, and is consequently unlikely to prove particularly effective.

But the implications of our thinking about needs cannot be restricted to CPD. For the more we think about tertiary education, the more we see close parallels with the issues we have identified by scrutinizing the structure of CPD.

Can Undergraduate Learning Respond to Fundamental Needs?

In the three years which have seen us heavily involved in CPD, we have also engaged in a radical innovation in the penultimate year of our undergraduate course. We have allocated four hours per week as a 'space' in which the students may select their own interdisciplinary objectives, plan their own programmes and evaluate their own progress. Our only declared expectation was the reasonable demand that each student should select objectives which (s)he considered important in terms of overall educational development, while at the same time being in an area in which development was possible.

In this scheme we presumed that some of the important fundamental needs of the learners would not be identified or satisfied in the conventional system, since the choice of objectives is made by others without an informed impression of the learners' priorities.

As facilitators we spent about half our time helping the students to process needs through the various stages of our model – until they were expressible. The remainder of our effort mainly went into supporting small group work; the interactions between the learners there led to exchanges of peer group perception, joint exploration of new issues, and mutual support in the face of difficult challenges and objectives. Through these experiences many previously unrecognized undergraduate needs were revealed and resolved.

Most of our students managed to perceive a wide range of needs, to formulate these in helpfully precise behavioural terms, and to expose them within a group where the assistance of fellow students and facilitator helped them to tackle the problem of effecting improvement.

We were impressed with the motivation and the purposefulness of the students – and with the objectivity which they brought to the process of self-appraisal. Members of study groups saw and heard dramatic improvement in unprepared oral communication. They read perceptive analyses of effective listening, which left them in little doubt about the analytical capacity of the writer, or the effect of that analysis on subsequent performance. They saw confidence develop, and noted the behavioural changes which were a consequence of that development.

What Lessons Have We Learnt?

In the two experimental situations we have mentioned:

1. A heavy commitment to facilitating the expression of needs led to statements of needs (and consequent course objectives) which were significantly different from those in similarly named courses with objectives drafted on behalf of the learners.
2. There were no problems in respect of commitment, motivation or shallow learning – provided the learners were able to express their needs with genuine sincerity.
3. The discrepancy between the needs which the learners declared as fundamental, and the needs diagnosed and published elsewhere, was even more marked than we had anticipated.

Conclusion

Facilitation of learning includes facilitation of the process by which the real underlying needs of the learner are perceived, formulated and expressed. Unless that happens, the objectives chosen by the learner (or chosen on behalf of the learner) are likely to be incomplete and unsatisfactory. Most learners find it extremely difficult to identify needs of which they have hitherto been unaware – without purposeful interaction with others.

That statement virtually concludes our paper. But the message which we wish to convey is not the calm and confidence of the above paragraph – but rather an impression of confusion and concern.

We are confused because we have been brought up in the belief that aims and objectives should be chosen by the system on behalf of learners, without much effort being made to identify unperceived and unformulated needs. And we are concerned – because our experiences over the last two or three years suggest to us that this approach leaves some important and very fundamental aims and needs totally disregarded, even if only for a minority of the learners in a group.

We feel that greater improvements can be brought about by approaching learning and development in the way we have outlined. But we are conscious that this would mean turning the whole system inside out.

We were therefore tempted to echo the words of the anonymous Belfast citizen who commented, in the early stages of the troubles in Northern Ireland, that 'Anyone who isn't confused here doesn't really understand what's going on'. But we prefer the constructive optimism of Adlai Stevenson (in a speech at Colombus, Ohio in 1952):

'Understanding human needs is half the job of meeting them'.

3.3 What Technologies Matter in Primary Education?

J Oakley
La Sainte Union College of Higher Education, Southampton

Abstract: Despite the widespread introduction of the microcomputer into primary education, a three-year survey involving postgraduate teacher trainees in a college of higher education revealed a surprisingly stable pattern of preference for some of the earlier technology, and a continuing heavy reliance on paper-based classroom resources for the bulk of the day-to-day work. Consideration is given to whether enough is done to support this level of trainee activity, and also to what extent the effects of constant technological innovation are beneficial to development and training in the older technologies.

Without doubt one of the most interesting and widespread developments in education and training over the past decade or so has been the use made of the microcomputer. Machines, software, experiments and case studies, expert advice and familiarization courses for teachers and instructors, have proliferated to the extent that one might be forgiven for supposing at first sight that the microcomputer had swept all before it, including sweeping many of the earlier technologies out of existence.

As is usual with any technical innovation of this magnitude, it is not hard to find supporters who seem to be suggesting that not only is this so, but that it should be so, and who enthusiastically present suggestions and even designs for quite sweeping changes in some sector or other of the educative or training process, based on the introduction of the new innovation. Primary education has not escaped the microcomputer phenomenon, and machines have been introduced into a large number of schools in the United Kingdom and elsewhere in the world, as acts of national or local policy, staff initiative or parental interest.

With any new innovation it always seems oddly difficult, once the initial period of highly reported and publicized euphoria is over, to find out in detail exactly what is going on in a consistent and well-established way. Answers to the really important professional questions are hard to come by, including such questions as: to what degree has the new innovation caused permanent changes in the teaching and learning modes employed in this sector or that institution? What percentage of the total workload is now mediated via the new technology? What is now the current state of the older technologies, and modes of teaching and learning? Which can now be regarded as obsolescent, obsolete, or totally redundant? In short, what is the degree of penetration of the new innovation, over what kind of area, and what else can now be regarded as dead or finished as a result?

Whilst not in any way being able to answer any of these questions fully with regard to the microcomputer, the author is in a position to throw some light on the kinds of technology and resources currently found most useful in primary education by teacher trainees, as a result of a three-year survey carried out in his own institution, and to pose certain questions as a result.

Since the survey was not designed in any way as a formal piece of research but rather emerged as a natural concomitant of current work within a teacher training institution, it will be necessary to sketch in a few background details before going on to consider the results and implications of the survey.

La Sainte Union College of Higher Education in Southampton has been running courses in educational technology for all its teacher trainees (both Bachelor of Education and Postgraduate Certificate of Education), since the early 1970s. The work of the college was used as a case study by the Council for Educational Technology (CET) at a series of national conferences, and was later published by them in *The Role of Educational Technology in Teacher Education* (Neville, 1977).

The courses have always been systems-based, and rather than write essays or take formal examinations, students have had to produce curriculum packages, called 'educational technology modules', as part of their assessment. These generally take the form of a fully designed programme of work lasting between five and ten weeks, for a class of primary schoolchildren, complete with all necessary resources and materials. University acceptance and encouragement of this mode of assessment was a powerful stimulus for the students, and work of a very high quality has been produced, much of which is stored on microfiche and serves as a college resource of considerable importance.

However it readily became apparent in the mid-1970s that to put pressure on students to produce usable classroom materials of this nature rather than asking them to write essays was decidedly unfair, and perhaps unethical, if at the same time the institution concerned made no arrangements for the provision of raw materials needed by the students, and instead left them to the mercies of the hard commercial world outside. There, for example, a single sheet of large card needed for a chart could cost as much as 80 pence, and thirty A4 workcards could cost at least £2.00.

With the College's initially somewhat nonplussed permission, the author expanded the work of the institution's media resources centre to include the provision and sale of all materials needed for curriculum work by the students. Extremely tight monitoring by the VAT authorities ensured that only materials of direct classroom use could be supplied; only at cost price; and only to students. We were not even allowed to sell such materials to college staff. Initial turnover was a few hundred pounds per annum. This year it will exceed thirty thousand pounds. The running of this aspect of the work of the media resources centre now demands one full-time appointment, and occupies a large amount of the author's time in constantly looking for items, materials and products which may have application in the primary classroom. Despite VAT constraints we carry a range of several hundred items and are constantly expanding the range.

Stock control in such a situation is necessary, and a chance meeting with Dr James Hartley at an earlier ETIC conference led to an interesting spin-off. Dr Hartley was researching into the nature and production of handouts and worksheets, and was endeavouring to get some idea of the quantities being produced in institutions of various kinds. We in La Sainte Union (LSU) knew, because of our stock control system, just how many sheets of spirit duplicator paper, A4 workcards, and large sheets of card we were supplying to students, and we knew when we were supplying them. It was unlikely that students were buying further large quantities from other sources, simply because of the unfavourable price differentials, and the distance they would have to go to get them. Making certain deductions on the basis that not all supplied would end up in the classroom, we still found that some 200 students had apparently used 125,000 sheets of A4 spirit duplicator paper, and 8,000 sheets of A4 card. (Hartley, 1979). Dr Hartley was to describe

'... producing worksheets and handouts (as) a cottage industry across the country.'

He went on

'... to my mind – from what I have seen – many of these sheets are churned out with little rational thought concerning their layout and design.'

With both of his statements I would totally agree. During 1985 in my college media resources sold at least 270,000 sheets of A4 spirit duplicator paper to students.

Deducting ten per cent for wastage and other possible uses, this leaves some 243,000 sheets used during 19 weeks of teaching practice by an average of 68 students out in schools at any one time. This is equivalent to one student distributing a handout to a class of thirty children six times a week. The students also purchased some 40,000 sheets of A4 card, which works out at each student using just over 30 a week. Last year we also used 96 rolls of laminating film or 14.4 kilometres. The mind rather boggles at a line of A4 workcards stretching for 7.2 kilometres, but that was in fact our verifiable production.

I mention lamination because initially we did not provide this facility. Many of our innovations come from suggestions from the students, and lamination was their suggested answer to protecting and lengthening the life of workcards and picture banks, which are a fundamental resource in primary education. Eventually it was decided not to rely on informal comment and suggestion, but at the end of each year to select a student group and give them a questionnaire to find out how effective the media resources centre has been in meeting their classroom needs; to find out which technologies they found most useful for a primary classroom; and to find out which materials stocked they relied on and needed most.

For the last three years the group so surveyed has been the PGCE Course. This group always numbers 40 or more students and so provides a useful sample of the total teacher trainee group. Since they are taught by the author it is easy to arrange for comprehensive completion and return of the questionnaires. Worth noting is the fact that teaching practice figures very largely in their intensive one-year course and they make very heavy use of the media resources centre. If things go wrong there, then it matters very much, and their comments, generated perhaps by their anxieties, are that much lengthier, sharper and pertinent.

The questionnaire they complete is a lengthy one, and covers such matters as the quality of supervisory and departmental assistance they receive on teaching practice; the quality of the service provided by the media resources centre, the college language/reading resources centre, and the college library; and finally the quality of the PGCE course as a whole.

Two questions from the questionnaire are germane to this paper. PGCEs are asked to list in order of importance the five pieces of technology available in the media resources centre which they found of most help to them on teaching practice in primary school. They are provided with a list of thirteen items of technology. Points are awarded (five, four, three, two, one) in descending order for each student's list of items. This enables a rank order of importance to be constructed by adding up the points given for each item of technology selected by all the students. In addition, note is taken of how many students include a particular item of technology in their lists, since in terms of demand, five students placing the same item in fifth position on their lists represents a greater demand for service than one student placing one item first on his list. In both cases the points total would be five.

Findings over the past three years have been remarkably consistent, as Figure 1 shows.

The second question concerns the provision of materials by the media resources centre. From a list of 63 types of item stocked, PGCEs are again asked to select the five kinds of materials which they made most use of on teaching practice. Findings again have been consistent over three years, as is shown by Figure 2.

Looking at such consistent results, as shown in Figures 1 and 2, and remembering the considerable increase in sales since we provided data for Dr Hartley, lead me to suggest that we are certainly turning out no less spirit duplicator handouts and workcards than we did before, that we are in fact certainly turning out more. Despite the introduction of the microcomputer into the primary classroom, and allowing for whatever inroads it has made, it does seem hard to support the idea that the older technologies as represented by the spirit duplicator, the heat copier, the photocopier and the laminator are somehow dead or even obsolescent. Our data suggests that they

	1983	1984	1985	*	**
1	spirit duplicator	spirit duplicator	spirit duplicator	165	36
2	laminator	laminator	photocopier	127	36
3	photocopier	photocopier	laminator	95	31
4	heat copier	heat copier	heat copier	73	27
5	fast audio tape copier	overhead projector	episcope	32	16

* Points total.
** Number of students placing this item on their list (N = 30)

Figure 1. *Most important items of technology in the media resources centre*

	1983	1984	1985	*	**
1	spirit duplicator materials	spirit duplicator run-off paper	spirit duplicator carbon paper	112	26
2	A4/A5 workcard	spirit duplicator carbon paper	spirit duplicator run-off paper	98	22
3	Sugar Paper	Large card	A4 workcard	81	25
4	Pens/Markers	A4 workcard	Large card	59	19
5	Large card	spirit duplicator master paper	spirit duplicator master paper	52	13

* Points total.
** Number of students placing this item on their list (N = 30)

Figure 2. *Most popular items of technology in the media resources centre*

are very much alive and kicking, and I would suggest that the bulk of the day-to-day teaching is still mediated through the paper-based technologies rather than a VDU, and that it is likely to continue to be so. Certainly, as far as PGCEs in my training institution are concerned, the workhorse technology of the primary classroom is the spirit duplicator with all its support materials, and then the hand-made A4 workcard, often subsequently photocopied several times. the heat copier is much favoured because it permits a spirit duplicator master to be made of already published material, so for example 30 copies of a useful textbook map can readily and quickly be acquired sometimes using the original map if detachable, or a photocopy of it, if not.

I would like to conclude by considering some of the implications of these findings, and posing certain questions. Firstly, I'm not at all certain that enough is done to train students in the production of classroom handouts and workcards, certainly not enough to support the level of activity that they display, and which Hartley suggests is merely part of a much wider 'cottage industry'. Virtually everything connected with handout production really matters from a professional point of view, from the choice and mix of colours, text layout, choice of typeface or writing style, the integration of visuals, graphics or tables with text, the placing and type of question, the adjustment of language and concept to suit the level of cognitive development of the learner, the variants needed for differing abilities or personalities, the quantity, the sequence, the provision of reinforcement and feedback. My institution certainly doesn't provide any kind of coherent in-depth course to cover that range of factors, though of course many tutors might make passing reference to some of them.

It might be that we have yet to amass the research and build a theory to underpin such a course. We certainly need more research of the kind done by Hartley and others, and it does need to be co-ordinated so that training institutions can build findings into courses, and then maintain those courses so that further developments can take place. But part of the problem could be that each innovation such as the microcomputer leads to a demand by those in authority for a course to be provided to familiarize trainees with the innovation. This inevitably eats up time that was formerly available elsewhere, and so something gets squeezed out, since the student's workload cannot be infinitely expanded. Each innovation can therefore exercise a 'choking-off' effect on ongoing work associated with an earlier innovation, however valuable that work might be, and however slow the increments of progress are. Curriculum change is now too often the order of the day, not curriculum development. This is often compounded by the attitude of some academic researchers who ought to know better, who move readily into the newest innovatory field often summarily dismissing work in earlier fields as 'completed', or 'outmoded', or just plain 'wrong', long before such work ever became known, current, taught, used or tried out on a large scale in the training institutions.

Programmed learning was a case in point. Much useful work of direct relevance to handout and workcard design was done, but it never had time to filter down to become general knowledge among the students I was teaching, before it was discarded in favour of the next innovation. Not all the findings were by any means useless, irrelevant, inapplicable or undeserving of professional attention. But very often it seems as if such knowledge is now 'lost', in the sense that one sees all the old mistakes one learned to avoid on paper happily reappearing on VDUs, and one wonders if the programme author has ever heard of the work of Brethower, Meyer Markle, Rowntree et al. To my total amazement I once won a cash prize from the magazine *Educational Computing* and had my piece starred as the 'letter of the month', for simply suggesting that that journal might republish some of the earlier research from the days of programmed learning for the benefit of latter-day computer software writers.

Publishers must bear some of the blame. They are still quite capable of turning out abominable materials, and probably will continue to do so, until teachers demand evidence that such materials have actually been tested and validated in classrooms, and performance data is actually included in the total package. This also presupposes that teachers have received either training in the production of good materials, or at least training in evaluation of materials. This too we have precious little time to do with trainees.

So, it is perhaps worth pondering, as each new technical innovation bursts upon us, and we rush to deal with it enthusiastically at the research and conference level, and support the introduction of yet more familiarization courses in the training institutions at whatever cost to existing courses, whether or not we are contributing to the expansion of the gap between what in reality is going on on a large scale, and what we hope, or think, ought to be going on. Do we also by this process, destroy or inhibit or leave unsupported many valuable developments which have slowly and quietly been coming to fruition?

For the PGCE students in my institution work in the primary classroom is still largely a matter of paper, card and the earlier technologies, not the micro or the videodisc, or whatever innovation is coming up next. It is salutary to me as an educational technologist to be told this so consistently and clearly. I'm fortunate in being able to support them in the provision of materials, but I do wish I could support such a large amount of their daily work with a commensurate amount of professional training, and to assure them that all the research connected with how you actually write teaching material on paper is coming along very nicely after all these years, and might soon constitute a coherent theory. Who knows? Such a theory might also benefit the microcomputer, the videodisc, and whatever is coming up next.

References

Hartley, J (1979) A reply to Robin Kinross. *Instructional Science*, 8, 291-294.
Neville, C (ed) (1977) *The Role of Educational Technology in Teacher Education*. CET, London.
Oakley, J (1982) Letter of the month. *Educational Computing* (May).

3.4 Flexible Learning Systems – Developments in Secondary Education

P Waterhouse and J Monaco
Council for Educational Technology
R Rainbow
Somerset TVEI Scheme

Abstract: This paper is in three distinct parts. Part 1 deals with the management of flexible learning in schools. The main argument is that the key to the successful development of flexible learning systems is good management. This implies that the teacher's main role in education is in the management of the learning process, and the implications of this deserve thorough investigation.

Part 2 deals with developments in the use of information technology and library services. As the benefits to learners of both information technology and supported self-study become better known, activities develop which integrate the two. The role of library/resource centres and their professional staff is crucial in the implication of such activities and in complementing the teacher's expertise and skills.

Part 3 deals with flexibility in the school organization and curriculum. A fully modular curriculum, flexible day arrangements, new learning strategies, and the use of information technology can develop independent library information and study skills in the learner. Supported self-study will add to this flexibility, either as an alternative means of study or to complement work carried out in the classroom.

Part 1: The Management of Flexible Learning (P Waterhouse)

There has been a sudden resurgence of interest in more flexible learning systems in the secondary schools. This is in response to a number of influences and pressures:

- new initiatives in the curriculum and in assessment stress the importance of more active forms of learning with the pupils taking greater responsibility;
- there is an emphasis on the acquisition of skills rather than the accumulation of factual knowledge and this is coupled with a realization that skills are acquired through practice and experience in real situations, not through artificially contrived simulations;
- Her Majesty's Inspectors have strongly criticized the 'spoon-feeding' which has been observed in many secondary schools;
- falling rolls have created problems in maintaining the breadth of curricula, especially for minority subjects where groups are regarded as non-viable.

However, flexible learning systems have in the past proved difficult to root inside the secondary schools. Contributory causes are:

- the fragmentation of the secondary school day;
- large classes in the lower and middle schools;
- pressure on space, making it difficult to provide for the independent learner;
- the pressure of external examinations, emphasizing memorization and verbal facility, not thinking or creativity;
- the problems of discipline and motivation of adolescents.

The main hope for the successful implementation of flexible learning systems rests on the concept of support. In the past this has been insufficiently emphasized and, as a result, pupils have floundered and the teacher has either accepted a more chaotic classroom, or returned to safer methods with the assertion that 'it' doesn't work! With the benefit of past experiences many teachers now see flexible learning systems as a form of *training* for independence. So the pupil's first encounters are with well-structured and controlled systems; greater choice and responsibility are gradually introduced as the pupil seems ready for them.

This is *supported* self-study, and the teacher's role is more important than in traditional teaching, not less. It is the teacher who arranges and provides the support for the pupil who is learning how to become an independent learner. This is substantially different from traditional teaching. The emphasis is on *managerial* tasks, and on *tutoring* as opposed to teaching.

Resources are the first kind of support. Extra care is needed in selection, since they have to provide a simple and clear support for those occasions when the pupil is required to work independently. The resources provide structure, enrichment, and guidance.

Good *structured* material forms the core of the resources system. It is usually organized in short blocks or chapters, with clear guidance on objectives for each heading. The writing is concise and direct with a disciplined use of typography, graphics and layout. There are devices to keep the learner active – things to do, problems to solve, self-assessment questions.

Additional *enrichment* material is also needed. This helps with motivation and inspiration. It is often in multi-media format. It provides the raw data and stimuli for the practice of study skills and information skills.

Where the resource base is rich and varied, the teacher may feel it necessary that the pupil should be supported by some kind of prepared *guidance*. This may be in the form of study guides, assignments or task cards. The fact that the teacher has prepared this in advance will help to take some of the pressure off when working with a large group of pupils, when detailed personal joint planning of each individual's tasks would be impossible.

Tutoring is the second kind of support. The case for a more sensitive, listening, conversational, interactive style is already part of the conventional wisdom of the day. There is however a big gap between the understanding of the verbal concept of tutoring and its achievement in practice. Even teachers who are very sensitive to the needs of pupils find it difficult to make the shift. We are all conditioned by the view of the teacher as a director, an organizer, a presenter, and when confronted by a group of young learners the urge to take control is very powerful. Yet the effort in making the shift towards the genuine tutorial is worth making, for the results can be startling.

Management is the third kind of support. Most of the early failures in resource-based learning and similar systems can be attributed to the neglect of the management implications for the teacher. The objective of a management system is to provide a firm framework of discipline and control which will, at the same time, make demands on the young learner and gradually lead towards greater independence and responsibility.

The first element in the management system is the grouping. Supported self-study cannot work if a large class is treated as the only unit for the organization of the work. Nor can it usually succeed where the teacher attempts to allow unrestricted self-pacing and deal with each pupil individually (the logistics problems are too great in all but the smallest of classes). So the small tutorial group has to be the basis of the system. The optimum size is probably about five, but numbers up to eight can be handled successfully. This implies that a large class may have to be operated, at least for some of the time, as three or four tutorial groups. In a small class fewer tutorial groups are required, and the very small class can be operated as a single group.

The second element in the management system is the set of procedures followed by a tutorial group. A cycle similar to the management by objectives (MBO) cycle seems particularly appropriate.

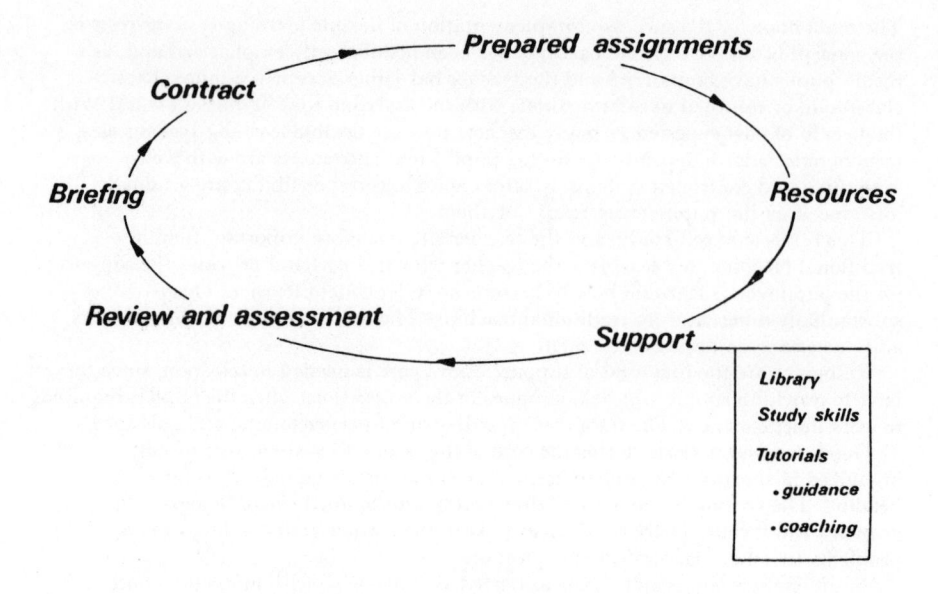

Figure 1. *A system for the management of supported self-study*

At first the group has a tutorial with the teacher. The tasks here are the tasks of *review* and *assessment*; *briefing* for the next phase of self-study; *negotiation* of all aspects of this with a view to arriving at a clear *contract*. The teacher, in the role of tutor, is aiming to get the benefits of economy of time and effort by dealing with a small group, not each individual in turn, but at the same time to individualize the guidance and support as much as possible.

The members of the group then proceed to the self-study phase. During this they are supported by the resources that have been specially chosen or prepared for them. In addition the support services of the school are brought to bear – the library, the workshops, and any other support of a personal kind that may be available within or outside the school. The self-study can be organized within the framework of the normal timetable and normal class grouping, or it can be on a more open basis, with the individual pupils given discretion as to the time and place for independent study. There are countless variations on these main themes.

The importance of a good management system cannot be sufficiently stressed. For those new to the concept of supported self-study, the advice is to get the basic tutorial grouping and the MBO cycle operating *first*, before attempting too great sophistication in resources. Pupils, as well as teachers, need lots of reassurance in the early stages. They need to be shown that there will be no loss of direction or discipline in the short term, even though the main benefits will mostly be long-term.

Part 2: Developments in the Use of Information Technology and School Library/Resource Centres (J Monaco)

Information Technology and Supported Self-Study

Teachers who have experience of implementing supported self-study schemes and at the same time feel confident about using new information technologies (IT) within such schemes, are at present in the minority. However, as the benefits to learners of both IT and supported self-study become better known, and as teachers acquire the necessary knowledge and skills in each area, so we are beginning to see activities develop which integrate the two.

There is no doubt that information technology can contribute significantly to supported self-study and outlined briefly below are some of the ways in which it can be (and increasingly is being) used.

Providing a means of communication between teachers and learners

Audioconferencing is one example of IT being used by some schools to provide tutorial sessions where they would previously have been difficult or impossible to arrange. It can be particularly valuable – and cost beneficial – in rural areas, where schools scattered across a large geographical area may each have only one or two pupils following a particular course of study. It can help where there is a shortage of subject specialist teachers too, since one specialist can provide tutorials simultaneously to groups of pupils in several different schools.

Experiments in the use of electronic mail are also underway to enable schools to exchange ideas and experience about supported self-study with schools in other parts of the country, and it will probably not be very long before electronic mail is used to facilitate some counselling and tutorial activities, such as transmissions of pupils' assignments and provision of feedback on assignments and other guidance from teachers.

Acting as a source of individualized teaching/learning material

Computer assisted learning (CAL) packages are purpose-designed to help learners learn on their own or in small groups and, when used in conjunction with other media, can help to provide the rich variety of stimuli that learners need, particularly during private study periods. Perhaps most importantly in the context of supported self-study, they can give learners some measure of control over their pace of learning, permit choice of route through the learning material, and provide instant feedback on progress.

Telesoftware (ie transmission of software programs from a central computer to another, down a telephone line) is not known to be used as an integral part of any supported self-study scheme at the moment, although it is being used by a number of schools and education authorities in other curricular contexts. However, its potential for allowing pupils who are studying on their own to 'download' learning material, as and when they need it, from a central library, is considerable.

Helping learners to develop information skills

All pupils engaged in supported self-study need information skills – the skills required to make effective use of all the sources of information at their disposal. IT-based information sources such as databases and videotex, and software which allows learners to create their own databases, pages of information, graphics, pictures, etc all offer particularly potent ways of helping learners to acquire the skills and underlying concepts associated with handling information.

Easing the administrative burden on teachers

In common with all programmes of 'individualized' learning, supported self-study brings with it the need to keep track of the progress of each individual. Given appropriate software (and there is quite a lot around), a microcomputer can be used to save time and take the tedium out of maintaining pupil records. Time is a precious commodity – not least in supported self-study – and time saved can be used by teachers to do what they have been trained to do – help learners to learn.

School Library/Resource Centres and Supported Self/Study

The role of library/resource centres, and their professional staff (referred to below as 'library/resource managers'), is extremely important, if not crucial, to the success of supported self-study. Library/resource managers not only have a part to play in implementing all the IT-related activities already outlined, but they also have other skills and knowledge which complement those of teachers, and which are needed in supported self-study schemes. Outlined below are just a few examples of how these facilities and this type of expertise are contributing at present.

The library/resource centre as a place to learn

During periods of private study, learners need suitable accommodation and access to a wide range of information, learning materials and associated equipment. Specially designated areas in, or adjacent to, the school library/resource centre are being provided in some schools for this purpose. They are equipped not only with microcomputers to give learners access to educational software, databases and other electronic information sources, but also with equipment for using learning materials in other media, such as video, slides, and audio tapes.

School databases of information about teaching/learning material

In collaboration with teachers, library/resource managers are beginning to develop computerized databases of information about teaching/learning material suitable for use in supported self-study. As pupils are amongst the intended users of these databases, they too are being involved in such developments, from helping to decide the database structure to inputting the necessary information, and thus also developing skills in using IT as an information handling tool.

Library/resource managers and information skills

Many library/resource managers are information experts by training and in such cases can make a particularly valuable contribution to information skills initiatives (see also above). They probably understand better than anyone else the skills that teachers, as well as learners, need to acquire to make the most effective use of information, in all its various shapes, forms and means of transmission. This puts them in a unique position not only to advise on ways and means of helping teachers and learners to acquire or extend their repertoire of information skills, but also to play an important, if not leading, role in implementing activities appropriate to the needs of the teachers and learners in their particular school.

A partnership between teachers and library/resource managers

If library/resource managers are to be expected and able to satisfy the needs of teachers and learners engaged in supported self-study, it is important for them to understand fully what the actual and potential implications of supported self-study are for their work.

This implies a closer involvement than at present in such matters as planning, curriculum development and the selection of appropriate teaching/learning materials. It demands a recognition by teachers of the potential contribution that the school library/resource centre and its staff can make to teaching and learning in general and to supported self-study in particular. It requires library/resource managers to make their expertise and its relevance to supported self-study well known to teachers, to be ready to make a good case for being involved, and to take initiatives, as well as be responsive to needs.

In short, supported self-study calls for a partnership in which the professional skills, knowledge and experience of both groups can be harnessed to benefit the learners concerned.

Part 3: Flexibility in the School Organization and Curriculum (R Rainbow)

Background

In most schools, the day is regulated by the period bell, signifying a change from one activity to another. The system offers the students little opportunity to make decisions for themselves about their use of time, patterns of work and rates of work, and yet it is expected that they will be able (and willing) to organize themselves and manage their own time as soon as they leave school.

In the traditional education system, the education process tends to be norm- rather than criterion-referenced. It is a system which is geared to what the average child can be expected to achieve within a given period, rather than a system which enables the individual to achieve given criteria in his/her own time. School should be defined in terms of what is learned rather than how much time is spent. A flexible timetable and supported self-study (SSS) may go some way towards achieving an educational environment in which students have some say in their own education and acquire the study and learning skills all schools claim to want for their pupils.

It should be stated at the outset, however, that I am neither advocating a completely flexible school timetable nor the adoption of supported self-study as the sole teaching method in schools.

The former would be impracticable and probably unworkable, while the latter should be seen as one of a whole range of teaching/learning strategies employed by teachers.

The School

Holyrood School, Chard, Somerset is a mixed, 11-18 comprehensive school with a population of 1,200 pupils and 70 staff. Holyrood is one of the two schools in the Somerset TVEI scheme and has undertaken some interesting experiments in: a flexible school day; a modular curriculm (14-18); supported self-study; and co-ordinated community use of the school. All four initiatives are part of an overall strategy to give greater support for the learners in the school while making more effective use of time, teaching staff and premises. The modular curriculum is simply a mechanism which offers students shorter, more easily obtainable learning goals and greater choice and flexibility of subject matter. Most modules are 40 hours in length and are assessed using grade-related criteria.

SSS is seen as both a means of bringing about changes in classroom management/teaching methods and as the most effective way of improving study and information skills for students. While it is recognized that SSS can and should be encouraged in secondary schools, the management of the school and the structure of the curriculum can facilitate its wider use.

Holyrood School Organization: Flexi-time

In the summer term of 1982 the school undertook an experiment in a flexible school day. The 'conventional' school day ended at lunchtime (after six 35-minute periods). The afternoon was given over to a wealth of optional activities, both recreational and academic. Since then, a more conservative arrangement has existed whereby flexi-time activities take place from 3.00-4.10 pm.

All members of staff are expected to run a flexi activity of their own choosing one afternoon each week. Courses can be short (1 term) or all year. Students are expected to take *one* course, but can take more. A free choice is given to all students when 'flexi' options are made in September, and a computer is used to allocate students to courses. Supported self-study is offered as an option within the flexi scheme and students are free to nominate any subject at all for study.

Use of Supported Self-Study

SSS is seen as a means of providing remedial help (in the widest sense of the term); enrichment for classroom activities; and extension work. While the majority of students electing to do SSS in flexi-time ask for help with their school work, a sizeable minority ask to work in subjects such as geology, Latin and sociology, which are not available on the school timetable. Flexi-time also gives staff a valuable opportunity to experiment with SSS with small, well-motivated groups of students without the pressures of exams, tight teaching schedules or the preparation of materials. In the process teachers have become more familiar with IT equipment and the resources available in the Resource Centre.

Flexi-time is a useful device for introducing support for learners without threatening 'normal' classes or teacher time. Moreover, the atmosphere is relaxed and purposeful and students have responded well. However, if SSS is to succeed, it must be incorporated in the mainstream of the school day. To do this teachers need to overcome their natural anxiety to govern children's behaviour and the belief that the 'teacher always knows best'. Experience at Holyrood school would suggest that this is a slow process despite an extraordinary willingness on the part of many teachers to incorporate some SSS into their teaching.

SSS is now firmly established as a means of handling small groups of students as well as whole classes. Conventional classes of 25-30 students are divided into smaller 'study groups' and their teacher acts as tutor. They work either in their normal classrooms or in the central school Resource Centre which is equipped with video recorders and televisions, cassette recorders, BBC computers, slides and filmstrips, as well as books and magazines. Whole classes use the Centre for assignment work, projects, workshop activities and 'clinics'.

Staff, in general, find the Centre provides a wider range of resources and support materials than are available in their departments. In addition, they have commented that the different environment helps to motivate the students.

Central to the SSS scheme in Chard has been the production of Study Packs. Each pack (over 1,300 have been produced) consists of a structured study guide, as well as a variety of other materials. The latter usually includes commercially produced texts as well as audio cassettes, video recordings, microsoftware etc. Our aim has been to suggest routes for students to follow and structures for programmes of work, not to write detailed texts or work books. The study packs, requested by and normally designed by the teaching staff, have proved useful as a starting point for courses of study as well as support for the learner and tutor.

As well as being used in class, SSS is used by students who are released from some timetabled lessons in small groups to carry out research unaided for two or three weeks. Their brief is to prepare a lesson which they will give when they return to class. Both dance and PE staff have used this approach.

Where subjects have not been available on the school timetable, where students have dropped out of courses, or where students have had 'clashes' in fourth/fifth form option boxes, SSS has been available to fill the gap. GCSE to 'O' level has been taken by students in geography, geology, sociology, English literature and human biology. Results are encouraging.

The Modular Curriculum

As part of the Somerset TVEI scheme, Holyrood school's curriculum (14-16) has been modularized in most subjects. A module is normally 40 hours in length and, wherever possible, 'freestanding'. Four modules can be aggregated to form one GCSE subject. While most students will choose to aggregate four modules in the same subject (eg four physics for a GCSE in physics), it is also possible to hybridize (eg physics with chemistry) as well.

The shorter learning goals provided by the modular curriculum offer us an opportunity to incorporate modules using SSS methods. Indeed, it may not be possible to timetable a modular scheme if a SSS scheme is not available. The modules and the introduction of GCSE grade-related criteria, have led to a dramatic change in the content and approach to most subjects in the fourth and fifth years. Many modules include assignment work, projects, field work, continuous assessment (including self-assessment) and research – the very stuff of supported self-study.

Conclusions

These developments, resulting from a more flexible school organization and curriculum, place new demands on both the student and the teacher. A well resourced, co-ordinated, supported self-study scheme, central to the school philosophy can offer support not only for the learner, but for the hard-pressed teacher as well.

3.5 Some Problems of Computers and the Individualization of Learning in Bulgarian Schools

A Pisarev and R Pavlova
Higher Institute of Mechanical and Electrical Engineering, Sofia, Bulgaria

Abstract: The Bulgarian national programme for introducing computers in education has provided so many microcomputers for schools that in primary and secondary education there is now about 1 micro for every 70 children. The microcomputers are concentrated in experimental schools, mainly in the larger towns and particularly in the capital, Sofia, where there are computer classrooms. There are also some experimental kindergartens with micros.

However, it is not sufficient just to introduce microcomputers into the schools. It is also necessary to introduce microcomputers to the teachers, and this is a rather larger problem. Bulgarian teachers are provided with in-service courses on computer literacy and, when they are familiar with the micro, some of them are invited to work with groups developing educational software. The teachers choose and structure the materials, which are then coded by programmers. This has resulted in courseware for subjects including mathematics, physics, chemistry and foreign languages. The next step is to use computers and to prepare educational software to support individualized and flexible learning, to improve the Bulgarian educational system. This is a major and important problem because the new strategy in Bulgarian secondary education requires new approaches.

Changes in Secondary Education

The main objectives of secondary education in Bulgaria are to provide:

- knowledge adequate for the modern achievements of science, technology and culture; and
- up-to-date vocational training based on a wide polytechnical background knowledge.

Secondary education is organized so as to achieve these objectives most effectively. In the eighth, ninth and tenth grades students acquire a core of general and vocational knowledge as compulsory basic training.

In the 11th and 12th grades there is a compulsory course in some general education subject and some vocational training, which is a requirement for the award of a certificate of secondary education. The new educational strategy which is currently being tried in Bulgaria allows the students in the 11th and 12th grades to have a choice of subjects, both in educational and vocational training. The subjects from which the students can choose fall into two groups.

The first group of subjects (optional/compulsory) are those in the compulsory basic training. Although the student can choose the subjects, there is a set curriculum for each. For students who do not intend to continue their education, the subjects can be chosen in such a way as to raise their educational qualifications. Alternatively, they can help the student to prepare for the entrance examinations for higher educational establishments.

The second group of subjects are non-compulsory, and the students can choose subjects to suit their personal interests and capabilities, either to improve their vocational training or to prepare for entrance examinations. Some subjects, such as music, drawing, aesthetics, etc, contribute to their development as a versatile personality.

Out of the 34 curriculum hours each week in the 11th and 12th grades, 28 are assigned to the common core, 4 to the optional/compulsory subjects in the first group, and 2 to the optional subjects in the second group.

This organization requires the extensive use of individualized learning in the compulsory classes, and especially in the optional subjects and extra-curricular work.

The new educational strategy in Bulgarian secondary schools has given rise to a number of problems of organization and finance, including

- the formation of classes of students with differing interests;
- the writing of suitable textbooks;
- the provision of adequate facilities, especially for subjects like physics and chemistry where laboratories are needed; and
- the selection of teachers with adequate training and qualifications.

All these requirements involve the schools. However, they are not always able to provide the funds themselves, particularly for the individualization of learning.

One possible solution to these problems is to make use of the existing information technology. The microcomputer, with its vast possibilities for storing, processing and transmitting data, for interactive dialogues and for presenting information in text and images, is a powerful aid for individualized education. In a computer classroom, students of various capabilities and differing interests can work simultaneously, so that they can master the compulsory subjects at their own pace and work with a mix of compulsory and optional subjects.

Computer Classrooms

A number of experimental schools have now been furnished with computer classrooms, using a Bulgarian-made computer called the PRAVETS, which is compatible with the Apple II micro.

A computer classroom consists of up to 18 student work stations and a lecturer's work station. Each student work station has a terminal desk (90 × 60cms), with a PRAVETS-8M personal computer, a monitor and up to two floppy disk drives, and a chair. There is also space left on the desk for writing. The teacher's work station has a larger desk (130 × 60cms) with the same PRAVETS-8M and monitor, but with between two and six disk drives. Two further colour monitors are connected to the computer and suspended from the ceiling so that the students can see them. The teacher may also have an easel and a video recorder.

This organization poses obvious difficulties for the teacher in following the progress of individual students and these are overcome by using local computer networks, such as the Bulgarian-made MICRONET.

The MICRONET local area network makes it possible for students to work individually with adaptive teaching programs developed for different levels, and with individual problems created for each student. MICRONET provides:

- centralized loading of identical or different teaching packages;
- feedback from the students to the teacher;
- control of the teaching process and online intervention;
- testing and control of students' knowledge;
- collection and processing of statistical information; and
- the sharing of peripherals.

The teacher's work station becomes the central microcomputer which handles requests for information and controls the shared resources. Every learner's personal microcomputer has its own computational capabilities that can be extended by using external storage devices and memory from other computers (including that of the teacher).

Problem Areas

There are three problem areas in individualizing learning;

- ☐ the development and selection of appropriate curriculum materials: that is, educational software development for both the compulsory and optional subjects;
- ☐ the efficiency of the computer-based lessons;
- ☐ the training of teachers to work in computer classrooms.

With the present rapid advances in information technology, when there is no problem of having computers in schools, the paramount and most difficult problem is that of developing educational courseware to cover the wide gamut of levels and subjects, to meet the requirements of the compulsory education at the same time as the students' individual interests. While taking into account the general and well-known criteria for developing good educational software, we must not forget the specific characteristics of secondary education in Bulgaria, so that:

- ☐ the computer-based learning material is structured in such a way as to avoid repeating the minimum compulsory basic knowledge; and that
- ☐ the new information is supplied at the rate best suited to the individual student.

This last requirement presupposes that data about each student is kept in the local network. Experience of this has already been amassed in the development of a series of computer packages in physics and mathematics.

Individualized computer-based learning needs a new type of teacher with a broad, almost encyclopaedic training in related subjects. This problem is being tackled through a programme of in-service courses at the higher teacher training institutes. In essence, the teacher takes on a managerial and pedagogical role, rather than that of an instructor. Specialized consultations can be provided by teachers who are experts in the various subjects. They will be on duty in the staff room and can talk to the students both during and after the computerized lesson, change the mode of instruction, and provide additional work.

Meanwhile for children in the primary school, the afternoon classes are devoted to self-education and are being stimulated and enriched by using the independence and increased flexibility of computer assisted learning materials.

This approach ensures that each child works individually at his or her own speed, in his or her own place in the course. Life is also made easier for the teacher who now maintains order and discipline, and directs the students' self-education in accordance with their abilities and capabilities.

3.6 How to Promote Student-Centred Learning with Simple Video Technology (Workshop Report)

D Eastcott and R Farmer
City of Birmingham Polytechnic

Abstract: The purpose of the session was to provide a packaged workshop for teachers and trainers who are interested in running workshops for their colleagues on the varied applications of cost-effective television in teaching and training, across a range of subject areas.

Participants not only experienced the workshop themselves, but were also given materials as a basis for running similar workshops in their own institutions.

The materials used were intended to encourage teachers to make flexible use of simple video technology to meet the needs of a variety of learners.

The emphasis was on low-cost techniques to promote student-centred learning, not on traditional studio-based television programmes and professional production techniques.

The workshop began by identifying a theoretical framework for considering the effective use of a television in educational practice.

This was followed by sharing a variety of practical examples and support materials on the use of video techniques.

Background to the Workshop

Recent developments in video technology, particularly the ownership of portable equipment for home use, are an incentive for trainers to employ low-cost video techniques in their own teaching. As tutors in the educational development unit at Birmingham Polytechnic, we are keen to promote such developments. However, we are also concerned with encouraging colleagues to adopt methods which are flexible, effective and technically simple. Video self-confrontation methods can help to provide such alternatives (Zuber-Skerritt, 1984) but in our experience some teachers simply use these techniques as a novelty, without considering the behavioural changes they hope to bring about or the stress and pain that such methods can sometimes inflict on individuals.

The purpose of the workshop was to provide a summary of these alternatives, to identify a theoretical framework for them and to describe an experiential model of learning through television which has been developed by the authors.

Workshop Organizer's Account

Workshop Materials

Workshop participants were each given a set of papers at the beginning of the workshop, which would provide a 'working tool' for those who wished to run the workshop in their own institutions. They included copies of the exercises and activities, and masters for producing overhead projector transparencies.

Theoretical Framework

Workshop participants were introduced to a spectrum of learning experiences and activities which involved the use of simple video techniques. The list of training styles was based on a continuum (after Boydell, 1976) ranging from learning activities which are carefully prepared in advance and designed by the tutor, to learning activities where participants are helped to identify their own learning needs.

The spectrum incorporated six learning activities, none of which are mutually exclusive.

(a) *Behaviour modelling.* In this activity the trainer organizes the showing of video models of the required skills (behaviours). The learner practises the skills and is recorded. Playback of the video is followed by feedback from the trainer and further practice. The method relies upon the interactive effects of feedback and modelling (Cooper and Alderfer, 1978).

(b) *Self-confrontation.* This is a widely employed technique which does not involve the use of video models. The learner's performance is recorded. During the playback the supervisor and peer group assist with the analysis of the learner's performance. This analysis is usually made on the basis of agreed and assumed models of 'good' performance.

(c) *Trigger films (cognitive).* A typical cognitive trigger film portrays a situation which focuses on an intellectual problem, perhaps raising a general issue. The film is very short and is directed at the viewer, who is involved as an active participant and problem-solver. The method is often used to initiate a brainstorming approach.

(d) *Trigger films (affective).* Here short portrayals of a situation are intended to elicit emotional as well as cognitive responses. Viewers are encouraged to think about how they would handle the situation. The method is then used as a stimulus for role play.

(e) *Stimulated recall.* In this activity the learner's performance is recorded. Playback is confined to the learner and a facilitator, and is used to stimulate recall of thoughts and feelings. The facilitator's purpose is to encourage self-discovery of feelings and motives; not to analyse behaviour or offer advice.

(f) *Experiential learning.* This method has been developed by the authors in training sessions which are concerned with both professional development and personal growth (Walter and Marks, 1981, Boot and Reynolds, 1983). In situations such as lecturing, being interviewed etc, the learner's performance is recorded. Playback is regarded as a 'learning experience', followed by reflection, which is facilitated by a variety of techniques including the use of stimulated recall. The learner identifies individual needs and goals and these form the basis of carefully planned experimentation and action learning which may include further video recordings.

Workshop Activities

The workshop contained three major sections which demonstrated a particular video technique and its place on the spectrum of learning experiences. For each of these sections the workshop activity and the focus of the discussion will now be described.

1. *The Use of Video 'Triggers'*

   At the beginning of the workshop each participant was asked to imagine him or herself as the head of media services at 'Plumstead Polytechnic'. The setting was that 'Dr Pain', a newly appointed head of department, had made an appointment to see the head of media services, bringing with her a long-established member of her department, 'Mr Smith'.

   A short video trigger was shown to the workshop participants. Dr Pain, in an

A SPECTRUM OF LEARNING EXPERIENCES AND ACTIVITIES

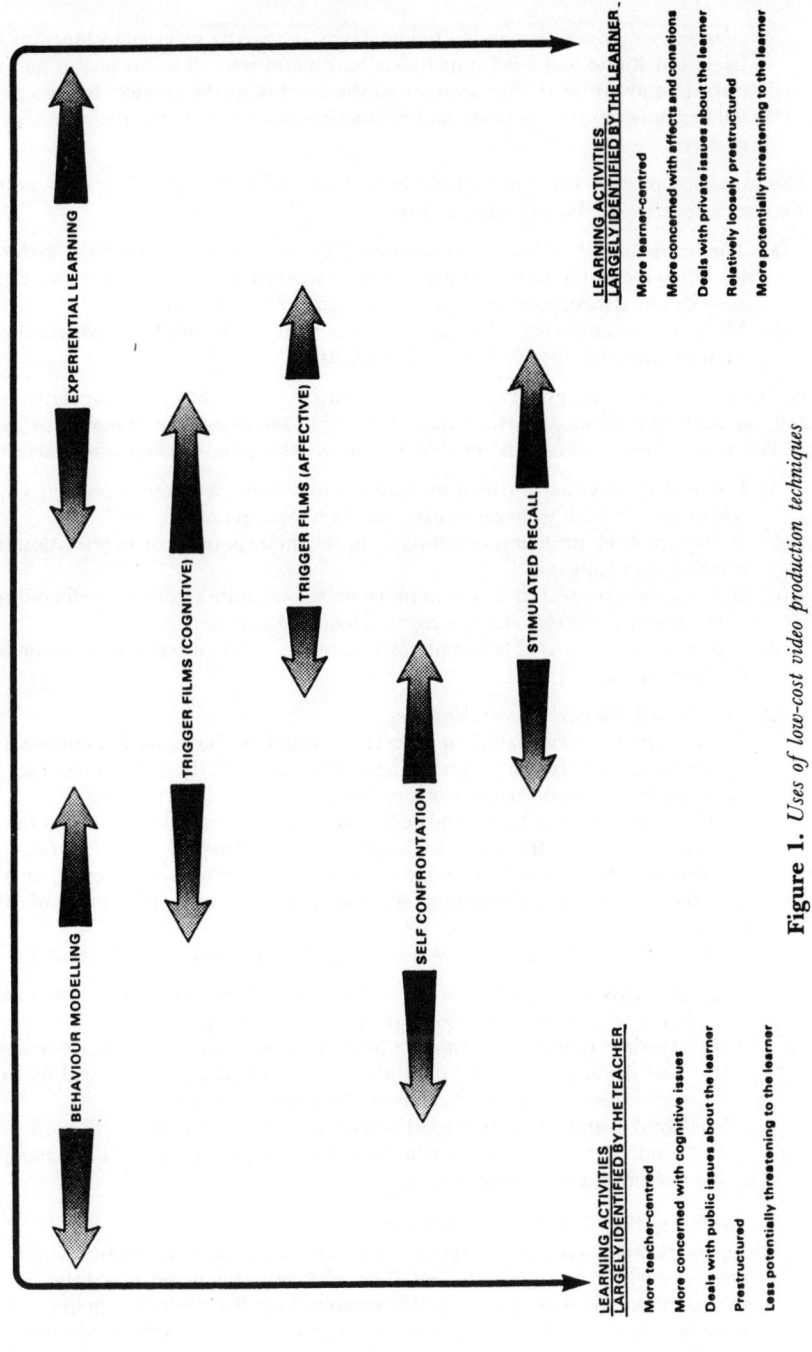

EXPERIENTIAL LEARNING

TRIGGER FILMS (COGNITIVE)

TRIGGER FILMS (AFFECTIVE)

BEHAVIOUR MODELLING

SELF CONFRONTATION

STIMULATED RECALL

**LEARNING ACTIVITIES
LARGELY IDENTIFIED BY THE TEACHER**

More teacher-centred

More concerned with cognitive issues

Deals with public issues about the learner

Prestructured

Less potentially threatening to the learner

**LEARNING ACTIVITIES
LARGELY IDENTIFIED BY THE LEARNER**

More learner-centred

More concerned with affects and conations

Deals with private issues about the learner

Relatively loosely prestructured

More potentially threatening to the learner

Figure 1. *Uses of low-cost video production techniques*

aggressive manner, demanded to know why the media services technicians in the television studio had been rude to Mr Smith and refused to work with him in recording group work. She stated that the head of media services had no right to tell her how to use television, and demanded to know how the problem could be resolved.

The workshop participants were asked how they would handle this situation and the discussion centred on the following points:

(a) The technicians had been rude because they were not clear about the purpose of the video recording and felt they had been wasting their time. They saw the exercises as a misuse of high-quality equipment in the studio.
(b) Mr Smith was not clear of his objectives in using video, and had not clarified what he intended the students to learn from it.

Workshop participants agreed that this is a situation which they have encountered, and, as workshop organizers, we called this use of television the 'amorphous model'.

We used a trigger film as an opening for the workshop for the following purposes:

(a) It initiated activities in which the participants were given the opportunity to reflect upon a highly charged situation (Weil and Schofield, 1984).
(b) It presented the problems resulting from the 'amorphous' use of television in teaching and learning.
(c) It provided a context in which to move on to our more rigorous model of the use of video which fits into the spectrum of learning experiences.
(d) It proved to be a useful 'icebreaking' activity as it generated discussion among the participants.

2. *The Use of Video in Behaviour Modelling*

The activity here was based on an exercise which we have used in our workshops on lecturing for polytechnic staff. These lecturing workshops often include microteaching based on the work of Borg (1970) and Perrott (1975).

The workshop organizers showed a short extract from the section on the 'exemplary lecturer' from the videotape *Styles of Lecturing: Research and Faculty Perspectives* (Brown, 1983). The participants were then asked to identify what they thought were good teaching techniques or behaviours on the part of the lecturer.

The following main points were made in the discussion which resulted:

(a) It is easy to criticize 'models' of behaviour for many reasons which can be quite trivial, and the models then lack credibility.
(b) 'Models' of poor performance (non-examples) are often easier to come by.
(c) Live demonstrations by the tutor of, for example, good and bad teaching techniques can be as effective as using video 'models'.
(d) Many people who have used video for skills training have not used 'models', but in doing so run the risk of not providing goals for change and perceived ways to change.

3. *The Use of Video in Experiential Learning*

The workshop participants were shown a video recording illustrating a job interview with a final year student. The workshop organizers asked the participants how they might use this video to help the student with her interviewing skills. The options already covered in the workshop, namely modelling or self-confrontation, were discussed briefly. As workshop organizers, we then described how we have used video in an experiential learning model based on the work of Kolb (Kolb and McIntyre, 1971) in workshops with final year students on interviewing skills.

The main features of the work are described in the diagram below; and are based on the features of the cycle identified by Boud (Boud, Keogh and Walker, 1985).

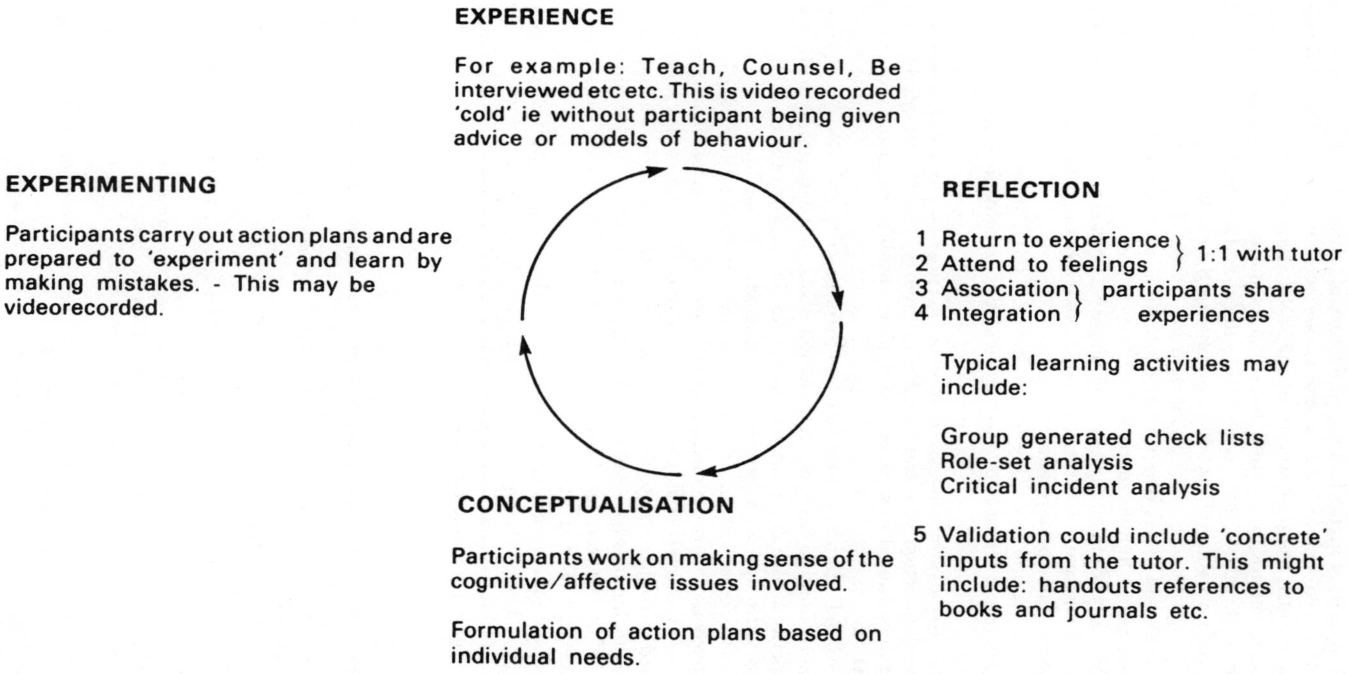

EXPERIENCE

For example: Teach, Counsel, Be interviewed etc. This is video recorded 'cold' ie without participant being given advice or models of behaviour.

REFLECTION

1 Return to experience ⎫ 1:1 with tutor
2 Attend to feelings   ⎭
3 Association ⎫ participants share
4 Integration ⎭ experiences

Typical learning activities may include:

Group generated check lists
Role-set analysis
Critical incident analysis

5 Validation could include 'concrete' inputs from the tutor. This might include: handouts references to books and journals etc.

CONCEPTUALISATION

Participants work on making sense of the cognitive/affective issues involved.

Formulation of action plans based on individual needs.

EXPERIMENTING

Participants carry out action plans and are prepared to 'experiment' and learn by making mistakes. - This may be videorecorded.

Figure 2. *Experiential learning*

Details of this work are as follows:

Firstly, the students had the experience of a role-played interview which was recorded 'cold' on video. On a 'one-to-one' basis with a facilitator, the students are then given the opportunity to reflect on the experience.

The facilitator used stimulated recall techniques to enable the student to return to the experience, attend to feelings, and evaluate the experience.

In the next stage of the reflection process the students met in a group to share their thoughts and feelings about their interviews. They generated checklists based on 'good things about today's interview' and 'things I would like to improve about today's interview'.

This association and integration phase was based on the student's own perceived needs and ways which were personally important to them about improving their performance.

The validation stage of reflection includes the first 'model' or factual input from the tutor. The students were provided with some fact sheets on interviewing skills.

The students then moved on to the conceptualization stage, when they prepared an action plan concerned with aspects of their own interviewing skills which they wanted to work on: being more enthusiastic, using more eye contact, and so on.

A second individual interview was then recorded on video giving the students the opportunity to carry out their action plans, and experiment with aspects of their performance in a relatively safe atmosphere. They then work through the second videotape on a 'one-to-one' basis with the facilitator.

The workshop organizers stated that they had found that the use of video in an experiential learning model was an extremely powerful technique, and had been very positively evaluated by the students. The individual student tapes are retained in confidence, so that students may return to them when they wish. Similar techniques have been used in the training of medical students (Robbins et al, 1978), the training of counsellors (Elliott, 1982) and in classroom management (Dowd, 1977).

Although this technique uses low-cost video equipment, it is very expensive in staff time. The workshop organizers felt that the way forward was to train students to work as facilitators and help each other (Kagan, 1975). Some workshop participants had tried this with success.

References

Boot, R and Reynolds, M (1983) *Learning and Experience in Formal Education*. Department of Adult and Higher Education, University of Manchester.

Borg, W A et al (1970) *The Mini Course: A Microteaching Approach to Teacher Education*. Collier-Macmillan, London.

Boud, D, Keogh, R and Walker, D (Eds) (1985) *Reflection: Turning Experience into Learning*. Kogan Page, London.

Boydell, T (1976) *Experiential Learning*. (Manchester Monographs 5) Department of Adult and Higher Education, University of Manchester.

Brown, G and Bakhtar, M (Eds) (1983) *Styles of Lecturing: Research and Faculty Perspectives*. ASTD Publication, Loughborough University of Technology.

Cooper, C L and Alderfer, C P (Eds) (1978) *Advances in Experiential Social Processes (Volume 1)*. Wiley, New York.

Dowd, E T (1977) Interpersonal process recall as a classroom management technique. *Elementary School Guidance and Counselling*, **11**, 4, pp 296-299.

Elliott, R et al (1982) Differential helpfulness of counselor verbal response modes. *Journal of Counselling Psychology*, **29**, 4, pp 354-61.

Kagan, N (1975) *Interpersonal Process Recall: A Method of Influencing Human Interaction*. Distributed by Mason Media Inc, Box C, Mason, Michigan 48854.

Kolb, D A, Rubin, I M and McIntyre, J M (1971). *Organizational Psychology: An Experiential Approach*. Prentice-Hall, Englewood Cliffs, New Jersey.

Perrott, E (1975) *Teacher's Handbook For Self-Instructional Microteaching Research Unit: University of Lancaster*.

Robbins, A S et al (1978) Teaching interpersonal skills in a medical residency training programme. *Journal of Medical Education*, **53**, 10, pp 988-90.

Walter, G A and Marks, S E (1981) *Experiential Learning and Change Theory, Design and Practice*. Wiley, New York.

Weil, and Schofield, A (1984) *Integrating Theory and Practice: The Use of 'Triggers' in Professional Education and Training*. Centre for Staff Development in Higher Education, University of London, Institute of Education.

Zuber-Skerritt, Ortrun (Editor) (1984) *Video in Higher Education*, Kogan Page, London.

3.7 Flexible Learning Systems: Another Gimmick or What? Implications for Nigerian Education

A Akinyemi
University of Ilorin, Nigeria

Abstract: Flexible learning systems (FLS) may be viewed as another gimmick by the sceptics. However, as a concept in education, it is not new in the developed world, including Nigeria. Its emphasis is on developing and encouraging learner autonomy and lifelong learning. This paper traces the history of flexible education, citing different forms in which it had been used in the pedagogical and andragogical domains since 1920. Its history in Nigeria dates back to the 1930s and it continues to be used in many ways in human resources development by many Nigerian universities. Nigeria's heavy reliance on educational technology makes it expedient for agencies to prepare the educational scene for future resumption of the suspended Open University of Nigeria. Some infrastructural problems may threaten the successful practice of FLS in Nigeria. However, it is certain that these problems are surmountable. Demand for higher education in Nigeria is great, and the existing 27 universities are unable to cope. Flexible education may be one answer.

Introduction

The title of this paper is not a reflection of the author's scepticism about flexible learning systems (FLS). Rather, it represents the probable reaction of some policy makers in developing countries who are often sceptical about educational innovations. Perhaps a recent example of these sceptics were those who 'contributed' to the demise of the Open University of Nigeria by going beyond the rational and economic considerations.

The traditional educational system of providing formal schooling from childhood (6 years +) to adulthood (18 years +) has been in existence for a long time and will continue to exist. It is evident, however, that it is not meeting the educational needs of nations, whether industrialized or developing. The problem of 'drop-ins' and 'drop-outs' in educational systems (Fafunwa, 1983) provide evidence of imperfection in a general sense. Even where people are deemed to have reached the apex of their career, the need to update knowledge in view of ever-changing technologies and acquire matching experiences or learn entirely new skills makes further education desirable. Cooper (1985) has stated that frequently key people in organizations cannot be spared to attend long courses which are sometimes rigid, inflexible for particular needs and not available at convenient locations or times. A solution to these educational problems lies in the design of a special education system that is relevant, flexible and accessible to different categories of people and needs.

What are Flexible Learning Systems?

'Flexible learning system' is a term sometimes used to describe a 'learner-do-as-you-can' or 'go-as-you-please' approach to education offering minimal constraints while enabling and encouraging learners to take responsibility for learning (Boud, 1981). It permits learners to pursue educational plans suitable for their development and capable of being achieved through an arrangement which suits peculiar circumstances.

FLS is not an entirely new concept or terminology. It belongs to the family of terminologies which includes distance education, open education, flexistudy, correspondence education, learning by tuition, external degree programmes, sandwich educational programmes, university of life, university of the air, continuing education, open university and university without walls (Ologunde, 1970; MacKenzie et al, 1975; Afigbo, 1983; Ojo, 1983). When all of these names are critically considered, it seems that flexible learning system is the most all-embracing and the one which offers its meaning readily even to the layman. It is a dynamic educational approach which re-opens the gateway to formal education otherwise considered closed. Birch and Latcham (1984) defined FLS as flexible learning opportunities which translate as the degrees of freedom allowed to the student to decide the what, when, how, and where of an educational pursuit. Flexibility mainly relates to the range of possibilities offered to the students and the degree of student autonomy in learning (Boud, 1981). Further, flexible learning is the adaptation of available learning opportunities to meet the needs of the learner in a way that optimizes the autonomy of the learner as well as the effectiveness of the process of learning.

Flexible Learning in Historical Perspective

The origin of flexible learning can be traced to the early activities of people like Dalton, Morrison and Washburn in the 1920s. The Dalton Laboratory Plan in the United Kingdom was designed as a way of educational reorganization which reconciles the twin activities of teaching and learning (Parkhurst, 1922). Two basic principles of the Dalton Plan were freedom to learn and co-operation in learning. The plan evokes in the child a spirit of self-reliance and initiative. It also avoids subjecting the child to constant direction and restraints. The flexible learning system which we now embrace is, in other words, just an adapted version of the Dalton Plan to suit adult learning in the 1980s, 60 odd years after!

The Keller Plan, known as the personalized, proctorial or programmed system of instruction (PSI) was conceptualized by Keller in 1963. In principle and practice, the PSI holds the learner responsible for his own learning, furnishing a full description of the what, how, where, who and when of instruction (Keller and Sherman, 1974). Individualized instruction (II) is an empirically-based system which gained popularity in the mid-1960s. It was designed to produce measurable learning objectives while allowing the learner to go at his own pace (Johnson and Johnson, 1974). The programmed instruction, also called a 'scrambled book', and again in the flexible learning category, became popular in the 1960s (Lysaught and Williams, 1963). Individually guided education (IGE) is a comprehensive alternative to schools organized in either age-graded self-contained classrooms or in subject-centred departments and it represents a change of great magnitude (Klausmeier et al, 1977).

The supported self-study (SSS) is a United Kingdom model of providing the supportive learning environment for young learners and allowing them to take control over their own learning (Lewis, 1981). The SSS is in effect a semi-flexible approach with definite boundaries on learner autonomy. Resource-based learning (RBL), yet another in the category of flexible approaches, is a situation in which learning is generated at least partly by the learner and in which he has his own individual work schedule (Davies, 1975) of flexible learning.

Trends in these cited approaches have shown two different modes of the flexible education systems as pedagogical and andragogical (Knowles, 1980). In the mainstream of all approaches cited as FLS-related, many characteristics and assumptions are common. One that seems most basic is that the learner has the will or can develop favourable attitudes to learning. Quite against the conventional practice of the teacher being the focus in the learning situation, the shift now is towards the learner (Percival and Ellington, 1984). Learning materials are designed to cater for learners' needs with less requirement of teacher support through the face to face contacts.

Trends in Flexible Education in Nigeria

FLS as a learning approach in Nigeria is new only as a terminology. The characteristics and assumptions are not new in the Nigerian educational scene. Traces of individualized instruction can be seen at different levels of education. A few nursery/primary schools in cities, staffed with qualified teachers, apply the II approach in the teaching of English and mathematics. Programmed instruction has been used in the teaching of geography to secondary school pupils in many Nigerian schools (Okunrotifa, 1970). The flexible learning system had been extensively used by many Nigerians in the forms of learning by tuition, external degree programmes and correspondence education plans. The Rapid Results College, Wolsey Hall, Bennet College and the University of London provided FLS opportunities for hard-working, dedicated and disciplined Nigerians. Ojo (1984) reported that by 1933 a handful of Nigerians had obtained bachelors degrees. All the avenues stated above are evidences of individual investments in self development activities (Ologunde, 1970). Many Nigerian adults continue to enrol in universities' extra-mural programmes to obtain professional qualifications in law, accountancy, and so on, or to obtain basic qualifications for university admissions.

Flexible educational programmes are established in almost all Nigerian universities in the form of sandwich education for one or more of the following qualifications: Associate Certificate in Education (ACE), National Certificate of Education (NCE) Bachelor of Arts, BEd (primary education), postgraduate degrees (PGDE, PGCE, MEd, etc). The University of Lagos has been running the Correspondence and Open Studies Unit (COSU) for almost a decade. The University of Ilorin has run graduate programmes in education on the sandwich format for five years and will start the BEd primary education degree programme in the summer of 1986. The Ahmadu Bello University, Zaria and the University of Nigeria, Nsukka specialize in running short programmes as well as other programmes leading to various certificates and degrees. The University of Ibadan initiated and continues to run an extra-mural programme. It also runs many long and short courses for the interested groups and organizations. In all these cases, each university has established strong and functional institutes of education to plan, design and execute the sandwich and other flexible learning systems with the approval of the university's governing authorities.

Trends in educational development in Nigeria have provided evidence of the need for alternative educational systems with flexible characteristics (Ojo, 1984; Afigbo, 1983; National Universities Commission, 1983 and Gana, 1984). For example the Joint Admissions and Matriculation Board (JAMB), which is the agency in charge of university admissions in Nigeria, is usually unable to offer admission to 80 per cent of its applicants. In 1979-80, only 13,675 students were offered admissions out of 114,397 applicants (barely 12 per cent).

Nigerians are adventurous when it comes to further education. Many have travelled abroad or 'stowed away', notably to Britain and America, for further education – 'in search of the golden fleece', so to speak. Several had subscribed to tuition and correspondence education programmes as previously mentioned, financing their programmes from their meagre salaries. The ultimate goals of these efforts were to attain better education as the key to a 'white-collar job', higher salaries and better living.

The development of university education dates back to 1948, when the first university was established at Ibadan. Since independence in 1960 the number of universities has increased at an astronomical rate. Today, there are 20 Federal Universities, and seven State Universities (Joint Admission and Matriculation Board, 1985) spread all over the country. Four federal universities of technology have been merged with some older universities since the military takeover in 1984, but existing private universities were abolished and prohibited through decree number 19 in 1984.

The national Open University, which represented innovation in university education and an alternative to the conventional universities, was suspended in May 1984 before the end of its first year because of the national economic crisis (Gana, 1985). Universities in Nigeria by now might be approaching 40, but for the mergers, prohibitions and suspension. In spite of this large number of universities, admissions are still very competitive among candidates across the university system. Flexible learning programmes such as are presently available in Nigeria will continue to serve at least until the Open University of Nigeria becomes a reality.

Implications of FLS for Nigerian Education

Demands of new technologies around the world dramatize the need for all countries to get educated or get retrained in order to be able to cope. The world of information technology is exploding, and changing the technological profile of manufacturing and the service industries. The effect of 'explosions' on the less developed countries like Nigeria is an increase in the rate of obsolescence of industries, services and development strategies (Rada, 1985). Computers, micros and mainframes are assuming smaller physical dimensions, with wider capacities. Top executives of multinational corporations now have their 'offices' anywhere they possibly can, be it in their bedroom, car or aeroplane, and all these are due to developments in telecommunications. These therefore call for everyone to learn the language and practice of the new technologies.

In order for many professionals to be able to cope with their work in the near future, the need for the flexible learning system cannot be overstated as a world wide approach. The suspension of the Open University is only a temporary measure and as soon as Nigeria's economy improves, its reopening will probably be followed by the inevitable re-orientation and restructuring of its programmes. The university will not only benefit from the emerging technologies but will also offer courses in information technology and the computer related programmes as weekend or holiday courses in Nigeria. Other universities will need to do the same.

The learner autonomy syndrome which is central to the underlying philosophy of the FLS is not a popular culture in learning at the lower levels of education in Nigeria. Students are new at it and teachers are not armed to inculcate it. Teachers have for a long time spoonfed their students. The new trend is 'learning how to learn', and producing a group of autonomous lifelong learners in all societies. What is required in Nigeria to promote learner autonomy is to re-orient the entire educational system and restructure it to promote 'self-learning'. A good starting point is a modification of the teacher education curricula at all levels (primary, secondary, tertiary and higher education). Through inculcating the discipline of autonomy in learning in teachers, they will be able to practise it in developing the attributes of 'self-directed learning' in their students, rather than spoonfeeding them.

Finally, an important implication is in developing and promoting educational technology in Nigeria. Educational technology is *sine qua non* to the success of FLS, since flexibility relies on a variety of resources and learner scheduling. Percival and Ellington (1984), in taking a glimpse into the future, much like Toffler, have predicted the shift towards a more student-centred approach to instruction. With this trend, the traditional teacher-centred approach which still dominates the educational scene at all levels in Nigeria will become obsolete. Recognition of the mythology of the teacher as the fountain of all knowledge then requires systems commitment to the practice of educational technology. The National Educational Technology Centre in Nigeria must play a leading role in promoting educational technology and obtaining the necessary governmental backing to conduct training programmes for teachers while also embarking on instructional resource development schemes. Flexible learning systems will flourish in a solid resource base where hardware, software, and other ancillary materials are available in abundance. The Nigeria Audio Visual Association (NAVA) is a functional professional association actively committed to the promotion of educational technology. It may be worth considering having NAVA conduct short workshops on developing materials which will enrich the pool of available resources to enhance learner autonomy among learners in Nigeria.

Conclusion

In response to the sceptical opening, it is now clear that FLS is neither 'just another gimmick' nor another cosmetic of education. It is a learner autonomy approach to lifelong education. It is a 'self-help technology' of learning, to put it in Schumacher's words. The main task therefore is to prepare learners from the lower levels to learn how to take responsibility for their learning and become self-directed. Some limitations of the flexible learning system in Nigeria have been recognized. However, the prospects are greater in the light of current infrastructural improvements and the favourable disposition of Nigerians to higher education and lifelong learning.

References

Afigbo, A E (1983) *Nigeria and the Open University*. New African Publishing Company, Owerri, Nigeria.
Birch, D W and Latcham, J (1984) *Flexible Learning in Action*. Further Education Unit, London.
Boud, D (1981) *Developing Student Autonomy in Learning*. Kogan Page, London.
Cooper, A (1985) Distance learning and management education. *Media in Education and Development*, **18**, 1, pp 25-28.
Council for Educational Technology (1984) *Supported Self-Study Project*. Council for Educational Technology, London.
Davies, W J K (1975) *Learning Resource? An Argument for Schools*. Council for Educational Technology, London.
Fafunwa, B (1983) drop-ins and drop-outs in the Nigerian educational system. In Adesina, S, Akinyemi, K and Ajayi, K (eds) *Nigerian Education: Trends and Issues*. University of Ife Press Ltd, Nigeria.
Gana, F Z (1985) Distance education: a Nigerian perspective. *Educational Media International*, **1**, 1, pp 12-13.
Johnson, S R and Johnson, R B (1970) *Developing Individualized Instructional Material*. Westinghouse Learning Press, California.
Joint Admission and Matriculation Board (1985) *JAMB Brochure*, Lagos, Nigeria.
Keller, F S and Sherman, J G (1974) *The Keller Plan*, Benjamin, Inc. California.
Klausmeier, H J, Rossmiller, R A and Saily, M (1977) *Individually Guided Elementary Education*. Academic Press, New York.
Knowles, M S (1980) *The Modern Practice of Adult Education*. Follett Publishing Company, Chicago (revised).
Lewis, R (1981) *How to Write Self-Study Materials*. Council for Educational Technology, London.
Lysaught, J P and Williams, C M (1963) *A Guide to Programmed Instruction*. John Wiley and Sons, Inc., New York.
MacKenzie, N, Postgate, R and Scupham, J (1975) *Open Learning, Systems and Problems in Post Secondary Education*. The UNESCO Press, Paris.
National Universities Commission (1983) *20 Years of University Education in Nigeria*. NUC, Lagos, Nigeria.
Ojo, G J A (1983) The Open University: an alternative to higher educational system. In Adesina, S, Akinyemi, K and Ajayi, K (eds) *Nigerian Education: Trends and Issues*. University of Ife Press Ltd., Nigeria.
Ojo, G J A (1984) *Distance Education in Nigeria and the Emergence of the National Open University*. Abuju, Nigeria.
Okunrotifa, P O (1970) Programmed learning and the teaching of geography. *West African Journal of Education*, **14**, 3, pp 203-208.
Ologunde, D A (1970) Correspondence instruction and education in Nigeria. *West African Journal of Education*. **45**, 3, pp 209-215.
Parkhurst, H (1922) *Education on the Dalton Plan*. Bell and Sons Ltd, London.
Percival, F and Ellington, H (1984) *A Handbook of Educational Technology*. Kogan Page, London.
Rada, J (1985) Information technology and the Third World. In Forester, T (ed) *The Information Technology Revolution*. Basil Blackwell Ltd., Oxford.

3.8 *Inside Information* – A Joint BBC and City and Guilds Study Course on Information Technology

C Loveland
BBC Education, Leeds

Abstract: *Inside Information* is the title of a multi-media study package produced by the British Broadcasting Corporation (BBC)'s education department as part of its well-established computer literacy project, which has the overall purpose of raising the general public's awareness and understanding of information technology. The package comprises ten 25-minute radio programmes, a substantial book and a suite of computer programs. *Inside Information* is designed to appeal to mature and young adults and to be used in a variety of formal and informal learning environments. Closely associated with the study materials is the assessment scheme devised by the City and Guilds of London Institute, Certificate 444. The assessment test, consisting of multiple choice questions, is taken on a computer which means that it can be taken, at a registered centre, by appointment.

Introduction

The speed and magnitude of change to so many aspects of daily life brought about by the technology of the microchip and its main instrument, the computer, meant that there was a substantial public education need to be met if people at large were to have any understanding of what was happening. Thus, in 1982, BBC Education launched its computer literacy project, whose aim was to raise the general awareness and understanding of the computer and what it could do. Television was the medium for a series of programmes, beginning with 'The Computer Programme', which looked at the computer and its uses. Closely associated with the programmes themselves were a number of publications, the BBC microcomputer system and a developing range of applications software and a nationwide network involving educational institutions and computer clubs, which offered practical support and tuition to the many thousands of viewers who were stimulated to find out more about information technology.

Inside Information is the title of a new self-learning package from BBC Continuing Education Radio designed to provide a basic introduction to information technology (IT) and to encourage systematic study. The package has been designed with both mature and young adults in mind and aims to allow the listener/student to pursue an interest in information technology to a variety of levels.

There are four parts to the *Inside Information* package:

- ☐ a ten-programme radio course, presented by Paul Heiney
- ☐ an *Inside Information* book from BBC Publications
- ☐ computer software for the BBC micro, also from BBC publications
- ☐ assessment and certification by the City & Guilds of London Institute.

The radio series presented by Paul Heiney offers a lively, general introduction to the whole field of IT while the book and the software pack enable the reader/user to explore this area in greater depth, to get 'hands-on' experience of computers and to gain some insight into their workings. Finally, the City & Guilds assessment provides an opportunity to gain a nationally recognized basic qualification in this field for vocational or other reasons.

It is hoped that the study package will be equally valuable in further education colleges and adult education centres, in ITeCs and in schools and will offer starting points to potential students of all ages.

The Radio Programmes

1. The series begins with a look at what 'information' is, and compares how computers handle and store information.
2. In this programme, Paul Heiney looks at some problems involved in setting up databases, at what computer software is, and at how it is written.
3. How computer networks have developed, and some new services like electronic mail and telesoftware.
4. The electronic office – examining the impact it has had, and will have, on all of us.
5. The many ways in which we can communicate with computers.
6. How computers are used in the world of design.
7. How computers are being used to control machines.
8. How computers are now being used in the classroom.
9. To look at some of the applications of principles discussed earlier in the series, Paul Heiney visits a car manufacturing plant and a car dealer, and discovers how computers are used in the sales, servicing and manufacture of modern vehicles.
10. Looking to the future, what computer developments lie ahead?
(For further details please write to BBC Education, 30 CE, London W1A 1AA.)

The Book

For listeners who want to learn about this rapidly expanding field, an illustrated book *Inside Information: Computers, Communications and People*, by Jacquetta Megarry, provides more detailed explanations of the underlying principles and gives examples of the application of the new information technologies in industry and commerce, in the home and in the high street.

This book covers the converging technologies of video, telecommunications and computing. It does not assume any previous knowledge of how computers work or of information technology. The book is divided into three sections.

Part 1 is mainly concerned with the basic principles underlying modern communications and information handling systems. This section includes several chapters on software. These set computers in the context of other developments in communications technology – the changing telephone and the video revolution. It therefore offers a basis for understanding the developing electronic communication networks, whether at very local level (in the home, factory, or office), or in the major national and international systems.

Part 2 concentrates directly on the commercial, industrial, and domestic applications of the new information technologies. It aims to show how and why the new technologies are being introduced, and to reveal some of their practical advantages and disadvantages. Examples cover the use of IT in the retail trade, in banking and commerce, in design and manufacture, in printing and the mass media as well as in the home.

Part 3 consists of a comprehensive reference section and glossary.

Inside Information: Computers, Communication and People is published by BBC Publications, price £7.95, and is available through bookshops.

The Software

When plans were being made for the *Inside Information* radio study course, it seemed logical for the package of supporting materials to include software; and indeed for the software to be of a kind which enabled the computer to explain itself.

The software is designed to run on a BBC Model B microcomputer system and includes a user guide which is designed to help and encourage the user to experiment and explore a range of typical computer applications. Ideally, the user, having acquired some understanding of how the computer does what it does, should seek the opportunity to experience purpose-designed software and equipment.

The software pack includes programs which explain how the computer works, how it handles text, how it models a spreadsheet, how it controls a lathe and how it stores and retrieves information. It is available from BBC Publications priced £12.95.

The Certificate

The City and Guilds of London Institute, more widely known as 'City and Guilds', is Britain's largest technical testing and qualifying body. An independent organization operating under a royal charter, it enjoys wide support from industry and works closely with the education service, the Manpower Services Commission (MSC) and government departments. Each year there are about half a million candidate entries in a wide range of subjects and the certificates awarded are accepted worldwide as evidence of achievement of recognized standards in technical skills.

The Joint City and Guilds/BBC certificate scheme (subject no 444) is intended to provide an introduction to information technology and the basic skills to cope with it in everyday situations. The scheme will also provide the opportunity for progression to specialist courses of education and training. It has been devised on the assumption that prospective candidates will be able to have access to 'hands-on' experience at their local college, school, training or adult education centre, or at their home or at work.

To enable centres offering this scheme City and Guilds publish a syllabus pamphlet and an assessment package. The assessment consists of a program of multiple choice questions and interactive simulation exercises. The City and Guilds Institute will recognize centres offering both 'hands-on' experience and the assessment under the Institute's Form 2 (Non-Series Tests and Examinations) Regulations. Currently there are 250 centres registered.

3.9 Peer Group and Self-Assessment of Essays: Their Correspondence with Tutor Assessments, and Their Possible Learning Benefits

N Falchikov
Napier College, Edinburgh

Abstract: Questions pertaining to assessment, such as its purposes and modes of execution, are discussed. The prevailing authoritarian model of assessment in higher education is examined, and its disadvantages elaborated. Particular problems associated with the marking of essays are discussed. Previous studies of self-assessment are reviewed.

Any student assessment procedure should meet a number of criteria. It should be 'valid, reliable, practicable, fair, and useful to students' (Percival and Ellington, 1984). The present study into peer group and self-assessment of essays attempts to meet these criteria.

The aim of the initial procedures of this study was to arrive at a clear, unambiguous set of criteria as to what constitutes a 'good essay'. Tutors involved in marking essays for particular groups first of all agreed on their criteria, and the relative importance of these. Next, the students carried out a similar procedure. The two sets of criteria generated in this way were remarkably similar. Finally, tutors and students collaborated and negotiated a common list. A marking schedule was drawn up from this list which was to be used by all assessors.

Students wrote their essays, marked them, and handed their mark to the tutor, together with two further copies of the essay. One of these was retained and marked by the tutor, the other given to a member of the peer group for marking. A procedure for resolving any large discrepancies between marks was agreed at the outset, as was a policy on how to award the final mark.

The results of a preliminary study are presented and discussed. Possible learning benefits and implications for future studies are elaborated.

Introduction

The prevailing model of assessment in higher education has been described as an authoritarian one, involving the unequal possession and exercise of power.

> 'Staff exercise unilateral intellectual authority: they decide what students shall learn, they design the programme of learning, they determine criteria of assessment and make the assessment of the student.' (Heron, 1981)

The student is clearly excluded from every stage of decision-making.

Not only is this authoritarian system of assessment disliked by many students and tutors, it also gives rise to a number of negative effects and generates a number of problems. The system tends to breed conformity in students, and militates against not only personal development, but also against development of interpersonal skills. Traditional authoritarian assessment practices clearly go no way towards developing increased student responsibility and autonomy.

Empirical studies of alternative methods of assessment, usually carried out in the United States, have tended to emphasize self-assessment.

Results of these studies vary widely. The highest rate of agreement between students and tutors, 80 per cent, was obtained in Stanton's study with graduate teachers (1978). This, at first, might be seen to support the superiority of self-grading of older students suggested by Filene (1969) and others. However, results of other studies cause this simple explanation to break down. Mueller's 'adult students', for example, (1970) achieved only a 33 per cent agreement rate with their tutors, while Larson's younger undergraduates (1978) were found to agree with their tutor assessments 70 per cent of the time. At least two factors other than age must be considered. First of all the level of learning and type of assessment must be taken into account, as well as use of and agreement over criteria of excellence.

These studies raise a number of important questions. First of all, what are 'accurate' measurements of student performance or achievement? Some writers argue that failures in agreement between student assessor and tutor may point to 'inaccuracies' in assessment on the part of the tutor rather than on the part of the student. Notorious lack of correspondence between marks awarded to the same piece of work by two different tutors also points to this question. Secondly, the studies also raise the question of criteria of excellence relating to each area of assessment.

The Present Study

The present study aimed to implement and evaluate a method of collaborative self- and peer group assessment. It arose from the premise that 'any student assessment procedure should be valid, reliable, practicable, and fair and useful to students'. (Percival and Ellington, 1984). Previous studies point to a number of important factors, namely explicitness and use of assessment criteria, age and experience of participants, and ability variation within the group.

The study addressed itself to a number of important questions.

1. Is collaborative self- or peer group assessment comparable with traditional methods of assessment?
2. To what extent do our student assessors tend to under- or over-grade?
3. Is there a relationship between accuracy of grading and either age or overall abililty?
4. Does collaborative self- or peer group assessment have any significant impact on learning?

Participants and Area of Assessment

Three psychology tutors and 50 first year students on the BSc Biological Sciences degree at Napier College, Edinburgh participated in this study. The mean age of students was 19 years five months.

The area assessment chosen was a psychology coursework essay on the topic of either perception, selective attention or memory.

Procedure

Tutors agreed on their criteria and made provisional rankings in terms of relative importance. This exercise was repeated by the students, and tutor-student comparisons were made. An essay marking schedule was devised, and tested by tutor 1. Students wrote and marked their own essay, and that of a peer group member on a different topic. Self, peer and tutor marks were compared at a tutorial. Each participant attempted to justify her/his marking, and a final mark was agreed by a method decided by the students. Finally, each student completed a feedback questionnaire.

Results

Product-centred results

- *Student self-marker – tutor comparisons*
  Comparing self-grading with tutor grading, we found that in 73.8 per cent of

cases the variation between these two marks was acceptably low (defined as less than or equal to 9 marks) being unacceptably high (greater than or equal to 10 marks) in the remaining 26.2 per cent of cases. There was no consistent tendency overall for students to either over- or under-mark in comparison with the tutor. Rather more students under-mark than over-mark (57.1 per cent compared with 42.9 per cent overall).

☐ *Peer-tutor comparisons*

In 60.6 per cent of cases there was acceptably low variation. There does, however, appear to be a tendency for peer group markers to over-grade in comparison with tutor markers. In 60.6 per cent of cases peer group over-marking was observed. Not only do peer group markers tend to over-mark in comparison with the tutors, the mean amount of over-marking is higher than the mean amount of under-marking.

☐ *Peer – self-marker comparisons*

In 60 per cent of all cases there was an acceptable degree of variation between peer and self-marker grades. Once again there is a tendency for peer group markers to over-mark in comparison with self-graders. In this case 70 per cent of over-marking was observed. Again it was observed that both the degree and magnitude of over-marking exceeded those of under-marking.

☐ *Age variation in degree of 'accuracy' achieved*

Figure 1 shows the degree of correspondence of self-marker with tutor against the age of the self-marker.

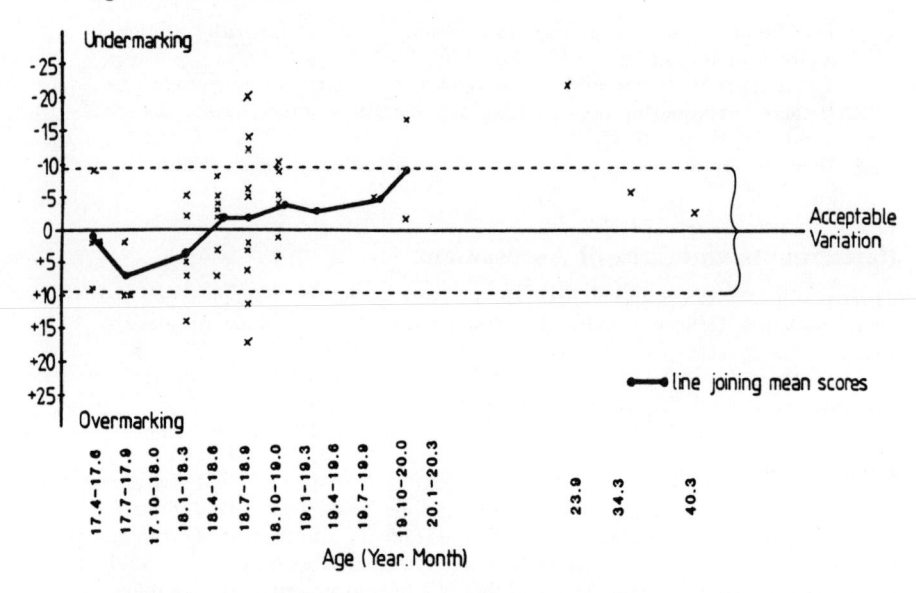

Figure 1. *Correspondence of self – with tutor marks against age of student*

Plots falling on either side of the zero line within the dotted horizontal lines fall within the range of acceptable variation. Note that no significant over-marking occurs after the age of 18 years and 9 months.

Note also the tendency of the line joining mean scores for each age group to rise with increasing age.

☐ *Ability variation in the degree of 'accuracy' achieved*

No clear relationship was found between the ability of the group (as measured by a cumulative entry requirement score) and the 'accuracy' of self-marking.

Process-centred results

☐ *Student ratings of the effects of the scheme*

It appears that students feel that the system of self-assessment makes them critical (94.1 per cent) makes them think more (91.2 per cent), makes them structured (79.4 per cent), and makes them learn more (58.8 per cent). The scheme of self-assessment is, furthermore, rated as challenging (82.4 per cent), helpful (70.6 per cent) and beneficial (64.7 per cent) in spite of being rated as hard (91.2 per cent) and time-consuming (61.8 per cent).

The results for peer group assessment, similarly, suggest that students feel that assessing a peer makes them think more (82.4 per cent), makes them critical (76.5 per cent) makes them learn more (61.8 per cent) and makes them structured (52.9 per cent). The ratings for the scheme of peer group assessment resemble those of the self-assessment scheme in that peer group assessment is also rated as challenging (79.4 per cent), beneficial (64.7 per cent) and helpful (71.8 per cent) as well as being hard (70.6 per cent) and time-consuming (58.8 per cent). Although the patterns of responses for self- and peer assessment are very similar, the experience of self-assessment seems to make students fractionally more independent, confident, critical and structured than the peer marking experience, which, however, enables students to learn even more than the self-assessment scheme. The scheme of self-assessment is found slightly more challenging and helpful than peer assessment and at the same time slightly harder, and more time-consuming to carry out. Both schemes are found equally beneficial.

☐ *Best and least liked features of the system*

36.1 per cent of respondents rated the *provision of an outline as an aid to their writing* as the best liked feature.

> 'It helped me to think more about what I was writing – thinking things through in a chronological order and creating a theme through the paragraphs.'

19.4 per cent found that the *increase in awareness* prompted by the study was the feature of the system they liked best.

> 'It made you realize how complex an essay is.'

The benefit of reading the peer essay was listed by 16.7 per cent of the sample as the best-liked feature. 11.1 per cent liked the *less biased mark* they perceived to result from the system.

> 'It allows you to argue a case if you think you have been marked down.'

Learning about mistakes and the possibilities of subsequent improvement were best liked by 8.3 per cent of students.

Finally, 8.3 per cent found the *guidelines provided for marking* the best-liked feature.

Most frequently listed least-liked feature concerned the difficulty of the task. 22.9 per cent of respondents cited *lack of knowledge about the peer topic* as the least-liked feature and a further 14.3 per cent listed some examples of *general difficulty*.

14.3 per cent felt that some of the *weightings on the marking schedule were wrong*.

The possibility of marking down or failing a peer was the least liked feature of 11.4 per cent of the sample.

> 'Marking someone else's (essay) is hard as the person may be annoyed if their assessment mark is lowered because of you.'

A number of characteristics of the marking schedule were listed as least-liked features of the system. *The system was too rigid/clinical* (8.6 per cent) and *the marking schedule was not comprehensive* (5.7 per cent). Finally, *criteria overlap* was listed by

2.9 per cent, *no ideal model provided for comparison* by a further 2.9 per cent. 14.3 per cent listed 'marking' either their own or peer group essay as the least-liked feature, but did not expand on any aspect of the process that they particularly disliked.

47.1 per cent of the sample agreed that the knowledge that they were to act as marker as well as writer influenced the writing process.

> 'It made you more aware of what you were writing, ie it wasn't just a case of getting the information down – you had to plan it.'

Tutors participating in the scheme were enthusiastic and felt the study to be of value both to themselves and to the students involved. They hope to employ the scheme again.

Discussion

Returning now to the questions addressed by this study, it seems that collaborative self-assessment does appear to be comparable to traditional tutor methods of assessment, while collaborative peer group assessment corresponds less well with either tutor or self-grading. Secondly, the present study found no consistent tendency to overgrade, as might have been predicted from the results of previous studies with students of comparable ages (Stover, 1976; Davis and Rand, 1980). In the present study an agreement rate of 73.8 per cent was found, together with a slightly greater tendency to under- than to over-mark overall. Thirdly, the present study points to an age or experience effect in the correspondence of tutor and student marks/grades (the older the student, the lesser the tendency to overgrade), but to no clear ability effect. While these findings must be regarded as provisional, due to the relatively small size of the sample of participants, both deserve further investigation.

Finally, collaborative self- and peer assessment appear to be beneficial to the student. Students found that the schemes of both self- and peer assessment made them think more, learn more, and be more critical and structured. Furthermore, they found the scheme challenging, helpful and beneficial in spite of being hard and time-consuming. Some modifications to the scheme have been suggested by the responses to the questionnaire. Future marking schemes will aim to be less rigid and allow credit to be given to creativity and originality. Further consultation on the subject of weightings will also take place. Some aspects of peer group assessment require modification. In this study the acknowledged beneficial effects of reading the peer's essay are balanced by negative effects of supplying a grade. In the future, the former could operate without the latter.

There is little doubt that this scheme of collaborative self- and peer group assessment increases student responsibility and autonomy, and allows for the development of both personal and interpersonal skills. It is clearly practicable, at least as a valid alternative, and it is also rated by users as fairer than the traditional method. The scheme appears to be successful in terms of both product and process.

References

Davis, J K and Rand, D C (1980) Self grading versus instructor grading. *Journal of Educational Research*, **73**, 4, pp 207-11.

Filene, P G (1969) Self grading: an experiment in learning. *Journal of Higher Education*, **40**, 6, pp 451-458.

Heron, J (1981) Assessment revisited. In Boud (1981) *Developing Student Autonomy in Learning*. Kogan Page, London.

Larson, M B (1978) Multiple copies of exams encourage self grading. *Engineering Education*, February, pp 435-437.

Mueller, R H (1970) Is self-grading the answer? *Journal of Higher Education*, **41**, 3, pp 221-224.

Percival, F and Ellington, H (1984) *A Handbook of Educational Technology*. Kogan Page, London.

Stanton, H E (1978) Self grading as an assessment method. *Improving College and University Teaching*, **24**, 4, pp 236-238.

Stover, R V (1976) The impact of self-grading on performance and evaluation in a constitutional law course. *Teaching Political Science*, **3**, 3, pp 303-310.

3.10 Directed Self-Learning in Liberal Studies for Science Undergraduates: An Experiment in the Management of Learning

S M Cox
Coventry (Lanchester) Polytechnic

Abstract: This paper describes the evolution and continuing evaluation of a liberal studies course for second-year undergraduates on a modular sciences course. There are now no formal lectures or 'traditional' classes on this course. Students rely for their information on a variety of sources:

- the set course text, which all students are required to buy;
- selected readings from texts located in the short loan collection in the library, available for all but for a matter of a few hours only;
- readings from a growing pile of clippings from newspaper journals and magazines, also on the short loan collection;
- videotape extracts from Open University and other materials, available on open access or request, but also replayed at set times during the year;
- periodic student-led seminars followed by plenary feedback sessions during which each group reports to all the others on their main findings.

In addition, there are unconventional assessment processes which involve four short (500-word) essays during the course, and a final examination for which a paper is predistributed.

Evaluation of the course during its evolutionary stages was by student feedback questionnaire at the halfway stage and at the end of the course.

Introduction

In 1982 the author agreed to run a liberal studies course on the modular sciences degree course at Coventry (Lanchester) Polytechnic. Teaching on the course involved contact with two different groups of students on two different days, because of timetabling difficulties. The response in these circumstances is often for the member of staff concerned to give the same lecture on two occasions, often during the same week.

As an alternative, the author decided to try to design a course which eliminated lectures, and which put the onus on the students for their own learning, whilst maintaining academic standards.

The course as it operated in 1985-86 now comprises the following elements, each of which will be dealt with in turn:

- detailed course programme
- introduction and study skills exercises
- course text
- selected further readings from associated texts
- clippings file, added to and updated by staff and students
- videotape extracts from Open University and other material
- periodic student-led seminars
- coursework
- final examination by predistributed paper
- student feedback on the course by interim and final questionnaire.

Detailed Course Programme

Since the students will be largely on their own during the course, it is vital to provide a clear overall structure or framework. The course leaflet is designed to enable students who wish to do so to study entirely independently without attending any of the plenary or seminar events on the course. It presents a complete guide to the set books, with the programme of various video extracts used, the readings which need to be covered and the dates of these and of the associated seminars. Objectives for the course are also provided. Some students do use the course programme to enable them to work entirely independently, borrowing the readings from the short loan collection and the videotapes from the media librarian or his staff.

Introduction and Study Skills Exercises

First, the students are given the lecturer's name and his room number. In exchange, they give the lecturer their names, their course, and the name of their personal tutor. On a course on which staff and students may not meet face-to-face for some weeks, it is vital that they have a direct route to contact one another at short notice if necessary.

Next, the course programme is looked at in detail, section by section. Students are told where they can obtain copies of the set book, and its cost. The details of using the short loan collection in the library are covered, and the clippings file produced for inspection. A copy of the final exam paper for a previous year is produced for inspection, and its nature and form emphasized. Dates are put to each weekly event on the programme.

Then follows an overview of the course, using extracts from some of the videotapes to sketch in the main structure, and to whet the appetite of the students for what is to come. This is the nearest that any session on the course comes to a lecture.

At the meeting in the second week, most time is devoted to study skills exercises to prepare students for the unusual requirements of the course.

For instance, an essay-marking task is given to students, in which they are asked to mark two contrasting essays on the same subject, making helpful suggestions to the author as to how they might improve. Students then discuss their findings with a partner, and then in groups of four to try to arrive at some consensus about the qualities and shortcomings of the essays. Then, in plenary, each group reports back on one of its main findings about the essays, until a list of the qualities of a well-written essay emerges. After many of these exercises, it seems true to say that many classes of students produce criteria for the excellent essay which compare well with those produced by departmental staff.

Using similar student-centred exercises, consideration is also given to developing student awareness about the processes of the seminar, and about learning from video and film.

Course Text

The course text is obviously an even more important component of this than more conventional courses. The work itself is not long, or particularly difficult, and as a first task the students are asked to read this all the way through. Since the course takes its name from the text, there is an obvious requirement for the student to become very familiar with the work, and in subsequent weeks they are directed by the course programme to read chapters relevant to particular sections of the course.

Selected Further Reading

These texts are selected to develop or question the assumptions and approach taken in the course text. An important element of the course is to evaluate critically the ideas put forward by the authors of the text, and these readings are selected with this in mind.

The short loan collection of the library in which these readings are kept restricts loans of the material to a matter of a few hours only, (morning, afternoon, evening). Alternatively, students can consult these works as they would reference materials, without taking them out of the library at all.

Clippings File

Over the years, this has become one of the most borrowed items on the short loan collection. Students seem to be stimulated by it, consisting as it does of relevant clippings from current journals such as *New Scientist* and *Nature*, and articles from the 'quality' press. Students are encouraged to add to this as a supplement to those already contributed. Also on the clippings file is a copy of an examination paper from a previous year.

Videotape Extracts

With the enthusiastic support of the media librarian, the author has been able to provide a great deal of material on videotape relevant to the main themes of the course. Recordings of programmes of the Open University, of Channel 4 under licence, and of the BBC and ITV by purchase, are made available in a lecture room at designated dates and times during the course to enable those students who wish to do so to see the material at regular times. The media unit in the library provides video replay facilities for those who wish to view the material independently, or in small groups.

Student-Led Seminars

The class is divided into groups of about eight to ten students for seminars on five occasions during the course. Each seminar is centred on a question which is printed in the course leaflet, and which is designed to summarize or set the scene for a particular aspect of the course. Each group elects its own chairperson and secretary at the beginning of each seminar session. The guidelines for effective discharge of these responsibilities were laid down in the introductory sessions at the beginning of the course. When the groups reconvene in plenary at the end of the seminar discussion, each secretary makes a brief summary report of the group's deliberations, which is recorded on the board.

Coursework

The questions which form the basis of the seminar discussions also become the subjects for the four short essays which comprise the coursework. Each essay is about 500 words, and is a summary of each student's position, having heard the views of the class and having read and watched the appropriate material. The coursework is an important part of the course because it often raises issues connected with presenting material in an academic, or in some cases a business, commercial or industrial setting. Because the essays are short, some selection of argument is required. Arguments without support become assertions, so that the necessity and conventions for presenting supporting evidence feature strongly.

Final Examination

Rather than set a conventional examination paper, the author looked for a mode which approximates more to the world outside academia. The outcome is a written two-hour examination, from a list of questions which the students receive three to four weeks

	Agree Strongly			Agree			Neither Agree nor Disagree			Disgree			Disagree Strongly		
	'82 %	'83 %	'84 %	'82 %	'83 %	'84 %	'82 %	'83 %	'84 %	'82 %	'83 %	'84 %	'82 %	'83 %	'84 %
1. I feel that the course is well organised	3	0	2	30	48	50	47	35	23	17	17	17	3	0	0
2. The seminar discussions are useful	3	4	18	39	45	35	19	24	30	25	23	7	11	4	4
3. The readings on short loan are easy to use	3	10	4	25	37	26	42	32	40	28	17	21	0	3	2
4. Student participation is encouraged	25	7	18	56	70	61	17	21	7	3	4	5	0	0	0
5. I find that the style of the course is appropriate	6	3	9	25	39	37	28	32	30	30	23	14	8	3	2
6. There is too much videotape	3	3	18	11	8	5	25	17	19	42	52	42	19	20	7
7. I would prefer to have lectures	28	10	11	25	17	12	17	13	19	14	32	25	17	20	26
8. I find the course enjoyable	3	1	11	17	46	44	56	42	30	22	4	5	3	1	4
9. I find the course difficult	0	1	2	8	8	16	47	32	12	42	48	54	6	7	9
10. There is not enough time to do all the work	28	7	19	42	33	12	17	21	19	11	31	33	3	7	7
TOTAL NUMBERS OF STUDENTS ON THE COURSE EACH YEAR							1982 36	1983 71	1984 86						

Figure 1. *Student assessment of a liberal studies course*

before the examination. This gives them the time to prepare their answers through reading, discussion and planning before the examination date. The expectation of the examiners is that given this preparation the papers will be written to a higher standard than those written on an unseen basis. The method gives the students the chance to pursue a particular aspect of the course in some depth after the regular 'classes' are over. It also gives the examiner greater scope in the range and relevance of his questions.

Student Feedback

The results obtained in answer to these questions over the three years in which the course has operated in this mode are shown in Figure 1.

3.11 Medical Text and Student Strategies of Learning

S C Driver
University of Melbourne, Australia

Abstract: A protocol recorder linked to a microcomputer was used to obtain a record of medical students' progress through a portion of anatomy text. This enabled us to follow each student's progress through the reading task and then obtain a printed record of it.
 Immediately on completion of the reading/learning task each student was individually interviewed about their strategies of study. During this interview each student described their approach to the reading task, and commented on where and why difficulties had occurred. This was directly related to the printed protocol record.
 The third and final phase of this experiment was a group discussion in which each student received feedback on their recording and subsequent interview. The students became more aware of their own and other students' strategies and reading habits. Many students experienced difficulty in interpreting diagrams.
 The ultimate aims are (a) to enable all students to develop appropriate strategies in *approaching* a reading task and to effectively implement these *during* the reading of a text, (b) to modify text materials so that they become more effective learning tools. The real challenge is to detect those students who are blissfully unaware of their limitations in approaching and performing a reading/learning task.

Introduction

Two questions were addressed by this study:

1) How can we design more effective printed learning materials for undergraduate medical students?
2) How can we optimally assist all medical students to develop appropriate strategies in *approaching* a reading task and effectively implement these during the *reading* of a text?

The second question is linked to, and grew out of, the first. The knowledge explosion resulted in an over-full curriculum for medical students and most have little free time to participate in experimental research. They are much more likely to become experimental subjects if there is some benefit for them in the experience. We therefore ensured that during phase three of this study all participating students were provided with advice and assistance to improve their study strategies. The students selected for this study were experiencing some difficulty with anatomy and were considered borderline in this subject. The offer of assistance with their study techniques was therefore especially welcome.
 Higher education students must often wonder why and how their lecturers select the texts that they do. The process of selecting a suitable text has far-reaching implications – not only for subject matter but also the manner of presentation and relative emphases. Upon what criteria do university departments and subject teams select a prescribed text? Often it is an *ad hoc* arrangement, simply because the text 'seems appropriate'. If the text has been written and selected with principles of structuring, graphic design and presentation in mind in addition to the content, then it will assist the student to locate, and organize the relevant information. To quote Parer (1983),

'the well designed book enables students to get an overview of arguments, interact with a maze of new information and follow directions. Just as we have all had the experience of being confronted with a proliferation of highway signs that lead to an utter confusion, and at the other extreme with total absence of signs and equal confusion, so too some text books and study guides confuse by too many distractions and others by too few directions. Work done in traffic highway signs has shown that well designed strategically placed signs are more easily understood. So too in the case of study guides, we have seen examples where good textual design enhances student learning.'

Overview of the Three Phases

In order to supply our students with the most appropriate textual materials we need to be aware of those textual factors which may enhance the reading/learning activity. One method of exploring these variables is to give a student precise learning goals and then electronically 'follow' his passage through a prescribed passage of text by means of a study protocol recorder (SPR). This was the first phase of the study. If an immediate in-depth interview with the student follows (second phase), then it is possible to gain a great deal of information about his perception of what he did and why he did it.

The interviews provided a valuable supplement to the printed SPR records. Because of the immediacy (within one minute of completing the reading/learning task on the SPR) of the interview, students were able to clearly describe and comment on the precise nature of difficulties encountered. These difficulties were then directly related to the printed record.

The third and final stage of this study was a group discussion in which each student received feedback on their SPR recording and subsequent interview. Students' queries were answered and suggestions for improving their reading/learning strategy were given. Students became more aware of their own and other students' strategies and reading habits. As students listened to others describing their techniques and relating how they dealt with problem areas in the text, their own repertoire of study skills was enlarged, and they began to understand that others often encountered similar problems, but sometimes had better solutions to the difficulties. Students who previously imagined they were alone (eg in being unable to interpret three-dimensional diagrams), now realized that others had the same difficulty. They gained sufficient confidence to discuss these problem areas with their peers and with the experimenter.

Individual Learning

It is, of course, a truism that all learning is an intensely individual activity. Yet students sometimes act as though others, be they students or lecturers, can do some of their learning for them. An important contribution that authors, tutors and lecturers can make, is to arrange the printed material in a manner that facilitates learning, to ask searching questions and to pose problems for the students' consideration. Associated activities, such as explaining the material to others, debating an issue or justifying a conclusion, will all tend to assist the learner by deepening the learning experience and providing an opportunity to practise manipulating the knowledge he has acquired. These tasks will deepen the 'memory trace'.

The student who studies in isolation (whether a medical student in his own study or a remote distance education student) is largely reliant upon his textual learning materials. Any vagueness, inadequate explanation or case of insufficient or poorly selected examples will hinder the student's progress. An inappropriate diagram or caption may disrupt a learner just as surely as a poorly expressed or inadequately presented passage of prose.

A diagram which contains too much detail may be as much a hindrance to learning as a simplistic diagram which lacks precision. Clearly, the decision about what to omit from a diagram or illustration is as important to the learning process as the decision about what to include. Due consideration should be given not only to the content of a diagram but also its optimum placement in the passage of text. For example, will a table or diagram provide an overview of the text, so that the learner benefits by studying it both before *and* after the text? If so, the learner will need to be referred to it on both occasions – but may be asked to study it with different questions or aims in mind. The caption will also need to take account of both functions. The framework and context which is provided by text is quite critical to the 'conditions of learning' which are established.

Also, because individual styles of learning vary so much, and we have such an inadequate understanding of these personal styles of learning, it may often be worthwhile to provide alternative tracks or choices in the learning programme. However, students are often unsure of which strategy is most beneficial and therefore hints and guidance will be necessary.

The study guide provided for each student in this project had the following attributes:

- an overview of material to be learned with a summary of the concepts and the task defined;
- provision of a logical order for gaining an understanding of the topic;
- subdivision of the learning task into sections;
- provision of *simple* diagrams illustrating basic concepts;
- indication of common student errors.

A study guide such as this is a particularly useful instrument when used before, during and after the study session. Of course, such a guide could only be designed by a teacher who was both familiar with the subject matter *and* was experienced in teaching and tutoring anatomy students.

The point which should be emphasized is that the medical student, learning alone in his study, has an experience more closely attuned to the isolated distance education student than is commonly acknowledged:

- Neither may obtain immediate assistance.
- They are both provided ideally with a study guide, or at least a statement of aims and objectives to provide guidance in dealing with their textual materials.
- They may be encouraged to submit periodic written work for assessment and/or comment.
- In most formal learning situations they will sooner or later be required to present for examination.

Sample

15 second-year anatomy students in the University of Melbourne were experiencing some difficulty with the subject. Their anatomy results from the previous year indicated that they were 'borderline' students in this subject. An anatomy lecturer invited these 15 students to participate in a reading/learning task, under controlled conditions, and all accepted. It is significant that the topic was core anatomy material. All students participated, with the intention of improving their method of approaching a reading task. All these students were experiencing difficulties of one kind or another in reading/learning the prescribed text.

In particular, the problems they had experienced were concerned with:

(a) time allotment to the various subsections, eg the balance between descriptive information and clinical applications;
(b) the order in which subsections were studied – the recommended sequence was provided in a study guide, which followed the same order that topics would be encountered in dissection.

Use of the Study Protocol Recorder (SPR) (Phase 1)

In the current study we were particularly concerned with the manner in which students approach a specific learning task. We were interested in discovering not only the path taken through the learning material, but the time taken on the subsections and the reasons for their choice.

The SPR is an electronic device, invented recently at the British Open University, which accepts A4 pages of text in a spiral binder and by means of infra-red signals and binary coded page markings, keeps a record of the time spent on each page of a text (to an accuracy of one-tenth of a second) and the patterns of page usage. The SPR interfaces with an Apple microcomputer and a printout may be obtained immediately each student completes his study session.

Students were set a realistic task to study. It was core material which closely approximated their usual study assignment. They were provided with a study guide and the required pages of their text, coded and mounted in the spiral binder as required by the SPR. The directions given were as follows:

> '*Time allowed 45 minutes*
> Topic a) The Root of the Neck. Moore p 1113-1146.
>   b) Cervical Viscera. Moore p 1146-1155.
>   c) Fascial Planes of the Neck. Moore p 1155-1158.
>
> *Theme*
> Review the important principles, essential information and applications regarding the above topics.
>
> *Study these topics as you would normally do in your own private study.*
>
> Take care to budget your time over the various sections. You will be allowed an uninterrupted study time of 45 minutes.'

It should be noted that the topics selected for study were central in their anatomy programme the following week.

In-Depth Personal Interview (Phase 2)

Immediately after each student's 45-minute period of study was complete and the printed record of his progress through the task was available, he was interviewed for 40 minutes and his study notes were examined. He was asked whether he had covered this topic in private study and for his estimate of time spent on the three topic areas (listed above). The set study material comprised four *distinct* types of printed information – text, diagrams, captions and clinically oriented comments. For example, the author clearly indicates clinical comments by printing them on a light grey background. It was therefore of interest to hear how much time students spent on the various sections and to find how they rated the importance of the subsections, both for end of second term assessment and for the long term – vocational usefulness and clinical relevance. Note-taking techniques, including questions such as whether they copied diagrams or consciously tried to restructure material, were explored with each student. They were asked if they used the guidelines, and if so, why and how, and did they pose questions to themselves? In particular, questioning centred on areas of difficulty they encountered and how they dealt with their problems. Finally some content questions were asked to determine how much they understood and retained from the pages studied.

Group Interview (Phase 3)

This was an opportunity for general discussion about the task and an exchange of experiences and strategies. The experimenter adopted the role of 'participant-observer'

as he advised the group about techniques to become more active learners. In this
session, with the assistance of SPR data, interview records and student notes, it was
possible to show groups of students where their strategy was faulty and how they could
improve. Some students found a conflict between the instructions 'study as you would
at home' and 'budget your time', because they were unaccustomed to budgeting their
time. Students found it useful to hear of the benefits on restructuring notes and
diagrams – not just passively copying what was in the text, but re-interpreting and
'writing their own text' as one student described it.

Results and Discussion

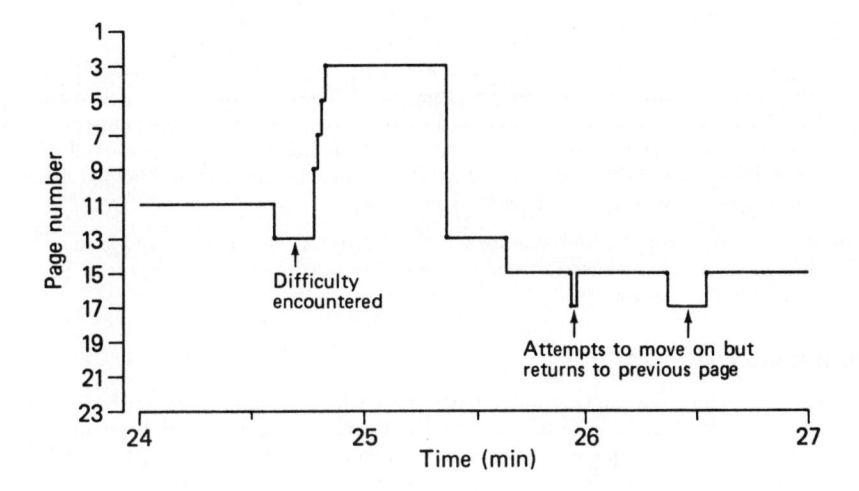

Figure 1. *Portion of an SPR record for an anatomy student*

No two students progressed through the 24 pages of set text in the same manner.
Figure 1 is a short extract of a typical SPR record. Notice where the student has
encountered difficulty and referred back several pages for clarification. During the
subsequent interview the student was questioned about this behaviour and he readily
recalled details of his problem – a term with which he was unfamiliar was used and a
conclusion he didn't follow was reached. In fact several students encountered
difficulties at this same point, which probably means the text requires modification.

The following points summarize the results and experiences of the group who
participated in this study:

  (a) 12 out of 15 students encountered considerable difficulty in interpreting and
      understanding three-dimensional diagrams. Several students revealed during the
      interview that they 'skip the diagrams and concentrate on the text'. Of those who
      do study diagrams, only a minority read the captions. This must be a
      considerable handicap in a visual subject such as anatomy.
  (b) Of the eight students who drew diagrams as part of their note-taking, only one
      structured his own diagram (rather than copying from the original) and *then*
      compared it with the original. Students agreed that diagrams reveal one's
      mistakes more, and therefore may be good for learning but more risky in
      examinations.
  (c) Only three students started the task by overviewing the learning material and
      then set priorities and budgeted their time. Most students devoted the same
      amount of time to each page of text.

(d) All students experienced a time pressure on the task – just as they encountered in their usual study practice. They found that all the variables encountered in their private study were present – except for two students who found the environment unduly quiet!
(e) One-third of students said they frequently faced a dilemma between studying material of clinical significance which was important in the long term (for their career) but not so relevant for the term examination. Several students consequently ignored clinical relevance and did not even read those sections. This was an error of judgement, because clinical relevance is not only esteemed by examiners but assists in the understanding, organization and intrinsic interest of the subject.
(f) All students subsequently said that they found the individual interview valuable. They felt it raised their awareness of their studying strategies.
(g) The group experience proved most useful and some are continuing to meet regularly for mutual help. The discussion of a range of strategies revealed that they were not alone in the problems they faced. They identified others who had similar problems and also wanted to do something about it. Feelings of isolation and alienation were therefore decreased. Students indicated that the overall experiences of the three phases had improved their perspective and helped them make better use of tools such as the study guide.

It must be remembered that our sample is one of borderline students. Many of the difficulties, errors and weaknesses listed above no doubt contribute towards their poor understanding of anatomy.

Conclusion

The detailed documentation of student experiences with the anatomy prescribed text has already resulted in a change of text for second-year anatomy in 1986. Students have had an opportunity to study a set passage of core text under controlled conditions with the SPR. Many of the difficulties and weaknesses that emerged became apparent during the individual interview. Nevertheless the SPR hardware was the trigger that initiated the revelations.

Most students participated in the programme with undue confidence in the SPR and microcomputer – it was going to 'tell them all about their study methods'. Hence, when they came to the interview they were particularly co-operative and revealing. This role of the hardware was totally unexpected, and there is little doubt that without the use of the SPR in Phase 1 the individual and group interviews would have been much less successful. Students probably would not have become as aware of their 'surface approach to learning' (Marton et al, 1984) without examining their SPR records and reflecting on their aims and methods of study.

This study has assisted students in two main ways:

(a) there is an increasing awareness on the part of the students of the elements of the text and the requirements of the task;
(b) there is increasing control over their own study – the rate, the sequence, the choice of the most appropriate strategy from an enlarged repertoire.

There is no single way to read or study a text, but it is vital to be aware of a range of strategies and our own strengths and weaknesses. It will be interesting to see how a stratified sample of anatomy students compare to borderline students in their text processing skills. The real challenge is not only to modify faulty portions of the text and/or diagrams, but to enable *all* students to develop appropriate strategies in *approaching* a reading task and to effectively implement these *during* the reading of a text.

References

Fleming, M and Levie, W H (1978) *Instructional Message Design*. Educational Technology Publications, Englewood Cliffs.
Hartley, J and Burnhill, P (1977) Fifty guide-lines for improving instructional text, *Programmed Learning and Educational Technology*, **14**, 2.
Hartley, J, Trueman, M and Burnhill, P (1980) Some observations on producing and measuring readable writing. *Journal of Programmed Learning and Educational Technology*, **17**, 3.
Hartley, J (ed) (1980) *The Psychology of Written Communication*. Kogan Page, London.
Hartley, J (1978) *Designing Instructional Text*. Nichols, London.
Huey, E B (1908) *The Psychology and Pedagogy of Reading and Writing of Methods, Texts, and Hygiene in Reading*. Republished MIT Press, 1968.
Marton, F, Hounsell, D, Entwistle, N (eds) (1984) *The Experience of Learning*. Scottish Academic Press, Edinburgh.
McDonald-Ross, M (1976) The quality of course materials. *Evaluating Teaching in Higher Education*. University of London Teaching Methods Unit, London.
Parer, M S (1983) *Distance Education*, **4**, 2, p 229.
Sless, D (1978) Image design and modification: an experimental project in transforming. *Information Design Journal*, **1**, 2.
Waller, R H W (1979) Dimensions of quality in educational texts. In Kolers, P A, Wrolstad, M E and Bouma, H (eds), *Proceedings of Visible Language*, **1**, Plenum Press.

Acknowledgements

Grateful appreciation is expressed for the assistance of Dr Norman Eizenberg for making the sample of anatomy students available, Professor Gordon Stanley for the provision of research facilities, and Dr Michael Parer for the use of the Student Protocol Recorder. The author is indebted to all three for valuable discussions and advice.

3.12 A Programme Development for Educational Technology Courses in Teacher Education

M Inoue, K Kojima and F Shinohara
Tokyo Gakugei University, Japan

Abstract: This paper discusses the current trends in research and development on the curricula regarding educational technology and its related fields conducted and offered in teacher training universities in Japan.

Introduction

As a result of recent progress and developments in aspects of information technology, research on improving educational methods and instruction in school education through the use of educational technology is becoming widespread. Reasons for this include: the development of instructional methods which bring instructional analysis, design and evaluation together into a unified whole; the introduction of new instructional aids such as video equipment and response analysers; and the development of educational data processing program packages resulting from improvements in microcomputer capabilities and quality, combined with a reduction in their costs.

The truth of the matter however is that except for only a few educational technology centres, teacher education institutions have done little, if anything, towards developing courses appropriate to the classroom. Since the early 1970s, however, various educational technology centres in Japan have been conducting systematic research aimed at developing teacher education courses involving educational technology – courses which aim to move towards the introduction of these new developments into classroom teaching. As a result, a number of teacher education institutions have been establishing and evaluating courses specifically related to educational technology. This paper outlines the situation in relation to those courses in educational technology now being developed at centres for educational technology and discusses future problems and prospects.

Problems and Future Prospects

Rapid progress has recently been made in information technology involving various combinations of video, computer, and communications technologies. Accompanying these developments in information technology, Japan has seen a remarkable diffusion of new information and educational technology systems into the classroom. This diffusion points out the need for looking afresh at classroom educational methods and contents, from a technical as well as an educational point of view. Specific areas include:

(a) Research on ways to stimulate the educational development and growth of each child and on instructional reform based upon development of individual study and diagnostic programmes designed for acquisition of basic knowledge and skills;

(b) Developmental research involving unified systems of analysis, design and evaluation of the teaching/learning process in group learning situations and action based upon these results;
(c) Video, computer and communications technologies, as well as comprehensive technological systems based upon combinations of these technologies are now becoming available to the schools. There is a need for developmental research aimed at producing effective teaching/learning processes through the application of these innovations.

As a result of these factors there are demands for new curricula in teacher education. These should give particular attention to educational technology and audiovisual media.

Imae et al (1984) conducted a questionnaire survey on the competencies expected of specialists in educational technology. From the results, he identified five basic competencies for educational technology specialists. In addition to showing that the competencies desired varied depending upon where the educational technologist is employed, he was also able to establish the primary and secondary competencies expected of such specialists employed either in schools or in universities (see Figure 1). The competencies for educational technology specialists in schools emphasize instructional design and analysis, and media preparation and equipment operation, while at the university level particular emphasis is placed upon an ability to conduct research. The introduction of new information media into the classroom has resulted in an increase in the production of courseware which makes use of educational technology methods and media, which in turn has created a sudden demand for the development of courses in educational technology.

Competency	School level	University level
Instructional design and research	P	S
Media preparation and equipment operation	P	S
Research	S	P
Educational system development	S	S
Basic knowledge of education		S

Figure 1. *Primary (P) and secondary (S) areas of competence expected of specialists in educational technology*

Reconsideration of Educational Technology Curricula in Teacher Education

To date, university courses in audiovisual education and educational technology have tended to emphasize theory and knowledge and to be lacking in practical activity and research. However, as a result of the introduction of the new information technologies into the classroom, there is now a need to adapt these courses to balance theory with practice. In-service training programmes require a corresponding modification.

Inoue et al (1982, 1984) reviewed the literature on research into educational technology and teacher education and divided the field of educational technology into three areas: instructional analysis, design and evaluation; development and use of instructional media, educational aids and media; and educational data processing. They further divided these into undergraduate and graduate levels. By establishing goals for each of these subdivisions, they devised a tentative framework for a comprehensive model curriculum for educational technology (Figures 2 and 3).

(1) The meaning and purposes of instructional analysis, design, and evaluation

   (a) Structuring and a model of instruction
   (b) Analysing instructional objectives and principles of organizing instructional content
   (c) Categorizing teaching/learning behaviours
   (d) Methods of interactional analysis of instruction
   (e) History and principles of programmed learning and educational psychology
   (f) Preparing lesson plans
   (g) Teacher perceptions and decision-making
   (h) Microteaching
   (i) Games and simulations

(2) Development and use of instructional media and equipment

   (a) Characteristics and functions of instructional media
   (b) Structuring curricula and the media
   (c) The instructional process and selection and use of instructional media
   (d) The significance of multimedia-based instruction
   (e) Preparing instructional materials (slides, overhead projectors, television, videotape recorders/equipment, individual and group teaching machines, language laboratories, and group response analysers)
   (f) Fieldwork (audiovisual centres, audiovisual libraries, libraries, media centers, etc) and assignment of a specific research project

(3) Educational data processing

   (a) Basics of data processing
   (b) Collection, organizing (categorizing), application and systematizion of educational data
   (c) Basics of educational statistics
   (d) Concepts of instructional evaluation
   (e) Computer languages and programming
   (f) Designing and evaluating the CAI teaching/learning process
   (g) Instructional evaluation, curriculum management and grade administration through CAI
   (h) Gathering and processing classroom data and assignment of a specific research project

Figure 2. *A proposed curriculum for educational technology*

Areas in Table 2	(1)	(2)	(3)	Credits
Graduate Level	(a), (b), (c) (d), (e), (f), (g), (h), (i)	(a), (b), (c), (d), (e)	(a), (b), (c), (d), (e), (f), (g)	6
Master's Degree Level	(f), (g), (h) (i), (j)	(e), (f)	(f), (g), (h)	12

Figure 3. *Relationships between items given in Figure 2 and undergraduate/postgraduate studies*

Their proposed curriculum incorporates the existing undergraduate and graduate level curricula. But in addition their goal is to bring about a synthesis of theory and practice by developing an awareness of the problems and relationships between educational methods, subject instruction and teaching.

Although teacher education still contains many unresolved problems, the point has now been reached when there are specialized teacher education universities offering master degrees aimed at in-service training. In addition there are now centres for educational technology, or centres for educational research and training, in a total of 36 national universities. A great deal is expected of these centres. They are not limited to inter-departmental, co-operative use but are also conducting independent educational research on methods of educational technology, and are promoting developmental research on practical teacher education programmes, thus combining theory and practice.

Development of Core-Material Videotapes for Teacher Education

In June 1984, representatives from a number of universities came together to discuss plans for the development of a series of common use instructional materials (both video and print) for teacher education and to organize the Council for the Study of Teacher Education Media.

A number of organizations, including the Japan Council for Educational Technology Centres, the Council of Private University Departments of Teacher Education, the Tokyo Area Liaison Council for Practice Teaching and others, had already begun deliberations on the need for a series of videotaped materials of this type. In particular, the Japan Council for Educational Technology Centres (composed of 36 national university centres for educational technology) in 1978 sanctioned a Committee for Research on Teaching Skills whose task was to promote research on improving practice teaching, primarily centered around the development of videotape materials. The work of this committee was particularly fruitful regarding development of a programme for pre-practice teaching guidance (designed as a two-credit university course).

Based upon this research, the Council for the Study of Teacher Education Media, in co-operation with the National Centre for Development of Broadcasting Education (a co-operative international university organization) has embarked upon a five-year programme, which began in 1984, for the development of a series of core-material videotapes for use in teacher education.

References

Imae, K *et al* (1984) Competency levels required of specialists in educational technology. *Japan Journal of Educational Technology*, **8**, 3.

Inoue, M *et al* (1982, 1984) *Development of a Teacher Education Curriculum Related to Educational Technology*. Part 2 and Part 3, 6th and 8th Conferences of the Japan Society of Science Education.

3.13 Some Recent Microcomputer-Based Innovations in a Well-Established Micro-Teaching Programme for Teacher Trainers

J Oakley and M Arrowsmith
La Sainte Union College of Higher Education, Southampton

Abstract: Re-equipping a closed circuit television studio in a college of higher education provided an opportunity to build in microcomputer facilities, which have since enabled exploratory innovations to be made in a well established microtraining programme for teacher trainees. One very flexible CAL program permits the addition of a wide range of comments to be made to any ongoing recording of a micro-lesson. A second program, combined with a network of keypads permits quite sophisticated rating of micro-lessons to be carried out.

Introduction

Micro-teaching, frequently described as a 'scaled-down teaching encounter' has been a valuable training technique used by all students on the Bachelor of Education, Postgraduate Certificate of Education, and Certificate in Further Education courses at La Sainte Union College of Higher Education, Southampton, for over ten years.

During that time a stable pattern of work has been established. Two classroom skills of importance, namely set induction and questioning, are practised. For the work on set induction, the procedure for each 90-minute session is that three students will each teach a micro-lesson, lasting some seven minutes, in succession. Each student has had one week to prepare the lesson and is in full charge of arrangements. As 'teacher', the student sets the scenario for his peers, nominates the age and abilities of his envisaged learners, the prerequisite knowledge he wants them to have, and so on, and the other students in the group are expected to role-play within the bounds of this scenario, though none of this need inhibit them from creating unexpected incidents or initiating behaviour not necessarily appreciated by the 'teacher'.

Three unmanned cameras are then positioned, one on the 'teacher' and two on the 'class', and these are remote-controlled from an annexe to the main studio. An extensive range of mixes, wipes, and other effects can be readily obtained via the use of a sophisticated effects generator. After the recordings are completed the students collect around a large monitor, hitherto blank, to review and analyse the recordings. The review session usually occupies the large part of each 90-minute session.

For the micro-lesson on questioning skills, one session is given over to establishing and reviewing theory, using explanatory tapes made by the author in conjunction with Wessex Educational Television, based at King Alfred's College, Winchester. The remaining sessions are used by the students to work through a series of graded exercises which are designed to highlight and permit practice of certain specific skills in turn.

Student work differs in two respects from their work with set induction. One is that they work at their own intellectual level rather than role playing, and the second is that all preparation is done during the sessions, not beforehand. Using passages from the top levels of the Scientific Research Associates reading kits as material, the 'teacher' and the others are first given time to read the passage, and in the case of the 'teacher' to prepare a series of questions with some object in mind. In the simplest exercise the intention might be solely to check how much of the passage can be recalled by the 'learners' in the absence of the printed material. From this elementary beginning, further skills are built up, each student in turn acting as 'teacher'. A stage is eventually reached when the passages are not removed, are quite lengthy and complex, and the 'teacher' is now trying to run a discussion, endeavouring to co-ordinate ideas, responses, and opinions, and in some cases elucidate a concept or principle from a context with which he may actually be unfamiliar. The work is far more complex than with set induction, and it is not unusual for one recording and its subsequent analysis to occupy a whole session.

The method of analysis has developed over the years until the position has been reached where for both set induction and questioning sessions the procedure is as follows. Prior to replaying his recording, the 'teacher' is requested to watch and note and report anything about his performance which he feels significant or important. He is asked for as full a self-evaluation as possible. The other students are asked to look at some specific aspect of the 'teacher's' performance, and to concentrate solely upon that aspect. Thus as regards set induction, one student might concentrate upon voice usage, another upon speech and language, a third upon posture and movement, etc. During a questioning session, one student might concentrate upon the types and frequencies of reinforcement used, another might plot the nature of the interactions with individual 'learners', a third analyse the types of response made by the 'teacher' to answers. In all cases frequent use is made of a variety of rating schedules.

The recording is then replayed and at the conclusion of the replay, the 'teacher' student has complete freedom to say what he likes and at any length. Then the other students, having listened to him, comment from their particular viewpoint, and finally the tutor comments. This might be done with the aid of notes taken during recording or replay, or by rerunning parts of the recording. Finally, the 'teacher' student has chance to comment once more in the light of all the feedback.

To understand the importance of the recent microcomputer innovations in this technique, it is of importance to review problems which have revealed themselves over the years in the running of the sessions as described.

The Problem of Complexity

Any micro-teaching session, whether concerned with set induction or questioning, is a complex affair. A multiplicity of interesting events, each worthy of considerable analysis and comment, can and do frequently occur, and moreover they occur at speed. Since the one available tutor is not only watching the recording while it is being made, trying to scribble useful notes at the same time for the later evaluation, and also doing the jobs of programme director and recording engineer, much of significance can easily be missed while switching cameras, checking sound levels, and making a note. We have long looked for some way of superimposing a comment onto a videorecording while it was being made, even at the elementary level of 'note that incident' simply to remind us that the incident was well worth talking about on replay.

Also during questioning sessions we had often wished for some way of describing what was going on, and again superimposing a terse comment at an appropriate place on the videorecording, such as 'that was an effective prompt', 'that needed a further probe', or 'why did you say that?'.

Normal superimposition techniques, needing a captions camera, telecine bench, and a whole range of graphics, were ruled out as cumbersome and slow – besides which, we didn't have the requisite equipment.

Problem with Rating Schedules

A second problem concerns the use of rating schedules by the students, and their reporting back in the evaluation session. Often while taking the time to use the schedule, or simply to refer to it (since they have very little time to get used to it), they too easily miss important events occurring on the playback monitor. In other words they can't maintain unbroken attention when using paper and pencil to log events or make judgements.

Also, because they report back in open session on the performance of a colleague, 'regression to the mean' becomes a significant factor. It is after all, very hard for a young student to say in open court to another 'your voice is harsh, monotonous, used mainly in an ineffective manner and my assessment of it is a straight "E" ', even if we are all thinking it. Likewise, they will rarely give 'A' grades for truly excellent performances.

Rating schedules have other problems also. It is often difficult to discriminate between behaviours which figure largely in a trainee's performance, and those he rarely engages in. Once placed on a rating schedule on some kind of continuum, behaviours tend to assume equal significance. Often the student 'looks for' them and grades accordingly in some way, even if the behaviour is only vestigially present on the playback. We had often looked for an easy procedure to 'weight' displayed behaviours in some way.

Microcomputer-Based Developments

A successful application to the Department of Education and Science (DES) to replace our ageing closed circuit television (CCTV) equipment, gave an opportunity to put into effect ideas involving the microcomputer, since the DES agreed to incorporate a BBC Model B into the system. A commercially available genlock system ensures that the video and BBC micro signals are synchronized, and that Mode 7 screens generated by the micro can be overlaid on the video signal. Once the hardware was proved to work satisfactorily it then became a matter of designing the correct software. What was needed was an 'all-purpose program' readily and quickly available and applicable to any micro-teaching situation. The key features needed were:

1. the ability to store in memory a series of short comments, each of which could be independently and randomly retrieved by a simple key press;
2. that comment could be immediately superimposed upon an ongoing video-recording;
3. the ability to edit any comment rapidly, if necessary during an actual recording session;
4. the ability to switch to a whole new series of comments quickly should the type of micro-teaching session change.

The college's department of computing, in the shape of its programmer Mike Arrowsmith, came up with a highly successful answer. The software allows the creation of files of ten messages, each message containing up to thirty-six letters. Initially, ten coloured 'slots' as it were, are displayed on the VDU, into which comments can be typed via the micro keyboard, edited, spaced, made to 'flash' if need be, and so on. When completed, a separate section of the program ensures that simply using the red function keys on the BBC keyboard allows each message to be displayed at the bottom of the VDU. Via the genlock board and the CCTV effects unit, the same message is displayed on the CCTV programme monitor and recorded upon the videotape. Pressing the space bar on the micro removes the message.

All the tutor has to do is to refer to a small *aide-memoire* which shows which comment is attached to which function key, and he is then in a position to add considerable information to the video recording that is being made.

Already three sets of messages are in use: one for set induction, one for story-telling, and one for questioning. Changing from one set to another is merely a question of using the ESCAPE key, returning to the main menu, and loading a new set of messages. With a double disc drive this is a matter of seconds only. Pressing one key on the CCTV effects unit isolates the computer so that an amendment can be made to a message being used, using the VDU to edit, and then returning the micro to the CCTV system without affecting an ongoing recording at all. Figure 1 shows a typical set of messages.

```
0  Remember that incident
1  Good point
2  Well explained
3  Smoothly organized
4  Don't do that!
5  Watch your class!
6  A bit awkward there
7  Nerves?
8  Confidently done
9  Not clear to your learners
```

Figure 1. *A typical set of computer-stored comments*

As regards the second problem, that of sharpening up playback, what I had long envisaged was a system which:

1. would permit any one of ten or more raters to assess as many as ten or so variables in a micro-teaching performance;
2. would enable each variable to be rated upon some kind of scale, as frequently as the rater felt necessary;
3. would permit each rater to act quite independently of any other rater, as regards the variable assessed, the frequency of assessment, etc;
4. would ensure total anonymity to any rater in the sense that the trainee could not identify 'exactly who had said what';
5. would permit all the ratings, on all the variables, by all the raters, to be rapidly stored, processed, and tabulated;
6. would allow such tabulations to be displayed upon a large CCTV monitor, not just a micro VDU;
7. would ensure that hard copy of the tabulation would be available to the trainee assessed, and to the tutor;
8. would enable tabulated data to be stored on disc for possible future and further analysis.

Again Mike Arrowsmith, this time with a little help from outside, came up with a solution. The hardware needed was designed by E Wingfield, a local teacher who works with the department on a variety of projects. The solution was electronically quite innovative and was not forthcoming from several commercial firms who had been approached. We call the system the 'Octopus' mainly as a result of the cabling needed. Sixteen keypads are connected via an interface to the user port of the BBC micro. Each keypad has sixteen keys labelled zero to nine and A–F.

The user port allows eight-bit parallel data to be processed, so cycling through all the possible eight-bit values identifies each of the 256 (16 × 16) individual keys on the pads in turn. The value returned on one of the user port 'handshake' lines indicates whether or not the identified key is being pressed.

Using the same idea as before, a file of ten messages can be created and displayed on the VDU. These messages are now variables to be used in assessing teacher performance rather than comments to be recorded upon the videotape. They can be displayed on a monitor as an *aide-memoire* during the evaluation session, or the rater can have them listed upon a small card. Figure 2 shows a set of variables.

excellent	0 *in toto* performance	weak
clear	1 questions	diffuse
attentive	2 interaction	inattentive
frequent	3 probing	infrequent
helpful	4 prompting	redirects
varied	5 reinforcement	stereotyped
logical	6 sequencing	poor
equal	7 participation	unequal
patient	8 manner	impatient
integrative	9 atmosphere	dominative
Grades A, B	Grade C	Grades D, E

Figure 2. *Sample rating assessments*

The rater is now in a position to view the recording of a micro-training session, and to rate the trainee's performance on as many as ten variables simply by pressing any key from zero to nine, each of which identifies a separate variable, and by pressing A–E, each of which represents a grade on a five-point scale. Key F cancels any currently selected grade, and is thus a correction facility. About all the rater has to do is remember to press the variable key before he presses the grading key, and of course to remember or check which key represents which variable.

During an evaluation session, the Octopus is used during the playback of the video recording. During the playback, all key presses are recorded and stored in a large buffer. When the rating is complete, the ESCAPE key is pressed and the micro then analyses all the data (rejecting any invalid key presses). The tabulated data can now be shown on the same monitor used for the playback, which is an obvious advantage over VDU display.

The table indicates the number of times each grade from A to E was used for each rater in rating each of the ten variables. It also gives the total number of times each grade was awarded for each variable by all the raters. It gives too the total number of times each variable was rated irrespective of grade, both as an absolute value, and as a percentage of all key presses. No averages are given, since *a priori* the spread or profile of grades both individually and collectively was seen as of more value.

One advantage is that the computer 'scrambles' the station/keypad numbers before tabulating the data, so preserving anonymity. Thus, although the micro tabulates all the grades given by the rater using keypad number five, and displays them on the monitor, it randomly allocates another keypad number to the display. The raters are told this before using the system, and are quite aware that if they use 'E' or 'A' keys heavily, they are unlikely to be identified by the trainee.

The Octopus has not been in operation long enough yet to permit other than some illuminative evaluation. I'm quite certain other problems will emerge. But my initial views are

1. that, despite the spaghetti-like appearance of the Octopus, it is easy to use, and it has certainly given an impetus to evaluation sessions. We are currently using it to rate questioning sessions, but by defining a new set of variables it can of course be readily applied elsewhere. Also it could be used to do a deep analysis of one variable such as 'reinforcement', by defining ten aspects or modes of that variable;
2. students' initial reactions appear favourable. A few quick polls during sessions have revealed no adverse reactions. Most questions concern whether the variables looked for are the best ones to use, etc;

3. that it does seem to change the nature of micro-teaching somewhat. If comments are attached to the video recording while the trainee is working, then the tape is definitely 'compromised' as far as the trainee's own self-evaluation is concerned later. But this might depend upon the nature of the predetermined message. One could envisage a simple set of messages designed solely to alert, such as 'remember that', 'what was the intention there?', 'was that an anticipated outcome?' etc, which might have less of an inhibiting effect than other more evaluative comments such as 'good technique there', etc;
4. that the two programs we have so far constructed and the Octopus are capable of being used in many other areas than teacher training and the normal micro-teaching skills relevant there. There are obvious applications in many other fields where any kind of human interaction takes place. One thinks of management, police work, nursing, consultancy, selling, and so on.

In conclusion, it is obviously early days as far as we are concerned, and we don't quite know where it will all lead. But we are certain that with the advent of microcomputer facilities in our CCTV studio, we have given a new lease of life to an old technique, and raised the possibility of several new and interesting extensions.

It remains to be seen where we get.

3.14 Reading Skills: A Psycholinguistic Approach to Computer Assisted Learning (CAL)

M D Vinegrad
Goldsmiths' College, University of London

Abstract: Reading is a prime skill, yet many individuals fail to achieve an adequate level of mastery. Reasons for failure are complex and are bound up with the language background and linguistic experiences of the individual concerned. The paper describes the development of a computer-based system designed to provide a means of analysing samples of oral reading. The system of analysing the reading and the creation of a database is described. The objective is to enable a tutor to interrogate the database so that he may develop insights into the nature of the reading problem of the individual concerned. Sample results are indicated. Methods of linking such a system to computer assisted learning (CAL) programs are indicated.

Introduction

In this paper I would like to present an outline of a computer-based system designed for the backward reader, both child and adult. To be truly responsive to the needs of the individual, such a system needs to be highly flexible, as no two problem readers are alike. The system described here works best for the individual who has started to read but is not doing very well, rather than for the individual just taking the first steps. Because of the great diversity of reading problems it seems desirable to have some form of assessment procedure to aid in the choice of appropriate tutorial methods. The procedure described here is based on the analysis of oral reading. First of all, the individual is asked to read a short story or passage between 100 and 200 words in length. This can be of his own choosing or provided by the tutor. It is important to know whether the story is being read for the first time or whether it has been previously practised. However, both kinds of reading are informative. Backward readers of all ages tend to be defensive about their performance and therefore care needs to be taken to prevent them failing too badly. This can be done by making sure that the initial choice of material is at an appropriate level. Where possible, the reader should begin with something easy and then move on to something challenging but not frustrating. A second technique that can be used to prevent excessive failure and to get the reader going is called 'paired reading'. Here the tutor says, 'I will read each word – repeat it after me. Whenever you can, try to beat me to the word.' The tutor adjusts his rate of reading to a suitable speed and where the reader has correctly anticipated the text, the tutor remains silent. This technique can work wonders, particularly for the reader who lacks confidence. All reading sessions are tape recorded and throughout, the reader is asked to concentrate on the meaning of what he is reading rather than on giving a good oral performance. At the end of the passage the reader knows he will be asked to say in his own words what the passage was about. Throughout, the focus is on comprehension, not on accurate oral rendition.

Once a sample of reading has been obtained, the tape is analysed and the performance coded in a variety of ways. The coded data is then entered into a computer to form a database. Once this has been done, the tutor is free to interrogate the database in a number of ways which allow him to test hypotheses about the reader's performance. The method of coding gives rise to a large amount of data. Even the single reading of a short passage can generate a lot of information. The task of analysis rapidly becomes unmanageable without the assistance of a computer. To date a mainframe VAX computer has been used. This supports a package called SPSSX, which allows a large range of analyses to be performed. Commands are entered by the tutor in a high-level language close to ordinary English.

Creation of the Database

In order to describe the creation of the database, it is necessary to outline briefly the coding procedure. The theoretical work on which this is based derives mainly from the work of an American psycholinguist called Kenneth Goodman. In fact most of the coding procedures employed have been pioneered by Goodman and his associates (Goodman and Burke, 1972).

First, the tape of the reader's performance is compared to the text and all alterations the reader has made are written in on the text. Following the lead of Goodman, alterations of all kind are referred to as 'miscues' (Gollasch, 1982). Once the text has been fully marked up, each sentence is read as the reader left it. The reader's performance may then be coded at several levels, each of which gives somewhat different information about the learning problem.

Coding at the Sentence Level

Four questions are asked about each sentence:

Question one: Does the sentence the reader has produced contain any miscues (ie alterations of any kind)? If the answer is 'yes', then:

Question two: Is the sentence grammatically acceptable?
Question three: Is the sentence semantically acceptable?
Question four: Does the sentence result in a change to the author's message?

Questions one to three are coded in terms of 'yes' or 'no' and question four in terms of 'yes', 'no' or 'partial'. In creating a database the first information to be entered consists of such essentials as the identity of the individual and of the passage being read. Other information may be added (if this is available) such as the difficulty level of the passage, the reader's age and reading level, and so on. The answers to the four questions indicated above are entered in the form of Figure 1.

| | Question | | | |
Sentence	1	2	3	4
1	Y	Y	Y	P
2	N	–	–	–
3	Y	Y	N	Y
etc				

Figure 1. *Entering sentence level coding into the database*

Obtaining Information from the Database

Whilst the information entered so far is not very great, certain features of performance may be examined. Interrogating the data base in SPSSX is a simple matter. It is only necessary to type in a simple command such as FREQUENCIES GENERAL = QUESTION 1. This produces a display like that in Figure 2. Similarly, the command FREQUENCIES GENERAL = QUESTION 4 produces a display like that in Figure 3.

Number of sentences read: 30	
without miscue	: 8
with miscues	: 12

Number of sentences read	: 30
change to author's message	: 18
partial change to author's message	: 7
no change to author's message	: 5

Figures 2, 3. *Sample answers to database enquiries*

The tutor may decide to break Figure 2 down further with a command such a CROSSTABS TABLES = QUESTION 2 BY QUESTION 3 BY QUESTION 4. This produces a display like Figure 4.

Change to author's message

		Semantically Acceptable	
		yes	no
Grammatically Acceptable	yes	3	–
	no	–	15

No change to author's message

		Semantically Acceptable	
		yes	no
Grammatically Acceptable	yes	7	1
	no	–	1

Figure 4. *Sample answer to a three-way database enquiry*

For reasons of space, only part of Figure 4 is shown. The section referring to 'partial change to the author's message' has been omitted. The upper section of Figure 4 suggests that this particular reader loses the author's message, as he is producing garbled sentences – grammatically and semantically unacceptable. This is by no means always the case. Sometimes the upper and lower sections of the table show the same pattern. In such cases, the reader may always produce grammatically and semantically sound sentences. Loss of the author's message is due to other factors and illustrates a different type of problem from that depicted in Figure 4. The tutor is not of course limited to the displays illustrated. The procedure is entirely flexible and a variety of different tables may be produced. In this way the tutor may explore the data from other points of view.

Coding of Individual Miscues

Further insights into the nature of the reading problem may be gained by coding individual miscues. This results in a greatly expanded database, giving wide scope for interrogation. The majority of individual miscues can be classified under six main headings.

Substitutions

As the term suggests, the reader makes changes to the text. For example, when reading 'swimming', the reader may say 'singing', or when reading 'river' may say 'lake'.

Refusals

These are really 'don't know' or 'won't say' responses. Refusals are accompanied by pauses, often of some length, and the reader may show signs of frustration.

Omissions/Insertions

Omissions are quite different from refusals. The reader makes no pause and shows no awareness of having left anything out. Insertions occur in the opposite direction. Once again the reader is usually unaware of having added to the text. These two types of miscue rarely involve a loss of comprehension and occur frequently in the performance of good readers.

Intonation Miscues

These always involve a loss of comprehension. The reader's intonation pattern does not correspond to the structure of the text, which is, so to speak, repunctuated.

Complex Miscues

In these, more than a single word is involved. For example, a whole phrase may be substituted for another, or a sentence may be grammatically reorganized.

Corrections

Finally, an important aspect of the reading process is whether or not miscues are spontaneously corrected. This feature is coded along with the type of miscue. All the codings are entered into the database as shown in Figure 5.

Once this has been done, a clearer picture of the reader's performance may be obtained. The tutor may for example, enter the following command: CROSSTABS TABLES = TYPE BY CORRECTION BY QUESTION 4. This produces a display

Sentence	Miscue	Reader	Text	Corrected	Type
3	1	which	that	yes	substitution
4	1	–	so	no	omission
4	2	on	no	no	substitution
6	1	–	I've	no	refusal
etc					

Figure 5. *Coding of miscues*

like the one in Figure 6. Only one-third of the total display is shown. There would in fact be corresponding sections for partial change and no change to the author's message. Comparison of the three sections in terms of type of miscue can often be very informative for the tutor involved.

Sentences with change to author's message: 18

Type of Miscue	Not Corrected	Corrected	Total
Substitution	12	5	17
Refusal	4	–	4
Omission	–	–	–
Insertion	–	–	–
Intonation	2	1	3
Complex	1	–	1
Total	19	6	25

Figure 6. *Assessment of a reader's total performance*

It will be obvious of course from a consideration of the database that a fairly large number of other tables could be printed out. What might prove useful would vary according to the case at hand.

Tutorial Models

In the preceding sections, two types of coding have been described to illustrate how the process works. There are other types of coding that may be entered into the database which portray other features of the reader's performance. Goodman and Burke (1972) suggested that to obtain an adequate diagnosis of the reading problem, nine questions should be asked about each individual miscue. In the system described in this paper, the tutor is free to ask as few or as many questions as he wishes, depending on the nature of the problems and the time available.

The system does not contain any mechanism for translating information about a reader's performance into a set of tutorial decisions. This depends upon the experience of the tutor. However, it should be stressed that the system is itself a training device for tutors. New insights and hypotheses about the nature of the reading process may be developed through its use.

Computer assisted learning programs would seem to constitute a logical corollary. A search has been made of existing programs within the field of reading. As far as possible these have been categorized in terms of their relevance to particular types of reading problem. In addition, a number of program ideas are being developed by the author along the lines of exercises to be found in remedial reading texts. Many of these exercises are highly suitable for the computer, but have been largely neglected by the developers of programs.

References

Gollasch, F V (ed) (1982) *Language and Literacy: The Selected Writings of Kenneth S Goodman. Volume 1 Process, Theory and Research.* Routledge and Kegan Paul, London.
Goodman, Y M and Burke, C C (1972) *Reading Miscue Inventory Manual.* Macmillan London.

3.15 Illustrative Characteristics of the Figures in Science Material and Construction of Educational Computer Graphics

I Kitagaki
Fukuoka University of Education, Japan

Abstract: Science teachers often have cause to use illustrative materials, eg transparencies, in their teaching. Often precise drawing is necessary, as in geometrical representations. However many figures share characteristics with others. The paper will discuss the use of educational computer graphics designed for use in science.

Introduction

Precise graphic representations are often required in science and science teaching. The paper describes a system in which a desired diagram is depicted on a computer screen and printed through an X–Y plotter. The system uses basic diagrammatic characteristics, and is intended to be flexible enough to allow the convenient modification of diagrams.

Characteristics of the Basic Diagram

In the system, elements of the basic diagram are depicted on the screen or printout and peripheral elements can be added later manually. For example, in Figure 1, the basic diagram consists of the tripod stand (U^1), the beaker (U 2) – and the reactants (U 3) – without the gas burner and flame.

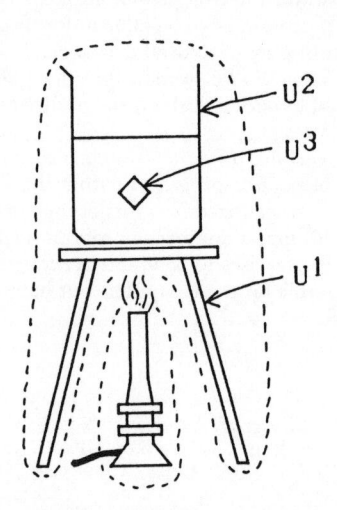

Figure 1. *A model used in science education*

The basic diagram is analysed as block B, unit U, principal unit V and element set E as shown in Figure 2.

```
            ┌─────────┐
            │ Block B │
            └────┬────┘
                 │
            ┌────┴────┐
            │ Unit U  │
            └────┬────┘
                 │
         ┌───────────┐       ┌──────────┐
         │ Principal │-------│ Element  │
         │ Unit V    │       │ Set E    │
         └───────────┘       └──────────┘
```

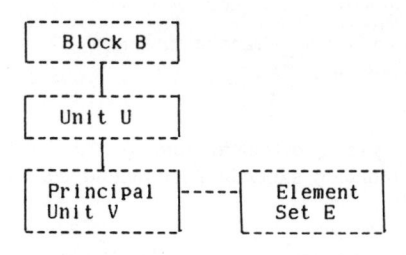

Figure 2. *Analysis of a basic diagram*

Principal unit V can be considered to be the apparatus used very often in experiments. In other words, since a diagram in a demonstration experiment is very often made by combining apparatus, V can be considered to be a logical diagrammatic element. On the other hand, element set E denotes the part(s) incidental to the apparatus (or, denotes apparatus not used very often); for example in Figure 1 the horizontal line indicating the water in the beaker corresponds to E. Therefore E can be considered to be the diagrammatic part, lacking in generality.

Unit U consists of not more than one principal unit or element set and constitutes also a logical diagrammatic unit. Block B consists of plural units and constitutes also a logical diagrammatic unit. It can be considered to be a set of units which are in physical contact with each other.

A characteristic of diagrams in science education is the geometric similarity between a set of principal units. In the depiction of a diagram in a demonstration experiment, dimensions of units are, in many cases, based approximately on the dimensions of the actual apparatus. For example, glass tubes with the same diameter and differing only in length can correspond with each other by expansion and contraction in a single direction. There is a parallel here to the relation between a square and a rectangle in mathematics.

System Construction

This system is composed of JOB 1 to JOB 4, as shown in Figure 3.

JOB 1

File register of principal units – ie principal units to be registered are examined and stored in the principal unit file. In order to clarify the role of each principal unit as an apparatus, two attributes (unit centre and unit axis) are given to it.

Some principal units which have the same configuration may be given different attributes and registered separately. For example, in Figure 4, (a) and (b) are test tubes of the same type, both of which are file-registered and selected in accordance with the role and operationality. In this case, (a) is a test tube to be held by a test-tube holder, while (b) is one to be inserted into a beaker or similar vessel. In the case where an electrode is to be covered by a test tube as shown in (c), the unit centre and axes of test tube (a) can be used more easily for fixing its position.

JOB 1: File register of principal units

JOB 2: Display of principal unit

JOB 3: Diagram depiction using stratified commands

    Block command (parallel transfer, turning, magnifying/reducing, etc)
    |
    Unit command (parallel transfer, turning, magnifying/reducing, expanding/contracting, etc.)
    |
    Principal unit command ———————— element command
    (calling up, giving
    Units relations, etc)

JOB 4: Depicting the diagram using a XY plotter

Figure 3. *System construction*

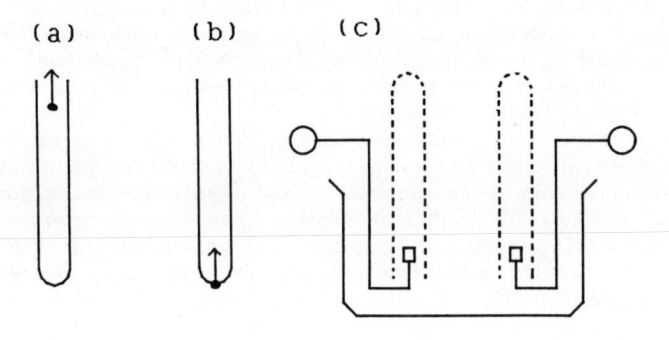

Figure 4. *Two test tubes of the same type and their usage*

JOB 2

Display of principal unit – ie principal unit stored in the file is displayed. This procedure is used to confirm the configuration and attributes of the registered principal unit. For improving the efficiency of diagram depiction a hard copy of principal units should be made.

JOB 3

Diagram depiction – ie a diagram is depicted by using stratified commands. The block command and unit command shown in Figure 3 are the commands to modify the relevant diagrammatic unit.

The principal unit command is the command to call up the desired principal unit on the screen, while the element command is the command to depict or delete lines, circles and the like.

A command is also provided which can give units the potential to superordinate and co-ordinate. Thus, when a unit is given an operation of parallel transfer or turning, all the units subordinate to it will be subjected to the same operation. Thus with this procedure modification of configurations is made easier.

By using this relationship between units, position adjustment of a principal unit can be done as follows. When a principal unit is called up on the screen, a unit on the screen is designated as the superordinate unit; and then the principal unit can be automatically depicted, as the unit centre and unit axis of it will correspond with those of the superordinate unit. For example, Figure 5, (a) shows the principal unit of a test-tube holder. Suppose it is inclined as in (b) and the test-tube (a) is called up on the screen. Now, if the test-tube holder is designated as the superordinate unit, the test-tube will be positioned automatically as in (c).

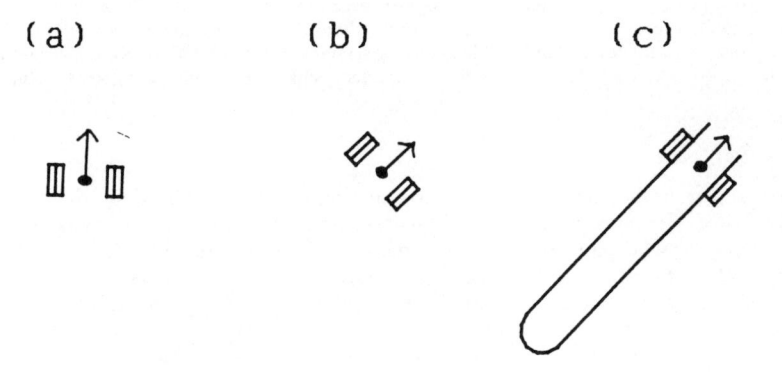

Figure 5. *How to call up a test-tube on the screen*

JOB 4

Diagram output – ie the basic diagram is depicted in colour on OHP transparency (or ordinary sheet) by using the X–Y plotter.

Discussion

This system aims at the flexible modification of configurations, and analyses of a diagram must be done initially. Commands are stratified and given a function to provide units with certain relations. However, these characteristics raise certain problems.

In the initial formulations, relations between units and the analysis of the diagram are difficult to display on the screen of a computer. Accordingly, confusion in the operational procedure has resulted with users when depicting a diagram. To help avoid these problems, we have roughly sketched the basic diagram beforehand on an auxiliary sheet and analysed the diagram. During the work of diagram depiction we have written in the information regarding relations between units on the sheet one after another. In addition, it is necessary for a new user to be given in advance a thorough briefing about the system.

Also, user training in diagram analysis and appropriate relationships between units is necessary to prevent the unnecessary combining of units and the resulting confusion in diagram depiction.

3.16 The Computer as a Learning Tool in University Physics Courses

H Kühnelt
University of Vienna, Austria

Abstract: Traditional courses in theoretical physics prove inadequate for student teachers because they centre on what can be computed with sophisticated mathematics, rather than on physics' relevance to their future. An attempt to improve the situation has been undertaken by integrating microcomputers in the lecture and problem-solving sessions. A number of program packages have been developed. These are described, with the experiences gathered from working with them.

Introduction

Besides research, the main duty of the Institute for Theoretical Physics at the University of Vienna is the teaching of theoretical physics to students of two kinds: physics majors, who want to enter a research career, and future high school physics teachers. A further task is the in-service training of physics teachers.

Traditional courses in theoretical physics (which start after a general introductory course) are intended to provide a better insight into the structure of physics. They concentrate to a large extent on those topics which can be treated through pencil and paper methods. (This is especially true of problem-solving sessions.) Since the language of physics is mathematics, the degree of required mathematical sophistication becomes very high, and sometimes the students' impression is that in every lecture a new mathematical 'trick' is used for solving some equation. The situation is exacerbated by the fact that only a small fraction of physical phenomena can be treated this way. All other effects become 'dirty effects'.

The dilemma may be characterized as follows: the laws of nature are rather simple as far as their mathematical representation is concerned. They are either dynamic laws, like Newton's or Maxwell's laws – describing changes of some quantities with time, or they are conservation laws, like conservation of energy or angular momentum – restricting the possible changes of the dynamic quantities.

But understanding physics means making predictions. For that purpose one needs a whole range of different tricks (which will soon be forgotten if not used regularly) which tend to hide the coherent structure of the underlying physics. Also problems of everyday life are excluded from the course. For teacher training students, with their short exposure to physics, this is a very unsatisfactory situation!

One unacceptable solution would be to drop all deductions of consequences of the laws of physics and to report only the results. However, some factors which point the way to an improved situation are listed below:

- reduction of the mathematical prerequisites;
- increase student interest by more realistic problems;
- enable the student to check his understanding, especially by allowing him to experiment in worlds with different laws of nature through the creation of 'microworlds';
- improve the teaching of difficult concepts by visualization;

☐ introduce new topics of high interest both in terms of current research and of relevance to our understanding of nature. Examples include dynamic systems, and questions of the formation of ordered structures and of transition to chaotic behaviour.

Our Approach

In an effort to provide an improved learning environment (especially the possibility for the student to explore the material presented in the lectures in depth on his own) the following solution has been adopted.

(a) Hardware

Audiovisual equipment, including a sufficient number of TV monitors, has been installed in the lecture room. An integral part is a microcomputer for teacher use during lessons. For student use a small microcomputer lab has been set up.

(b) Software

A set of computer simulation programs has been developed. In the first programs, emphasis has been put on visualization of abstract ideas:

   (i) motion in phase space instead of ordinary space, *paradoxa* of special relativity, etc;
  (ii) topics with high motivational content: physics in sports;
 (iii) new topics: order and chaos.

Students' assignments consisted partly of traditional problem-solving, partly of using the program packages, and partly of a small program project.

An additional benefit for the students was the introduction to computing they obtained in this way. Our students still belong to the generation who did not get any education on computers in their school days, but will have to use them in their professional life.

Success?

Students were forced to use computers and to think about them. This led to polarization and mixed acceptance, as many of them (about 50 per cent in the first term) saw the new possibilities as an additional burden. Acceptance improved in the second term to about 75 per cent.

A second relevant observation showed that the tool character of computer programs has not really been acknowledged by the students. Instead of using programs to study the behaviour of the model system, they wanted to analyse the program. This may be due to the relative novelty of computers and the idea that computers have to be programmed.

In terms of staff acceptance, the two-term course covering mechanics, electrodynamics, thermodynamics and quantum mechanics has been delivered by a member of the development team, who has put great efforts into this course. But lecturers change, and everybody prefers his personal style. In order to be used by lecturers outside the development team software

   (a) has to be very flexible to be adaptable to different teaching styles,
   (b) must be very user friendly, self-explanatory and fault tolerant, and
   (c) must cover the full course (which has not yet been achieved).

Packages Developed So Far

Programs are considered of limited usefulness if they are not accompanied by support material in printed form. This is especially true if programs are to be used for independent study by students and in in-service training. One could provide all information as HELP files on the computer, but then its use is restricted to log-on time.

The printed documentation includes background information about the physics content, information on the numerical methods used, problems for using the program with varying parameters, problems suggesting modification of the underlying models or even of the program, and information about the structure of the program. Useful parameter ranges have to be given as well as typical results. The less familiar a topic is, the more information is needed.

The programs have been developed in BASIC for Apple II with support routines for graphics written in machine language. We are now transferring them to GW-BASIC for MS-DOS machines, but future work will use PASCAL to improve portability.

A Short Description of the Physics Content of the Packages

(a) *Einstein's world (paradoxa of special relativity). Light clocks. Simultaneity. Synchronization. Moving systems of reference. Addition of velocities. Travel through space. Nonexistence of rigid bodies. Appearance of fast-moving objects.* Relativity can be treated with different levels of abstraction (Sexl, 1985) ranging from popular science to differential calculus. As a theoretical framework it is a coherent system, but to grasp the coherence it is necessary to ask about the consequences of leaving out a piece. This can be done in computer simulation, whereby the origin of certain *paradoxa* of special relativity become apparent.

(b) *Physics in sports.* Physics applied to tennis, golf, sailing, and soccer.

(c) *Order and chaos. The complicated behaviour of simple mappings: the logistic growth law.* Non-linear systems with deterministic behaviour, which nevertheless show the limits of predictability: the Lorenz equations of Benard convection, and the chaotic behaviour of a model for the earth's magnetic field.

(d) *Numerical approximation methods for differential equations.* A laboratory for exploring different methods of confronting students with physics problems, not with the usual problems from courses on numerical mathematics.

Reference

Sexl, R U (1985) Einstein's world on computer. In Marx, G and Szücs, P (eds) *Proceedings of International Workshop on the Use of Microcomputers in Science Education*. International Centre for Educational Technology, Veszprem, Hungary.

Acknowledgement

The work reported in this paper has been done by the members of the working unit Microcomputers in Physics Education, ie RU Sexl, A Pflug, H Rupertsberger, M Kugler, P Jakesch and the author. We thank the Austrian Ministry for Science and Research for its financial support.

3.17 Learning Linear and Integer Programming in a Mathematics Laboratory

T D Scott
Napier College, Edinburgh

Abstract: In this paper a new approach to learning linear and integer programming is described. The method involves a specially developed computer package for use in a mathematics microcomputer laboratory. The standard linear programming problem is stated, together with an economic interpretation; and in this context, an example is given of the type of investigation for which the laboratory is ideally suited. A description of the package is included with an explanation of its various facilities. In Appendix I, the mathematical background of the linear programming problem is given. Appendix II contains a worked example which illustrates the use of the package in analysing the behaviour of a firm; and, in Appendix III, consideration is given to the role of the package in solving integer and mixed integer programming problems by the branch and bound method.

Introduction

In many undergraduate courses, linear programming is introduced as a topic within the mathematics syllabus, and usually commands only a small proportion of the total time available. With conventional teaching methods it is therefore virtually impossible to progress beyond an elementary treatment of the concepts and algorithms used.

At Napier College, in the department of mathematics, a new approach has been successfully developed. With the advent of the mathematics microcomputer laboratory, it has become possible to extend the student's learning quite considerably. The method involves the use of the computer package LINPROG, which has been developed on a BBC microcomputer, together with worksheets which direct the student towards specific learning objectives.

Having introduced the student to linear and/or integer programming (either within or outside the laboratory), the package can first be used to reinforce the user's understanding of the algorithms involved. Second, with an appropriate worksheet, a single laboratory session is sufficient to allow useful and realistic problems to be explored. Finally, the student is encouraged to experiment with problem parameters and investigate their effect on particular solutions. It is this latter analysis, in particular, which enhances the student's learning; and the laboratory environment is essential for the work involved.

The Standard Linear Programming Problem

The 'primal' problem takes the form

$$\left. \begin{array}{l} \text{Maximize } I = c_1x_1 + c_2x_2 + \ldots + c_nx_n \\ \text{subject to } x_1, x_2, \ldots, x_n \geq 0 \\ \quad a_{11}x_1 + a_{12}x_2 + \ldots + a_{1n}x_n \leq b_1 \\ \quad a_{21}x_1 + a_{22}x_2 + \ldots + a_{2n}x_n \leq b_2 \\ \quad \cdots\cdots\cdots\cdots\cdots\cdots\cdots\cdots\cdots\cdots\cdots\cdots\cdots \\ \quad a_{m1}x_1 + a_{m2}x_2 + \ldots + a_{mn}x_n \leq b_m \end{array} \right\} \ldots \text{I}$$

and the corresponding 'dual' problem is

$$\begin{rcases}
\text{Minimize } Z = b_1\lambda_1 + b_2\lambda_2 + \ldots + b_m\lambda_m \\
\text{subject to } \lambda_1, \lambda_2, \ldots, \lambda_m \geq 0 \\
\quad a_{11}\lambda_1 + a_{21}\lambda_2 + \ldots + a_{m1}\lambda_m \geq C_1 \\
\quad a_{12}\lambda_1 + a_{22}\lambda_2 + \ldots + a_{m2}\lambda_m \geq C_2 \\
\quad \ldots\ldots\ldots\ldots\ldots\ldots\ldots\ldots\ldots\ldots\ldots\ldots\ldots\ldots \\
\quad a_{1n}\lambda_1 + a_{2n}\lambda_2 + \ldots + a_{mn}\lambda_m \geq C_n
\end{rcases} \ldots \text{II}$$

A derivation of the standard problem is given in Appendix I.

An Economic Interpretation

The primal problem above models a firm which produces n outputs $(x_1, x_2, \ldots, x_n)$, with n associated selling prices $(c_1, c_2, \ldots, c_n)$. There are m factors of production, of which the firm has on hand b_1 units of the first, b_2 units of the second, etc. The firm has a technology represented by the matrix A: that is, the production of one unit of good i requires a_{1i} units of factor 1, a_{2i} units of factor 2, and so on. The problem facing the firm is to maximize its gross revenue

$$c^T x = c_1 x_1 + c_2 x_2 + \ldots + c_n x_n \text{ subject to the production constraints } Ax \leq b.$$

In this model, λ is a vector of factor prices (often referred to as 'shadow prices') which reflect the value that the firm places on its resources. If factor i is not completely utilized in the production programme which maximizes revenue, then its imputed price λ_i must be zero. Similarly, if, at the imputed factor prices λ, the unit cost of producing one unit of good j is greater than its selling price c_j, then the output x_j will be zero. For this model, the value of output at market prices equals the cost of production in terms of the shadow prices. An example of this type of problem, and its solution using LINPROG, is given in Appendix II.

Post-Optimal Analysis

An analysis of the effects of changes in the problem formulation, after the optimal solution has been found, is usually as important as (and often more interesting than) solving the original problem. Such an analysis typically involves the following types of investigation:

(a) *Sensitivity analysis*, to determine the range of values of some parameter over which the optimal solution remains optimal, and
(b) *Parametric programming*, to decide how the optimal solution changes as some parameter of the problem is varied through a given range.

In the context of the economic interpretation given above, three important cases lend themselves to laboratory investigation.

Case 1 (Playing with Prices)

It is obviously useful to know how sensitive an optimal solution is to changes in market prices. The following questions may be explored:

(i) For a given change in one price, or in a number of prices, does the production plan remain unchanged? If so, in which way and by how much is the firm's revenue altered?
(ii) Holding all other factors equal, over what price range for a given output will the original optimal basis stay the same?
(iii) If changes in the prices of goods result in a different production schedule, what is the new optimal solution, and how are the factor prices affected?

Case 2 (Fiddling with Factors)

First, it is worth noting that the analysis for the resource vector entries is entirely symmetric with that of the objective function coefficients. In the light of duality, precisely the same questions (as in Case 1 above) can be applied to the firm's dual problem of minimizing production costs.

However, the most common requirement is the optimal solution to the primal problem as a function of the availability of one (or more) of the firm's resources. For example, the supply of factor i may be uncertain, even though its price was fixed at the time of contract. In this case, it would be useful to know the optimal production combinations for *any* amount of factor i, from some lower limit (perhaps zero) to some upper limit (possibly unlimited).

Case 3 (Tinkering with the Technology)

Another reason for exploring changes in problem formulation is that the elements of the matrix A may be best estimates, with the actual values unknown. It would, therefore, be useful to know how sensitive the optimal solution is to changes in any of these 'technical coefficients', $\{a_{ij}\}$. Analyses where two or more coefficients vary together as a function of a parameter are also possible.

(c) *Adding Variables or Constraints*
In many real situations it is necessary, after obtaining a preliminary solution, to alter the problem by adding variables or constraints not previously considered. Increasing the number of the firm's outputs by one provides a new dimension and increases the solution space, so that all previously available production plans are still feasible, with the addition of some new possibilities. Hence, the firm's maximum revenue cannot be lowered by the introduction of another product, and it may well be increased. Conversely, by adding another constraint, no new options are made available. Indeed, some of the previously feasible solutions may become infeasible. Therefore the firm's maximum revenue cannot be improved with the addition of a new constraint, and it is likely to decrease.

Some illustrations of the above analyses are described in Appendix II.

The Package

LINPROG is structured in such a way that the investigations of the previous section can be carried out easily and efficiently. Prior to its availability, too much of the student's time was spent on computational aspects, and correspondingly less time was devoted to modelling and analysing realistic problems. With the introduction of the package, in the environment of a laboratory, the user has, at his disposal, a flexible piece of 'apparatus' with which he can confidently conduct reasonable 'experiments' in linear programming.

The program has been developed by Mrs D Mackie, a member of the Mathematics Department at Napier College, in collaboration with the author (who is *not* a computer programmer).

It has clearly defined objectives, is easy to use and does not require a user manual. The user selects from a range of facilities, each of which is clearly explained at the appropriate stage. If the user is unclear as to how he should proceed, or if he fails to answer a question correctly, the program leads him in an appropriate direction.

The aims of LINPROG include:

- □ the enhancement of the user's understanding of linear programming, and, in particular, the Simplex method;
- □ the provision of a useful tool for solving linear programming problems;

☐ an efficient implementation of the branch and bound method for solving integer programming problems (Appendix III);
☐ a promotion of the investigative work which arises in linear programming problems, typically sensitivity analysis and/or parametric programming.

The package copes with three main classes of problem:

(a) *Standard linear programming problems* of the type described previously. There are many realistic problems of this nature. For these problems the user can follow a tableau-by-tableau display through the Simplex method. The user is asked to select the pivot element, to decide when the solution is optimal and to extract the solution from the final tableau.
    Minimization problems are solved by first forming the dual problem.
(b) *General linear programming problems* where any combination of constraints is allowed. To facilitate a post-optimal analysis of the solution, the user may change a coefficient in the objective function, alter the right-hand side of one of the constraints, update the coefficients of the original constraints, or simply add a further constraint. In each of these cases, it is not necessary to retype the original problem.
(c) *Integer and mixed integer programming problems*. The initial problem is solved as for a general linear programming problem. The user can then add further constraints and solve the new problem thus formed or return to the initial set of constraints. Thus the branch and bound method can be implemented with ease.

Appendix I

The Kuhn-Tucker theorem (Kuhn and Tucker, 1951) proves that maximizing a concave function $f(x)$ on a convex constraint set $C = \{x: g_i(x) \geq 0\}$ is equivalent to the Lagrangian function $G(x,\lambda) = f(x) + \lambda_i g_i(x)$ having a saddle point, $(x°,\lambda°)$. Linear programming is merely a special case in which $f(x) = c^T x$ and $g_i(x) = b_i - a^i x$, where a^i is the ith row of an (m × n) matrix A, so that $c \in R^n$, $a^i \in R^n$ and $b_i \in R$ (ie the constraints are hyperplanes). We can, therefore, state the linear programming problem as:

$$\left. \begin{array}{l} \text{Maximize } c^T x \\ \text{subject to } Ax \leq b \end{array} \right\} \quad \cdots\cdots\cdots \quad \text{I}$$

Furthermore, if $x°$ maximizes $c^T x$ on the set $C = \{x: Ax \leq b\}$, then $\lambda°$ minimizes $b^T \lambda$ on the set $C^* = \{\lambda: A^T \lambda \geq C\}$. This property is called 'duality' (Bunday, 1984), and problem I may be referred to as the 'primal' problem with the corresponding 'dual' problem:

$$\left. \begin{array}{l} \text{Minimize } b^T \lambda \\ \text{subject to } A^T \lambda \geq C \end{array} \right\} \quad \cdots\cdots\cdots \quad \text{II}$$

Given that $G(x,\lambda) = c^T x + \lambda^T(b - Ax)$, and defining $G^*(\lambda,x) = -b^T \lambda + x^T(A^T \lambda - c)$, it follows that $G^*(\lambda,x) = -G(x,\lambda)$, and, in particular, $G^*(\lambda°,x°) = -G(x°,\lambda°)$. Therefore,

$$c^T x° = b^T \lambda°,$$

since $(Ax° - b)^T \lambda° = 0 = (A^T \lambda° - c)^T x°$. (This is known as the complementary slackness condition.)

Appendix II

A firm produces four products, X_1, X_2, X_3 and X_4, using three factors of production F_1, F_2 and F_3. The firm's technology is given by the matrix

$$A = \begin{bmatrix} 1 & 2 & 3 & 0 \\ 2 & 3 & 0 & 1 \\ 1 & 1 & 3 & 2 \end{bmatrix}$$

Given that the unit prices of the four products are $c_1 = £300$, $c_2 = £500$, $c_3 = £700$ and $c_4 = £200$ respectively, and that the weekly supplies of the three factors are $b_1 = 100$, $b_2 = 70$ and $b_3 = 80$, the firm requires a weekly production schedule which maximizes its total revenue.

The firm's problem can be stated as:

Maximize $300x_1 + 500x_2 + 700x_3 + 200x_4$, where $x_1, x_2, x_3, x_4 \geq 0$ are the weekly outputs of the four products, subject to the constraints

$$\begin{aligned} x_1 + 2x_2 + 3x_3 &\leq 100, \\ 2x_1 + 3x_2 + x_4 &\leq 70, \\ x_1 + x_2 + 3x_3 + 2x_4 &\leq 80, \end{aligned}$$

which has the solution

$$\begin{aligned} x_1 &= 0, \\ x_2 &= 22.9, \\ x_3 &= 18.1, \\ x_4 &= 1.43, \end{aligned}$$

giving a gross revenue of £24380.95 with shadow prices for F_1, F_2 and F_3 of $\lambda_1 = £152$, $\lambda_2 = £38.10$ and $\lambda_3 = £81$ respectively.

If the selling price c_2 is increased to £700, say, the production plan remains unchanged, although the revenue naturally increases to £28952.38. In fact, as the price of X_2 is increased further, the amounts produced do not alter for $c_2 \leq £1000$. When $c_2 = £1000$, the revenue is £35809.52, and the shadow prices become $\lambda_1 = £224$, $\lambda_2 = £181$ and $\lambda_3 = £9.52$.

However, if the price of X_2 goes as high as £1070, it becomes profitable for the firm to stop producing X_4, reduce its production of X_3 to 17.8 and increase production of X_2 to 23.3. With this schedule, the revenue is £37411.11 and the shadow prices are $\lambda_1 = £233$, $\lambda_2 = £201$ and $\lambda_3 = £0.00$. Notice that $\lambda_3 = 0$ suggests that the third constraint of the primal problem has become 'slack', which is indeed the case (thus confirming the principle of complementary slackness).

At the other end of the price range, c_2 has to decrease by no more than £17 before the production plan changes. For $c_2 = £483$, the optimal solution is

$$\begin{aligned} x_1 &= 5, \\ x_2 &= 20, \\ x_3 &= 18.3, \\ x_4 &= 0, \end{aligned}$$

with a revenue of £23993.33, and shadow prices $\lambda_1 = £150$, $\lambda_2 = £33.30$ and $\lambda_3 = £83.70$. This completes one example of a sensitivity analysis.

If none of factor F_2 is available, while b_1 and b_3 remain fixed, the firm will produce 26.7 units of X_3 only. As soon as F_2 becomes available in any quantity, production of X_2 begins with a consequent reduction in x_3. x_1 and x_4 remain at zero until $b_2 > 60$. When $b_2 = 60$, $x_2 = x_3 = 20$ and the firm's revenue is £24000. As b_2 increases from 60 to 165, the production of X_4 increases from zero, x_2 continues to rise and x_3 decreases towards zero. At $b_2 = 165$, the firm produces only X_2 and X_4 in quantities of 50 and 15, respectively, for an income of £28000, and increasing the supply of F_2 further has no effect on this final solution. This is an application of parametric programming.

Suppose that, during a particular week, total output has to be restricted to 50 units. The effect of this is the introduction of the additional constraint $x_1 + x_2 + x_3 + x_4 \leq 50$. However, in this case, the extra constraint is redundant, since $x_1 + x_2 + x_3 + x_4 = 42.43$ at the optimum, so that the new constraint is already satisfied. If the restriction is to 40 units, this time the new constraint is $x_1 + x_2 + x_3 + x_4 \leq 40$, and the new solution is

$x_1 = 0,$
$x_2 = 20,$
$x_3 = 20,$
$x_4 = 0,$

giving a total revenue of £24000.

Finally, suppose that the firm has the opportunity to extend its range of products, the new technology being

$$A = \begin{bmatrix} 1 & 2 & 3 & 0 & 2 \\ 2 & 3 & 0 & 1 & 4 \\ 1 & 1 & 3 & 2 & 1 \end{bmatrix}$$

Given that the price of the new product is c_5, the firm will only produce positive amounts of X_5 if c_5 is high enough. For example, if $c_5 = £300$, then X_5 will not be produced, but, if $c_5 = £800$, then the solution becomes

$x_1 = 0,$
$x_2 = 0,$
$x_3 = 20.8,$
$x_4 = 0,$
$x_5 = 17.5,$

giving a gross revenue of £28583.33. In fact, x_5 remains non-basic if $c_5 \leq £538$.

The above results by no means exhaust the production possibilities of the firm, but rather they provide some insight into the post-optimal analyses that are possible, and easily implemented, using LINPROG.

Appendix III

The standard integer programming problem is given in the text with the added condition that $x_1, x_2, \ldots, x_n$ must be integer valued. If only some of the x_i have to be integers, problem I becomes a mixed integer programming problem. Both types of problem, and indeed any general integer/mixed integer programming problem, can be solved using the branch and bound method. This algorithm typically involves adding constraints to a previously solved linear programming problem, or returning to a previous solution; and, since both these options are available with LINPROG, the method can be used very efficiently.

For example, the firm described in Appendix II might require some or all of its outputs to be integers for the solution to be sensible. In this case, the problem becomes a (mixed) integer programming problem, requiring the implementation of the branch and bound method. In particular, if x_1, x_2, x_3 and x_4 take only integer values, the solution becomes

$x_1 = 0$
$x_2 = 23$
$x_3 = 18$
$x_4 = 1,$

giving a gross revenue of £24300.00.

Reference

Kuhn, H W and Tucker, A W (1951) Non-linear programming. In Neyman, (ed) *Proceedings of the Second Berkeley Symposium on Mathematical Statistics and Probability*. University of California Press, Berkeley.

3.18 An 'Intelligent' Approach to Computer Aided Learning: G

M F W Meurrens
Free University of Brussels, Belgium

Abstract: G is a methodology and a system based on seven intelligent learning concepts.
   It is a microcomputer package, now available on most PC compatibles, using computer graphics and taking advantage of artificial intelligence concepts. G is designed to fulfil scientific requirements as well as human sciences; it is used in elementary schools as well as for graduate students in many areas of education (physics, law, etc).
   Its strategy, based on a distinct modelization of (a) the knowledge, (b) the pedagogical approach, (c) the student's 'profile', allows really fast production of scenario-less courseware.

Introduction

Computer aided learning (CAL) can be viewed as a way to fill in the gap between the computer and the educational process. Classical approaches can be viewed as a step from the computer in the direction of the learning process: they use several tools, such as programming languages or tutorial systems, and provide satisfactory answers to computing problems, screen management, etc. However, algorithmic methods start to fail when natural languages or really complex reasoning methods are involved. Furthermore, the number of hours spent by the teacher, expert or programmer to produce one hour of dialogue with the student often reaches 100 or more.
   G's approach is based on a modelization of the learning process. It starts from this model and moves in the direction of the computer. This implies that it is well suited for natural languages processing or for reasoning simulation. However, G was not designed to provide full screen control, and access to programming languages is still restricted.
   One of the main features of G is that no pre-programmed scenario is needed or *even allowed*. The absence of a pre-programmed scenario guarantees an individual approach for each student.
   Furthermore, G only handles data (eg text) but no programming is involved at all and G does not include instructions such as 'run this screen' or 'branch to that step' or 'goto this module', etc. This leads to a production ratio of 15 teacher hours per one student hour.

Seven Intelligent Learning Concepts

1. The most important word in the phrase 'computer assisted learning' is 'learning' not 'computer'.
   CAL helps the learning process in allowing the pupil to discover, doubt, understand, verify, progress, etc. Multiple choice or endless repetition are definitively outside G's goals.

2. Building a CAL system involves three basic questions: *what* are the topics to be learned? *how* to teach it? *who* is learning?

3. Building computer-based courseware must be as easy (as difficult), as cheap (as expensive) and as time-consuming in comparison with other conversational and multimedia course preparations.

Computer-based courseware must take account of a conversation between three units: the student, the teacher, the computer. Each of them provides questions or answers; each of them uses natural languages. Errors, mispelling, mistyping, etc must be processed.

4. What is to be learned? The basic structure of the learning is a set of concepts (knowledge, facts, attitudes). This set must be easily extended, modified or revised. These concepts are mutually independent (each concept may be directly accessed by a student) and are bounded (the access to a given concept implies an interest in accessing one or more other concepts).

These concepts are defined, in G, as 'C object'; they are implemented as a set of records (of one to ten fields). Data entry is realized through a full screen editor.

5. How is it taught? The learning process implies the existence of a set of *elementary* tools. These tools must be available to let G organize a dialogue with the student but all are not necessarily used within a given dialogue. Examples of tools are demonstrations, examples, questions, discussions, etc.

This set of tools must be easily extended, modified or revised. These tools are totally independent: G does not provide the opportunity to branch from one to another (just as one could imagine with steps within a pre-programmed dialogue).

Each tool has an 'external definition' similar to the description of a rule: *prerequisites* are the C objects the student must know before using this tool; *objectives* are the C objects the student must 'desire' in order to use this tool.

Each tool also has an 'internal definition': the sentences of a short dialogue and the rules for analysis of the answers.

These tools are defined, in G, as 'P object'; they are implemented as a set of records. Data entry is realized through a full screen editor.

6. Who is learning? Each individual or student is unique. No scenario has to be pre-programmed.

G records for each student all that he already knows, all that should be learned in the future (with priorities), and all that was already performed so that unexpected repetitions are automatically excluded.

Real time dialogue (ie which P object must now be used) is organized by G, taking into account the student *profile*, which C objects the student already knows, which objects he should now learn, which P objects were already used, etc.

Sometimes, no P object is available for immediate use and G computes the best path. Often, however, more than one solution exists; G makes a choice by posing alternatives and/or random choices. In any case, this leads to personalized dialogue including unattempted, but well justified, situations.

7. A CAL system must operate in real educational situations: tricky problems, hazardous solutions, incomplete knowledge, memory lapses, etc.

Implementation

G is a microcomputer package well suited for the teaching of complex courses, using case studies, text discussions, 'learn by doing' strategies, etc. While G was not designed for game-like screen control, it can be used in place of other teaching methods and for the evaluation of the student by himself or by the teacher.

G is a full system including many features such as:

- ☐ intelligent management of messages;
- ☐ management of unexpected answers and unexpected situations;

- graphic capabilities to visualize the learning process;
- natural languages (G is multilingual) processing (allowing mispelling), and so on.

3.19 A Competence-based Learning Strategy

P M Roxburgh
Hartlepool College of Further Education

Abstract: Competence is a student-centred concept. It has a structure of knowledge and skill set in a matrix of attitudes and relationships. A competence record for individual students will require a large data storage facility. An effective competence-based learning strategy, therefore, requires the establishment of a computer-based system of record keeping. This must be simple and provide a picture of individual student progress. The system must encompass career roles and assignments; profiles and feedback; and administration. The career roles are negotiable contracts between the learner and the sponsor. They are computerized packages of weighted skill areas, attainable through individualized assignments.

The computerized profiles have learning as the predominant feature, achieved through supportive feedback. This feedback is formative at the objectives focus and summative at the skill competence focus and skill area focus.

The administration is a recording and reporting computerized system. It has provision for a large data storage system with a facility to carry forward summative statements to the next stage of learning.

In order to manage a competence-based learning resource, together with its computerized support system, the traditional specialist teacher must acquire the counselling and facilitating skills required in the management of learning.

Introduction

The Hartlepool Project is concerned with improving the effectiveness of student learning, while utilizing the data handling capacity of a microcomputer support facility. We have investigated student-centred learning through extended contact with a large number of students/trainees over the past ten years, identifying the barriers to learning which they have actually experienced. This project is designed to remove some of these barriers.

The system attempts to alleviate some of the data handling problems resulting from the introduction of a student-centred learning strategy. It is designed to answer some of the questions arising from the following:

- ☐ profiling for all the learners by 1990
- ☐ negotiation between learners, teachers and employers during the learning and assessment
- ☐ assessments, both formative and summative
- ☐ profiling being undertaken on top of heavy teaching commitment
- ☐ significant changes necessary in almost every aspect of the learning provision
- ☐ the role identification of counsellor, curriculum evaluator, action researcher
- ☐ negotiation of the career roles of the individual learner with employers
- ☐ the preparation of the learners for their involvement in formative assessment and profiling
- ☐ enabling learners to develop their capacity to review and reflect upon their learning.

Background

The present system of education is a teacher-centred system with a norm referenced assessment strategy, requiring a large administrative role.

This strategy, which is examination-driven, consists essentially of comparing a student's/pupil's attainments with that of others, and establishing an examinee's relative position. Normative scores do not tell what a pupil/student knows or can do, they only tell whether they know or can do more than the others. There is within the strategy very little opportunity for the individual students/pupils to learn at their own rate.

The aim of a norm referenced approach is to provide assessments that will be used as widely as possible, and are therefore unlikely to be congruent with any given college/school curriculum reference. In looking for a common factor across the curricula, their construction fails to emphasize the particular content and skill which characterize individual courses against which student's/pupil's capabilities should be assessed. The outcomes from such an approach might well provide an administratively satisfactory system, but do very little for the individual learner.

The following indicates some of the frailties of the present position in education.

1. Items in the assessment instrument which all students/pupils get correct, for whatever reason, are rejected. These may be the best items for measuring what the student/pupil has achieved.
2. There is no indication given of the nature of the help needed as a result of an assessment.
3. A student/pupil assessment score signifies relative performance on a haphazard collection of test items.
4. A student's/pupil's total mark may be attained by the student/pupil in many different ways, but the total, together with the rank order, is all that is recorded.
5. The norm referenced approach has a direct effect on the student's/pupil's motivation to learn. They appreciate very quickly that what matters is not their own achievements, but how they compare with others. A succession of poor comparative grades can have serious effects on a student's/pupil's motivation and self-esteem.
6. There is an assumption that there is a normal distribution of achievement among students/pupils, rather than groupings of students/pupils who have mastered different levels of work.
7. There is scant use being made of the process whereby assessments are used to identify weak aspects of instruction.
8. There is very little use being made of the assessment purpose of facilitating and improving the quality of communication of information about what students/pupils can or cannot do, among teachers, employers, parents, local authorities, government and the students/pupils themselves.
9. Although colleges/schools should not necessarily be concerned with selecting students/pupils for employment or further study, they have the responsibility to provide profiles of student/pupil attainments that will enable those who do have to make a selection to do it on a more valid basis than the present system allows.

Statistical evidence has been provided by a large number of surveys and research projects, resulting in significant moves away from a norm referenced teacher-centred approach in the educational provision to a criterion referenced student/pupil-centred strategy, with a major shift of emphasis to 'learning to learn' and the identification of the needs of the individual learner.

The pressure to develop a system such as that proposed in the Hartlepool Project exists because, if a criterion referenced strategy is to be effective, it is necessary to establish a system of record-keeping that is simple, short, and provides a picture of each student's/pupil's progress and the progress of the class, but that is unencumbered by other information that may be wanted for other purposes by the teacher, the college, the local authority or any other body. Moreover if the criterion referenced strategy is to be effective, administration and curriculum developers must be allowed the time and training needed to implement them. Most of all, there must be support systems that make it possible for teachers to use them in an effective and efficient manner.

Outcomes

Competence is a student-centred concept, with a structure of knowledge and skills set in a matrix of attitudes and relationships. If such a strategy is to succeed, a system must be developed to allow access to the attitudes and relationships element of the matrix. Records arrived at using competence objectives for individual students will require a large data handling facility. An effective competence-based learning strategy therefore requires the establishment of a computer-based system of record keeping. This, for the Hartlepool project, is entitled the REULL system.

The REULL system must be simple to use, and provide a picture of individual student progress.

The outcomes of the project will be fourfold.

(a) Career Roles and Assignments

Career roles are negotiable contracts between the learner and sponsor. They will be computerized packages of weighted skill areas attainable using individualized assignments.

Roles:
(VENUS)
This program enables the assembly of individualized career roles, from prepared catalogues of related skill areas.

The career role is an agreement of intent, which is assembled in consultation with the learner and the sponsor, and indicates the required bias for each of the skill areas of the role.

The career role is held in a program file, available for modification and update at any time during the learning period.

The program output is in the form of bar charts which indicate the following:

(i) the initial career role as an agreement of intent (projection);
(ii) a sequence of amended career roles as dated modifications made to the initial role (progressive);
(iii) the final career role presented at the completion of the learning period.

Satellite 1 (Projects)
This program enables the construction of work-based or simulated projects.

The projects are designed within the following parameters:

(i) a selection of skill areas drawn from a library;
(ii) an identification of the number and discipline of the personnel involved in the project;
(iii) a declared recommended time for completion of the project.

A project is the vehicle for achieving competence in the various skill areas of the career role.

Assignments:
(MERCURY)
An assignment is an individual student's response to a group project, where all the responses of the group members are complementary to the solution of the project.

The relationship and attitudinal responses of the assignments are those resulting from the interaction of group members, and will require a more subjective assessment.

The program enables the assembly of multi-discipline packages of learning objectives. These packages will contain all of the objectives necessary to design a task-based response to the problems set by a work-based project. The tasks and their objectives are selected in consultation with the learner and the sponsor. They are held in a program file, available for modification and updating, in response to any career role changes.

The scope and standard/level of the assignment is determined by the objectives selected for the tasks.

To provide a learning support and record of achievement, the following feedback is available for each assignment:

(i) a series of 'formative profiles' (tier I) from the 'transaction' program of REULL, with supporting statements, for the individual learner;
(ii) a list of summative responses to satisfy both the sponsor (competence statements) and the certificating bodies (grades of achievement). These particular responses are available from the 'profiles' program of REULL.

(b) Learning Profiles

These support the learning process with adequate feedback. The feedback will be formative at the competence objective focus, and summative at the task competence and skill area focus.

Transactions: (EARTH)
This is the program which identifies the formative focus of the package. It is an easy to use program which is designed to accept individual student scores, achieved against the agreed objectives. This output (the first of three tiers of profiles available from the package) is the 'objective profile', in the form of bar charts, and provides immediate feedback to the student/trainee. Additional information is provided for the lecturer/instructor in the form of an analysis of the student/trainee groups' response to an assessment and the assessing material. This is necessary for curriculum review. All assessment resits are catered for by this program.

Satellite 1 (Groups):
This program enables the setting up of day files on which data relative to specific groups of students in register/class form may be stored, and subsequently used relative to their day of attendance/assessment, for retrieval of information.

EARTH with its SATELLITE is the work-horse of the package.

Profiles: (JUPITER)
This is a program that provides on demand the two other tiers of student profiling. JUPITER summarizes the individual student's/trainee's score/competence for each phase test/skill area assessment, and presents a cumulative tier II profile as a list of competence statements – thus providing an immediately available snapshot of student/trainee achievements.

A further summary of assessment scores/competences for each unit/module, is presented as a tier III summative profile using feedback material drawn from a bank of achievement statements. JUPITER will provide the index of the individual student's/trainee's log book.

(c) Administration

This will be an administrative support system for recording learning achievements and managing strategy. It will have provision for a large data storage, with facility to carry forward summative statements to the next stage of learning.

Package Administration: (SUN)
: This program was designed specifically to provide support and guidance in the creation of the system's files and directories. SUN is the housekeeping program with responsibility for care and maintenance, including modification and deletion facilities across the system.

Registration: (URANUS)
: This is a user-friendly program designed specifically for facilitating an accurate registration of students/trainees on a unit/module-based programme of learning. It enables the storage of individual student/trainee study profiles, student/trainee – employer lists, and student/trainee group lists for units/modules. URANUS is the enrolment program.

(d) Staff Development

Activity here will prepare outline staff training packages to allow the project outcomes to be used in the YTS/CPVE and Technical and Vocational Educational Initiative (TVEI) schemes.

In order to manage a competence-based learning strategy, together with a computerized support system, the traditional specialist teacher must acquire skills in the counselling and facilitating required of such a strategy.

Closing Address
The Significance of Flexible Learning Systems

N E Paine
Assistant Director (Learning Systems), Scottish Council for Educational Technology (SCET), Glasgow

Unlike the other keynote speakers whose eminence demands originality in thought and presentation, the person chosen for the closing address has the strength of eclecticism. He has the great advantage of being able to borrow the good ideas that have emerged from the conference and share those with delegates with complete impunity. If we look at this in its most favourable light we can call it, according to Bloom's taxonomy, a higher level cognitive skill: synthesis.

Many of the ideas which have been shared at ETIC 86 are not original ideas. Many of the themes, philosophies and experiments undertaken have new target groups, new media and perhaps new methods, but the overall underpinning philosophy – to create increasing choice and autonomy for the learner – has been with us for a long time.

Why then are we not simply going round in circles and why is the theme for ETIC 86 important and well chosen?

The answer to that lies in a formula put forward by Tom Foggo, an independent consultant, but once a senior manager with ICI. He explained that:

$$C = f[A,B,C,] > I$$

This formula might not have mathematical credibility but I feel it has tremendous educational validity.

C = change or innovation.

Change or innovation will occur in both the education system and in industry when the factors of $[f]$:

  A: the perceived need for change
  B: the ultimate vision or goal is clear, and
  C: we know what first steps to take

are seen to be greater than the investment 'I' required to implement that change. This investment can be in terms of cash or people.

The three factors are not absolute criteria, but relative criteria. If the investment is *perceived* to be too great, change will not occur.

It is perhaps that formula which explains why the tremendous interest in innovation and change embraced by the delegates at ETIC 86 is not change for change's sake or innovation to justify activity. It is a reflection of the genuine feeling that we live in a changing world and that both the education and training systems will have to move to keep pace with that world and to remain relevant. For once, the need for change outweighs the required investment.

Even a diligent conference-goer could not have attended more than 15 or 20 per cent of the sessions at this conference. It would be possible for two delegates to come away with an entirely different perception of what was being said, but for the first time at an ETIC conference that I have attended, there was a degree of common ground between sessions that was striking. The theme of the conference was picked up again and again in sessions, and points made in keynote addresses were used by parallel session leaders to reinforce their own points and philosophies.

ETIC 86 had a genuine and deeply felt theme that struck a chord for the vast majority of people in attendance.

It is also true to say that many conference speakers actually 'put their philosophies into action', in other words the kinds of presentations that we were subject to moved a long way from the conventional delivery of a written paper. There was a new confidence in the speakers; and the groups were involved and receptive.

I attended a presentation looking at open learning in an industrial context via a detailed case study of Lucas Industries and their use of open learning systems.

The actual lessons learned by Lucas were developed by delegates via small group work, looking at the factors that Lucas had to take into account and asking the group to develop their own model to implement open learning. This was compared with the eventual model that Lucas implemented.

I attended a session which was looking at the constraints of introducing flexibility into the educational curriculum. This was covered by a game (or more appropriately a simulation) which allowed people present to make decisions about which aspects of the curriculum they would open and assess the resource implications of this.

The game was played twice, firstly as a naive user and secondly as a more experienced practitioner aware of some of the resource implications. The difference between the two sessions was then discussed and the lessons learned by each group was shared.

Both of these presentations could have been delivered as conventional papers. They would have been less exciting, made less of an impact and not illustrated their message in nearly as stark a way as they did. For most people at the conference the lesson seemed patently obvious: participation meant greater learning, greater enjoyment and greater stimulus.

Couple this with sessions that used media intelligently, colourfully and illustratively and a second lesson emerged: the more you stimulate your audience, the more they will learn.

These are simple points which have been ingrained within the educational technology philosophy for many years. But they were graphically illustrated during the course of this conference. If learning should be more student-centred then clearly the message for a successful conference should be to become more delegate-centred.

I think it is important that the components of that student-centredness ought to be explored in a little more detail. We are really talking about a series of general shifts along continua. We are not talking about movement from one extreme to another, but nevertheless the overall picture is of a move

From:	To:
Passive absorption of knowledge	Active participation in the learning process
The focus on teaching	The focus on learning
Institution/teacher centred	Learner centred
Content handed out	Content discovered
Teacher at centre	Resources at centre

This shift has created a number of new models of education and training innovation. I will share one with you which I helped develop for a publication called *The Open Learning Toolkit*.

Here the learner is at the centre of the model and the model seeks to balance the use of learning resources with the need to support and help the learner through the learning process. This in turn generates the necessity for an effective management and administrative system around which the learning can be structured. All of these three areas – package, support and management – can be negated by poor planning. As the toolkit model implies careful development prior to delivery, it is clear that careful planning and analysis are necessary.

But even if we get that model right, if we ignore what lies behind it – the organizational context, the culture of the company, the ethos of the school or college – then innovation will still fail.

We can only build on the resources that exist. We have to operate within the constraints imposed upon us. Far too few models of educational innovation have taken that organizational context into account. So where do you begin? What are the first steps in moving into a more flexible provision?

There are a whole series of choices, including:

who your learners are:
what they should learn;
where they should learn;
when they should learn;
how they should learn;

and whether you are interested in purely *product* outcomes, or you are more concerned with *process*.

Each of these choices can be seen as a continuum from open to closed for a particular course or a particular part of a course, as illustrated in the model below.

      Open   Closed

Who?
What?
Where?
When?
How?
Outcomes?

It is up to the manager, developer, trainer, educator to decide which of those continua he or she wants to open and why. It is probably impossible to move to a model that is entirely open on every choice. It would be unworkable and undesirable. The skill lies in opening up just enough according to the criteria that matter in your context.

For some institutions the question of access (*who* can learn) is of prime importance; for others the emphasis must be on *how* people learn or *what* people learn. There are many choices that are possible, and these need proper management and proper exploration.

The Further Education Unit (FEU) offers an alternative model (see Figure 1). It is necessary to decide on which of the possible permutations of the factors listed you wish to act on *before* developing some kind of flexible learning system. (The FEU model is taken from their publication entitled *Tutoring*.)

The previous model is simpler but this one unpacks the how? continuum into a variety of learning processes, and is therefore worthy of note.

What I am advocating however is not an academic model, but a needs-driven model. The decision to move ahead should be taken with reference to what educational outcomes are required rather than beginning with the idea that a particular model has to be implemented rigidly. Thus open learning is much more a philosophy and an approach rather than a rigid model. As a rigid model it deserves to die. As an underpinning philosophy it has yet to come of age.

Much of what I have said underpinned the educational innovation of the 16+

```
┌─────────────────────────────────────────────────────────┐
│  THE AIMS AND CONTENT OF THE LEARNING                   │
│  WHO IS THE LEARNER?                                    │
│                                        mode of attendance│
│  THE PROCESS OF LEARNING               resources of learning│
│                                        mode of learning │
│                                        pace of learning │
│                                        interaction with others│
│  THE METHOD OF ASSESSMENT                               │
└─────────────────────────────────────────────────────────┘
```

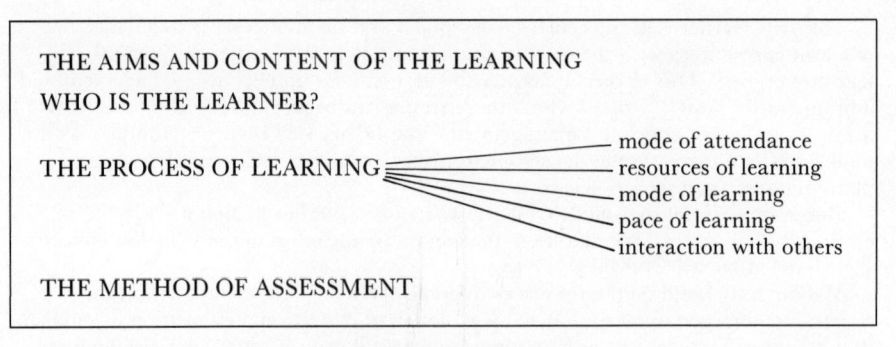

Figure 1. *The FEU model*

Action Plan. It was designed first and foremost to create a relevant curriculum and a flexible delivery that was capable of infinite development and extension. This can be illustrated by two brief quotations from the original report:

> 'A new educational framework is required, which will take account of the needs of all young people, will reflect today's occupational requirements and will provide a sound base on which to build for the later acquisition or updating of skills and knowledge to meet the challenges of the future.'

> 'The aim of the proposals in this Action Plan is to improve the quality and flexibility of curricular provision in schools and further education. By developing a system based on modules and check certification, the Government's intention is to facilitate more rational use of available resources for education.' (Scottish Education Department, 1983)

But there are countless examples where small-scale developments have occurred without massive public debate or injections of resources, to the benefit of learners.

One example is in Wester Hailes community education centre, where the social subjects teachers have worked as a team to develop resources allowing a very judicious and skilful mixture of resource-based learning and conventional teaching for second-year secondary students.

Using the second world war as the theme, mixed ability groups explore a wide range of resources on paper, slide and audio cassette and record their experiences singly or in groups.

This is not necessarily a model to follow. There are many constraints imposed upon the learner that others might wish to open and much of the development in Wester Hailes implies a different kind of management and organization of staff than happens in many conventional schools. But it does show that it is possible to move forward in this area in a quiet and sensible way.

I am immensely proud of some of the developments that have occurred in Scotland and further afield. I was particularly impressed by details of the BBC Domesday Project, where vast amounts of local and national information will be stored on each side of the two video data disks. This will become a detailed, in-depth resource for schools and other educational users for a long time to come.

Access to that data will be provided in a large variety of ways using a combination of hardware and software still to be fully developed.

I wonder ultimately if a lesser development which took account only of existing technology rather than potential technological developments yet to be tested would have been such a tribute to British inventiveness.

I firmly believe that flexibility in terms of education and training delivery is not just a good idea, but is absolutely essential for producing the kind of adults capable of adapting to a society caught up in vast change. The pressure to fit the education and training system to that world is increasing past a point of no return. Change is balanced with the resources necessary to achieve that change.

Flexible learning systems take account of the multitude of learning styles which adults develop to survive in a complex world.

We are not just talking about learning in an institution, but the interface between the world outside and the various components of the education system. I think most engineers are aware that the problems often occur at the interfaces between materials rather than within the materials themselves, and this is no less true within education.

If we are going to move into a learning society where inventiveness and imagination are stimulated and develop, then the ways in which people learn from the very earliest – experiences in school through to regular adult updating, re-skilling, re-educating and training – then flexibility is surely the key.

We might not have come very far in terms of brand new models, but we have come a long way in terms of why and how we use those models. This conference addressed issues which are central to and crucial for the future of our society. That is a tribute to the organizers and the planners who put this conference together.

Just under half a century after he wrote them, T S Eliot's words still ring true:

> We shall not cease from exploration
> And the end of all our exploring
> Will be to arrive where we started
> And know the place for the first time.
>
> From *Four Quartets: Little Gidding*

Reference

Scottish Education Department (1983) *16-18s in Scotland. An Action Plan.* Scottish Education Department, Edinburgh.